Praise for *Cultural Studies:
From Theory to Action*

"It is vitally important to explore the relations between cultural studies and practical politics. This edited collection does so admirably by bringing together a huge variety of material. The sheer diversity of intellectual and political engagement is mapped with great respect for difference. Moments are also considered when differences are subsumed but not obliterated in a shared project of emancipation."

Jim McGuigan, Loughborough University

"Cultural studies has always claimed a certain practical and political relevance for itself, but this orientation has often been submerged in the preoccupation with theoretical fluency. This collection provides a much-needed reminder that any theoretical practice in cultural studies is also, in important ways, a political intervention, as well as a contribution to critical reflection of practical politics on the ground – wherever in the world."

Ien Ang, University of Western Sydney

"This is a very comprehensive and inclusive project. It will make a strong impact and considerable contribution to global critical theory and praxis."

Joy James, Brown University

"This anthology is a major scholarly contribution to cultural studies. Leistyna's text is extremely well articulated, organized, and developed. The stress throughout on agency is a productive one, as is the emphasis on the politics of cultural studies and activism. The juxtaposition of theoretical and more practical articles provides more practical urgency to theoretical texts and more empirical and activist efforts with theoretical sophistication and guidance. This volume will be a popular classroom text, especially among those younger scholars who crave more contemporary and activist applications to cultural studies – and as the years go by, they will be the ones teaching and doing cultural studies. In addition, the text will find a popular audience among both those engaged in cultural studies, as well as those engaged in social movements."

Douglas Kellner, University of California at Los Angeles

"Both culture and cultural studies have always occupied a contested terrain. Pepi Leistyna has brought together some of the best exponents of this burgeoning tradition not only to show why culture is worth studying, why cultural studies is worth defending, and why cultural studies educators threaten the political status quo in universities and other public spaces, but also to reveal the urgent role cultural studies has to play in our everyday lives, especially at this particular historical juncture of revitalized US imperialism and the struggle over the meaning and direction of democracy. Leistyna's volume is a must-read for all educators interested in challenging the devolution of human rights throughout the world and engaging in the continuing struggle for liberation."

Peter McLaren, University of California at Los Angeles

This book is dedicated to all those unsung people who have lost their lives in the struggle to radicalize democracy. It is also dedicated to Pierre Bourdieu, 1930–2002, and Edward Said, 1935–2003.

Cultural Studies

From Theory to Action

Edited by
Pepi Leistyna

Blackwell
Publishing

BLACKWELL PUBLISHING
350 Main Street, Malden, MA 02148-5020, USA
108 Cowley Road, Oxford OX4 1JF, UK
550 Swanston Street, Carlton, Victoria 3053, Australia

First published 2005 by Blackwell Publishing Ltd

Library of Congress Cataloging-in-Publication Data

Cultural studies: from theory to action / edited by Pepi Leistyna.
        p. cm.
    Includes bibliographical references and index.
    ISBN 0-631-22437-8 (hardcover: alk. paper)—ISBN 0-631-22438-6 (pbk.: alk. paper) 1. Social justice. 2. Social movements. 3. Culture—Study and teaching—Political aspects. I. Leistyna, Pepi.

    HM671.C85 2005
    306′.071—dc22
                                                            2004006270

A catalogue record for this title is available from the British Library.

Set in 10/12.5pt Minion
by Kolam Information Services Pvt Ltd., Pondicherry, India

For further information on
Blackwell Publishing, visit our website:
http://www.blackwellpublishing.com

Contents

Part IV: Gendered Identities in the Realm of Patriarchy   319

Part V: Heterosexism and Homophobia: Critical Interventions   409

Preface: *How To Use This Book*

Cultural Studies: From Theory to Action is the first text of its kind in Cultural Studies that gives both theory and political action center stage. Moving beyond the descriptor *Studies*, which perhaps implies that analysis alone, and not social interventions, is the goal of Cultural Studies, this anthology is designed to encourage a wide audience of readers, especially undergraduate, graduate, and postgraduate students throughout the humanities and social sciences, to begin a dialogue between contemporary critical social theories and progressive activist practices.

Instead of rendering Cultural Studies an abstract discipline, this anthology grounds theory in actual life experiences and struggles for social justice around the globe. Through the voices of international scholars and activists, this book demonstrates how critical and inclusive publics can effectively challenge oppression from economic, political, techno- logical, and cultural fronts. The kind of Cultural Studies that this text embraces consists of more then simply thinking culture politically – it is also connected to finding better ways for making sense of and acting upon the contemporary social world. Theory is thus understood as being strategic, performative, concrete, and directed towards solving important pressing social and political problems – hence the book's title, *Cultural Studies: From Theory to Action.*

The chapters herein showcase groups actually engaged in cultural and political reflec- tion, struggle, and projects of social transformation. Confronting a myriad of social injustices, each individual contribution to this book demonstrates at least one facet, or a combination, of consciousness-raising, coalition-building, resistance, activism, and structural change. These provocative juxtapositionings of theoretical with activist works are pedagogically instructive because they highlight for students that Cultural Studies is as much a practical, political enterprise as it is a theoretical concern.

A central goal for readers moving through the following materials is to explore and begin to build upon some of the infinite ways in which concerned individuals and groups from diverse geopolitical locations have worked towards critical awareness and more just and effective responses to current unjust and debilitating economic and sociopolitical conditions. *Cultural Studies: From Theory to Action* aims for the kinds of reader partici- pation in which individuals and groups can begin to examine whether or not the theories, organizational strategies, coalitions, and moments of activism presented in each section of this book emerge out of different/similar conditions and circumstances, are on target with their professed goals, in contradiction with each other, relevant to one another's local predicaments, and/or applicable globally. Readers are encouraged to evaluate, based on their own experiences, expertise, and insight, the strengths and weaknesses of the conceptual and practical movements presented in this volume, and recontextualize and reinvent their possibilities for one's own predicaments, while also considering expanding such efforts in order to create new global coalitions and collective responses. Readers are also encouraged to consider relations between sections as the analytic distinctions that subdivide this book should not inhibit examining the multiple and interpenetrating relationships that these categories have with other issues and concerns. Throughout this book, students are encouraged to understand emergent political struggles and pose and address questions about how to develop routine activities of resistance and agency, how to develop and support efforts at institutional realignments, and how to realize counter-hegemonic strategies and revolutionary practices.

Cultural Studies: From Theory to Action is divided into 6 sections and 38 chapters. Its organization allows for easy insertion into a semester-long course of study. The Introduction – Revitalizing the Dialogue: Theory, Coalition-Building, and Social Change – works to reconcile some of the obstacles that have blocked the way of theory informing practice: the rift created between modern and postmodern theories, how to bridge the local/global divide when it comes to activist concerns, how to combine theoretical forces such as political economy and representation, and how to balance the demands of political unity and cultural diversity.

The chapters in Part I, The Politics of Economic Oppression: Anticolonialism Meets Globalization, provide theoretical and practical insights about understanding the logic of capitalism, class structure, and antagonistic social relations. These chapters illustrate some of the ways that it is possible to challenge the global hegemony of neoliberalism, and unite activists by working through a politics of location, area-specific traditions and economic interests, and overcoming language barriers. The authors raise issues and questions for readers about how to bring about demilitarization and decolonization, how to develop counterinsurgency movements, ways to organize labor, ways to combat privatization and the assault on public life, how to develop effective environmental movements, and how to invoke community renewal. They also speak to what can be learned from old/new political alliances and organizations, and ways to strategize agitation and demonstrations in the public sphere.

Part II, Representational Politics: Making Up Your Own Mind by Minding the Popular Media, is concerned with the political economy of the mass media, text production and analysis, and audience reception and consumption. Readers are challenged to consider how to develop antico-optation movements in popular culture, how activists can forge alternative media and attract audiences, how people can continue to effectively use music, theater, and other arts as resistance and for social change (articulating new dimensions of aesthetics, fashion, expression, and meaning), and how activists can use cyberspace to forge global solidarity.

The next three Parts of the anthology deal with issues of identity and oppression. In Part III, Identity and Ethnicity in the Face of Discrimination and Racism, readers are exposed to particular struggles against bigotry in various parts of the world, as well as how such diverse conditions and concerns can be brought together in a conference to combat global discrimination. Readers are invited to consider how to develop ways to fight against racism and ethnocentrism and forge antiviolence campaigns.

Part IV, Gendered Identities in the Realm of Patriarchy, examines many of the concerns, limitations, and contradictions of the women's movement so as to be able to create local solidarities across race, class, and sexual borders and transnational feminist networks. Part V, *Heterosexism and Homophobia: Critical Interventions*, strategically uses the analytic distinction "sexuality" while moving beyond the traditional parameters of identity politics and into the terrain of coalition-building. All three of these sections demand of readers serious contemplation about how to have both a politics of identity and a politics of difference, how to develop public policy that supports and sustains civil rights, and how to develop popular education and classroom practices and curricular transformations that can lead to critical literacy.

The last section of this book, *Getting Informed, Getting Involved: Places to Turn To*, provides readers with some supplementary resources: a collection of activist organizations and web resources with contact information, and an alphabetized list of international, progressive journals. Readers are encouraged to explore these resources in the creative process of addressing the social and institutional ills revealed in this book.

Extensive reading lists are provided at the end of the book. Included are dictionaries, introductory texts, classics, readers, and cutting-edge theoretical, research, and activist literature. In order to provide the reader with access to the past – given that this text focuses on contemporary work – the suggested readings are chronologically organized to offer access to a vast history of critical social theories and activism. Readers are encouraged to do additional reading and research in order to more fully contextualize and understand the area-specific moments of activism included in this anthology.

This anthology, designed to be used in a variety of settings and at a variety of educational levels, begs the central question: How can theorizing in Cultural Studies be used as a form of social practice that inspires people to not only read the world critically, but to also act within it? Facilitating the dialogue, this book provides a volume introduction that invites readers into the basics of Cultural Studies; it is organized around useful thematic categories within Cultural Studies; and it helps readers find their way into and around this interdisciplinary terrain with such tools as lists of further reading for each section and activist resources. In addition, this anthology offers a picture of Cultural Studies that is truly international; it uses contemporary essays and concrete examples of practice to ground complex and abstract theoretical ideas; and it provides practical pieces that can be theorized by readers. The emphasis of *Cultural Studies: From Theory to Action* is on making Cultural Studies practical as part of a broader discourse of democratic change.

Pepi Leistyna

Acknowledgments

This project could not have been realized without the flexibility, insight, and tenacity of Jayne Fargnoli and her tireless crew at Blackwell Publishing. I would also like to thank the advisory board for their critical guidance throughout this long process: Ien Ang, Arif Dirlik, David Theo Goldberg, Ann Gray, Doug Kellner, John Erni, and Joy James; with special thanks to John Frow, who generously offered his energy and insight up until the final seconds of the book's completion. I also want to thank Henry Giroux for responding to my endless emails, at all hours, looking for advice. There were many other people who helped me along the road and I am forever indebted to them: Noam Chomsky, Peter McLaren, Valerie Walkerdine, Robert McChesney, Sut Jhally, Jackson Katz, Vijay Prashad, Ken Saltman, Robin Truth Goodman, Gautan Premnath, Joan Roelofs, Victoria Bernal, Mariam Meynert, L. Muthoni Wanyeki, Jack Shaheen, Ayse Gul Altinay, Sasha Torres, Fred Cooper, Shyamala Raman, Gregory Martin, Tim Seiber, Nikki Jordan, and Wendy Harcourt. I am also grateful to Paulo Freire, whose spirit always keeps me hopeful and whose advice of being "patiently impatient" I hold to tightly during such enduring times. I would also like to express my appreciation and love to the entire Kubik family, especially Susan – without her support, humor, and heart, none of this would have been possible.

The editor and publisher gratefully acknowledge the permission granted to reproduce the copyright material in this book:

1   Samir Amin, "Unity and Changes in the Ideology of Political Economy," pp. 27–47 from *Spectres of Capitalism: A Critique of Current Intellectual Fashions*. New York: Monthly Review Press, 1998. © 1998 by M.R. Press. Reprinted by permission of Monthly Review Foundation.

2   Arif Dirlik, "The Postcolonial Aura: Third World Criticism in the Age of Global Capitalism," pp. 501–27 from Anne McClintock, Aamir Mufti, and Ella Shohat (eds.), *Dangerous Liaisons: Gender, Nation, and Postcolonial Perspectives*. Minneapolis: University of Minnesota Press, 1997. Reprinted by permission of University of Minnesota Press.

3   Zygmunt Bauman, "Time and Class," pp. 6–26 and 128–9 from *Globalization: The Human Consequences*. Cambridge: Polity Press and New York: Columbia University

Press, 1998. Reprinted by permission of Blackwell Publishing Ltd. and Columbia University Press.

4   Brooke G. Schoepf, Claude Schoepf, and Joyce V. Millen, "Theoretical Therapies, Remote Remedies: SAPs and the Political Ecology of Poverty and Health in Africa," pp. 91–125 and 440–57 from Jim Yong Kim, Joyce V. Millen, Alec Irwin, and John Greshman (eds.), *Dying for Growth: Global Inequality and the Health of the Poor.* Monroe, ME: Common Courage Press, 2000. Reprinted by permission of Common Courage Press.

5   Fernanda Navarro, "A New Way of Thinking in Action: The Zapatistas in Mexico – A Postmodern Guerrilla Movement?" pp. 155–65 from *Rethinking Marxism: A Journal of Economics, Culture, and Society* 10:4 (1998), http://www.tandf.co.uk/journals/titles/08935696.html. Reprinted by permission of Taylor & Francis Ltd.

6   Anita Chan, "Workers' Resistance," pp. 206–22 in *China's Workers under Assault: The Exploitation of Labor in a Globalizing Economy.* Armonk, NY: M. E. Sharpe, 2001. Copyright © 2001 by M. E. Sharpe, Inc. Reprinted with permission.

7   Üstün Reinart, "Life Against Gold," *Z Magazine* (June 2001), pp. 19–21. Reprinted by permission of the author.

8   Richard Appelbaum and Peter Dreier, "The Campus Antisweatshop Movement." Reprinted with permission from *The American Prospect*, vol. 10, no. 46: Sept. 1, 1999–Oct. 1, 1999. The American Prospect, 5 Broad Street, Boston, MA 02109. All rights reserved.

9   Sangeeta Kamat, "The NGO-ization of Grassroots Politics," pp. 152–68 from *Development Hegemony: NGOs and the State in India.* New Delhi: Oxford University Press, 2001. Reproduced by permission of Oxford University Press India, New Delhi.

10   Robert W. McChesney, "Global Media, Neoliberalism, and Imperialism," *Monthly Review*, vol. 52, no. 10 (March 2001). Copyright © 2001 by M.R. Press. Reprinted by permission of Monthly Review Foundation.

11   David Morley, "Theoretical Orthodoxies: Textualism, Constructivism and the 'New Ethnography' in Cultural Studies," pp. 121–37 from M. Ferguson and P. Golding (eds.), *Cultural Studies in Question.* London: Sage, 1997. Reprinted by permission of Sage Publications Ltd.

12   Henry A. Giroux, "Disney, Southern Baptists, and Children's Culture: The Magic Kingdom as Sodom and Gomorrah?" *Z Magazine* (Sept. 1997). Reprinted by permission of the author.

13   Jennifer David, "Seeing Ourselves, Being Ourselves: Broadcasting Aboriginal Television in Canada," *Cultural Survival Quarterly* (Summer 1998), pp. 36–9.

14   Stephen Duncombe, "Zines," pp. 1–16 and 199–200 from *Notes from the Underground: Zines and the Politics of Alternative Culture.* New York: Verso, 1997. Reprinted by permission of Verso.

15   Kekula P. Bray-Crawford, "The Ho'okele Netwarriors in the Liquid Continent," pp. 162–72 from Wendy Harcourt (ed.), *Women Internet: Creating New Cultures in Cyberspace.* London: Zed Books, 1999. Reprinted by permission of Zed Books.

16 Richard Kahn and Douglas Kellner, "Internet Subcultures and Political Activism" (2003). Reprinted by permission of the authors.

17 Rosemarie Garland Thomson, "Staring Back: Self-Representations of Disabled Performance Artists," *American Quarterly*, vol. 52, no. 2 (June 2000), pp. 334–8. © The American Studies Association. Reprinted with permission of The Johns Hopkins University Press.

18 Johnny Temple, "Noise From Underground: Punk Rock's Anarchic Rhythms Spur a New Generation to Political Activism," *The Nation*, vol. 269, no. 12 (Oct. 18, 1999), pp. 17–22.

19 Nancy Fraser, "Rethinking Recognition," *New Left Review*, no. 3 (May–June 2000), pp. 107–20. Reprinted by permission of New Left Review.

20 Fidel Castro, "The Roots of International Racism," *Monthly Review*, vol. 53, no. 7 (Dec. 2001), pp. 24–7. Copyright © 2001 by M.R. Press. Reprinted by permission of Monthly Review Foundation.

21 Edward Said, "Invention, Memory, and Place," *Critical Inquiry* (Winter 2000), pp. 175–92. Reprinted by permission of The University of Chicago Press and The Wylie Agency.

22 Pepi Leistyna, "White Ethnic Unconsciousness," *Cultural Circles*, vol. 2 (Spring 1998), pp. 33–51. Reprinted by permission of Elementary Education and Specialized Studies, Boise State University.

23 Bhikhu Parekh, "Racial Justice in a Multi-Ethnic Society," *Economic and Political Weekly* (Sept. 15, 2001).

24 Elizabeth "Betita" Martinez, "Where Was the Color in Seattle? Looking for Reasons Why the Great Battle Was So White," *ColorLines*, vol. 3, no. 1 (Spring 2000). Reprinted by permission of ColorLines.

25 Nancy Murray, "Sharing the Story of the Movement: The Project HIP-HOP Experience," *Radical Teacher*, no. 57 (2000), pp. 8–15. Reprinted by permission of Center for Critical Education, Inc., Radical Teacher, 466 Putnam Ave. #2, Cambridge, MA 02139.

26 A. S. Narang, "World Conference Against Racism: Prospects and Challenges," *Economic and Political Weekly* (July 7, 2001).

27 Chandra Talpade Mohanty, "Women Workers and Capitalist Scripts: Ideologies of Domination, Common Interests, and the Politics of Solidarity," pp. 3–29 and 355–8 from Jacqui Alexander and C. T. Mohanty (eds.), *Feminist Genealogies, Colonial Legacies, Democratic Futures*. New York: Routledge, 1997. Copyright © 1997. Reproduced by permission of Routledge/Taylor & Francis Books, Inc.

28 Joy James, "Radicalizing Feminism from 'The Movement' Era," pp. 73–94 and 200–4 from *Shadowboxing: Representations of Black Feminist Politics*. New York: Palgrave, 1999. Copyright © Joy James. Reprinted with permission of Palgrave Macmillan.

29 Leonie Pihama, "Mana Wahine Theory: Creating Space for Mäori Women's Theories" (2002). Reprinted by permission of the author.

30 Tahmeena Faryal (2002), "Revolutionary Association of Women in Afghanistan (RAWA): Women Working for Freedom," *Against the Current*, vol. XVI, no. 6 (Jan.–Feb. 2002), pp. 5–8. Reprinted by permission of Against the Current.

31 Miriam Ching Yoon Louie, "*Minjung* Feminism: Korean Women's Movement for Gender and Class Liberation," *Women's Studies International Forum*, vol. 18, no. 4 (2000), pp. 417–30. Copyright © 1995, reprinted with permission from Elsevier.

32 Jackson Katz, "Reconstructing Masculinity in the Locker Room: The Mentors in Violence Prevention Project," *The Harvard Educational Review*, vol. 65, no. 2 (Summer 1995), pp. 163–74. Copyright © 1995 by the President and Fellows of Harvard College. All rights reserved.

33 Dennis Altman, "The Globalization of Sexual Identities," pp. 86–105 and 188–93 from *Global Sex*. Chicago: University of Chicago Press, 2001. Reprinted by permission of University of Chicago Press and Dennis Altman.

34 Jewelle Gomez, "Black Lesbians: Passing, Stereotypes, and Transformation," pp. 161–77 from *Dangerous Liaisons: Blacks, Gays, and the Struggle for Equality*. New York: The New Press, 1999.

35 Pat Califia, "Trashing the Clinic and Burning Down the Beauty Parlor: Activism Transmutes Pitiable Patients into Feisty Gender Radicals," pp. 221–4 from *Sex Changes: The Politics of Transgenderism*. San Francisco: Cleis Press, 1997. Reprinted by permission of Cleis Press.

36 Mazibuko K. Jara, Naomi Webster, and Gerald Hunt, "At a Turning Point: Organized Labor, Sexual Diversity, and the New South Africa," pp. 191–205 from G. Hunt (ed.), *Laboring for Rights: Unions and Sexual Diversity Across Nations*. Princeton: Temple University Press, 1999. Reprinted by permission of Temple University Press. © 1999 by Temple University. All rights reserved.

37 Doug Ireland, "Gay Teens Fight Back: A New Generation of Gay Youth Won't Tolerate Harassment in Their Schools," *The Nation* (Jan. 31, 2000), pp. 21–3.

38 Ien Ang, "Who Needs Cultural Research?" (2001). Reprinted by permission of the author.

Every effort has been made to trace copyright holders and to obtain their permission for the use of copyright material. The publisher apologizes for any errors or omissions in the above list, and would be grateful if notified of any corrections that should be incorporated in future reprints or editions of this book.

Revitalizing the Dialogue:
Theory, Coalition-Building, and
Social Change

I come back to theory and politics, the politics of theory. Not theory as the will to truth, but theory as a set of contested, localized, conjunctural knowledges, which have to be debated in a dialogical way. But also as a practice which always thinks about its intervention in a world in which it would make some difference, in which it would have some effect.[1]

Stuart Hall

Cultural Studies: From Theory to Action is intended to inspire, provoke, and revitalize dialogues among all members of the global society who are concerned with issues of social and economic justice and the current crisis in democracy. This book has been forged with those thousands of people in mind that I've taught and worked with over the years who have exclaimed, "I realize that there are major social problems, but how can I fully understand them, and what can I do to make change?" As an educator my response has always been the same: "I cannot tell you what to think or what to do, but I can facilitate a participatory dialogue that calls for exploration, that reaches for understanding, and that works to instigate both individual and collective social activism."

It is to the spirit of Paulo Freire's work that this new book turns for a working definition of *dialogue*. The late Brazilian critical pedagogue, who profoundly believed that any participatory democracy has to be dialogical, argued, "Dialogue is not simply another word for a mere conversation among people about everyday matters. Dialogue, from an epistemological perspective, requires approaching and examining a certain object of knowledge."[2] At its heart, this type of discursive practice is encouraged to facilitate critical interaction that focuses on the kinds of analyses of knowledge and experience that can lead to social awareness, debates over organizational strategies, political innovations, coalition-building, and mass citizen actions capable of working towards eradicating oppressive economic, political, and cultural institutions and structures, identities, social practices, public policies, and governments.

However, even from this working definition of *dialogue*, the question remains: Where should such critical discussions begin? In order to assist readers in taking up the reins of coalition-building and social change within the myriad of controversial and contradictory areas that make up the complex exploratory terrain of critical social theory, *Cultural Studies: From Theory to Action* is designed to move the active participant through some of the central discouraging stumbling blocks that can inhibit creative and constructive interactions and productive articulations – that is, a coming together – of theory and practice.

Embracing praxis: the ongoing relationship between reflection and action

I have come to understand *theory* as how people interpret, critique, and draw generalizations about *why* the social world spins the economic, cultural, political, and institutional webs that it does. From this working definition, theory is the ability to make sense of all levels of the everyday – that is, the *why* and *how* of what has been happening in people's lives, and not simply a focus on *what* is occurring and how to effectively respond.

Unfortunately, in many forms of human mobilization, theory is disconnected from practice, denying that practices are always undergirded by particular theoretical perspectives and assumptions. This denial is reflected in mainstream and more progressive pedagogical models and activist movements that inspire a search for materials, methods, and strategies for direct action, without sufficiently and continuously exploring the sociohistorical, economic, cultural, and institutional realities that generate the particular political and material conditions that invoke the need for such active responses. There is often a premature demand for "how tos," or uncritical calls for empirical research to replace rather than complement theory – as if descriptive or numerical patterns of behavior in the data will interpret themselves.

There are a number of reasons why this disconnection of theory from practice has occurred. One of the most frequently expressed rejections of theory that I've experienced among students and activists pertains to the "inaccessible" conceptual and lexical complexity of many of the social and cultural theories emanating from the academy. The sophisticated and intertextual theoretical discourses that have emerged from the university, that do require a healthy amount of apprenticeship in order to meaningfully decode their significance, are often described by activists and students alike as ivory tower elitism that has little or nothing to do with the real world. Theory is thus unfortunately pushed aside for not being in touch with the everyday.

On the one hand, there is without doubt work out there that consists of little more than polysyllabic gymnastics which often "pile up one sophisticated theoretical construction on top of another... without ever once touching ground and without reference to a single concrete case or historical example."[3] Henry Giroux describes this as "forms of theorizing that do little more than instrumentalize, polemicize, obscure, or insulate – and of course, this is a discourse and pedagogy that generally threatens no one."[4] Instead of rendering Cultural Studies an abstract discipline, this anthology grounds theory in tangible life experiences and struggles for social justice around the globe.

On the other hand, any blanket dismissal of critical theoretical work as simply being "jargon" and "inaccessible" is troubling. Inherent in so many notions of "unintelligible language" is the assumption that there is a universal medium of clarity that *we* all understand. However, as multiple audiences read and comprehend the world differently, the question is who is the inferred "we"?

Educators and cultural workers do need to problematize the basis of our own linguistic privilege so that we can work to generate the necessary conditions in which language provides a vehicle for opening up different spaces for people to speak to and be aware of multiple voices and audiences. But at the same time, when my graduate students complain about the density of critical social theories, I often turn the argument around by asking them why they think that after over 16 years of formal education, they have rarely if ever been exposed to such work. I subsequently offer them a number of introductory texts and sociological dictionaries that can help to scaffold the active reader into ongoing discussions and debates around these complex economic, political, sociocultural, and psychological issues (for an extensive list of such heuristic devices, see the Suggested Reading list at the end of the book).

Consciously working against objectifying readers by promoting the semi-literacy of "clarity," or infantilizing readers by assuming that they are only able to deal with simple language that masks the intricacies of the social reality being examined, the language used for this introduction, as well as in the selected readings that follow, although demanding, is intended to provide signposts into these complex debates. While by no means dismissing other intricate and many-faceted theories which do play a significant role in dissecting multilayered social phenomena (many of which are included in the suggested reading lists at the end of the book), the chapters that have been chosen for this anthology are those that I thought, in conjunction with reader-initiated intrigue and effort, would be both inviting and challenging to as wide an audience as I could imagine.

The basic strategy for organizing this edited collection has been to either find research that illustrates the relationship between theory and practice, or to juxtapose theoretical with practical works that focus on similar issues; for example, placing side by side chapters that attempt to explain the formation and trajectory of neoliberalism, with those that describe particular geopolitical movements that are trying to combat the oppression that ensues from such economic practices. As this book confronts a vast array of social injustices, each individual contribution demonstrates at least one facet, or a combination, of consciousness-raising, coalition-building, resistance, activism, and structural change. The chapters strive to exemplify what Raymond Williams referred to throughout his work as "knowable communities" by showcasing groups actually engaged in cultural and political reflection, struggle, and projects of social transformation.

It is important to note here that while the idea of "knowable communities," as it pertains to political projects, is both appealing and useful, neither Williams nor this anthology aspire to essentialize geographies and identities by assuming that there are biologically determined or culturally fixed thoughts and practices at play that are easily identifiable, readily accessible, and necessarily indicative of what other groups are experiencing and how they are responding. The following chapters that attend to the specific, the local, or the regional context, simply introduce and provide an international readership with access to a multiplicity of complex problems that offer working examples for analysis and a place to initiate dialogue about praxis and democratic social change. A central goal in moving through the following materials is to explore and begin to build upon some of the infinite ways in which concerned individuals and groups from diverse geopolitical locations have worked towards critical awareness and more just and effective responses to current unjust and debilitating economic and sociopolitical conditions.

With that in mind, this book is designed to be pedagogically instructive as it aims for the kinds of reader participation in which individuals and groups can begin to examine whether or not the theories, organizational strategies, coalitions, and moments of activism presented in each Part emerge out of different/similar conditions and circumstances, are on target with their professed goals, in contradiction with each other, relevant to one another's local predicaments, and/or applicable globally.

In calling for this type of interaction, it is important to note here that *theory* and *theorizing* are not being considered as one and the same. While understanding the ways in which existing theories explain social reality is enormously important, *theorizing* is the ability to actively and meaningfully engage bodies of knowledge and human practices for the logics, histories, economic conditions, values, and beliefs that inform them so that they can be reworked. Rather than simply treating this as a recipe book to be followed to the exact detail, readers are encouraged to evaluate, based on their own experiences, expertise, and insight, the strengths and weaknesses of the conceptual and practical movements presented in this volume and recontextualize and reinvent their possibilities for one's own predicaments, while also considering expanding such efforts in order to create new global coalitions and collective responses. It is important to emphasize that while engaged in this exploratory and creative process, one's own subject position – the place that a person occupies within a set of social relationships often shaped by such factors as nation, locale, social class, gender, race, language, religion, sexual orientation, age, and physical ability – should always be held in a critical light, not only for the purposes of continued self-actualization, but also so that the ethical stances that are taken on an issue allow a person to speak to particular problems and in solidarity *with* others rather than *for* people from different backgrounds.

The act of theorizing embraced here is also ongoing and pliable: as societies and lived experiences change within shifting social landscapes, theories as well as social activism should always be subjected to further critical exploration and recontextualization. Praxis of this type presents a constant challenge to imagine and materialize alternative political spaces, identities, and economic, social, cultural, and technological relations capable of generating area-specific constituencies, and when possible, transnational activist networks and movements. In such undemocratic times, it's not surprising that theorizing along these lines is often discouraged.

The assault on theorizing is in part connected to ways in which the university has been used as a major indoctrinating force to deskill students by working to mold them into uncritical receivers and consumers of existing theory, but rarely viewing them as active and creative participants in the generative process of understanding.[5] This is especially evident as globally the academy is falling prey to the kinds of corporate logic that package thought as a commodity for exchange in the marketplace rather than inspiring the kinds of inquiry that probe that very logic and use of public energy and space.[6] Within these corporate models of public education the production of technicians in all disciplines (areas of study which are artificially disconnected from one another) comes at the expense of transdisciplinary thinkers and producers of social knowledge about the world. As students are distracted or lured away from critically reading historical and existing social formations, especially those that maintain abuses of power, they so often become the newest wave of exploited labor power and reproducers, whether they are conscious of it or not, of oppressive social practices.[7]

The form of Cultural Studies that this anthology embraces is that which takes seriously the connection between the university and everyday life, one that understands that the projects that drive Cultural Studies should be established in light of how the larger social order affects people's lives, and not inspired by the imperatives of disciplinary profession-alism. As Ien Ang states, in support of university/public partnerships, in her closing chapter of this anthology:

I do firmly believe that the world needs Cultural Studies more than ever. But if so, then we will have to find practical ways of convincing others that the intricate knowledges and understandings we are capable of producing have some relevance to them.

What is being offered here is in many ways a revitalization of the 1960s political ethos of the Centre for Contemporary Cultural Studies at the University of Birmingham, England, where theory was understood as being strategic, performative, and directed towards solving important, pressing economic, social, and political problems. In order to benefit from the cracks of radical agency that still exist in the academy, though few and far between, *Cultural Studies: From Theory to Action* is intended to pry open the gates of progressive theoretical camps that have created great insight, but also rigid and insular boundaries. The task at hand is to find ways to revitalize conceptual soil and connect and recultivate the theoretical problematics of modernism and postmodernism – in particular, their concerns with political economy and cultural and identity politics – and transform them into fertile grounds for practical political innovation.

Bridging the local/global divide

The theoretical minds, movements, and debates that have emerged from Enlightenment/ modernist thought, and more recently postmodern critique, have made vast contributions to ways of thinking about democracy and social and economic justice. However, after years of deliberation and dispute, both inside and outside of the academy, the potential for theorizing connections between these worldviews has been suffocating in the deeply dug trenches that separate modernist claims to universalism from the postmodern embrace of particularism.

It is not within the means of this introduction to fully elaborate on the plethora of theories that shape the terms *modernity* and *postmodernity*. In fact, no one actually agrees on the parameters of these complex concepts and there are endless and even contradictory meanings for both. Nonetheless, David Harvey's working definitions are helpful in detailing where some of the major tensions exist:

> Generally perceived as positivistic, technocratic, and rationalistic, universal modernism has been identified with the belief in linear progress, absolute truths, the rational planning of ideal social orders, and the standardization of knowledge and production. Postmodernism, by way of contrast, privileges heterogeneity and difference as liberative forces in the redefinition of cultural discourse. Fragmentation, indeterminacy, and intense distrust of all universal or totalizing discourses (to use the favored phrase) are the hallmark of postmodern thought.[8]

For many modern theorists, there is a single, centered, and essentialized route to human rights and emancipation outside of history, economics, ideology, and the powers of hegemony.[9] Unfortunately, as has been examined for centuries, the search and imposition of ultimate rationality and order has historically perpetuated theoretical orthodoxies and relations of domination.[10]

At the same time, postmodernism's embrace of particularism, discontinuity, and difference at the expense of any attempt to make grander analyses that thread together world events through narratives that connect the local to the global,[11] has made it epistemologically unpopular within some strains of Cultural Studies to map out the world, collapsing into a language of fragmentation, ambiguity, relativism, and primal chaos which reduces theorizing and politics to the impossible.[12] As David Morley points out in his chapter in this book, "It is hard to mobilize around a political platform of principled uncertainty, especially if one of those principles is that it is ultimately impossible to know what is going on."

Rather than discourage theorizing as an active and creative process, dismiss camps of thought at face value, or be limited by the paralyzing extremities of closed theoretical systems, the dialogue that this book entertains is one that searches for ways of pursuing modernity as an unfinished project, where the concepts and potential implications of liberty, human rights, and equality are debated, while also examining the role of contingency and the specificities within which power is wielded. All of the chapters throughout this edited collection present constructive and yet fluid strategies that people use to understand and combat existing inequalities in specific places and situations. At the same time, the collection addresses the complexities of an historical conjuncture characterized both by a long history of colonialism and by rapid globalization that leaves no society entirely isolated. Readers are exposed, in each of the five major sections of this anthology, to how different social agents within particular locations and conditions, including struggles in South Africa, China, Mexico, Afghanistan, Rwanda, the United States, India, Canada, Turkey, Aotearoa/New Zealand, Israel, Palestine, Korea, and England, collide with and are influenced by other cultures, ideological structures, and social movements. In trying to bridge the local/global divide, it is important for readers to compare chapters by looking for differences and commonalities in the conditions, enemies, and obstacles that activists face, and to strategize about building larger collective responses that have both local and global dimensions. Hence, the exploratory intent of this book isn't to discover universal mechanisms or processes that explain human behavior in some extreme, modernist, structuralist way. Rather, the goal is for readers to examine social justice movements, expand upon their possibilities, and whenever possible, extend their geographical reach.

For example, in Part III, *Identity and Ethnicity in the Face of Discrimination and Racism*, readers are exposed to particular struggles against bigotry in various parts of the world, as well as how such diverse conditions and concerns can be brought together in a conference to combat global discrimination: Nancy Fraser rethinks the relationship between "recognition" and "redistribution"; Fidel Castro explores the roots of international racism; Edward Said takes up some of the ways in which Palestinians are misrepresented and oppressed; I examine the links between white supremacy and ethnicity in the United States; Bhikhu Parekh evaluates the negotiations and compromises of antiracist policy development in the UK; Elizabeth "Betita" Martinez takes a look at why the anti-WTO coalition movement is predominantly white; Nancy Murray addresses how youth in public schools can fight bigotry; and A. S. Narang outlines the challenges of the "World Conference against Racism."

Readers are also beckoned to consider relations between Parts, as the analytic distinctions that subdivide this book should not inhibit examining the multiple and interpenetrating relationships that these categories have with other issues and concerns. Exploring a wide range of theoretical and political movements, readers are invited to find ways of creating unity without denying specificity, and becoming politically flexible without collapsing into a pluralism of indifference.

Of course the idea of "practical politics" embraced here comes with no guarantees. Identifying adversaries, articulating a clear collective agenda, and drawing new political frontiers presupposes defining the concepts of political "Left" and "Right," progressive thought and social agency, as well as hegemonic and antihegemonic sociocultural practices. In engaging with and reinventing the theories and activism presented in this anthology, readers are positioned to question whether or not these movements are progressive, reactionary, or both. Addressing this dilemma, Sangeeta Kamat, in her contribution to this project, problematizes what happens when nongovernmental organizations (NGOs), which in many respects have taken over the functions of leftist parties in much of the world, can actually keep the capitalist system going by providing limited and limiting provisions that work to subvert mass upheaval. Similarly, Anita Chan in her chapter takes up the realities of China's exploitation of labor under the old-guard articulation of communism within the new global economy.

Defining terms and teasing out contradictions in political thought and practice is especially important given the extensive history of such cases (many of which are directly addressed or touched upon in the following chapters), where feminist movements, working-class struggles, gay and lesbian groups, antiracist efforts, and antiglobalization movements have experienced exclusionary, discriminatory, and conservative tendencies; and where some struggles for national sovereignty have turned fascist, mass revolutions have become totalitarian, or social democracies have capitulated to capitalist demands.

In this effort to revitalize the dialogue about ways to radicalize democracy and democratize local and global decision-making, my working definition of *progressive/Leftist* thought and action pertains to any fight against all forms of exploitation and oppression, and any effort to democratize global technologies, environmental resources, and media, information, and financial systems. This democratizing project would include, but not be limited to, a battle against the social class structures and agenda of dominant capital, racism, sexism, homophobia and heterosexism, discrimination against persons with disabilities, and ethnocentrism.

In order to actualize the potential of this working definition, *Cultural Studies: From Theory to Action* hopes to open up dialogues that bridge the important modernist and postmodern concerns over political economy, culture, representation, and identity. As all of these points of analysis are intertwined and fundamental to democratic struggle, the objective is to transcend the inhibiting walls that have been erected between what is referred to as "real" versus "cultural" politics, and "real" versus "identity" politics.

Combining theoretical forces

Rather than limiting one's theoretical focus to either political economy (i.e., concerns over material conditions, relations of production and distribution, and political regulation), or to cultural/representational politics, which are primarily occupied with how meaning is produced, circulated, legitimated, and consumed in society, this volume demonstrates how a critical and inclusive public can effectively wage war against oppression from economic, political, technological, and cultural fronts. Readers are exposed to ways in which people come to understand and fight to transform how these categories currently organize society.

In considering how meaning, consumption, and leisure are not mutually exclusive to production, labor, and institutions, a central challenge for readers is to examine the current state of systems of production and distribution and theorize how they may complement or conflict with (or both) political and cultural logics. There are three important ways in which this relationship has already been considered.

Karl Marx argued that the material foundation of a society – with its fundamental economic structure – provides a "base" on which all other elements, which are referred to as the "superstructure," can be established: a legal system, political processes and government, religion, aesthetics and art, education, the family, and other cultural phenomena. Ideology – the ideas of a society that serve to validate the power of the ruling social class – is part of this superstructure. From this perspective, social phenomena, including social relations between classes and corresponding forms of social consciousness, have their roots in relations of production. In other words, for Marx the mode of production conditions social, political, and intellectual life. He insisted that any shifts in the economic base would have to be accompanied by shifts in the superstructure.

Louis Althusser suggests that the co-determination of economic determinants, and those that govern politics, ideology, and culture all work in the same direction and consequently "overdetermine" developments in a society. Samir Amin proposes a theory of "underdetermination" in which each of the determining factors is governed by its own logic and these factors are in a constant battle of subordinating others, or being subordinated.[13]

While readers are encouraged to consider these three positions, the intent of this anthology is not to create a hierarchy of influence or a schematic of fixed determinants that subordinate politics and culture to economics or vice versa. The approach of *Cultural Studies: From Theory to Action* is to examine moments of political articulation in order to identify the leading reactionary or transformative forces and their relationships with other social factors.

This anthology takes very seriously the material, structural, political, and cultural effects of capitalism; especially when only about 500 transnational corporations control 80 percent of global investment and 70 percent of trade, and imperialist governments in the name of neoliberalism and deregulation are applying diplomatic and military pressure on other nations in order to secure unlimited access to cheap labor, raw materials, and new areas of investment. The virtual elimination of national sovereignty in many countries makes it that much easier for invading corporate interests to smash democratic grassroots movements, environmental protections, and social policies and institutions developed to help secure the public's well being. Analyses of, and actions against, this kind of imperialism are especially important since the horrifying events of 9/11, as the United States government, guided by corporate imperatives, is using, *ad nauseam*, the words "freedom," "democracy," and "security" to continue to exploit the planet.

The chapters in Part I, *The Politics of Economic Oppression: Anticolonialism Meets Globalization*, provide theoretical and practical insights about understanding and challenging the global hegemony of neoliberalism. Samir Amin examines historical changes in the ideology of political economy; Arif Dirlik looks at the effects of, and responses to, global capitalism on the "Third World"; Zygmunt Bauman discusses the human consequences of globalization; Brook Schoepf, Claude Schoepf, and Joyce Millen reveal the horrific consequences of, and counter-measures to, structural adjustment and corporate global expansion on poverty and health in various parts of Africa; Fernanda Navarro reviews the struggles and coalitions of the Zapatistas against economic oppression and indigenous subordination; Anita Chan analyzes labor activism in communist China; Reinart Ustun covers an environmental protest in Turkey against transnational corporate exploitation; Richard Appelbaum and Peter Dreier explore the global impact of antisweatshop mobilization in the United States; and Sangeeta Kamat evaluates collective struggles to deal with neoliberalism in India.

These chapters illustrate some of the ways that it is possible to unite activists by working through a politics of location, area-specific traditions and economic interests, and overcoming language barriers. Such solidarity, as opposed to isolated localized efforts, may present the only way of combating transnational corporations that no longer need to negotiate with local labor organizations for living wages and realistic environmental protections, or with area-specific human rights groups – they just go elsewhere, leaving trade restrictions, unemployment, poverty, and political chaos in their path. In moving through the theoretical and activist moments and movements presented in this volume, readers are asked to simultaneously explore and envision different ways of organizing social relations that can work to restore the centrality of politics over the tyranny of market forces.

But political consciousness and action do not take place in a vacuum. Globalization not only consists of a structural reality built on political and economic processes and relationships, it also relies on symbolic systems to shape the kinds of meaning, identity, desire, and subjectivity that can work to ensure the maintenance of what Antonio Gramsci referred to as the hegemony of "common sense" and consent.[14] This volume thus exposes readers to the pedagogical terrain of representation and encourages theorizing about how culture shapes our sense of political agency and mediates the relations between everyday struggles and structures of power. This entails understanding culture as a pedagogical force in which the multiplicity of aural and visual signifying systems that people are inundated with everyday, through language, TV, advertising, radio, print journalism, music, film, and so on, are ideological and formative, rather than merely vehicles for expression or reflections of reality. They are the conduits through which dominant values and beliefs that work to shape how people see, interpret, and act as socialized and political beings, can be promoted.

Complementing rather than competing with Part I, Part II of this book – *Representational Politics: Making Up Your Own Mind by Minding the Popular Media* – is concerned with the political economy of the mass media, text production and analysis, and audience reception and consumption. However, this focus on language and representation does not reduce theorizing and acting upon the social world to polysemic interpretations (taking to the extreme the possibility of infinite meanings of texts that neutralizes theorizing about the cumulative effects of intended and motivated messages), or to a mere populist celebration of media culture. Instead, this section combines Robert McChesney's analysis of the political economy of global media, David Morley's critique of the pitfalls of ethnographic audience research, and Henry Giroux's examination of the power and representational ploys of Disney, with Jennifer David's discussion of the critical role of Aboriginal television, Stephen Duncombe's investigation of the rise of Zines as alternative newspapers, Kekula Bray-Crawford's exploration of using cyberspace to create subversive cultures, Richard Kahn and Douglas Kellner's look into internet subcultures and political activism, Rosemarie Garland Thomson's use of performance art to fight against the negative and imposed representations of persons with disabilities, and Johnny Temple's illustration of the role of protest music in consciousness-raising and social change.

As this volume reveals, all cultural terrain is worth fighting over. If it weren't, then colonizers and fascists alike wouldn't immediately go after schools, media, and other public spheres that produce and disseminate knowledge. As clearly expressed in the work of many of the early anticolonial theorists/revolutionaries, imperialists have always understood the relationship between knowledge and power and its central role in controlling the psyche of people, public opinion, and consequently in maintaining systems of oppression.[15] They recognized how material conditions, politics, and culture are inter-laced and how subordination, resistance, and opposition take place in both the physical and symbolic realm.

In order to interrogate dominant discourses, confront the oppressive values and beliefs that have come to inform mainstream social and political practices, and continuously forge and work to secure economic and political rights within the endless antagonisms that feed the ongoing democratic process, this anthology encourages readers to not only think about culture politically, but also to think about politics culturally. As many of the contributions illustrate, culture and politics coexist in a symbiotic relationship in which effective political mobilization can create new cultural spaces, and such transformative political movements emerge out of progressive cultural shifts.

In addition, as many of the chapters reveal, social justice movements not only encompass already existing forms of consciousness, interest, and concern, but they also actively generate political subjects once participants are engaged in the process of struggle. Readers are thus invited to explore the ways in which activists throughout this book constantly reflect upon their actions and develop new understandings that inform novel strategies and tactics. Crucial to recognize in such developments is the move to formulate more inclusive and effective political subjects and democratizing networks.

Balancing the demands of political unity and cultural diversity

Cultural Studies: From Theory to Action aspires to move beyond the walls that limit theorizing the relationships between political economy/"real" politics and "identity" politics. Identity politics refers to an exploration of the lived experiences and political responses of individual groups; for example, women, gays, indigenous populations, particular ethnic backgrounds, the working class, and so on. While these and other categories have helped to mobilize people to achieve certain civil rights in many countries around the world – rights that are currently under attack – such analytic distinctions and political bonds need to transgress the divisive, limiting theories and practical applications that they have come to engender.

A major flaw of identity politics is that it has a tendency to essentialize and thus objectify and stereotype subject positions. Essentialism ascribes a fundamental nature or a biological determinism to groups through fixed ideas about the experience, knowledge, and attitudes that they wield. The category of race, for example, from a racist point of view appears as a gross generalization and single-cause explanation for individual charac-ter and behavior. From the limited stance of identity politics, issues, concerns, and experiences based on group identification are also homogenized – of course for very different reasons. Nonetheless, such an analysis is inclined to ignore important intragroup differences and internal divisions across geography, social class, language, health, religion, age, sexuality, and so forth. On the other hand, when a politics of difference is taken to its extreme, postmodern fragmentation disarms the political subject and collapses into a form of individualism that defuses the powers of collective identity.

An additional recurring problem with identity politics is that experience with discrim-ination is often left at the level of description; that is, narratives are welcomed at the expense of theoretical analysis. Such an atheoretical posture gives the erroneous percep-tion that subject position is inherently linked to critical consciousness. In other words, when a subordinated person shares the pains of social injustice, this narration, in and of

itself, is thought to necessarily bring about the intra- and interpersonal political understanding of such oppressive acts. Peter McLaren warns of this pitfall:

> Either a person's physical proximity to the oppressed or their own location as an oppressed
> person is supposed to offer a special authority from which to speak...Here the political is
> often reduced only to the personal where theory is dismissed in favor of one's own personal
> and cultural identity – abstracted from the ideological and discursive complexity of their
> formation.[16]

Countering this tendency to conflate location and consciousness, *Cultural Studies: From
Theory to Action* encourages the kinds of critical dialogue that work to explain why it is
that something (a particular experience) occurred in the first place, so as to be able to act
upon and change the very material, political, and symbolic conditions that have given it
life.

Another major theoretical limitation that identity politics has succumbed to is the
general disregard of the influences of political economy. With the exception of social class,
other analytic distinctions are often decoupled from an analysis of the effects of economics on identity development. At the same time, identity within traditional Marxist
categories is often reduced to the "superstructural" results of the capitalist mode of
production.

Many theorists have equated Marx's work with economic determinism, where all social
and cultural processes are held to be directly reducible to underlying economic and
material relations. Limited by these theoretical walls, such a position disregards the
complexities of other interconnecting battles over identity and meaning. As Ernesto
Laclau and Chantal Mouffe argue:

> Many social antagonisms, many issues which are crucial to the understanding of contempor-
> ary societies, belong to fields of discursivity which are *external* to Marxism, and cannot be
> reconceptualized in terms of Marxist categories – given, especially, that their very presence is
> what puts Marxism as a closed theoretical system into question, and leads to the postulation
> of new starting points for social analysis.[17]

Encouraging critical appropriation and reinvention of Marxist ideas, this anthology sets
forth the position, as previously argued, that any approach to understanding and countering oppression should include a profound engagement with the interrelationships of
economics, politics, and culture, and their influence on identity development. For
example, women constitute 70 percent of the 1.3 billion people living in absolute poverty,
and two-thirds of the world's illiterate population.[18] In this case, readers are encouraged
to theorize, but not conflate, the multiple and interpenetrating relations among economics, sexism, and racism that produce such appalling statistics and existential realities. In
this way, social agency is based on an ongoing effort to grasp the politics and production
of identity, rather than on economic determinants, or fixed notions of authenticity
embedded in identity politics. Again, such an analysis would take into account the
specificities and area-specific conditions and experiences that generate different concerns
– e.g., women from various world regions frame their predicaments and responses in
different ways.

As previously stated, the idea is not to create a hierarchy of oppression that renders
insignificant certain struggles, rather the intention is to analyze political moments,
identify influential factors, and consequently develop critical responses that have both

local and global dimensions. In other words, the goal is to work towards group recognition and self-representation (allowing theoretical flexibility as such identities shift and have internal diversity), and movement interrelationships that can actually realize the redistribution of resources and the guarantee of public access and democratic rights.

From a quick glance at the table of contents, it may appear that this anthology is set up in much the same way as the traditional approach to identity politics, as the book is subdivided by capitalism and social class, race, gender, sexuality, etc. Indeed, this typology is intended to continue to identify analytic distinctions that are readily used to oppress. Instead of completely destabilizing these categories, and giving in to the infinite influences that shape subjectivity, the goal here is to still search out larger oppressive patterns of human behavior that are linked to relations of power. However, within the present plurality of antagonisms, readers are simultaneously asked to conceptualize novel approaches that bring together multiple social justice concerns, identities, and movements, so as to balance the demands of political unity and cultural diversity. The idea is to search out new forms of democratic and revolutionary identification rather than collapse into closed orthodoxies. Orthodoxies of any type inevitably lead to an extremely limited sense of community, solidarity, citizenship, and agency. By disregarding all differences in experience, opinion, and perspective, the idea of *community involvement* and *public deliberation* collapses into a paradigm of containment. Instead, this anthology embraces open-ended interaction among all people, where a plurality of perspectives based on differences, antagonisms, and dissent are experienced as productive rather than disruptive and unacceptable.

Recognizing the need for new kinds of identification, the chapters that follow this introduction were selected and assembled to reveal how different social groups are presently defining and redefining themselves as agents of global democratic change. In similar fashion to the way that Part III takes up a diversity of issues related to racism, Part IV of this book – *Gendered Identities in the Realm of Patriarchy* – examines many of the concerns, limitations, and contradictions of the women's movement so as to be able to create local solidarities and transnational feminist networks across a politics of identity and difference. Chandra Mohanty analyzes the possibilities of bringing race, capitalism, and feminism to the table for developing coalitions among women globally; Joy James differentiates between "neoconservative," "neoliberal," "neoradical," and "revolutionary" feminist theory and action; Leonie Pihama discusses the pros and cons of Maori women appropriating from Western feminists while combating both sexism and imperialism; Tahmeena Faryal, from the Revolutionary Association of Women in Afghanistan, elaborates on the effects of an Afghan women's movement in the face of internal and international conflict; Miriam Ching Yoon Louie explores the gender and social class coalitions that have developed to battle exploitation in Korean factories; and Jackson Katz presents some strategies for how men can work towards eradicating patriarchal violence against women.

Along these same lines, Part V – *Heterosexism and Homophobia: Critical Interventions* – strategically uses the analytic distinction "sexuality" while moving beyond the traditional parameters of identity politics and into the terrain of coalition-building. Dennis Altman takes up the globalization of sexual politics; Jewelle Gomez exposes her own personal struggles to reconcile the rifts between black, feminist, and lesbian subject positions; Pat Califia illuminates the much-neglected category of transgendered identity and activism; Mazibuko Jara, Naomi Webster, and Gerald Hunt explore coalition-building in South Africa among labor unions and activists concerned with sexual politics; and Doug Ireland examines the efforts of gay, lesbian, and bisexual teens to gain support from their elders.

Once again, the intention of such juxtapositionings is to have readers grapple with these works in order to recognize differences and commonalities within such struggles, critically appropriate from the theories and practices, and begin dialogues about developing alliances across issues and interests.

Some additional tools

Cultural Studies: From Theory to Action provides readers with some supplementary resources: suggested reading lists, a collection of activist organizations and web resources with contact information, and an alphabetized list of international, progressive journals.

There is an endless number of books in the areas of social theory, cultural studies, and critical pedagogy that one could spend multiple lifetimes reading. The list provided at the close of this anthology is intended to scaffold the up-and-coming reader into the bounty of works available. Included are dictionaries, introductory texts, classics, readers, and cutting-edge theoretical, research, and activist literature. Because of space considerations, fiction, while enormously important, has for the most part been excluded.

As the lists are extensive, the stars next to particular titles represent a shorter path of recommended readings. I apologize for any important contributions to the literature that are not included. Hopefully the books that were chosen will act as bridges to other existing works.

While considering possible directions that this anthology could go in, and wanting to put together a collection of work that encourages dialogue between contemporary critical social theories and progressive activist practices, I was constantly reminded that the past offers important insights into the mistakes and victories of democratic struggle. An indispensable part of praxis is to study historically significant activist movements that have worked toward social justice; for example, the Abolitionist Movement, the First and Second International, the Cuban, Mexican, and Russian Revolutions, Anarcho-syndicalism, experiments in social democracy around the globe, first- and second-wave feminism, the Situationists, the 1968 rebellions in France, the United States, Spain, Mexico, Japan, Germany and Czechoslovakia, and the revolutionary efforts of Jose Marti, Emiliano Zapata, Rosa Luxemburg, Che Guevara, Augusto Caesar Sandino, Mohandas Gandhi, Malcolm X, and Nelson Mandela. There is also much to learn from the histories of trade union revivals, labor and environmental coalitions, antinuclear-weapons activism, and the global networks that have developed in the fight against AIDS. The intent here is not to look to historical struggles as a form of nostalgia, but rather as a way to critically appropriate and reinvent revolution.

However, as the reader will note, after a brief look over the table of contents, all of the selections in this anthology (with the exception of Samir Amin's elaboration of the developments of political economy) deal with current theories, issues, and acts – that is, the chapters specifically address what people are doing at this particular juncture. Given this focus, an historical approach to social justice movements is simply beyond the scope of this book. In order to provide the reader with access to the past, the suggested readings for each section, at the back of the book, are chronologically organized to offer access to a vast history of critical social theories and activism.

The body of contemporary democratizing movements is also immense, and choosing which theories and stories to include was extremely difficult. The selections that I've made are by no means definitive, they are simply stepping-stones into the kinds of dialogue embraced by this book around the diverse ways that people struggle for justice and human rights. They also reflect an effort to speak to international issues and to be inclusive in terms of the subject positions of authors. But there is a plethora of other significant movements that should be taken up in conjunction with this edited collection: the important efforts of Mexican workers resisting exploitation in Maquiladoras, establishing child labor laws globally, the developments of the International Tribunal on Violation of Human Rights, liberation fronts in East Timor, Eritrea, Burma, Tibet, the Philippines, Puerto Rico, and Columbia, the liberatory efforts of the Kurds, the drafting of the Declaration on the Rights of Indigenous Peoples, the work of liberation theology, the African Women's Anti-War Coalition, the East Asia–US Women's Network against Militarism, environmental protests against Monsanto and other biotechnology corporations, heading off of the Multilateral Agreement on Investment, and a vast array of other revealing struggles. An extensive list of the organizations responsible for many of these important efforts and events can be located in the last section of this book – *Getting Informed, Getting Involved: Places to Turn To*.

While they are making use of all of the tools provided herein, a central question asked of readers is: Can Cultural Studies be used to effectively commit to the idea of *praxis*? In other words, how can theorizing be used as a form of social practice that inspires people to not only read the world critically, but to also act within it? It is important to be clear about the idea of *praxis* engendered in this anthology, as it is not intended to simply instigate forms of resistance – which are conscious political projects that reject existing structures of power. While resistance is important, it is not predicated here on the insuperability of systems of domination. In other words, this book is not about crisis management; the goal herein is to work towards political consciousness and short- and long-term strategies and policies directed at radical but achievable democratic change. Thus it is not simply an attempt to give in to centrist notions of reforming existing social formations and practices; rather, its intent is transformative.

This book is built on the basic premise that politics has to be done on many levels. As the tension between equality and liberty cannot be fully reconciled within a liberal democracy,[19] *Cultural Studies: From Theory to Action* invites a dialogue about what kinds of public spheres, policies, and institutional practices can be forged that move beyond mere accommodations and compromises to existing power structures. For example, can the kind of critical and creative interaction called for here be institutionalized and yet remain fluid, and if so how?[20]

This anthology is intended to better equip readers with the necessary skills to interpret, problematize, draw meaningful generalizations about, and act upon the economic, sociocultural, and political realities that shape the historical present. Indeed, the approach of this book hopes to contribute to a dialogue about what current problems exist in society, how they have evolved, and what the future holds. On the basis of this dialogue, together we can more effectively struggle to realize and radicalize democracy.

Notes

1   Hall, S. (1996). "Cultural Studies and its Theoretical Legacies." In: *Stuart Hall: Critical Dialogues in Cultural Studies*. (Eds.) Morley, D. and Chen, K. H. New York: Routledge, p. 275.

2   Freire, P. (1999). "Presence of Mind in the Process of Learning and Knowing: A Dialogue with Paulo Freire." In: Leistyna, P. (1999). *Presence of Mind: Education and the Politics of Deception.* Boulder, CO: Westview, p. 46.

3   Hall, S. (1988). "The Toad in the Garden: Thatcherism among the Theorists." In: (Eds.) Nelson, C. and Grossberg, L. *Marxism and the Interpretation of Culture.* Basingstoke: Macmillan, p. 35.

4   Giroux, H. (2000). *Impure Acts: The Practical Politics of Cultural Studies.* New York: Routledge, p. 14.

5   In the fields of business and the natural sciences, the ability to theorize about new profitable social relations and technologies is encouraged. Of course, such theorizing is disarticulated from ideological and ethical analysis.

6   See Aronowitz, S. (2001). *The Knowledge Factory: Dismantling the Corporate University and Creating True Higher Learning.* Boston: Beacon Press; Reading, B. (1997). *The University in Ruins.* Cambridge, MA: Harvard University Press; Giroux, H. and Myrsiades, K. (Eds.) (2001). *Beyond the Corporate University.* Lanham, MD: Rowman & Littlefield.

7   For an example of this, see my chapter "Veritas: The Fortunes of My Miseducation at Harvard." In: *Presence of Mind: Education and the Politics of Deception.* Boulder, CO: Westview Press.

8   Harvey, D. (1990). *The Condition of Postmodernity.* Oxford: Blackwell, pp. 8–9. It is important to note that Harvey's working definition is in part taken from the editors of the architectural journal *PRECIS* 6 (1987), pp. 7–24.

9   For a working example of this view of modernity, see Habermas, J. (1987). *The Philosophical Discourse of Modernity.* Cambridge, MA: MIT Press.

10 See for example, Adorno, T. and Horkheimer, M. (1944/1973). *Dialectic of Enlightenment.* New York: Schocken.

11 See for example, Lyotard, J.-F. (1984). *The Postmodern Condition: A Report on Knowledge.* Minneapolis: University of Minnesota Press; Foucault, M. (1972). *Power/Knowledge: Selected Interviews and Other Writings – 1972–1977.* New York: Pantheon; Baudrillard, J. (1983). *Simulations.* New York: Semiotext(e).

12 For an analysis of this manifestation in the 1990s, see McGuigan, J. (1997). "Cultural Populism Revisited." In: *Cultural Studies in Question.* (Eds.) Ferguson, M. and Golding, P. London: Sage.

13 See, Marx, K. (1859). *A Contribution to the Critique of Political Economy.* London: Lawrence & Wishart; Althusser, L. (1965). *For Marx.* New York: Vintage; Amin, S. (1998). *Spectres of Capitalism: A Critique of Current Intellectual Fashions.* New York: Monthly Review Press.

14 *Hegemony,* as derived from the work of Italian theorist Antonio Gramsci, is used to express how certain groups manage to dominate others. An analysis of hegemony is especially concerned with how the imposition of particular ideologies and forms of authority results in the reproduction of social and institutional practices through which dominant groups maintain not only their positions of privilege and control, but also the consensual support of other members (even those subordinated) of society. See, Gramsci, A. (1971). *Selections from the Prison Notebooks.* New York: International Publishers.

15 See for example, Memmi, A. (1965). *The Colonizer and the Colonized.* Boston: Beacon Press; Fanon, F. (1967). *Black Skin White Masks.* New York: Grove Press; and Cabral, A. (1973). *Return to the Source: Selected Speeches by Amilcar Cabral.* New York: Monthly Review Press.

16 Mclaren, P. (1995). *Critical Pedagogy and Predatory Culture: Oppositional Politics in a Postmodern Era.* New York: Routledge, p. 125.

17 Laclau, E. and Mouffe, C. (2001). *Hegemony and Socialist Strategy: Towards a Radical Democratic Politics.* London: Verso, pp. ix–x.

18 Basu, A. (2000). "Globalization of the Local/Localization of the Global: Mapping Transnational Women's Movements." In: *Meridians: Feminism, Race, Transnationalism* 1(1) (Autumn), p. 82.

19 For a thorough discussion of the tension between liberty and equality, see Mouffe, C. (2000). *The Democratic Paradox.* London: Verso.

20 For an interesting read on this, see Bennett, T. (1993). "Putting Policy into Cultural Studies." *The Cultural Studies Reader.* New York: Routledge.

Part I

The Politics of Economic Oppression: Anticolonialism Meets Globalization

CHAPTER 1

Samir Amin

Unity and Changes in the Ideology of Political Economy

As with all social sciences, the history of economic theory has not proceeded along a course like that taken by the natural sciences. In the natural sciences new theories – fuller, more complex, more accurate – ultimately take the place of formerly dominant theories, which are then completely abandoned. Of course, this development is shaped by conflicts among schools of thought, and sometimes the victory of a theory is but temporary. Nevertheless, as Kuhn has shown so well, the deepening of knowledge always ends up with the imposition of a new paradigm. The concept of science, closely linked to this progression, here takes on its full meaning.

Things stand quite differently in regard to knowledge of social reality, where schools of thought constantly oppose each other without ever attaining a definitive predominance. Such schools are defined by different – and sometimes diametrically opposed – conceptions of the real nature of their common object of analysis: society. And these oppositions transgress reality; they outlive all the changes in social reality itself. Of course, the best analysts in each of these schools are well aware of these changes and sharpen their observations and analytic techniques to take account of the new questions posed, but even so they always remain within the bounds of their own chosen paradigm.

This difference, then, characterizes the different status of scientific analysis in the fields of nature and society: it reminds us that human beings, as individuals and as social actors, make their own history, while they can merely observe the history of the natural world. In regard to society, science (in the sense of a respect for facts) and ideology (in the sense of a point of view justifying social conservatism or social transformation) are inseparable. And that is why I prefer to speak of "social thought" (without implying any evasion of the requirements of scientific method) rather than of "social science."

Concerning the modern history of capitalism, we have had for the last two centuries two opposing lines of argument, and never will the partisans of one of them succeed in convincing those of the other. On one side is the conservative line of discourse, which justifies the capitalist social order, and on the other is that of socialism with its radical

Samir Amin, "Unity and Changes in the Ideology of Political Economy," pp. 27–47 from *Spectres of Capitalism: A Critique of Current Intellectual Fashions*. New York: Monthly Review Press, 1998. © 1998 by M.R. Press. Reprinted by permission of Monthly Review Foundation.

critique of that order. This is not to say that they dispute in a circle, tirelessly repeating the same arguments. For the capitalism about which they argue is itself in constant evolution, and at each of its phases the requirements for its further development call for different policies. The most interesting point of view within the conservative (pro-capitalist) current is that which succeeds in justifying these necessary policies and in showing the most effective means for their implementation. On the other side of the tracks, the social problems created by this development are themselves changed, some lessening or vanishing, others newly arising or becoming intensified; the most effective point of view within the radically critical current is that which best sizes up the new challenges.

Social thought, accordingly, is always closely linked to the question of social power, either by justifying a given established system of power or by challenging it by proposing a different one. Among the entirety of conceptions making up bourgeois thought, that one which responds best to the demands posed by the particular phase of capitalist development under consideration easily wins its place of intellectual dominance; it becomes the "single thought" of the moment. In contrast, ideological pluralism tends to be the rule to the extent that the intellectual critique of capitalism relates only oppositionally to established power. Nevertheless, precisely because there was, from 1917 to 1990, a really existing system of established power claiming the status of socialist alternative, a dominant social ideology inextricably linked to the Soviet power structure was also imposed within the socialist ranks. An alternative "single thought," expressed in language inspired by vulgar Marxism, coexisted with the succeeding forms of capitalist single thought – liberal nationalist, Keynesian, neoliberal globalist – that have held the stage during this period. With the collapse of the Soviet alternative, the "single thought" of "really existing socialism" vanished. Into its place have swarmed radical critiques of a diverse scope. These have not yet crystallized into coherent alternative projects, formulated as renewed systems of critical thought that would be sufficiently powerful to give effective answers to the challenges of the contemporary world. The bourgeois single thought of the moment thus holds universal sway, without the need to share that influence as it did during the period of ideological dualism. However, this is not a new situation: dominant bourgeois thought, in the forms appropriate to the requirements of the 1800–1914 expansion of capitalism, was also, by and large, the universal single thought for each successive stage of that expansion.

Thus the dominant line of thought of capitalism is displayed as a succession of forms which, beyond the diversity of their modalities of expression, remain organized around an unchanging core of basic conceptions and methods. To point out the permanence of this hard core and to identify the real scope of the successive and varied modalities of capitalist discourse is to understand both what is permanent in capitalism and what is specific to each phase in its blossoming. Thus we can see the place of each successive "single thought" in the history of capitalist society.

The characteristic ideology of capitalism has always been economic determinist. This gives a dominant position to the subject matter of what has become economic theory. Yet this (and the autonomy that economic theory derives from it) does not fully comprise it. For it is also the product of a social and political philosophy that underlies the concept of individual freedom and defines the limits within which modern political democracy is practiced. The characteristics and contradictions of conventional economic theory flow from this ambiguous position in the ideological rhetoric of capitalism. Indeed, this economic theory is strung out between two extreme positions. At one pole its practitioners seek to construct a "pure economics" (according to their own terminology) that follows only its own self-contained set of laws, free from such dimensions of social reality as the organization of societies as nations, political practice, and state intervention. This perpetual tendency in conventional economic theory thus seeks to formulate a rigorous theory (by its own specific criteria) of how a general equilibrium is produced through the self-regulating nature of the market. But at its other pole these economists choose deliberately to put themselves at the service of the really existing power structure, in order to suggest effective actions to regulate the market and to enhance their nation's position in the world system. However, these really existing power structures are not at all identical to each other irrespective of space and time. To say that they all maintain the power of the bourgeoisie is quite insufficient, even though the statement is not false. For this power is imposed through hegemonic social coalitions specific to particular countries and historical periods, a fact which requires state policies that maintain the compromises among social classes that define such coalitions. Economic theory is then formulated in terms suited to these objectives, and stays far away from the abstract preoccupations of pure economics.

The single thought is generally expressed through successive formulations of this second type, with "pure economics" relegated to the status of academic palaver without any bearing on real life. The fact remains that at certain exceptional times – and the grounds for these exceptions demand explanation – the single thought comes close to the propositions of pure economics or even merges into them. We are currently in one of those periods.

I will not at this point hark back to the reasons why the capitalist worldview is naturally economic determinist. This characteristic follows from an objective requirement, without which capitalism cannot function: the inversion of the relation between politics and economics characteristic of precapitalist social systems so that politics becomes subordinate to economics. This objective requirement creates the space for the establishment of an "economic science" whose laws govern the reproduction process of capitalist society which really appears – and it is in this that it breaks with its past – to be determined by those laws. It is this reversal of the relationship between politics and economics that of necessity demands the formulation of "pure economic theory."

Nor will I dwell long on the history of this theory's establishment. It took place just as soon as capitalism – with the Industrial Revolution at the start of the nineteenth century – took on its completed form. It was at first expressed in a clumsy form that (as in Bastiat) represented little more than unconditional praise for the "market" – a form that Marx for this very reason rightly termed vulgar economics. Later, mathematical techniques would be used (as in Walras) to express the interdependence of markets in a theory of general equilibrium.

To show that capitalism can function (that it does function is a matter of fact) is not the sole concern of this theory, which remains the inescapable hard core of capitalist rhetoric. It is equally necessary to prove that this rational functioning answers to the expectations of individuals and peoples, which in turn makes capitalism not only legitimate but even "eternal." It represents "the end of history." Such a proof necessarily requires re-establishment of the linkage between economic theory and social and political philosophy. Economic discourse would thus be enriched to become the general discourse of capitalism, transcending the economic basis of its argument.

The relationship linking conventional economic theory to its underlying social philosophy spreads over numerous subjects. I will here deal with two of them, the theory of value and the concept of individual freedom.

The choice to base the concept of value on social labor or on individual and subjective estimation of utility is itself the result of the opposition between two concepts of social reality. The second of these choices, which became crystallized into a theory of pure economics only at a late stage, after (and in response to) Marx, defines society as a collection of individuals, nothing more. It seems to me that, despite being formulated in ever more sophisticated ways, the attempt to formulate on this basis the theorems that would allow proof both that the system functions and reproduces itself (general equilibrium) and that it simultaneously is the best possible (by maximizing individual gratifications), fails to reach its objective. But that is not what concerns us here. In contrast, the first choice, because it is based on measurable quantities, has fed into a succession of positivist depictions of capitalist reality, from Walrasian general equilibrium which has been taken up again and reformulated by Maurice Allais (in an attempt to synthesize the positive interdependence of markets with subjective valuation) to the purely positivist system of Piero Sraffa.

The positivist mentality inspiring the evolution of this current within conventional economic theory allows for the possibility of communication between the economic discourse of capitalism and that of its critics, or at least, as we will see further on, with one possible line of critical thought.

No less important is the relationship between the theory of pure economics, in all its variants, and the bourgeois philosophy of individual freedom. We here have a philosophy that was produced by the bourgeoisie both as an act of self-affirmation in the face of the ancien régime and as the basis of its own social and economic system. This system is of course not summed up by the single notion of individual freedom, although it holds a decisive position in economic theory. *Homo oeconomicus* is a free individual who chooses whether to sell his labor or refrain from work, whether to innovate or to conform, whether to buy or to sell. The exercise of such freedom requires that society be organized on the basis of generalized markets – for labor, for products, for business firms.

This principle has as a logical consequence that social reality should produce all the conditions, and only the conditions, for the exercise of this freedom – in other words, this logic rejects as irrational any association of these individuals into communities (for example, into nations), rejects the historically constituted state, and even, as we will see, rejects private property. Under these conditions all the individuals comprising the population of the planet can meet in the marketplace to negotiate their mutual relationships on terms of perfect equality, since none of them would hold a privileged position through ownership of even the smallest capital. A state/administration/bank positioned above these individuals, on a world scale of course, would be charged with managing this generalized marketplace. Would-be entrepreneurs would propose their projects for its judgment. The state/bank would lend capital to those favored by its judgment. Other individuals would negotiate the sale of their labor to these entrepreneurs, and all products would be bought and sold by fully informed participants on open markets. This logic, when pushed to an extreme, frightens defenders of capitalism, and for this reason it is rarely expressed (although Walras, like his successor Allais, did begin to give it consideration). In contrast, some social thinkers critical of capitalism found themselves comfortable with this logic. They accordingly have imagined a market that would be planned in this way so as to be perfect, unlike that of really existing capitalism – and, what is more, would be perfectly equitable because it would be based on the equality of all citizens (of a single country or of the world). This sort of socialism, of which Barone was a theoretical precursor, looks very much like capitalism – a capitalism without (private) capitalists or, more exactly, without hereditary owners of capital. But it belongs within that line of critical thought which does not call into question capitalism's inherent economic determinism (the alienated form of economic life inseparable from the market). This tendency likewise accepts the arguments of the positivist general-equilibrium analysis as expressed in labor-value terms. In this way it provided elements for the conception of what was to become socialist economic planning. We will return to this point later.

The bourgeois conception of individual freedom as accepted by pure economics (whether capitalist or socialist) is that of right-wing anarchism – hostile to the state, to organizations (including trade unions), and, in principle, to monopolies. It thus has wide appeal among small businessmen and, as is well known, was a component in the attraction of the 1920s fascist and protofascist movements for these confused sections of the middle class. But it can also turn into statism, as was the case for all historic forms of fascism. These waverings stem from the fact that "pure economics" (and the "market-governed society" inspired by it) is a utopia. It is, in reality, dependent on hypotheses that exclude all those aspects of really existing capitalism that trouble its rhetoric, such as states, nations, social classes, and global interdependencies, just as it abstracts from the exclusive ownership of the means of production by a minority, from the forms of real competition (like oligopolies), and from the rules limiting access to the use of natural resources. But reality, excluded from this ideological discourse, gets its own back and, in the end, prevails.

Behind the abstract discourse on pure market economics lurks a real, and very different, model of the market. This model, to begin with, is dualistic: integrated in its three dimensions (markets for products, labor, and capital) at the national level, but curtailed and reduced to only two of these three (markets for products and capital, but not for labor) at the global level. Accordingly, this duality manifests as conflict among nations within the global system and so compels the rhetoric of right-wing anarchism to merge into that of nationalism. Moreover, the economic determinist alienation at the source of the capitalist utopia we are discussing likewise leads to treating natural resources as mere objects of market trading, with all the consequences that follow from this reduction.

Because pure capitalism does not exist, and because really existing capitalism is not an approximation of it but an altogether different sort of thing, the theorems characteristic of pure economics are meaningless and its behavioral rules and propositions have no application. So our ideologues have to accept that contesting states and nations exist, that competition is oligopolistic, that the distribution of property determines the distribution of income, and so forth. To hold onto the rhetoric of pure economics, they extend it with proposals for concrete economic policies that allegedly meet the criteria for a "second best" optimization, even though they are nothing of the sort. These proposals quite simply express the demands of politicians at the service of interests whose very existence pure economics denies in principle: the nation, the ruling classes, or some ruling-class faction, depending on the balance of social power characterizing one or another stage in the history of capitalism.

It must thus be understood that the bourgeois single thought generally does not take on the extreme, virtually absurd, forms of the capitalist utopia. This single thought is expressed most frequently, and most forcefully, in realistic forms appropriate to concrete situations. It brings together the market, the state, and the nation to serve the social compromises needed for the functioning of coalitions among dominant class interests.

I am not going to put forward here a history of the successive forms of the capitalist single thought. I will merely consider a few of its broad features, relevant to the modern period.

From the latter part of the nineteenth century, from about 1880 – when monopoly capitalism became established in the sense given that term by Hobson, Hilferding, and

Lenin – to 1945, the capitalist single thought could well be called "monopolistic nationalist liberalism." "Liberalism" here signifies a double affirmation: affirmation on the one hand of the predominant role of markets (oligopolistic markets, to be sure) in a self-regulating economy within the structure of appropriate public policies applied during this period, and on the other hand, of bourgeois-democratic political practices. Nationalism was a regulating fact within this liberal model able to legitimize the public policies underlying competition within the global system. Those policies hinged on local hegemonic coalitions (alliances with middle-class and aristocratic strata) that backed up the dominant power of capitalist monopolies and kept the industrial working class in political isolation. Notable examples were the British and German regulatory systems, based on protection of aristocratic privilege and of Junker landholdings, and the French system, based on support to peasant farming and family-scale small business. Likewise, these alliances were generally rounded out and reinforced through colonial privileges. Electoral democracy, based on these alliances, allowed ongoing flexible adjustment of the terms for their maintenance. This model, without being statist, was nevertheless at the opposite pole from the antistate right-wing anarchist approach. The state was needed for management of the hegemonic coalition by organizing and regulating markets appropriately (for example, by subsidizing agriculture) and for directing its international competitive strategy (through protective tariffs and monetary regulation). Its active intervention in this sense was considered perfectly legitimate, even necessary. A whole world separated the single thought of that epoch from the utopia of pure capitalism. The latter's votaries could survive only by retreating into the academic world, where as always they went on accusing history of being wrong because it was unfolding without regard to the logic of pure economics. By that very fact they had no influence at all.

The monopolistic nationalist liberal single thought fell into crisis when the system it underlay entered into the crisis that began in 1914, as economic competition turned into world war. I regard its fascist deviation of the interwar period as within this same structure. Fascism abandoned the politically democratic aspect of the system, but renounced neither nationalism (which, on the contrary, it aggravated) nor the internal social compromises that bolstered the power of the monopolies. Fascist thought was thus a component, even though a sick one, of the ruling single thought of this long phase in the history of capitalism.

During this period, the liberal single thought was not based on an anarchist conception of individual freedom. To the contrary, freedom was supposed to need laws and a law-based state in order to flourish properly. Nevertheless, the notion of democracy remained limited: the rights of the individual were those guaranteeing formal juridical equality, freedom of expression, and, up to a certain point, freedom of association. But nothing more: still embryonic were the rights that later would show up (in the countermodel of really existing socialism after 1917 as well as in the later stage of capitalism after 1945) as special social rights required to give real effect to the general rights.

The liberal nationalist single thought entered into crisis when the claim of economic theory to maintain a harmoniously working society was contradicted by reality. This economic theory, which was made into a comprehensive and integrated whole (of which Alfred Marshall undoubtedly gave the fullest account) at exactly this moment in history, was "a rhetoric of universal harmonies." In substance, it claimed to prove that markets (structured through adequate public policies) were self-regulating (in the sense that their workings correct for all imbalances between supply and demand). But it was not, in this regard, limited to an abstract and general proof. It applied to all the dimensions of economic reality. For example, it presented a theory of the business cycle that filled out, by applying it concretely, the general theory of the self-regulating ability of the market. The parallel to this was a theory of fluctuations in the balance of payments that provided for automatic maintenance of equilibrium at the global level. The picture was completed by a theory of monetary management as determined by the requirement of maintaining the regulatory power of the market mechanisms.

But starting exactly in 1914, all of these promises of harmony became inoperative. Nevertheless, throughout the interwar years this single thought continued to prevail and its prescriptions, such as national protectionism, competing strong currencies, and cuts in wages and government spending in response to recession, went on being imposed. Was this a case of simple mental inertia? The answer to this question is not to be sought in the debates over economic theories but is to be found at the level of the real balance of social forces underlying the policies prevailing during this period. Until the New Deal in the United States and the Popular Front in France, the working class remained weak and isolated. Under those conditions, why indeed should capital have made any concessions to it? In the debate over economic ideas, it was specifically Keynes who indicted the single thought of the interwar period, proving that it prompted the economic policies that worsened the slump. Nevertheless, this critique had no impact on policy. It took the Second World War, which upset the balance of social forces in favor of the working classes and oppressed peoples, for its message to be understood and to become central to the new version of the single thought.

This explains why a new single thought, starting in 1945, took the place of liberal nationalism and prevailed on the world scene until 1980. Indeed, the Second World War, through the defeat of fascism, changed the relationship of forces in favor of the working classes in the developed countries of the West (these classes gained a legitimacy and status that they had never theretofore possessed), of the colonial peoples who freed themselves, and of the countries of "really existing socialism" (which I would rather call Sovietism). This new relationship is behind the threefold construction of welfare states based on national Keynesian policies, of development states in the Third World, and of planned state socialism. I would therefore describe the single thought of the 1945–80 period as "social and national," operating within the framework of a controlled globalization.

Karl Polanyi was the first to understand the nature and bearing of the crystallization of this new thought, which was to become the single thought of the postwar period. I will not dwell here on his critique of the 1880–1945 liberalism that was responsible for the catastrophe. In a frontal attack on the capitalist utopia he showed that labor, nature, and money could be treated as commodities only at the cost of the alienation and degradation of human beings, the pitiless destruction of the planet's resources, and the subversion of the government–money relationship to the profit of financial speculators. These three basic features of liberalism's irrationality were to surface again after 1980.

The dominant single thought of the 1945–80 years was thus built, at least in part, on the critique of liberalism. That is why I described it as "social and national," intentionally omitting the word "liberal" in order to underline this fact. The new single thought, often simplistically called "Keynesian," remained, of course, a capitalist way of thinking. That is why it did not make a radical break with the basic dogmas of liberalism, but merely rearranged them incompletely. Labor was still treated as a commodity, but the severity of its treatment was mitigated through the three principles of collective bargaining, social insurance, and wage increases proportional to productivity increases. Contrariwise, natural resources remained the object of systematic and aggravated wastage, which is the inescapable consequence of the absurd "discounting of the future" characteristic of "rational" short-run economic calculation (whereas what we need is the exact contrary – to give greater value to the future). Money, on the other hand, was thereafter subject to political control at both governmental and global levels. (The purpose of Bretton Woods was to maintain stable exchange rates.)

The two adjectives "social" (not socialist) and "national" express well the essential political objectives operative during this period and, consequently, the methods employed for those purposes. It was held that solidarity – which was expressed in a remarkable stability of income distribution, in full employment, and in continual increases in social expenditures – needed to be maintained on the national level through policies of systematic state intervention (described as "Keynesian" or, rather, "neo-Keynesian" policies). Reformulation of these policies in terms of (Fordist or welfarist) "regulation" allowed specification of the grounds for the validity and effectiveness of state intervention as thus conceived. Nevertheless, this nationalism, indubitable, never amounted to all-out nationalism. For it was circumscribed within a general climate of regionalization (as the building of "Europe" attests) and of an accepted, even desired, but controlled globalization through such efforts as the Marshall Plan, the expansion of multinational corporations, UNCTAD, GATT, and the organization of collective North–South discussions within the UN framework.

The basic aims of these welfare state practices were analogous to those of modernization and industrialization for the newly independent countries of the third world, which I call the Bandung project for Asia and Africa with its parallel, *desarrollismo* (developmentalism) in Latin America. We can thus characterize this single thought as dominant on the global scale, excluding only the zone of Sovietism. For the third world countries, an equally important objective was to overcome their backwardness through effective and controlled entry into a world system undergoing sustained growth.

Thus, the single thought of the 1945–80 phase was not merely an "economic theory" (that of Keynesianism and the macroeconomic management flowing from it) but was likewise the expression of a true corporate project which, though capitalist, was also "social." And within this framework, it must be understood, substantial progress was realized in regard to specific social rights that gave concrete expression to general rights. The right to work and the rights of workers; the rights to education, health, and welfare assistance; the establishment of pension and retirement funds; and the readjustment of pay scales in favor of working women – all these were always presented as the very objectives of economic growth and development. Of course, the actual achievements in these domains were uneven and generally dependent on the strength of progressive social movements.

Four decades after the end of the Second World War this model had used up its potential for expansion. It is this evolution, with its parallel in the exhaustion of the Sovietist countermodel, that lies at the origin of the overall crisis of the system which began in 1980 and accelerated throughout the next decade to end in 1990 with the generalized collapse of the three component subsystems of the prior phase (the welfare state, the Bandung project, and the Sovietist system). It was this crisis, unfolding on the level of reality, that caused the collapse of the "social and national" single thought which had been operative in the framework of the "controlled globalization" of the postwar phase. This collapse was obviously not the result of debates about "economic theory" in which "young" neoliberals (pupils of Von Hayek, Chicago-school monetarists, etc.) were opposed by "socialist dinosaurs," as is sometimes suggested by the polemicists who currently hold the stage.

The new period, which opened with the collapse of the prior phase's real-growth models, has itself not yet had enough time to become stabilized. That is why I have analyzed it in terms of "chaos" rather than a new national or global order, and why I have analyzed its practices in terms of "crisis management" and not of a new growth model.

This observation informs the description I have here put forward of the new crisis-impelled single thought. This thought, which is put forward as "globalized neoliberalism," can be more precisely characterized as a social neoliberalism, operative within globalization gone wild. By that very fact, it is impracticable, incapable of any sort of actual or full realization. Its constituent dogmas (privatization, free trade, flexible exchange rates, cuts in public spending, deregulation) are too well known to need discussion here. They cannot last because they shut capitalism into a fatal stagnation, shutting all the doors that might let it overcome the slump and begin a new growth period. I have given elsewhere the grounds for this judgment, which I share with Paul Sweezy and Harry Magdoff, namely that the single-minded pursuit of profit maximization, even were it not to clash with antisystem forces representing the aspirations of workers and oppressed peoples, would inescapably involve a structural disequilibrium in which supply exceeded demand. In other words, contrary to the pseudotheoretical dogma of capitalist utopia (the theory of pure economics), markets are not self regulating. To work, they need government regulation.

The hard choices imposed by the new single thought do not stem from some intellectual waywardness that allowed their advocates to win a theoretical debate. They are the product of a new relationship of forces, extremely favorable to capital, since the working classes and the peripheral nations have steadily lost the positions of strength they had held at the moment when fascism was defeated. The development models on which they based themselves having become worn out, the popular forces have not yet had time to regroup around new social projects that would be adequate, possible, and acceptable to them. This imbalance is at the origin of the sway of speculative capital markets, an analysis of which I have put forward elsewhere.

Though these hard choices are generally dominant in rhetorical discourse, the reality is that they are applied in a way that at times flagrantly contradicts the dogmas from which they stem. The vaunted globalization remains curtailed to the detriment of labor markets and, to an ever-increasing extent, by strengthened restrictions against immigration; rhetoric about the virtue of competition barely hides how in practice monopolies are systematically defended (as is visible in the dealings of the new World Trade Organization, or WTO); and insistence on discounting the future reduces to zero the significance of environmentalist discourse. Finally, belying their affirmation of internationalist principles, the Great Powers (conspicuously the United States) continually apply raw power in all domains, whether military (the Persian Gulf War) or economic (the "Super 301" clause in the US foreign trade law).

Of course, the new single thought and the policies following from it are directed at systematically dismantling the specific rights that had been achieved by the workers and lower classes. Given this, all its discourse about democracy is exposed as empty rhetoric, unrelated to reality. In practice, democracy based on an organized citizenry is being replaced by the right-wing anarchist utopia. Reality then lashes back through the emergence of communal, ethnic, and fundamentalist religious particularisms, confronting an ineffectual state and a disruptive marketplace.

The current single thought has no future. As a symptom of the crisis, it offers no solutions but is itself part of the problem.

The single thought of capitalist political economy has always been based on an imperialist world view, in accord with the development of capitalism which, by its very nature, has always been uneven and polarizing on the world scale. During the monopolistic nationalist liberal phase (from 1880 to 1945), imperialism was (or rather imperialisms were) synonymous with conflict among imperialist powers, in the Leninist sense. In contrast, the social and national postwar phase (1945 to 1980) was characterized on the one hand by the strategic convergence of national imperialisms under the discipline of a hegemonic United States, and on the other by a retreat of imperialism, which was forced to withdraw from the regions of "real socialism" (the USSR, Eastern Europe, China) and to bargain with national liberation movements over the terms under which it would maintain its position in its Asian, African, and Latin American peripheries. Now that "really existing socialism" and third world radical populism have met their ruin, imperialism is once again on the offensive. The "globalization" thesis proclaimed so arrogantly by the current ideology is nothing but a new way in which the inherently imperialist nature of the system asserts itself. In this sense, it can be said that "globalization" is a euphemism for that forbidden word, imperialism.

Of course, the permanently imperialist dimension of the capitalist political economy is never admitted. The material advantages associated with imperialism – notably the superprofits enjoyed by dominant capitalists – are always buried under the vaguest possible rhetoric about "international competition." Assertions about such age-old competition, which antedates the modern system of global capitalism, can mean everything or nothing. For this competition is governed not by purported natural laws (such as racial inequality) or pseudonatural laws (such as the uniqueness of cultures, or the laws of the market as alleged by economic theory), but by the strategic options of nations and peoples within the logical framework specific to each successive historical system.

Can we hope to see the reconstitution of a coherent and effective anticapitalist discourse, in confrontation with the capitalist rhetoric whose major features, expressed simultaneously in its singular character and its successive adaptations, I have outlined? I will not here try to answer this question, which goes beyond our topic. I will merely say that anticapitalist discourse is truly radical only when it deals with the basic and permanent features of capitalism, and in the first instance with the alienated nature of economic behavior. That, in my opinion, was the meaning of Marx's project.

Yet there have been partially anticapitalist discourses developed during the real history of the last two centuries, which, despite their limits, have proven effective in some ways. Without them, neither Western social democracy, nor Eastern state socialism, nor the Southern project of national liberation could have existed. These anticapitalist discourses were able to impose on the dominant sectors of capital those historic compromises which forced it to adapt to the popular and working-class demands expressed in the above-mentioned three instances. The Sovietist alternative model stemmed from this sort of unradical critique of capitalism, with the result that in reality it led to "capitalism without capitalists." But here also, as always, that evolution was not the result of a special theoretical outlook (not even though it could be considered a "deviation" from Marxist proposals) but was the result of real challenges confronting the societies at issue and real relationships of social forces marking them. As always, the theory was produced by reality, not the other way around.

CHAPTER 2

Arif Dirlik

The Postcolonial Aura: Third World Criticism in the Age of Global Capitalism

"When exactly...does the 'post-colonial' begin?" queries Ella Shohat in a discussion of the subject.[1] Misreading the question deliberately, I will supply here an answer that is only partially facetious: "When Third World intellectuals have arrived in First World academe."

My goal in the discussion below is to review the term "postcolonial," and the various intellectual/cultural positions associated with it, within the context of contemporary transformations in global relationships and the reconsiderations these transformations call for of problems of domination and hegemony, as well as of received critical practices. "Postcolonial" is the most recent entrant to achieve prominent visibility in the ranks of those "post" marked words (seminal among them, "postmodernism") that serve as signposts in(to) contemporary cultural criticism. Unlike other "post" marked words, "postcolonial" claims as its special provenance the terrain that in an earlier day used to go by the name of "Third World" and is intended, therefore, to achieve an authentic globalization of cultural discourses: by the extension globally of the intellectual concerns and orientations originating at the central sites of Euro-American cultural criticism; and by the introduction into the latter of voices and subjectivities from the margins of earlier political and/or ideological colonialism, which now demand a hearing at those very sites at the center. The goal, indeed, is no less than the abolition of all distinctions between center and periphery, and all other "binarisms" that are allegedly a legacy of colonial(ist) ways of thinking, and to reveal societies globally in their complex heterogeneity and contingency. While intellectuals who hail from one part of that terrain, India, have played a conspicuously prominent role in its formulation and dissemination, the appeals of "postcoloniality" would seem to cut across national, regional, and even political boundaries, which on the surface at least would seem to substantiate its claims to globalism.

My answer to Shohat's question is only partially facetious because the popularity that the term "postcolonial" has achieved in the last few years has less to do with its rigorousness as a concept, or the new vistas it has opened up for critical inquiry, than it does with

Arif Dirlik, "The Postcolonial Aura: Third World Criticism in the Age of Global Capitalism," pp. 501–27 from Anne McClintock, Aamir Mufti, and Ella Shohat (eds.), *Dangerous Liaisons: Gender, Nation, and Postcolonial Perspectives*. Minneapolis: University of Minnesota Press, 1997. Reprinted by permission of University of Minnesota Press.

the increased visibility of academic intellectuals of Third World origin within the area of cultural criticism. I suggest below that most of the critical themes of which postcolonial criticism claims to be the fountainhead predated in their emergence the appearance, or at least the popular currency, of the term "postcolonial" and, therefore, owe little to it for inspiration. Whether or not there was a "postcolonial consciousness" before it was so termed, a consciousness that might have played a part in the production of those themes, is a question to which I will return below. As far as it is possible to tell from the literature, however, it was only from the mid-1980s that the label "postcolonial" was attached to those themes with increasing frequency, and that in conjunction with the use of the label to describe academic intellectuals of Third World origin, the so-called postcolonial intellectuals, who themselves seemed to acquire an academic respectability they did not have before.[2] A description of a diffuse group of intellectuals, of their concerns and orientations, was to turn by the end of the decade into a description of a global condition, in which sense it has acquired the status of a new orthodoxy both in cultural criticism and in academic programs. Shohat's question above refers to this global condition; given the ambiguity imbedded in the term "postcolonial," to redirect her question to the emergence of "postcolonial intellectuals" seems to be justifiable in order to put the horse back in front of the cart. It is intended also to underline the First World origins (and situation) of the term.

My answer is also facetious, however, because pointing to the ascendancy in First World academia of intellectuals of Third World origin and to the role they have played in the propagation of "postcolonial" as a critical orientation begs the question of why they and their intellectual concerns and orientations have been accorded the respectability that they have. The themes that are now claimed for postcolonial criticism, both in what they repudiate of the past and in what they affirm for the present, I venture to suggest, resonate with concerns and orientations that have their origins in a new world situation that has also become part of consciousness globally over the last decade. I am referring here to that world situation created by transformations within the capitalist world economy – by the emergence of what has been described variously as global capitalism, flexible production, late capitalism, and so on – that has "disorganized" earlier conceptualizations of global relations, especially relations comprehended earlier by such binarisms as colonizer/colonized, First/Third Worlds, or the "West and the rest," in all of which, furthermore, the nation-state as the unit of political organization globally was taken for granted. It is no reflection on the abilities of "postcolonial critics" to suggest that they, and the critical orientations that they represent, have acquired respectability to the extent that they have answered to the conceptual needs of the social, political, and cultural problems thrown up by this new world situation. It is, however, a reflection on the ideology of postcolonialism that except for a rare nod in this direction,[3] postcolonial critics have been largely silent on the relationship of the idea of postcolonialism to its context in contemporary capitalism; indeed, they have suppressed the necessity of considering such a possible relationship by repudiating a "foundational" role to capitalism in history.

A consideration of this relationship is my primary goal in the discussion below. I argue, first, that there is a parallel between the ascendancy in cultural criticism of the idea of postcoloniality and an emergent consciousness of global capitalism in the 1980s and, second, that the appeals of the critical themes in postcolonial criticism have much to do with their resonance with the conceptual needs presented by transformations in global relationships due to changes within the capitalist world economy. This also explains, I think, why a concept that is intended to achieve a radical revision in our comprehension of the world should appear to be complicit in "the consecration of hegemony," as Shohat has put it.[4] If postcolonial as a concept has not necessarily served as a fountainhead for the criticism of ideology in earlier ways of viewing global relationships, it has nevertheless helped concentrate under one term what had been earlier diffuse criticisms. At the same time, however, postcolonial criticism has been silent about its own status as a possible ideological effect of a new world situation after colonialism. "Postcolonial" as a description of intellectuals of Third World origin needs to be distinguished, I suggest below, from "postcolonial" as a description of this world situation. In this latter usage, the term mystifies both politically and methodologically a situation that represents not the abolition but the reconfiguration of earlier forms of domination. The complicity of "postcolonial" in hegemony lies in postcolonialism's diversion of attention from contemporary problems of social, political, and cultural domination and its obfuscation of its own relationship to what is but a condition of its emergence: a global capitalism that, however fragmented in appearance, serves nevertheless as the structuring principle of global relations.

Postcolonial intellectuals and postcolonial criticism

The term "postcolonial" in its various usages carries a multiplicity of meanings that need to be distinguished for analytical purposes. Three uses of the term seem to be especially prominent (and significant). (1) It is used as a literal description of conditions in formerly colonial societies, in which case the term has concrete referents, as in "postcolonial societies" or "postcolonial intellectuals." It should be noted, however, that colonies here include both those encompassed earlier in the Third World and settler colonies usually associated with the First World, such as Canada and Australia. (2) The term is employed as a description of a global condition after the period of colonialism, in which case the usage is somewhat more abstract in reference, comparable in its vagueness to the earlier term "Third World," for which it is intended as a substitute. (3) The word is used to describe a discourse on the above conditions that is informed by the epistemological and psychic orientations that are products of those conditions.

Even at its most concrete, the term "postcolonial" is not transparent in meaning because each meaning is overdetermined by the others. Postcolonial intellectuals are clearly the producers of a postcolonial discourse, but who exactly are the postcolonial intellectuals? Here the contrast between "postcolonial" and its predecessor term, "Third World," may be revealing. The term "Third World," postcolonial critics insist, was quite vague because it encompassed within one uniform category vastly heterogeneous historical circumstances and because it locked in fixed positions, structurally if not geographically, societies and populations whose locations shifted with changing global relationships. While this objection is quite valid, the fixing of societal locations, misleadingly or not, permitted the identification of, say, Third World intellectuals with the concreteness of places of origin. "Postcolonial" does not permit such identification. I wondered above whether there might not have been a postcolonial consciousness even before it was so labeled, by which I mean the consciousness that postcolonial intellectuals claim as a hallmark of postcoloniality. The answer is: probably there was, although it was invisible because it was subsumed under the category "Third World." Now that postcoloniality has been released from the fixity of Third World location, the identity of the postcolonial is no longer structural but discursive. "Postcolonial" in this perspective represents an attempt to regroup intellectuals of uncertain location under the banner of "postcolonial discourse." Intellectuals in the flesh may be the producers of the themes that constitute postcolonial discourse, but it is participation in the discourse that defines them as postcolonial intellectuals nevertheless. Hence it is important to delineate the discourse so as to identify postcolonial intellectuals themselves.

Gyan Prakash frames concisely a question that provides the point of departure for postcolonial discourse: How does the Third World write "its own history"?[5] Like other postcolonial critics, such as Gayatri Spivak, he finds the answer to his question in the model of historical writing provided by the work on Indian history of the *Subaltern Studies* group,[6] which also provides, although it does not exhaust, the major themes in postcolonial discourse.

These themes are enunciated cogently in an essay by Prakash that, to my knowledge, offers the most condensed exposition of postcolonialism currently available. Prakash's introduction to his essay is worth quoting at some length:

> One of the distinct effects of the recent emergence of postcolonial criticism has been to force a radical rethinking and reformulation of forms of knowledge and social identities authored and authorized by colonialism and Western domination. For this reason, it has also created a ferment in the field of knowledge. This is not to say that colonialism and its legacies remained unquestioned until recently: nationalism and Marxism come immediately to mind as powerful challenges to colonialism. But both of these operated with master-narratives that put Europe at its [sic] center. Thus, when nationalism, reversing Orientalist thought, attributed agency and history to the subjected nation, it also staked a claim to the order of Reason and Progress instituted by colonialism; and when Marxists pilloried colonialism, their criticism was framed by a universalist mode-of-production narrative. Recent postcolonial criticism, on the other hand, seeks to undo the Eurocentrism produced by the institution of the West's trajectory, its appropriation of the other as History. It does so, however, with the acute realization that postcoloniality is not born and nurtured in a panoptic distance from history. The postcolonial exists as an aftermath, an after – after being worked over by colonialism. Criticism formed in the enunciation of discourses of domination occupies a space that is neither inside nor outside the history of Western domination but in a tangential relation to it. This is what Homi Bhabha calls an in-between, hybrid position of practice and negotiation, or what Gayatri Chakravorty Spivak terms catachresis; "reversing, displacing, and seizing the apparatus of value-coding."[7]

It will be helpful to elaborate on these themes. (1) Postcolonial criticism repudiates all master-narratives and, since the most powerful current master-narratives are Eurocentric, as the products of the post-Enlightenment European constitution of history, takes the criticism of Eurocentrism as its central task. (2) Foremost among these master-narratives to be repudiated is the narrative of modernization, both in its bourgeois and its Marxist incarnations. Bourgeois modernization (developmentalism) represents the renovation and redeployment of "colonial modernity...as economic development."[8] Marxism, while it rejects bourgeois modernization, nevertheless perpetuates the teleological assumptions of the latter by framing inquiry within a narrative of modes of production in which postcolonial history appears as a transition (or an aborted transition) to capitalism.[9] The repudiation of the narrative of modes of production, it needs to be added, does not mean the repudiation of Marxism – postcolonial criticism acknowledges a strong Marxist inspiration.[10] (3) Needless to say, Orientalism, in its constitution of the colony as Europe's other, in which the other is reduced to an essence without history, must be repudiated. But so must nationalism, which, while challenging Orientalism, has perpetuated the essentialism of Orientalism (by affirming a national essence in history) as well as its procedures of representation.[11] (4) The repudiation of master-narratives is necessary to dispose of the hegemonic Eurocentric assumptions built into those master-narratives that have been employed in the past to frame Third World histories. It is necessary also to resist all spatial homogenization and temporal teleology. This requires the repudiation of all foundational historical writing. According to Prakash, a foundational view is one that assumes "that history is ultimately founded in and representable through some identity – individual, class, or structure – which resists further decomposition into heterogeneity."[12] The most significant conclusion to follow from the repudiation of foundational historiography is the rejection of capitalism as a "foundational category" on the grounds that "we cannot thematize Indian history in terms of the development of capitalism and simultaneously contest capitalism's homogenization of the contemporary world."[13] (Obviously, given the logic of the argument, any Third World country could be substituted here for India.) (5) "Postfoundational history," in its repudiation of essence and structure and a simultaneous affirmation of heterogeneity, also repudiates any "fixing" of the "Third World subject" and, therefore, of the Third World as a category:

> [T]he rejection of those modes of thinking which configure the third world in such irreducible essences as religiosity, underdevelopment, poverty, nationhood, non-Westernness... unsettles the calm presence that the essentialist categories – east and west, first world and third world – inhabit in our thought. This disruption makes it possible to treat the third world as a variety of shifting positions which have been discursively articulated in history. Viewed in this manner, the Orientalist, nationalist, Marxist and other historiographies become visible as discursive attempts to constitute their objects of knowledge, that is, the third world. As a result, rather than appearing as a fixed and essential object, the third world emerges as a series of historical positions, including those that enunciate essentialisms.[14]

It might be noteworthy here that with the repudiation of capitalism and structure as foundational categories, there is no mention in the above statement of a capitalist structuring of the world, however heterogeneous and "discrepant" the histories within it, as a constituting moment of history. (6) Finally, postfoundational history approaches "third-world identities as relational rather than essential."[15] Postfoundational history (which is also postcolonial history) shifts attention from "national origin" to "subject-position." The consequence is that

> the formation of third-world positions suggests engagement rather than insularity. It is difficult to overlook that all the third-world voices identified in this essay speak within and to discourses familiar to the "West" instead of originating from some autonomous essence, which does not warrant the conclusion that the third-world historiography has always been enslaved, but that the careful maintenance and policing of East–West boundaries has never succeeded in stopping the flows across and against boundaries and that the self-other opposition has never quite been able to order all differences into binary opposites. The third world, far from being confined to its assigned space, has penetrated the inner sanctum of the First World in the process of being "third-worlded" – arousing, inciting, and affiliating with the subordinated others in the First World. It has reached across boundaries and barriers to connect with the minority voices in the first world: socialists, radicals, feminists, minorities.[16]

It will help to underline the affirmations in the above statement, which are quite representative of the postcolonial stance on contemporary global relations (and of its claims to transcending earlier conceptualizations of the world). (*a*) attention needs to be shifted from national origin to subject-position; hence a "politics of location" takes precedence over politics informed by fixed categories (in this case the nation, but quite obviously referring also to categories such as Third World and class, among others). (*b*) While First/Third World positions may not be interchangeable, they are nevertheless quite fluid, which implies a necessity of qualifying, if not repudiating, binary oppositions in the articulation of their relationship. (*c*) Hence local interactions take priority over global structures in the shaping of these relationships, which implies that they are best comprehended historically in their heterogeneity rather than structurally in their "fixity." (*d*) These conclusions follow from the "hybridness" or "in-betweenness" of the post-colonial subject which is not to be contained within fixed categories or binary oppos-itions. (*e*) Finally, since postcolonial criticism has focused on the postcolonial subject to the exclusion of an account of the world outside of the subject, the global condition implied by postcoloniality appears at best as a projection onto the world of postcolonial subjectivity and epistemology; this is a discursive constitution of the world, in other words, in accordance with the constitution of the postcolonial subject, much as it had been constituted earlier by the epistemologies that are the object of postcolonial criticism.

If postcolonial criticism as discourse is any guide to identifying postcolonial intellec-tuals, the literal sense of "postcolonial" is its least significant aspect, if not altogether misleading. Viewed in terms of the themes that I have outlined above, on the one hand, "postcolonial" is broadly inclusive; on the other hand, as intellectual concerns these themes are by no means the monopoly of postcolonial criticism, and one does not have to be post*colonial* in any strict sense of the term to share in them, for which the most eloquent evidence is that they were already central to cultural discussions before they were so labeled. Crucial premises of postcolonial criticism, such as the repudiation of post-Enlightenment metanarratives, were enunciated first in poststructuralist thinking and the various postmodernisms that it has informed.[17] Taking the term literally as "post*colonial*," some practitioners of postcolonial criticism describe societies such as the United States and Australia as postcolonial. It is pointed out that regardless of their status as First World societies and as colonizers themselves of their indigenous populations (to be fair, the latter could also be said of many Third World societies), these societies did, after all, start off as settler colonies. According to Bill Ashcroft, Gareth Griffiths, and Helen Tiffin, three enthusiastic proponents of the postcolonial idea, postcolonial covers

> all the cultures affected by the imperial process from the moment of colonization to the present day, . . . so the literatures of African countries, Australia, Bangladesh, Canada, Caribbean coun-tries, India, Malaysia, Malta, New Zealand, Pakistan, Singapore, South Pacific Island countries, and Sri Lanka are all postcolonial literatures. The literature of the USA should also be placed in this category. Perhaps because of its current position of power, and the neo-colonizing role it has played, its postcolonial nature has not been generally recognized. But its relationship with the metropolitan centre as it evolved over the last two centuries has been paradigmatic for postcolonial literatures everywhere. What each of these literatures has in common beyond their special and distinctive characteristics is that they emerged in their present form out of the experience of colonization and asserted themselves by foregrounding the tension with the imperial power, and by emphasizing their differences from the assumptions of the imperial centre. It is this which makes them distinctly post-colonial.[18]

At the same time, the themes of postcolonial criticism have been outstanding themes in the cultural discourses of Third World societies that were never, strictly speaking, colonies, and/or conducted successful revolutions against Euro-American domination, such as China. There are also no clear temporal boundaries to the use of the term because the themes it encompasses are as old as the history of colonialism. To use the example of China again, such themes as the status of native history vis-à-vis Euro-American conceptualizations of history, national identity and its contested nature, the national-historical trajectory in the context of global modernization, and even the subjectivity created by a sense of "in-betweenness" are as old as the history of the Chinese encounter with the Euro-American West.[19] One might go so far as to suggest that, if a crisis in historical consciousness, with all its implications for national and individual identity, is a basic theme of postcoloniality, then the First World itself is postcolonial. To the extent that the Euro-American self-image was shaped by the experience of colonizing the world (since the constitution of the other is at once also the constitution of the self), the end of colonialism presents the colonizer as much as the colonized with a problem of identity. The crisis created by the commemoration of the five-hundredth anniversary of Columbus's adventure comes to mind immediately. Indeed, some postcolonial critics have gone so far to claim for postcoloniality all of modern history, substituting postcoloniality as a condition for everything from imperialism to revolution. To quote Ashcroft, Griffiths, and Tiffin again:

> European imperialism took various forms in different times and places and proceeded both through conscious planning and contingent occurrences. As a result of this complex development something occurred for which the *plan* of imperial expansion had not bargained: the immensely prestigious and powerful imperial culture found itself appropriated in projects of counter-colonial resistance which drew upon the many indigenous local and hybrid *processes* of self-determination to defy, erode and sometimes supplant the prodigious power of imperial cultural knowledge. Post-colonial literatures are a result of this interaction between imperial culture and the complex of indigenous cultural practices. As a consequence, "post-colonial theory" has existed for a long time before that particular name was used to describe it. Once colonised peoples had cause to reflect on and express the tension which ensued from this problematic and contested, but eventually vibrant and powerful, mixture of imperial language and local experience, post-colonial "theory" came into being.[20]

Never mind the awkward statements about "theory" in this passage. What is important is that "postcolonialism" is coextensive with "colonialism," which not only confounds what we might mean by these terms but also abolishes any possibility of drawing distinctions between the present and the past or the indigenous oppressed and the oppressor settlers. If postcoloniality is a set of discursive attributes, moreover, there is no reason why in its extension to the past we should stop with the beginnings of modernity. Indeed, a recent work has carried this logic to its conclusion, claiming for postcoloniality all of human history, since "hybridity" and "in-betweenness" have been characteristics of cultural formation throughout![21]

In contrast, the term "postcolonial," understood in terms of its discursive thematics, excludes from its scope most of those who inhabit post*colonial* societies or hail from them. It does not account for the attractions of modernization and nationalism to vast numbers in Third World populations, let alone those marginalized by national incorporation in the global economy. Prakash seems to acknowledge this when he observes that "outside the first world, in India itself, the power of Western discourses operates through its authorization and deployment by the nation-state – the ideologies of modernization and instrumental science are so deeply sedimented in the national body politic that they neither manifest themselves nor function exclusively as forms of imperial power."[22] It excludes the many ethnic groups in post*colonial* societies (among others) who, obviously unaware of their "hybridity," go on massacring one another. It also excludes radical "postcolonials," who continue to claim that their societies are still colonized and believe that the assertion of integrated identities and subjectivities is essential to their ability to struggle against colonialism. Of particular note are indigenous radical activists who refuse to go along with the postcolonial repudiation of "essentialized" identities. When faced with this kind of challenge, some postcolonial critics are quick to forget their claims to openness and playfulness, as in the following statement by a Canadian "postcolonial critic," Diana Brydon:

> While post-colonial theorists embrace hybridity and heterogeneity as the characteristic post-colonial mode, some native writers in Canada resist what they see as a violating appropriation to insist on their ownership of their stories and their exclusive claim to an authenticity that should not be ventriloquized or parodied. When directed against the Western canon, post-modernist techniques of intertextuality, parody and literary borrowing may appear radical or even potentially revolutionary. When directed against native myths and stories, these same techniques would seem to repeat the imperialist history of plunder and theft.... Although I can sympathize with such arguments as tactical strategies in insisting on self-definition and resisting appropriation, even tactically they prove self-defeating because they depend on a view of cultural authenticity that condemns them to a continued marginality and an eventual death.... Ironically, such tactics encourage native peoples to isolate themselves from contemporary life and full citizenhood.[23]

In other words, be hybrid or die! Brydon's attitude is also revealing of the tendency of most postcolonials to take for granted the present economic and political organization of the world.

The problem of the relationship between postcoloniality and power is not restricted to its manifestations in the response to postcoloniality of people, such as the indigenous peoples of Australia or the Americas, about whose continued oppression there is little question. Intellectuals in India ask Spivak to explain "questions that arise out of the way you perceive yourself ('The post-colonial diasporic Indian who seeks to decolonize the mind'), and the way you constitute us (for convenience, 'native' intellectuals)," to which Spivak's answer is: "[Y]our description of how I constituted you does not seem quite correct. I thought I constituted you, equally with the diasporic Indian, as the post-colonial intellectual!" The interrogators are not quite convinced: "Perhaps the relationship of distance and proximity between you and us is that what we write and teach has political and other actual consequences for us that are in a sense different from the consequences, or lack of consequences, for you." They express doubts in another sense as well: "What are the theories or explanations, the narratives of affiliation and disaffiliation that you bring to the politically contaminated and ambivalent function of the non-resident Indian (NRI) who comes back to India, however temporarily, upon the wings of progress?"[24] As phrased by Prakash, it is not clear that even the work of the *Subaltern Studies* collective, which serves as the inspiration of so much of the thematics of postcoloniality, may be included under "postcolonial." I have no wish to impose an unwarranted uniformity on *Subaltern Studies* writers, but it seems to be that their more radical ideas, chief among them the idea of class, are somewhat watered down in the course of their representation in the enunciation of postcolonial criticism.[25] It is also misleading, in my opinion, to mention in the same breath as "postcolonial critics" intellectuals as widely different politically as Edward Said, Aijaz Ahmad, Homi Bhabha, and Gyan Prakash (and even

Gayatri Spivak and Lata Mani). In a literal sense, they may all share in postcoloniality, and some of its themes. Said's situation as a Palestinian intellectual does not permit him to cross the borders of Israel with the ease that his in-betweenness might suggest (which also raises the question for postcoloniality of what borders are at issue). Aijaz Ahmad, vehemently critical of the Three Worlds concept, nevertheless grounds his critique within the operations of capital, which is quite different from the denial of a foundational status to capitalism in the understanding of postcoloniality by Prakash.[26] Spivak and Mani, while quite cognizant of the different roles in different contexts that in-betweenness imposes upon them,[27] nevertheless ground their politics firmly in feminism (and, in the case of Spivak, Marxism).

Finally, examining the notion of postcoloniality in a different geographical context, Africa, Kwame A. Appiah points to another pitfall in the literal use of postcoloniality as post*colonial*, this time a temporal one. Appiah shares in the understanding of postcolonial as postmodernization, post-Third World, and postnationalist and points out that while the first generation of African writers after the end of colonialism were nationalists, the second generation of writers have rejected nationalism.[28] In a recent discussion (a response to the controversy provoked by his criticism of postcolonial Sub-Saharan Africa), Achille Mbembe hints at an answer as to why this should be the case when he states that "the younger generation of Africans have no direct or immediate experience" of colonization, whatever role it may have played as a "foundational" event in African history.[29] "Postcolonial," in other words, is applicable not to all of the post*colonial* period but only to that period after colonialism when a "forgetting" of its memories has begun to set in, among other things.

What, then, may be the value of a term that includes so much beyond it and that excludes so much of its own postulated premise, the colonial? What it leaves us with is what I have already hinted at: postcolonial, rather than a description of anything, is a discourse that seeks to constitute the world in the self-image of intellectuals who view themselves (or have come to view themselves) as postcolonial intellectuals; to recall my initial statement above, these are Third World intellectuals who have arrived in First World academe and whose preoccupation with postcoloniality is an expression not so much of agony over identity, as it often appears, but of newfound power. Two further questions need to be addressed before I elaborate further on this proposition; one concerns the role intellectuals from India have played in the enunciation of postcolonial discourse; the other concerns the language of this discourse.

Spivak comments (in passing) in an interview that "in India, people who can think of the three-worlds explanation are totally pissed off by not being recognised as the centre of the non-aligned nations, rather than a 'Third-World' country."[30] This state of being "pissed off" at categorization as just another Third World country is not restricted to Indian intellectuals (and others in India) but could be found in any Third World country (my country of origin, Turkey, and the country I study, China, come to mind immediately), which speaks to the sorry state of Third World consciousness, if there is one. It is also impossible to say whether or not Indian intellectuals being "pissed off" at such categorization has anything to do with the themes that appear in postcolonial discourse, in particular the repudiation of Third World as a category. Nevertheless, intellectuals from India, as I noted above, have been prominent in identifying themselves as postcolonial intellectuals, as well as in the enunciation of postcolonial criticism. There is nothing wrong with this, of course, except in a certain confusion that has been introduced into the discourse between what are specific problems in Indian historiography and general problems of a global condition described as "postcolonial," and the projection globally of subjectivities that are (on the basis of the disagreements among Indian intellectuals to which I alluded above) representative only of very few among the intellectuals in India. Most of the generalizations that appear in the discourse of postcolonial intellectuals from India may appear novel in the historiography of India but are not novel "discoveries" from broader perspectives. It is no reflection on the historical writing of *Subaltern Studies* historians that their qualifications of class in Indian history, their views on the nation as contested category, and their injunction that the history of capitalism must be understood not just as a triumphal march of a homogenizing capital but also in terms of the resistance to it at both the national and the local level (which rendered its consequences quite fractured and heterogeneous) do not represent earth-shattering conceptual innovations; as Said notes in his foreword to *Selected Subaltern Studies*, these approaches represent the application in Indian historiography of trends in historical writing that were quite widespread by the 1970s, under the impact especially of social historians such as E. P. Thompson, Eric Hobsbawm, and a host of others.[31] All this indicates is that historians of India were participants in the transformations in historical thinking in all areas – transformations in which Third World sensibilities were just one among a number of factors, which also included new ways of thinking about Marxism, the entry into history of feminism, and poststructuralism. To be sure, I think it very important that Third World sensibilities must be brought into play repeatedly in order to counteract a tendency toward cultural imperialism of First World thinkers and historians, who extend the meaning of concepts of First World derivation globally without giving a second thought to the social differences that must qualify those concepts historically and contextually, but this is no reason to inflate a postcolonial sensibility, especially one that is itself bound by national and local experiences, indefinitely. And yet such a tendency (for which *Subaltern Studies* writers may themselves not be responsible at all) is plainly visible in the exposition of postcoloniality by someone like Prakash who writes of Indian historiography in one sentence and projects his observations globally in the very next one.

These observations are not intended to single out postcolonial intellectuals from India, which would be misleading not only about Indian intellectuals in general but also about postcolonial intellectuals in general; the appeals of postcoloniality are not restricted to intellectuals of any one national origin, and the problems to which I pointed above are problems of a general nature, born out of a contradiction between an insistence on heterogeneity, difference, and historicity and a tendency to generalize from the local to the global, all the while denying that there are global forces at work that may condition the local in the first place. What my observations point to is a new assertiveness on the part of Third World intellectuals that makes this procedure possible. Another example may be found among Chinese intellectuals, in the so-called Confucian revival in recent years. The latter obviously do not describe themselves as postcolonial, for their point of departure is the newfound power of Chinese societies within global capitalism, which, if anything, shows in their efforts to suppress memories of an earlier day when China, too, suffered from Euro-American hegemony (though not colonialism). In their case the effort takes the form of articulating to the values of capitalism a "Confucianism" that in an earlier day was deemed to be inconsistent with capitalist modernization; this Confucianism has been rendered into a prime mover of capitalist development and has found quite a sympathetic ear among First World ideologues who now look to a Confucian ethic to relieve the crisis of capitalism.[32] While quite different from "postcoloniality" in its urge to become part of a hegemonic ideology of capitalism, it does share with the latter a counterhegemonic self-assertiveness on the part of another group of formerly Third World intellectuals. And it may not be a coincidence that Chinese intellectuals in First World academia have played a major part in the enunciation of this Confucian revival, although it is by no means restricted to them.

A somewhat different but parallel observation could be made with regard to the appeals of postcoloniality to intellectuals from settler colonies. A changing global situation in recent years has transformed earlier identifications with Euro-America in these societies to new kinds of regional affinities – most clearly in the case of Australia, which seeks to remake itself as an "Asian" society, but also in Canada, which seeks to become part of a new Asia-Pacific economy. While it would be erroneous to say that settlers earlier did not have an awareness of being colonized or lacked all identification with the Third World (witness Canada's relationship with the United States, for example), it is also misleading to erase memories of racist exclusion and oppression practiced by the settlers themselves toward nonwhite immigrants or the indigenous populations. It is difficult to escape the observation, in light of what I have written above, that in these societies "postcoloniality" serves to erase such memories – on the one hand, it allows the settlers to identify more explicitly than earlier with Third World victims of colonialism, and, on the other hand, it helps them to counteract indigenous demands for authenticity and, even more radically, for land and political sovereignty.

The second question that needs to be considered concerns the language of postcolonial discourse, which is the language of First World poststructuralism, as postcolonial critics readily concede themselves, although they do not dwell too long on its implications. Prakash's statement (which I quoted above) that "all the third-world voices identified in this essay...speak within and to discourses familiar to the 'West'" acknowledges this problem but goes on to conceal its implications in his conclusion that all this proves is that "the maintenance and policing of East–West boundaries has never succeeded in stopping the flows across and against boundaries," as if the flows in the two directions have been equal in their potency. This is important not just for the inequalities disguised by assertions of flows, hybridity, and so on. More importantly, I think, it enables us to place temporally a postcoloniality that otherwise may stretch across the entire history of colonialism. Here, once again, a comparison with China may be instructive, this time over the issue of Marxism. Postcolonial critics insist that they are Marxists, but Marxists who reject the "nineteenth-century heritage" of Marxism, with its universalistic pretensions that ignored historical differences.[33] This is a problem that Chinese Marxist revolutionaries faced and addressed in the 1930s: how to articulate Marxism to Chinese conditions (and vice versa). Their answer was that Marxism must be translated into a Chinese vernacular, not just in a national but, more importantly, in a local sense: the language of the peasantry. The result was what is commonly called "the Sinification of Marxism," embodied in so-called Mao Tse-tung Thought.[34] In the approach to a similar problem of postcolonial critics, the translation takes the form not of translation into a national (as that is rejected) or local (which is affirmed) vernacular but of a rephrasing of Marxism in the language of poststructuralism, where Marxism is "deconstructed," "decentered," and so on. In other words, a critique that starts off with a repudiation of the universalistic pretensions of Marxist language ends up not with its dispersion into local vernaculars but with a return to another First World language with universalistic epistemological pretensions. It enables us, at least, to locate postcolonial criticism in the contemporary First World.

This is not a particularly telling point. Postcolonial critics recognize that the "critical gaze" their studies "direct at the archeology of knowledge enshrined in the west arise[s] from the fact that most of them are being written in the first-world academy."[35] Rather, in drawing attention to the language of postcolonial discourse, I seek to "deconstruct" the professions of hybridity and in-betweenness of postcolonial intellectuals. The hybridity that postcolonial criticism refers to is uniformly a hybridity between the post*colonial* and the First World – never, to my knowledge, between one post*colonial* intellectual and another. But hybridity and in-betweenness do not serve very revealing purposes in the former case either. While postcolonial criticism quite validly points to the "overdetermined" nature of concepts and subjectivities (and I am quite sure that the postcolonial subjectivity is overdetermined, while less sure that it is "more" overdetermined than any other), it conveniently ignores how location in ideological and institutional structures gives direction to the resolution of contradictions presented by hybridity – and the consequences of location in generating vast differences in power.[36] If the language of postcolonial discourse is any guide to its ideological direction, in this case the contradictions presented by hybridity would seem to be given direction by the location of postcolonial intellectuals in the academic institutions of the First World. However much postcolonial intellectuals may insist on hybridity and the transposability of locations, it is also necessary to insist that not all positions are equal in power – as Spivak's interrogators in India seem to recognize in their reference to the "wings of progress" that brought her to India. To insist on hybridity against one's own language, it seems to me, is to disguise not only ideological location but also the differences of power that go with different locations. Postcolonial intellectuals, in their First World institutional location, are ensconced in positions of power not only vis-à-vis the "native" intellectuals back at home but also vis-à-vis their First World neighbors here. My neighbors in Farmville, Virginia, are no match in power for the highly paid, highly prestigious postcolonial intellectuals at Columbia, Duke, Princeton, or the University of California at Santa Cruz; some of them might even be willing to swap positions with the latter and take the anguish that comes with hybridity so long as it brings with it the power and the prestige it seems to command.[37]

"Postcoloniality," Appiah writes, "has become…a condition of pessimism,"[38] and there is much to be pessimistic about the world situation of which postcoloniality is an expression. This is not the message of postcolonialism, however, as it acquires respectability and gains admission in US academic institutions. While this discourse shares in the same themes as postcolonial discourses everywhere, it rearranges these themes into a celebration of the end of colonialism, as if the only tasks left for the present were to abolish the ideological and cultural legacy of colonialism; this sounds convincing only to the extent that, with its gaze fixed on the past, it avoids confrontation with the present. The current global condition appears in the discourse only as a projection of the subjectivities and epistemologies of First World intellectuals of Third World origin; this is another way of saying that the discourse constitutes the world in the self-image of these intellectuals: which makes it an expression not of powerlessness but of newfound power. Postcolonial intellectuals have "arrived" in the First World academy not just because they have broken new intellectual ground (although they *have* rephrased older themes) but because intellectual orientations that earlier were regarded as marginal or subversive have acquired a new respectability. Postcoloniality, it has been noted, has found favor even among academic conservatives who prefer it to less tractable vocabulary that insists on keeping in the foreground contemporary problems of political division and oppression.[39]

Postcoloniality has already been the subject of some telling criticism. Critics have noted that, in spite of its insistence on historicity and difference, postcoloniality mimics in its deployment the "ahistorical and universalizing" tendencies in colonialist thinking.[40] "If the theory promises a decentering of history in hybridity, syncretism, multi-dimensional time, and so forth," Anne McClintock writes, "the *singularity* of the term effects a recentering of global history around the single rubric of European time. Colonialism returns at the moment of its disappearance."[41] In a world situation in which severe inequalities persist in older colonial forms or in their neocolonial reconfigurations, moreover, "the unified temporality of 'postcoloniality' risks reproducing the colonial discourse of an allochronic other, living in another time, still lagging behind us, the genuine postcolonials."[42] The spatial homogenization that accompanies a "unified temporality" not only fails to discriminate between vastly different social and political situations but also, to the extent that it "fails to discriminate between the diverse modalities of hybridity," may end up in "the consecration of hegemony."[43] Rosalind O'Hanlon and David Washbrook observe that divorced from such discrimination, and without a sense of totality, "postcoloniality" also ends up mimicking methodologically the colonialist epistemology that it sets out to repudiate:

> [T]he solutions it offers – methodological individualism, the depoliticising insulation of social from material domains, a view of social relations that is in practice extremely voluntaristic, the refusal of any kind of programmatic politics – do not seem to us radical, subversive or emancipatory. They are on the contrary conservative and implicitly authoritarian, as they were indeed when recommended more overtly in the heyday of Britain's own imperial power.[44]

Postcolonialism's repudiation of structure and totality in the name of history, ironically, ends up not in an affirmation of historicity, but in a self-referential "universalizing historicism" that reintroduces an unexamined totality by the back door by projecting globally what are but local experiences. The problem here may be the problem of all historicism without a sense of structure, a web of translocal relationships without which it is impossible in the first place to determine what is different, heterogeneous, and local. In his critique of "essentializing" procedures (of India, of the Third World), Prakash offers as a substitute an understanding of these categories in terms of "relationships" but does not elaborate on what these relationships might be. The critique of an essentialist fixing of the Third World is not novel; Karl Pletsch's eloquent critique of "Three Worlds" theory (without the aid of postcoloniality), published more than a decade ago, enunciated clearly the problem of ideological essentializing in modernization "theory."[45] Further, Prakash's conceptual "innovation" (i.e., relationships) is not novel. Pletsch himself pointed to the importance of global relationships to understanding problems of development (as well as in understanding the conceptual underpinnings of modernization theory); and an understanding of modern global history in terms of relationships, needless to say, is the crucial thesis of world-system analysis.

The difference between the latter and Prakash's postfoundational understanding of relationships rests on his rejection of foundational categories, chief among them capitalism. What O'Hanlon and Washbrook say on this issue is worth quoting at some length because of its relevance to the argument here:

> What his [Prakash's] position leaves quite obscure is what this category of "capitalist modernity" occupies for him. If our strategy should be to "refuse" it in favour of marginal histories, of multiple and heterogeneous identities, this suggests that capitalist modernity is

nothing more than a potentially disposable fiction, held in place simply by our acceptance of its cognitive categories and values. Indeed, Prakash is particularly disparaging of Marxist and social historians' concern with capitalism as a "system" of political economy and coercive instrumentalities. Yet in other moments Prakash tells us that history's proper task is to challenge precisely this "homogenization of the world by contemporary capitalism." If this is so, and there is indeed a graspable logic to the way in which modern capitalism has spread itself globally, how are we to go about the central task of comprehending this logic in the terms that Prakash suggests?[46]

Prakash's answer to his critics simply evades the issues raised in this passage (while coming close to acknowledging a central role to capitalism) because to recognize them would make his postfoundational history untenable.[47] The political consequences of postcolonialist repudiation of the totality implied by metanarratives have been drawn out by Fernando Coronil in his observation that the opposition to metanarratives produces disjointed mininarratives, which reinforce dominant worldviews; reacting against determinisms, it presents free-floating events; refusing to fix identity in structural categories, it essentializes identity through difference; resisting the location of power in structures or institutions, it "diffuses it throughout society and ultimately dissolves it."[48] It also relieves this "self-defined minority or subaltern critics," O'Hanlon and Washbrook note, of the necessity of "doing what they constantly demand of others, which is to historicise the conditions of their own emergence as authoritative voices – conditions which could hardly be described without reference of some kind to material and class relations."[49]

Finally, the postcolonial repudiation of the Third World is intimately linked with the repudiation of capitalism as constituting "foundational categories" and of the capitalist structuring of the modern world. Once again, essentialism serves as a straw man, diverting attention from radical conceptualizations of the Third World, which are not essentialist but relational, as in world-system approaches. The latter comprehends the Third World as a structural position within a capitalist world order – a position that changes with changing structural relationships – rather than "fixing" it ahistorically, as Prakash would have it. To be sure, world-system analysis is as discursive in its location of the Third World as one based on modernization, but, as I have argued above, so is post-colonialist analysis. The question then becomes one of the ability of competing discourses to account for historical changes in global relationships and the oppositional practices to which they point. I will say more on the former below. As for oppositional practices, postcoloniality by its very logic permits little beyond local struggles and, without reference to structure or totality, directionless ones at that. For all its contradictions, Shohat writes, "'Third World' usefully evokes structural commonalities of struggles. The invocation of the 'Third World' implies a belief that the shared history of neo/colonialism and internal racism form[s] sufficient common ground for alliances among . . . diverse peoples. If one does not believe or envision such commonalities, then indeed the term 'Third World' should be discarded."[50]

The denial to capitalism of "foundational" status is also revealing of a culturalism in the postcolonialist argument that has important ideological consequences. This involves the issue of Eurocentrism. Without capitalism as the foundation for European power and the motive force of its globalization, Eurocentrism would have been just another ethnocentrism (comparable to any other ethnocentrism from the Chinese and the Indian to the most trivial tribal solipsism). An exclusive focus on Eurocentrism as a cultural or ideological problem, which blurs the power relationships that dynamized it and endowed it with hegemonic persuasiveness, fails to explain why this particular ethnocentrism was able to define modern global history, and itself as the universal aspiration and end of that history, in contrast to the regionalism or localism of other ethnocentrisms. By throwing the cover of culture over material relationships, as if the one had little to do with the other, such a focus diverts the task of criticism from the criticism of capitalism to the criticism of Eurocentric ideology, which helps disguise its own ideological limitation but also, ironically, provides an alibi for inequality, exploitation, and oppression in their modern guises under capitalist relationships. I will say more below on the contemporary circumstances of capitalism that enable such a separation of capitalism from Eurocentrism (the deterritorialization of capital under global capitalism). Suffice it to note here that the postcolonialist argument projects upon the past the same mystification of the relationship between power and culture that is characteristic of the ideology of global capitalism – of which it is a product.

These criticisms, however vehement on occasion, do not necessarily indicate that postcolonialism's critics deny to it all value; indeed, critics such as Coronil, McClintock, and Shohat explicitly acknowledge some value to the issues raised by postcolonialism and postcolonial intellectuals. There is no denying, indeed, that "postcolonialism" is expressive of a current crisis in the conceptualization of the world – not just a crisis in the ideology of linear progress but a crisis in the modes of comprehending the world associated with such concepts as the "Third World" and the "nation-state." Nor is it to be denied that as the global situation has become blurred with the disappearance of socialist states, the emergence of important differences economically and politically among so-called Third World societies, and the diasporic motions of populations across national and regional boundaries, fragmentation of the global into the local has emerged into the foreground of historical and political consciousness. Crossing national, cultural, class, gender, and ethnic boundaries, moreover, with its promise of a genuine cosmopolitanism, is appealing in its own right.

Within the institutional site of the First World academy, fragmentation of earlier metanarratives appears benign (except to hidebound conservatives) because of its promise of more democratic, multicultural, and cosmopolitan epistemologies. In the world outside the academy, however, it shows in murderous ethnic conflict; continued inequality between societies, classes, and genders; and the absence of oppositional possibilities that, always lacking in coherence, are rendered even more impotent than earlier by the fetishization of difference, fragmentation, and so on.

The predicament to which this gap points is rendered more serious in the confounding of ideological metanarratives with actualities of power – that is, mistaking fragmentation in one realm with fragmentation in the other, ignoring the possibility that ideological fragmentation may represent not the dissolution of power but rather its further concentration. It is necessary, to account for this possibility, to retain a sense of structure and totality in the confrontation of fragmentation and locality; the alternative to this may be complicity in the consolidation of hegemony in the very process of questioning it. "Postcoloniality," while it represents an effort at adjusting to a changing global situation, for the same reason appears as an exemplary illustration of this predicament. Critics have hinted at its possible relationship to a new situation in the capitalist transformation of the world without examining this relationship at length. I would like to look at this relationship more closely.

David Harvey and Fredric Jameson, among others, perceive a relationship between postmodernism and a new phase in the development of capitalism that has been described variously as late capitalism, flexible production or accumulation, disorganized capitalism, or global capitalism.[51] I would like to suggest here that as a progeny of postmodernism, postcolonialism is also expressive of the "logic" of this phase of capitalism, this time on Third World terrain.

First, fundamental to the structure of the new global capitalism (the term I prefer) is what F. Frobel and others have described as "a new international division of labor": in other words, the transnationalization of production whereby, through subcontracting, the process of production (of the same commodity even) is globalized.[52] The international division of labor in production may not be entirely novel, but new technologies have expanded the spatial extension of production, as well as its speed, to an unprecedented level. These same technologies have endowed capital and production with unprecedented mobility, so that the location of production seems to be in a constant state of change, seeking for maximum advantage for capital against labor, as well as to avoid social and political interference (hence, flexible production). For these reasons, analysts of capitalism perceive in global capitalism a qualitative difference from similar practices earlier – and a new phase of capitalism.

Second, there is the "decentering" of capitalism nationally. In other words, it is increasingly difficult to point to any nation or region as the center of global capitalism. More than one analyst (in a position of power) has found an analogue to the emerging organization of production in the northern European Hanseatic League of the early modern period – that is, the period before the emergence of nation-states (one of these analysts described the new situation as a "high-tech Hanseatic League"); in other words, this is a network of urban formations, without a clearly definable center, whose links to one another are far stronger than their relationships to their immediate hinterlands.[53]

Third, the medium linking this network is the transnational corporation, which has taken over from national markets as the locus of economic activity – not just as a passive medium for the transmission of capital, commodities, and production but as a determinant of the transmission and its direction. In other words, while the analogy with the Hanseatic League suggests decentralization, production is heavily concentrated – behind this facade – in the corporation. One articulate spokesman for the new economic order suggests that when it comes to decision making regarding production, the corporation has roughly 70 percent of the say-so, and the market has roughly 30 percent.[54] With power lodged in transnational corporations, which by definition transcend nations in organization and/or loyalty, the power of the nation-state to regulate the economy internally is constricted, while global regulation (and defense) of the economic order emerges as a major task. This is manifested not only in the proliferation of global organizations but also in efforts to organize extranational regional organizations to give coherence to the functioning of the economy.[55]

Fourth, the transnationalization of production is the source at once of unprecedented unity globally and of unprecedented fragmentation (in the history of capitalism). The homogenization of the globe economically, socially, and culturally is such that Marx's predictions of the nineteenth century, premature for his time, finally seem to be on the point of vindication. At the same time, however, there is a parallel process of fragmentation at work – globally, in the disappearance of a center to capitalism and, locally, in the fragmentation of the production process into subnational regions and localities. As supranational regional organizations, such as the European Economic Community, the Pacific Basin Economic Community, and the North American Free Trade Zone (to mention some that have been realized or are the objects of intense organizational activity), manifest this fragmentation at the global level, localities within the same nation competing with one another to place themselves in the pathways of transnational capital represent it at the most basic local level. Nations, themselves, it is arguable, represented attempts historically to contain fragmentation, but under attack from the outside (transnational organization) and the inside (subnational economic regions and localities), it is not quite clear how this new fragmentation is to be contained.[56]

A fifth important (perhaps the most important) consequence of the transnationalization of capital may be that for the first time in the history of capitalism, the capitalist mode of production appears as an authentically global abstraction, divorced from its historically specific origins in Europe. In other words, the narrative of capitalism is no longer a narrative of the history of Europe, so that, for the first time, non-European capitalist societies make their own claims on the history of capitalism. Corresponding to economic fragmentation, then, is cultural fragmentation or, to put it in its positive guise, "multiculturalism." The most dramatic instance of this new cultural situation may be the recent effort to appropriate capitalism for the so-called Confucian values of East Asian societies, which is a reversal of a long-standing conviction (in Europe and East Asia) that Confucianism was historically an obstacle to capitalism. I think it is arguable that the apparent end of Eurocentrism is an illusion, because capitalist culture as it has taken shape has Eurocentrism built into the very structure of its narrative, which may explain why even as Europe and the United States lose their domination of the capitalist world economy, culturally European and American values retain their domination. It is noteworthy that what makes something like the East Asian Confucian revival plausible is not its offer of alternative values to those of Euro-American origin but its articulation of native culture into a capitalist narrative. Having said this, it is important to reiterate nevertheless that the question of world culture has become much more complex than in earlier phases of capitalism. The fragmentation of space and its consequences for Eurocentrism also imply a fragmentation of the temporality of capitalism: the challenge to Eurocentrism, in other words, means that it is possible to conceive of the future in ways other than those based on Euro-American political and social models. Here, once again, it is difficult to distinguish reality from illusion, but the complexity is undeniable.

Finally, the transnationalization of production calls into question earlier divisions of the world into First, Second, and Third Worlds. The Second World, the world of socialism, is, for all practical purposes, of the past. But the new global configuration also calls into question the distinctions between the First and Third Worlds. Parts of the earlier Third World are today on the pathways of transnational capital and belong in the "developed" sector of the world economy. Likewise, ways of life in those parts of the First World marginalized in the new global economy are hardly distinguishable from what used to be viewed as Third World ways of life. It may not be fortuitous that the North–South distinction has gradually taken over from the earlier division of the globe into the three worlds, so long as we remember that "North" and "South" designate not merely concrete geographic locations but also metaphorical referents: "North" denoting the pathways of transnational capital; "South" denoting the marginalized populations of the world, regardless of their location (which is where "postcoloniality" comes in!).

Ideologues of global capital have described this condition as "global regionalism" or "global localism," adding quickly, however, that global localism is 70 percent global and only 30 percent local.[57] They have also appropriate for capital the radical ecological slogan, "Think globally, act locally."[58]

The situation created by global capitalism helps explain certain phenomena that have become apparent over the last two to three decades, but especially since the 1980s: global motions of peoples (and, therefore, cultures), the weakening of boundaries (among societies, as well as among social categories), the replications in societies internally of inequalities and discrepancies once associated with colonial differences, simultaneous homogenization and fragmentation within and across societies, the interpenetration of the global and the local, and the disorganization of a world conceived in terms of "three worlds" or nation-states. Some of these phenomena have also contributed to an appearance of equalization of differences within and across societies as well as of democratization within and between societies. What is ironic is that the managers of this world situation themselves concede the concentration of power in their (or their organizations') hands as well as their manipulation of peoples, boundaries, and cultures to appropriate the local for the global, to admit different cultures into the realm of capital only to break them down and remake them in accordance with the requirements of production and consumption, and even to reconstitute subjectivities across national boundaries to create producers and consumers more responsive to the operations of capital. Those who do not respond and the basket cases that are not essential to those operations – four-fifths of the global population by these managers' count – need not be colonized; they are simply marginalized. The new "flexible production" has made it no longer necessary to utilize explicit coercion against labor, at home or abroad (in colonies); those peoples or places that are not responsive to the needs (or demands) of capital or that are too far gone to respond "efficiently" simply find themselves out of its pathways. And it is now easier even than in the heyday of colonialism or modernization theory to say convincingly: "It's their own fault."

I began this essay with Shohat's question, "When exactly...does the 'post-colonial' begin?" I can now give it a less facetious answer consistent with her intention: It begins with the emergence of global capitalism, not in the sense of an exact coincidence in time, but in the sense that the one is a condition for the other.

There is little that is remarkable about this conclusion, which is but an extension to postcolonialism of the relationship Harvey and Jameson have established between postmodernism and developments within capitalism. If postcolonialism is a progeny of postmodernism, then these developments within capitalism are also directly or indirectly pertinent to understanding postcolonialism. Postcolonial critics readily concede the debt they owe to postmodernist poststructuralist thinking; indeed, their most original contribution would seem to lie in their rephrasing of older problems in the study of the Third World in the language of poststructuralism. What is remarkable, therefore, is not my conclusion here but that a consideration of the relationship between postcolonialism and global capitalism should be absent from the writings of postcolonial intellectuals; this is all the more remarkable because this relationship is arguably less abstract and more direct than any relationship between global capitalism and postmodernism, since it pertains not just to cultural/epistemological but to social and political formations.

Postcoloniality represents a response to a genuine need: the need to overcome a crisis of understanding produced by the inability of old categories to account for the world. The metanarrative of progress that underlies two centuries of thinking first in Europe and then globally with the expansion of Europe is in deep crisis; this is not just because of a loss of faith in progress or because of its disintegrative effects in actuality but more importantly because over the last decade in particular our sense of time has been jumbled up: as conservatism has become "revolutionary" (the "Reagan revolution") while revolutionaries have turned first into conservatives and then into reactionaries (as in formerly socialist countries such as the Soviet Union and China); as religious millenarianisms long thought to be castaways from the Enlightenment have made a comeback into politics, sometimes allied to high-tech revolutions, as in the United States; and as fascism has been reborn out of the ashes of communist regimes. The crisis of progress has brought in its wake a crisis of modernization, more in its Marxist than its bourgeois guise, and has called into question the structure of the world as conceived by modernizationists and radicals alike in the decades after World War II: that is, the structure of "the Three Worlds." The Three Worlds as fixed in social theory (bourgeois or Marxist) geographically or structurally are indeed no longer tenable, as the globe has become as jumbled up spatially as the ideology of progress is temporally: with the appearance of Third Worlds in the First World and First Worlds in the Third; with the diasporas of people that have relocated the self there and the other here, and the consequent confounding of borders and boundaries; and with the culture flows that have been at once homogenizing and heterogenizing, where some groups share in a common global culture regardless of location even as they are alienated from the culture of their "hinterlands," and others are driven back into cultural legacies long thought to be residual, to take refuge in cultural havens that are as far apart from one another as at the origins of modernity – even though they may be watching the same television shows.

Politically speaking, the Second and the Third Worlds have been the major casualties of this crisis. The Second World, the world of socialist states, is already, to put it bluntly, "history." What has happened to the Third World (the immediate subject of "postcoloniality") may be less apparent but no less significant. We may note here that the two major crises of the early 1990s that are global in implication are the crises occasioned by Iraq's invasion of Kuwait and the situation in Somalia. In the Gulf crisis, a Third World country appeared as the imperialist culprit against a neighbor (a socially and politically reactionary but economically powerful neighbor) and had to be driven back by the combined armies of the First, Second, and the Third Worlds, led by an imperial power now turned into a paradigm of righteousness. The "invasion" (I borrow the word from a television report) of Somalia, if anything, was more revealing: if in the case of the Gulf crisis one "Third World" country had to be saved from another, in Somalia a Third World country had to be saved from itself. The Third World, viewed by radicals only two decades ago as a hope for the future, now has to be saved from itself. The crisis could not get much deeper.

"Postcoloniality" addresses this situation of crisis that eludes understanding in terms of older conceptualizations,[59] which may explain why it should have created immediate "ferment" in intellectual circles. But this still begs the questions of Why now? and Why has it taken the intellectual direction it has? After all, there is more than one conceptual way out of a crisis, and we must inquire why this particular way has acquired immediate popularity – in First World institutions. To put it bluntly, postcoloniality is designed to *avoid* making sense of the current crisis and, in the process, to cover up the origins of postcolonial intellectuals in a global capitalism of which they are not so much victims as beneficiaries.

Postcoloniality resonates with the problems thrown up by global capitalism. As the crisis of the Third World became inescapably apparent during the 1980s, so did the effects of global capitalism: the Reagan (and Thatcher) revolution was not so much a revolution heralding a new beginning as a revolution aimed at reorganizing the globe politically so as to give free reign to a global capitalism straining against the harness of political restrictions that limited its motions. The overthrow of socialist states was one part of the program. Another part was taming the Third World, if necessary by invasion, preferably by encirclement: economically or by "Patriot" missiles. But these are at best options of the last resort. By far the best option is control from the inside: through the creation of classes amenable to incorporation into or alliance with global capital.

I use "control" here advisedly; under conditions of global capitalism, control is not to be imposed: it has to be negotiated. Transnational capital is no longer just Euro-American, and neither is modernity just Euro-American modernity. The complicated social and cultural composition of transnational capitalism makes it difficult to sustain a simple equation between capitalist modernity and Eurocentric (and partiarchal) cultural values and political forms. Others who have achieved success within the capitalist world-system demand a voice for their values within the culture of transnational capital; the East Asian Confucian revival to which I referred above is exemplary of this phenomenon. Eurocentrism, as the very condition for the emergence of these alternative voices, retains its cultural hegemony; but it is more evident than ever before that, in order for this hegemony to be sustained, its boundaries must be rendered more porous than earlier, to absorb in its realm alternative cultural possibilities that might otherwise serve as sources of destructive oppositions – the mutual "bashing" between Japan and the United States in recent years, which revives racist and Orientalist vocabulary, attests to the dangers of conflict among the very ranks of transnational capital. And who knows, in the end, what values are most functional to the needs of a changing "capital"? Commentator after commentator has remarked in recent years that the "communitarian" values of "Confucianism" may be more suitable to a contemporary managerial capitalism than the individualistic values of an entrepreneurial capitalism of an earlier day. What is clear is that global capitalism is (and must be) much more fluid culturally than a Eurocentric capitalism.

This is also the condition of postcoloniality and the cultural moves associated with it. Obscurantist conservatives, anxious to explain away cultural problems by substituting the machinations of subversives for systemic analysis, attribute the cultural problems that became apparent in the 1980s (most recently, multiculturalism) to the invasion of academic institutions (and politics in general) by Marxists, feminists, ethnics, and so on. What they ignore is the possible relationship between the Reagan economic revolution and these cultural developments – in other words, the cultural requirements of transnational corporations that, in their very globalism, can no longer afford the cultural parochialism of an earlier day. Focusing on "liberal arts" institutions, they conveniently overlook how much headway multiculturalism has made in business schools and among the managers of transnational corporations, who are eager all of a sudden to learn about the secrets in "Oriental" philosophies that might explain the East Asian economic success, who cannibalize cultures all over the world in order better to market their commodities, and who have suddenly become aware of a need to "internationalize" academic institutions (which often takes the form not of promoting scholarship in a conventional sense but rather of "importing" and "exporting" students and faculty). While in an earlier day it might have been Marxist and feminist radicals, with the aid of the few ethnics, who spearheaded multiculturalism, by now the initiative has passed into the hands of "enlightened" administrators and trustees who are quite aware of the "manpower" needs of the new economic situation. Much less than a conflict between conservatives and radicals (although that, too, is there, obviously), the conflict shapes up now as one between an older elite (and a small-business sector threatened from the inside and the outside) and the elite vanguard of international business. The *Harvard Business Review* is one of the foremost and earliest (in the United States) advocates of transnationalism – and multiculturalism.

The Reaganites may have been misled by visions of many Dinesh D'Souzas, who were not forthcoming. Their failure to grasp the social and political consequences of the economic victory for transnationalism they had engineered became apparent during the 1992 elections when, against the calls from right-wingers for a return to such "native" American values as Eurocentrism, patriarchalism, and racism, George Bush often looked befuddled, possibly because he grasped much better than right-wingers such as Pat Buchanan the dilemmas presented by the victory of transnationalism over all its competitors in the Second and Third Worlds. The result has been the victory of high-tech yuppies who are much better attuned to the new world situation and aware of the difficulties it presents. It is no coincidence that Robert Reich, frequent contributor to the *Harvard Business Review*, keen analyst of developments within the capitalist world economy, and an advocate of the "borderless economy," is a close confidant of President Clinton.

This is also the context for the emergence of postcoloniality and its rapid success in academic institutions as a substitute for earlier conceptualizations of the world. Postcoloniality, in the particular direction it has taken as a discourse, also resonates with the problems of the contemporary world. It addresses issues that, while they may have been issues all along in global studies, are now rephrased in such a way that they are in tune with issues in global capitalism: Eurocentrism and its relationship to capitalism; the kind of modernity that is relevant to a postmodern/postsocialist post-Third World situation; the place of the nation in development; the relationship between the local and the global; the place of borders and boundaries in a world where capital, production, and peoples are in constant motion; the status of structures in a world that more than ever seems to be without recognizable structure; interpenetrations and reversals between the different "worlds"; borderland subjectivities and epistemologies (hybridity); homogeneity versus heterogeneity; and so forth.

Postcoloniality, however, is also appealing because it disguises the power relations that shape a seemingly shapeless world and contributes to a conceptualization of that world that, while functional for the consolidation of hegemony, is also subversive of possibilities of resistance. Postcolonial critics have engaged in valid criticism of past forms of ideological hegemony but have had little to say about its contemporary figurations. Indeed, in their simultaneous repudiation of structure and affirmation of the local in problems of oppression and liberation, they have mystified the ways in which totalizing structures persist in the midst of apparent disintegration and fluidity. They have rendered concrete and material problems of the everyday world into problems of subjectivity and epistemology. Because capital in its motions continues to structure the world, refusing "foundational" status to capital renders impossible the "cognitive mapping" that must be the point of departure for any practice of resistance, while any cognitive mapping there is remains in the domain of those who manage the capitalist world economy.[60] Indeed, in projecting the current state of conceptual disorganization upon the colonial past, postcolonial critics have also deprived colonialism of any but local logic, so that the historical legacy of colonialism (in an Iraq or a Somalia or, for that matter, any Third World society) appears irrelevant to the present, which shifts the burden of persistent problems on to the victims themselves.

"Postcoloniality," Appiah writes, "is the condition of what we might ungenerously call a *comprador* intelligentsia."[61] I think this is missing the point because the world situation that justified the term *comprador* no longer exists. I would suggest, rather, that postcoloniality is the condition of the intelligentsia of global capitalism. Ahmad is closer to the mark when he states, with characteristic bluntness, that "post-coloniality is . . . like most things, a matter of class."[62] While the statement is not entirely fair in ignoring that postcoloniality also has its appeals for many among the oppressed who would rather forget past oppression in order to be able to live in the present,[63] it is an uncompromising reminder nevertheless of the continued importance, albeit reconfigured on a global basis, of class relations in understanding contemporary cultural developments. The question, then, is not whether or not this global intelligentsia can (or should) return to national loyalties but whether or not, in recognition of its own class position in global capitalism, it can generate a thoroughgoing criticism of its own ideology and formulate practices of resistance against the system of which it is a product.

Notes

My being (more or less) one of the Third World intellectuals in the First World academy does not privilege the criticism of postcolonial intellectuals that I offer below, but it does call for some comment. It is not clear to me how important the views I discuss (or the intellectuals who promote them) are in their impact on contemporary intellectual life. "Postcolonial" has been entering the vocabulary of academic programs in recent years, and there have been a number of conferences/symposia inspired by this vocabulary ("Postcolonialism," "After Orientalism," etc.), as well as special issues devoted to the subject in periodicals such as *Social Text* and *Public Culture*. Given the small number of intellectuals directly concerned with "postcoloniality" and the diffuseness in their use of the term, it might make more sense to study the reception of the term. What makes it important to study as a concept, I argue in this essay, is that the ideas associated with postcoloniality are significant and widespread as concerns, even if they predate in their emergence the appearance of the term "postcolonial" itself. It is not the importance of these ideas that I question, in other words, but their appropriation for "postcoloniality." Meanwhile, a "Third World" sensibility and mode of perception have become increasingly visible in cultural discussions over the last decade. I myself share in the concerns (and even some of the viewpoints) of "postcolonial intellectuals," though from a somewhat different perspective than those who describe themselves as such; this is evident most recently in my *After the Revolution: Waking to Global Capitalism* (Hanover, NH: University of New England Press for Wesleyan University Press, 1994).

For their assistance with sources/comments, I would like to thank the following, while relieving them of any complicity in my views: Harry Harootunian, Roxann Prazniak, Rob Wilson, and Zhang Xudong. The present essay is a slightly revised version (to take account of recent literature) of an essay that was published first in *Critical Inquiry* 20:2 (winter 1994): 328–56. Since the essay was first published, I have had occasion to discuss the ideas in it in seminars at Duke University, the University of California at Santa Cruz, the University of Hawaii, Washington University in St. Louis, and the Humanities Institute at Stony Brook. It would be impossible to name the participants in these various seminars. I extend my gratitude to them all.

1 Ella Shohat, "Notes on the 'Post-colonial'" *Social Text* 31/32 (1992): 103.
2 In 1985, Gayatri Chakravorty Spivak insisted in an interview that she did not belong to the "top level of the United States Academy" because she taught in the South and the Southwest whereas "the cultural elite in the United States inhabit the Northeastern seaboard or the West coast." See Gayatri Chakravorty Spivak, *The Post-colonial Critic: Interviews, Strategies, Dialogues*, ed. Sarah Harasym (New York: Routledge, 1990), 114. Since then Professor Spivak has moved to the northeastern seaboard.

3 Ibid., *Passim*. See also Arjun Appadurai, "Global Ethnoscapes: Notes and Queries for a Transnational Anthropology," in Richard G. Fox ed., *Recapturing Anthropology: Working in the Present* (Santa Fe: School of American Research Press, 1991), 191–210. Aijaz Ahmad, whom I do not include among the postcolonial critics here, does an excellent job of relating the problems of postcoloniality to contemporary capitalism, if only in passing and somewhat differently from what I undertake in this essay. See his "Jameson's Rhetoric of Otherness and the 'National Allegory,'" *Social Text* 17 (fall 1987): 3–25 and his more recent book *In Theory: Classes, Nations, Literatures* (London: Verso Books, 1992).

4 Shohat, "Notes," 110.

5 Gyan Prakash, "Writing Post-Orientalist Histories of the Third World: Perspectives from Indian Historiography," *Comparative Studies in Society and History* 32:2 (1990): 383.

6 Ibid., 399. See also Gayatri Chakravorty Spivak, "Subaltern Studies: Deconstructing Historiography," in Ranajit Guha and Gayatri Chakravorty Spivak, eds., *Selected Subaltern Studies* (New York: Oxford University Press, 1988), 3–32.

7 Gyan Prakash, "Postcolonial Criticism and Indian Historiography," *Social Text* 31/32 (1992): 8. I use Prakash's discussions of postcoloniality as my point of departure here because he has made the most systematic attempts at accounting for the concept and also because his discussions bring to the fore the implications of the concept for historical understanding. As this statement reveals, Prakash himself draws heavily for inspiration on the characteristics of postcolonial consciousness delineated by others, especially Homi Bhabha, who has been responsible for the prominence in discussions of postcoloniality of the vocabulary of "hybridity" and other terms. Bhabha's work, however, is responsible for more than the vocabulary of postcolonialism, as he has proved himself to be something of a master of political mystification and theoretical obfuscation, of a reduction of social and political problems to psychological ones, and of the substitution of poststructuralist linguistic manipulation for historical and social explanation – which show up in much postcolonial writing, but rarely with the same virtuosity (and incomprehensibility) that he brings to it. For some of his more influential writings, see "Of Mimicry and Man: The Ambivalence of Colonial Discourse," *October* 28 (1984): 125–33; "The Comment to Theory," in Jim Pines and Paul Willemen, eds., *Questions of Third World Cinema* (London: BFI, 1989), 111–32; "The Other Question: Difference, Discrimination and the Discourse of Colonialism," in F. Barker et al., eds., *Literature, Politics and Theory* (New York: Methuen, 1986), 148–72; his essays in Homi Bhabha, ed., *Nation and Narration* (New York: Routledge, 1990); and, most recently, *The Location of Culture* (New York: Routledge, 1994). Bhabha may be exemplary of the Third World intellectual who has been completely reworked by the language of First World cultural criticism. This is not to deny, to rephrase what I said above, his enormous linguistic talents, which may be inseparable from his conviction to the priority of language, his conversion of material problems into metaphorical ones, and his apparent concern for aesthetic playfulness over clarity in his writing.

8 Prakash, "Post-Orientalist Histories," 393.

9 Ibid., 395. See also Dipesh Chakrabarty, "Post-coloniality and the Artifice of History: Who Speaks for 'Indian' Pasts?" *Representations* 37 (winter 1992): 4.

10 Prakash, "Postcolonial Criticism," 14–15. See also Spivak, *Post-colonial Critic, passim*. As the term "subaltern" would indicate, Antonio Gramsci's inspiration is readily visible in the works of subaltern historians.

11 Prakash, "Post-Orientalist Histories," 390–1.

12 Ibid., 397.

13 Prakash, "Postcolonial Criticism," 13.

14 Prakash, "Post-Orientalist Histories," 13.

15 Ibid., 399.

16 Ibid., 403.

17 Indeed, Lyotard has "defined" postmodern as "incredulity toward metanarratives" (Jean-François Lyotard, *The Postmodern Condition: A Report on Knowledge* [Minneapolis: University of Minnesota Press, 1984], xxiv).

18 Bill Ashcroft, Gareth Griffiths, Helen Tiffin, *The Empire Writes Back: Theory and Practice in Post-colonial Literatures* (London: Routledge, 1989), 2. Note that in this instance, the postcolonial concerns itself with literature, although the implications obviously go beyond the literary realm, which is characteristic of much of these discussions. Also, in case the reader might wonder why Latin American literatures, which may be more "paradigmatic" than any, are not included in the list, it is noteworthy that in the writings of Australian and Canadian postcolonials, "postcolonial" more often than not is associated with the former Commonwealth countries, rather than with the Third World in general – and this in spite of immense differences economically and politically between countries comprising the Commonwealth. This is indicated by Stephen Slemon, "Unsettling the Empire: Resistance Theory for the Second World," in Bill Ashcroft, Gareth Griffiths, and Helen Tiffin, eds., *The Post-colonial Studies Reader* (New York: Routledge, 1995), 104–10; reprinted in abridged form from *World Literature Written in English* 30:2 (1990).

19 For discussions of similar problems in Chinese historiography, see Joseph Levenson, *Confucian China and Its Modern Fate* (Berkeley: University of California Press, 1968); Rey Chow, *Woman and Chinese Modernity* (Minneapolis: University of Minnesota Press, 1991); Arif Dirlik, *Revolution and History: Origins of Marxist Historiography in China, 1919–1937* (Berkeley: University of California Press, 1978); idem, "The Globalization of Marxist Historical Discourse and the Problem of Hegemony in Marxism," *Journal of Third World Studies* 4:1 (spring 1987): 151–64.

20 Ashcroft, Griffiths, and Tiffin, *The Post-colonial Studies Reader*, 1.

21 Frederick Buell, *National Culture and the New Global System* (Baltimore: Johns Hopkins University Press, 1994).

22 Prakash, "Postcolonial Criticism," 10.

23 Diana Brydon, "The White Inuit Speaks: Contamination as Literary Strategy," in Ashcroft, Griffiths, and Tiffin, *The Post-colonial Studies Reader*, 140–1; originally published in Ian Adam and Helen Tiffin, eds., *Past the Last Post: Theorizing Post-colonialism and Post-modernism* (New York: Harvester Wheatsheaf, 1991). Similar warnings toward Australian aboriginal claims to "authenticity," although phrased much more gently, are to be found in Ashcroft, Griffiths, and Tiffin, *The Empire Strikes Back*, and Gareth Griffiths, "The Myth of Authenticity," in Chris Tiffin and Alan Lawson, eds., *De-scribing Empire: Post-colonialism and Textuality* (New York: Routledge, 1994), 70–85.

24 Spivak, *Post-colonial Critic*, 67–8.

25 This is at any rate a question that needs to be clarified. It seems to me that Prakash's denial of foundational status to class goes beyond what is but a *historicization* of class in the work of *Subaltern Studies* historians, in the same way that, say, E. P. Thompson historicizes the concept in *The Making of the English Working Class* (New York: Random House, 1966). For a note on the question of class, see Dipesh Chakrabarty, "Invitation to a Dialogue," *Subaltern Studies* 4 (1985). The procedure of generalization may also play a part in the deradicalization of *Subaltern Studies* ideas by removing them from their specific historiographical context, where they *do* play an innovative, radical role. For instance, the qualification of the role of colonialism in Indian history is intended by these historians to bring to the fore the mystifications of the past in nationalist histories, which is a radical act. Made into a general principle of "postcolonialism," this qualification turns into a downplaying of colonialism in history. For an acknowledgment of doubt concerning the "success" attributed to *Subaltern Studies* historiography, see Chakrabarty, "Postcoloniality and the Artifice of History."

26 Note not just the ideas but the tone in the following statement by Ahmad: "But one could start with a radically different premise, namely the proposition that we live not in three worlds but in one; that this world includes the experience of colonialism and imperialism on both sides of Jameson's global divide...; that societies in formations of backward capitalism are as much

constituted by the division of classes as are societies in the advanced capitalist countries; that socialism is not restricted to something called the second world but is simply the name of a resistance that saturates the globe today, as capitalism, itself does; that the different parts of the capitalist system are to be known not in terms of binary opposition but as a contradictory unity, with differences, yes, but also with profound overlaps" ("Jameson's Rhetoric of Otherness," 9).

27 Spivak, "Can the Subaltern Speak?" in Cary Nelson and Lawrence Grossberg, eds., *Marxism and the Interpretation of Culture* (Urbana: University of Illinois Press, 1988), 271–313; Lata Mani, "Multiple Mediations: Feminist Scholarship in the Age of Multinational Reception," in James Clifford and Vivek Dhareshwar, eds., *Travelling Theories Travelling Theorists* (Santa Cruz, CA: Center for Cultural Theory, 1989), 1–23.

28 Appiah, "Is the 'Post-' in 'Postmodernism' the 'Post-' in 'Postcolonial'?" *Critical Inquiry* 17 (winter 1991): 353.

29 Achille Mbembe, "Prosaics of Servitude and Authoritarian Civilities," *Public Culture* 5:1 (fall 1992): 137.

30 Spivak, *Post-colonial Critic*, 91.

31 Edward Said, foreword to Guha and Spivak, *Selected Subaltern Studies*.

32 For a sampling of essays, see Joseph P. L. Jiang, *Confucianism and Modernization: A Symposium* (Taipei: Freedom Council, 1987). Scholars such as Tu Wei-ming and Yu Ying-shih have played a major part in efforts to revive Confucianism, while the quasi-fascist regime of Singapore (especially under Lee Kuan Yew) has been a major promoter of the idea.

33 Prakash, "Postcolonial Criticism," 14–15.

34 For a discussion of this problem in detail, see Arif Dirlik, "Mao Zedong and 'Chinese Marxism,'" *Encyclopedia of Asian Philosophy* (London: Routledge, 1993).

35 Prakash, "Postcolonial Criticism," 10.

36 Althusser recognized this problem, with specific reference to Mao Tse-tung Thought. See his "Contradiction and Overdetermination," in *For Marx*, trans. Ben Brewster (New York: Vintage Books, 1970), 87–128. For the "molding" of ideology, see Althusser's "Ideology and Ideological State Apparatuses," in *Lenin and Philosophy*, trans. Ben Brewster (New York: Monthly Review Press, 1971), 127–86. Lata Mani gives a good (personal) account of the contextual formation of ideology in her "Multiple Mediations." The risk in contextual ideological formation, of course, is the transformation of what is a problem into what is a celebration: game playing. This is evident throughout in Spivak's "playfulness" in The Post-colonial Critic as well as in, say, James Clifford's approach to the question of ethnography and culture. For a brief example of the latter, among Clifford's many works, see "Notes on Theory and Travel," in *Travelling Theory Travelling Theorists*, 177–88. My objection here is not to the importance of immediate context in ideology formation (and the variability and transposability of roles it implies) but to the mystification that such emphasis on the local causes regarding the larger contexts that differentiate power relations and suggest more stable and directed positions. No matter how much the ethnographer may strive to change places with the native, in the end the ethnographer returns to the First World academy and the native back to the "wilds." This is the problem with postcoloniality, and it is evident in the tendency of so much postcolonial criticism to start off with a sociology of power relationships only to take refuge in aesthetic phraseology.

37 Conversely, absence from powerful institutions may lead to silence. This is an explanation that Nicholas Thomas has offered for the obliviousness of postcolonial criticism to the problem of indigenous peoples who, to the extent that they are present in the academy, are only marginally so. See Thomas, *Colonialism's Culture: Anthropology, Travel, and Government* (Princeton, NJ: Princeton University Press, 1994), 172.

38 Appiah, "Is the 'Post-' in 'Postmodernism' the 'Post-' in 'Postcolonial'?" 353.

39 See the example Shohat gives of his experiences at CUNY ("Notes," 99).

40 Ibid.

41 Anne McClintock, "The Angel of Progress: Pitfalls of the Term 'Post-colonialism,'" *Social Text* 31/32 (1992): 86. Recall the statement I quoted above from Diana Brydon.

42 Shohat, "Notes," 104.

43 Ibid., 110.

44 Rosalind O'Hanlon and David Washbrook, "After Orientalism: Culture, Criticism, and Politics in the Third World," *Comparative Studies in Society and History* 34:1 (January 1992): 166.

45 Karl Pletsch, "The Three Worlds, or the Division of Social Scientific Labor, circa 1950–1975," *Comparative Studies in Society and History* 23:4 (1981).

46 O'Hanlon and Washbrook, "After Orientalism," 147.

47 Prakash, "Postcolonial Criticism," 13–14.

48 Fernando Coronil, "Can Postcoloniality Be Decolonized? Imperial Banality and Postcolonial Power," *Public Culture* 5:1 (fall 1992): 99–100.

49 O'Hanlon and Washbrook, "After Orientalism," 165–6.

50 Shohat, "Notes," 111.

51 David Harvey, *The Condition of Postmodernity* (Cambridge, MA: Blackwell, 1989), and, Fredric Jameson, "Postmodernism or, the Cultural Logic of Late Capitalism," *New Left Review* 146 (July/August 1984).

52 F. Frobel, J. Heinrichs, and O. Kreye, *The New International Division of Labour* (Cambridge: Cambridge University Press, 1980). The term "disorganized capitalism" comes from Claus Offe, *Disorganized Capitalism* (Cambridge, MA: MIT Press, 1985), while "global capitalism" is the term used by Robert J. S. Ross and Kent C. Trachte, *Global Capitalism: The New Leviathan* (Albany: State University of New York Press, 1990). Other noteworthy books on the subject are Leslie Sklair, *Sociology of the Global System* (Baltimore: Johns Hopkins University Press, 1991), which spells out the implications for the Third World of global capitalism, and, especially in light of what I say below about the Clinton presidency, Robert Reich, *The Work of Nations* (New York: Alfred A. Knopf, 1991). Reich's book incorporates his contributions to the *Harvard Business Review* and contains pieces with suggestive titles like "Who Is US?" and "Who Is Them?" For "subcontracting," see Gary Gereffi, "Global Sourcing and Regional Divisions of Labor in the Pacific Rim," in Arif Dirlik, ed., *What Is in a Rim? Critical Perspectives on the Asia-Pacific Idea* (Boulder, CO: Westview Press, 1993).

53 Riccardo Petrella, "World City-States of the Future," *New Perspectives Quarterly* (fall 1991): 59–64. See also "A New Hanseatic League?" *New York Times*, February 23, 1992, E3.

54 Kenichi Ohmae, "Beyond Friction to Fact: The Borderless Economy," *New Perspectives Quarterly* (spring 1990): 21.

55 While I stress transnational corporations here, it is important to note that the functioning of corporations is made possible by a whole gamut of transnational organizations, from state-led ones, such as the World Bank and International Monetary Fund, to what might be described as organizations of a global "civil society," from nongovernmental organizations to professional associations. Taking note of these organizations also serves as a reminder that, in spite of the appearance of decentralization and the dispersion of power, the powerful of the First World, through their immense concentration of wealth as well as the influence they exert on these organizations, continue to dominate the world, albeit at a greater distance (especially in terms of social and public responsibility) from their own societies.

56 This phenomenon is addressed in most of the works cited above n. 52.

57 Ohmae, "Beyond Friction." See, also, James Gardner, "Global Regionalism," *New Perspectives Quarterly* (winter 1992): 58–9.

58 "The Logic of Global Business: An Interview with ABB's Percy Barnevik," *Harvard Business Review* (March–April 1991): 90–105.

59 See Achille Mbembe, "The Banality of Power and the Aesthetics of Vulgarity," *Public Culture* 4:2 (spring 1992): 1–30, and the discussion provoked by that essay in *Public Culture* 5:1 (fall 1992).

60 For "cognitive mapping," see Fredric Jameson, "Cognitive Mapping," in Cary Nelson and Lawrence Grossberg, *Marxism and the Interpretation of Culture* (Urbana: University of Illinois

Press, 1988), 347–57. Jameson has been a forceful advocate of retaining a sense of totality and structure in a socialist politics. His own totalization of the global structure has come under severe criticism (see Ahmad, "Jameson's Rhetoric"). I should stress here that it is not necessary to agree with his particular mode of totalization to recognize the validity of his argument.

61 Appiah, "Is the 'Post-' in 'Postmodernism' the 'Post-' in 'Postcolonial'?" 348.

62 Aijaz Ahmad, "The Politics of Literary Postcoloniality," *Race and Class* 36:3 (1995): 16. See also Benita Parry, "Signs of Our Times: Discussion of Homi Bhabha's *The Location of Culture*," *Third Text* 28/29 (autumn/winter 1994): 3–24.

63 This is an aspect of postcoloniality, and of its appeals, that clearly calls for greater attention. A historian of the Pacific, Klaus Neumann, writes that "these days Papua New Guineans . . . do not appear overtly interested in being told about the horrors of colonialism, as such accounts potentially belittle today's descendants of yesterday's victims" ("'In Order to Win Their Friendship': Renegotiating First Contact," *The Contemporary Pacific* 6:1 [1994]: 122). Likewise, Deirdre Jordan notes the complaints of adult aboriginal students in Australia about emphasis on white oppression, "which seems designed to call forth in them responses of hostility and racism and which, they believe, causes a crisis of identity" ("Aboriginal Identity: Uses of the Past, Problems for the Future?" in Jeremy R. Beckett, ed., *Past and Present: The Construction of Aboriginality* [Canberra: Aboriginal Studies Press, 1994], 119). There are others, needless to say, who would suppress memories of the past for reasons of self-interest.

CHAPTER 3

Time and Class

Zygmunt Bauman

'The company belongs to people who invest in it – not to its employees, suppliers, nor the locality in which it is situated.'[1] This is how Albert J. Dunlap, the celebrated 'rationalizer' of modern enterprise (a *dépeceur* – 'chopper', 'quarterer', 'dismemberer' – in the juicy yet precise designation of the CNRS sociologist Denis Duclos)[2] summarized his creed in the self-congratulating report of his activities which Times Books published for the enlightenment and edification of all seekers of economic progress.

What Dunlap had in mind was not, of course, the simple question of 'belonging' as just another name for the purely legal issue of ownership, an issue hardly contested and even less in need of restating – let alone such an emphatic restating. What Dunlap had in mind was, mostly, what the rest of the sentence implied: that the employees, the suppliers and the spokesmen of the community have no say in the decisions that the 'people who invest' may take; and that the true decision-makers, the investors, have the right to dismiss out of hand, and to declare irrelevant and invalid, any postulates which such people may make concerning the way they run the company.

Let us note: Dunlap's message is not a declaration of intent, but a statement of fact. Dunlap takes it for granted that the principle it conveys has passed all the tests which economic, political, social and any other realities of our times might have set or made proper to examine its viability. It has by now entered the family of self-evident truths which serve to explain the world while themselves needing no explanation; which help to assert things about the world while themselves no longer being seen as assertions, let alone contentious and arguable assertions.

There were times (one would say 'not so long ago', if not for the fast shrinking span of collective attention, which makes even a week not just a long time in politics, but an exceedingly long stretch in the life of human memory) when Dunlap's proclamation would have seemed by no means obvious to all; when it would have sounded more like a war-cry or a battlefield report. In the early years of Margaret Thatcher's war of annihilation launched against local self-government, businessman after businessman felt the need to climb rostrums of the Tory Annual Conference to hammer out again and

Zygmunt Bauman, "Time and Class," pp. 6–26 and 128–9 from *Globalization: The Human Consequences*. Cambridge: Polity Press and New York: Columbia University Press, 1998. Reprinted by permission of Blackwell Publishing Ltd. and Columbia University Press.

again a message they must have thought to be in need of hammering out because of sounding uncanny and bizarre to yet untuned ears: the message that companies would gladly pay local taxes to support road building or sewage repairs which they needed, but that they saw no reason to pay for the support of the local unemployed, invalids and other human waste, for whose fate they did not feel like carrying a responsibility or assuming an obligation. But those were the early years of the war which has been all but won a mere two dozen years later, at the time Dunlap dictated his credo, which he could rightly expect every listener to share.

There is not much point in debating whether that war was malevolently and surreptitiously plotted in smoke-free company boardrooms, or whether the necessity of war action was visited on unsuspecting, peace-loving leaders of industry by changes brought about by a mixture of the mysterious forces of new technology and the new global competitiveness; or whether it was a war planned in advance, duly declared and with its goals clearly defined, or just a series of scattered and often unanticipated warlike actions, each necessitated by causes of its own. Whichever of the two was the case (there are good arguments to be advanced for each, but it may well be that the two accounts only seem to be in competition with each other), it is quite probable that the last quarter of the current century will go down in history as the Great War of Independence from Space. What happened in the course of that war was a consistent and relentless wrenching of the decision-making centres, together with the calculations which ground the decisions such centres make, free from territorial constraints – the constraints of locality.

Let us look more closely at Dunlap's principle. Employees are recruited from the local population and – burdened as they might be by family duties, home ownership and the like – could not easily follow the company once it moves elsewhere. Suppliers have to deliver the supplies, and low transport costs give the local suppliers an advantage which disappears once the company changes its location. As to the 'locality' itself – it will, obviously, stay where it is and can hardly change its location, whatever the new address of the company. Among all the named candidates who have a say in the running of a company, only 'people who invest' – the shareholders – are in no way space-tied; they can buy any share at any stock-exchange and through any broker, and the geographical nearness or distance of the company will be in all probability the least important consideration in their decision to buy or sell.

In principle there is nothing space-determined in the dispersion of the shareholders. They are the sole factor genuinely free from spatial determination. And it is to them, and to them only, that the company 'belongs'. It is up to them therefore to move the company wherever they spy out or anticipate a chance of higher dividends, leaving to all others – locally bound as they are – the task of wound-licking, damage-repair and waste-disposal. The company is free to move; but the consequences of the move are bound to stay. Whoever is free to run away from the locality, is free to run away from the consequences. These are the most important spoils of victorious space war.

Absentee landlords, mark II

In the post-space-war world, mobility has become the most powerful and most coveted stratifying factor; the stuff of which the new, increasingly world-wide, social, political, economic and cultural hierarchies are daily built and rebuilt. And to those at the top of the new hierarchy freedom to move brings advantages far beyond those short-listed in

Dunlap's formula. That formula takes note of, promotes or demotes only such competitors who may make themselves audible – those who can, and are likely to, voice their grievances and forge their complaints into claims. But there are other – also locally bound, cut-off and left-behind connections, on which Dunlap's formula keeps silent because they are unlikely to make themselves heard.

The mobility acquired by 'people who invest' – those with capital, with money which the investment requires – means the new, indeed unprecedented in its radical unconditionality, disconnection of power from obligations: duties towards employees, but also towards the younger and weaker, towards yet unborn generations and towards the self-reproduction of the living conditions of all; in short, freedom from the duty to contribute to daily life and the perpetuation of the community. There is a new asymmetry emerging between exterritorial nature of power and the continuing territoriality of the 'whole life' – which the now unanchored power, able to move at short notice or without warning, is free to exploit and abandon to the consequences of that exploitation. Shedding the responsibility for the consequences is the most coveted and cherished gain which the new mobility brings to free-floating, locally unbound capital. The costs of coping with the consequences need not be now counted in the calculation of the 'effectiveness' of investment.

The new freedom of capital is reminiscent of that of the absentee landlords of yore, notorious for their much resented neglect of the needs of the populations which fed them. Creaming off the 'surplus product' was the sole interest the absentee landlords held in the existence of the land they owned. There is certainly some similarity here – but the comparison does not give full justice to the kind of freedom from worry and responsibility which the mobile capital of the late twentieth century acquired but the absentee landlords never could.

The latter could not exchange one land estate for another and so remained – however tenuously – tied to the locality from which they drew their life juices; that circumstance set a practical limit to the theoretically and legally unconstrained possibility of exploitation, lest the future flow of income might thin out or dry up completely. True, the real limits tended to be on the whole more severe than the perceived ones, and these in their turn were all too often more severe than the limits observed in practice – a circumstance which made absentee land-ownership prone to inflict irreparable damage upon soil fertility and agricultural proficiency in general, and which also made the fortunes of absentee landlords notoriously precarious, tending to decline over the generations. And yet there were genuine limits, which reminded of their presence all the more cruelly for being unperceived and not complied with. And a limit, as Alberto Melucci put it, 'stands for confinement, frontier, separation; it therefore also signifies recognition of the other, the different, the irreducible. The encounter with otherness is an experience that puts us to a test: from it is born the temptation to reduce difference by force, while it may equally generate the challenge of communication, as a constantly renewed endeavour.'[3]

In contradistinction to the absentee landlords of early modern times, the late-modern capitalists and land-brokers, thanks to the new mobility of their by now liquid resources, do not face limits sufficiently real – solid, tough, resistant – to enforce compliance. The sole limits which could make themselves felt and respected would be those administratively imposed on the free movement of capital and money. Such limits are, however, few and far between, and the handful that remain are under tremendous pressure to be effaced or just washed out. In their absence there would be few occasions for Melucci's 'encounter with otherness'. If it so happened that the encounter were enforced by the other side – the moment 'otherness' tried to flex its muscles and make its strength felt, capital would have little difficulty with packing its tents and finding an environment that was more hospitable – that is, unresistant, malleable, soft. There would therefore be fewer occasions likely to prompt either attempts to 'reduce difference by force' or the will to accept 'the challenge of communication'.

Both attitudes would have implied recognition of the irreducibility of otherness, but, in order to be seen as irreducible, 'otherness' must first constitute itself into a resistant, inflexible, literally 'gripping', entity. Its chance to do so is, however, fast shrinking. To acquire a genuinely entity-constituting capacity the resistance needs a persistent and effective attacker – but the overall effect of the new mobility is that, for capital and finances, the need to bend the inflexible, to push the hurdles aside or to overcome or mitigate resistance hardly ever arises; if it does arise it may well be brushed aside in favour of a softer option. Capital can always move away to more peaceful sites if the engagement with 'otherness' requires a costly application of force or tiresome negotiations. No need to engage, if avoidance will do.

Freedom of movement and the self-constitution of societies

Looking backward in history, one can ask to what extent the geophysical factors, the natural and the artificial borders of territorial units, separate identities of populations and *Kulturkreise*, as well as the distinction between 'inside' and 'outside' – all the traditional objects of the science of geography – were in their essence merely the conceptual derivatives, or the material sediments/artifices of 'speed limits' – or, more generally, of the time-and-cost constraints imposed on freedom of movement.

Paul Virilio suggested recently that, while Francis Fukuyama's declaration of the 'end of history' looks grossly premature, one can with growing confidence speak presently of the 'end of geography'.[4] The distances do not matter any more, while the idea of a geophysical border is increasingly difficult to sustain in the 'real world'. It suddenly seems clear that the divisions of continents and of the globe as a whole were the function of distances made once imposingly real thanks to the primitiveness of transport and the hardships of travel.

Indeed, far from being an objective, impersonal, physical 'given', 'distance' is a social product; its length varies depending on the speed with which it may be overcome (and, in a monetary economy, on the cost involved in the attainment of that speed). All other socially produced factors of constitution, separation and the maintenance of collective identities – like state borders or cultural barriers – seem in retrospect merely secondary effects of that speed.

This seems to be the reason, let us note, why the 'reality of borders' was as a rule, most of the time, a class-stratified phenomenon: in the past, as they are today, the elites of the wealthy and the powerful were always more cosmopolitically inclined than the rest of the population of the lands they inhabited; at all times they tended to create a culture of their own which made little of the same borders that held fast for lesser folk; they had more in common with the elites across the borders than with the rest of the population inside them. This seems also to be the reason why Bill Clinton, the spokesman of the most powerful elite of the present-day world, could recently declare that for the first time there is no difference between domestic and foreign politics. Indeed, little in the elite's life experience now implies a difference between 'here' and 'there', 'inside' and 'outside', 'close by' and 'far away'. With time of communication imploding and shrinking to the no-size of the instant, space and spatial markers cease to matter, at least to those whose actions can move with the speed of the electronic message.

The 'inside' vs. 'outside', 'here' vs. out there', 'near' vs. 'far away' opposition recorded the degree of taming, domestication and familiarity of various fragments (human as much as inhuman) of the surrounding world.

Near, close to hand, is primarily what is usual, familiar and known to the point of obviousness; someone or something seen, met, dealt or interacted with daily, intertwined with habitual routine and day-to-day activities. 'Near' is a space inside which one can feel *chez soi*, at home; a space in which one seldom, if at all, finds oneself at a loss, feels lost for words or uncertain how to act. 'Far away', on the other hand, is a space which one enters only occasionally or not at all, in which things happen which one cannot anticipate or comprehend, and would not know how to react to once they occurred: a space containing things one knows little about, from which one does not expect much and regarding which one does not feel obliged to care. To find oneself in a 'far-away' space is an unnerving experience; venturing 'far away' means being beyond one's ken, out of place and out of one's element, inviting trouble and fearing harm.

Due to all such features, the 'near–far' opposition has one more, crucial dimension: that between certainty and uncertainty, self-assurance and hesitation. Being 'far away' means being in trouble – and so it demands cleverness, cunning, slyness or courage, learning foreign rules one can do without elsewhere, and mastering them through risky trials and often costly errors. The idea of the 'near', on the other hand, stands for the unproblematic; painlessly acquired habits will do, and since they are habits they feel weightless and call for no effort, giving no occasion to anxiety-prone hesitation. Whatever has come to be known as the 'local community' is brought into being by this opposition between 'here' and 'out there', 'near' and 'far away'.

Modern history has been marked by the constant progress of the means of transportation. Transport and travel was the field of particularly radical and rapid change; progress here, as Schumpeter pointed out a long time ago, was not the result of multiplying the number of stage-coaches, but of the invention and mass production of totally new means of travel – trains, motorcars and airplanes. It was primarily the availability of means of fast travel that triggered the typically modern process of eroding and undermining all locally entrenched social and cultural 'totalities'; the process first captured by Tönnies' famous formula of modernity as the passage from *Gemeinschaft* to *Gesellschaft*.

Among all the technical factors of mobility, a particularly great role was played by the transport of information – the kind of communication which does not involve movement of physical bodies or involves it only secondarily and marginally. Technical means were steadily and consistently developed which also allowed information to travel independently from its bodily carriers – and also from the objects of which the information informed: means which set the 'signifiers' free from the hold of the 'signifieds'. The separation of the movements of information from those of its carriers and its objects allowed in its turn the differentiation of their speed; the movement of information gathered speed on a pace much faster than the travel of bodies, or the change of the situations of which the information informed, was able to reach. In the end, the appearance of the computer-served World Wide Web put paid – as far as information is concerned – to the very notion of 'travel' (and of 'distance' to be travelled) and renders information, in theory as well as in practice, instantaneously available throughout the globe.

The overall results of the latest development are enormous. Its impact on the interplay of social association/dissociation has been widely noted and described in great detail. Much as one notices the 'essence of hammer' only when the hammer has been broken, we now see more clearly than ever before the role played by time, space and the means of saddling them in the formation, stability/flexibility, and the demise of socio/cultural and political totalities. The so-called 'closely knit communities' of yore were, as we can now see, brought into being and kept alive by the gap between the nearly instantaneous communication *inside* the small-scale community (the size of which was determined by the innate qualities of 'wetware', and thus confined to the natural limits of human sight, hearing and memorizing capacity) and the enormity of time and expense needed to pass information *between* localities. On the other hand, the present-day fragility and short life-span of communities appears primarily to be the result of that gap shrinking or altogether disappearing: inner-community communication has no advantage over inter-communal exchange, if *both* are instantaneous.

Michael Benedikt thus summarizes our retrospective discovery and the new under-standing of the intimate connection between the speed of travel and social cohesion:

> The kind of unity made possible in small communities by the near-simultaneity and near-zero cost of natural voice communications, posters and leaflets, collapses at the larger scale. Social cohesion at any scale is a function of consensus, of shared knowledge, and without constant updating and interaction, such cohesion depends crucially on early, and strict, education in – and memory of – culture. Social flexibility, conversely, depends on forgetting and cheap communication.[5]

Let us add that the 'and' in the last quoted sentence is superfluous; the facility to forget, and cheapness (as well as the high velocity) of communication, are but two aspects of the same condition and could hardly be thought of separately. Cheap communication means quick overflowing, stifling or elbowing away the information acquired as much as it means the speedy arrival of news. The capacities of 'wetware' remaining largely un-changed since at least palaeolithic times, cheap communication floods and smothers memory rather than feeding and stabilizing it. Arguably the most seminal of recent developments is the dwindling differences between the costs of transmitting information on a local and global scale (wherever you send your message through the Internet, you pay by the tariff of the 'local call', a circumstance as important culturally as it is economically); this, in turn, means that the information eventually arriving and clamouring for atten-tion, for entry to, and (however short-lived) staying in the memory, tends to be originated in the most diverse and mutually autonomous sites and thus likely to convey mutually incompatible or mutually cancelling messages – in sharp contradiction to the messages floating inside communities devoid of hardware and software and relying on 'wetware' only; that is, to the messages which tended to reiterate and reinforce each other and assist the process of (selective) memorizing.

As Timothy W. Luke puts it, 'the spatiality of traditional societies is organized around the mostly unmediated capacities of ordinary human bodies':

> Traditional visions of action often resort to organic metaphors for their allusions: conflict was chin-to-chin. Combat was hand-to-hand. Justice was an eye-for-an-eye, a-tooth-for-a-tooth. Debate was heart-to-heart. Solidarity was shoulder-to-shoulder. Community was face-to-face. Friendship was arm-in-arm. And, change was step-by-step.

This situation had changed beyond recognition with the advance of means which allowed the stretching of conflicts, solidarities, combats, debates or the administration of justice well beyond the reach of the human eye and arm. Space had become 'processed/centred/organized/normalized', and above all emancipated from the natural constraint of the human body. It was therefore the capacity of technics, the speed of its action and the cost of its use which from then on 'organized space': 'The space projected by such technics is radically different: engineered, not God-given; artificial, not natural; mediated by hardware, not immediate to wetware; rationalized, not communalized; national, not local.'[6]

Engineered, modern space was to be tough, solid, permanent and non-negotiable. Concrete and steel were to be its flesh, the web of railway tracks and highways its blood vessels. Writers of modern utopias did not distinguish between social and architectural order, social and territorial units and divisions; for them – as for their contemporaries in charge of social order – the key to an orderly society was to be found in the organization of space. Social totality was to be a hierarchy of ever larger and more inclusive localities, with the supra-local authority of the state perched on the top and surveilling the whole, while itself protected from day-to-day invigilation.

Over that territorial/urbanistic/architectural, engineered space a third, *cybernating* space of the human world has been imposed with the advent of the global web of information. Elements of this space, according to Paul Virilio, are 'devoid of spatial dimensions, but inscribed in the singular temporality of an instantaneous diffusion. From here on, people can't be separated by physical obstacles or by temporal distances. With the interfacing of computer terminals and video-monitors, distinctions of *here* and *there* no longer mean anything.'[7]

Like most statements pronouncing on the 'human' condition as such – one and the same for all humans – this one is not exactly correct. The 'interfacing of computer terminals' has had a varied impact on the plight of different kinds of people. And some people – in fact, quite a lot of them – still can, as before, be 'separated by physical obstacles and temporal distances', this separation being now more merciless, and having more profound psychological effects, than ever before.

New speed, new polarization

To put it in a nutshell: *rather than homogenizing the human condition, the technological annulment of temporal/spatial distances tends to polarize it.* It emancipates certain humans from territorial constraints and renders certain community-generating meanings exterritorial – while denuding the territory, to which other people go on being confined, of its meaning and its identity-endowing capacity. For some people it augurs an unprecedented freedom from physical obstacles and unheard-of ability to move and act from a distance. For others, it portends the impossibility of appropriating and domesticating the locality from which they have little chance of cutting themselves free in order to move elsewhere. With 'distances no longer meaning anything', localities, separated by distances, also lose their meanings. This, however, augurs freedom of meaning-creation for some, but portends ascription to meaninglessness for others. Some can now move out of the locality – any locality – at will. Others watch helplessly the sole locality they inhabit moving away from under their feet.

Information now floats independently from its carriers; shifting of bodies and re-arrangement of bodies in physical space is less than ever necessary to reorder meanings and relationships. For some people – for the mobile elite, the elite of mobility – this means, literally, the 'dephysicalization', the new weightlessness of power. Elites travel in space, and travel faster than ever before – but the spread and density of the power web they weave is not dependent on that travel. Thanks to new 'bodylessness' of power in its mainly financial form, the power-holders become truly exterritorial even if, bodily, they happen to stay 'in place'. Their power is, fully and truly, not 'out of this world' – not of the physical world in which they build their heavily guarded homes and offices, themselves exterritorial, free from intrusion of unwelcome neighbours, cut out from whatever may be called a *local* community, inaccessible to whoever is, unlike them, confined to it.

It is this new elite's experience of non-terrestriality of power – of the eerie yet awesome combination of ethereality with omnipotence, non-physicality and reality-forming might – which is being recorded in the common eulogy of the 'new freedom' embodied in electronically sustained 'cyberspace'; most remarkably, in Margaret Wertheim's 'analogy between cyberspace and the Christian conception of heaven':

> Just as early Christians envisaged heaven as an idealized realm beyond the chaos and decay of the material world – a disintegration all too palpable as the empire crumbled around them – so too, in this time of social and environmental disintegration, today's proselytizers of cyberspace proffer their domain as an ideal 'above' and 'beyond' the problems of the material world. While early Christians promulgated heaven as a realm in which the human soul would be freed from the frailties and failings of the flesh, so today's champions of cyberspace hail it as a place where the self will be freed from the limitations of physical embodiment.[8]

In cyberspace, bodies do not matter – though cyberspace matters, and matters decisively and irrevocably, in the life of bodies. There is no appeal from the verdicts passed in the cyberspatial heaven, and nothing that happens on earth may question their authority. With the power to pass verdicts securely vested in cyberspace, the bodies of the powerful need not be powerful bodies nor need they be armed with heavy material weapons; more than that, unlike Antheus, they need no link to their earthly environment to assert, ground or manifest their power. What they need is the isolation from locality, now stripped of social meaning which has been transplanted into cyberspace, and so reduced to a merely 'physical' terrain. What they also need is *the security of that isolation* – a 'non-neighbourhood' condition, immunity from local interference, a foolproof, invulnerable isolation, translated as the 'safety' of persons, of their homes and their playgrounds. Deterritorialization of power therefore goes hand in hand with the ever stricter structuration of the territory.

In a study with the telling-it-all title 'Building Paranoia', Steven Flusty notes the breathtaking explosion of ingenuity and a most frenetic building boom in a field new to the metropolitan areas: that of the 'interdictory spaces' – 'designed to intercept and repel or filter would-be users'. Flusty deploys his unique knack for coining precisely targeted and poignantly suggestive terms to distinguish several varieties of such spaces which supplement each other and combine into a new urban equivalent of the moats and turrets that once guarded medieval castles. Among such varieties, there is 'slippery space' – 'space that cannot be reached, due to contorted, protracted, or missing paths of approach'; 'prickly space' – 'space that cannot be comfortably occupied, defended by such details as wall-mounted sprinkler heads activated to clear loiterers or ledges sloped to inhibit sitting'; or 'jittery space' – 'space that cannot be utilized unobserved due to active monitoring by roving patrols and/or remote technologies feeding to security stations'. These and other 'interdictory spaces' serve no other purpose than to re-forge the social exterritoriality of the new supra-local elite into the material, bodily isolation from locality. They also put a final touch on the disintegration of locally grounded forms of together- ness and shared, communal living. The exterritoriality of elites is assured in the most material fashion – their physical inaccessibility to anyone not issued with an entry permit.

In a complementary development, such urban spaces where the occupants of different residential areas could meet face-to-face, engage in casual encounters, accost and chal- lenge one another, talk, quarrel, argue or agree, lifting their private problems to the level of public issues and making public issues into matters of private concern – those 'private/ public' agoras of Cornelius Castoriadis's – are fast shrinking in size and number. The few that remain tend to be increasingly selective – adding strengths to, rather than repairing the damage done by the push of disintegrating forces. As Steven Flusty puts it,

> traditional public spaces are increasingly supplanted by privately produced (though often publicly subsidized), privately owned and administered spaces for public aggregation, that is, spaces of consumption... [A]ccess is predicated upon ability to pay... Exclusivity rules here, ensuring the high levels of control necessary to prevent irregularity, unpredict- ability, and inefficiency from interfering with the orderly flow of commerce.[9]

The elites have *chosen* isolation and pay for it lavishly and *willingly*. The rest of the population *finds itself* cut off and *forced* to pay the heavy cultural, psychological and political price of their new isolation. Those unable to make their separate living the matter of choice and to pay the costs of its security are on the receiving side of the contemporary equivalent of the early-modern enclosures; they are purely and simply 'fenced off' without having been asked their consent, barred access to yesterday's 'commons', arrested, turned back and facing a short sharp shock when blundering into the off-limits regions, failing to note the 'private property' warning signs or to read the meaning of the non-verbalized, yet no less resolute for that reason, the 'no trespassing' hints and clues.

Urban territory becomes the battlefield of continuous space war, sometimes erupting into the public spectacle of inner-city riots, ritual skirmishes with the police, the occasional forays of soccer crowds, but waged daily just beneath the surface of the public (publicized), official version of the routine urban order. Disempowered and disregarded residents of the 'fenced-off', pressed-back and relentlessly encroached-upon areas, respond with aggressive action of their own; they try to install on the borders of their ghettoized home ground 'no trespassing' signs of their own making. Following the eternal custom of *bricoleurs* they use for the purpose any material they can lay their hands on – 'rituals, dressing strangely, striking bizarre attitudes, breaking rules, breaking bottles, windows, heads, issuing rhet- orically challenges to the law'.[10] Effective or not, these attempts have the handicap of non- authorization and tend to be conveniently classified, in the official records, as issues of law and order, rather than what they are in fact: attempts to make their territorial claims audible and legible and so merely to follow the new rules of the territoriality game everyone else is playing with gusto.

The fortifications built by the elite and the self-defence-through-aggression practised by those left outside the walls have a mutually reinforcing effect clearly predicted by Gregory

Bateson's theory of 'schismogenetic chains'. According to that theoretical model, schism is likely to emerge and deepen beyond repair when a position is set up in which

> the behaviour X, Y, Z is the standard reply to X, Y, Z ... If, for example, the patterns X, Y, Z include boasting, we shall see that there is a likelihood, if boasting is the reply to boasting, that each group will drive the other into excessive emphasis of the pattern, a process which if not restrained can only lead to more and more extreme rivalry and ultimately to hostility and the breakdown of the whole system.

The above is the pattern of 'symmetrical differentiation'. What is its alternative? What happens if group B fails to respond to the X, Y, Z kind of challenge by group A with an X, Y, Z type of behaviour? The schismogenetic chain is not then cut – it only assumes the pattern of 'complementary', instead of symmetrical, differentiation. If, for instance, assertive behaviour is not responded to in the same currency, but meets with submissiveness, 'it is likely that this submissiveness will promote further assertiveness which in turn will promote further submissiveness'. The 'breakdown of the system' will follow all the same.[11]

The overall effect of the choice between the two patterns is minimal, but for the sides tied by the schismogenetic chain the difference between the patterns is one between dignity and humiliation, humanity and its loss. One can safely anticipate that the strategy of symmetrical differentiation would be always preferred to the complementary alternative. The latter is the strategy for the defeated or for those who accepted inevitability of defeat. Some things, though, are bound to emerge victorious, whatever strategy is chosen: the new fragmentation of the city space, the shrinkage and disappearance of public space, the falling apart of urban community, separation and segregation – and above all the exterritoriality of the new elite and the forced territoriality of the rest.

If the new exterritoriality of the elite feels like intoxicating freedom, the territoriality of the rest feels less like home ground, and ever more like prison – all the more humiliating for the obtrusive sight of the others' freedom to move. It is not just that the condition of 'staying put', being unable to move at one's heart's desire and being barred access to greener pastures, exudes the acrid odour of defeat, signals incomplete humanity and implies being cheated in the division of splendours life has to offer. Deprivation reaches deeper. The 'locality' in the new world of high speed is not what the locality used to be at a time when information moved only together with the bodies of its carriers; neither the locality, nor the localized population has much in common with the 'local community'. Public spaces – agoras and forums in their various manifestations, places where agendas are set, private affairs are made public, opinions are formed, tested and confirmed, judgements are put together and verdicts are passed – such spaces followed the elite in cutting loose their local anchors; they are first to deterritorialize and move far beyond the reach of the merely 'wetware' communicative capacity of any locality and its residents. Far from being hotbeds of communities, local populations are more like loose bunches of untied ends.

Paul Lazarsfeld wrote of the 'local opinion leaders', who sift, evaluate and process for other locals the messages which arrive from the 'outside' through the media; but to do so, the local leaders must first have been heard by the locality – they needed an agora where the locals could come together to talk and listen. It was that local agora which allowed the voice of the local opinion leaders' to compete with the voices from afar and gain conviction able to outweigh the much more resourceful authority, thinned as it was by its distance. I doubt whether Lazarsfeld would come to the same conclusion were he to repeat his study today, a mere half-century later.

Nils Christie has recently tried to encapsulate, in an allegory, the logic of the process and its consequences.[12] Since the text is not yet easily available, I will quote the story at length:

> Moses came down from the mountains. Under his arm he carried the rules, engraved in granite, dictated to him by one even further up than the mountains. Moses was only a messenger, the people – the populus – were the receivers... Much later, Jesus and Mohammed functioned according to the same principles. These are classical cases of 'pyramidal justice'.
>
> And then the other picture: females gathering at the water-fountain, the well, or at natural meeting places along the river... Fetch water, wash the clothes, and exchange informations and evaluations. The point of departure for their conversation will often be the concrete acts and situations. These are described, compared to similar occurences in the past and somewhere else, and evaluated – right or wrong, beautiful or ugly, strong or weak. Slowly, but far from always, some common understanding of the occurrences might emerge. This is a process whereby norms are created. It is a classical case of 'equalitarian justice'....
>
> ...[T]he water well is abolished. We had in modernized countries for a while some small shops with coin-operated Laundromats where we could come with our dirty linen and leave with the clean ones. In the intervals, there was some time to talk. Now the Laundromats are gone... Huge shopping malls might give some opportunities for encounters, but mostly they are too large for the creation of horizontal justice. Too large to find the old acquaintances and too busy and crowded for the prolonged chats needed to establish standards for behaviour...

Let me add that the shopping malls are so constructed as to keep people moving, looking around, keep them diverted and entertained no end – but in no case for too long – by any of the endless attractions; not to encourage them to stop, look at each other, talk to each other, think of, ponder and debate something other than the objects on display – not to pass their time in a fashion devoid of commercial value...

Christie's allegorical account has the extra merit of bringing to the surface the ethical effects of the demotion of public spaces. The meeting places were also the sites in which norms were created – so that justice could be done, and apportioned horizontally, thus reforging the conversationalists into a community, set apart and integrated by the shared criteria of evaluation. Hence a territory stripped of public space provides little chance for norms being debated, for values to be confronted, to clash and to be negotiated. The verdicts of right and wrong, beauty and ugliness, proper and improper, useful and useless may only descend from on high, from regions never to be penetrated by any but a most inquisitive eye; the verdicts are unquestionable since no questions may be meaningfully addressed to the judges and since the judges left no address – not even an e-mail address – and no one can be sure where they reside. No room is left for the 'local opinion leaders'; no room is left for the 'local opinion' as such.

The verdicts may be completely out of touch with the way life runs locally, but they are not meant to be tested in the experience of people on whose conduct they pronounce. Born out of a kind of experience known to the local receivers of the message through hearsay at best, they may rebound in more suffering even if they intend to bring joy. The exterritorial originals enter locally-bound life only as caricatures; perhaps as mutants and monsters. On the way, they expropriate the ethical powers of the locals, depriving them of all means of limiting the damage.

Notes

1   See Albert J. Dunlap (with Bob Andelman), *How I saved Bad Companies and Made Good Companies Great* (New York: Time Books, 1996), pp. 199–200.

2   Denis Duclos, 'La cosmocratie, nouvelle classe planétaire', *Le Monde Diplomatique*, August 1997, p. 14.

3   Alberto Melucci, *The Playing Self: Person and Meaning in the Planetary Society* (Cambridge: Cambridge University Press, 1966), p. 129.

4   See Paul Virilio, 'Un monde surexposé: fin de l'histoire, ou fin de la géographie?', *Le Monde Diplomatique*, August 1997, p. 17. The idea of the 'end of geography' was first advanced, to my knowledge, by Richard O'Brien (see his *Global Financial Integration: The End of Geography* (London: Chatham House/Pinter, 1992)).

5   Michael Benedikt, 'On Cyberspace and Virtual Reality', in *Man and Information Technology*, (lectures from the 1994 international symposium arranged by the Committee on Man, Technology and Society at the Royal Swedish Academy of Engineering Sciences (IVA) (Stockholm, 1995), p. 41.

6   Timothy W. Luke, 'Identity, Meaning and Globalization: Detraditionalization in Postmodern Space-Time Compression', in *Detraditionalization*, ed. Paul Heelas, Scott Lash and Paul Morris (Oxford: Blackwell, 1996), pp. 123, 125.

7   Paul Virilio, *The Lost Dimension* (New York: Semiotext(e), 1991), p. 13.

8   Margaret Wertheim, 'The Pearly Gates of Cyberspace', in *Architecture of Fear*, ed. Nan Elin (New York: Princeton Architectural Press, 1997), p. 296.

9   See Steven Flusty, 'Building Paranoia', in *Architecture of Fear*, ed. Nan Elin, pp. 48–9, 51–2.

10 See Dick Hebdige, *Hiding in the Light* (London: Routledge, 1988), p. 18.

11 Gregory Bateson, *Steps to an Ecology of Mind* (Frogmore: Paladin, 1973), pp. 41–2.

12 Nils Christie, 'Civility and State' (unpublished manuscript).

CHAPTER 4

Theoretical Therapies, Remote Remedies: SAPs and the Political Ecology of Poverty and Health in Africa

Brooke G. Schoepf, Claude Schoepf, and Joyce V. Millen

Beset by grinding poverty, AIDs, drought, rampant malnutrition, genocide, and war, the world's poorest continent has suffered a quarter century of profound, multiplex crisis. The policies proposed to remedy Africa's[1] ills and the theories upon which they rest are vigorously contested. Neoclassical economists, sometimes dubbed the "Washington Consensus," attribute the region's decline primarily to internal factors, such as misguided policies, mismanagement, and corruption of African governments.[2] Under the sway of Washington Consensus dicta, in the early 1980s the international financial institutions (IFIs) began to impose a series of structural adjustment programs (SAPs) which they claimed would restore health to stagnant African economies. The institutions' neutral-sounding, technical economic calculus actually re-presented policies that had been discredited in the late 1960s and 1970s by extensive scholarly research.

Critical social scientists acknowledged the destructive effects of internal patterns within African countries. They argued, however, that these must not be understood narrowly as the "irrational" policies or individual failings of African leaders. Rather, the destructive effects of policies and practices must be understood in the context of Africa's "chains of history" and the continent's place in the world political economy.[3] The cumulative consequences of the slave trade, violent colonial conquest, and the brutal extraction of natural resources by imperial powers created an enduring legacy of structural imbalances: entrenched asymmetries between Africa and the West, and between rich and poor within Africa. In this perspective, economic recovery depends upon transformation of distorted production and power structures and on reversing Africa's role in the world economy as a supplier of cheap labor and cheap raw materials.

Such critiques, however, were either systematically ignored or dismissed as "ideological" by the Washington Consensus. The claim of neoclassical economists to authoritative wisdom rests upon the power embodied in the conservative alliances that won

Brooke G. Schoepf, Claude Schoepf, and Joyce V. Millen, "Theoretical Therapies, Remote Remedies: SAPs and the Political Ecology of Poverty and Health in Africa," pp. 91–125 and 440–57 from Jim Yong Kim, Joyce V. Millen, Alec Irwin, and John Greshman (eds.), *Dying for Growth: Global Inequality and the Health of the Poor.* Monroe, ME: Common Courage Press, 2000. Reprinted by permission of Common Courage Press.

elections in the United States and Western Europe in 1980. This political shift delegitimated social welfare and undermined policies designed to meet the basic needs of poor people. In the aftermath, the IFIs imposed SAPs on 42 governments in sub-Saharan Africa in the 1980s and 1990s as a condition for new loans.

This chapter examines the health consequences of SAPs. We present evidence to show that after two decades, more Africans are poorer and less healthy than at the beginning of the SAP era. The growth that *did* occur failed to "trickle down" to ordinary people. Not only have SAPs failed to remedy the deep causes of Africa's crises; they have visited the brunt of austerity measures on the most vulnerable and powerless people. We explore how and why this has happened.

Countrywide health data are lacking for some African countries, and are inaccurate for others. Accordingly, we supplement findings of epidemiological studies with personal narratives collected in our field research. Together, these provide a vivid sense of how SAPs have worked in African contexts to undermine the health of the poor.

Our first narrative, the story of Nsanga, a poor woman struggling to survive in Kinshasa, capital of the Democratic Republic of Congo (DRC, called Zaire from 1971 to 1996), illustrates relations between power (or powerlessness), poverty, and disease. Disease epidemics result from social processes; the spread of infection is propelled by history, political economy, and culture. The HIV disease and AIDS strike with particular severity in poor African communities that are struggling under the burdens of continentwide economic crises and two decades of SAPs.[4] Following Nsanga's story, we review historical studies and then integrate historical perspectives into our analysis of current political and economic configurations. We seek to achieve a broad understanding of SAPs and their consequences, especially their impact on the health of the rural and urban poor, the majority of whom are women.

Nsanga's story: a survival strategy gone awry

In 1987 Nsanga was 26 years old and very poor. She and her two children, a bright and mischievous 8-year-old boy and a loquacious 5-year-old girl, lived in a sparsely furnished room, one of eight such rooms grouped around a communal courtyard. The families living in the compound shared a water tap, a latrine, and a roofless bathing stall. The electric company had disconnected the hookup because the landlord failed to pay the bill for six months. The women cooked on charcoal braziers made by local artisans. When money for charcoal ran out, they reverted to the village method, setting their pots on three stones over fires of scrap wood and cardboard scavenged by the children.

Sanitation in most of Kinshasa was dilapidated or absent. Nsanga and her friends knew their neighborhood was unhealthy. Waste ran into open drains. Flies, cockroaches, and mosquitoes were ubiquitous. In the dry season, dust containing fecal matter blew about and settled on water containers and food. In the rainy season, latrines sometimes overflowed into the courtyards. Malaria, gastrointestinal disorders, malnutrition, and persistent coughs were common. Many mothers without money for adequate food or medicine had lost at least one young child to illness. A number of Nsanga's neighbors delivered their babies at home because they could not pay maternity fees.

Nsanga hadn't always been the head of her household. She grew up in a village and married Lelo, a schoolteacher, when she was 18. She joined him in Kinshasa, where even on his meager salary, and despite galloping inflation, Nsanga managed to feed her family two meals a day. But soon their lives began to change.

In 1983, the international financial institutions, IFIs, instituted a series of "economic recovery" measures designed to reduce Zaire's public expenditures so that its corrupt government, which had borrowed heavily in the 1970s, could make payments on its foreign debt. The government removed price controls and sharply cut social service budgets, raising user fees for health services and education. In 1984, as an additional way to cut expenses, it fired more than 80,000 teachers and health workers, further reducing poor people's access to education and health care. Without a powerful patron to intercede for him, Lelo lost his job. The family lost his income, health insurance, and the subsidized rice allotted to government employees.

After six fruitless months waiting in offices in an attempt to obtain another position, Lelo's morale fell. He began to drink, selling off household goods to pay for beer and then for lutuku, a cheap but potent home-distilled alcohol. Nsanga berated him for wasting money; their relationship deteriorated. Often drunk and despondent, Lelo beat his wife and son.

Nsanga tried many things to earn money. Like most poor women in Kinshasa, she had had only a few years of formal schooling. She lacked well-connected friends and family who could help her find a job cleaning offices. Forced into the "informal" economic sector, Nsanga prepared meals for the men who worked in her neighborhood. She also sold food such as dried fish when she could walk several miles across town to obtain such items cheaply. Meanwhile, prices rose with currency devaluation, unemployment mounted, and real wages fell sharply. Even men still working had little money to spend, and many skipped the noon meal. Week by week, Nsanga had fewer customers. She also faced heightened competition from other women attempting to sell similar goods. Her best efforts at petty trade brought in only pennies at a time. She grew vegetables in a vacant lot, but soldiers stole her crop. Nsanga was forced to find another way to provide money for food and rent.

One day early in 1986, after walking the downtown streets selling mangoes, Nsanga returned home to discover that Lelo had left. Stunned, because she had performed the duties of a "good, faithful wife," Nsanga rationalized Lelo's abandonment: "Good riddance! At least he won't beat me any more, and besides, now there is one less mouth to feed."

When Nsanga's children ate the food she had intended to sell, she went into debt to the landlord. She begged her elder brother for a loan, but he had a large family and no savings to lend despite his steady job on the docks. Wage freezes and sharply rising prices made it difficult for workers to stretch their incomes to the end of the month. Insulted by her brother's failure to "understand" and to help her, Nsanga ceased visiting his family. The breach of relations with her only relative in the city left her alone and vulnerable. Asked why she did not return to her parents' village, Nsanga responded:

> That's unthinkable! My relatives there are old and very poor; they barely scrape by. They would expect gifts from the city, but they would not be able to help me clear land and build us a house. Where would I get food for the children to tide us over until next year's harvest? Go to the village? Impossible! Something might happen to my children . . . .

Desperate for cash, and without money to start a business, exchanging sex for subsistence appeared to be Nsanga's only recourse. In the first year of this new strategy Nsanga thought she was lucky. She became the second (unrecognized) wife of a government official, who paid her rent and provided regular support. She also had occasional "spare tires" to buy medicine when one of her children became sick. But then she got pregnant. Shortly thereafter, this "husband" told her his salary could not stretch farther, and he, too, left.

Nsanga had to take on more sexual partners. The rate for a "quickie" in her poor neighborhood was less than 50¢. On a good day she might find two or three partners.

By comparison, the average salary for a hospital nurse at the time was about $30 per month. Nsanga and her children lived precariously, sometimes on the very edge of survival.

In mid-1987, the government and media began to acknowledge publicly the threat of AIDS. A leaflet warned men against visiting prostitutes. Most of Nsanga's clients, however, were neighborhood men who came to her each month. As her friends or "husbands," they did not label her a prostitute. Nor was Nsanga stigmatized as a "bad woman." On the contrary, as a mother fallen on hard times through no fault of her own, neighbors admired her for trying her best to "break stones" (kobeta libanga) in order to meet family obligations. In the presence of HIV, however, this survival strategy had become a death strategy.

In 1989, Nsanga grew very thin. She believed that people whispered about her. Indeed, neighbors were sure that she had AIDS. "But then," Nsanga reasoned, "people say this about everyone who loses weight, even when it is just from hunger and worry. All these people who are dying nowadays, are they really all dying from AIDS?"

Nsanga died in 1991. While her neighbors believed that she had been infected in the course of her "sex work," the time frame casts doubt on this assumption. Until the end of 1986, Nsanga had had sex with only one partner: her husband. Thus, given the long incubation period between infection with HIV and manifestation of symptoms, Nsanga's husband was more likely the source of her infection.

Many married women were disarmed by public health advice that assured people that marital fidelity would protect them from AIDS. However, most married women throughout Africa infected with HIV acquired the disease from husbands who had multiple sex partners and failed to use condom protection. Nevertheless, when men fall sick, their wives are often blamed.

Nsanga's story is significant not only because it records the courageous struggle and premature death of a unique human being, but also because it mirrors conditions of life and death for millions in Africa today. Dying obscurely in a Kinshasa courtyard, Nsanga may not seem like a "historical" figure. Yet her personal tragedy embodies that of Africa, with its legacy of systematic structural and corporeal violence.

The SAP policies that played such a crucial role in Nsanga's destiny do not break with the logic of colonial exploitation. Instead, they perpetuate many of colonialism's destructive features. To understand the political and economic patterns that bring suffering and death to people like Nsanga, we must gain a sense of the background from which these patterns emerge.

Colonialism, violence, and health

Conquest and colonial rule

African history has been decisively shaped by the colonial ambitions of the industrialized powers of Europe and the United States. In 1885, the western European nations carved up Africa, often creating artificial boundaries that divided peoples of the same cultures and kingdoms into subjects of different colonial states. For more than two decades Africans resisted conquest, but the superior military technology of the imperial powers prevailed. In some places entire peoples were wiped out by armed violence and "scorched earth" policies, or by famine when driven from their homes. In the early 1890s, rinderpest, a virulent infectious disease of cattle, killed 95 percent of the cattle herds of East and

Southern Africa. Milk and meat disappeared from the diet; grazing land reverted to bush that provided a habitat for tsetse flies. A deadly sleeping sickness epidemic followed. Increased contact with Europeans, army movements, and widespread population displacement introduced new human diseases (and new strains of old diseases) that caused severe epidemics in populations unprotected by immunity. Tremendous social disruption resulted.

Colonization of Africa took place during the heyday of Western monopoly capitalism and emergent dominance of the institutions of finance capital.[5] Extensive tracts of land were expropriated to establish plantations and mines. Colonial states conceded vast monopoly production zones and trading territories to large European and American corporations. Many firms were multinationals, some with interlocking directorates that extended over wide areas. State and company administrators used violence to commandeer low-cost African labor. African raw materials and crops fueled European industrial development, while little of the profit was re-invested in Africa. In some areas, officials requisitioned peasants' crops or forced them to collect forest products. Men in "labor reserve" areas distant from European work sites were conscripted as porters, migrant laborers, and soldiers. Roads and railways needed to evacuate exports were built at great cost to African lives. When paid, wages were extremely low, and living conditions unhealthy and dangerous. Overworked and underfed, African workers suffered high death rates. Fatal work-related accidents were common, especially among underground miners.[6]

As young men were forced to leave their homes, women's work burdens greatly increased, while their social position and autonomy declined. Elder men who remained in rural villages might marry several young women, who, with their children, were put to wielding the hoe. Women in many places protested increased workloads, often by escaping to towns. As planting cycles were disrupted and agriculture suffered from a lack of labor, African food production declined in many areas.

Widespread hunger and periodic famines ensued, rendering populations susceptible to epidemic outbreaks of infectious disease. Colonial responses to disease often involved coercive measures, such as forced removal of populations. In 1918–19 military conscripts returning to their villages brought the influenza pandemic. The movement of soldiers and migrant laborers over large land areas led to the spread of sexually transmitted diseases (STDs), which lowered fertility. While earlier Western writers depicted Africa as rife with disease from time immemorial, in fact the "unhealthiest period in all African history was undoubtedly between 1890 and 1930," the era of colonialists' primary capital accumulation. In some areas, population declined until the end of World War II.

The economic growth generated during this period mainly benefited colonial states and the European-owned plantations, mines, and trading firms. Because colonial sovereignty required total subjugation through overwhelming force, no political space remained for "civil society."[7] Colonial social relations enshrined a racist hierarchy rooted in discourses of biological supremacy, with whites on top. Africans' taxes and export produce paid for continuation of the colonial endeavor on the continent, but brought few of the benefits usually granted a tax-paying citizenry. When colonial governments introduced health services, they did so first to protect European agents, then to maintain those Africans directly useful to the regime, such as soldiers and overseers.

Rigid "color bars," supported by a public culture of exclusionism, operated in every area of life. African workers were paid below-subsistence wages, while skilled jobs were monopolized by whites. In many cities, Africans' houses (mainly crowded shacks) remained segregated from the low-density European settlements. Racism kept most Africans who obtained primary education from advancing to upper secondary schools and universities. Those who did succeed were barred from higher levels of the civil service. Thus, much of Africa was deprived of critical technical and policy-making skills, and deprived of models of democratic governance, both of which would be needed upon achieving political independence.

Following World War II, trade union activity and the "rural radicalism" of poor peasants increased. International pressures led western European governments to open limited political space to the colonized.[8] African war veterans, miners, and railway and civil service unions agitated for a family wage and social security, then, along with educated elites and peasants, demanded independence. Bent on using African materials to rebuild war-torn Europe, the colonial powers attempted to deflect popular demands. In the final phase of colonial rule, colonial states implemented limited reforms with "development" and welfare goals. Peasants' forced labor and crop-planting quotas eased, nutrition improved, and limited biomedical health services were extended to rural areas. The new African elites obtained special status, and better-off peasants received improved agricultural services. Not yet resigned to African independence, colonial rulers sought to create a co-opted middle stratum uninterested in political independence. The majority of poor Africans, however, still lacked access to primary education and health care.

In sum, colonial rule came later in Africa than elsewhere. It coincided with the era of finance capitalism and multinational monopolies. Although differences existed in strategies of rule, all colonizing powers used their superior weaponry and military force to extract local resources and exploit African labor. Foreign business ventures concentrated on mines, plantations, and export-import trade. The companies, owned by white settlers and colonial states, blocked accumulation by Africans, who also were denied political and legal rights. Autocratic states created a culture of systematic violence and humiliation,[9] crafting "a set of policies and a texture of relationship with subject peoples portending the difficulties . . . that beset African societies today."[10]

Early independence

Most of sub-Saharan Africa won independence in the 1960s; it was the last region of the world to do so. The continent's independence is regarded by many as an achievement "of epochal dimensions."[11] Yet two closely related sets of problems were to shape Africa's future. One was political – the state and class structures broached in the preceding section – the other economic.

African governments were left dependent upon revenue generated from the export of a limited number of raw materials. Commodity prices on the world market, however, routinely encounter "boom-and-bust" cycles, over which African states have no control. During the 1960s and 1970s, many African leaders therefore sought to diversify their economies and alter their countries' place in the international economy. They increased processing of domestic raw materials, created import substitution industries (ISIs) to reduce imports of manufactured goods, and taxed foreign-owned businesses to provide resources for development.

Most African governments also sought to meet popular expectations of expanded access to jobs, education, health care, and other services. Urban middle class constituents were favored, and urban hospitals absorbed the largest share of health budgets. In some countries, many rural people also benefited; expanded services and increased food production led to lower child death rates and gains in life expectancy. Still, most rural poor had little or no access to modern preventive and primary health care. Lacking a sufficient domestic revenue base to sustain outlays for human services and development, African governments resorted to borrowing money from abroad. Private commercial banks were eager to lend, especially because lenders' home-country governments guaranteed their loans.

But whether African governments chose statism and nationalization of foreign firms or "liberalism" and "Africanization" of management, independence failed to alter European economic domination. Multinational firms extracted profitable concessions from fledgling African governments and continued to repatriate their profits, leaving relatively little surplus capital for national investment.

The hopeful nationalist project in newly independent African states was of short duration. As many leaders became removed from the struggles of their people, they became increasingly dependent on the "metropolitan powers," as the imperialist states are often called.[12] Foreign debt rose rapidly in the 1960s as loans funded infrastructure development. Huge sums were expended on unproductive "white elephant" prestige projects. Few of the funds disbursed in loans went to poor Africans, or to programs that would have ameliorated their plight: as much as 80 percent of loan funds are estimated to have remained in the hands of Western suppliers of capital goods, management, and technical assistance.

Political patterns in the newly independent countries were deeply impacted by these economic factors. Members of African countries' new "political class" had an interest in creating their own economic resource base; with most of the economy in foreign hands, their road to wealth was the state. Many individuals privatized public resources by manipulating licenses, foreign exchange, land acquisition, credit, and scarce commodities for their own enrichment. Much of their ill-gotten wealth went to foreign banks and tax shelters. Representatives from the World Bank and other members of the international financial community, critical of corruption in Africa, failed to acknowledge their own complicity; the loans they disbursed fueled the misuse of funds by wealthy elites, thereby creating debts that poor Africans must now repay.

Widening disparities in wealth and failure to meet popular expectations for a better life brought political dissent and popular rebellions. As governments were threatened with loss of control, authoritarian bureaucracy and "clientelism" won out over declarations of populist and socialist intent. Often, competing elites mobilized mass ethnic constituencies to support their claims to power.[13] In some countries populist leaders and peasants sought a "second independence" through civil war. As the colonizers before them had done, newly independent central governments met rebellions with force rather than negotiation. Military coups, sometimes aided by Western troops, became common.

Where governments maintained control, peasants increased production for market. Many countries saw modest growth during the period; a few, such as Côte d'Ivoire, were considered growth "miracles," without regard for the inequalities engendered. Relatively high rates of growth, however, failed to "trickle down" to the poor, as governments held down wages and social spending. Instead, resources generated by peasants and laborers were "sucked up" by local and foreign capitalists, and drained into the world economy. Studies conducted during early independence linked life in local communities with macro-level political economies and thus *underscored the tenacity of colonial processes and the difficulty of decolonialization.*

Debt crisis: African initiatives and IFI response

In the mid-1970s, as a result of quadrupled oil prices, Western banks received an abundance of "petro-dollars" from oil-producing countries. Eager to lend the petro-dollars, banks lowered their interest rates substantially, fueling further borrowing by African governments. Beginning in the same period, commodity prices became increasingly volatile. From the mid-1970s, prices of copper and agricultural commodities fell, especially in "terms of trade" – a measure that compares the prices of commodity exports with prices paid for imported manufactured goods from the industrialized countries. Hard-pressed governments stepped up extraction of "rents" from the peasant sector, where farmers were often coerced to grow marketed crops for low returns. As governments confronted overwhelming payments on massive foreign loans, debts were rescheduled at higher interest rates.[14] Prior to this time, African governments seldom had borrowed capital to expand production and to achieve balanced national (or regional) economies.[15]

Faced with deepening crisis, African governments, under the leadership of the Organization of African Unity (OAU) and the UN Economic Commission for Africa (ECA), recognized many past policy errors. They advocated a development strategy combining broadly based growth with social justice. Known as the "Lagos Plan," the strategy's long-term aims included regional food security, to be realized via support for increased production by small farmers, and satisfaction of basic needs of the population through decentralized government services and local self-help. Investments would be directed toward alleviating poverty, and broadening access to health services and education. Together, these measures would slow population growth. The Lagos Plan also recommended regional integration to create wider markets for African industries using local resources. Africa-centered scholars emphasized the need for redistribution of resources on a global scale. Human betterment in Africa was perceived as crucial, both for social justice and for the advancement of world peace.[16]

These perspectives, however, were of little interest to international financial and corporate power holders. Instead of consulting with governments that signed the Lagos Plan, the World Bank in the same year proposed its own strategy for Africa. The multiplex African crisis, exacerbated by global economic stagnation, gave the framers of the Washington Consensus an opportunity to re-create conditions for debt reimbursement and for more profitable resource extraction. These conditions would include easing foreign corporations' access to Africa's profitable oil and mineral resources and lowering import tariffs to facilitate foreign companies' access to African markets.

The key document signaling this shift in policy was the World Bank's 1981 *Agenda for Action in Sub-Saharan Africa*. This report, known by the name of its senior author, Elliot Berg, shed African leaders' mid-1970s concern for social justice and "basic needs." It sought to justify "production first" export policies on the grounds of economic efficiency and comparative advantage. The Berg Report linked further loans to governments' acceptance of policy reforms, and required African states to devalue their currencies to make exports more competitive. Governments were told to remove price controls and end subsidies for food crops to stimulate local production. The Bank demanded concessions to foreign capital, along with privatization of government-owned enterprises and public services. New investment codes included tax incentives, free repatriation of profits, elimination of tariff protection for local industries, and an end to minimum wages and labor protections.

The IFIs pressed African governments to trim their budgets, reduce the civil service, and recover costs by charging "user fees" for public health and education. These measures, the building blocks of SAPs, were supposed to lead to new private foreign investment and stimulate economic growth. The IFIs and governments withheld loans from African states until they signed SAP agreements. Funds previously committed were shifted away from countries that refused to sign the agreements or that insisted on designing their own SAPs rather than accepting the official models. The pattern shows how the power of the Washington Consensus rests on its command of discourse as well as financial assistance. During this period, as in the colonial era, wealthy countries and their experts claimed a monopoly of expert knowledge and exerted their power to specify the limits of policy.[17] Rather than being aided by superior weaponry and using direct military force, however, this time the metropolitan countries were buttressed by superior wealth, the promise of large loans, and the threat of Africa's further marginalization in the global economy.

The results of SAP implementation in the 1980s bore little resemblance to the predictions initially offered by IFI experts. Poor countries' economies stagnated while their debt burdens continued to increase. By the end of the 1980s, debt levels were so high that governments of most non-oil-producing countries used 30 to 70 percent of export revenues for debt service.[18] Governments required new adjustment loans in order to remain even minimally operative, while recession politics in the West diminished the amount of funds for development. Few private foreign investors appeared, except in the oil and mining industries. Commodity prices crashed. Even in adjusting countries, more capital flowed out of Africa during the 1980s than went in. The effects of structural adjustment further widened the gap between rich and poor nations. Within poor nations, costs fell most heavily on poor and vulnerable segments of the population. The 1980s, called "the debt decade," were a "lost decade for Africa."

Crushing debt burdens and SAP conditions for new loans, coupled with the threat of popular unrest, gave foreign capital enormous leverage over policy-making. The decline in national sovereignty led some to write (and many more to speak) of the "re-colonization of Africa." "The state in Africa is being recast . . . the power apparatus locally is increasingly being turned exclusively into an apparatus of repression . . ."[19]

Omissions of the Berg Report

The destructive results of SAPs came as little surprise to many African and Africanist scholars. Immediately following the Berg Report's appearance, and while acknowledging the pertinence of many of its criticisms, scholars argued that the deep historical and structural reasons for crisis in African political economies would remain untouched by Berg's prescriptions. Critics of the Report foresaw further decline in terms of trade for African agriculture largely because similar advice to increase tropical crop exports was being given to the whole of the Third World. Reliance on market forces, privatization, and low-cost labor *would* allow a small number of "progressive" farmers and export-oriented large farms to increase production and profits, at least initially. However, it could be foreseen that peasants with a shrinking resource base would not benefit from increased crop prices. Prices of consumer goods would rise, while diminishing access to cheap credit (where available) and the removal of subsidies for fertilizer and improved seeds, would escalate costs of production. Because rising prices and unemployment prevent urban workers from sending *cash* remittances to *poor* rural relatives, the latter would suffer reduced food production, and with less income, would be unable to pay for essential food and social services.

These predictions proved all too accurate.

Meanwhile, and just as foreseeably, devaluation and price "liberalization" raised the prices of imported agricultural inputs and undermined poor-country producers by exposing them to competition from larger and wealthier foreign companies. Impact fell not only on industries that, on advice from an earlier generation of experts, used many imported components. Small farmers who produced for market also faced heightened competition from cheaper imported food, including subsidized grains. Food security, recognized as a priority following disastrous droughts of the 1970s, was undermined by export-first policies.

In addition, although SAP policies appeared to be gender-blind, they were not gender-neutral. Women's work burdens increased as they were pressed to supply an increasing share of family incomes, their earnings crucial to support children's nutrition and health as well as their own. Thus, poor women and children bore the brunt of SAP austerity. The IFIs proposed to trade "short-term pain for long-term gain." They failed to acknowledge that for already vulnerable populations short-term pain could mean devastating long-term health consequences affecting future generations, and that those least responsible for the crisis would be its primary victims.[20] Yet such failure cannot be explained as mere oversight. As one critic has observed:

> Anthropologists often point to the unforeseen consequences of policies [that arise] when these are actually implemented. Sometimes the consequences are more properly viewed as undeclared goals. Critiques of the Berg Report emerged immediately following its publication [in 1981]. [Yet the policies continued.] [H]ence, we can assume that its policy prescriptions were intended to accomplish just what their results have shown.[21]

The principal goal of the original Bretton Woods Charter that established the IFIs was not to reduce poverty but to safeguard investments and profits of metropolitan firms. Because this is what SAPs actually did, it is undoubtedly what the IFIs, in fact, sought to achieve.[22]

By the mid-1980s, criticism of SAPs began to be voiced in many quarters. Independent researchers and development workers across the continent documented the suffering of communities gripped by deepening poverty and declining health. Case studies by the UN agencies concerned with children's health and social and economic development spurred advocacy for "adjustment with a human face."[23]

In 1989, a new analysis by the World Bank recognized that SAPs had not helped the African poor and that special compensatory poverty alleviation measures were needed. A new "African Initiative" sponsored by African leaders proposed substantial debt cancellation and arms reduction, the savings to be invested in health, education, and essential economic sectors. The IFIs, however, were still reluctant, both to address structural imbalances or to resolve the debt issue. Leading IFI economists continued to advocate reliance on markets and privatization, although some acknowledged that much new local private economic activity was in trade and speculation, rather than in diversified production, and that moreover, privatization had created new opportunities for corruption.[24] New foreign investment continued to be slow, except in extractive sectors that create few linkages to local industry – and in which foreign firms traditionally expatriate most of the profits. In some countries, SAP conditions and resources were used by members of the dominant classes to reposition themselves economically and to co-opt opposition leaders as clients.[25]

Poor Africans continued under the first two decades of SAPs – and continue today – to struggle courageously and creatively to earn livelihoods. Contrary to perceptions current in rich countries, Africans do not simply accept poverty fatalistically as their foreordained condition. Yet grinding misery in the 1980s stretched and then – for many – tore apart the fabric of kinship and other social relations that serve as safety nets in times of need. The impacts have included further subordination of women, more homeless children, higher rates of malnutrition and disease, and worsening domestic and social violence.[26]

Though necessarily schematic, our survey of the historical background of Africa's current economic ills indicates the enduring forces generated by colonial conquest and the ways that recent IFI policies toward the continent perpetuate the logic of colonial exploitation. We now examine some of the consequences of SAP-enhanced economic exploitation on the health of the African poor.

Paying the price: SAPs' impact on the health of the poor

How do SAPs and persistent historical patterns of injustice and inequality degrade the health of Africa's poor? We examine five key areas in which SAPs, and the underlying power relations they reinforce, undermine poor people's health. First, we look at rising social and political violence, with the 1994 genocide in Rwanda as a key example. Second, we return to the spread of HIV/AIDS. Third, we document poor people's reduced access to biomedical health care. Fourth, we show the deteriorating quality of health care available to the poor and middle classes. Finally, we document the consequences of SAPs' effects on food production and nutrition. Throughout the discussion we note how SAPs have affected gender relations and have had a different impact on women than on men.

We begin by examining the most obvious challenge to health and survival for the poor: overt, systematic violence unleashed as a result of social destabilization.

From structural to corporeal violence

Violence arising from political tensions and the disintegration of the social fabric constitutes one very direct way in which the health of the poor is menaced by Africa's multiplex crisis. State tyranny and civil conflict have their roots in the legacy of European colonialism, in the structural violence of poverty, and in the competition among privileged groups.[27] Anticolonial and anti-Apartheid struggles in the 1970s and 1980s were bitter and bloody, as Europeans sought to retain a monopoly of power. White minority governments in southern Africa intervened to destabilize their neighbors.

As the impoverishing effects of SAPs began to be felt across the continent, strikers and street demonstrators protested rising prices and lower real wages. Termed "IMF riots," most of these actions have been met by a varying mix of force and concessions. Protesters find that even new "reform" governments deploy force against them as rulers strive to meet SAP conditions and maintain credibility with international financial institutions and donor governments.

Fear of organized social unrest ("disorder") leads some power-holders to scapegoat ethnic and regional minorities in order to weaken opposition and retain their hold on power. Coalition-building by democracy movements is thereby rendered difficult. Few political elites are strongly linked to the rural poor, although some parties have included organizations of peasants, urban workers, local NGOs, and university students.

Africa's violent disputes, its civil wars, ethnic cleansing, and genocide, are not throwbacks to "centuries of tribalism," as many in the news media would have it. They are similar to strategies of political and economic competition in other parts of the world. Their specific forms help to explain the level of violence in Africa over the past two decades. Struggles for control of the state as a site of enrichment have led to the "implosion" of states in civil wars; some of these have spread to encompass entire regions.[28] The conflicts have brought millions of civilian deaths, tens of thousands of rapes, and massive population displacements.

The genocide of Tutsi by extremists bent on exclusive "Hutu Power" in Rwanda in 1994 is the best-known example. Extremist leaders' extensive ideological preparations, the scale of the killings, and the speed with which they were carried out were unprecedented in Africa. The organizers' basic aims, however, were not unique. State and ethnic violence is a predictable result of what has come to be known as "structural violence." As an illustration of how economic and political conflicts nourished by the legacy of colonialism can unleash murder on a vast scale, the case of Rwanda demands detailed consideration.

Rwandan genocide: an economic genealogy

While US news media continue to view genocide in Rwanda in 1994 as the result of a "centuries-old tribal conflict" between Hutu and Tutsi, the direct cause lay in political struggles. Faced with having to share power, government officials used a barrage of racist propaganda and practices to mobilize their partisans. Many people were motivated to kill their neighbors by manipulation of ethnic identities; others by promises of gain.[29] Economic factors played a crucial and insufficiently acknowledged role in driving the violence. Evidence for this comes from the patterns of the atrocities themselves: houses were looted before being burned; corpses were stripped; cattle were stolen. Rather than be hacked to death by machetes, some victims with cash paid their murderers to shoot them.[30] The conflict was by no means a "purely" ethnic clash between "The Tutsi" and "The Hutu" as monolithic entities.

Ironically, in 1989 Rwanda was cited as one of the World Bank's success stories. Agricultural production had risen by 4.7 percent each year between 1966 and 1982, 1.3 percent faster than the population, and cultivated area had expanded by 37 percent. With more than 90 percent of the population living in the countryside, "Rwanda avoided the urban bias."[31] Moreover, growth was said to have taken place "without the inequities that have sometimes accompanied development elsewhere."[32]

But what the World Bank saw as an "absence of inequity" was viewed quite differently by many Rwandans. The Bank ignored violations of human, economic, and political rights. Rwandan peasants chafed under decrees that in 1976 reinstituted restrictions on freedom of movement. Rwanda had "avoided the urban bias" by hampering urban growth. By the mid-1980s, an estimated one million landless and near-landless people were held "down on the farm" by pass laws. Systematic discrimination against Tutsi was instituted in 1973. Tutsi were barred from the army and limited in their access to government posts. Tutsi children's ability to gain entrance to tax-supported secondary schools and higher education was restricted by quotas. Top jobs in government and *parastatals* (state-owned enterprises) went to people from the president's network and those of his wife and her brothers, without concern for competence.

In reporting on Rwanda during this era, the World Bank approvingly cited the country's erosion control programs. Yet forced labor had been used for soil protection and road building by the colonial administration. Hated by peasants, such compulsory labor (*umuganda*) was abolished at independence, but reinstated in 1976. In praising

Rwanda's soil conservation efforts, the Bank had not listened to peasants who, in 1990, took advantage of weakened state power to destroy many detested anti-erosion works.[33]

With an average farm size of 1.2 hectares per family in 1984, Rwanda may have appeared from the outside to be more egalitarian than most African economies. However, averages can mask significant resource disparities, even in rural areas. Most reclaimable land was already cultivated. With annual population growth at 3.7 percent and with most Rwandans confined to living on small farms, even the insufficient yields of the mid-1980s could not be sustained. The result was a looming threat of hunger.

The rural crisis could only be remedied by intensifying agricultural production, redistributing resources, and reordering government priorities to include creation of labor-intensive off-farm employment.[34] The government, however, actively discouraged informal artisan production, viewing it as competition for formal sector businesses in which the political class had an interest.

The World Bank praised the fact that crop purchasing was left to private merchants and that "market forces fixed the level of food prices, which rose by 10–17 percent annually during the 1970s." Government officials, among others, found trade quite lucrative. By 1989, under the combined onslaught of land shortage and food price rises, rural incomes had fallen by 30 percent from their 1975 level.[35] A small industrial sector emerged, built by the petty *bourgeoisie*, who garnered capital from trade and corruption.

The World Bank and other foreign lenders provided funds to expand export production on large parastatal tea estates and cattle ranches. Projects, including those led by the Bank, often expropriated peasants' land. Improved land was redistributed to government and army officials, their clients, and to the growing rural petty *bourgeoisie*, rather than to needy peasants. Thus, foreign assistance contributed to an accelerating crisis in the rural economy.[36] The plethora of development projects also brought conspicuous inequality: one-third of funds spent for projects in-country went to pay the salaries of technical assistants; half the remaining funds went to build these technical advisors' houses, and another one-quarter to purchase vehicles. Visible inequality heightened many peasants' sense of social exclusion – a form of structural violence.[37] Without employment in the rural areas, children of the rural poor flocked to the towns, where they tried to avoid police controls.

Government agricultural agents tended to work not with resource-poor farmers (72 percent of the population in 1984) but with better-endowed "progressive farmers" owning at least 1.5 hectares.[38] Most research and extension resources went toward increasing exports, about 90 percent of it to coffee. Except for trials of climbing coffee bean varieties and potatoes for high altitudes, little yield-increasing technology for food crops emerged from agricultural research. Peasants' processing and storage problems received scant attention.

From the mid-1970s, a chain of Swiss-funded rural banking cooperatives, intended to benefit peasants, expanded their operations. However, although their savings typically made up 80 percent of their total holdings, the majority of peasants were without collateral and therefore could not qualify for loans. Two-thirds of loans were made for trade and building activities of townsmen, thus de-capitalizing agriculture.[39]

An observer in the early 1980s described how some poor peasants fell victim to usury.[40] Beans are the preferred food staple throughout Rwanda; but poor peasants with little land cannot produce enough to last the season. When they exhaust their supply, they borrow from a trader, who brings five bags of beans worth 5,000 francs. Peasants agree to repay him after the coffee harvest with five bags of coffee worth 30,000 francs. The trader reaps profits equal to five times his initial outlay.

Health conditions reflected the deepening crisis. In 1988, one-third of rural children showed stunted growth, indicating chronic malnutrition, while 40 percent of women and children consumed too few calories. An estimated 80 percent of women delivered their babies at home without a trained attendant. Maternal deaths were estimated at 1,530 per 100,000, among the highest rates in Africa. Starting in 1978, health expenditures began to decline as a percentage of the national budget. By 1987, training and management absorbed 65 percent of public health funds.[41]

The World Bank's upbeat 1989 report on Rwanda is difficult to understand. In contrast, the Rwandan government's 1988 Development Plan recognized the imminent crisis. Its authors called for massive job creation in order to reduce growing inequality and social unrest among landless youth. A 1992 evaluation found that very little had been done.

In 1989, at the World Bank's insistence, the "floor price" paid to coffee growers by the parastatal *Caisse de Stabilisation* was withdrawn. Then the world market price for coffee crashed. Peasants responded by uprooting coffee and planting food crops, as they had following an earlier crash. As a result, cash incomes of the peasant majority declined still further, with consequent worsening of nutrition and health.[42]

By the late 1980s, the absence of political rights in Rwanda's single-party state was under challenge from many quarters. Leaders of clandestine opposition parties who sought political representation, the rule of law, and socioeconomic justice were harassed, and some assassinated. Years of negotiation by Tutsi refugees who had fled state-orchestrated pogroms and ethnic cleansing in the period from 1959 to 1973, failed to secure the right to return to their homeland. In October 1990, refugee soldiers living in Uganda crossed Rwanda's northern frontier in an attempt to claim by force what they had failed to achieve through negotiation.[43] Calling themselves the Rwanda Patriotic Front (RPF), they were joined by other exiled opponents of the dictatorial regime. The government in response straightaway arrested some 10,000 Tutsi and Hutu political opponents living inside Rwanda, many of whom were held without charge for eight months. Beatings and torture were common; sick prisoners were left untreated and many developed lasting illnesses.

While these deadly human rights violations took place, international donors continued to fund development projects and to support the government financially.[44] Increasing tensions still further, Rwanda signed a new SAP agreement in November 1990. The World Bank insisted upon 40 percent currency devaluation. Prices rose and the debt grew; production stagnated, then fell. As unrest mounted, the government blamed all difficulties on the RPF invasion; officials scapegoated the Tutsi inside Rwanda. Still, sophisticated hate propaganda, pogroms led by local officials, and assassination of political opponents received little international notice, despite the plethora of resident Western development project staff. A second currency devaluation, of 15 percent, took place in June 1992; coffee prices fell again.[45] With new foreign loans, the government expanded the army, and bought weapons and equipment. Extremist parties associated with the government recruited 20,000 to 30,000 unemployed young men into militias. The government bought them arms; the army taught them to kill Tutsi "cockroaches" without mercy. Violence grew in both rural and urban areas.

Conditions in the rural areas continued to deteriorate. As population grew, farm size declined and the fertility of the soils that had been cultivated without fallow periods or fertilizers was exhausted. Poorer peasants switched from cultivating beans and maize to manioc and sweet potatoes. While the 1989 World Bank report placed a positive spin on this change, because it led to "more calories per hectare," the nutritional quality of diets suffered. A longitudinal study of a commune in rural Butare Province found that the cash incomes of 75 percent of peasants declined by 35 percent each year from 1990 through 1992. In the latter year, coffee prices fell below the level of the 1989 crash. One-fourth of peasants incurred debts and risked losing their farms. The government instituted *umuganda* work projects to drain marshes for growing rice in the dry season. While all peasant households were made to contribute labor, only officials, businessmen, and loyal peasant clients were awarded access to these plots. In 1992, only rice-growing peasants reported increased incomes.

A peace accord reached in August 1993 provided for power-sharing among government and opposition leaders. Hard-liners in government and the army rejected the accords, however, and prepared, in the words of one leader, "the Apocalypse." A plane crash that killed the presidents of Rwanda and Burundi served as a pretext for a military coup that unleashed a preplanned bloodbath against all Tutsi, as well as Hutu members of opposition parties and their families. The United Nations and leaders of Western governments, warned in advance of plans for genocide, refused to honor their obligations under the Geneva Convention. On television news, the world watched unarmed people hacked and beaten to death. The worldwide audience was told that tribal violence had broken out, when in fact it was genocide and political murder, planned and executed by a self-appointed rump government, whose delegate sat on the UN Security Council. *The extreme violence did not erupt unforeseeably, out of irrational "ethnic hatreds." It was the culmination of a long history of economic deterioration and political conflict,* every stage of which in Rwanda had been observed by representatives of international financial institutions – some of whom mandated the very processes and policies that led to the bloodshed.

The structural violence of AIDS

The destructive impact of ongoing economic crisis on the health of poor communities takes forms less dramatic than genocide yet just as devastating. Structural and social violence have contributed decisively to the dissemination of HIV on the African continent.[46] As economic crisis intensified in the late 1970s, the HIV epidemic silently spread. Seemingly unrelated, the two phenomena are in fact intimately entwined: the effects of poverty accelerate the spread of the virus. The ravages of AIDS in turn plunge afflicted regions deeper into economic crisis.

With just 10 percent of the world's population, Africa is home to 70 percent of past and present AIDS victims in the world: 35 million people. An estimated 22 million African adults and more than 1 million children currently live with HIV/AIDS. Sub-Saharan Africa was the first region to experience the effects of the prolonged crisis and, to date, remains the most vulnerable to the pandemic.[47]

Nearly 90 percent of HIV infections in Africa are transmitted during heterosexual intercourse. Untreated, classic STDs facilitate the sexual transmission of HIV, especially to women, who make up more than half of those infected.[48] In parts of Africa, cultural factors appear to limit the ability of women, married or single, to refuse sex with a steady partner, even if they suspect he may be infected. Moreover, studies in a variety of contexts have shown that women's agency in determining condom use is often severely constrained.

The spread of AIDS has devastated economic and social structures in the areas hardest hit. Ninety percent of AIDS deaths in sub-Saharan Africa occur in adults aged 20 to 49, the prime working years; more than half those infected are aged 15 to 24. As the disease proliferates, industrial firms in southern Africa face shortages of trained personnel. The impact on rural economic activities – particularly season-sensitive, labor-intensive agriculture and food processing – and on family life in affected areas is severe. Despite the efforts of extended families, most are unable to cope with the material and psychological burdens of the disease or with the millions of newly orphaned children. Rather than strengthening families and communities to confront the AIDS onslaught, SAP policies, by failing to reduce poverty and often increasing it, have contributed to accelerating the pandemic.[49] In severely affected countries, three decades of achievement in health – including longer life expectancies and reduced mortality among infants and young children – were annulled in the 1990s due to the mutually reinforcing effects of poverty and AIDS.

Response to AIDS is political in Africa as elsewhere. Public health action takes place on a terrain of contested meanings and unequal power, where different forms of knowledge struggle for control. Epidemiologists and health planners in the development agencies greatly underestimated the potential magnitude of HIV/AIDS in Africa. The disease was initially "constructed" as an urban plight from which "traditional" rural areas, home to a majority of the population, would be spared. Dismissing those who foresaw a catastrophic pandemic, health officials proposed to control AIDS by targeting most prevention efforts to "core transmitters." These included sex workers and long-haul transporters, recognized as having multiple sex partners.

The poor themselves soon grasped the epidemic's economic roots. In 1986, people in Kinshasa dubbed AIDS (SIDA, in French) "an imaginary syndrome to discourage lovers" (*Syndrome Imaginaire pour Décourager les Amoureux*). They were aware that westerners stigmatized Africans for "having too much sex." By 1987, however, another phrase captured popular understanding of AIDS' social epidemiology: "*Salaire Insuffisant Depuis des Années.*" In anglophone Africa, the same causal relationship was expressed as, "the Acquired Income Deficiency Syndrome."

Poverty and gender inequality make women particularly vulnerable to AIDS. The story of Nsanga, which introduced our chapter, shows the risks taken by a poor urban woman struggling to feed her children, her struggles sharpened by SAP policies. Nsanga's fate reflects living conditions and changes in social relations in the era of AIDS. In situations of dire poverty, the limits of "the economy of affection" are quickly reached. Family ties that might once have provided enduring support give way under the combined assault of poverty and disease. People unable to count on family solidarity incur various risks as they struggle to fend for themselves economically.

Specific SAP measures, such as currency devaluation, not only shrink resources that could improve AIDS prevention and the treatment and care of persons with AIDS; they also precipitate social upheavals that accelerate the rate of HIV transmission. Poverty and SAPs have undermined the viability of rural economies, promoted mass labor migration and urban unemployment, worsened the condition of poor women, and left health systems to founder. As a result of these shifts, vast numbers of people in Africa are at increased risk for HIV infection.[50] Such economic and social factors, rather than raging hormones or a special "African sexuality," explain why HIV spreads so rapidly on the continent.

The World Bank, one of the foremost architects of SAPs, is now the single largest lender for AIDS prevention efforts in Africa. Somewhat belatedly, the Bank has acknowledged AIDS as a key development issue, not simply a health problem. According to a 1998 Bank report on the worldwide AIDS situation, HIV/AIDS is exacerbating poverty and inequality, and is projected to further slow the already unfavorable per capita income growth of many countries in sub-Saharan Africa through its effects on savings and productivity. The deleterious effects of SAPs led a long-time AIDS policy advisor to ask: "Given the increased needs in terms of health on the continent, largely due to the prevalence of AIDS, why didn't the World Bank make *increasing* health budgets a condition for their loans?"

Reproductive and sexual health

African women are greatly concerned about reproductive and sexual health: the social status of many depends on producing healthy children. They are more likely than women elsewhere to die in childbirth and from pregnancy-related conditions, especially when they deliver their children unattended by trained health workers. Those at highest risk are poor women, young women under age 20, women bearing children over age 34, and women who have had five or more pregnancies. In the poorest African countries 60 to 80 percent of women give birth with little or no assistance from health providers. Despite the well-known problem of high maternal mortality, many SAP countries *increased* fees for child delivery and other maternity services. In Zimbabwe, studies have shown that when maternity fees are increased, more women risk the dangers of delivering their children at home unattended by health providers.[51]

Small but growing numbers of poor women and men began to use biomedical contraceptive methods in some countries in the late 1970s. By the 1990s, that increase was threatened wherever SAP-restricted health policies took hold. Family planning services were reduced, and user fees prevented many poor women from taking advantage of the services that did exist. Deprived of preventive care, including health education and contraception, poor women, especially adolescents, will produce more, rather than fewer, children. As the dangers connected with unattended pregnancy and childbirth combine with poverty, malnutrition, and STDs, women's already high risks of death climb still higher.

Sexual health includes freedom from STDs, which in addition to pain and increased risk of acquiring HIV, also lead to reproductive failures and serious health problems in children.[52] Women, and especially adolescent females, are more vulnerable than men to STDs, for both biological and social reasons.[53] They are also heavily stigmatized if their affliction becomes known. Because many health services primarily target married women or mothers, and are unable to provide private examining spaces, or even treat women courteously, at-risk women are often discouraged from seeking care. User fees are an even greater deterrent to successful STD treatment.

Declining access to health care

The lack of health provider discretion and the imposition of user fees, however, are not the only barriers confronting poor Africans who seek biomedical health care. A person's ability to reach a health-care facility, to be treated by a health-care provider, or to obtain needed medicine is dependent on many factors, including proximity to the facility, transportation costs, ability to pay service and medicine fees, and sociocultural factors such as language, class, and gender.[54] Generally, the more numerous and widely dispersed health facilities and health-care providers are, the greater people's access to health care. This is especially true in Africa where the majority of poor people live in villages far from urban centers. In remote areas, distance is the most crucial determinant of health-care access.

In the 1960s and 1970s, African countries made enormous strides toward bringing health facilities and personnel to the rural majority. Since the early 1980s, however, this progress has slowed and even halted, due in large part to the economic constraints imposed by SAPs and to the costs of the AIDS pandemic. During the SAP era, governments have found it expedient to cut expenditures on services for those with little political influence. Public health outlays for the poor all too often provide such a strategy, where budget austerities are attended by only minimal political risks. As a result, public hospitals and clinics in many parts of Africa are now desperately understaffed and poorly equipped. Budget compression under SAPs reduced support for health in most countries to about 2 percent of GDP.[55]

Moreover, medical doctors and nurses throughout much of Africa either moonlight to survive or leave their countries to find employment or better salaries elsewhere. The emigration of health professionals further exacerbates the personnel shortages caused by SAP-guided government hiring freezes, salary cutbacks, and early retirement for civil servants, including health workers. In Ghana, according to a World Bank paper, the number of doctors decreased from 1,782 in 1985 to 965 in 1991. In already underserved rural areas, these employment shifts have greatly increased the workload of the remaining doctors and nurses. At the same time that user fees were imposed, devaluation increased prices for imported medicines and supplies. Thus, SAPs "helped to precipitate a catastrophe in which virtually all economic, social, educational, and public health gains made in the 1960s and 1970s have been wiped out."[56]

Wide-ranging health, economic, agricultural, and industrial policy changes mandated by SAPs complicate access to health care for men as well as women. Inability to obtain needed health care is another way that poverty and inequality translate into suffering and premature death for the already vulnerable. The tragic effects of this pattern are illustrated in the story of Aseffa Okoso.

Okoso was a strong, imposing Ghanaian man of 43 from a small town 165 kilometers northwest of the capital city. Okoso had a wife, five children in school, and many good friends with whom he shared his extensive repertoire of jokes and songs. Beloved by neighborhood children, despite his rugged appearance and deep voice, Okoso was usually at the center of Sunday gatherings when he was at home.

Proud of his strength and skill, Okoso had worked for eight years as a manual laborer at an American-owned gold-mining company located two hours by bus from his home. In the mining town, he stayed with workmates in a rented room. So as not to spend too much on bus fare, he returned home every other Saturday after work. On alternate Saturday nights, he joined his mates at a local beer joint, where they competed to impress the young waitresses.

In January 1996, Okoso suffered from extended bouts of diarrhea, with fever and night sweats. At first he thought his sickness might be due to bad water in the compound. While still on the job, he was able to pay for medicines to relieve his diarrhea. But it kept coming back. Okoso grew thin, coughed a lot, and eventually became too sick to keep up the hard physical labor his job required. He also became frightened. As his illness progressed, he was forced to leave the mine without severance pay.

At home, Okoso's condition worsened, but care at the local clinic became very expensive. When the financial burdens of Okoso's illness began to overwhelm his family, friends generously helped him cover the costs of care. But because his friends, too, were struggling, Okoso stopped asking for their assistance. Just three months after leaving the mine, Okoso gave up on his illness, choosing instead to remain at home. When asked why he no longer sought care from the clinic located just a few miles from his urban home, he responded with conviction:

> *If I went to the clinic, they would make me pay this new fee which, frankly, my family and I cannot afford. I have no work, no salary. We live day to day on what my wife can make selling vegetables in the local market or what my sons can bring home from selling things on the streets. Some days we eat only one meal and we often go to bed hungry.*

Okoso knew that the clinic nurse would give him a prescription to purchase medicines that, once again, would be too expensive. In conversation, Okoso showed a lucid awareness that his inability to afford treatment was related to the vast and rapid economic changes his country had undertaken over the preceding 13 years.

Friends suggested that he consult an African healer, but Okoso rejected that option as futile, for he was coughing blood. Miners' folklore in Africa had familiarized him, an open pit miner, with the symptoms of tuberculosis. Okoso died just seven months after being diagnosed with AIDS. His two youngest children began to cough, leading the researcher to suspect that they, too, had become infected with tuberculosis.[57]

Deteriorating quality of health care

Okoso's story illustrates the effects of reduced health access on people struggling simultaneously against poverty and deadly disease. Joined with the erosion of public health-sector budgets and salaries, the proliferation of such cases has had predictably negative effects on staff morale, professionalism, practitioner-patient relations, and quality of care in African countries affected by the social fallout of SAPs. The poor find less health care available to them, and the quality of the care that exists is declining.

In Côte d'Ivoire, attendance at the university teaching hospital in the country's capital, Abidjan, declined by about 50 percent following currency devaluation in 1994; the price of medicines meanwhile rose 30 to 70 percent. Physicians expressed their demoralization as, powerless to provide adequate care to poor patients, they sent them home to die.[58] Sick people consulted "traditional" practitioners, whose numbers expanded markedly.[59] While many healers have knowledge of specific herbal remedies and can treat a limited range of ailments, the claims of others to treat diseases such as cancers, tuberculosis, and AIDS suggest charlatanism.

In practice, for the poor who do access state health-care facilities, nurses deliver most of the curative as well as preventive services, usually without physician supervision. Nurses' patient loads have increased dramatically, even in poor rural and urban areas where many cannot afford services. The story of Demba Djemay, a nurse from Senegal, reflects the frustration even highly motivated health-care providers feel when facing the impossible working conditions resulting from SAP-mandated economic austerity measures in the public sector.

Djemay considers nursing more than just a job; for him it is a calling. Thirty-five in 1993, he had trained for three years following primary school to become a nurse. He works in a small hospital near his hometown in Senegal. But now Djemay is unable to use his skills to care adequately for patients. His regional health center is seriously underequipped, lacking medicines and the most basic medical supplies – including disinfectants, gloves, masks, and disposable syringes. It is also short-staffed, with only one other nurse and a part-time physician. Together, these two-and-a-half professionals serve a population of more than 150,000 people. Djemay and his nurse colleague are overworked, barely compensated, and each often sees 70 patients a day – many of whom die of readily treatable diseases. Treatable, that is, were medicines and equipment available. "My work is one frustration after another," Djemay lamented. "Under these conditions, I simply cannot provide my patients the kind of care they urgently need."

Patients may wait all day, sometimes into the following day, to see him. When they finally enter his small examining room, they receive a brief, if sympathetic, audience and a prescription. Djemay said: "Most patients would have to trade away the family's food supply to purchase the medicines. Many have already sold livestock to pay for their transport to town and their hospital admission fee. So often after losing a day or more of work, patients go home empty-handed."

Djemay's patients are fortunate that he has kept his professional conscience despite adversity. His frustration reflects a grim statistic: between 1980 and 1993, the number of people per nurse in Senegal rose more than six times, from 1,931 to 13,174. Many other countries registered increases of two to nine times during the same period. Meanwhile, health coverage was quite uneven, with a few countries admitting declines and some making doubtful claims of improvement. Botswana, with diamonds, peace, and effective governance, was the only country with both credibly improved health coverage and a lower number of people per nurse.

Shrinking access to health care and deteriorating quality of care available, both direct results of SAP policies, leave the poor increasingly exposed to suffering and death that relatively modest health expenditures could prevent. The impact of SAPs and related policy measures on food production and nutrition constitutes another critical channel through which the accumulated heritage of colonial and postcolonial economic exploitation influences the health of Africa's poor.

Food, nutrition, and health

Nutrition may be the single most important determinant of health. Poor nutrition is *synergistic* with disease; that is, the presence of either increases the likelihood of the other. Indeed, the strongest predictors of child health are, first, broad, equitable distribution of food and primary health services, and, second, the education of women. These factors are interrelated and depend less on gross national product (GNP) figures than on governments' political choices in allocating resources to different segments of the population. To show the interrelation between economic patterns, political choices, nutrition, and health, we consider data on malnutrition among poor women and children. Then we focus on World Bank agricultural policies in Africa and assess these policies' results.

Both adequate energy (calories) and "micronutrients" are required for growth and health. Even moderate malnutrition increases the risk of sickness and death in young children by about 50 percent. Stunting (low height for age, indicative of chronic malnutrition) affects the health of the entire body and may prevent children from ever being able to "catch up" developmentally, even if calorie intake later improves. Prolonged severe nutrient deprivation may lead to mental retardation.[60] Women who had been chronically malnourished in childhood often fail to develop the bone structure needed for safe childbirth; they also give birth to more underweight babies, as do those who perform strenuous work late in pregnancy. Undernourished women also produce poor quality breast milk. The consequence of these interwoven patterns is that poorly fed mothers and their infants risk chronic illness and death.[61]

Effects of economic recession and structural adjustment on the health and lives of children are monitored by UNICEF. A longitudinal study undertaken in Brazzaville, the capital of Congo, used body measurements to assess nutritional status before and during the implementation of structural adjustment. As adjustment took hold, the proportion of underweight children rose, including those in families considered non-poor.[62] Among children of the poor, both acute malnutrition and stunting rose. The percentage of low birth-weight babies, considered evidence of maternal nutritional stress, almost doubled. The proportion of poor mothers with chronic energy deficiency increased; nearly 20 percent of mothers under age 18 did not get sufficient calories. Researchers concluded that the effects of economic decline and SAPs on the health of the poor will continue to be manifested during the course of the next 20 to 30 years.[63]

Another time series comes from rural and urban samples in Côte d'Ivoire, where nutritional status worsened as poverty incidence increased between 1988 and 1993. The rural poor registered the sharpest declines: child stunting rose as incomes declined. The poorest households were concentrated among small farmers in the northern savannah zone.[64] These are the people left out of the earlier growth "miracle."[65]

Most researchers did not disaggregate their data. That is, they failed to separate measurements made on children of the poor from those on children in better-off households. Even so, a study that surveyed children born in Lusaka, the capital of Zambia, found that in just two years (from 1986 to 1988), SAP policies had measurable negative effects on child nutrition and health.

Increased food prices and poverty are conspicuous in big cities. However, malnutrition is generally more prevalent in rural areas, where more poor people live. Food production and rural incomes have declined since the late 1970s in most of sub-Saharan Africa. Inequality widened not only in incomes but in wealth and property, as ownership and access to fertile land became increasingly concentrated. Women, especially, lost land rights.

Laws to encourage the privatization of land have reinforced a multilayered landholding pattern in regions where fertile land is in short supply. At the top, large agribusiness estates produce for market, increasingly for export, using the labor of the landless or near-landless rural poor. The largest estates are owned by transnational corporations (TNCs); European, Asian, or local businessmen; and government officials. Since the 1980s, SAP policies have enhanced the profitability of these large export-oriented businesses, while making economies that followed SAP prescriptions even more dependent upon fewer primary products than before.

The peasant (or small farm) sector is also differentiated. It includes those farmers with sufficient resources to invest in technology and labor, who produce mainly for market, and hire migrants or their poorer neighbors as temporary laborers. To the extent that government and donor programs have helped small farmers at all, in most countries it is these "progressive" or small-scale commercial farmers who have been the main beneficiaries. Middle-level peasant families are able to grow most of their food and sell the surplus. Both these types of better-off peasants have sought to educate at least one family member sufficiently to obtain a civil service job. However, as access to government employment has narrowed with SAP budget cuts, many graduates join the unemployed.

At the bottom of the land-holding pattern are peasants who produce some crops for sale but are too poor in resources to fully meet family food and other basic requirements.

These households must send out members to work for wages, sometimes on farms, but also as migrant labor. In many countries, the numbers and percentage of households in this category of poor peasants expanded in the 1980s and 1990s as access to fertile land grew increasingly restricted.

Structural adjustment programs require governments to remove subsidies on food as well as on agricultural inputs such as fertilizer and fuel. Food subsidies were reduced gradually in many countries, while subsidies on fertilizer and other inputs to small farmers were removed more rapidly. International advisors, nevertheless, expressed confidence that higher crop prices would create incentives for farmers to produce more. The advisors believed that farmers aiming for higher yields would continue to use fertilizer even if they had to borrow money to purchase it. The errors in this notion are demonstrated by field studies. Research with women farmers is especially telling.

Even where credit is available, small producers are apprehensive about making use of it. They cannot risk being unable to reimburse loans if their crop yields suffer due to insufficient rainfall. Indebted farmers may lose their land and be forced to work on others' farms. Determined to avoid this fate, small farmers struggling on the edge of survival are unwilling to adopt the entrepreneurial mentality the SAP-mandated programs assume as the "natural" inclination.

The increased vulnerability of poor farming families under the impact of SAP-mandated policies is illustrated by the story of Bintu, a 45-year-old Jola woman, and her family, in their village in southwestern Senegal.

Bintu has difficulty pulling her slight frame out of bed each day. She explains: "When you open your eyes in the morning knowing that your day will be filled with hardship and humiliation, your desire to begin the day may wane." Before this year (1994), Bintu had considered herself fortunate. Though she had lost two children in childbirth, she had two grown children from a previous marriage who looked after her. Her daughter Sali, living in the Senegalese capital Dakar, regularly sent Bintu money, and every year after the harvest her son gave her a portion of the money he earned from selling his peanut crop. With this income, Bintu was able to meet her expenses. She was praised in the village for her cooking and for the hearty meals she served her husband and his extended family.

Bintu also felt fortunate because, despite unreliable rainfall, her husband managed to grow enough peanuts to sell in order to cover the monthly cost of purchasing subsistence grains once the familial rice stocks ran out, usually five or six months after the harvest. When Bintu was a young girl, the rice the women cultivated would last well into the next harvest season, and surplus rice could be bartered for other household necessities. But in recent decades, the rains come late and end early, and the rice fields are slowly taking on salt from nearby saline waters. Despite such trends, Bintu considered herself relatively lucky.

But in 1994 one seemingly minor incident in Bintu's household shattered the fragile balance on which the family's livelihood depended. The 4-year-old son of Bintu's brother-in-law accidentally sliced his thumb with a knife. The wound became infected, and the boy fell seriously ill. The family collected enough money to send the boy and his father to see a nurse or doctor in the hospital 45 kilometers away. At the hospital, as Bintu's brother-in-law tells the story, the boy looked dreadfully ill, barely conscious. The doctor insisted on keeping him in the hospital. He ordered the boy's father to go to the local pharmacy to purchase medicines for his son's treatment, as the hospital did not have the medicines in stock. Having spent most of the money on transportation and hospital entrance fees, the boy's father was obliged to return to the village for more money so that he could fill the prescription. After ten days, and approximately $64 in medicines, hospital fees, and transportation costs, Bintu's brother-in-law returned to the village with a healthy son.

Most of the money for the young boy's treatment (approximately $50) came from Bintu's husband, who had stashed away half of the previous year's peanut proceeds to be able to buy rice when the family's grain stock was depleted at the end of the dry season. His remaining savings could purchase only one 50 kilo sack of rice, enough to feed the family for about 27 days. With the government's devaluation of the currency and removal of transportation subsidies for grain, the price of rice was at an all-time high. For the following two months, Bintu and her sister-in-law contributed their meager savings to purchase rice. But then with two more months remaining before the harvest, the extended household was forced to begin selling off their modest livestock.

To make matters worse, when the two men of the household went to prepare for the peanut season, they learned that the government had also ended two long-standing programs designed to encourage farmers to produce peanuts: input subsidies and a credit system that enabled farmers to receive credit for seed, fertilizer, and equipment purchases. Now, for the first time since the peanut cash crop was introduced to the area toward the beginning of the century, it was up to the individual farmers to procure their own agricultural inputs. The government promised that farmers would be paid a higher price for their peanuts after the harvest. But with no money for seeds and other inputs, Bintu's husband and brother-in-law were forced to go into debt. The family now wonders if they will break even once they sell their crop. Next year, if they incur any extraordinary expenses, the entire household is likely to "go under" altogether.

Meanwhile, the financial support Bintu had previously received from urban relatives ceased. Bintu's daughter Sali and son-in-law Bocar, living in Dakar with their baby son, had themselves fallen on desperate times, due to layoffs directly resulting from Senegal's SAP. At a time when their aid was critical, they were unable to continue sending remittance money to Bintu and the family in their rural village.

The story of Bintu and her family shows how SAP policies have worked at multiple levels to increase the economic vulnerability and health risks faced by poor rural families. Bintu's family members cultivate the family's own land. Poor peasants who must work on others' land also find themselves in desperate situations. As previously noted, farm workers' wages are extremely low; for women in particular they are often insufficient to support families, even in good times. Under such conditions, any sort of health emergency can rapidly take on catastrophic proportions, forcing a family to pledge or sell their productive assets to obtain cash. By selling off their land or farm animals, families exacerbate their current plight, and dim their future prospects. Single events requiring an unexpected outlay of money can push entire families to abandon the land and flock to urban squatter settlements.

The international financial institutions have imposed the privatization of agricultural marketing in the belief that state marketing boards are inherently less efficient than private sector traders.[66] Certainly, arguments could be made in defense of this claim. Parastatal marketing boards were originally designed by colonial rulers to assist white settlers in marketing their produce. They also served to tax peasant producers by holding prices down. Following independence, many such boards continued to function to the advantage of officials who not only collected the state's "rent" from peasants, but also seized opportunities for corruption. Nevertheless, the better-run agencies brought goods and services not otherwise available to farmers in remote areas. These goods included fertilizer and seeds, often supplied with low-cost or interest-free loans, or for the promise of a percentage of a farmer's future harvest. In Tanzania, Zambia, and Senegal in the late 1960s, and Zimbabwe in 1980, a system of state subsidies and "pan-territorial" prices enabled peasants far from markets to increase their production and to earn cash without having to migrate in search of employment. However, the elimination of these structures in response to IFI pressure in favor of "free market" models imposed from outside has worked to the disadvantage of poor farmers in remote areas. The case of Zimbabwe shows how SAPs can exacerbate social inequality within a country (see Box 4.1).

Box 4.1: Free Markets and "Free Fall" in Zimbabwe

Zimbabwe's history of struggles for control of land has been long and bitter. In the late nineteenth century, conquest by European settlers was vigorously resisted for decades. When Africans lost, they were pushed off the best land and made to work the settlers' farms. In 1965, seeking to avoid Black majority rule, Europeans unilaterally declared independence (UDI) from Britain. During the UDI period of white minority rule, new land laws reconfirmed white settlers' possession of 45 percent of the total land area – including the most fertile and well-watered land. Black Africans, 95 percent of the population, were confined to just half the land, much of it arid and unsuitable for cultivation. Much of the white settlers' land remained uncultivated.

The white minority government pursued policies, including subsidized credit, prices, and infrastructure, to support the white-owned, large-scale commercial farms (LSCFs). The policies further marginalized the black peasant majority, many of whom became supporters of the protracted armed struggle for liberation from white domination. In the mid-1970s, indebtedness overtook many white settler farmers, and South Africa-based TNCs gained control of the sector. By the time of independence in 1980, TNC farms garnered 75 percent of profits derived from agriculture; they prospered in part by reducing workers' wages. Zimbabwe had joined the "Global Big House."

The Mugabe government's ability to carry out land reform was hampered by a British-brokered peace agreement stipulating that any redistribution must compensate settler farmers at market rates. Some farm purchases and redistribution took place in the early 1980s, but not enough to meet popular expectations. A 1983 survey found that 60 percent of rural households were still without land. Twenty percent of the labor force worked on plantations, with the lowest wage rates of the formal sector, the worst living conditions, and the worst health status to be found in Zimbabwe.[67] In 1982, despite a pay raise, the minimum wage was 25 percent less than the cost of a bare subsistence diet. By 1990, the large farm sector employed 300,000 workers, more than any other sector. Real wages fell. Migrants could no longer send home remittances; wives and children were pressed into work.

The parastatal grain marketing board (GMB), originally set up to aid LSCFs, expanded its collecting points into African farmers in communal areas (the old "tribal" reserves). The GMB provided peasants with inputs and collected the maize crop in a timely fashion, reducing post-harvest losses. For the first time, many peasants gained access to fertilizer and hybrid seeds adapted to low-potential agro-ecological zones. Production rose among African small-scale commercial

(*continues*)

Box 4.1 (*cont'd*)

farmers (SSCFs) and among peasants in the communal areas. Between 1980 and 1985, small holders nearly doubled the area planted with white maize, the staple food, as the government raised the farm price by 80 percent. In order not to increase urban wages beyond what employers would accept, however, the government subsidized the price of white maize. Small farmers could sell shelled grain to the GMB and purchase milled maize in local shops at subsidized prices. As a result of these favorable conditions, despite two years of drought (1982 and 1983), maize collected by the GMB tripled between 1980 and 1985.

Gender inequality persisted. As "heads of households," men were awarded land titles and cooperative memberships, and the attention of extension agents.[68] Men, even those working in towns, received payment for crops grown by women, despite the women's heavy cash needs for household expenses, school uniforms, and clothing. Women from the new cooperative resettlement areas agitated for change, particularly for the right to hold land in their own names. Peasants in the communal areas were still poor, but from their experience in the protracted war for liberation they remained organized as communities taking active part in local and national life. Free government-supported rural schools and primary health care lightened the load. Infant mortality dropped by half. Some NGOs assisted with water supply and maize storage facilities, without expecting reimbursement. Production was unevenly distributed, however, varying with rainfall, soil quality, labor, and access to machinery.

The LSCFs still occupied nearly one-third of all cultivated land – including most of the best. Transnational corporations became the major producers of export crops. Employers provided miserable camp housing and some clinics, but health services were poor in both accessibility and quality. Prices for food and basic goods (salt, oil, soap, and so on) were higher in the shops in LSCF areas than elsewhere.[69]

In 1991, Zimbabwe signed a new SAP agreement that mandated "liberalization." Controls were removed from foreign exchange prior to devaluation. This led to speculative imports of expensive consumer goods that drained hard currency reserves. The World Bank delayed loan disbursement, apparently to hasten further policy changes. Maize and fertilizer subsidies were removed and activities of the GMB restricted. The rural poor, affected by sharply rising costs of fertilizer, food, and basic necessities, became still poorer. Zimbabwe's 1991 SAP "sent a previously moderately successful economy into free-fall."[70]

In 1991, the worst drought ever recorded struck the region. The maize crop was ruined over most of the country and prices shot up, though few small farmers could benefit. Introduction of "user fees" at health centers and hospitals led to sharp declines in attendance, because people could not afford to pay.[71] The worst health and living conditions were on the large farms. Conditions for women workers were even worse than for men.

By 1998, the government had laid off 7,000 nurses. Many physicians left the public system for private practice. In the early 1980s, Zimbabwe's formal sector workers had quite adequate health insurance for themselves and their families, but with so many unemployed due to SAP de-industrialization, the percentage of

(*continues*)

Box 4.1 (*cont'd*)

people covered dwindled. One-quarter of the adult population reported being infected with HIV, and AIDS killed 1,200 people each day. Life expectancy declined dramatically, from 60 years in 1991 to 49 years in 1997.[72]

Beginning in 1997, the urban population became more active in expressing its anger at the widening gap between their own poverty and the wealth of the political class. Strikes, stay-at-homes, and street demonstrations protested sharp consumer price hikes, government corruption, and profiteering. While President Mugabe blamed SAPs for the country's economic problems, others saw his inner circle grow wealthier by manipulating foreign exchange, import speculation, and privatization. Costly intervention in the Congo civil war, apparently to defend assets conceded to Zimbabwe officials by Congo President Kabila, is also extremely unpopular. The Congo government refused dialogue, and instead responded with force. Leaders of trade unions and religious and other civic groups called for a new constitution and began to form a new political party.

Struggles over conditions of production and exchange traced in earlier sections continue across the continent today. Studies by social scientists who have observed market transactions and interviewed peasants find that, in many countries, unregulated private sector marketing has resulted in a lack of available inputs for small farmers, and in some areas, lower prices for their produce. Currently, the rural poor are socially powerless, "surrounded by a dense network of public and private actors reducing their freedom of action and draining what few resources they do have."[73] Relying solely on unrestricted markets is *not* a rational policy for Africa. The solution to the inefficiency and abuses of parastatals is not to eliminate these organizations entirely but to restructure them so as to make their bookkeeping transparent and their managers accountable to peasants. Improving life for poor rural Africans will be less a matter of liberating free market forces than of liberating and empowering the poor themselves. The examples of Zimbabwe, Zaire, and Rwanda show that politics in peasant communities and relations between states and peasants lie at the heart of rural economic transformation.

To be effective and just, rural revitalization must also consider gender equity in land use, food production, and marketing. In most of Africa, the majority of people are farmers, and women are overrepresented among farming populations. Women produce, transport, and process between 70 and 90 percent of food grown in many areas of Africa. They also work on husbands' cash-crop fields. Women spend long hours in the fields and also may walk for miles to procure wood and water, returning to prepare meals and care for children. Women's average workdays are 30 to 50 percent longer than men's, often lasting from 10 to 12 hours in slack seasons and 14 to 16 hours in peak periods, such as during field preparation, weeding, and harvests.

Rural women's cash incomes, derived mainly from their own produce sales, purchase food and other family necessities such as soap, salt and oil, medicines, and school uniforms and supplies. Where women control a significant share of household resources, they and their children are more likely to eat as well as men.[74] Generally, however, when families are unable to grow or purchase enough food to meet the nutritional requirements of all members, children's and women's health is the first to be sacrificed.[75]

In regions where men migrate in search of paid employment, 25 to 60 percent of household heads may be female. Unless men are able to send home remittances, these households may be very poor. Beyond these generalities, however, there exist many differences. Both rural and urban women's situations vary with age, reproductive status, education, and the wealth of their families.

As women's vital role in production became recognized in the 1970s, it was noted that women farmers had less access to land, labor, tools, and credit than did men. Furthermore, women were neglected by the agricultural extension services their taxes went to support.[76] Analysts urged that women be given greater access to resources, not only as an equity issue but to increase food production and national food security.[77] Pilot projects showed that women could increase their productivity when provided with small amounts of credit, training, and technology.[78] However, these promising demonstrations were not enlarged into nationwide programs. Instead, in the 1980s most women's access to resources declined as a result of economic crisis and structural adjustment.[79] More women became unpaid laborers on their husbands' fields or low-paid workers on the fields of others.[80]

Structural adjustment policies favor export crops grown on farms controlled by senior men.[81] As in the colonial period, pressure to grow export crops has meant heavier work burdens for wives and daughters. Women's time and access to land, labor, and other inputs for their own independent agricultural projects have decreased. Crops controlled by women receive less fertilizer.[82] Yields of vegetable gardens and maize fields are reduced because women cannot afford to buy improved seeds. They must often choose between family meals and cash sales. Either choice may mean a decline in the quality of the family's diet and health, because women's cash is most often used to buy foods not grown at home, along with products such as soap, salt, cooking oil, fish, and other items essential to health.[83]

Tools produced with imported steel are too expensive, so women use inferior hoes made from recycled scrap. Meanwhile, bicycles, wheelbarrows, or oxcarts for daily transport of water and materials are now an impossible dream for most poor and medium-scale peasants. The absence of wheeled conveyances means still more toil for women. Men, who often would cooperate when wheeled transport was available, generally define head-loads as "women's work." Many African peasant women bitterly attribute their declining status to "recolonization by SAPs."[84]

Reforming SAPs: rhetoric and reality

Right words, wrong actions

Widespread criticism of SAPs' deleterious effects on vulnerable populations in the late 1980s led the World Bank to design new loans and programs ostensibly intended to protect the poor during the years Bank officials label the "transition period" from state-planned to market economies. Yet these short-term compensation packages, or *social safety nets*, failed in most cases to mitigate the hardships of the poor. Instead, in many African countries, they became political tools used primarily to placate SAPs' vocal and politically organized opponents. In Senegal, for example, safety net projects were created after violent protests erupted in the aftermath of a national election in the late 1980s, that threatened to derail the government's compliance with SAPs. The projects provided small business management training and credit to educated, voting urbanites, *not* the rural poor.[85] Compensatory reductions in school and health service fees were often so badly publicized or cumbersome to access that little assistance actually reached those most in need. The World Bank's 1995 Africa Poverty Reduction Task Force found that poverty-alleviation programs in most countries failed to adequately identify and target the neediest – the peri-urban and rural poor. Nor was the impact of such programs on poor communities adequately monitored.[86]

Poverty alleviation campaigns were potent rhetorical tools for assuaging SAPs' critics, but they were feeble in realizing their own stated objectives. Even though farm-level studies have shown that poor farmers can, with policy support, increase their production, contribute to food security, and reduce dependence on imports, the World Bank "still has not internalized or programmed enhanced production by poor people as a significant strategic element."[87] Without first altering the fundamental relationship between the IFIs and the people and governments of Africa, it is unlikely that "band-aid" remedies such as safety nets will go far in raising vulnerable populations out of poverty. What policies might induce meaningful change? Debt forgiveness offers one option.

Dogged debt

After two decades of SAPs, the debt burdens of many African countries are unsustainable. In the 1980s, Africa, the world's poorest continent, was a net *supplier* of capital to the industrialized countries. Still, in 1993, for every dollar given to Africa in aid, rich nations took back three in debt repayments.[88] The amount of interest paid by poor countries to multilateral banks has already exceeded the original sums of money borrowed, yet the countries are still in debt.[89] In the 1980s and early 1990s, SAP-directed currency devaluation raised debt levels by 40 to 50 percent in most African countries. The effects continue to be felt. In 1996, sub-Saharan Africa received $15 billion in loans but paid out $12 billion in debt service. Despite some debt relief in the mid-1990s, debt service payments by African governments averaged 31 percent of exports.

The obligation to spend so much of national budgets on debt service hinders governments' capacity to invest in health and social development. In 1994, over four-fifths of Uganda's export earnings – $162 million – went to debt and interest payments. By comparison, the country was able to spend a total of just $120 million on health and education services.[90] Between 1990 and 1993, sub-Saharan Africa transferred $13.4 billion annually to its external creditors. This is four times as much as governments in the region currently spend on health services.[91] Debt also impedes direct foreign investment, stifles employment creation, and ultimately inhibits economic growth. (See Box 4.2.)

Heavily Indebted Poor Countries (HIPC) that meet SAP "conditionalities" can, in time, obtain some relief from debt service payments and IFIs. Debt relief is not the same as outright cancellation. Relief may also include rescheduling payments on loans made by foreign governments and private banks. By allowing debtor countries a longer time to pay, and given probable inflation, drawing out the debt period should reduce total expense. While private and bilateral loans rescheduled in the 1980s and 1990s required higher rates of interest than the original loans made in the 1970s, the IFIs will lower their rates to offer "concessional" terms.

Uganda spearheaded the call by African leaders for debt cancellation. The first (and only) African HIPC to conduct successful debt relief negotiations with the IFIs to date, Uganda obtained approximately a 20 percent reduction in overall external debt service payments. Burkina Faso, Côte d'Ivoire, and Mozambique are the other African countries that met debt relief conditions in April 1998. Their SAP compliance will be monitored for

Box 4.2: Uganda's Promise

In the 1990s, Uganda was considered to be one of the most successful adjusting countries. An initial, failed adjustment program in 1981–5 exacerbated the suffering wrought by more than a decade of death and destruction under autocratic rulers. In 1986, a guerrilla force calling itself the National Resistance Movement (NRM) won power after protracted struggle. The new government, headed by President Museveni, pledging to bring reconciliation and reconstruction, attracted substantial amounts of foreign aid.

The major contribution to growth in food production and agricultural exports in Uganda in the early 1990s was made by small-scale producers, rather than by large farms.[92] Peasants made up more than 70 percent of the population. Improved crop prices reduced the cross-border smuggling for which Uganda had been famous under dictatorial regimes. At the same time, favorable credit and other terms for South Asian owners ousted in 1972 encouraged those now returning to Uganda to revitalize sugar and tea plantations, cotton gins, and factories, as well as trading enterprises. African-owned firms also expanded. Amelioration of public sector salaries meant that peasants no longer had to send food to urban relatives.[93] Uganda regained its position as Africa's largest coffee producer. Growth in the gross domestic product averaged 6 percent annually over the period 1987–97. It included not only agriculture, but a building boom in Kampala and new manufacturing, as well as collection and processing of peasant-grown crops. Renewed hope and restored public order over much of the country appear to have been as important as policy shifts in restarting Uganda's economy.

Uganda is by no means out of difficulty. With average per capita income at $330 in 1997 and 50 percent of people living on less than two-thirds of that amount, the majority of Ugandans are still among the world's poorest people. A few Ugandans and some foreigners have grown conspicuously wealthy. According to Uganda's vigorous opposition press, a recent boom in banking and urban construction (led largely by TNCs) fueled corruption in government and business. Rapid privatization of publicly owned assets also brought new opportunities for corruption.

Prices of Uganda's major exports – coffee, cotton, and tea – are highly volatile. Crop diversification involves exports of flowers and vegetables air-freighted to Europe. Agricultural growth slowed to 1.3 percent in 1997, well below the 3.1 percent increase in population. Food production levels are precarious. Inequality in land ownership and land shortages are severe. Insurgents terrorize peasants living along the borders of Sudan and Congo and abduct children to serve them. In western Uganda, insurgents, operating from bases in Congo, include remnants of the army and militias that carried out genocide in Rwanda, and unemployed Ugandan youth.[94]

While donors have expressed concern about corruption and increased military expenditures, they appear willing to make concessions in hopes that President Museveni can maintain the stability necessary to sustain Uganda's growth.[95] A documentary film crew followed several months of SAP negotiations in 1997. Their video shows the African leader making his country's loan priorities prevail over those of the World Bank advisory team.[96]

three additional years, however, before action is taken. A portion of bilateral and private loans made to African nations may yet actually be cancelled, rather than merely stretched out. If creditor governments agree to buy up private debts at current market value (an estimated 10 percent of face value), thereby in effect bailing out the banks, Africans could benefit. To date, there has been more talk than action.

Growth for whom?

From the late 1970s, the IFIs gave optimistic assurances of prospects for short- and medium-term economic recovery through SAPs. Yet despite two decades of adherence to IFI-designed programs, sustainable economic growth continues to elude many African countries. The IFIs are themselves forced to concede that the current situation gives little grounds for hope.

The World Bank's 1995 Africa Poverty Reduction Task Force estimated that at least 7 percent annual GDP growth would be needed to make "a substantial impact" on poverty. What did the authors mean by "substantial"? The Task Force calculated that at that rate, it would take 30 years or more to double average per capita incomes from their present levels. In 30 years, debts now being rescheduled may be paid off, but debt service on new loans will remain. Growth of the magnitude needed to substantially reduce poverty and harmful inequality requires debt cancellation, economic transformation, and institutional measures of resource redistribution.

By their own admission, the IFIs were overly optimistic about short- and medium-term growth recovery in Africa. The World Bank's 1998 poverty report found that the limited recovery that took place in the 1990s was not sufficient to reverse the spread of poverty. Across the continent, GDP growth remained very fragile at between 4 and 5 percent, just 1 to 2 percent greater than population growth. "The outlook for sub-Saharan Africa in 1998 and beyond is more uncertain than was the case in 1997," the Bank reported. It recognized that where growth has occurred, its benefits have been unevenly distributed. The report also emphasizes that gender makes a difference: women have borne the brunt of SAP-induced poverty. Bank analysts are silent, however, about the effects on African food producers, most of them female, when Western agribusiness firms dump food exports onto African markets.

The 1998 Bank report offers a new list of factors that limit growth in African economies. These include weak governance, high policy volatility, poor public services, high transport costs, poor soils, disease, climatic risk, export concentration in commodities, and violent conflict. There is little explicit recognition of the crippling effect of debt or the stubborn heritage of colonial abuses, and no acknowledgment of advisors' policy errors. No mention is made of the need to transform Africa's distorted structures of production. The study does not discuss how the pressure brought to bear on poor countries by powerful international corporations restricts African governments' capacity to protect their citizens or effectuate meaningful economic change.

Studies focused on the actual effects of policies, rather than policy-makers' rhetorical justifications, reveal SAPs' principal goals and hidden agenda. The first goal is debt reimbursement. The World Bank used the notion of "comparative advantage" to press for increased export production rather than for diversification. Though exports and budgetary austerity have helped governments make debt service payments, government expenditures continue to exceed revenues. Hence the need for new loans. Consequently, no surplus remains to invest in human or economic development.

The Washington Consensus has demonstrated little concern for family or regional food security. This suggests a second, unstated goal associated with SAPs. American, Canadian, and European agribusiness firms are major exporters of grain and meat. Their lobbyists seek wider, unprotected markets for agricultural products aborad. Exports to Africa, including sales of food aid, are especially attractive to the industrialized nations, in the face of today's shrunken markets in Asia. That region's current crisis and SAPs have reduced Asian consumers' incomes and ability to purchase imported food. Supplying their governments with food to aid Africa is a profitable alternative for agribusiness.

A third goal of SAPs is to improve the "investment climate" – in fact, to enhance the profitability and security of TNCs in Africa. Most such firms are involved in extraction of oil and minerals, others in the sale of technology and capital equipment, and some in manufacturing. In the future, more manufacturing firms may find Africa to be an attractive outlet for surplus capital. This once again bodes ill for the poor in Africa, as private investment requires guarantees of high profits, low taxes, an end to worker protection, publicly financed infrastructure, and free repatriation of capital.

The studies cited in the present chapter show that growth under these conditions cannot bring long-term socioeconomic improvements to the majority of Africans. The World Bank's remedies prescribe more of the same SAP-with-poverty-reduction advice. Yet neither credit to support survival strategies in the urban informal sector nor free rural health services and schools can remedy the structural conditions that breed poverty, disease, powerlessness, hopelessness, and violence.[97] Given that the governments of wealthy nations wield financial and political power within the World Bank and the IMF, their objectives, rather than those of the African poor, guide these institutions' decisions with respect to Africans' futures.[98]

Conclusion

In this chapter we have examined the complex crises of African economies and societies over the past quarter century. We demonstrated how Africa's exploitation by the European powers shattered earlier social patterns and governance institutions. Colonialism established new economic and political relations based on authoritarianism, brutality, racism, and ethnic and class stratification to ensure the profits of multinational firms and white settlers' ventures. Although Europeans claimed a "civilizing mission," Africans were forced to finance their own domination through taxes and forced labor. The roots of the economic crisis that predated SAPs reside in a combination of internal and international processes that continue to shape the realities of life in Africa today. Crises in the world economy have had deep and lasting effects on an Africa made vulnerable by colonialism's legacy of distorted internal production structures and authoritarian states that extract wealth from Africa.

Africa's ills are, of course, not only externally derived. Unable to achieve economic independence, many leaders of the new states acquired a vested interest in maintaining the old relations of domination. In order to accumulate capital and enjoy lifestyles commensurate with ruling classes elsewhere, they squeezed poor producers and plundered their countries. In the process, leaders rendered operating conditions less profitable for foreign firms. Forced to share their profits, many companies shifted operations elsewhere. In the 1980s, international financial and corporate interests sought to regain their ascendancy in Africa through SAPs. We have shown how SAPs help re-create internal and international conditions that had earlier led to economic growth without development. Africa's working poor have been made to endure wage freezes, unemployment, hunger, and ill-health so that funds might be directed to pay foreign debts and restore or enhance corporate profitability. With emphasis on export-led growth and reliance on private firms subsidized by public investment, SAPs benefit TNCs and their partners, the wealthy few within Africa.

This complex weave of history and SAPs has rendered poor Africans more vulnerable to disease and more likely to die unnecessarily. Low levels of health and education restrict the capacity of societies to develop, and undermine the long-term future of poor families. The heavy social costs of failure force increasing numbers of Africans to live in abject poverty, worse off at the end of the century than at any time since 1960. Nearly two decades of SAPs that were supposed to trade "short-term pain for long-term gain" have not halted the deterioration. Although presented by the IFIs as the only road to growth, SAPs in fact embody political choices. Deregulation and privatization are technocratic, neutral-seeming ways to redistribute wealth upward and outward.

This chapter demonstrates that the "short-term pain" of SAPs means that for many poor Africans *there will be no long term*. Case studies of hunger, malnutrition, and disease show the silent struggles for survival unfolding daily on the African continent. The 1994 genocide in Rwanda illustrates an extreme consequence of Africa's colonial legacy, as this heritage interweaves with contemporary political and economic crises exacerbated by the immediate effects of SAPs. Nsanga's story reveals how, in the deadly synergy between poverty and disease, AIDS inflicts further tragedy on poor Africans and devastates already vulnerable communities.

In order for positive economic and political transformations to take root, it is essential to cancel debt, increase investment in public services, expand productive employment at a living wage, and support sustainable, high-yield production by small-scale cultivators. These shifts would enable poor Africans to focus on something *other* than mere survival. Yet in the absence of a still more profound transformation of African economies and of the ways African wealth is redistributed, even these reforms can do little but extend the agony to future generations. However, structural transformation enabling hundreds of millions of struggling poor people to truly improve their lot would mean there would be lower profits for foreign and local firms. Therein lies the problem: conflict, as yet unresolved, between the health needs and human aspirations of poor people, and the economic agenda of the IFIs, corporate interests, and their allies among African rulers.

Acknowledgments

The authors are grateful to Alec Irwin for his advice on successive versions of this chapter, his reworking of several sections, and his careful editing of the endnotes. Evan Lyon shifted our extensive references to the general bibliography and helped locate missing reference data. Jim Kim, Julie Rosenberg, Jon Welch, Aaron Shakow, Joel Brenner, Heather Rensberry, and Cassis Henry also provided valuable assistance. We thank them all.

Notes

1   In this chapter, we use "Africa" to refer to sub-Saharan Africa (SSA).

2   The "Washington Consensus" refers to a loose alliance including leading international financial institutions (IFIs) such as the World Bank and the International Monetary Fund (IMF); the US Government, as the IFIs' major financier; and the network of scholars and development experts whose work defined the conventional economic wisdom of the SAP era and translated that wisdom to policy.

3   The phrase is from Moore, 1958.

4   Schoepf, 1988, 1991; Schoepf, Rukarangira, and Schoepf, 1988.

5   Young, 1996.

6   Leys, 1973; Gann, 1963; First, 1982; van Onselen, 1976; Perrings, 1979; Painter, 1987; Cooper, 1996.

7   Mamdani, 1996.

8   Davies, 1966.

9   Cooper, 1996; Ake, 1996; Mamdani, 1996; Young, 1996.

10   Young, 1996.

11   Young, 1996.

12   Ake, 1992.

13   C. Leys, 1978, for Kenya; Vail, 1991, p. ix, for Malawi.

14   Adedeji, 1989.

15   Seidman, 1974.

16   Skinner, 1981.

17   Cooper, 1996.

18   George, 1988; George, 1992; Onimode, 1989; Adedeji, 1990; Adedeji, 1996.

19   Mkandawire, 1992, p. 45, comment on presentation by the late Claude Ake, 1992.

20   J. Millen, interview with A. Edward Elmendorg, the World Bank's lead health specialist for Africa, March 1998.

21   Schoepf, Walu, and Russel, 1991.

22   Southall, 1988.

23   Cornia, Jolly, and Stewart, 1987.

24   Mazrui, 1991; Goheen, 1991; Raikes and Gibbon, 1996.

25   Beckman, 1992.

26   Obbo, 1992; Dedy and Tape, 1995.

27   Young, 1996.

28   Chretien, 1991.

29   Mukagasana, 1997.

30   African Rights, 1995.

31   World Bank, 1989.

32   World Bank, 1989.

33   Ntezilyayo, 1995.

34   Ntezilyayo, 1986.

35   Marysse, de Herdt, and Ndayambaje, 1994a, p. 35, T.2.9.

36   Ntezilyayo, 1986.

37   Schoepf, 1996; Uvin, 1998.

38   Bart, 1993.

39   Bezy, 1990.

40   Runyinya, 1985, in a thesis on Butare Prefecture, cited in Bezy, 1990.

41   UNICEF, 1988.

42   UNICEF, 1992.

43   Watson, 1991.

44   B. G. Schoepf, interviews, 1996; Uvin, 1998.

45   Marysse, de Herdt, and Ndayambaje, 1994a, 1994b.

46   Schoepf, Rukarangira, and Schoepf, 1988.

47   Mann, Tarantola, and Netter, 1992.

48   Cohen, Plummer, and Mugon, 1999.

49   Lurie, Hintzen, and Lowe, 1995.

50   Lurie, Hintzen, and Lowe, 1995.

51   Bijlmakers, Bassett, and Sanders, 1996.

52   Schultz, Cates, and O'Mara, 1994.

53   Voeller and Anderson, 1992.

54   Moses, Manji, and Bradley, 1992.

55 World Bank, 1997.
56 Evans, 1995.
57 J. Millen, interviews, Ghana, March 1989 and March 1992.
58 B. G. Schoepf, interviews, Abidjan, May 1997; Professor Seri Dedy, personal communication to B. G. Schoepf, June 1997.
59 B. G. Schoepf, interviews, Abidjan, May 1997; Professor Seri Dedy, personal communication, June 1997.
60 UNICEF, 1990.
61 UNICEF, 1990.
62 Cornu, Massamba, and Trissac, 1995.
63 Costello, Watson, and Woodward, 1994.
64 Kanbur, 1990.
65 Campbell, 1984.
66 Bates, 1981a, 1981b.
67 Chinemana and Sanders, 1993.
68 Cheater, 1981.
69 B. G. Schoepf, C. Schoepf, field observations, 1983; Chinemana and Sanders, 1993.
70 Green, 1993.
71 Chinemana and Sanders, 1993.
72 WHO, 1998.
73 Jazairy, 1992.
74 Schoepf, 1987.
75 Schoepf and Schoepf, 1988.
76 Boserup, 1970.
77 Afonja, 1986; Staudt, 1987; Davison, 1988; Peters, 1991.
78 Anderson, 1985.
79 Mikell, 1997; Gladwin, 1991; Mbilinyi, 1990, 1994.
80 Meena, 1991; Zuidberg and Djire, 1992; Steady, 1992.
81 Schoepf, Walu, and Russell, 1991; Gladwin, 1991.
82 Gladwin, 1991; Goheen, 1991.
83 Schoepf, 1987.
84 Schoepf, Walu, and Russell, 1991; Tanzania Gender Networking Programme, 1994.
85 Graham, 1994.
86 World Bank, 1995.
87 Green, 1993.
88 Watkins, 1995.
89 Watkins, 1995.
90 Simmons, 1995.
91 Watkins, 1995.
92 Brett, 1996.
93 B. G. Schoepf, fieldnotes, February 1992.
94 Prunier, 1998.
95 Prunier, 1998.
96 Leymaire, 1998.
97 We are mindful that we have not adequately pursued considerations of the state in our analysis. We recommend that readers consult Seidman and Anang, 1991; Mamdani, 1996; Ake, 1992; and Ake, 1996.
98 Stott, 1999.

References

Adedeji, Adebayo (1989). *Towards a Dynamic African Economy*. London: Frank Cass.
Adedeji, Adebayo (1990). *The African Alternative*. Addis Ababa: Economic Commission for Africa.
Adedeji, Adebayo (1996). "Institutional Restitution, Renewal and Restructuring." *Development*, June 2, pp. 68–72.

Afonja, Semi (1986). "Land Control: A Critical Factor in Yoruba Gender Stratification." In *Women and Class in Africa*. Claire Robertson and Iris Berger, eds. New York: Africana Publishing, pp. 78–91.

African Rights (1995). *Rwanda: Death, Despair and Defiance*, 2nd ed. London: African Rights.

Ake, Claude (1992). "The Legitimacy Crisis of the State." In *Structural Adjustment and the Crisis in Africa: Economic and Political Perspectives*, David Kennett and Tukumbi Lumumba-Kasongo, eds. Lewiston, ME: Edwin Mellen Press, pp. 29–47.

Ake, Claude (1996). *Democracy and Development in Africa*. Washington, DC: Brookings Institute.

Anderson, Mary B. (1985). "Technology Transfer: Implications for Women." In *Gender Roles in Development Projects: A Casebook*, Catherine Overholt, Mary B. Anderson, and Kathleen Cloud, eds. West Hartford, CT: Kumarian Press, pp. 57–78.

Bart, Francois (1993). *Terres d'Afrique, Montagnes Paysannes: Le Cas du Rwanda*. Bordeaux: Université de Bourdeaux, p. 508.

Bates, Robert H. (1981a). "Agricultural Policy in Africa: Political Origins and Social Consequences." In *The Role of US Universities in Rural and Agricultural Development*, Brooke G. Schoepf, ed. Tuskegge, AL: Tuskegee Institute, Center for Rural Development, pp. 51–60.

Bates, Robert H. (1981b). *Markets and States in Tropical Africa*. Berkeley: University of California Press.

Beckman, Bjorn (1992). "Empowerment or Repression? The World Bank and the Politics of Adjustment." In *Authoritarianism, Democracy and Adjustment: The Politics of Economic Reform in Africa*," Peter Gibbon, Yusuf Bangura, and Arye Ofstad, eds. Uppsala: Scandinavian Institute for African Studies.

Bezy, Fernand (1990). *Rwanda: 1962–1989: Bilan Socio-Economique d'un Régime*. Louvain-la-Neuve, Belgium: Institut d'Etudes du Development.

Bijlmakers, Leon, Mary Bassett, and David Sanders (1996). "Health and Structural Adjustment in Rural and Urban Settings in Zimbabwe: Some Interim Findings." In *Structural Adjustment and the Working Poor in Zimbabwe*, Peter Gibbon, ed. Uppsala: Nordiska Afrikaininstitutet, pp. 215–82.

Boserup, Ester (1970). *Women's Role in Economic Development*. New York: St. Martin's Press.

Brett, Edward A. (1996). "Uganda." In *Limits of Adjustment in Africa*, Poul Engberg-Pedersen, Peter Gibbon, and Phil Raikes, eds. London: James Currey, pp. 309–46.

Campbell, Bonnie (1984). "Inside the Miracle: Cotton in Ivory Coast." In *The Politics of Agriculture in Tropical Africa*, Jonathan Barker, ed. Berkeley: Sage Publications, pp. 143–72.

Cheater, Audrey (1981). "Women and Their Participation in Commercial Agricultural Production: The Case of Medium-Scale Freehold in Zimbabwe." *Development and Change* 12(3): 349–77.

Chinemana, Frances, and David Sanders (1993). "Health and Structural Adjustment in Zimbabwe." In *Social Change and Economic Reform in Africa*, Peter Gibbon, ed. Uppsala: Scandinavian Institute of African Studies.

Chrétien, Jean-Pierre (1991). "Les Racines de la Violence Populaire en Afrique." *Politique Africaine* 92: 15–27.

Cohen, Craig R., Francis A. Plummer, and Maclean Mugon (1999). "Increased Interleukin-10 in the Endocervical Secretions of Women with Non-ulcerative Sexually Transmitted Diseases: A Mechanism for Enhanced HIV-1 Transmission?" *AIDS* 13(3): 327–32.

Cooper, Fredrick (1996). *Decolonization and African Society: The Labor Question in French and British Africa*. Cambridge: Cambridge University Press.

Cornia, Giovanni Andrea, Richard Jolly, and Frances Stewart (1987). *Adjustment with a Human Face: Protecting the Vulnerable and Promoting Growth*, 2 vols. Oxford: Clarendon Press.

Cornu, A., J. P. Massamba, and P. Trissac (1995). "Nutritional Change and Economic Crisis in an Urban Congolese Community." *International Journal of Epidemiology* 24(1): 155–64.

Costello, Anthony, Fiona Watson, and David Woodward (1994). *Human Face or Human Facade? Adjustment and the Health of Mothers and Children*. London: Centre for International Child Health, University of London.

Davies, Ioan (1966). *African Trade Unions*. Harmondsworth, UK: Penguin Books.

Davison, Jean, ed. (1988). *Agriculture, Women and Land: The African Experience.* Boulder, CO: Westview Press.

Dedy, Seri and Goze Tape (1995). *Famille et Education en Côte d'Ivoire: Une Approche Socio-Anthropologique.* Abidjan: Editions des Lagunes.

Evans, Imogen (1995). "SAPping Maternal Health." *Lancet* 346(8982): 1046.

First, Ruth (1982). *Studies in Black and Gold: The Mozambiquan Miner from Peasant to Proletarian.* Sussex, UK: Harvester Books.

Gann, Lewis, H. (1963). *A History of Northern Rhodesia: Early Days to 1953.* London: Chatto and Windus.

George, Susan (1988). *A Fate Worse than Debt: A Radical New Analysis of the Third World Debt Crisis.* Harmondsworth, UK: Penguin Books.

George, Susan (1992). *The Debt Boomerang: How Third World Debt Harms Us All.* Boulder, CO: Westview Press.

Gladwin, Christina H., ed. (1991). *Structural Adjustment and African Women Farmers.* Gainesville: University of Florida Press.

Goheen, Miriam (1991). "The Ideology and Political Economy of Gender: Women and Land in Nso, Cameroon." In *Structural Adjustment and African Women Farmers,* Christina H. Gladwin, ed. Gainesville: University of Florida Press, pp. 239–56.

Graham, Carol (1994). *Safety Nets, Politics, and the Poor: Transitions to Market Economies.* Washington, DC: National Academy Press, pp. 116–47.

Green, Reginald H. (1993). "The IMF and the World Bank in Africa: How Much Learning?" In *Responses to Africa's Economic Decline,* Thomas Callaghy and John Ravenhill, eds. New York: Columbia University Press, pp. 54–89.

Jazairy, Idriss (1992). *The State of the World Rural Poverty.* New York: International Fund for Agricultural Development/NYU Press.

Kanbur, Ravi (1990). *Poverty and the Social Dimensions of Adjustment in Côte d'Ivoire.* Washington, DC: World Bank.

Leymaire, Philippe (1998). "Review of 'Nos Amis de la Banque' by Peter Chappell." *Le Monde Diplomatique,* February, p. 12.

Leys, Norman (1973). *Kenya,* 4th ed. London: Frank Cass. Original 1924.

Leys, Colin (1978). "Capital Accumulation, Class Formation and Dependency: The Significance of the Kenyan Case." *The Socialist Register* 1978: 241–66.

Lurie, Peter, Percy Hintzen, and Robert A. Lowe (1995). "Socioeconomic Obstacles to HIV Prevention and Treatment in Developing Countries: The Roles of the International Monetary Fund and the World Bank." *AIDS* 9(6): 539–46.

Mamdani, Mamoud (1996). *Citizen and Subject: Contemporary Africa and the Legacy of Late Colonialism.* Princeton, NJ: Princeton University Press.

Mann, Jonathan, Daniel Tarantola, and Thomas Netter, eds. (1992). *AIDS in the World.* Cambridge, MA: Harvard University Press.

Marysse, Stefaan, Tom de Herdt, and Elie Ndayambaje (1994a). *Revenus Ruraux Avant l'Ajustement Structurel.* Cahiers du CIDEP, March 19, p. 35, T.2.9.

Marysse, Stefaan, Tom de Herdt, and Elie Ndayambaje (1994b). *Rwanda: Apauvrissement et Ajustement Structurel.* Paris: L'Harmattan.

Mazrui, Ali (1991). "Privatization Versus the Market: Cultural Contradictions in Structural Adjustment." In *Changing Uganda: The Dilemma of Structural Adjustment and Revolutionary Change.* Holger Bernt Hansen and Michael Twaddle, eds. London: James Currey, pp. 351–78.

Mbilinyi, Marjorie J. (1990). "Structural Adjustment, Agribusiness and Rural Women in Tanzania." In *The Food Question: Profits Versus People.* Henry Bernstein ed. London: Earthscan, pp. 111–24.

Mbilinyi, Marjorie J. (1994). "Gender and Structural Adjustment." In *Structural Adjustment and Gender: Empowerment or Disempowerment.* Tanzania Gender Networking Programme (TGNP), pp. 25–62.

Meena, Ruth (1991). "The Impact of Structural Adjustment Programs on Rural Women in Tanzania." In *Structural Adjustment and African women Farmers*, Christina H. Gladwin, ed. Gainesville: University of Florida Press, pp. 169–89.

Mikell, Gwendolyn ed. (1997). *African Feminism: The Politics of Survival in Sub-Saharan Africa*. Philadelphia: University of Pennsylvania Press.

Mkandawire, Thandika (1992). "The Political Economy of Development with a Democratic Face." In *Africa's Recovery in the 1990s: From Stagnation and Adjustment to Human Development*. Giovanni Andre Cornia, Rolph van der Hoeven, and Thandika Mkandawiree, eds. New York: St. Martin's Press, pp. 296–311.

Moore, Barrington (1958). *Political Power and Social Theory: Six Studies*. Cambridge, MA: Harvard University Press.

Moses, Stephen, Firoze Manji, and J. E. Bradley (1992). "Impact of User Fees on Attendance at a Referral Centre for Sexually Transmitted Diseases in Kenya." *Lancet* 340(8817): 463–6.

Mukagasana, Yolande (1997). *La Mort Ne Veut Pas de Moi*. Paris: Editions Fixot.

Ntezilyayo, Anastase (1986). "L'Agriculture a l'Horizon 2000 ou Comment Doubler la Production Vivrière au Rwanda." *Revue du Tiers Monde* 27(106): 395–417.

Ntezilyayo, Anastase (1995). "L'Agriculture: Une Priorité dans la Reconstruction Nationale." In *Les Crises Politiques au Burundi et au Rwanda (1993–1994)*, Andre Gichaoua, ed. Paris: Karthala, pp. 319–38.

Obbo, Christine (1992). *Needs, Demands and Resources in Relation to Primary Health Care in Kampala*. Save the Children Foundation.

Onimode, Bade, ed. (1989). *A Future for Africa: Beyond the Politics of Adjustment*. London: Earthscan.

Painter, Thomas (1987). "Making Migrants: Zarma Peasants in Niger 1900–1920." In *African Population and Capitalism: Historical Perspectives*, Dennis D. Cordell and Joel W. Gregory, eds. Boulder, CO: Westview Press, pp. 122–33.

Perrings, Charles (1979). *Black Mineworkers in Central Africa: Industrial Strategies and the Evolution of an Industrial Proletariat in the Copperbelt, 1911–1941*. London: Heinemann.

Peters, Pauline (1991). "Debate on the Economy of Affection. Is It a Useful Tool for Analysis?" In *Structural Adjustment and African Women Farmers*, Christina H. Gladwin, ed. Gainesville: University of Florida Press, pp. 307–20, 324–8.

Prunier, Gerard (1998). "Forces et Faiblesses du Modèle Ougandais." *Le Monde Diplomatique*, February, pp. 12–13.

Raikes, Phil and Peter Gibbon (1996). "Tanzania." In *Limits of Adjustment in Africa*, Paul Engberg-Petersen, Peter Gibbon, and Phil Raikes, eds. Copenhagen: Centre for Development Research (in association with Oxford: James Currey and Portsmouth, NH: Heinemann), pp. 215–308.

Schoepf, Brooke G. (1987). "Social Structure, Women's Status and Sex Differential Nutrition in the Zairian Copperbelt." *Urban Anthropology* 6(1): 73–102.

Schoepf, Brooke G. (1988). "Women, AIDS and Economic Crisis in Zaire." *Canadian Journal of African Studies* 22(3): 625–44.

Schoepf, Brooke G. (1991). "Ethical, Methodological and Political Issues of AIDS Research in Central Africa." *Social Science and Medicine* 33(7): 749–63.

Schoepf, Brooke G. (1996). "When Structural Violence Goes Corporeal: The Political Ecology of Genocide in Rwanda." Paper presented at the American Anthropological Association 95th Annual Meeting. San Francisco, November 20–4.

Schoepf, Brooke G., Rukarangira wa Mkera, Claude Schoepf (1988). "AIDS and Society in Central Africa: A View from Zaire." In *AIDS in Africa: Social and Political Dimensions*, Norman Miller and Richard Rockwell, eds. Lewiston, ME: Edwin Mellen, pp. 211–35.

Schoepf, Brooke G., and Claude Schoepf (1988). "Land, Gender, and Food Security in Eastern Kivu." In *Agriculture, Women and Land: The African Experience*, Jean Davison, ed. Boulder, CO: Westview Press, pp. 106–30.

Schoepf, Brooke, G., Engundu Walu, and Diane Russell (1991). "Women and Structural Adjustment in Zaire." In *Structural Adjustment and African Women Farmers*, Christina H. Gladwin, ed. Gainesville: University of Florida Press, pp. 151–68.

Schultz, K. F., W. Cates, Jr., and P. R. O'Mara (1994). "Pregnancy Loss, Infant Death and Suffering: Legacy of Syphilis and Gonorrhea in Africa." *Genitourinary Medicine* 63: 191–5.

Seidman, Ann (1974). *Planning for Development in Sub-Saharan Africa.* Dar es Salaam: Tanzania Publishing House.

Seidman, Ann and Fred Anang, eds. (1991). *Twenty-First Century Africa: Towards a New Vision of Self-Sustainable Development.* Trenton, NJ: Africa World Press.

Simmons, Pat (1995). *Words into Action: Basic Rights and the Campaign against World Poverty.* Oxford: Oxfam, p. 20.

Skinner, Elliott, P. (1981). "The Global Economic Order and the Poor Villages." In *The Role of US Universities in Rural and Agricultural Development*, Brooke G. Schoepf, ed. Tuskegee, AL: Tuskegee Institute, Center for Rural Development, pp. 8–18.

Southall, Aidan (1988). "'The Rain Fell on its Own' – The Alur Theory of Development and Its Western Counterparts." *African Studies Review* 31(2): 1–16.

Staudt, Kathleen (1987). "Uncaptured or Unmotivated? Women and the Food Crisis in Africa." *Rural Sociology* 52(1): 37–55.

Steady, Filomina Chioma, ed. (1992). *Women and Children First: Environment, Poverty, and Sustainable Development.* Rochester, VT: Schenkman Books.

Stott, Robin (1999). "The World Bank: Friend or Foe to the Poor?" *British Medical Journal* 318(7187): 822–3.

UNICEF (1988). *Analysis of the Situation of Women and Children in Rwanda.* Kigali: UNICEF, p. 83.

UNICEF (1990). *Children and Development in the 1990s: A UNICEF Sourcebook.* New York: UNICEF.

UNICEF (1992). *Situation of Women and Children in the Republic of Rwanda.* Kigali: UNICEF.

Uvin, Peter (1998). *Aiding Violence: The Role of Foreign Assistance in the 1994 Genocide in Rwanda.* West Hartford, CT: Kumarian Press, p. 146.

Vail, Leroy, ed. (1991). *The Creation of Tribalism in Southern Africa.* Berkeley: University of California Press.

Van Onselen, Charles (1976). *Chibaro: African Mine Labor in Southern Rhodesia 1900–1933.* London: Pluto Press.

Voeller, Bruce and Deborah J. Anderson (1992). "Heterosexual Transmission of HIV." *Journal of the American Medical Association* 267(14): 1917.

Watkins, Kevin (1995). *The Oxfam Poverty Report.* Oxford: Oxfam, p. 179.

Watson, Catherine (1991). *Exile from Rwanda: Background to an Invasion.* Washington, DC: US Committee for Refugees.

WHO: World Health Organization (1998). *Report on the Global HIV/AIDS Epidemic (Slideshow).* Geneva: World Health Organization.

World Bank (1989). *Sub-Saharan Africa, Status Report.* Washington, DC: World Bank, p. 105.

World Bank (1995). *Taking Action for Poverty Reduction in Sub-Saharan Africa: Draft Report of an Africa Region Task Force.* Washington, DC: Technical Department of Poverty and Human Resources Division, p. 77.

World Bank (1997). *Health, Nutrition, and Population Sector Strategy.* Washington, DC, pp. 74–5.

Young, Crawford (1996). *The African Colonial State in Comparative Perspective.* New Haven: Yale University Press.

Zuidberg, Lida and Tata Djire (1992). *Les Paysannes du Mali-Sud: Vers une Meilleure Intégration au Program de la CMDT.* Amsterdam: Royal Tropical Institute, Bulletin 326 and Sikaso, Mali: CMDT.

CHAPTER 5

A New Way of Thinking in Action: The Zapatistas in Mexico – A Postmodern Guerrilla Movement?

Fernanda Navarro

First of all I would like to thank the organizers for the invitation to participate in this conference on "The Languages and Politics of Contemporary Marxism."[1] It is a great pleasure to be here with you today at the University of Massachusetts: a great pleasure and a great surprise to see the growing interest in rethinking Marxism, especially in this country. Ten or fifteen years ago we could have said, "Here, in the heart of the beast." Now, the beast is everywhere; it is *global*. There is no fixed address. But we are global too, or rather we are all over the *globe*... in an *age* which reminds me of that atmosphere described by Giordano Bruno at the end of the Renaissance, when "the center is everywhere and the circumference is nowhere."

My intention in this paper is to address a peripheral movement, a marginal movement, but one that is based on universal grounds and values: the Zapatista movement in Chiapas, Mexico. I will do this with reference to Althusser's last ideas on political philosophy and also with regard to postmodernism.

Among Althusser's unedited writings there are some that refer to the modern spaces, or what he called interstices, that have emerged all over the world, bringing some hope with their different way of functioning and organizing, with no intention of instituting new pyramids with dominating structures. He referred to the social and popular movements and the struggles of marginalized people that are taking place all over the planet with a growing vitality and success, such as the pacifist, ecological, feminist, gay, student, and immigrant movements as well as the liberation theology movement in Latin America, whose renewed impulse of religious feeling, Althusser said, has made the Vatican tremble. These movements, without knowing it, he added, followed the line of Rosa Luxemburg and not that of Lenin. Althusser was convinced of their priority, as opposed to those with rigid, vertical structures that make the practice of democracy difficult, if not impossible. I would like to quote a few eloquent lines that Althusser wrote:

Fernanda Navarro, "A New Way of Thinking in Action: The Zapatistas in Mexico – A Postmodern Guerrilla Movement?" pp. 155–65 from *Rethinking Marxism: A Journal of Economics, Culture, and Society* 10:4 (1998), http://www.tandf.co.uk/journals/titles/08935696.html. Reprinted by permission of Taylor & Francis Ltd.

Everything in this world is in a constant, unpredictable flow. If we want to give an image of it we must go back to Heraclitus or Epicurus. Yet, if we want a more recent image, we can follow Deleuze in order to avoid Descartes's hierarchical representation of the world as a tree and think of it as a rhizome instead: that is, a horizontal root.

Yet, I still prefer Marx's image; "the gods exist in the interstices of the world of Epicurus. In the same way that mercantile relations existed already in the Interstices of the slave world."[2]

All these groups and movements announce and represent a new positive dislocation... allowing the undetermined, the relative, the aleatory to arise, giving place to possibility as a category. The last Althusser believed that these organized minorities coexist already at a microscale and are working on an alternative platform seeking a different kind of politics that may allow a different kind of human practice and human relations, one sharing a common goal: to build a more just society, free from ideological manipulation, misery, and oppression. Althusser believed that the key to their success is "organization" with a democratic conception and starting from within, in a self-governed manner. He criticized those who, for having read Marx and Lenin, feel themselves capable of and with the right to direct these movements. He concluded that they should be not centralized but local, not international but regional. Their unity should be given by objective intersecting lines, by communitarian forms with transversal relations. To go further, he added, any dream of an international liberational movement would be utopian. The most we can do is to conceive of a Center for International Liberation whose main task would be that of providing information, not direction – since that corresponds to the militants of each region; an open Center where active revolutionary groups and alternative movements might meet and exchange experiences and strategies for transforming society. Althusser stressed his conviction about the primacy of a materialist philosophy as a basis for any action; otherwise, he feared, "we are bound to remain in the dark night of theory and of practice." As for the basic theoretical instruments for the analysis of any concrete situation or struggle, Althusser mentioned his last thesis: aleatory materialism and Marx's scientific instruments.

With this background, I now turn to one of the concrete spaces or interstices: a regional, marginal movement that is part of our present living history – the Zapatista movement in Mexico today.

On 1 January 1994, a few hours before the implementation of the North American Free Trade Agreement, the unexpected uprising began. The armed group came from Chiapas, one of the most miserable southern states of Mexico and one of the richest in natural resources. The Ejército Zapatista de Liberación Nacional (Zapatista National Liberation Army), composed mainly of native Indians, shook the whole country and its apparently peaceful state as if to remind us, Mexicans, that to enter the promised first world takes more than a signature, more than a treaty, that our place and condition, for quite some time, is still that of the Third World.

From the very first day the Zapatistas published their First Declaration of the Lacandonas Jungle, explaining the reasons for their uprising and making it clear that the indigenous question was central. The indigenous, the Indians, the first inhabitants of our country, of our hemisphere, the poorest of the poor, the most forgotten ones, they remind us that no country can pretend to enter the first world building from the top down, from the penthouse down. They have to start from the bottom, from the roots. Thus, they presented eleven Basic Demands, such as the right to have land to cultivate; the right to adequate health care, food, education; and so on. The last demand had a universal scope: the right to dignity, justice, freedom, and democracy (not merely electoral democracy). What happened was – as we have read somewhere in political theory – that they had reached the saturation point, or the point of no return; and their situation was lived and felt by them as *unbearable*. The decision to *act* was then taken. "*Ya basta!* Enough!" they said, and they meant it. They had tried all other possible paths (even as they were training themselves as a clandestine armed group). Their last peaceful attempt was a march of over 746 miles (1,200 kilometers) from Chiapas to Mexico City on foot to present their main problems to the government. They went back, as everybody does in my country when dealing with the high authorities, empty-handed and with mouthfuls of promises never to be fulfilled. As Marcos, one of the leaders wrote: "What country is this where you must kill and be killed in order to be heard?" Their "Ya basta" included their decision to choose their own destiny (even if that destiny was death): "Better to die from a bullet than from misery or an unattended curable disease." (There's one doctor for every 1,500 people in Chiapas.)

From bullets to dialogue (logos)

One of the astonishing things was the length of time that the war lasted. What had taken decades of bloodshed and death in other countries of South and Central America, here took only 12 days. The pressure of an emerging civil society, the president's shock at the sight of his image collapsing, and the Zapatistas' aim not really being to win a war but to be heard and to be taken seriously, all helped to bring about a quick cease-fire. By the third week of January a "Dialogue" began between the Zapatistas and the government of Mexico at the Cathedral of San Cristobal, with Bishop Ruiz from the liberation theology movement present. (In contrast to the church's hierarchy, the priests in this movement are on the side of, and live with, the people.) Days before, the then-President Salinas (who is now a fugitive and doesn't dare come back because he would be swallowed by the people) had awkwardly announced a "pardon" in an arrogant Olympian attitude which finally ended in an amnesty. Subcomandante Marcos answered the pardon with a poem:

> Why do we have to ask for forgiveness:
> for not dying of hunger,
> for not hiding our misery,
> for having shown the world
> that human dignity still lives in its poorest inhabitants,
> for having learned to fight
> before fighting
> – after having found all other paths closed . . .
> Who is to forgive and who to be forgiven?

(This text, with others, was chosen by some Mexican writers for a national prize in literature. Of course, he didn't get it.)

From then on a peaceful revolution of an armed movement began and language and ideas took the place of weapons, as Marcos wrote to Carlos Fuentes, one of our best writers. From the beginning there was something surprising: the language and paradoxes of the Zapatistas that had nothing to do with the style of previous revolutionary speeches and conceptions of people talking to posterity with solemn phrases. No, it had a different quality. Subcomandante Marcos, one of the best-known leaders – the only mestizo in the Head Indian Revolutionary Committee – was assigned by them to be their speaker, their "voice," silenced for so long. He has managed to intertwine the Indian way of speaking and conceiving of the world with his talent and intelligence as a writer and a thinker.

Instead of the dull, flat messages or declarations of the typical politician, right or left, he writes short stories and plain literature and invents characters such as Durito, the beetle philosopher, or Eva and Heriberto, two native kids in the jungle, or writes poetic prose to get messages through, as well as brilliant analyses of the country's political and economic situation. He is also known for his sense of humor – completely absent in all traditional revolutionary leaders who speak for posterity. One of the first pages we read from him was, "We screamed Ya Basta! We screamed we are here! And strangely enough, to be seen, we covered our faces, and to be named, we denied ourselves a name, and to live fully, we were willing to die." He later added, "Behind our ski mask, there is an I who is a you." (This willingness to die meant a decision to live.)

An identity and a name revealed

In February 1995, Subcomandante Marcos's identity was supposedly discovered. A huge mobilization was then geared up to apprehend him. In the press and on TV, Marcos's double picture appeared, with and without the ski mask. But an astonishing thing for us was the following clipping: "*Rafael Sebastian Guillen* [his supposed name]: *An Althusserian Philosopher.*" Obviously he has neither accepted nor denied any identity attributed to him.

A ruthless military invasion followed his persecution in the jungle. Soldiers committed terrible atrocities against people in the Zapatista liberated zones because the Zapatista movement is not an armed movement only – there are a lot of Mexicans, especially in Chiapas, who are Zapatistas. Those who supported them in clandestinity, those who fed them, and those who kept their secret – these people suffered. There are videos that show the army's cruelty and destructiveness. In response, thousands of Mexican citizens protested. In Mexico City, within one week there were three huge demonstrations ending up at the Zocalo Plaza (which holds some 120,000 people), almost filling it. People were yelling "Todos somos Marcos" ("we are all Marcos"). "If you want to apprehend Marcos you must put us all in jail and you will never have enough jails for us." Many articles in the press also condemned the military invasion and hundreds of signatures from all over the world were published in several newspapers. All this pressure made the government decide to order the withdrawal of troops from the Zapatista areas, but not from the state of Chiapas. To this date, of the 150,000 soldiers that make up the Mexican army, 60,000 are in Chiapas – one third!

The impact on society

To many of us this movement has brought us reason to believe again, although we had been so skeptical and we had said, "never again." A second "Dialogue" with the next (and present) government was restarted in April 1995 (and interrupted in September 1996), but the Zapatistas' bet has been with society, the citizens, what they call the civil society in general. They proposed that in this Dialogue there would not be a "secret talk" but a public talk in newspapers and by inviting as counselors many people known for their work and their contributions in certain fields. They invited over one hundred counselors to be part of the talk. The government agreed to this, but the government had only 20 bureaucratic counselors who had little to say. The interesting thing was the way the Zapatistas behaved before the government with such dignity, as equal to equal, and that was unusual. They were all native Indians talking to the government. Marcos was not there. He is never there in these dialogues. To show the racist government that native Indians also think and are capable of discussing was very important, and they did this brilliantly and with reason and cause.

The Zapatistas have addressed and involved people from civil society far beyond the scope of the Left: mainly the nonorganized, nonmilitants in political parties, common citizens and intellectuals fed up with traditional politics. This is new. With great creativity and imagination the Zapatistas have organized all kinds of meetings, forums, and encounters inviting people from different political positions, from Mexico, and from other countries. The first was the National Convention in August 1994. Six thousand people attended! Three kilometers of buses going to the rain forest, one after the other, to find a way for a civilized world in Mexico. Another great event was the Intercontinental or Intergalactic Encounter in August 1996. Five thousand people from 43 countries gathered and discussed different subjects such as new policies, peaceful roads to democracy, the need for a new constitution in Mexico, culture and mass media, and how we all have been affected by and suffer with neoliberalism. This Encounter was named "For Humanity and Against Neoliberalism." Every night after the plenary sessions, in every event, we all ended up dancing with the Zapatistas of the community; men, children, women with incredible gaiety shared hour on end with us and the village's band. They have learned to integrate their struggle into their daily lives and they manage to smile, dance, die, and fight any Sunday, Wednesday, or Friday.

I would like to mention one talk we had with one of the Zapatistas, not a leader. A friend and I were very angry with the Mexican government and he came and said, "Wait, wait, they have *their* reasons. The thing to do is to talk and talk until they understand that there are other reasons, too – ours, for example." That was a lesson in tolerance, I thought.

Another impact is that many civilian groups have appeared since then, more than ever before. Although this started with the terrible earthquake of 1985, the number of civilian groups grew immensely after the Zapatistas' uprising. These groups have a common aim: to participate independently in affairs that concern society and not to leave politics in the hands of politicians only, which is always a calamity. This is unheard of in Mexico where there is no tradition of civil protest. As an example, there is an all-embracing group called Convergencia, which gathers 104 groups. Among them I'll just mention two outstanding ones: Alianza Civica and El Barzón. The first is respected and known for its serious, professional independent work in public polling and consultations on civilian issues. The Zapatista National Liberation Army asked them to undertake a nationwide survey on "peace and democracy" regarding its own future: whether to become a political and not a military force. More than a million answered. (President Zedillo had carried out a survey on the "new economy" shortly before with only 300,000 answers.) The second, El Barzón, has gained massive support from those indebted in all classes. After the last devaluation, when interest rates went up to 150 percent, people lost their property, the houses and cars they were buying. Many enterprises went broke. El Barzón simply said, "We won't pay. We can't pay." Its advice is now being solicited in other countries of Latin America.

The impact in the countryside, however, has been different. Many peasants offered to take up their own arms and join the Zapatistas' fight in Chiapas. Marcos explained that the thing to do was for everybody to face their own conflicts in their own locales with their own weapons, which are not only armed weapons and open fire but to face their conflicts by organizing. There are other ways of fighting besides that of open fire.

Not only adults have been touched. Many young people and even children are involved. In all the regular work, especially for the big public meetings or forums, the young take over many important tasks of organization and security. You find even the punks! It's quite unusual in Mexico to see the young interested in any political work. I'll mention a few lines that Marcos wrote in answer to a 12-year-old who had sent him a letter: "We, the professionals of hope – not the professionals of violence as the government calls us – realized we had to become soldiers so that in the future there will be no more need of soldiers." A strange guerrilla whose intention is to disappear as such.

International support has been incredible. From the United States many compañeros have participated and shown their support. Noam Chomsky is one of them. From abroad many people have not only supported the Zapatistas but have organized themselves into solidarity committees. Many artists and intellectuals have also given their support in writings and with signatures and they have traveled to Chiapas, from Oliver Stone and Eddie Olmos to Regis Debray and Mme Mitterrand and the right-wing sociologist Alain Tourrain who afterwards wrote an article in *Le Monde* called "Marcos, the armed democrat." An impressive testimony came from two Latin American guerrilla leaders of the 1960s and 1970s at the August 1996 Intercontinental Meeting, "For Humanity and Against Neoliberalism," in Chiapas. I summarize. Douglas Bravo (Venezuela) said, "In the heart of the rain forest where poetry, memory, dance, and weapons coexist, one feels the emergence of a new sort of State of Law, founded on a new spirit of Laws, where the main actor is the vanquished of 1492. For us who had lost all Utopias with the fall of the Berlin Wall, this is a reason for regaining hope." And Hugo Blanco (Peru) said:

> The Zapatistas deserve our recognition. They do not address themselves only to the Left but to everyone. The meeting here cannot be valued only in terms of numbers but in the quality of the ideas put forth. They are radical democrats. Something we, in the Left, never learned. It is said that the Left made mistakes. No! We simply were defeated. A defeat is all my generation has to offer. And the main cause is that we did not know how to be democratic. All the old style based on the "Vanguard" and revolutionary elites has proved to be wrong. All I hope for is that you, Zapatistas, may be capable of turning the defeat that we bequeath you into history.

There is one key concept that stands out in the Zapatistas' thought: the reformulation of their conception of power. What did they mean when they said "no" to the seizure of power? – a statement that has enflamed the Left in my country and has evoked the admiration of many who are looking beyond the traditional political spectrum. They mean a different way of relating to power. Marcos has said that "the only virtue of Power is that, in the end, it inevitably produces a revolution against itself."

History has taught us that even in the outstanding cases when tyranny or dictatorships were overthrown by revolutionary liberating forces, disillusionment sooner or later follows when we witness that the basic principles of justice and freedom, which led the struggle, begin to decay. It is as if there were some dominating traits inherent to power itself which gradually end up in a repetition, *ressemblance*, or reproduction of – not an alternative to – the rigid, arbitrary governments which were overthrown. And at what price in blood and death (this has been done)!

Another reason for choosing a different road and saying no to the seizure of power is that it is incompatible with real democracy (not only in electoral terms) since power implies domination, hierarchy, authority, and imposition, and is unable to listen to others. These are all the opposite of equality which is one of the main traits of democracy. Here, however, an interesting distinction comes out: "equality" is not to be identified with "uniformity" or "standardization," since one of the Zapatistas' principles is to respect the differences of opinion, ideas, political positions, beliefs, sexual preferences, and so on. One of their mottos is "*Queremos un Mundo donde quepan muchos Mundos*" (We want a world which holds many worlds).

In short, their conception of power is closer to the verb than to the noun (which is the same word in Latin languages: *poder, pouvoir*) – that is, a faculty, a strength that you conjugate in the plural, collectively, not that heavy weight of an unalterable noun: Power, imposing, appalling, domineering. Thus, they have made it possible for "politics" to go hand in hand with ethics, something unheard of in many decades.

Another big issue has been that of women's role in this movement. Something that is barely known outside Mexico is that women made their own revolution a month before the uprising of January 1994. It was in December 1993 that the women in the Zapatista army got together to discuss and decide their participation in their own terms. They set out a few laws regarding their own lives and rights. Some of the most relevant were their demand to have the right to have the number of children they choose and when they choose; to have the right to fight on terms equal with men and not to go to the battlefield as cooks or feminine company; and to have the right to choose their compañero! (In Indian communities it is still common for parents to choose their daughters' husbands.)

Thus, in the Zapatista National Liberation Army there are presently women comandantas, majors, and lieutenants. Some of them have been in top posts in military operations, like that of Ramona. Here again a few explanatory words are necessary. This demand for "equality" in the battlefield reflects a "limit situation," a "borderline" situation which does not claim to be desirable for anybody. It is not ideal, but we must remember that we are not talking about a peaceful situation. It refers to a transitory stage until the Indian communities achieve their right to live as human beings. Marcos wrote a few words explaining why they had to become soldiers: "So that soldiers shall no longer be necessary in a near future... but meanwhile, it is necessary for us, for Ana Maria, Ramona, and Hortensia to take up arms instead of becoming doctors, engineers, or teachers: Until a just social structure is achieved."

One of the actual, concrete achievements of the Zapatista National Liberation Army is to have gathered 38 of the 56 ethnic groups in the country in a historic meeting in Chiapas, in the Congreso Nacional Indigena. Never had so many Indian groups met and discussed their common problems and their strength in their traditions and languages. They planned to keep in touch and organize common actions. A beautiful cry resulted from that meeting: "*Nunca Más Un México Sin Nosotros*" (Never again a Mexico without us; that is, we will no longer be forgotten). After over a year's work the Zapatistas, with a Congress committee and some personalities from the church (the liberation theology movement), wrote a Law on Indian Culture and Autonomy to be passed by Congress and added to the Constitution. The government's delegation signed this paper, accepting its terms but, in the end, the president did not acknowledge it. Marcos remarked then, "This nation must acknowledge that it is not made up of equals, but of others. We are different and, therefore, it is vital to respect our differences." This is a concrete conquest, even though we know that our government often infringes the Constitution. But still, this is something important. And this is the real reason the Dialogue between the Zapatistas and the government has been cut off. This is also the reason they will not give up their arms, even though they have kept them quiet since 12 January 1994.

I will finish these lines by addressing a major subject: the Fourth Declaration of the Lacandonas Jungle issued in January 1996, where Marcos calls upon civil society to organize itself – not the Left in particular, not the proletariat or the masses in general. It is mainly addressed to those who do not belong to political parties. It is an open invitation to all members of society. Membership is individual, not by organizations, groups, or associations.[3] The invitation is to form and construct the Frente Zapatista de Liberación (Zapatista National Liberation Front), which is to be based on three main principles: (1) not to seek power, (2) not to seek government posts, and (3) not to become a political party.

This Declaration was like an explosion; it created a scandal. Beginning with the Left, criticisms fell like stones. "How can you not fight for power? What can you do without power?" What else to expect from old mental schemes or fixed ideas? It simply revealed they are not on the same wavelength. The Zapatistas have gradually been explaining that their main goal is not to take over power but something a bit more ambitious: a different world. And, to succeed in that, you must first open the road to democracy. And, democracy cannot be declared from above or signed in the high spheres of power. It has to be woven from below in a nationwide growing network of Comités de Diálogo (Dialogue Committees): the basic units, the backbone of the Zapatista Front.

The Dialogue Committees are being formed according to their specific problems, conditions, and even geographical situations. They are self-regulated. Their main purpose is not only to support the Zapatistas but to organize themselves as part of society, following the Zapatistas' principles and values: "to represent others, not to supplant them or take over," "to serve others, not to serve oneself," "to convince, not to impose," and "to demand that whoever 'governs' must obey the governed in their needs, their demands, their proposals and desires." Membership is individual and the prerequisite for participating is "to want to reinvent the world." Dialogue, as well as a willingness to listen to others, is basic. For that reason there should not be more than 20 people in each committee (made up mainly of persons with similar activities or links such as students, women, and workers). Leadership is to be avoided. Personal responsibility is taken for each specific task at a time. Rotation takes place and revocation is possible. There is to be a link among the committees at the municipal, state, regional and, finally, national levels. The idea is to link together as many Dialogue Committees as possible in one area in order to press the corresponding authorities in one city or town to solve a common problem – that is, to make them fulfill their duties as public servants, for which they are paid, and gradually to establish a different kind of relationship between those who govern and those who are governed – in other words, a different relationship with power.

It was not until 13 September 1997 that the Zapatista Front was formally founded, with members from all over the country present except for one state. It was a peculiar founding congress because the Front had been born many months before. At the moment of the formal celebration, 349 Dialogue Committees had been formed in the country, responding to the invitation of January 1996. Thus we witness an interesting phenomenon: Zapatismo is not only an army (the Zapatista National Liberation Army) but has become a popular movement in Mexico with tremendous international support. The Second Intercontinental (Intergalactic) Meeting, "For Humanity and Against Neoliberalism," was held in Spain from 27 July to 3 August 1997. Over 3,000 people from all over the world attended and participated in various workshops. The 100 videos made on the Zapatistas, the more than 20 books written by national and foreign writers, the three books on Communiqués and Testimonies mainly written by Marcos (the voice of the Zapatistas) and translated into 13 languages, and the Zapatistas' Internet page all show the widespread interest in the Zapatistas that has arisen and some of the reasons they have been called "postmodern guerrillas." Many foreign visitors to Zapatista territories soon became ambassadors of this movement which, rooted in its own particular reality of misery and wants, has been able to transcend its sphere and to touch on worldwide issues like justice, freedom, and dignity. They claim that they cannot prevail in the globe until poverty, unemployment, and inequality are faced and solved. Thus, from their corner they are resisting globalization and indicating new paths and new alphabets to interpret the world under a different light.

To many of us this announces the beginning of a new political culture in Mexico, one based on an ethics that contrasts sharply with the corrupt, demagogic and inefficient administration that marks one of the most trying moments in our modern history. Amidst this darkness many of us feel that the Zapatista movement is opening up a new horizon.

Postscript

Three years and 9 months after their uprising, 1,111 people from Zapatista communities entered Mexico City on 12–18 September 1997. Not one of the known "leaders" was there; all were "from the bottom." From Chiapas to Mexico City, in hundreds of buses, thousands of other people, mainly Indians, gathered and joined in the march so that 5,000 arrived at the big city. At the march thousands of Mexicans awaited them in the Zocalo Plaza with euphoric cries. The plaza was overflowing; not a pin would fit!

They came to celebrate the National Indigenous Congress and to be present at the founding of the Zapatista National Liberation Front. The welcome was so overwhelming that the government could not but accept it without interfering. Food, "housing," and transportation were organized mainly by "civil society" using a bank account for funds and hundreds of women cooking enormous meals for all. The anonymous, quiet, collective effort it all meant was beyond words. The loudest cry that could be heard was "*No están solos*" (You are not alone), and someone added, "We are not alone."

Five years after the initial uprising, the movement continues. Most recently, the Zapatistas called for a Consulta (a national referendum) on Indigenous Rights and Culture. On 14–21 March 1999, 5,000 Zapatistas – unarmed; half men, half women; many of them with babies – spread out over the country. We, the civilian Zapatistas, together with other organized groups that support the movement and "civil society," decided to organize ourselves so that in each state of the republic they were met by us, all expenses covered – transportation, housing, and meals.

The Consulta was called because of the Mexican government's refusal to fulfill the Agreements signed three years ago. This time the Zapatistas decided to undertake a dialogue with civil society, not with the government. There were programmed activities in universities, at schools, in public plazas, on radio stations, and so forth. This was unheard of, and with such a good response from the people! After hearing the Zapatistas speak with such simple, authentic language, people were impressed and, on the day of the Consulta (Sunday, 21 March), a lot of votes in support of it were obtained: in Michoacan, for instance, 122,390 and, in the whole country, with 85 percent of the votes counted, there were 2.5 million in favor. This was an enormous turnout! a big success! The final results will be delivered to Congress, which means another mobilization will be coming!

Acknowledgments

I would like to thank Antonio Callari for his invitation to participate in Rethinking Marxism's December 1996 conference, "The Languages and Politics of Contemporary Marxism," and Carole Biewener for her help in preparing this plenary talk for publication.

Notes

1   This essay was first presented as a plenary talk at "Politics and Languages of Contemporary Marxism," a December 1996 conference sponsored by Rethinking Marxism and held at the University of Massachusetts-Amherst.
2   All references to Althusser's work are from Fernanda Navarro's interview with Althusser, *Filosofía y Marxismo*, which was first published in Mexico by Siglo XXI. Over 100 pages in length, this interview was Althusser's last. It has been published in Japanese by Ohmura Shotten and in French by Gallimard.
3   An important point is being touched on here which I intend to develop sometime regarding the qualitative difference between the term "mass" as indicating an unreflexive, tumultuous, gregarious group more keen on following the leader than on identifying with the compañeros alongside each other, and the somewhat more reflexive term "individuals" that make up a "civil society," who supposedly have a more conscious response inasmuch as they "choose" and decide for themselves to become involved in the collective "we" or not.

CHAPTER 6

Workers' Resistance

Anita Chan

In a political climate that suppresses all forms of activities that smack of autonomous trade unionism, workers seek to protect their rights by either legal or illegal means. This chapter shows three ways in which workers have struggled for social justice: by collectively resorting to outbursts of violence, by protesting on the streets, and by seeking legal solutions. The legal path, as will be seen, seems to be increasingly accepted by the authorities. It is encouraging that China's new legal structure, which has gradually evolved over the past two decades, is beginning to help workers,[1] notwithstanding the widespread assaults on workers' rights that we have documented in this volume [Chan's *China's Workers Under Assault*]. Increasingly, the authorities have come to realize that a legal system can serve as a useful mediating mechanism to resolve labor disputes and preempt social disturbances. The authorities seem particularly amenable to allowing disputes over industrial accidents to come to court.

Case 21

To a certain extent, this case is quite similar to case 10, in which migrant construction workers exploded in uncontrollable anger and rose up in a riot against local police and local authorities. In case 21, however, the workers are not migrants; they are former state workers. The riot was on a small scale, and instead of the local authorities, it was the Taiwanese bosses who were injured in the mayhem.

The upheaval was organized by none other than the chair of the work-place union. He had the temerity to organize the workers because he had the backing of the Chinese factory director, who also happened to be a person of some local importance as a delegate to the county-level people's congress. Indeed, the incident even had the tacit approval of the local city government. The report suggests that the animosity between the two partners of the joint venture ran deep. It was not clear why the Chinese managers and the Taiwanese managers were at loggerheads, but the workers took advantage of this division to vent their anger.

The case involves a number of people, and it is not always easy to follow who belongs to which side of the joint venture. The following is a list of the protagonists:

On the Chinese side:
- Director Wu Caigeng
- Deputy General Manager Tang Mingqi
- Head of Labor and Wage Department Wu Haiying
- Trade Union Chair Chen Zhaoyuan
- Finance Manager Da Zuxing
- Production Manager Zhang Kouhua

On the Taiwanese side:
- Deputy Director Zhou Guiliang
- His wife, Wang Meifang
- General Manager Fang Zhongjun
- Deputy General Manager Zhu Zhenlong

This report received full-page coverage in Taiwan's main newspaper, the Central Daily. *As might be expected, it is totally biased toward the Taiwanese managers.*

SEVERAL DOZEN WORKERS BESIEGED AND TAIWANESE BUSINESSMEN INJURED; THE VICTIMS' PAINFUL ACCOUNT

Workers Beat Up and Injure Zhou Guiliang, Fang Zhongjun, and Two Others of the Far East Concrete Factory[2]

One year after the Qiandao Lake Boat Incident,[3] on March 6, the Far East Concrete Factory [Yuandong shuini chang], a joint venture operated by Taiwan businessman Zhou Guiliang and the Jurong county Concrete Factory in Zhenjiang city of Jiangsu province, yet another violent incident took place. Workers beat up and threatened the management of the Taiwanese partners when they demanded an increase in their "floating wages." They even said they would "drive the Taiwanese businessmen out with a broomstick." The violence raised serious concern among members of the Taiwanese business community about their own and their spouses' personal safety and the fate of their businesses on the mainland.

In the incident, the deputy head of the board of directors, Zhou Guiliang, and his wife, Wang Meifang, General Manager Fang Zhongjun, and Deputy General Manager Zhu Zhenlong were all beaten, injured, and forced to sign a "treaty." That evening, Zhou, Wang, and Zhu gave up protecting the factory and moved out of the factory compound to stay temporarily at the Zhenjiang Hotel. General Manager Fang flew back to Taipei to seek help.

Subsequently, the victims filed letters of complaint to the Jurong county, Zhenjiang city, and Jiangsu province governments, to the PRC Taiwanese Affairs Office, and the Overseas Chinese Association. But as of today, they had not received any reasonable response.

In addition, Wang Meifang, who also holds US citizenship, filed a complaint with the US consulate in Nanjing. It was reported that the consulate had expressed its concern to the Chinese authorities, but nothing else has happened since. The three who retreated to stay in the hotel are actually captives. All they can do each day is to act as the Chinese party's rubber stamp. They have completely lost their rights to manage the factory.

The Far East Concrete Factory has 1,000 staff members and workers. At the time of the incident about half of them, led by the trade-union chair and some important cadres, participated in besieging and beating up the Taiwanese businessmen.

* * *

"Don't beat my wife. She is pregnant. No, you can't beat her! Don't beat her anymore!" Just then, a metal spittoon flew across the room, hit Zhou on the head, and cut short his plea.

That morning, Zhou had sensed a strange atmosphere already brewing in the factory. Very early, Zhou Guiliang finished drawing up the wage-scale table and handed it to Finance Manager Da Zuxing. Zhou also instructed Da to get ready to go into Zhenjiang city to remit some of the foreign party's money out of the country. Da's response astonished Zhou: "Last Saturday, the director told me that I could not send money out."

"Why?"

"Let us wait until the director comes back from the county people's congress meeting." It was only later Zhou realized that this unusual behavior was the initial shot fired in a whole series of actions taken by workers against the managerial staff. Later, Zhou bumped into Trade-Union Chair Chen Zhaoyuan and Wu Haiying of the Labor and Wage Department, and saw them deeply absorbed in conversation. But the moment they spotted Zhou they stopped talking.

At about 9:00 a.m., Trade-Union Chair Chen brought Zhou and Deputy General Manager Zhu Zhenlong to General Manager Fang Zhongjun's office. Chen told the three: "The trade union and the cadres are of the opinion that the wage-scale table is not correct."

Fang therefore checked the wage-scale table, which had been drawn up by the Financial Department and which had been approved by the board of directors, against that of the Labor and Wage Department. He found no discrepancy. A bit later, Deputy General Manager Tang Mingqi and Finance Manager Da Zuxing of the Chinese side joined in. Da Zuxing held up an old wage-scale table and pointed out that the company has "left out one level of floating wages." An argument ensued. The Taiwanese side insisted that it was all done in accordance with the decision made at the last board of directors meeting; the other side disagreed. The argument went on for some time without resolution.

At about noon, a rumor was spreading in the factory: "The company is not paying out wages today."

When Fang heard this, he was furious. He went to question Da: "Why are you not paying the workers today? Whose decision was it?" Da could not give any reason. Under Fang's insistence, Da went to the bank to withdraw money for the payroll.

Fang and Zhou Guiliang discussed among themselves what had gone wrong: "In the beginning, Da said he was under orders not to withdraw money, but later, he did go to get the money. Something fishy is going on."

At about 1:15 p.m., Director Wu came back from the county people's congress meeting and immediately called a board meeting to discuss the decision on the "wage reform" that was made on February 28. In addition to the four representatives from the foreign party, the Chinese party included Director Wu, Trade-Union Chair Chen, and Tang Mingqi. When General Manager Zhou left the room to go to the restroom, he saw a lot of workers walking toward the administration building.

"Deputy Director Zhou, this strike is organized. It was planned by Trade-Union Chair Chen two days ago," a worker divulged to Zhou when he was in the restroom.

Zhou was furious. He rushed back to the conference room and berated Trade-Union Chair Chen right there, "You have to take responsibility for this strike."

Chen's face changed color. He shoved Zhou out of the room to the corridor and yelled, "Tell me who told you this!"

By then, about 300 workers were already gathered downstairs. When they saw the scuffle, some rushed upstairs. About 50 of them were blocking the staircase. When Zhou realized that the situation had become serious, he went back into the conference room. Workers were now crowding outside the room yelling, "Why are you not giving out wages!"

Director Wu took this opportunity to press Zhou and his cohorts to give in. But they refused to capitulate. Meanwhile, the workers outside the room were becoming more and more agitated. Suddenly, "Bang!" A worker had punched his fist through the window. Glass was scattered all over. An explosive atmosphere was hanging in the air. Director Wu asked Chen to call all the mid-level managerial staff to a meeting. Within 10 minutes, everyone had arrived. The efficiency was impressive. Normally, it takes half an hour to gather everybody.

Zhou and his associates were told to go to the other end of the room while Wu and the Chinese cadres convened for about 20 minutes. He then came over to Zhou and said "The cadres all want you to agree to the pay raise. What I said as the director is not good enough."

Braving the storm, General Manager Fang insisted, "I am just following the decision made at the board of directors' meeting. The decision is that wages will go up 62 percent. I do not have the authority to decide on anything that was not a board decision."

The production manager, Zhang Kouhua, who was also present, immediately said, "In that case, there is not much I can do [to calm the workers down]. If something untoward happens, I will not intervene."

Meanwhile, the workers outside were roaring: "We have been here for more than an hour! Let's force our way in!" Zhang then led the mid-level cadres out of the conference room. In doing so they raised the curtain for the violent scene to take place.

* * *

The four Taiwanese businesspeople were beaten by the workers, placed under arrest, and victimized for more than 10 hours. It was only at 9:00 p.m. that people from the labor bureau and the police arrived. But the first thing they asked the Taiwanese was not whether their personal safety had been in jeopardy or their rights had been violated. They merely asked, "Now that you have agreed to the demands of the workers, how are you going to implement them?"

When Zhou and his company heard this, their hearts sank. They knew that under such circumstances, it was impossible to ask for more. "Please escort us back to our dormitories," they requested. All they could hope for at that moment was to leave the scene.

Comments

The incident was taken very seriously by the Taiwanese newspaper, which gave it the "date name" of the "March 6 Incident." By Chinese convention, only events of historical significance normally merit a "date name." This is certainly too weighty a title for this particular incident, but behind the news-media hype lay the Taiwanese business community's deep anxieties about their personal safety when operating factories in China.[4] The report suggested that the Taiwanese managers were victims of a devious plot, and that the violence was instigated by Chinese officials. The report did not delve into the root causes of the Chinese workers' anger against the Taiwanese managers. The immediate cause was said to be a disagreement between the two sides of management over a wage increase. But such a dispute could have been settled peacefully in the boardroom. For it to explode as it did, the workers' resentment and antagonism must have run deep. Taiwanese managers on the mainland have a poor reputation, and it was likely that the Taiwanese leadership in this concrete factory had been abusive. When the trade-union chair stoked the fire, so to speak, the workers felt no inhibition in venting their anger against the Taiwanese. To Taiwanese investors, who were accustomed to enjoying the support of Chinese managers and local authorities, this incident touched off alarm bells. It was obvious that when Chinese authorities sided with workers, the consequences for investors could be disastrous.

Notably, the Jiangsu provincial government did not lend the city authorities and the factory director any public support. There was a news blackout to protect Jiangsu's good investment climate. There was not even a single reference to the incident in the Jiangsu Daily and the Jiangsu Workers' News.[5] The Taiwanese vehemently lodged complaints to a number of Chinese bureaucracies, including the provincial governor, and were informed that the officials and workers involved in the incident had been reprimanded.[6]

Case 22b

The workers at this factory vented their anger against management in a manner very different from the previous case. Workers at a Beijing factory owned by the People's Liberation Army had been pressured to sign one-year employment contracts that would have effectively stripped them of their jobs when the contracts expired. They planned to air their grievances in public and to stage a legal demonstration. Their insistence that they be granted a permit by the police, as stipulated by the Demonstration Law, shifted the focus of their struggle from employment contracts to the right to demonstrate. When the workers insisted on playing by the rules, the authorities did likewise, by finding technical loopholes in the law that prevented the workers from protesting on the streets.[7]

Here, we see workplace collective action emerging that begins to resemble actions taken by an autonomous trade union, with an organizing committee formed to renegotiate employment contracts. The natural leader, Zhu Rui, had an unusual personal history. She was active in the Democracy Wall Movement 20 years ago in 1979–80, when a schoolteacher at this factory. Because of her activities, she was demoted to the shop floor.[8] Under her leadership the organizing committee took a bold and unusual step, informing the Hong Kong news media of their application to demonstrate.[9]

Three items are included for this case. The first two are undated open letters issued by the organizing committee, calling for solidarity and updating readers on the latest status of the application to stage a street demonstration. The third was written by "a sacked worker from Factory 3501" to the general public, detailing the step-by-step battle the committee fought with the local authorities. Ultimately the demonstration did take place.

OPEN LETTER TO ALL THE STAFF AND WORKERS AT FACTORY 3501[10]

Fellow 3501 Workers,

Our application to hold a demonstration is a fundamental right of all citizens of China. How could anyone approve of the policies and decisions of the management at Factory 3501? They are using their powers of office to force us to sign one-year contracts. If we refuse to sign, they hide behind the law and say that "the contract has expired and the law is now effective." This is just a weapon to force us to be unemployed. In this manner, they are even denying us the right to claim allowances as laid-off workers.[11] Is this the spirit of the law that the Party Central Committee talks about in the newspapers and on television every day? They are not talking realistically or reasonably. They don't care if the workers have enough to eat, so why shouldn't we use the law to protect our constitutional rights? Everyone here has put the best years of their lives into the factory. Some of us started working here on the military-uniform assembly line on piece rates, earning just 18 yuan a month. We have worked hard for many years to the point that many of us now suffer from serious work-related illnesses. Yet now that we are nearing retirement age, they want to kick us out. Is it not understandable that these experiences have left all of us at 3501 feeling bitter? How many older workers here have put up with this endless hard work? If we were to start all over again, had known how matters would have ended up, none of us would have been prepared to do it again, even if they paid us 100 times over and there weren't half the hardships which we have endured in the past.

Now that China is moving into a new age, those of us over 40 have already given our best and are too exhausted to keep up. The 10,000 yuan that management has offered in redundancy is nothing more than charity, and anyway, with prices rising the way they are, what's the use of that kind of money? It's simply not enough to exist on. Fellow workers, our past experiences here at 3501 should be a lesson to all of us – young and old.

All the steps we have taken regarding the planned demonstration are in accordance with the legal procedures: if the authorities ratify our application, then the demonstration will be totally legal. We understand that some people are very nervous about taking part, and that not everyone feels the same as we do. However, anyone who contacts the organizing committee can do so anonymously, and will count as one more person opposed to management.

If we are going to change the unreasonable management policies of 3501, and struggle for our own individual interests, we must pull together and make a concerted effort by relying on our collective strength. It is not guaranteed that we will obtain a total victory, but it is guaranteed that the interests of everyone is the first concern, and no one is putting their own interests above the collective interests of all 3501's workers. If people try to drive a wedge between us, anyone at the factory should feel free to check out the whole situation.

If anyone is thinking that we are just doing this as a way of getting more money, then the answer is simple: our financial situation is not good. The factory officials have made it perfectly clear that if we don't take the redundancy money on offer, we will be sacked anyway because our contracts have expired. The paper, ink, and banners for the demonstration are all paid for out of our own pockets, and some people have therefore had to take the money on offer in order to protect their own interests. No one can dare say we haven't put our own sweat and blood into Factory 3501. No one can deny our years of hard work with the factory. No one should deprive us of our rights in such a manner.

Fellow workers, our interests are the same – no one is going to just put on a platter what we are due. We have to stand up and fight for our rights. We have worked for years to win our retirement and pension rights, and management is doing all they can to take them away from us. If just one or a few of us stand up against them, we don't have a chance. But if we all stand together, then they will have to listen to us. We must unite and get the issue solved.

Sacked Workers of Factory 3501
Tel: 62930909
Beeper: 191–2981921

Case 22b

Second Letter to the Staff and Workers at Factory 3501

To All Workers of Factory 3501:

Twenty days have passed since we applied for permission to hold a demonstration. So far we still have not been given permission. Despite this delay, we have already gained a major victory. Why?

First, more and more people, at all levels of society, are increasingly aware of the situation at Factory 3501 and know that the management's policies are unreasonable. Moreover, as attention focuses on the factory, management and officials at 3501 are beginning to examine their own behavior.

This is at least a step in the right direction! Our sincerity in trying to solve the problems confronting us is also well known. How can the authorities refuse to grant us permission to demonstrate when we apply again?

We hope to achieve a satisfactory settlement to the problems. However, management has acted in a totally insincere manner thus far. They are worried that they will not be able to implement their plans for the factory – plans that threaten the interests of every single one of us. No wonder we all feel that this is an urgent problem requiring immediate action. We need to learn from the mistakes of the past and unite in order to protect our interests; we must get everything ready so that we can hold a street demonstration as soon as we get permission from the police.

If we want to solve the problems, we have to have our say! If they do not give us a say, then we have to adopt another way of firmly expressing our opposition to their unreasonable policies. The organizing committee has already won the support of many people.

Demonstration time: 18 January, 1998. 10:00 a.m.

Slogans:.
- 3501 Workers and our Families Demand the Right to Welfare
- No to Unemployment! Yes to Retirement Rights!
- Kick Out the Unreasonable Policies at 3501
- Protect the Right to Demonstrate

Route:. 3501 Hujialou gate–Dabeiyao–Shuangjing–Dajiaoting–Back to the Factory
Contact Person: Zhu Rui, Tel: 62930909
Beeper: 191–2981921

Case 22c

News From Beijing Factory 3501

At 3:00 p.m. on December 8, 1997, we distributed several dozen copies of our "Application to Hold a Demonstration" and "Complaint of the Staff and Workers at Factory 3501" to employees at the factory. We also sent materials and information to various newspaper offices, government organizations, and the general office of the Central Committee of the Communist Party of China. At the same time, Zhu Rui went to the

Beijing Public Security Bureau (PSB) to complete the application procedures to hold a demonstration. However, because the site for the demonstration was incorrect, she was unable to register.

The following morning, Zhu Rui again went to the PSB office No. 13 in Gongdelin district to complete the procedures. While she was waiting in the office, a police officer from Chaoyang district rushed in and took Zhu Rui to Factory 3501's security office for talks. Their purpose was to bring the application procedures to a halt.

According to the provisions in China's constitution, citizens have the right to freedom of speech, publication, assembly, association, procession, and demonstration (Chapter 2, Article 35). The same section of the constitution also guarantees citizens' labor rights, rest days, the right to existence, as well as material assistance to the aged, those who are ill, or suffer from loss of the capacity to work. Moreover, "the constitutional provisions for the basic rights of citizens are the legal foundation for the rights of all citizens." In light of these rights, Zhu Rui persisted with our application to hold a demonstration.

On the afternoon of December 9, the leader of the Chaoyang district office, along with leaders from the Beijing PSB, held a meeting at Factory 3501. Zhu Rui waited for the results of the talks, but by 8:00 p.m. they still had not persuaded her to withdraw the application. Finally, they decided that those who wanted to demonstrate could continue with their application in accordance with the law, but that they should cease handing out any information to the public about the protest.

While preparing our application to hold a demonstration, we reported the situation at the factory to Party committees at all levels, National People's Congress committees, and government organizations. We also made use of news agencies and other channels of communication to expose the irrational policies of the management at Factory 3501. We made personal visits and sent letters to national bodies and government offices to express our views in the hope of obtaining the support of as many people as possible.

At 11:20 a.m. on December 10, the general office of the Party Central Committee telephoned us and inquired about the problems. They said they would make preparations to visit the factory to find out more about the situation.

On the morning of December 11, Zhu Rui handed over the notice for holding a demonstration to the No. 13 office. The officer-in-charge said that the problems could be solved through the relevant government departments. If they still weren't happy with the results, then they could resume their application to hold a demonstration.

On the morning of December 17, we went to the Beijing Public Security Bureau No. 13 office to inquire about the situation. An office worker, who did not want to reveal her name, said that the officer-in-charge was not present and asked us to return after two days.

On December 19, we again went to the No. 13 office. The same office worker said that the officer-in-charge was not there and asked us to return the following Monday.

On December 22, we went to No. 13 office for the third time and were received by the officer-in-charge. He told us that the matter concerning Factory 3501 had already been passed on to a higher government level. We replied that at no time had anyone from the government come to talk to us, and the problems at the factory itself were far from being solved. We demanded that we be allowed to formally complete the procedures for holding a demonstration. Because 11 days had already passed and the problems at the factory were nowhere near being resolved, our patience was proof of our sincerity. We said: "Since you have not solved the problems, we want to make use of our rights as citizens and express our opinions to society in general. All we are demanding is our right to survive, not golden handshakes or positions on high-ranking Party committees. We feel that it is our own sweat and blood that has gone into the factory, and now even our rice bowls have been taken away."

As our labor insurance has been expropriated by Factory 3501 [in itself an illegal act – Ed.], we believe the opinions which we expressed are entirely within legal means and are rational. The officer-in-charge was sympathetic to our plight and explanations, asked us to wait another day, and he would personally go to the central authorities to encourage them to deal with the issues. As a further expression of goodwill, we again promised to wait.

On December 24, we were again received by the officer-in-charge. He told us that over the previous two days, they had been in constant talks with the relevant departments: the government, Factory 3501, and the higher government office responsible for Factory 3501. The problems could definitely be solved. Over the past few days, the person responsible from the factory's Party committee, the factory head, and the factory security department had also been holding meetings to study the situation, and had made a report to the government office expressing their sincerity in finding solutions to the problems.

The officer-in-charge also said that further visits to the factory over the next two days were planned and urged us to wait patiently. Our position was clear: the aim of the planned demonstration depended on finding solutions to the problems. With the above assurance of the factory management's good-will, we would again wait.

On December 25, the officer-in-charge telephoned us, and told Zhu Rui to go to No. 13 office the following day.

On December 26, Zhu Rui went to the office feeling reasonably optimistic. The officer-in-charge picked up the December 24 edition of "News" and started to speak: "They are not happy with this type of news bulletin. However, the PSB has no business interfering in the internal business of an enterprise. We are already fully aware of the situation at the factory, and if you want to express your opinions about it through a demonstration, then fill in the forms."

Zhu Rui replied, "Why didn't you tell us earlier? There are now only two days before the day fixed for the demonstration. Also, when you rang yesterday, you asked me to come to the office and talk about the situation 'in general,' so I haven't brought the information for the application forms."

The officer said, "Check your demonstration route. If the march is in Chaoyang, then you must apply for permission at the Chaoyang police station. Here we can only deal with [routes] that cross districts."

It had taken nearly three weeks, from December 8 until December 26, to get permission to hold a demonstration!

The following day, a reporter from Hong Kong Cable TV interviewed Zhu Rui at the factory gate. That same afternoon, she was taken away to Hujialou police station by four policemen who said that the interview tape had already been confiscated.

On December 28, Zhu Rui was allowed to go home. The attitude of the police toward her had been polite at all times. On January 1, 1998, the sacked staff and workers from Factory 3501 formally applied for permission to hold a demonstration.

A sacked worker from Factory 3501,
January 4, 1998.

This is the case of a migrant from Sichuan province who became a legal advocate for workers claiming industrial injury compensation in Guangdong province. His career pattern did not suggest he would be a likely person to fight for migrant worker rights. He had first been in the army, then in the police force, and later he had worked as a private security guard in a factory in Guangdong. His empathy with the workers launched him into a new career as a mentor for injured migrant workers in the area.

Had the local authorities not tolerated his activities, he could not have openly practiced his profession. That he was able to do so was a reflection of the changed political and social environment in Guangdong province in the late 1990s. It is now possible to litigate, especially for compensation for industrial accidents. The rate of accidents has become so abominably high that the authorities have realized there is a need to curb the problem.

THE MIGRANT "LAWYER" WHO SPECIALIZES IN "SPEAKING OUT" FOR OTHER MIGRANTS[12]

After migrant worker Deng Yuguo's two fingers were chopped off by a cutting machine in Jianghui Footwear Company in Panyu city in Guangdong province, the company would not compensate him a cent. Just as he was feeling helpless, he got in touch with Liao Xiaofeng. Liao made use of the law to fight hard on his behalf. In seven days, the boss handed over to Deng 65,000 yuan in cash.

Liao Xiaofeng, while being considered by some as a troublemaker, has become the savior of the migrants around Panyu area.

Fired after Four Years of Working for a Boss

It is not hard to get hold of Liao Xiaofeng. Many migrants know his pager number.

This stout and sharp-looking youngster from Sichuan is only 28 years old. After graduating from middle technical school, he joined the army, where he became a news reporter in one of the corps of the Beijing Army District. There, he gained a third-level merit. After being discharged in 1991, he worked as a team leader in the police station of Langzhong city in Sichuan province, and then as a public security subdivisional head at North Chengdu Railway Station.

In 1993, he quit those fairly decent jobs in the interior provinces and came south to Panyu city, where he took up several jobs in a row: as a deputy private security guard and then as a public security team leader in a few companies in Lianhua Shan Tax-Free Processing Zone. The pay was only a pitiful few hundred yuan and he could not stand having to be accommodating all the time. It was under such circumstances that he developed a profound empathy for the plight of migrants.

In 1996, when he was working as a security guard in Jidelong Company, a fellow villager, Zeng Guojian, came to him for help. Zeng had been working in a Hong Kong-invested coconut-candy factory and had two fingers cut off while sawing coconuts. The Labor Bureau had classed it as a ninth-level injury, and the factory gave him 6,000 yuan in compensation. Zeng felt cheated, and so went to his friend Liao for help. When Liao could not get anywhere after going to talk to the factory boss, he looked up the labor laws and regulations in some Panyu city bookstores and discovered that for a ninth-level injury, the compensation should be 10,000 yuan. So he stayed up the whole night and composed a letter of complaint addressed to the labor-arbitration committee of the labor bureau, demanding a higher compensation. Twenty-five days later, Zeng was awarded 12,000 yuan.

This was the first time that Liao Xiaofeng had gotten involved in a case, and surprisingly, he was successful. But it had not occurred to him then to take this up as a "profession."

Life passed by quickly and uneventfully until April 13, 1997, a day that was unforgettable for Liao. When the management committee of Lianhua Shan Tax-Free Processing Zone inspected the workers' dormitory of Jidelong Company and uncovered some 70 gas burners, security guard Liao Xiaofeng got the sack, all because he was too softhearted to confiscate the gas burners from the workers.

This incident changed Liao's life.

Twenty Cases: All Successful

Unemployed for a while, Liao felt lost and anxious. A friend came up with an idea for a way out – learn more about the labor laws and help people to file charges.

So Liao rented a room in Shiliu township and went to a Guangzhou bookshop to buy a whole lot of books on labor law, civil law, criminal law, civil litigation, marriage law, and so on. He studied them on his own, seeking some help from people in the legal profession, and began putting what he had learned into practice. Within a month, acting in the capacity as an authorized representative, he successfully helped several migrant workers involved in labor disputes. He started accumulating experience.

On May 22 last year, an arbitration case over an industrial injury was brewing in Shangfei Garment Factory in Lingxing Industrial District. A migrant worker in the factory, Zhang Donghua, slipped and broke her right leg as she came down the unlit staircase of the factory at 11:00 p.m. after working overtime. The next morning, she authorized her husband to go and claim work insurance. But not only did the company refuse to pay, it made her terminate her employment on June 9, giving her 200 yuan as compensation.

After Liao took up Zhang's case as her representative, he consulted a large number of laws and regulations. But when negotiations with the company broke down, he brought the case to the Panyu City Labor Arbitration Committee. On October 5, the arbitration committee ruled in Zhang's favor and demanded the company compensate Zhang with more than 13,000 yuan.

Last February migrant worker Chen Jizhao's foot was crushed by a pile of shoe lasts on the shop floor, but the company refused to pay her any compensation after taking care of her medical expenses. Liao fought on her behalf and got 12,000 yuan for her.

That year, Liao took up 20 cases. Most of them were related to disputes over compensation for workplace injuries, traffic accidents, marriage problems, and unpaid wages. In all cases, the complainants were awarded with some sort of compensation. Now, it is not only in Panyu city that people know of Liao, he is much sought after by migrant workers from Zhuhai, Dongguan, and even Hainan. People call him asking for legal advice or for him to take up their cases. Each day he receives up to 20 phone calls. He has become so busy that, except for when he is asleep, he is out all day.

Only He Himself Knows the Difficulties

For a young person coming from a faraway province, and without any connections, the difficulties Liao has encountered in fighting for justice for migrant workers are simply too numerous to count.

The greatest obstacle Liao faces comes from none other than the labor bureau's departments. Because of a lack of staff, their attitude is: the less trouble, the better. To them, Liao is nothing but a troublemaker.

Of course, obstacles also come from the companies. Bosses and managers refuse to see him, give him the cold shoulder, or treat him rudely. Once, a boss even called in the local police to arrest him. For his personal safety, Liao is careful not to tell others where he lives.

When it comes to the sensitive question of fees, Liao said he asks for very little, usually 200 yuan for a case. After the case is won, then it is up to the clients to give him as much as they want, and usually is it around 500 to 1,000 yuan. The largest amount he has ever received for one case was Deng's case mentioned in the very beginning of this report. Out of the 65,000 yuan Deng got, Liao got 2,000 yuan. "Making money is not my goal; it is redressing social justice. The compensation the migrant workers get after industrial accidents is for their blood and sweat. I feel bad taking it, but then I also have to make a living."

Liao Xiaofeng's present ambition is to become a certified lawyer, a real people's lawyer. He hopes his work can give migrant workers hope that their problems will have a silver lining.

Comments

Liao never became a certified lawyer, and in 1999, a non-governmental labor organization in Hong Kong received news that "he was driven out of Guangdong province."[13] But advocacy work for victims of industrial accidents did not disappear with Liao's departure. Soon, a certified lawyer, Zhou Litai, also from Sichuan province, became even better known. Zhou went further – he set up a shelter for his clients, who were all injured workers. Since 90 percent of injured workers get dismissed and are penniless and homeless, Zhou provides them with shelter while they file compensation claims in court. These claims can take months, even up to a couple of years. Zhou's home (comprised of two apartments) is an extended family of young men and women who are all disabled in one way or another, mainly by losing arms or fingers.[14] Thus far, he has handled about 200 cases, including those in process. Of these, about 40 are on behalf of women workers.[15] Males are more likely to be employed in physically hazardous jobs, and are therefore more likely to be maimed through workplace injuries.

Like Liao, Zhou finds that his main antagonists are local bureaucracies. The bureaucracies connive to undercompensate workers who are covered by local government industrial-insurance schemes by paying compensation at rates that have not kept up with inflation.

Zhou's actions have started to attract nationwide publicity. In 1999, he appeared on numerous Chinese television programs and in the Chinese and Hong Kong press,[16] and was even interviewed by the Washington Post.[17] *Publicity is probably his best protection against revenge and suppression. But he still has to walk a fine line to avoid the same fate as Liao.*

Notes

1 Li Yuwei, "Lawyers in China – A 'Flourishing' Profession in a Rapidly Changing Society," *China Perspectives*, No. 27 (January–February 2000), pp. 20–34.

2 Zhuang Ronghong, "Jiangsu 'Yuandong shuini chang' taishang Zhou Guiliang, Fang Zhongjun deng siren zao gongren oushang. Shushi gongren chengbao weiou. Shouhai taishang tongshu shimo. Yuji youcun," *Zhongyang ribao* (Central Daily) (Taipei), March 30, 1995. Translated by Anita Chan.

3   In this incident, a boatload of Taiwanese tourists visiting China were slaughtered on a lake in the middle of the night.

4   When I conducted field research with Taiwanese owners/managers in Dongguan city in Guangdong province in 1996, they expressed fears for their personal safety. Many of the Taiwanese managers had hired bodyguards.

5   In the editions of March 30 and 31, and all the April issues of these two newspapers, there was not a single word about the incident.

6   *Central Daily*, March 31, 1995.

7   "Organizing Against All Odds," *China Labor Bulletin*, Issue 40 (January–February, 1998), p. 2.

8   Ibid.

9   Jin Yi, "Gongchao – dalu de dingshi zhadan" (Strike Waves – The Time Bomb of Chinese Mainland), *Dongxiang* (The Trend), no. 2, 1998, pp. 28–31.

10 Reprinted with permission, from the *China Labor Bulletin*, Issue 40 (January–February 1998), pp. 3–6.

11 To be unemployed (*shiye*) means a worker's relationship is completely severed from the work unit and the worker is no longer entitled to any subsidies or benefits from the work unit. To be "laid off" or to be "taken off the post" (*xiagang*) is technically a suspension from work. A worker continues to be an employee of the work unit, and so is entitled to *xiagang* subsidies and other benefits, including a pension. By making the workers sign year-long contracts, the management would have been able to make the workers unemployed a year later.

12 From the Chinese text: Zeng Huafeng and Tan Yangchun, "Zhuan wei dagongzai tao 'shuofa' de dagongzai 'lushi,'" *Laodong daobao* (Labor News), May 5, 1998. Translated by Anita Chan.

13 I was not able to acquire more information about Liao.

14 In August 1999, I was able to interview Zhou Litai at the shelter and met about a dozen workers there.

15 However, women workers are more likely to contract chronic occupational safety and health diseases caused by toxic chemicals, such as in case 11 of the shoe factory workers in Putian.

16 Yu Bin, "Cangtian zai shang, ti tequ dagongzu daguansi de 'zhuanye' – Chongqing lushi Zhou Litai zai Shenzhen de zhuanqi gushi" (Heaven From On High Provides the Migrant Workers in Shenzhen Special Economic Zone with Someone Who Litigates on Behalf of the Workers – the Story of Chongqing Lawyer Zhou Litai), *Jiayuan* (Home), vol. 13, no. 1 (1999), pp. 13–16. Zhang Shen, "Dagongzai yingong zhican chuangao wumen, Zhou lushi pai an erqi baoda guansi" (Migrant Workers Handicapped by Industrial Accidents Have Nowhere to Appeal. Lawyer Zhou Rose to the Occasion to Take Their Cases to Court), *Xin bao* (New News), August 19, 1999. Wang Xiaoding, "Youxia Zhou lushi, Shenzhen chuangguan ji" (Lawyer Zhou, the Robin Hood of Shenzhen), *Fazhi zongheng* (Crisscrossing the Legal System), March 30, 1999, pp. 4–11. Lun Gu, "One Man's Bid for Workers' Justice," *South China Morning Post*, March 26, 2000, p. 9.

17 John Pomfret, "In China, No Workers' Paradise: Lawyer Fights for Clients Injured in Factories Placing Money Before Safety," *Washington Post*, January 11, 2000, pp. A11 and A13.

CHAPTER 7

Üstün Reinart

Life Against Gold

An aging man with a white mustache, wearing a peaked cap walks on the stage of an auditorium at Turkey's Middle East Technical University (METU), followed by 10 peasant women. More than 1,000 students filling the auditorium rise to their feet and give a standing ovation to the unlikely assembly on the stage: peasant women and elderly man, standing hand in hand. The faces of the women are sunburned and lined. The roaring ovation continues.

The aging man turns to the women, "Are you going to let Eurogold poison your lands?" He asks them. The women shout in unison: "No, we are not."

"Are you going to sell your children's future to foreigners?"

"No," the women call out to thundering applause, "We'll resist."

The women on the stage are only ten of the thousands of peasants fighting Eurogold, a transnational company planning to use cyanide to extract gold from the hills of Bergama on the Aegean coast of Anatolia. The man is their leader in civil disobedience: Oktay Konyar, nicknamed Asterix for his drooping mustache. Konyar has just been sentenced to 21 months in prison.

The oldest of the women, Sahsine *nine* (granny) from the village of Yenikent near Bergama calls out, "We won't let them take our leader to prison. They'll have to take us with him."

The hills on the Northern Aegean coast are covered with fertile fields, olive groves, nut-bearing pines, and fig orchards. In spring, blood-red poppies and wild daisies bloom on the roadsides, and the wind is scented with oregano and lavender. Today's town of Bergama was a thriving Roman city and healing center named Pergamon 2,000 years ago. With its thermal springs and its fragrant air, it was the city of Asclepios, the God of health. Today, tourists visit the remains of the Acropolis, the Temples of Athena, Zeus, Serapis, and Trajan, the steep amphitheatre, and the health center, Asclepion, where patients were cured by the sound of water and music in Pergamon. But if "the New World Order" has its way, Pergamon will become a wasteland.

In 1992, Eurogold obtained a license from the Turkish Ministry of Energy to look for gold on the hills of Bergama. Ten villages were located within a 5-kilometer radius of the mine site. At first, the villagers thought the mine would provide them with jobs. But soon they learned that Eurogold would leach the metal with a deadly poison: cyanide.

Üstün Reinart, "Life Against Gold," *Z Magazine* (June 2001), pp. 19–21. Reprinted by permission of the author.

They began to research gold mines. They learned that cyanide leaching had caused environmental disasters in the US, China, Guyana, Bolivia, Philippines, and Zimbabwe. Scientists told them the gold would be taken out of the country and leave the land contaminated with cyanide, that nothing would remain alive within a 30-kilometer radius of the mine. Cyanide leaching would also release other poisons such as arsenic, lead, cadmium, and mercury into the environment. What's more, a fault line passing through Kaynarca, only 1.5 kilometers away from the mine, posed an earthquake risk that could be catastrophic.

Bergama's peasants met with their mayor and held a news conference to announce these findings. They said they did not want the gold mine on their hills. Eurogold officials replied that the cyanide would be kept in strong clay pools and that it would evaporate under the sun.

The peasants organized under the leadership of Oktay Konyar to dismiss Eurogold from their olive groves. Konyar had grown up in Bergama, worked in various non-government organizations, and had served as the regional leader of the social democratic *Cumhuriyet Halk Partisi*, Republican People's Party. "I knew how un-democratic this country could be," he says, "but I also knew that violence would never be a solution. So we vowed never to violate laws, never to commit any crimes."

In November 1994, 652 people from the villages of Camkoy, Ovacik, and Narlica launched three lawsuits at the Court in Izmir, to get the mine's license canceled. But the regional court ruled in favor of Eurogold and the peasants took their case to the Court of Appeal.

Eurogold did not wait for the ruling. In 1996, they cut 2,500 pines and 800 olive trees and began constructing a mine surrounded with barbed wire and watchtowers.

The villagers launched civil disobedience. On November 16, 1996, 500 of them sat on an arterial highway close to the mine for 5 hours. "We don't want to die from cyanide," they chanted. They set tires on fire and performed traditional dances on the road. On December 23, 1996, thousands of people from 17 nearby villages protested Eurogold. The men stripped to the waist and marched under heavy rain. In January 1997, the people of Bergama held a referendum and voted against the mine. But Eurogold declared it illegal. In April that same year, 5,000 peasants from 17 villages occupied the mine, forcing the regional governor to close it for a month.

On May 13, 1997, after 10 years of court battles, the Court of Appeal ruled in favor of the peasants saying Eurogold was violating the article in the Turkish Constitution, guaranteeing all citizens' right to life and right to protect their health and their environment. It declared Eurogold's licenses invalid and said the mine should be closed. Under the Constitution, the country's law enforcement agencies had to comply with the court decision.

The peasants of Bergama danced in circles to the music of pipes and drums. "Get Out Eurogold," they chanted. "This land belongs to our ancestors and our children." But the mine remained. The Ministry of Energy and Natural Resources commissioned a new environmental report from a scientific institution called TUBITAK, and obtained a report saying Eurogold had installed new safety equipment after the Appeal Court ruling, and the cyanide would no longer pose a threat to the environment.

The peasants kept demanding that the court order be enforced. On July 1, 1997, they got word that cyanide trucks were on their way. They occupied the mine and burned some trucks and a social hall belonging to Eurogold. On August 26, 1997, three busloads of people went to Istanbul with Oktay Konyar, and tied themselves to the bridge parapets to stop traffic. In February 1998, 9 months after the Court of Appeal ruling, Eurogold blatantly violated the laws by using 3 tons of cyanide to obtain 1.5 kilograms of gold.

Early in 1999, the people of Bergama learned that 18 tons of cyanide had been delivered to the mine. Hundreds of people hit the mountain roads to demand that the poison be removed. On April 2, 1999, the cyanide was taken away from the mine and delivered to an unknown place.

The police laid charges against Oktay Konyar and 80 of the peasants, accusing them of forming a secret, illegal organization.

Eurogold seemed confident that it would have its way. The company had tied its hopes to an imminent Multilateral Agreement on Investment (MAI), which would introduce international arbitration to overrule national courts in disputes involving transnational investors. But in 1999, MAI talks collapsed. Still, the IMF pressured Turkey to accept international arbitration anyway. "The only way to encourage foreign investors," they said. In the fall of 1999, while Turkish people were reeling from a killer earthquake, the government rapidly changed the country's Constitution to allow international arbitration. Now, a foreign board sympathetic to business interests would overrule national courts. This was what Eurogold had been waiting for.

The company bought full-page advertisements in major Turkish newspapers, saying gold would enrich Turkey and provide jobs. It began to distribute job-application forms, and circulated rumors that ordinary miners would be paid upwards of US $1,000 a month.

The fight against Eurogold now became a fight against neo-liberalism. The peasants of Bergama compared their struggle to that of the aboriginal peoples of Chiapas, Mexico. They vowed to oppose international arbitration, and the New World Order. They became the guests of honor at rallies against nuclear energy, against the IMF, McDonald's, Cargill, and all the others set to plunder Anatolia.

On the morning of November 28, 1999, hundreds walked from the village of Camkoy towards the village of Ovacik, carrying placards reading "*Eurogold gidecek, bu is bitecek*" (this job will end when Eurogold leaves our lands). That morning, Eurogold launched a complaint against Oktay Konyar and the police charged the leader of the peasants with organizing an illegal demonstration.

"We are demonstrating against the violation of Turkish laws," said Konyar, "I am being charged for protesting the violation of our Constitution."

The charges stood. On March 30, 2001, under laws passed during the 1980s by a military junta in Turkey, Bergama's Court of first instance sentenced Konyar to 21 months in prison.

Oktay Konyar has appealed his sentence. He continues to travel across Anatolia with groups of peasants from Bergama to call for resistance. In his leather briefcase, he carries a stethoscope and pills for high blood pressure and heart disease. "I have health problems," he says. "It's the stress."

Then, he turns to granny Sahsine, whose own blood pressure rose to 24–12 during the METU rally, and who barely escaped a stroke.

"No dying before we get rid of Eurogold, eh granny?" he jokes. "I'll dance with you yet, when it's time to celebrate."

CHAPTER 8

The Campus Antisweatshop Movement

Each year of the past five, the annual survey of national freshman attitudes conducted by the University of California at Los Angeles has hit a new record low with students who say it is important to keep up with political affairs. At 26 percent this year, it was down from 58 percent when the survey was first done in 1966.

— Boston Globe, February 15, 1999

From: Arne David Ekstrom <ekstrom@NSMA.Arizona.EDU>
To: usas@listbot.com [United Students Against Sweatshops listserve]
Date: Thursday, April 29, 1999
Subject: U of Arizona STUDENTS AGAINST SWEATSHOPS SIT-IN CONTINUES

For those of you who are wondering, the University of Arizona sit-in is STILL GOING ON! We have reached a USAS record of 200 hours and still counting. Negotiations are still going slowly although progress is being made. We could still most definitely use your support in the form of emails, phone calls, and letters. Morale tends to go up and down but support ALWAYS keeps it high!

    our cell phone: (520) 400-1066 (somewhat unreliable)
    our email: akolers@u.arizona.edu (avery), lsnow@u.arizona.edu (laura)
    our President's email: President Likins at plikins@lan.admin.arizona.edu
    our President's phone: (520) 621-5511

If University of Arizona activist Arne Ekstrom was aware of today's widely reported student apathy, he certainly was not deterred when he helped lead his campus antisweatshop sit-in. Nor, for that matter, were any of the other thousands of students across the United States who participated in anti-sweatshop activities during the past academic year, coordinating their activities on the United Students Against Sweatshops (USAS) listserv (a listserv is an online mailing list for the purpose of group discussion) and Web site.

Richard Appelbaum and Peter Dreier, (1999), "The Campus Antisweatshop Movement." Reprinted with permission from *The American Prospect*, vol. 10, no. 46: Sept. 1, 1999–Oct. 1, 1999. The American Prospect, 5 Broad Street, Boston, MA 02109.

Last year's student antisweatshop movement gained momentum as it swept westward, eventually encompassing more than 100 campuses across the country. Sparked by a sit-in at Duke University, students organized teach-ins, led demonstrations, and occupied buildings – first at Georgetown, then northeast to the Ivy League, then west to the Big Ten. After militant actions at Notre Dame, Wisconsin, and Michigan made the *New York Times, Business Week, Time,* National Public Radio, and almost every major daily newspaper, the growing student movement reached California, where schools from tiny Occidental College to the giant ten-campus University of California system agreed to limit the use of their names and logos to sweatshop-free apparel. Now the practical challenge is to devise a regime of monitoring and compliance.

The antisweatshop movement is the largest wave of student activism to his campuses since students rallied to free Nelson Mandela by calling for a halt to university investments in South Africa more than a decade ago. This time around, the movement is electronically connected. Student activists bring their laptops and cell phones with them when they occupy administration buildings, sharing ideas and strategies with fellow activists from Boston to Berkeley. On the USAS listserv, victorious students from Wisconsin counsel neophytes from Arizona and Kentucky, and professors at Berkeley and Harvard explain how to calculate a living wage and guarantee independent monitoring in Honduras.

The target of this renewed activism is the $2.5 billion collegiate licensing industry – led by major companies like Nike, Gear, Champion, and Fruit of the Loom – which pays colleges and universities sizable royalties in exchange for the right to use the campus logo on caps, sweatshirts, jackets, and other items. Students are demanding that the workers who make these goods be paid a living wage, no matter where in the world industry operates. Students are also calling for an end to discrimination against women workers, public disclosure of the names and addresses of all factories involved in production, and independent monitoring in order to verify compliance.

These demands are opposed by the apparel industry, the White House, and most universities. Yet so far students have made significant progress in putting the industry on the defensive. A growing number of colleges and clothing companies have adopted "codes of conduct" – something unthinkable a decade ago – although student activists consider many of these standards inadequate.

In a world economy increasingly dominated by giant retailers and manufacturers who control global networks of independently owned factories, organizing consumers may prove to be a precondition for organizing production workers. And students are a potent group of consumers. If students next year succeed in building on this year's momentum, the collegiate licensing industry will be forced to change the way it does business. These changes, in turn, could affect the organization of the world's most globalized and exploitative industry – apparel manufacturing – along with the growing number of industries that, like apparel, outsource production in order to lower labor costs and blunt worker organizing.

The global sweatshop

In the apparel industry, so-called manufacturers – in reality, design and marketing firms – outsource the fabrication of clothing to independent contractors around the world. In this labor-intensive industry where capital requirements are minimal, it is relatively easy to open a clothing factory. This has contributed to a global race to the bottom, in which there is always someplace, somewhere, where clothing can be made still more cheaply. Low wages reflect not low productivity, but low bargaining power. A recent analysis in *Business Week* found that although Mexican apparel workers are 70 percent as productive as US workers, they earn only 11 percent as much as their US counterparts; Indonesian workers, who are 50 percent as productive, earn less than 2 percent as much.

The explosion of imports has proven devastating to once well-paid, unionized US garment workers. The number of American garment workers has declined from peak levels of 1.4 million in the early 1970s to 800,000 today. The one exception to these trends is the expansion of garment employment, largely among immigrant and undocumented workers, in Los Angeles, which has more than 160,000 sweatshop workers. Recent US Department of Labor surveys found that more than 9 out of 10 such firms violate legal health and safety standards, with more than half troubled by serious violations that could lead to severe injuries or death. Working conditions in New York City, the other major domestic garment center, are similar.

The very word "sweatshop" comes from the apparel industry, where profits were "sweated" out of workers by forcing them to work longer and faster at their sewing machines. Although significant advances have been made in such aspects of production as computer-assisted design, computerized marking, and computerized cutting, the industry still remains low-tech in its core production process, the sewing of garments. The basic unit of production continues to be a worker, usually a woman, sitting or standing at a sewing machine and sewing together pieces of limp cloth.

The structure of the garment industry fosters sweatshop production. During the past decade, retailing in the United States has become increasingly concentrated. Today, the four largest US retailers – Wal-Mart, Kmart, Sears, and Dayton Hudson (owner of Target and Mervyns) – account for nearly two-thirds of US retail sales. Retailers squeeze manufacturers, who in turn squeeze the contractors who actually make their products. Retailers and manufacturers preserve the fiction of being completely separate from contractors because they do not want to be held legally responsible for workplace violations of labor, health, and safety laws. Retailers and manufacturers alike insist that what happens in contractor factories is not their responsibility – even though their production managers and quality control officers are constantly checking up on the sewing shops that make their clothing.

The contracting system also allows retailers and manufacturers to eliminate much uncertainty and risk. When business is slow, the contract is simply not renewed; manufacturers need not worry about paying unemployment benefits or dealing with idle workers who might go on strike or otherwise make trouble. If a particular contractor becomes a problem, there are countless others to be found who will be only too happy to get their business. Workers, however, experience the flip side of the enormous flexibility enjoyed by retailers and manufacturers. They become contingent labor, employed and paid only when their work is needed.

Since profits are taken out at each level of the supply chain, labor costs are reduced to a tiny fraction of the retail price. Consider the economics of a dress that is sewn in Los Angeles and retails for $100. Half goes to the department store and half to the manufacturer, who keeps $12.50 to cover expenses and profit, spends $22.50 on textiles, and pays $15 to the contractor. The contractor keeps $9 to cover expenses and profits. That leaves just $6 of the $100 retail price for the workers who actually make the dress. Even if the cost of direct production labor were to increase by half, the dress would still only cost $103 – a small increment that would make a world of difference to the seamstress in Los Angeles, whose $7,000 to $8,000 in annual wages are roughly two-thirds of the poverty level. A garment worker in Mexico would be lucky to earn $1,000 during a year of 48 to 60 hour workweeks; in China, $500.

At the other end of the apparel production chain, the heads of the 60 publicly traded US apparel retailers earn an average $1.5 million a year. The heads of the 35 publicly traded apparel manufacturers average $2 million. In 1997, according to the *Los Angeles Business Journal*, 5 of the 6 highest-paid apparel executives in Los Angeles all came from a single firm: Guess?, Inc. They took home nearly $12.6 million – enough to double the yearly wages of 1,700 LA apparel workers.

Organizing workers at the point of production, the century-old strategy that built the power of labor in Europe and North America, is best suited to production processes where most of the work goes on in-house. In industries whose production can easily be shifted almost anywhere on the planet, organizing is extremely difficult. Someday, perhaps, a truly international labor movement will confront global manufacturers. But in the meantime, organized consumers may well be labor's best ally. Consumers, after all, are not as readily moved as factories. And among American consumers, college students represent an especially potent force.

Kathie Lee and Robert Reich

During the early 1990s, American human rights and labor groups protested the proliferation of sweatshops at home and abroad – with major campaigns focusing on Nike and Gap. These efforts largely fizzled. But then two exposés of sweatshop conditions captured public attention. In August 1995, state and federal officials raided a garment factory in El Monte, California – a Los Angeles suburb – where 71 Thai immigrants had been held for several years in virtual slavery in an apartment complex ringed with barbed wire and spiked fences. They worked an average of 84 hours a week for $1.60 an hour, living 8 to 10 persons in a room. The garments they sewed ended up in major retail chains, including Macy's, Filene's and Robinsons-May, and for brand-name labels like B. U. M., Tomato, and High Sierra. Major daily papers and TV networks picked up on the story, leading to a flood of outraged editorials and columns calling for a clamp-down on domestic sweatshops. Then in April 1996, TV celebrity Kathie Lee Gifford tearfully acknowledged on national television that the Wal-Mart line of clothing that bore her name was made by children in Honduran sweatshops, even though tags on the garments promised that part of the profits would go to help children. Embarrassed by the publicity, Gifford soon became a crusader against sweatshop abuses.

For several years, then Labor Secretary Robert Reich (now the *Prospect's* senior editor) had been trying to inject the sweatshop issue onto the nation's agenda. The mounting publicity surrounding the El Monte and Kathie Lee scandals gave Reich new leverage. After all, what the apparel industry primarily sells is image, and the image of some of its major labels was getting a drubbing. He began pressing apparel executives, threatening to issue a report card on firms' behavior unless they agreed to help establish industry-wide standards.

In August 1996, the Clinton administration brought together representatives from the garment industry, labor unions, and consumer and human rights groups to grapple with sweatshops. The members of what they called the White House Apparel Industry

Partnership (AIP) included apparel firms (Liz Claiborne, Reebok, L. L. Bean, Nike, Patagonia, Phillips-Van Heusen, Wal-Mart's Kathie Lee Gifford brand, and Nicole Miller), several nonprofit organizations (including the National Consumers League, Interfaith Center on Corporate Responsibility, International Labor Rights Fund, Lawyers Committee for Human Rights, Robert F. Kennedy Memorial Center for Human Rights, and Business for Social Responsibility), as well as the Union of Needletrades, Industrial and Textile Employees (UNITE), the Retail, Wholesale, and Department Store Union, and the AFL-CIO.

After intense negotiations, the Department of Labor issued an interim AIP report in April 1997 and the White House released the final 40-page report in November 1998, which included a proposed workplace code of conduct and a set of monitoring guidelines. By then, Reich had left the Clinton administration, replaced by Alexis Herman. The two labor representatives on the AIP, as well as the Interfaith Center on Corporate Responsibility, quit the group to protest the feeble recommendations, which had been crafted primarily by the garment industry delegates and which called, essentially, for the industry to police itself. This maneuvering would not have generated much attention except that a new factor – college activism – had been added to the equation.

A "sweat-free" campus

The campus movement began in the fall of 1997 at Duke when a group called Students Against Sweatshops persuaded the university to require manufacturers of items with the Duke label to sign a pledge that they would not use sweatshop labor. Duke has 700 licensees (including Nike and other major labels) that make apparel at hundreds of plants in the US and in more than 10 other countries, generating almost $25 million annually in sales. Following months of negotiations, in March 1998 Duke President Nannerl Keohane and the student activists jointly announced a detailed "code of conduct" that bars Duke licensees from using child labor, requires them to maintain safe workplaces, to pay the minimum wage, to recognize the right of workers to unionize, to disclose the locations of all factories making products with Duke's name, and to allow visits by independent monitors to inspect the factories.

The Duke victory quickly inspired students on other campuses. The level of activity on campuses accelerated, with students finding creative ways to dramatize the issue. At Yale, student activists staged a "knit-in" to draw attention to sweatshop abuses. At Holy Cross and the University of California at Santa Barbara, students sponsored mock fashion shows where they discussed the working conditions under which the garments were manufactured. Duke students published a coloring book explaining how (and where) the campus mascot, the Blue Devil, is stitched onto clothing by workers in sweatshops. Activists at the University of Wisconsin infiltrated a homecoming parade and, dressed like sweatshop workers in Indonesia, carried a giant Reebok shoe. They also held a press conference in front of the chancellor's office and presented him with an oversized check for 16 cents – the hourly wage paid to workers in China making Nike athletic shoes. At Georgetown, Wisconsin, Michigan, Arizona, and Duke, students occupied administration buildings to pressure their institutions to adopt (or, in Duke's case, strengthen) antisweatshop codes.

In the summer of 1998, disparate campus groups formed United Students Against Sweatshops (USAS). The USAS has weekly conference calls to discuss their negotiations with Nike, the Department of Labor, and others. It has sponsored training sessions for student leaders and conferences at several campuses where the sweatshop issue is only part of an agenda that also includes helping to build the labor movement, NAFTA, the World Trade Organization, women's rights, and other issues.

Last year, antisweatshop activists employed the USAS listserv to exchange ideas on negotiating tactics, discuss media strategies, swap songs to sing during rallies, and debate the technicalities of defining a "living wage" to incorporate in their campus codes of conduct. In May, the USAS listserv heated up after the popular Fox television series *Party of Five* included a scene in which one of the show's characters, Sarah (played by Jennifer Love Hewitt), helps organize a Students Against Sweatshops sit-in on her campus. A few real-life activists worried that the mainstream media was trivializing the movement by skirting the key issues ("the importance of unionized labor, the globalization of the economy, etc.") as well as focusing most of that episode on the characters' love life. University of Michigan student Rachel Paster responded:

> Let's not forget that we ARE a student movement, and students do complain about boy-friends and fashion problems. One of the biggest reasons why USAS and local student groups opposing sweatshops have been as successful as we have been is that opposition to sweatshops ISN'T that radical. Although I'm sure lots of us are all for overthrowing the corporate power structure, the human rights issues involved are what make a lot of people get involved and put their energies into rallies, sit-ins, et cetera. If we were a "radical" group, university adminis-trations would have brushed us off. . . . The fact that they don't is testament to the fact that we have support, not just from students on the far left, but from students in the middle ground who don't consider themselves radicals. Without those people we would NEVER have gotten as far as we have.

Indeed, the antisweatshop movement has been able to mobilize wide support because it strikes several nerves among today's college students, including women's rights (most sweatshop workers are women and some factories have required women to use birth control pills as a condition of employment), immigrant rights, environmental concerns, and human rights. After University of Wisconsin administrators brushed aside antisweat-shop protestors, claiming they didn't represent student opinion, the activists ran a slate of candidates for student government. Eric Brakken, a sociology major and antisweatshop leader, was elected student body president and last year used the organization's substantial resources to promote the activists' agenda. And Duke's student government unanimously passed a resolution supporting the antisweatshop group, calling for full public disclosure of the locations of companies that manufacture Duke clothing.

The labor connection

At the core of the movement is a strong bond with organized labor. The movement is an important byproduct of the labor movement's recent efforts, under President John Sweeney, to repair the rift between students and unions that dates to the Vietnam War. Since 1996, the AFL-CIO's Union Summer has placed almost 2,000 college students in internships with local unions around the country, most of whom work on grassroots organizing campaigns with low-wage workers in hotels, agriculture, food processing, janitorial service, and other industries. The program has its own staff, mostly young organizers only a few years out of college themselves, who actively recruit on campuses, looking for the next generation of union organizers and researchers, particularly minorities, immigrants, and women. Union Summer graduates are among the key leadership of the campus antisweatshop movement.

UNITE has one full-time staff person assigned to work on sweatshop issues, which includes helping student groups. A number of small human rights watchdog organizations that operate on shoestring budgets – Global Exchange, Sweatshop Watch, and the National Labor Committee – give student activists technical advice. (It was NLC's Charles Kernaghan, an energetic researcher and publicist, who exposed the Kathie Lee Gifford connection to sweatshops in testimony before Congress.) These groups have helped bring sweatshop workers on speaking tours of American campuses, and have organized delegations of student activists to investigate firsthand the conditions in Honduras, Guatemala, El Salvador, Mexico, and elsewhere under which workers produce their college's clothing.

Unions and several liberal foundations have provided modest funding for student antisweatshop groups. Until this summer USAS had no staff, nor did any of its local campus affiliates. In contrast, corporate-sponsored conservative foundations have, over the past two decades, funded dozens of conservative student publications, subsidized student organizations and conferences, and recruited conservative students for internships and jobs in right-wing think tanks and publications as well as positions in the Reagan and Bush administrations and Congress, seeking to groom the next generation of conservative activists. The Intercollegiate Studies Institute, the leading right-wing campus umbrella group, has an annual budget over $5 million. In comparison, the Center for Campus Organizing, a Boston-based group that works closely with antisweatshop groups and other progressive campus organizations, operates on a budget under $200,000.

This student movement even has some sympathizers among university administrators. "Thank God students are getting passionate about something other than basketball and bonfires," John Burness, a Duke administrator who helped negotiate the end of the 31-hour sit-in, told the *Boston Globe*. "But the tone is definitely different. In the old days, we used to have to scramble to cut off phone lines when they took over the president's office, but we didn't have to worry about that here. They just bring their laptops and they do work."

At every university where students organized a sit-in (Duke, Georgetown, Arizona, Michigan, and Wisconsin) they have wrested agreements to require licensees to disclose the specific location of their factory sites, which is necessary for independent monitoring. Students elsewhere (including Harvard, Illinois, Brown, the University of California, Princeton, Middlebury, and Occidental) won a public disclosure requirement without resorting to civil disobedience. A few institutions have agreed to require manufacturers to pay their employees a "living wage." Wisconsin agreed to organize an academic conference this fall to discuss how to calculate living-wage formulas for countries with widely disparate costs of living, and then to implement its own policy recommendations. [See Richard Rothstein, "The Global Hiring Hall: Why We Need Worldwide Labor Standards," *TAP*, Spring 1994.]

The industry's new clothes

Last November, the White House-initiated Apparel Industry Partnership created a monitoring arm, the Fair Labor Association (FLA), and a few months later invited universities to join. Colleges, however, have just one seat on FLA's 14-member board. Under the group's bylaws the garment firms control the board's decision-making. The bylaws require a "supermajority" to approve all key questions, thus any three companies can veto a proposal they don't like.

At this writing, FLA member companies agree to ban child and prison labor, to prohibit physical abuse by supervisors, and to allow workers the freedom to organize unions in their foreign factories, though independent enforcement has not yet been specified. FLA wants to assign this monitoring task to corporate accounting firms like Pricewaterhouse-Coopers and Ernst & Young, to allow companies to select which facilities will be inspected, and to keep factory locations and the monitoring reports secret. Student activists want human rights and labor groups to do the monitoring.

This is only a bare beginning, but it establishes the crucial moral precedent of companies taking responsibility for labor conditions beyond their shores. Seeing this foot in the door, several companies have bowed out because they consider these standards too tough. The FLA expects that by 2001, after its monitoring program has been in place for a year, participating firms will be able to use the FLA logo on their labels and advertising as evidence of their ethical corporate practices. [See Richard Rothstein, "The Starbucks Solution: Can Voluntary Codes Raise Global Living Standards?" *TAP*, July–August 1996.]

The original list of 17 FLA-affiliated universities grew to more than 100 by midsummer of this year. And yet, some campus groups have dissuaded college administrations (including the Universities of Michigan, Minnesota, Oregon, Toronto, and California, as well as Oberlin, Bucknell, and Earlham Colleges) from joining FLA, while others have persuaded their institutions (including Brown, Wisconsin, North Carolina, and Georgetown) to join only if the FLA adopts stronger standards. While FLA members are supposed to abide by each country's minimum-wage standards, these are typically far below the poverty level. In fact, no company has made a commitment to pay a living wage.

The campus movement has succeeded in raising awareness (both on campus and among the general public) about sweatshops as well as the global economy. It has contributed to industry acceptance of extraterritorial labor standards, something hitherto considered utopian. It has also given thousands of students experience in the nuts and bolts of social activism, many of whom are likely to carry their idealism and organizing experiences with them into jobs with unions, community and environmental groups, and other public interest crusades.

So far, however, the movement has had only minimal impact on the daily lives of sweatshop workers at home and abroad. Nike and Reebok, largely because of student protests, have raised wages and benefits in their Indonesian footwear factories – which employ more than 100,000 workers – to 43 percent above the minimum wage. But this translates to only 20 cents an hour in US dollars, far below a "living wage" to raise a family and even below the 27 cents Nike paid before Indonesia's currency devaluation. Last spring Nike announced its willingness to disclose the location of its overseas plants that produce clothing for universities. This created an important split in industry ranks, since industry leaders have argued that disclosure would undermine each firm's competitive position. But Nike has opened itself up to the charge of having a double standard, since it still refuses to disclose the location of its nonuniversity production sites.

Within a year, when FLA's monitoring system is fully operational, students at several large schools with major licensing contracts – including Duke, Wisconsin, Michigan, North Carolina, and Georgetown – will have lists of factories in the US and overseas that produce university clothing and equipment. This information will be very useful to civic and labor organizations at home and abroad, providing more opportunities to expose working conditions. Student activists at each university will be able to visit these sites – bringing media and public officials with them – to expose working conditions (and, if necessary, challenge the findings of the FLA's own monitors) and support organizing efforts by local unions and women's groups.

If the student activists can help force a small but visible "ethical" niche of the apparel industry to adopt higher standards, it will divide the industry and give unions and consumer groups more leverage to challenge the sweatshop practices of the rest of the industry. The campus antisweatshop crusade is part of what might be called a "conscience constituency" among consumers who are willing to incorporate ethical principles into their buying habits, even if it means slightly higher prices. Environmentalists have done the same thing with the "buy green" campaign, as have various "socially responsible" investment firms.

Beyond Consumer Awareness

In a global production system characterized by powerful retailers and invisible contractors, consumer action has an important role to play. But ultimately it must be combined with worker organizing and legislative and regulatory remedies. Unionizing the global apparel industry is an organizer's nightmare. With globalization and the contracting system, any apparel factory with a union risks losing its business.

Domestically, UNITE represents fewer than 300,000 textile and garment industry workers, down from the 800,000 represented by its two predecessor unions in the late 1960s. In the low-income countries where most US apparel is now made, the prospects for unionization are dimmer still. In Mexico, labor unions are controlled by the government. China outlaws independent unions, punishing organizers with prison terms. Building the capacity for unfettered union organizing must necessarily be a long-term strategy for union organizers throughout the world. Here, the student antisweatshop movement can help. The independent verification of antisweatshop standards that students want can also serve the goal of union organizing.

Public policy could also help. As part of our trade policy, Congress could require public disclosure of manufacturing sites and independent monitoring of firms that sell goods in the American market. It could enact legislation that requires US companies to follow US health and safety standards globally and to bar the import of clothing made in sweatshops or made by workers who are denied the basic right to organize unions. In addition, legislation sponsored by Representative William Clay could make retailers and manufacturers legally liable for the working conditions behind the goods they design and sell, thereby ending the fiction that contractors are completely independent of the manufacturers and retailers that hire them. Last spring the California Assembly passed a state version of this legislation. Student and union activists hope that the Democrat-controlled state senate and Democratic Governor Gray Davis – whose lopsided victory last November was largely attributed to organized labor's get-out-the-vote effort – will support the bill.

Thanks to the student movement, public opinion may be changing. And last spring, speaking both to the International Labor Organization in Geneva and at the commencement ceremonies at the University of Chicago (an institution founded by John D. Rockefeller and a stronghold of free-market economics, but also a center of student antisweatshop activism). President Clinton called for an international campaign against child labor, including restrictions on government purchases of goods made by children.

A shift of much apparel production to developing countries may well be inevitable in a global economy. But when companies do move their production abroad, student activists are warning "you can run but you can't hide," demanding that they be held responsible for conditions in contractor factories no matter where they are. Students can't accomplish this on their own, but in a very short period of time they have made many Americans aware that they don't have to leave their consciences at home when they shop for clothes.

CHAPTER 9

Sangeeta Kamat

The NGO-ization of Grassroots Politics

Politics in fact is at any given time the reflection of the tendencies of development in the structure, but it is not necessarily the case that these tendencies must be realised. A structural phase can be concretely studied and analysed only after it has gone through its whole process of development, and not during the process itself, except hypothetically and with the explicit proviso that one is dealing with hypotheses.

Gramsci, 1971: 408

Theorizing the basis of new struggles

The contemporary situation brings a certain urgency to the task of theorizing the role and historical character of non-party Left formations. At the time of writing this book, the BJP (Bharatiya Janata Party or Indian National Party), a Hindu fundamentalist party, governs the Indian state, with the support of various regional parties. Add to this the wave of economic liberalization that is sweeping the country and the globe, and the picture is indeed a bleak one for people's movements for social justice and democracy. Far from an unequivocal opposition to economic liberalization, Left parties have been, at best, ambivalent and at worst, supportive of the new economic policies. Given the dismal condition of political parties in India, it is the activity of non-party Left formations that gives many of us hope. But this hope is, at the same time, mixed with despair. The voices of despair point to the extreme fragmentation within these formations, and their inability to move from single issues and local struggles to form a unified movement.[1] No doubt, these are significant problems, but such criticisms have been largely unproductive in providing an analysis of why and how this situation has not only come to prevail, but also intensified over the past two decades.

As I explained in the preface, this intellectual project was motivated by certain practical questions about the nature of our involvement with the grassroots sector. The rapid growth of grassroots organizations in the country, the persuasive critiques against

Sangeeta Kamat, "The NGO-ization of Grassroots Politics," pp. 152–68 from *Development Hegemony: NGOs and the State in India*. New Delhi: Oxford University Press, 2001. Reproduced by permission of Oxford University Press India, New Delhi.

development ideology, and the ensuing conflict between popular movement building and 'project' work has made it difficult for many of us to know, with any certainty, the nature of our praxis and the possible effects of our work. This study is a beginning towards theorizing an area of political, practical, and ideological activity that has been discussed extensively, but has remained undertheorized, particularly in the context of the Third World. I hope to stimulate dialogue among activists as well as academics on the issues and analysis presented here because I, like many others, believe that grassroots organizations are one of the most significant forces in the continuing struggles for justice and democracy.

In the Introduction, I suggested that our ambiguity and conflict over the role of the grassroots sector is partly caused by the homogeneous unified representation of non-party political formations characterized as either 'non-governmental organizations', the 'voluntary sector' or 'new social movements' in much of academic and policy discourse. This homogenizing discourse merges the disparate and contradictory efforts of civil society into one singular wind of 'democracy' sweeping the country. While the growth of civil society as separate from, and often in opposition to, the sphere of the state is cause for much optimism, we need to be equally attentive to how capitalist institutions deploy various mechanisms to control and regulate radical popular initiatives. A necessary step to lay open the mechanisms of determination is to fragment this false homogeneity and to begin to analyse the complex and differentiated logics that make for the different kinds of organizations, their location within the dominant political economy, their articulation with particular discourses, and their creation of new ones.

A more complete conceptualization of the field of popular struggles can only come about through more extensive research on the different kinds of organizations and movements that are continually emergent across the world today. What I have offered is an analysis of one organization that represents a certain tendency within this field, from which we can tentatively propose its effects on other, real and potential, transformative forces in society.

The particular organizational structure presented in this book represents a significant trend among grassroots organizations in India that emerged out of a unique historical conjuncture of the politicization of development and the weakening of Left party organizations. The analysis of certain transformative moments leading to a dual organizational structure provide some important insights into the fundamental problem facing all non-party Left formations: that is, what are the necessary conditions for their development as a political force that can help construct the basis for counter-hegemonic struggles? The circumstances that compelled the activists to set up a dual structure – a development agency and a trade union – are extremely revealing of the structures that systematically impede the formation of counter-hegemonic forces.

In this chapter, I consolidate some of my key analytical insights about the divergent discourses of the Sansad and Sanghatna to further theorize their effects on the formation of subjectivities of struggle that are necessary for any radical political movement. I begin by briefly touching upon some of the major conclusions of the previous chapters, which I analyse in terms of the political culture that is established within such grassroots organizations. The construction of subjectivities and subject-positions, of social practices that reorganize relations within and between classes, determine the nature of the political culture cultivated. The kind of political culture that is fostered and developed by intellectual activists is central to creating the conditions within which transformative movements may be conceived and sustained. The impact of the political culture of grassroots organizations needs to be understood in terms of its articulation with other diverse political formations that exist today – namely, the rise of the Hindu right forces, the increasing power of neoliberal institutions (World Bank, IMF, WTO, etc.), the decrease in popular support for people's movements, and the growth of specialized NGOs. The simultaneity of these seemingly disparate phenomena is transforming the culture of politics as we know it, engendering a 'structural adjustment' of the political space that is not unlike the structural adjustment of the economy.[2] My concern here is to situate the emergence of a 'local' culture of politics that I have described in the preceding chapters within a dramatically altered national/global political landscape.

Collectivism versus corporatism

The state act of declaring political work as illegal within development organizations is a powerful instance of how the discourse of development is ordered at the local level. Political activity is defined by the legal statutes, as that which seeks to influence the legislature, and as such, cannot be determined as serving 'general public utility'. Here we can see the idea of the state working, in that it is presumed that the state apparati are organized to serve public interests. Conversely, activities that are defined as legitimate development activity are presumed to serve the general public interest. This definition of politics suppresses the other more lived nature of politics – as 'the discourse and the struggle over the organization of human possibilities' (see Held, 1984: 1). The ongoing discourse and struggle over the organization of social relations is made invisible and illegitimate within development practice, and instead, politics comes to abstractly reside in the state.

The evolution of the Sansad/Sanghatna's development activities illustrates precisely this discursive structuring. Class conflict, which is what the relation between the *adivasis* and the landlords represents, could not be taken up as class conflict within the development agency; it would have implied a struggle for redistribution of land, for fair working conditions and wages, as well as struggle over forests and forest products, water and all the elements that are the forces of production and reproduction. Instead, the organization stayed within the legal framework of development by posing the problem as one of class position, which can be transformed through certain inputs and did not involve the reorganization of social relations between people. The apolitical approach to class conflict leads logically to a discourse of 'needs' and 'absences' with no reference to the social relations that give rise to these 'needs' and 'absences', thus objectifying the social body, giving it a 'thing like' quality. The economy itself assumes a natural character that acts according to natural laws disconnected from the social relations of production and distribution. It is not surprising that again and again development programmes are focused on providing the poor with 'things' that make the economy – money in the form of development credit and grants, technological inputs in the form of hybrid cows and seeds, knowledge of the market – 'things', which in the words of Lukács (1971: 83) 'acquire a "phantom objectivity"', an autonomy that seems so strictly rational and all embracing as to conceal every trace of its fundamental nature: the relation between people'.

The reification of economic relations impacts even those development organizations that have no apparent link with the state development bureaucracy, but which exist under the law as charitable organizations, and hence, are subject to its statutes. Thus, it is not personal ideologies that are at stake here, but the discursive structuring of development which can compel even the most committed Left activists to focus on the individual as the problem and not the social relations of which s/he is a part. It also explains why modern technology, rather than the development of a critical consciousness, assumes pre-eminence in the development process. The discursive structuring creates an ideal space for the assertion of liberal values – that is, hard work, education, and the magical gifts of modern science in the form of hybrid cows and seeds are the only ways by which the poor can expect to alter their situation.

Nevertheless, politics can hardly be made to disappear through ideological structuration. Under the aegis of the law, the expression of class conflict within civil society is contained, only to find expression within the realm of the state. In other words, the space for legitimate political action is granted to the tribals only upon assuming their legitimate place within the political apparatus of society – that is, as subject-citizens of the state via the trade union. For many, this may seem a legitimate or necessary mechanism by which contradictory interests are resolved. However, at this point, the discursive structuring of the political apparatus comes to determine the relations between people, with the state as the legitimate arbiter of the rights of people. The social relations that give rise to the economic inequality between tribals and landlords are negotiated and settled within a discourse of equal rights and equal protection under the law, giving rise to its own contradictions. To begin with, it brings them 'freedom' from debt bondage but simultaneously it also binds them to the 'unfreedom' of wage labour. This contradiction is brought on by the separation of the economy from politics, in that the massive division between those who own and control the means of production, and those who must live by wage labour is regarded as the outcome of free private contracts, and not a matter for the state. The state's promise of equal protection under the law in the midst of actual inequality translates into a promise to protect these inequalities. The process of becoming clients of the development apparatus is thus premised on certain necessary illusions where the economy is reified and the state becomes the aegis under which political issues are resolved.

When we move from the single problem of bonded labour to the more extensive work of changing the social and economic situation of the *adivasis*, the effects of this law are even more far reaching. The 'unfreedom' of free labour compels the activists to take on certain income-generation schemes, such as dairy and poultry projects (not to forget that this infusion of 'inputs' is itself effected by the depoliticized nature of the economy) with the heavy involvement of technical experts to supervise and manage these projects. I show two main effects that proceed from this. One is the technical determinism that pervades the interactions and concerns of the members. Meetings between the Sansad workers and the 'beneficiaries' are devoted almost exclusively to imparting technical knowledge and skills such as amount of feed, the precise time of insemination to produce calves, the importance of vaccines and other injectibles to enable the cow to produce higher quantities of milk, and so on and so forth. Further, the technical experts establish a paternalistic relationship with the 'beneficiaries' wherein they see their role as educating the 'beneficiaries' in the bourgeois norms of hard work, discipline, hygiene, and surplus accumulation.

The second is the individualization of the subject–object of development wherein subsidies and loans are given to individual members, dividing the working class into some who benefit and many who do not. Those who have the means and the will to effectively operate within bourgeois capitalist practices consolidate their status as *sudharit adivasis*, who become the cultural models for the *adivasi* community. The success of the schemes requires the values of instrumentality and economic rationality, which competes with collective struggle. As members of a co-operative, those who are part of the economic projects have to learn to give primacy to their role as producers and sellers. Carried to the extreme in this direction, the only strategy legitimately available to the *adivasis* is to become capable competitors in the market by forming small producers' associations leading to a more corporatist identity among them.

The individualization of needs and benefits has a logical connection to the fetishism of the state engendered by the development discourse. Insofar as the *adivasis* secure their needs for income and land as individuals, that having established itself as the legitimate mode of social change, they have no 'real' need to resolve the contradictions between their individual interests and their collective identity, to ask questions about what forms the basis of their collective solidarity or what their mutual obligations are to the community. The resolution of these contradictions requires intensive and ongoing collective dialogue and reflection on the part of the organization's members. These questions imply a renegotiation of each individual member's interests in ways that bring them in confluence with the collective identity of the members.

This is not to say that collective identity is an already formed 'thing'; rather collective identity is always emergent, and it is through dialogue and the deliberate social practices of the members that it stabilizes. Quite likely, interests as they are now expressed – namely, to become beneficiaries of development schemes – would be substantially altered in this process. In the event that no such negotiation of individual versus collective interests is taking place, the state becomes the only reliable apparatus that can provide for the individual interests of members, according it a privileged role in their lives. As I have explained in previous sections, the methods of state patronage remain mystified, their effects paradoxical, and the state assumes an enigmatic persona.

The power of the trade union which is directly related to the strength of the collective identity of its members is seriously undermined by the corporatist identity engendered by development programmes. The formation of a collective identity depends upon consensus about collective interests and the creation of social practices that represent these collective interests. The process of building consensus, which is necessarily an involved one, is pre-empted when a significant number of individuals can meet their interests by becoming clients of the development apparatus. Identity is formed on the basis of an individual tribal's relation to the forces of production. Thus, one who has land, access to water and grass, and the help of household labour can afford to become a member of the dairy cooperative, whereas the one who depends on wage labour can only struggle for better wages. Further, this struggle is carried out with minimal support from those whose interests are being met through the development schemes. The difficulty the union activists experience in involving the organization's members in collective struggle is a consequence of this disunity. Collective struggle becomes a receding space of action, with only sporadic campaigns against individual transgressors of the law.

The identity of the organization's members is circumscribed, not only by their relation to the reified economy but also by their narrowly defined relation to the state. With the state as the proper arena for resolving political conflict, the political education of the trade union is directed towards knowledge of the state – its functions, laws, and policies. The main thrust of these educational programmes is to convince the *adivasis* that the state's role is to guarantee equal protection under the law and equal rights to all its citizens, and that these guarantees needed to be understood and used effectively to secure their rights. On the one hand, the activists see state agents as internalizing the contradictions of society, and on the other, they regard the abstract expressions of the state as being more objective and universal in their intent. The locus of action is individual functionaries whose behaviour needs to be brought in line with the 'ethical' state. This itself can be a highly empowering experience, but an empowerment which is conjunctural and immediate, rather than organic and systematic.[3]

The entrapment of politics in form

This analysis makes possible certain insights. First, that development discourse anchors human action for change in the permanence of existing structures and social relations. It interprets and mediates the will towards transformative praxis in ways that articulate with the prevailing hegemony of ideas and practices. Second, this articulation takes place by producing consent over the *forms* of political action which structures the content of political action (Offe and Wiesenthal, 1980).[4] The former, I hold to be immanent in the latter, and I explicate these insights below.

The separation of the economic realm from the political presents to the organization certain forms within which it can legitimately pose solutions to the economic problems of the tribals. These forms, to which is given the name 'development', prevent the conceptualization of alternative forms by which people can struggle for social justice. In other words, development is the political form granted to civil society to resolve its economic and social conflicts. But development discourse posits these, not as conflicts but as 'needs' which are universally binding on all, and hence, 'neutral.' The construction of material conflicts as 'universal human needs' is produced through the form of development. Needs, of course, are real, but the nature and meaning of needs are specific to the organization of social relations in a particular place and time. The 'needs discourse' though, cannot be reproduced without economic relations being simultaneously constructed as fixed and universal, and herein lies the significance of the law. Within this fixed economy, development is one among many other forms (for example, private investment) through which things of 'value' can be exchanged, and as such it validates this particular construction of the capitalist economy. The exponential growth of development agencies indicates that this form has become extremely normalized within the social imaginary.

Equally, social and economic struggles are represented through state forms which structure the means and ends of these struggles. On the one hand, the 'state-as-every-day-practice' is a point of contestation, but one in which the 'ethical state' is the point of reference. The struggle is subsumed within a state form of individual rights and equal protection under the law, providing little space for manoeuvring a reinterpretation of these rights. A reinterpretation implies that someone else's rights to secure their welfare will be violated. Arjun's cautious response to Kishna reflects that this understanding has been internalized to some extent. In a particularly low moment, Kishna confided that he was increasingly convinced of the need for violence, that all this lawful protest was not going to take them anywhere. To which Arjun replied, 'we cannot simply take away the rich man's wealth, he has his rights too'. To work with this understanding is the mark of the liberal citizen–subject who accepts the state forms – including the sanctity of private property – as valid and universally binding.

When analysed in terms of systematic relations of power, an acceptance of the forms for resolving fundamental conflicts leads to a status quo of power relations. The forms within which economic citizenship and political citizenship are expressed are universally binding on all, which gives them an air of neutrality, and therefore, fairness. The political action that results from this has much to do with securing the rights and needs guaranteed through these forms, and as such, functions at the level of 'normal' politics – a politics that is legitimately permitted within a liberal democratic framework. Certain fundamental issues are marginalized in this process. Politics is completely reduced to an issue of distribution with no negotiation over what it is that is being distributed. The 'what' is presupposed to be a question that is already answered through the existing political forms and the preferences that are revealed through them. The more fundamental issue of how an organization decides what it is they want to get does not become part of the struggle. The consequences of this for a radical praxis are profound.

The production of consent over given political forms for the resolution of conflict is central to preserving unequal relations. This consent is produced not only through the work of the state (its schools, the repressive apparatus, development apparatus, etc.) but also through the work of the numerous voluntary initiatives within civil society, which engage in political work, regardless of whether it is development or collective action. The ideological positioning of the leadership class within grassroots organizations, therefore, is not an insignificant matter to the state. Organizations that resist incorporation into the development apparatus are of special concern to the state. Premised as they are, on direct political action on social and economic issues, such organizations can, in all possibility, challenge the prevailing state structures which channel working class political activity. It becomes imperative for the state and capitalist interests to control and limit those groups which tend to challenge state forms of conflict resolution, and simultaneously encourage and support the expansion of those organizations that cohere with state structures. In terms of enforcing control, two main strategies are deployed by the state: first, outright repression of organizations that do not subscribe to the political forms of the liberal capitalist state, and second, persuasion and coercion of organizations to adopt develop-ment programmes. The history of the Sansad/Sanghatna is indicative of the latter strategy.

The Sansad/Sanghatna is largely ineffective in sustaining collective identities inasmuch as it works within available state forms and does not generate radically alternative social practices. Also, by not giving much consideration to the place of *adivasi* culture in building solidarity, the Sansad/Sanghatna is not able to facilitate a culturally grounded class identity. The state forms engender a modern individualistic identity which becomes difficult to transcend, since it is normalized by the dominant discourses. 'When an *adivasi* gets 20–5 acres of land, and all he can think of is how to get more out of them (labourers) for less, then how are we different from the *Patils*?' asks Deepak with a wry laugh. The crisis of identity that Deepak implies is a result of the modern individualized identity that state forms and economic relations (within capitalism) engender. Tribal activists associated with Sansad/Sanghatna were concerned, and rightly so, that members seemed to pursue their own private gain. These observations on the part of the tribal activists raised a vital issue for them. When collective solidarity is based on a history of oppositional identities of an exploiter and exploited class, the erosion of these identities disrupts the formation of collective struggle. Further, these identities cannot simply call upon past history, but need to find expression through ongoing material practices. The practices of modern subject production directly counter this fundamental principle of movement building.

NGOs as state formations

The above analysis makes it possible to arrive at a definition of NGOs that is based, not so much on formal criteria (such as non-governmental or foreign-funded), but on the kind of political praxis that organizations facilitate in contrast to the political praxis of certain other organizations. By political praxis I mean an organization's relation to the state, the mobilization of certain kinds of identities, the nature of its development activity, and its relation to the development apparatus. Accordingly, we may give the label NGO to those organizations that engender a corporatist identity among their members, that work within the existing political forms of the state, and do not facilitate a reinterpretation of the material basis for a collective identity. This definition enables us to differentiate between the varied number of grassroots organizations in India (and perhaps elsewhere) that organize poor communities to resist and recreate social, political, and economic relations.

The compromised nature of non-party Left activity is a function, not only of the repressive apparatus of the state and capital, but also of the growth of NGOs. Increasingly, as NGOs (as defined above) have come to dominate non-party Left activity, international capital and the state have not only supported their growth, but have also sought a collaborative relationship with them. At stake here is a complex of political interests that are quite explicit. The interest of international capital in aiding development in the Third World has always been clearly stated: '[T]o start the more than a billion people now living in the less developed areas up the road toward rising production and consumption while maintaining the growth of the industrialized areas' (See Gendzier, 1985, citing *Rockefeller Report*, 1958). To achieve this, capital needs to be constantly expanding, finding new producers and producing new consumers – what Marx (1983) abstractly called 'value in motion'. The perpetual insecurity and upheaval caused by the dynamic nature of capital creates the need for a system to co-ordinate the power of capital for its successful fruition – a stable power to co-ordinate a fluid power (see Harvey, 1996).

The development apparatus serves this function by seeking out, locating and harnessing marginal communities to realize the productive power of capital. Indirect colonization comes to replace direct colonization. In the contemporary period, these interests are unabashedly expressed, even in popular media. At a recent conference on International Development, World Bank President Wolfensohn and US Treasury Secretary Rubin reaffirmed their interests in financing development programmes in India: 'Development institutions offer the United States a cost-effective vehicle for addressing global issues such as environmental degradation, poverty, and political instability – as well as building open markets and democracy... Economic development abroad increase markets for US products and ideas' (cited in Haniffa, 1997).

The Sansad's dairy project and the Sanghatna's educational programmes on law discussed earlier are certainly doing both – building a market for multinational products such as hybrid cows, vaccines, fertilizers, cattle feed, as well as a respect for the law of the land. The stability of the liberal democratic capitalist order is possible only through this process of 'disciplining' individuals in the fetishization of modern technology and bourgeois values.

It is only proper that the state, as a sovereign disinterested organization of rules and activities, performs the function of disciplining and regulating the social body – and here we have to do away with a conceptualization of the state as a separate political body, and instead put in its place a conception of the state as 'that ensemble of organisms commonly called "private"' (see Gramsci, 1971: 12). For how else is each individual to be incorporated into the national-popular will, and how is pressure to be applied to single individuals 'so as to obtain their consent and collaboration, turning necessity and coercion into freedom'? (ibid.: 242).[5] These 'private organisms' serve to normalize state forms as the legitimate forms for resolving class conflict, facilitate corporatist identities and an ahistorical modern subjectivity, and in so doing, perform the work of the state. Today, NGOs comprise a critical part of such 'private organisms' which are placed in a particularly efficacious position to mediate and direct the subjectivities of individuals towards the necessities of the capitalist economy.

This view directly contradicts the public discourse on grassroots organizations as representing the progressive, if not radical face of society (see Omvedt, 1993, Bhatnagar and Williams, 1992). What about grassroots organizations themselves, and their identity as political actors, consciously and actively negotiating and challenging the state, and expanding the practice of democracy to include the marginalized groups in civil society? What about their agency, or consciousness of their role in society? Do we conclude from this that NGOs suffer from 'false consciousness'? I argue that the political discourse in India about grassroots organizations does not afford us such an easy dismissal. On the contrary, there is much serious reflection and debate on the nature and role of grassroots organizations within the current political economy. There are a few instances of organizations disbanding their state-related development activity in an effort to rearticulate their politics in new ways. Numerous activists who have worked several years in an NGO have left these organizations, although they made a comfortable living from it. Some activists have restricted themselves to working in advocacy or research-based NGOs, rather than grassroots NGOs, highlighting some of the same concerns raised here. Some have even registered as private organizations to escape the restrictions over political activity. So also, for the leadership of national movements that integrate the issues of diverse marginalized groups, a main point of contention has been whether to include or exclude NGOs from such an alliance. (Of course, a problem that continually surfaces in these discussions has been the lack of appropriate criteria to decide which organizations qualify as NGOs and which do not.) The debates have been resolved, superficially I believe, by defining NGOs as those organizations that accept foreign aid and are therefore seen as not accountable to their constituency.

On the basis of my analysis of the Sansad/Sanghatna, I suggest that there are other fundamental aspects of an organization that are crucial in determining their character and function within the broad range of new social movements. Two elements that define an organization's politics are its consent to the social construction of development as apolitical, and its consent to state structures, evident not so much in their public rhetoric, but in their organizational policies and practices. Analysing grassroots organizations in this manner, I suggest, will enable activists within these movements to grasp more fully and accurately the political sensibilities and visions that differentiate NGOs from non-party Left formations and build alliances on the basis of the philosophy and practice of organizations rather than on formal features (that is, funding, infrastructure, etc.) which may have little to do with constituting their practice or ideology.

As I have argued in Chapter 5 [of her *Development Hegemony*], an organization's conception of, and relation to, the state can be partly explained through the specific social class of the activists, whose ideological and historical location in Indian society *vis-à-vis* other social classes creates the conditions for the reproduction of hegemonic ideologies. I shall summarize and extend this argument to better represent the political agency of these actors. Both the structural location and the nationalist sentiments of the petit-bourgeois class of activists produce their consent to state structures. Their nationalist ideology and their location in-between the two opposing classes requires that their political vision be articulated through the most neutral and universal forms. The state, to whatever degree, best represents that form. Thus, it is believed that *adivasi* culture cannot serve as a basis for collective unity, because not only does it tend towards a particularistic identity, but it can also encourage anti-nationalism.

The criticisms by NGOs of the state as being imperfect and biased towards certain class interests can be understood within this light. They do not misunderstand the nature of the state as such, but within the conceivable forms through which to regulate class conflict, state forms are preferred, because these equally seek to maintain national unity by positing the modern, secular national subject as the vehicle for progress and prosperity. Their consent, therefore, is not so much to state structures as it is to the idea of the state. Their practice may be marked by both a collaboration and a contestation of state structures with the objective of preserving the idea of the state. Leading from this, my theoretical proposition is that NGOs may differ in the extent to which they contest state structures, but they will tend to affirm the national secular ethos that is contained in the idea of the state. The state as an idea refers to the implicit existence of a dispassionate disinterested Being that transcends individual and group interests to represent the will of all, the common good, the universal interests of the nation. Phil Abrams (1988: 73) makes this insightful observation on the power of this idea:

> There *is* a state-system: a palpable nexus of practice and institutional structure centred in government and more or less extensive, unified, and dominant in any given society. There *is*, too, a state-idea, projected, purveyed, and variously believed in different societies at different times. We are only making difficulties for ourselves in supposing that we have also to study the state – an entity, agent, function, or relation over and above the state-system and state-idea. The state comes into being as a structuration within political practice; it starts its life as an implicit construct; it is then reified – as the *res publica*, the public reification, no less – and acquires an overt symbolic identity progressively divorced from practice as an illusory account of practice. The ideological function is extended to a point where conservatives and radicals alike believe that their practice is not directed at each other but at the state; the world of illusion prevails.

NGOs in the era of globalization

The relation of NGOs to the state raises some crucial questions with regard to their role in the expanding global capitalist economy. At the dawn of the twenty-first century, scholars and activists are seriously reconsidering the political function of NGOs in the context of a state that is 'withering away'. Trade liberalization and the debt crisis is greatly limiting the autonomy of Third World states to formulate economic and social policy. Certainly, domestic and international interests appear to have a greater role in regulating the Indian state than was the case in previous decades. Consequently, NGOs are acquiring a more explicit quasi-state nature, in that their assistance in implementing social and economic policy is being sought by international bodies such as the World Bank and the United Nations, but with the consent of the state (see also Demirovic, 1996; MacDonald, 1994). They do not constitute, in this sense, an authority above the state, but operate within the sovereignty of the state.

This emergent context signifies certain important changes in their role. It may mean that their 'relative autonomy' – that is, their capacity to sustain themselves and determine their own projects and strategy – is greatly circumscribed by their increased dependence on the interests of international capital and the state. Conversely, it appears that grassroots NGOs may become more autonomous from those classes whose interests they claim to represent. A recent article by a prominent NGO activist in India reflects an awareness of the changed stature, and their need to prepare for it. To quote: 'NGOs need to decide whether they seriously want to be in this field, and if so, necessarily specialize in the LEIG (Livelihood, Employment and Income Generation) field' (Mahajan, 1994: 176).[6] The author adds that in LEIG activities, it is necessary that NGOs surrender their dependence on government and foreign grants, and instead, raise capital from mainstream sources such as development financial institutions and banks. He argues that to be effective, community-based NGOs must adopt the models and attitudes of business enterprises and learn to manage employment generation schemes on a 'for profit' basis. He admits that relief and welfare services are still required, but when it comes to the 'economy' there can be no 'free riders'. The re-orientation calls for changes at an organizational level, as well as at an ideological level. At the organizational level, Mahajan advocates employing people with business skills, paying them market salaries, accepting 'beneficiaries' who are credit worthy, and specializing in ventures that are viable. In short, they propose that all decisions, from organizing cooperatives to selecting appropriate technology, must be made on the basis of economic viability. At the ideological level, it is stated that NGOs must stop viewing the economic system as unequal and unfair to the poor, and must instead focus on the 'unused opportunities' that exist (ibid.: 177).

In the context of economic liberalization, this aggressive new proposition on the part of some NGOs is extremely disturbing, but nevertheless, quite predictable. Not only are state subsidies being cut, but also soft loans and grants for development programmes are being minimized by the fiat of the IMF and World Bank via the Structural Adjustment Programme. Investment in social sectors (such as education and health) are being subject to the same financial laws as is the economic sector (see Bhaduri and Nayyar 1996). While previously social sectors, such as primary education, were financed through interest-free loans and grants, today they form part of the infamous Third World debt.

It is, therefore, crucial for the state that NGOs manage these programmes on a profitable basis. It appears that NGOs that wish to survive this fiscal crisis may need to approach banks and lending institutions for loans which, in turn, will force them to tailor their projects to economies of scale. In the not too distant future, we may see many smaller NGOs folding up, and even declaring bankruptcy, replaced by what are being termed 'network NGOs' – large corporate-like structures with a highly professional staff and low paid 'grassroots workers' which coordinate select economic enterprises over several different regions. As Gramsci reminds us, it is possible for the state to function as 'night watchman' that is, a state whose functions are limited to the safeguarding of public order and respect for the laws, but only when 'hegemony over its historical development belongs to private forces, to civil society – which is "state" too, indeed is the state itself' (Gramsci, 1971: 261).

Recently, some scholars have forwarded a similar view of NGOs and the state (see Alvarez, 1998; Petras, 1997; Wood, 1997). For instance, according to Wood, the term 'franchise state' best characterizes the new relation of NGOs and the state in the neoliberal context wherein NGOs subcontract the management and administration of essential social services from the state. Alvarez traces the transformation of radical feminist movements in Latin America to the 'NGOization of feminism' wherein women's issues are professionally managed, much like state institutions are likely to do (1998: 306).

However, within the analysis I have proposed, this break can actually be understood as reflecting continuities. The philosophy of change which has been latent in the existing discourse of empowerment and more explicit in the emergent one of corporatization is that of 'vulgar Marxism', wherein the full realization of the productive forces of society is idealized as the appropriate mode of transformation. In this view, both state and civil society need to work together to direct and manage the productive forces of society (including people), so that the whole nation may 'progress'. As a consequence, state and civil society are equally in need of structural and moral disciplining for the productive forces of the nation to be actualized. The realization of productive forces requires that all classes produce to the best of their capacity, and that the poor need special assistance in order to do so. The downsizing of the welfare state may, therefore, be acceptable to many NGOs as long as state institutions and the international community remain committed to the development of productive forces.

In the final analysis, my study of the Sansad/Sanghatna explains why 'popular democratic' forms cannot automatically be seen to represent an expansion of democracy. Rather, in the contemporary political economy, these 'popular democratic' organizations need to be analysed within the context of the process of state formation in which the hegemonic ideologies of nationalism, modernization, and capitalism articulate with each other to stabilize the unequal and exploitative relations of modern political economies. Contrary to many scholars of new social movements who suggest that autonomous organizations of civil society reflect a devolution of power from the state to the public, I have explicated how the structure and praxis of particular grassroots organizations may contribute to reproducing the state, particularly in the era of capitalist globalization. My analysis identifies one specific tendency – which I have called the 'NGO-ization' of grassroots struggles – within the sphere of the 'new politics' of state and civil society.

However, this attempt to structure political culture at the grassroots to better fit with neoliberal imperatives is by no means a finished historical project. Within the context of this study, clearly the tribal activists are far from being under the hegemonic powers of development. Nor is it clear to what extent the intellectual–activists exercise a moral intellectual leadership over the tribals, over and above the political leadership that they maintain. It is the former element, according to Gramsci, that is essential to establishing hegemony over any social group. On a broader scale, the number of oppositional movements in the South and the North against the new global compact, and the numerous grassroots struggles that attempt to construct a new cultural politics that creatively engages with the institutions and ideologies of modernity belie the hegemony of development (Alvarez et al., 1998; Fraser, 1993; Mignolo, 2000). The plurality of struggles that assert the indivisibility of social life, and thereby, construct a new discourse of substantive democracy, and justice may no doubt produce new tendencies. The ways in which these forces align themselves and articulate with each other, leading to unexpected collaborations and conflicts is yet to be determined. The extent to which the neoliberal political tendency of grassroots NGOs will be reinforced and elaborated, or weakened and attenuated will no doubt play a decisive role in this determination. Only contextualized analysis of the praxis of these multifarious struggles and their (dis)articulation with dominant national and international discourses will enable scholars and activists to determine the liberatory potential of different political movements.

Notes

1 Efforts by some leading activists such as Medha Patkar of the Save the Narmada Movement to form a national movement (National Alliance of Peoples Movements) have borne some important results.

2   Structural adjustment refers to the set of conditionalities imposed by the IMF and the World Bank on approximately 70 countries of Asia, Africa, Latin America, the Caribbean, and Eastern Europe. In brief, the conditionalities enforce privatization of public sector industries and 'free market' capitalism. Here I suggest that these structural alterations of the economic sector have their corollary in the political sphere, where entrepreneurial citizenship and individual self-improvement are emphasized as primary modes of political expression. Elaborating on this thesis is beyond the scope of this book, though I hope the contours of this argument will be discernable to the reader. See Dagnino, 1998 and Schilds, 1998 for a more detailed exploration of this point in the context of Latin America.

3   Here I use Gramsci's notions of 'conjunctural' versus 'organic' (1971: 177). A struggle is conjunctural when the movement is not defined simultaneously in moral, cultural, political, intellectual, and economic terms; that is, it does not properly connect the relationship between base and superstructure. The effect of conjunctural movements is to preserve the economic structure by overcoming its contradictions in an immediate way. Organic movements have far-reaching historical significance in which enduring and structural contradictions are revealed (see Sassoon, 1987).

4   Offe and Wiesenthal (1980) have theorized this difference between political activity within state forms and political activity about state forms with respect to trade unions in the German Democratic Republic. Much of the debate on this issue has taken place in German language publications to which, unfortunately, I have no access.

5   With the freeing of bonded labour and the institution of development schemes, we saw how 'freedom' translated into necessity. This necessity, or in Marx's phrase, 'the dull compulsion of hunger' once again comes to be masked as 'freedom' by development's discourse on 'empowerment'.

6   LEIG is a fairly recent term used by NGOs as well as bureaucrats to refer to development programmes (including training) that are directed at creating stable income opportunities for poor communities. The incorporation of the term 'livelihood' is a result of NGO pressure on government to create development projects that would enable poor communities to create sustainable livelihoods in farm-based or craft industries such as bee-keeping or weaving, rather than rely on short-term cash schemes. The problem of 'finding' a profitable market continues to be the main problem faced.

References

Abrams, Phil (1988). 'Notes on the Difficulty of Studying the State', *Journal of Historical Sociology* 1(1), pp. 58–89.

Alvarez, Sonia (1998). 'Latin American Feminisms "Go Global": Trends of the 1990s and Challenges for the New Millennium', in Sonia Alvarez, E. Dagnino and A. Escobar (eds.), *Cultures of Politics, Politics of Cultures: Revisioning Latin American Social Movements*. Boulder, CO: Westview Press.

Alvarez, Sonia, Evelina Dagnino, and Arturo Escobar (eds.) (1998). *Cultures of Politics, Politics of Cultures: Revisioning Latin American Social Movements*. Boulder, CO: Westview Press.

Bhaduri, Amit and Deepak Nayyar (1996). *The Intelligent Person's Guide to Liberalization*. New Delhi: Penguin.

Bhatnagar, B. and A. Williams (1992). 'Participatory Development and the World Bank', World Bank Discussion Papers. Washington, DC: World Bank.

Dagnino, Evelina (1998). 'Culture, Citizenship and Democracy: Changing Discourses and Practices of the Latin American Left', in Sonia Alvarez, E. Dagnino and A. Escobar (eds.), *Cultures of Politics, Politics of Cultures: Revisioning Latin American Social Movements*. Boulder, CO: Westview Press.

Demirovic, Alex (1996). 'NGOs: Social Movement in Global Order?', Paper Presented at Annual American Sociological Association Meeting, New York.

Fraser, Nancy (1993). 'Rethinking the Public Sphere: A Contribution to the Critique of Actually Existing Democracy', in B. Robbins (ed.), *The Phantom Public Sphere*. Minneapolis, MN: University of Minnesota Press.

Gendzier, Irene (1985). *Managing Political Change: Social Scientists and the Third World*. Boulder, CO: Westview Press.

Gramsci, Antonio (1971). *Selections from the Prison Notebooks*, eds. Q. Hoare and G. Smith. New York: International Publishers.

Haniffa, Aziz (1997). 'Rubin and Wolfensohn Call for Development Aid', *India Aboard*, 24 Jan., p. 6.

Harvey, David (1996). *Justice, Nature and the Politics of Difference*. Malden, MA: Blackwell.

Held, David (1984). *Political Theory and the Modern State: Essays on State, Power and Democracy*. Cambridge: Polity Press.

Lukács, Georg (1971). *History and Class Consciousness: Studies in Marxist Dialectics*, tr. Rodney Livingstone. London: Merlin Press.

MacDonald, Laura (1994). 'Globalizing Civil Society: Interrupting International NGOs in Central America', *Millennium: Journal of International Studies* 23(2), pp. 267–85.

Mahajan, Vijay (1994). 'What NGOs Have to Learn', *Indian Journal of Social Work*, LV(2), pp. 174–82.

Marx, Karl (1983). *Capital: Volume 1*. New York: International Publishers.

Mignolo, Walter (2000). *Local Histories/Global Designs: Coloniality, Subaltern Knowledge and Border Thinking*. Princeton: Princeton University Press.

Offe, Claus and Helmut Wiesenthal (1980). 'Two Logics of Collective Action: Theoretical Notes on Social Class and Organizational Form', *Political Power and Social Theory* 1, pp. 67–115.

Omvedt, Gail (1993). *Reinventing Revolution: New Social Movements and the Socialist Tradition in India*. Armonk, NY: M. E. Sharpe.

Petras, James (1997). 'Imperialism and NGOs in Latin America', *Monthly Review* 49(3), pp. 10–27.

Sassoon, Anne (1987). *Gramsci's Politics*. Minneapolis, MN: University of Minnesota Press.

Schilds, Veronica (1998). 'New Subject Rights? Women's Movements and the Construction of Citizenship in the "New Democracies"', in S. Alvarez, E. Dagnino and A. Escobar (eds.), *Cultures of Politics, Politics of Cultures: Re-visioning Latin American Social Movements*. Boulder, CO: Westview.

Wood, Geof (1997). 'States without Citizens: The Problem of the Franchise State', in David Hulme and Michael Edwards (eds.), *NGOs, States and Donors: Too close for Comfort?* New York: St. Martin's Press.

Part II

Representational Politics:
Making Up Your Own Mind
by Minding the Popular
Media

CHAPTER 10

Robert W. McChesney

Global Media, Neoliberalism, and Imperialism

In conventional parlance, the current era in history is generally characterized as one of globalization, technological revolution, and democratization. In all three of these areas media and communication play a central, perhaps even a defining, role. Economic and cultural globalization arguably would be impossible without a global commercial media system to promote global markets and to encourage consumer values. The very essence of the technological revolution is the radical development in digital communication and computing. The argument that the bad old days of police states and authoritarian regimes are unlikely to return is premised on the claims that new communication technologies along with global markets undermine, even eliminate, the capacity for "maximum leaders" to rule with impunity.

For capitalism's cheerleaders, like Thomas Friedman of the *New York Times*, all this suggests that the human race is entering a new Golden Age. All people need to do is sit back, shut up and shop, and let markets and technologies work their magical wonders. For socialists and those committed to radical social change these claims should be regarded with the utmost skepticism. In my view, the notion of globalization as it is commonly used to describe some natural and inexorable force, the telos of capitalism as it were, is misleading and ideologically loaded. A superior term would be neoliberalism; this refers to the set of national and international policies that call for business domination of all social affairs with minimal countervailing force. Governments are to remain large so as to better serve the corporate interests, while minimizing any activities that might undermine the rule of business and the wealthy. Neoliberalism is almost always intertwined with a deep belief in the ability of markets to use new technologies to solve social problems far better than any alternative course. The centerpiece of neoliberal policies is invariably a call for commercial media and communication markets to be deregulated. What this means in practice is that they are "re-regulated" to serve corporate interests.

Understood as one of neoliberalism rather than simply globalization, the current era seems less the result of uncontrollable natural forces and more as the newest stage of class struggle under capitalism. The antidemocratic implications, rather than being swept under the rug as they are in conventional parlance, move to the front and center. Here, I should like to sketch out the main developments and contours of the emerging global media system and their political-economic implications. I believe that when one takes a close look at the political economy of the contemporary global media and communication industries, we can cut through much of the mythology and hype surrounding our era, and have the basis for a much more accurate understanding of what is taking place, and what socialists must do to organize effectively for social justice and democratic values.

The global media system

Prior to the eighties and nineties, national media systems were typified by domestically owned radio, television and newspaper industries. There were major import markets for films, TV shows, music and books, and these markets tended to be dominated by US-based firms. But local commercial interests, sometimes combined with a state-affiliated broadcasting service, predominated within the media system. All of this is changing, and changing rapidly. Whereas previously media systems were primarily national, in the past few years a global commercial-media market has emerged. To grasp media today and in the future, one must start with understanding the global system and then factor in differences at the national and local levels. "What you are seeing," says Christopher Dixon, media analyst for the investment firm PaineWebber, "is the creation of a global oligopoly. It happened to the oil and automotive industries earlier this century; now it is happening to the entertainment industry."

This global oligopoly has two distinct but related facets. First, it means the dominant firms – nearly all US-based – are moving across the planet at breakneck speed. The point is to capitalize on the potential for growth abroad – and not get outflanked by competitors – since the US market is well developed and only permits incremental expansion. As Viacom CEO Sumner Redstone has put it, "Companies are focusing on those markets promising the best return, which means overseas." Frank Biondi, former chairman of Vivendi's Universal Studios, asserts that "99 percent of the success of these companies long-term is going to be successful execution offshore."

The dominant media firms increasingly view themselves as global entities. Bertelsmann CEO Thomas Middelhoff bristled when, in 1998, some said it was improper for a German firm to control 15 percent of both the US book-publishing and music markets. "We're not foreign. We're international," Middelhoff said. "I'm an American with a German passport." In 2000 Middelhoff proclaimed that Bertelsmann was no longer a German company. "We are really the most global media company." Likewise, AOL-Time Warner's Gerald Levin stated, "We do not want to be viewed as an American company. We think globally."

Second, convergence and consolidation are the order of the day. Specific media industries are becoming more and more concentrated, and the dominant players in each media industry increasingly are subsidiaries of huge global media conglomerates. For one small example, the US market for educational publishing is now controlled by four firms, whereas it had two dozen viable players as recently as 1980. The level of mergers and acquisitions is breathtaking. In the first half of 2000, the volume of merger deals in global media, Internet, and telecommunications totaled $300 billion, triple the figure for the first 6 months of 1999, and exponentially higher than the figure from 10 years earlier. The logic guiding media firms in all of this is clear: get very big very quickly, or get swallowed up by someone else. This is similar to trends taking place in many other industries. "There will be less than a handful of end-game winners," the CEO of Chase Manhattan announced in September 2000. "We want to be an end-game winner."

But in few industries has the level of concentration been as stunning as in media. In short order, the global media market has come to be dominated by seven multinational corporations: Disney, AOL-Time Warner, Sony, News Corporation, Viacom, Vivendi, and Bertelsmann. None of these companies existed in their present form as media companies as recently as 15 years ago; today nearly all of them will rank among the largest 300 non-financial firms in the world for 2001. Of the 7, only 3 are truly US firms, though all of them have core operations there. Between them, these 7 companies own the major US film studios; all but one of the US television networks; the few companies that control 80–5 percent of the global music market; the preponderance of satellite broadcasting worldwide; a significant percentage of book publishing and commercial magazine publishing; all or part of most of the commercial cable TV channels in the US and worldwide; a significant portion of European terrestrial (traditional over-the-air) television; and on and on and on.

By nearly all accounts, the level of concentration is only going to increase in the near future. "I'm a great believer that we are going to a world of vertically integrated companies where only the big survive," said Gordon Crawford, an executive of Capital Research & Management, a mutual fund that is among the largest shareholders in many of the 7 firms listed above. For firms to survive, *Business Week* observes, speed is of the essence: "Time is short." "In a world moving to five, six, seven media companies, you don't want to be in a position where you have to count on others," Peter Chernin, the president of News Corporation states. "You need to have enough marketplace dominance that people are forced to deal with you." Chernin elaborates: "There are great arguments about whether content is king or distribution is king. At the end of the day, scale is king. If you can spread your costs over a large base, you can outbid your competitors for programming and other assets you want to buy." By 2000, massive cross-border deals – like Pearson merging its TV operations with CLT (Compagnie Luxembourgeoise de Télédiffusion) and Bertelsmann, or Vivendi purchasing Universal – were increasing in prominence.

Chernin's firm, Rupert Murdoch's News Corporation, may be the most aggressive global trailblazer, although cases could be made for Sony, Bertelsmann, or AOL-Time Warner. Murdoch has satellite TV services that run from Asia to Europe to Latin America. His Star TV dominates in Asia with 30 channels in 7 languages. News Corporation's TV service for China, Phoenix TV, in which it has a 45 percent stake, now reaches 45 million homes there and has had an 80 percent increase in advertising revenues in the past year. And this barely begins to describe News Corporation's entire portfolio of assets: Twentieth Century Fox films, Fox TV network, HarperCollins publishers, TV stations, cable TV channels, magazines, over 130 newspapers, and professional sport teams.

Why has this taken place? The conventional explanation is technology; i.e. radical improvements in communication technology make global media empires feasible and lucrative in a manner unthinkable in the past. This is similar to the technological explanation for globalization writ large. But this is only a partial explanation, at best. The real motor force has been the incessant pursuit for profit that marks capitalism, which has applied pressure for a shift to neoliberal deregulation. In media this means the relaxation or elimination of barriers to commercial exploitation of media and to concentrated media ownership. There is nothing inherent in the technology that required neoliberalism; new digital communication could have been used, for example, to simply enhance public service media had a society elected to do so. With neoliberal values, however, television, which had been a noncommercial preserve in many nations, suddenly became subject to transnational commercial development. It has been at the center of the emerging global media system.

Once the national deregulation of media began in major nations like the United States and Britain, it was followed by global measures like the North American Free Trade Agreement (NAFTA) and the formation of the World Trade Organization (WTO), all designed to clear the ground for investment and sales by multinational corporations in regional and global markets. This has laid the foundation for the creation of the global media system, dominated by the afore-mentioned conglomerates. Now in place, the system has its own logic. Firms must become larger and diversified to reduce risk and enhance profit-making opportunities, and they must straddle the globe so as to never be outflanked by competitors. This is a market that some anticipate having trillions of dollars in annual revenues within a decade. If that is to be the case, those companies that sit atop the field may someday rank among the two or three dozen largest in the world.

The development of the global media system has not been unopposed. While media conglomerates press for policies to facilitate their domination of markets throughout the world, strong traditions of protection for domestic media and cultural industries persist. Nations ranging from Norway, Denmark, and Spain to Mexico, South Africa, and South Korea keep their small domestic film production industries alive with government subsidies. In the summer of 1998, culture ministers from 20 nations, including Brazil, Mexico, Sweden, Italy and Ivory Coast, met in Ottawa to discuss how they could "build some ground rules" to protect their cultural fare from "the Hollywood juggernaut." Their main recommendation was to keep culture out of the control of the WTO. A similar 1998 gathering, sponsored by the United Nations in Stockholm, recommended that culture be granted special exemptions in global trade deals. Nevertheless, the trend is clearly in the direction of opening markets.

Proponents of neoliberalism in every country argue that cultural trade barriers and regulations harm consumers, and that subsidies inhibit the ability of nations to develop their own competitive media firms. There are often strong commercial media lobbies within nations that perceive they have more to gain by opening up their borders than by maintaining trade barriers. In 1998, for example, when the British government proposed a voluntary levy on film theater revenues (mostly Hollywood films) to benefit the British commercial film industry, British broadcasters, not wishing to antagonize the firms who supply their programming, lobbied against the measure until it died.

If the WTO is explicitly a pro-commercial organization, the International Telecommunication Union (ITU), the global regulatory body for telecommunications, has only become one after a long march from its traditional commitment to public service values. The European Commission (EC), the executive arm of the European Union (EU), also, finds itself in the middle of what controversy exists concerning media policy, and it has considerably more power than the ITU. On the one hand, the EC is committed to building powerful pan-European media giants that can go toe-to-toe with the US-based giants. On the other hand, it is committed to maintaining some semblance of competitive markets, so it occasionally rejects proposed media mergers as being anticompetitive. Yet, as a quasi-democratic institution, the EU is subject to some popular pressure that is unsympathetic to commercial interests. As Sweden assumed the rotating chair of the EU in 2001, the Swedes began pushing to have their domestic ban on TV advertising to children made into the law for all EU nations. If this occurs it will be the most radical attempt yet to limit the prerogatives of the corporate media giants that dominate commercial children's television.

Perhaps the best way to understand how closely the global commercial media system is linked to the neoliberal global capitalist economy is to consider the role of advertising. Advertising is a business expense incurred by the largest firms in the economy. The commercial media system is the necessary transmission belt for businesses to market their wares across the world; indeed globalization as we know it could not exist without it. A whopping three-quarters of global spending on advertising ends up in the pockets of a mere 20 media companies. Ad spending has grown by leaps and bounds in the past decade, as TV has been opened to commercial exploitation, and is growing at more than twice the rate of GDP growth. Latin American ad spending, for example, is expected to increase by nearly 8 percent in both 2000 and 2001. The coordinators of this $350 billion industry are 5 or 6 super-ad-agency-owning companies that have emerged in the past decade to dominate totally the global trade. The consolidation in the global advertising industry is just as pronounced as that in global media, and the two are related. "Mega-agencies are in a wonderful position to handle the business of megaclients," one ad executive notes. It is "absolutely necessary...for agencies to consolidate. Big is the mantra. So big it must be," another executive stated.

There are a few other points to make to put the global media system in proper perspective. The global media market is rounded out by a second tier of six or seven dozen firms that are national or regional powerhouses, or that control niche markets, like business or trade publishing. Between one-third and one-half of these second-tier firms come from North America; most of the rest are from Western Europe and Japan. Many national and regional conglomerates have been established on the backs of publishing or television empires. Each of these second-tier firms is a giant in its own right, often ranking among the thousand largest companies in the world and doing more than one billion dollars per year in business. The roster of second-tier media firms from North America includes Tribune Company, Dow Jones, Gannett, Knight-Ridder, Hearst, and Advance Publications, and among those from Europe are the Kirch Group, Mediaset, Prisa, Pearson, Reuters, and Reed Elsevier. The Japanese companies, aside from Sony, remain almost exclusively domestic producers.

This second tier has also crystallized rather quickly; across the globe there has been a shakeout in national and regional media markets, with small firms getting eaten by medium firms and medium firms being swallowed by big firms. Compared with 10 or 20 years ago, a much smaller number of much larger firms now dominate the media at a national and regional level. In Britain, for example, one of the few remaining independent book publishers, Fourth Estate, was sold to Murdoch's HarperCollins in 2000. A wave of mergers has left German television – the second largest TV market in the world – the private realm of Bertelsmann and Kirch. Indeed, several mergers have left all of European terrestrial television dominated by 5 firms, 3 of which rank in the global first tier. The situation may be most stark in New Zealand, where the newspaper industry is largely the province of the Australian-American Rupert Murdoch and the Irishman Tony O'Reilly, who also dominates New Zealand's commercial radio broadcasting and has major stakes in magazine publishing. Murdoch also controls pay television. In short, the rulers of New Zealand's media system could squeeze into a closet.

Second-tier corporations, like those in the first-tier, need to reach beyond national borders. "The borders are gone. We have to grow," the Chairman of CanWest Global Communication stated in 2000. "We don't intend to be one of the corpses lying beside the information highway.... We have to be Columbia or Warner Brothers one day." The CEO of Bonnier, Sweden's largest media conglomerate says that to survive, "we want to be the leading media company in Northern Europe." Australian media moguls, following the path blazed by Murdoch, have the mantra "Expand or die." As one puts it, "You really can't continue to grow as an Australian supplier in Australia." Mediaset, the Berlusconi-owned Italian TV power, is angling to expand into the rest of Europe and Latin America. Perhaps the most striking example of second-tier globalization is Hicks, Muse, Tate and Furst, the US radio/publishing/TV/billboard/movie theater power that has been constructed almost overnight. Between 1998 and 2000 it spent well over $2 billion purchasing media assets in Mexico, Argentina, Brazil, and Venezuela.

Second-tier media firms are hardly "oppositional" to the global system. This is true as well in developing countries. Mexico's Televisa, Brazil's Globo, Argentina's Clarin, and Venezuela's Cisneros Group, for example, are among the world's 60 or 70 largest media corporations. These firms tend to dominate their own national and regional media markets, which have been experiencing rapid consolidation as well. They generate much of their revenue from multinational corporate advertising. Moreover, they have extensive ties and joint ventures with the largest media multinationals, as well as with Wall Street investment banks. In Latin America, for example, the second-tier firms work closely with the US giants, who are carving up the commercial media pie among themselves. What Televisia or Globo can offer News Corporation, for example, is local domination of the politicians and the impression of local control over their joint ventures. And like second-tier media firms elsewhere, they are also establishing global operations, especially in nations that speak the same language. As a result, the second-tier media firms in the developing nations tend to have distinctly pro-business political agendas and to support expansion of the global media market, which puts them at odds with large segments of the population in their home countries.

Together, the 70 or 80 first- and second-tier giants control much of the world's media: book, magazine, and newspaper publishing; music recording; TV production; TV stations and cable channels; satellite TV systems; film production; and motion picture theaters. But the system is still very much evolving. The end result of all this activity by second-tier media firms may well be the eventual creation of one or two more giants, and it almost certainly means the number of viable media players in the system will continue to plummet. Some new second-tier firms are emerging, especially in lucrative Asian markets, and there will probably be further upheaval among the ranks of the first-tier media giants. And corporations get no guarantee of success merely by going global. The point is that they have no choice in the matter. Some, perhaps many, will falter as they accrue too much debt or as they enter unprofitable ventures or as they face intensified competition. But the chances are that we are closer to the end of the process of establishing a stable global media market than to the beginning. And as it takes shape, there is a distinct likelihood that the leading media firms in the world will find themselves in a very profitable position. That is what they are racing to secure.

The global media system is only partially competitive in any meaningful economic sense of the term. Many of the largest media firms have some of the same major shareholders, own pieces of one another or have interlocking boards of directors. When *Variety* compiled its list of the 50 largest global media firms for 1997, it observed that "merger mania" and cross-ownership had "resulted in a complex web of interrelationships" that will "make you dizzy." The global market strongly encourages corporations to establish equity joint ventures in which two or more media giants share ownership of an enterprise. This way, firms reduce competition and risk and increase the chance of profitability. As the CEO of Sogecable, Spain's largest media firm and one of the 12 largest private media companies in Europe, expressed it to *Variety*, the strategy is "not to compete with international companies but to join them." In some respects, the global media market more closely resembles a cartel than it does the competitive marketplace found in economics textbooks.

This point cannot be overemphasized. In competitive markets, in theory, numerous producers work their tails off largely oblivious to each other as they sell what they produce at the market price, over which they have no control. At a certain level, it is true these firms compete vigorously in an oligopolistic manner. But they all struggle to minimize the effects of competition. Today's media firms are what Joseph Schumpeter called "core-spective" competitors typical of situations with high levels of monopolization rather than classical competitors in an anonymous dog-eat-dog world as assumed in much of economic theory. The leading CEOs are all on a first name basis and they regularly converse. Even those on unfriendly terms, like Murdoch and AOL-Time Warner's Ted Turner, understand they have to work together for the "greater good." "Sometimes you have to grit your teeth and treat your enemy as your friend," the former president of Universal, Frank Biondi, concedes. As the head of Venezuela's huge Cisneros group, which is locked in combat over Latin American satellite TV with News Corporation, explains about Murdoch, "We're friends. We're always talking." Moreover, all the first- and second-tier media firms are connected through their reliance upon a few investment banks like Morgan Stanley and Goldman Sachs that quarterback most of the huge media mergers. Those two banks alone put together 52 media and telecom deals valued at $450 billion in the first quarter of 2000, and 138 deals worth $433 billion in all of 1999.

This conscious coordination does not simply affect economic behavior; it makes the media giants particularly effective political lobbyists at the national, regional, and global levels. The global media system is not the result of "free markets" or natural law; it is the consequence of a number of important state policies that have been made that created the system. The media giants have had a heavy hand in drafting these laws and regulations, and the public tends to have little or no input. In the United States, the corporate media lobbies are notorious for their ability to get their way with politicians, especially if their adversary is not another powerful corporate sector, but that amorphous entity called the "public interest." In 2000, for example, the corporate media giants led the lobbying effort to open up trade with China, and fought against those who raised concerns about free speech and free press. Everywhere in the world it is the same, and the corporate media have the additional advantage of controlling the very news media that would be the place citizens would expect to find criticism and discussion of media policy in a free society. The track record is that the corporate media use their domination of the news media in a self-serving way, hence cementing their political leverage.

Finally, a word should be said about the internet, the two-ton gorilla of global media and communication. The internet is increasingly becoming a part of our media and telecommunication systems, and a genuine technological convergence is taking place. Accordingly, there has been a wave of mergers between traditional media and telecom firms, and by each of these with internet and computer firms. Already companies like Microsoft, AOL, AT&T and Telefonica have become media players in their own right. It is possible that the global media system is in the process of converging with the telecommunications and computer industries to form an integrated global communication system, where anywhere from 6 to a dozen supercompanies will rule the roost. The notion that the Internet would "set us free," and permit anyone to communicate effectively, hence undermining the monopoly power of the corporate media giants, has not transpired. Although the internet offers extraordinary promise in many regards, it alone cannot slay the power of the media giants. Indeed, no commercially viable media content site has been launched on the internet, and it would be difficult to find an investor willing to bankroll any additional attempts. To the extent the internet becomes part of the commercially viable media system, it looks to be under the thumb of the usual corporate suspects.

Global media and neoliberal democracy

In the introduction I alluded to the importance of the global media system to the formation and expansion of global and regional markets for goods and services, often sold by the largest multinational corporations. The emerging global media system also has significant cultural and political implications, specifically with regard to political democracy, imperialism, and the nature of socialist resistance in the coming years. In the balance of this review I will outline a few comments on these issues.

In the area of democracy, the emergence of a such a highly concentrated media system in the hands of huge private concerns violates in a fundamental manner any notion of a free press in democratic theory. The problems of having wealthy private owners dominate the journalism and media in a society have been well understood all along: journalism, in particular, which is the oxygen necessary for self-government to be viable, will be controlled by those who benefit by existing inequality and the preservation of the status quo.

The two traditional recourses to protect democratic values in media – neither of which is the "answer" by any means – no longer apply. First, marketplace competition is of the oligopolistic variety, and even there it is quite weak by comparative or historical standards. It is virtually unthinkable for a citizen, even a wealthy capitalist, to launch a commercially viable company that can go toe-to-toe with the media giants. The market is effectively closed off to outsiders. And even a more competitive marketplace has clear limitations for generating democratic media. Second, the traditional means the commercial media system has provided to account for the lack of competition has been the idea that its journalism would be subject to the control of trained professional journalists who would be neutral and nonpartisan. This was always a flawed construct, because power remains in the hands of the owners, and what little professional prerogative existed to go against the political and commercial interests of owners has diminished in the past decade. This process was documented in *Monthly Review* in the November 2000 "Review of the Month."

The attack on the professional autonomy of journalism that has taken place is simply a broader part of the neoliberal transformation of media and communication. All public service values and institutions that interfere with profit maximization are on the chopping block. In media, this has been seen most dramatically in the fall from grace of public service broadcasting in much of the world. It is only because of the tremendous goodwill these services have built up over the years that they survive, because they go directly counter to the neoliberal logic that states profits should rule wherever they can be generated. The EU is in the position of condemning some of the traditional subsidies to public service broadcasters as "noncompetitive," as it is now assumed that broadcasting is first and foremost the province of capitalists. Public service broadcasting, once the media centerpiece of European social democracy, is now on the defensive and increasingly reduced to locating a semi-commercial niche in the global system. The pathetic and toothless US system of public broadcasting – a quasi-commercial low budget operation aimed at a sliver of the upper-middle class – is the model for public broadcasting under neoliberal auspices.

Neoliberalism is more than an economic theory, however. It is also a political theory. It posits that business domination of society proceeds most effectively when there is a representative democracy, but only when it is a weak and ineffectual polity typified by high degrees of depoliticization, especially among the poor and working class. It is here that one can see why the existing commercial media system is so important to the neoliberal project, for it is singularly brilliant at generating the precise sort of bogus political culture that permits business domination to proceed without using a police state or facing effective popular resistance.

This argument may seem to contradict the fairly common view of those who assert global conglomerates can at times have a progressive impact on culture, especially when they enter nations that had been tightly controlled by corrupt crony media systems (as in much of Latin America) or nations that had significant state censorship over media (as in parts of Asia). In fact, the global commercial media system is radically bourgeois in that it respects, on balance, no tradition or custom if it stands in the way of profits. But ultimately, once capitalist relations have become preeminent, the global corporate media system is politic-ally conservative, because the media giants are significant beneficiaries of the current social structure around the world, and any upheaval in property or social relations – particularly to the extent that it reduces the power of business – is not in their interest.

Sometimes the bias is explicit, and corporate overlords like Rupert Murdoch simply impose their neoliberal political positions on their underlings. More often, however, the bias is subtle and is due purely to commercial concerns. With concentration comes hypercommercialism, as media firms have more ability to extract profit from their activities; this generates an implicit political bias in media content. Consumerism, class inequality and so-called "individualism" tend to be taken as natural and even benevolent, whereas political activity, civic values, and antimarket activities are marginalized. The best journalism is pitched to the business class and suited to its needs and prejudices; with a few notable exceptions, the journalism reserved for the masses tends to be the sort of drivel provided by the media giants on their US television stations. In India, for example, influenced by the global media giants, "the revamped news media . . . now focus more on fashion designers and beauty queens than on the dark realities of a poor and violent country." This slant is often quite subtle. Indeed, the genius of the commercial-media system is the general lack of overt censorship. As George Orwell noted in his unpublished introduction to *Animal Farm*, censorship in free societies is infinitely more sophisticated and thorough than in dictatorships, because "unpopular ideas can be silenced, and inconvenient facts kept dark, without any need for an official ban."

Lacking any necessarily conspiratorial intent and acting in their own bottom line interest, media conglomerates gradually weed out public sphere substance in favor of light entertainment. In the words of the late Emilio Azcarraga, the billionaire founder of Mexico's Televisa: "Mexico is a country of a modest, very fucked class, which will never stop being fucked. Television has the obligation to bring diversion to these people and remove them from their sad reality and difficult future." The combination of neoliberal-ism and corporate media culture tends to promote a deep and profound depoliticization. One need only look at the United States to see the logical endpoint.

The global media and imperialism

The relationship of the global media system to the question of imperialism is complex. In the 1970s, much of the Third World mobilized through UNESCO to battle the cultural imperialism of the Western powers. The Third World nations developed plans for a New World Information and Communication Order (NWICO) to address their concerns that Western domination over journalism and culture made it virtually impossible for newly independent nations to escape colonial status. Similar concerns about US media domination were heard across Europe. The NWICO campaign was part of a broader struggle at that time by Third World nations to address formally the global economic inequality that was seen as a legacy of imperialism. Both of these movements were impaled on the sword of neoliberalism wielded by the United States and Britain.

Global journalism is dominated by Western news services, which regard existing capitalism, the United States, its allies, and their motives in the most charitable manner imaginable. As for culture, the "Hollywood juggernaut" and the specter of US cultural domination remain a central concern in many countries, for obvious reasons. Exports of US films and TV shows increased by 22 percent in 1999, and the list of the top 125 grossing films for 1999 is made up almost entirely of Hollywood fare. When one goes nation by nation, even a "cultural nationalist" country like France had nine of its top ten grossing films in 1999 produced by the Hollywood giants. "Many leftist intellectuals in Paris are decrying American films, but the French people are eating them up," a Hollywood producer noted. Likewise, in Italy, the replacement of single-screen theaters by "multiplexes" has contributed to a dramatic decline in local film box office. The moral of the story for many European filmmakers is that you have to work in English and employ Hollywood moviemaking conventions to succeed. In Latin America, cable television is overwhelmed by the channels of the media giants, and the *de facto* capital for the region is Miami.

But, with the changing global political economy, there are problems with leaving the discussion at this point. The notion that corporate media firms are merely purveyors of US culture is ever less plausible as the media system becomes increasingly concentrated, commercialized and globalized. As I note above, the global media giants are the quintessential multinational firms, with shareholders, headquarters, and operations scattered across the globe. The global media system is better understood as one that advances corporate and commercial interests and values and denigrates or ignores that which cannot be incorporated into its mission. There is no discernible difference in the firms' content, whether they are owned by shareholders in Japan or France or have corporate headquarters in New York, Germany, or Sydney. In this sense, the basic split is not between nation-states, but between the rich and the poor, across national borders.

As the media conglomerates spread their tentacles, there is reason to believe they will encourage popular tastes to become more uniform in at least some forms of media. Based on conversations with Hollywood executives, *Variety* editor Peter Bart concluded that "the world filmgoing audience is fast becoming more homogeneous." Whereas action movies had once been the only sure-fire global fare – and comedies had been considerably more difficult to export – by the late nineties comedies like *My Best Friend's Wedding* and *The Full Monty* were doing between $160 million and $200 million in non-US box-office sales.

When audiences appear to prefer locally made fare, the global media corporations, rather than flee in despair, globalize their production. Sony has been at the forefront of this, producing films with local companies in China, France, India, and Mexico, to name but a few. India's acclaimed domestic film industry – "Bollywood" – is also developing close ties to the global media giants. This process is even more visible in the music industry. Music has always been the least capital-intensive of the electronic media and therefore the most open to experimentation and new ideas. US recording artists generated 60 percent of their sales outside the US in 1993; by 1998 that figure was down to 40 percent. Rather than fold their tents, however, the four media multinationals that dominate the world's recorded-music market are busy establishing local subsidiaries in places like Brazil, where "people are totally committed to local music," in the words of a writer for a trade publication. Sony, again, has led the way in establishing distribution deals with independent music companies from around the world.

But it would be a mistake to buy into the notion that the global media system makes nation-state boundaries and geopolitical empire irrelevant. A large portion of contemporary capitalist activity, clearly a majority of investment and employment, operates primarily within national confines, and their nation-states play a key role in representing these interests. The entire global regime is the result of neoliberal political policies, urged on by the US government. Most important, not far below the surface is the role of the US military as the global enforcer of capitalism, with US-based corporations and investors in the driver's seat. Recall the approving words of Thomas Friedman: "The hidden hand of the market will never work without a hidden fist. McDonald's cannot flourish without McDonnell Douglas, the designer of the F-15. And the hidden fist that keeps the world safe for Silicon Valley's technologies is called the US Army, Air Force, Navy and Marine Corps." In short, we need to develop an understanding of neoliberal globalization that is joined at the hip to US militarism – and all the dreadful implications that that suggests – rather than one that is in opposition to it.

This core relationship between the US military and the global neoliberal project, one of the central political issues of our times, also is virtually unknown to the journalism of AOL-Time Warner's CNN and the other corporate media giants, who increasingly are the providers of substantive news concerning international politics. The very notion of imperialism has been dismissed as a historical artifact or a rhetorical ploy of desperate opportunists and the feeble-minded. In view of the corporate media's interdependence with the global neoliberal regime, any other outcome would be remarkable.

Prospects

It would be all too easy, given the above conditions, to succumb to despair or simply acquiesce to changes from which there seems no escape. Matters appear quite depressing from a democratic standpoint, and it may be difficult to see much hope for change. As one Swedish journalist noted in 1997, "Unfortunately, the trends are very clear, moving in the wrong direction on virtually every score, and there is a desperate lack of public discussion of the long-term implications of current developments for democracy and accountability." But the global system is highly unstable. As lucrative as neoliberalism has been for the rich, it has been a disaster for the world's poor and working classes. Latin America, a champion of market reforms since the eighties, has seen what a World Bank official terms a "big increase in inequality." The number of people worldwide living on less than $1 per day increased from 1.2 billion in 1987 to 1.5 billion in 2000, and looks to continue to rise for years to come. The "me first, screw you" ethos promoted by neoliberalism has contributed to widespread governmental corruption, as notions of principled public service are difficult to maintain. The stability of the entire global economy looks increasingly fragile. While the dominance of commercial media makes resistance more difficult, widespread opposition to these trends has begun to emerge in the form of huge demonstrations across the planet, including the United States. It seems that the depoliticization fostered by neoliberalism and commercial media is bumping up against the harsh reality of exploitation, inequality, and the bankruptcy of capitalist politics and culture experienced by significant parts of the population. Just as all organized resistance to capitalism appeared to be stomped out it now threatens to rise again from the very ground.

This leads to my final point. What is striking is that progressive antineoliberal political movements around the world are increasingly making media issues part of their political platforms. From Sweden, France, and India, to Australia, New Zealand, and Canada, democratic left political parties are giving structural media reform – e.g. breaking up the big companies, recharging nonprofit and noncommercial broadcasting, creating a sector of nonprofit and noncommercial independent media under popular control – a larger role in their platforms. They are finding out that this is a successful issue with the broad population. Other activists are putting considerable emphasis upon developing independent and so-called "pirate" media to counteract the corporate system. Across the board on the antineoliberal and socialist left there is a recognition that the issue of media has grown dramatically in importance, and no successful social movement can dismiss this as a matter that can be addressed "after the revolution." Organizing for democratic media must be part of the current struggle, if we are going to have a viable chance of success.

CHAPTER 11

David Morley

Theoretical Orthodoxies: Textualism, Constructivism and the 'New Ethnography' in Cultural Studies

My concern here is to offer an overview of some recent debates concerning ethnographic audience research within the field of cultural studies. Substantively, one of the major issues concerns the extent to which 'active audience theory' has produced an improperly romanticized image of the media consumer, which tends to ignore institutional questions of cultural power. Its critics have variously dismissed this work as a form of 'new revisionism' (Curran, 1990) or even as 'pointless populism' (Seamann, 1992). In the recent backlash against 'cultural populism', critics such as Frith (1991), Harris (1992) and McGuigan (1992) have tended towards a 'post hoc ergo propter hoc' structure of argument, in which, having identified some particular case in which subcultural/consumer/audience 'activity' is uncritically celebrated by an author with cultural studies allegiances, they then retrospectively declare that this is the kind of (bad) thing to which cultural studies, in general, was bound to lead and that therefore (conveniently reversing the terms of the argument) the whole cultural studies enterprise was, from the start, misconceived, as it has (in fact) led to whatever example of bad practice they have identified.

For my own part, I am happy to agree that some proponents of 'active audience theory' may have (mis)taken evidence of audience activity as an index of audience power (see Ang, 1990, on this point). However, my position is that the arguments of many of the recent critics of cultural studies are misconceived – not least because their criticisms seem designed principally to prepare the ground for a call for a return to the eternal verities of political economy (or classical sociology) as a way out of the blind alley into which cultural studies is said to have (misguidedly) led us. To argue that way is simply to ignore the very real advances made in many branches of cultural studies over the last 20 years. However, this is by no means to argue that cultural studies work on media audiences (or anything else) is problem-free. On the contrary, my other concern here, moving to a more methodological focus, is with the gradual institutionalization of what I view as a damaging set of theoretical/methodological orthodoxies, within some parts of cultural studies.

David Morley, "Theoretical Orthodoxies: Textualism, Constructivism and the 'New Ethnography' in Cultural Studies," pp. 121–37 from Marjorie Ferguson and Peter Golding (eds.), *Cultural Studies in Question*. London: Sage, 1997. Reprinted by permission of Sage Publications Ltd.

In recent years, much work in cultural studies has been influenced by debates originating in anthropology, concerning what has been described as 'postmodern' or 'self-reflexive' ethnography (Clifford and Marcus, 1986). Ethnography has become a fashionable buzz-word within the field, and the virtues of its postmodern inflection are now widely assumed to be self-evident, as are those of a constructivist epistemology, and a heavily textualist form of discourse theory, which has little regard for questions of socio-economic determination. This chapter offers a critical examination of these orthodoxies, and argues for a form of cultural studies based on a combination of sociological materialism, epistemological realism and methodological pragmatism. I shall begin with some orienting comments, concerning the recent development of the overall field of cultural studies.

Certainly, as cultural studies becomes increasingly codified and institutionalized, issues of orthodoxy are posed in a particularly sharp manner. Most problematically, in my view, in the context of the North American academy, cultural studies has become almost synonymous with a certain kind of postmodern, deconstructionist literary theory (often referred to, by those involved in it, by the interestingly ex-nominated form, 'Theory'). It is the particular content of the current theoretical orthodoxies of cultural studies with which I am here concerned. Going to conferences in the field, glancing at journals, or talking to graduate students involved in the newest work in cultural studies, one could be forgiven for presuming that all the difficult age-old debates, concerning questions of epistemology which have long bedevilled philosophers, have in fact finally been solved. It would seem, curiously enough, that within much of cultural studies, relativism has been absolutely victorious, to speak oxymoronically.

One part of the motivation for the development of the relativist, self-reflexive ortho-doxy which has come to dominate the field has been a quite proper concern with the politics of knowledge, and with taking into account the power relations between subject and object of knowledge. Unfortunately, in my view, the overall effect of much of this has in the end been a disabling one, as a result of which it becomes pretty hard for anyone to say anything about anyone (or anything) else, for fear of accusation of ontological imperialism. Apart from any other considerations, and despite the declared political credentials (and intentions) of much of this kind of work, within cultural studies, this is in fact, politically disabling. It is hard to mobilize around a political platform of principled uncertainty, especially if one of those principles is that it is ultimately impos-sible to know what is going on.

It is this set of difficulties which this chapter attempts to unravel, by working through current debates concerning both the 'new revisionism' in media audience research and the associated turn towards postmodern ethnography in cultural studies, more broadly. This, I would argue, is a crucial terrain on which to pursue these arguments as, within cultural studies, the employment of a particular self-reflexive form of ethnography has become almost emblematic of the field itself. A commitment to this particular set of epistemo-logical and methodological principles has come to be the doctrinal test of membership of those who are Saved. My argument here is deliberately intended in the spirit of heresy.

From my perspective, one of the crucial features of the American (and predominantly literary) appropriation of British cultural studies has been the loss of any sense of culture and communications as having material roots, in broader social and political processes and structures, so that the discursive process of the constitution of meanings often becomes the exclusive focus of analysis, without any reference to its institutional or economic setting. As Hall (1990b) observes, what we often see is a textualization of cultural studies, which constitutes power and politics as (exclusively) matters of language (or discourse). As Hall notes, in this respect, 'textuality is never enough' and cultural studies must learn to live with 'the tension which Said describes as its affiliations with institutions, offices, agencies, classes, academies, corporations, groups, ideologically defined parties and professions, nations, races and genders ... questions that ... can never be fully covered by critical textuality and its elaborations' (Hall, 1990: 16–17).

Of course, at this point, I have to declare my own position – as one trained initially as a sociologist who has, by virtue of that fact, always had substantial reservations about the successive dominant paradigms (culturalist, structuralist, psychoanalytic, poststructuralist or postmodern) within cultural studies. Thus, from within cultural studies, the major critique of much of my own work has been that it is too essentialist or reductionist, in its sociological emphasis. From my own point of view, the prime objective of the work has been to analyse processes of culture and communication within their social and material settings. I am personally much more worried by what I see as the tendency towards the textualization of cultural studies, which often allows the cultural phenomena under analysis to drift entirely free from their social and material foundations, and it is in this context that I now turn to the consideration of recent debates about media audiences within cultural studies.

The 'new' audience research

As Evans (1990) notes, recent audience work in media studies can be largely characterized by two assumptions: (a) that the audience is always active (in a non-trivial sense) and (b) that media content is always polysemic, or open to interpretation. The questions are what these assumptions are taken to mean exactly, and what their theoretical and empirical consequences are.

Hall's (1980) original formulation of the encoding/decoding model of communications contained, as one of its central features, the concept of the preferred reading (towards which the text attempts to direct its reader), while still acknowledging the possibility of alternative, negotiated or oppositional readings. This model has subsequently been quite transformed, to the point where it is often maintained that the majority of audience members routinely modify or deflect any dominant ideology reflected in media content, and the concept of a preferred reading, or of a structured polysemy, drops entirely from view. In this connection, I have to confess a personal interest, as I have been puzzled to find some of my own earlier work (Morley, 1980) invoked as a theoretical legitimation of various forms of 'active audience theory'. For any author to comment on the subsequent interpretation of his or her work is plainly an awkward enterprise, and when that work itself is substantively concerned with the ways in which audiences interpret texts, the irony is manifest. Nonetheless, I shall take this opportunity to comment on some recent debates in audience studies, and will argue that much 'active audience' theory is in fact premised on a heavily negotiated reading (if not a misreading) of some of the earlier work which is often invoked as its theoretical basis (see Derrida, 1989; Norris, 1991; and Richards, 1960 for the relevant distinctions between variant readings and misreadings).

For my own part, while I would argue that work such as the 'Nationwide' Audience project (along with that of Ang, 1985; Liebes and Katz, 1990; and Radway, 1984) offers counter-evidence to a simple minded 'dominant ideology' thesis, and demonstrates that any hegemonic discourse is always necessarily insecure and incomplete, this should not lead us to abandon concern with the question of media power – or as Martín-Barbero puts it, 'how to understand the texture of hegemony/subalternity, the interlacing of resistance and submission, opposition and complicity' (Martín-Barbero, 1988: 462). That was (and remains) precisely the point of studying audience consumption of media texts, a point which now, as the pendulum of media theory swings again (this time towards a dismissal of the more romantic versions of 'active audience theory'), is in great danger of being obscured.

I would agree with Corner (1991) that much recent media audience work is marred by a facile insistence on the polysemy of media products and by an undocumented presumption that forms of interpretive resistance are more widespread than subordination, or the reproduction of dominant meanings (see Condit, 1989, on the unfortunate current tendency towards an overdrawn emphasis on the 'polysemous' qualities of texts in media studies). To follow that path, as Corner (1991) correctly notes, is to underestimate the force of textual determinacy in the construction of meaning from media products, and not only to romanticize improperly the role of the reader, but to risk falling into a 'complacent relativism, by which the interpretive contribution of the audience is perceived to be of such a scale and range as to render the very idea of media power naive' (Corner, 1991: 281).

In a similar vein to Corner, Curran (1990) offers a highly critical account of what he describes as the 'new revisionism' in mass communications research on media audiences. In brief, his charge is that while this 'revisionism presents itself as original and innovative [it] ... is none of these things' (Curran, 1990: 135), but rather amounts to 'old pluralist dishes being reheated and presented as new cuisine' (ibid.: 151). The history Curran offers is an informative one, alerting us to the achievements of scholars whose work has been unrecognized or neglected by many (myself included) in the past. However, my contention is that this is a particular history which could not have been written (by Curran or anyone else) 15 years ago, before the impact of the 'new revisionism' (of which Curran is so critical) transformed our understanding of the field of audience research and thus transformed our understanding of who and what was important in its history. I would argue that it is precisely this transformation which has allowed a historian such as Curran to go back and re-read the history of communications research in such a way as to give prominence to those whose work can now, with hindsight, be seen to have 'pre-figured' the work of these 'new revisionists'.

However, despite my differences with him about the general terms of his critique, I would agree with Curran that recent reception studies which document audience autonomy and offer optimistic/redemptive readings of mainstream media texts, have often been, wrongly, taken to represent not simply a challenge to a simple-minded effects or dominant ideology model, but rather as, in themselves, documenting the total absence of media influence, in the 'semiotic democracy' of postmodern pluralism.

Budd et al. (1990) argue that much contemporary media audience research now routinely assumes that 'people habitually use the content of dominant media against itself, to empower themselves' (Budd et al., 1990: 170) so that, in their analysis, the crucial message of much contemporary American cultural studies media work is an optimistic one: 'whatever the message encoded, decoding comes to the rescue. Media domination is weak and ineffectual, since the people make their own meanings and pleasures' (ibid.: 170).

While we should not fall back into any form of simplistic textual determinacy, nonetheless we must also avoid the naive presumption that texts are completely open, like 'an imaginary shopping mall in which audience members could wander at will, selecting whatever suits them' (Murdock, 1989: 236). The equivalence that Newcomb and Hirsch (1987) assert between the producer and consumer of messages, in so far as they argue that the television viewer matches the creator (or the programme) in the making of meanings is, in effect, a facile one, which ignores de Certeau's (1984) distinction between the strategies of the powerful and the tactics of the weak (or, as Silverstone and I have argued elsewhere (1990), the difference between having power over a text and power over the agenda within which that text is constructed and presented). The power of viewers to reinterpret meanings is hardly equivalent to the discursive power of centralized media institutions to construct the texts which the viewer then interprets, and to imagine otherwise is simply foolish.

Between the micro and the macro

The boom in ethnographic media audience research in the 1980s was, in part, the result of the critique of overly structuralist approaches, which had taken patterns of media consumption to be the always-ready-determined effect of some more fundamental structure – whether the economic structure of the cultural industries (Murdock and Golding, 1974), the political structure of the capitalist state (Althusser, 1971) or the psychic structure of the human subject (Lacan, 1977). However, a number of authors (Curran, 1990 and Corner, 1991) have recently argued that the pendulum has now swung so far that we face the prospect of a field dominated by the production of micro (and often ethnographic) analyses of media consumption processes, which add up only to a set of micro-narratives, outside any effective macro-political or cultural frame. Despite my reservations above, concerning much 'active audience theory', I nonetheless hold that the developing backlash against micro-ethnography is in danger of encouraging a return to macro-political issues which is, in fact, premised on a mal-posed conception of the relation between the micro and the macro.

Thus, Corner argues that, in recent research on the media audience, the question of media power has tended to be avoided, and that much of this 'new audience research' amounts to 'a form of sociological quietism ... in which increasing emphasis on the micro-processes of viewing relations displaces ... an engagement with the macro-structures of media and society' (Corner, 1991: 269). My own contention would be that this formulation is problematic, in so far as Corner implicitly equates the macro with the 'real' and the micro with the realm of the epiphenomenal (if not the inconsequential). In the first place, Corner's analysis fails to recognize the gendered articulation of the divisions macro/micro, real/trivial, public/private, masculine/feminine, which is what much of the work which he criticizes has, in various ways, been concerned with (see for example, Gray, 1992; Morley, 1986; Radway, 1984). More centrally, Corner seems to invoke a notion of the macro which is conceptualized in terms of pre-given structures, rather than (to use Giddens's phrase) 'structuration', and which fails to see that macro structures can only be reproduced through micro-processes.

It was precisely that realization that drove the initial shift (see Hall, 1977) in cultural studies work, away from any notion of a mechanically imposed 'dominant ideology' towards the more processual model of 'hegemony' – as a better theoretical frame within which to analyse the reproduction of cultural power in its various forms. (Interestingly, neither Harris (1992) nor McGuigan (1992) quite seem to grasp this distinction, and both replicate the confusion instituted by Abercrombie and Turner's (1984) conflation of Althusser and Gramsci.) One important motivation of that shift was to attempt to find better ways to articulate the micro and macro levels of analysis, not to abandon either pole in favour of the other. Nor, as Massey (1991) argues, should we fall into the trap of equating the micro (or local) with the merely concrete and empirical, and of equating the macro (or global) with the abstract or theoretical. In all of this, we could do worse than heed Wright-Mills's (1959) strictures on the need to address the interplay of biography and history, in the 'sociological imagination'.

All of this is, of course, particularly vital in the realm of media consumption, given the media's key role in articulating the public and the private, the global and the local, and in articulating global processes of cultural imperialism with local processes of situated consumption – where local meanings are so often made (see Miller, 1992) within and against the symbolic resources provided by global media networks.

To say that is not to offer any *carte blanche* defence of 'ethnography-as-where-it's-at'. If, as Marcus and Fisher observe, the value of ethnography lies in reshaping our dominant macro-frameworks for the understanding of some structural phenomenon (such as the capitalist world-system, for example) so that we can 'better represent the actual diversity and complexity of local situations' for which our theoretical frameworks try to account in general terms (Marcus and Fisher, 1986: 88) yet, as Fiske cautions, any ethnography 'runs the risk, which we must guard against at all costs, of allowing itself to be incorporated into the ideology of individualism' (Fiske, 1990a: 9). If ethnography is concerned to trace the specifics of general, systemic processes, for instance, the particular tactics which various members of a given society have developed in order to 'make do' with the cultural resources which it offers them still, as Fiske notes, our concern must be with interpreting such activities in the broader context of that 'larger system through which culture and politics intersect' (Fiske, 1990b: 98).

In this context, recent debates within feminist media research and feminist theory offer some interesting parallels. The work of Ang and Hermes (1991), for example, is concerned to criticize essentialist tendencies with feminism, which would too readily invoke the category of gender as an explanatory device, in such a way as to blur all the cross-cutting differences that necessarily exist within that category. At the same time, Walby (1992) and Barrett (1992) raise questions about the potentially negative consequences of a post-structuralist destabilization of categories (such as that of gender) which leads only to the accumulation of micro-narratives of the local, specific and particular, which are theoretic-ally precluded from transposition into any broader form of macro-analysis. While the poststructuralist critique of essentialist tendencies to invoke social categories (whether those of gender, class or race) as the explanatory framework of individual action, functions as a useful corrective to any 'super-structuralist' form of determinism, that critique, nonetheless, itself always runs the risk of falling back into a form of methodological individualism (see Knorr-Cetina, 1981, for an account of a methodological situationist alternative) which leaves one, in the end, able only to tell individual stories of (logically) infinite differences.

From my own perspective, our objective must not be to substitute one (micro *or* macro) level of analysis for the other, but rather to attempt to integrate the analysis of the broader questions of ideology, power and politics (what Hall (1988b) has described as the vertical dimension of communications) with the analysis of the consumption, uses and functions of television in everyday life (the horizontal dimension of communications, in Hall's terms). It is not a question, finally, of understanding simply television's ideo-logical (or representational) role, or simply its ritual (or socially organizing) function, or the process of its domestic (and more broadly social) consumption. It is also a question of how to understand the articulation of micro and macro issues and processes.

Questions of methodology, self-reflexivity and epistemology

The substantive focus in recent years on media consumption as an active process has also had one particularly important methodological consequence, in so far as work in this field has come to employ principally qualitative, and often ethnographic, techniques of enquiry as a means of investigating this process in its natural settings. In the case of American cultural studies, in particular, the identification of qualitative methods with the progressive (politically correct?) wing of communications studies seems to be almost complete, and ethnography, as Lull (1987) has argued, has come to be a fetishised buzz-word in the field.

For my own part, while I have often (though not exclusively) employed ethnographic techniques in my own work, I would want to insist that ethnography, in fact, holds no exclusive claim to methodological adequacy, in so far as it, like any other methodological choice, involves what an economist would call 'opportunity costs'. I would agree with Murdock (1989) that analytical work can neither be guaranteed nor damned by its methodological choices alone, and I share Corner's (1991) anxieties about the assumption that the provision of 'more context' is always, in itself, the solution to methodological problems, as some proponents of ethnography would seem to believe (see Morley, 1992, chapter 8 for a fuller version of this argument).

However, despite these disclaimers, I would also want to argue that some of the theoretical debates which have surrounded the practice of ethnography in recent years (cf. Clifford and Marcus, 1986; Geertz, 1988; Marcus and Fisher, 1986) are of considerable importance, not just to anthropology, but also for scholars in the field of media research. In the first place, these debates (initially concerning the relations of power, as well as of knowledge, between representor and represented) concern not only the dilemmas of the white anthropologist who produces forms of knowledge of 'exotic' or 'tribal' peoples. They also concern media researchers, in so far as they too are in the business of investigating and representing others, whether or not those others wear exotic tribal dress: working-class audiences, youth audiences, gendered audiences, ethnic audiences. To that extent, media researchers can also easily fall prey to the dangers of an Orientalism (Said, 1979) in which, as Ang puts it, 'the audience is relegated to the status of exotic "other"...objects of study, about whom "we" have the privilege to know the perfect truth' (Ang, 1991: 10), or as Hartley puts it, such audiences 'become the "other" of [our] powerful imperial discourses' (Hartley, 1987: 125). In this context, Trinh T. Minh-Ha's (1989) comments on anthropology as itself an 'anthropophagous' (cannibalistic) discourse, concerned to 'grasp the marrow of native life', or Fiske's comments on the behaviour of the 'ethnographer who descended as a white man [sic] into the jungle and bore away, back to the white man's world, [the] meanings of native life' (Fiske, 1990b: 90) should also give media researchers pause for thought, as they consider their relations with the audiences they research.

Postmodern ethnography

Since the turn towards qualitative, and especially ethnographic, methods of research took hold in cultural studies' work on media consumption, for example, there has been an increasing interest in anthropology as a source of methodological correctives to the perceived dead-ends of the quantitative tradition of social science communications research. The irony here, however, is that, as Probyn observes, 'just as practitioners in other disciplines seem to be drawn to ethnography because of its promise to delve into the concrete (in the hope of finding real people living "real" lives), ethnography is becoming increasingly textual' (Probyn, 1993: 61). Probyn's reference is, centrally, to the influence within anthropology of Clifford and Marcus's collection *Writing Culture* (1986). This book, and the debates which it engendered, laid the basis for a heavily textualist approach to (postmodern) ethnography which has, latterly, also become extremely influential within cultural studies. This approach is heralded as being politically sensitive to questions of representation, to relations of power between researcher and researched, and to the possibility that anthropology as a whole, as the late Bob Scholte put it, may have simply been 'a way Europeans have invented of talking about their darker brothers or sisters' (Scholte, 1987: 25–36). As Fabian (1990: 758) notes, ethnography itself is a word that carries an ideological burden, in so far as, if its denotative meaning can be defined innocently as 'the description of peoples', connotatively, the implication is always that the peoples to be described are Others – non-writers, non-Europeans, non-Christians – 'Them', and not 'Us'.

The contributors to *Writing Culture*, along with Clifford and his collaborators, and their associated works (Crapanzano, Taussig, Nash, Rabinow, Rosaldo, et al.) are centrally concerned with the fact that ethnographies are written: that they are forms of writing and representation which must be scrutinized as such. However, to anticipate my later argument, if it is true that ethnography is a form of writing, it does not follow that it is *only* a form of writing; nor that an address to its textual characteristics will solve all its problems. This emphasis on textuality may well, in fact, also serve to blind us to the non-textual aspects of the frequently oppressive relations between the ethnographer and his or her subjects. As Fabian notes, it is not simply the fact that the would-be postmodern ethnographer's stress on self-reflexivity will not necessarily 'guarantee that [the] oppressors will be less oppressive, just because they are self-conscious' (Fabian, 1990: 768). It is also deeply problematic if 'awareness of the political dimension of writing remains limited to insights about the political character of aesthetic standards and theoretical devices. . . . To be dominated, it takes more than to be written about. . . . Conversely, to stop writing about the other will not bring liberation' (Fabian, 1990: 760). This is Grossberg's point when he notes that one can all too easily 'deconstruct the other into the productivity of the ethnographer's subjectivity – [a deconstruction in which – D.M.] – the very facticity of the other is erased, dissolved into the ethnographer's semiotic constructions' (Grossberg, 1988: 381–2). As Gewertz and Errington argue, it is but a small step from there to a position in which the other is seen as an entirely discursive phenomenon, a position in which, as they put it 'we think, therefore they are' (Gewertz and Errington, 1991: 80), as material otherness is reduced to semiotic difference. As the Native American Indian artist Jimmie Durham scathingly puts it: 'You think you own us. . . . You think I am *your* Other' (Durham, 1993: 138–9).

In saying all this, I am not wanting to decry the importance of the self-reflexive, textual questions posed by much of this recent anthropological work. I would entirely agree that questions of how ethnographic texts are fashioned, constructed and projected, what rhetorical strategies they use to appear persuasive and how their authority is authenticated and legitimated are important issues. Indeed, notwithstanding Geertz's (1988) criticisms of Clifford et al.'s stress on textuality, Hamer (1989) offers a fascinating analysis of the crucial role played by rhetorical and stylistic devices in Geertz's own writing. Equally, the questions Clifford raises as to 'Who speaks? Who writes? When and where? With or to whom? Under what institutional and historical constraints?' (Clifford, 1986: 13) are vital ones. However, while we must take due note of them, they are not the only, or indeed, necessarily the most important, questions. There remains the question of what these ethnographies say and what relation, if any, it is claimed they have to the world outside the text.

Similarly, I would not wish to deny the importance of the questions raised in contemporary anthropological debates concerning the staging of the voices of the ethnographer's subjects, and the relation between these voices and the meta-narrative of the ethnographer who edits and marshalls them. Thus, Marcus (1986) offers a very interesting discussion of the dangers of a kind of ventriloquism in ethnographic writing, using as his example Paul Willis's *Learning to Labour* (1977), in which Marcus argues that, in an undeclared fashion, Willis orchestrates the voices of the 'lads' he studies, in such a way as to give the impression that his analytic discourse is validated and authenticated by being grounded in the voices of his subjects.

Certainly, this is a question to be handled with some circumspection, and self-reflexivity is a useful antidote to any easy naturalization of the particular analytic account offered as the basis of any ethnographic evidence. However, it should be noted that, as Ernest Gellner (1970) argued many years ago in his debate with Peter Winch (1958), the fact that the analyst finally produces an account of his subjects' activities which is not expressed in their own terms, and which may in fact be different from the account they would offer of their own activities, hardly invalidates it, but is perhaps precisely the necessary responsibility of the analyst and this point remains, even if it can be argued that this is a responsibility which Willis himself attempts to displace on to his respondents. The question Marcus poses: 'Does Willis' articulated critical theory of capitalism really come from the lads?' (Marcus, 1986: 184) can, in fact, be answered in the negative – without that necessarily having any of the damning consequences for Willis's work which Marcus seems to presume this would have.

Moreover, as Ullin notes, the response of some contemporary ethnographers to this problem – to choose to foreground their informants' voices, 'does not settle the issue of authority, as these voices are not autonomous, but rather stand mediated by the social conditions of their production' (Ullin, 1991: 81) – conditions in which it is still the ethnographer who chooses, edits and sequences the (often implicit) meta-narrative of the material presented. In this respect it is surely better that the analyst's role in this procedure be explicit, rather than obscured in the editing process, while remaining nonetheless powerful. As Fabian notes 'dialogue, perceived vaguely as an alternative to isolating or domineering monologue' is now much in vogue in anthropological circles, and has 'acquired a non-specific ethical behavioural, oozing goodwill. . . . Who could be against dialogue?' (Fabian, 1990: 763). The problem is that, as Geertz (1988) puts it, the descriptions are still the describer's descriptions and the 'dialogue' is still edited, constructed and presented by the ethnographer – the burden or critical responsibility is, in this sense, inescapable, whether the material is finally presented in monologic or dialogic form. To have recourse to a rhetoric of polyphony, decentred texts, and the principled fragmentation of all meta-narrative, does not necessarily have any of the progressive ethical or political consequences which are often assumed to follow. It can also produce a disempowering incoherence, even if the analyst, in disburdening him – or herself of the responsibility of producing an explicit meta-narrative, is able to step more lightly the while.

Fabian raises the interesting possibility that much early ethnographic writing was not in fact so much realist as 'naively naturalist' (Fabian, 1990: 762) and argues further that 'ethnographic representations that are (or pretend to be) isomorphic with that which is being represented should be met with suspicion; more likely than not, they lack what distinguishes knowledge from mimickry' (ibid.: 765). The point here is parallel to that made by Borges in his story 'Of exactitude in Science' (1972). Purporting to come from an old travel book, the story describes how:

> In that Empire, the craft of Cartography attained such perfection that the map of a single Province covered the space of an entire city, and the map of the Empire itself an entire Province. In the course of time, these extensive maps were found somewhat wanting, and so the College of Cartographers evolved a map of the Empire that was of the same scale as the Empire and that coincided with it point for point. (Borges, 1972: 141)

Unfortunately, of course, while the map was now perfect and complete, it proved a little cumbersome, and soon fell into disuse.

To make these points is, on the one hand, to argue for realism against naturalism, but it is also to argue that the much-discussed "crisis of representation" in contemporary anthropology (and cultural studies) has to be met by the development of better forms of representation, rather than a rejection of the necessarily realist epistemology of the project of representation itself. As Fabian notes, the only logical alternative is finally 'non-representation, including its most radical form: not-writing, graphic silence' (Fabian, 1990: 761).

At this point, it is of some interest to return to what, for instance, Marcus and Fisher actually claim for their own ethnographies. Despite their espousal of a variety of textual concerns, even they, finally, are concerned with representation. Not only do Marcus and Fisher argue that ethnographies still must refer to and reflect an external reality, but they argue that if they do not, they are without ethnographic value: the value of ethnographic texts, they argue (see Pool, 1991: 321), is finally to be found precisely in their capacity to reflect an external reality. Similarly, notwithstanding the appropriation of the project of *Writing Culture* to a kind of 'anything goes' relativism, in his introduction to that volume, Clifford states clearly that 'the authors in this volume do not suggest that one cultural account is as good as another. If they espoused so trivial and self-refuting a relativism, they would not have gone to the trouble of writing detailed, committed critical studies' (Clifford and Marcus, 1986: 24). This returns us to the question of the relation between the textual and the real. Ullin rightly observes that 'there is much that we can learn from the critical appropriation of communicative or literary metaphor – an appropriation that discloses, as postmodernists and culture theorists alike have agreed, the proximity of [the discipline of anthropology – D.M.] to the art of storytelling' (Ullin, 1991: 82). We are necessarily involved in the telling of stories, and that clearly involves us in questions of rhetoric, textuality and writing. This brings us to the question of Deconstruction, or more precisely, to the theoretical consequences of the observation that philosophy is a kind of writing, which constitutes the theoretical foundation of these recent debates about the implications of the recognition of the necessarily textual status of ethnography itself, as one form of writing.

Textuality, rhetoric and the value of truth

In his account of 'Deconstructionist' theory, Norris (1991) offers us an illuminating analysis, which is quite at odds with that, increasingly accepted, reading of the work of Derrida and others which seems to underpin so much postmodern theorizing, in anthropology and elsewhere. Norris argues that, in the writings of 'post-analytical' philosophers such as Richard Rorty (1989), 'Deconstruction' comes to figure as a handy cover-term for everything that points beyond the 'old dispensation of reason, knowledge and truth' (Norris, 1991: 149) and Derrida comes to play the role of the arch-debunker, who dances rings round the earnest philosophical seekers-after-truth. Hence the title of Rorty's essay on Derrida, 'Philosophy as a Kind of Writing' (1978) where he urges that we should give up thinking of philosophy as a specialized activity of thought, with privileged claims on standards of argumentative validity and truth, and think of it simply as just another voice in the 'ongoing cultural conversation of mankind', but one with delusions of grandeur, that can easily be cut down to size by insisting on its necessarily textual status and by pointing to the final 'contingency' of *all* specialist vocabularies, that of philosophy included.

Norris's point is not simply that Rorty has got Derrida wrong; has *mis*-read him, in Richards's (1960) terms. One could not intelligibly even raise questions of interpretative validity and truth if the postmodern, pragmatist argument won out, and philosophy was reduced to the status of just another form of writing (see Gellner's (1992) trenchant critique of 'post-modern relativism' from the point of view of what he calls 'Enlightenment Rationalist Fundamentalism'). More directly, Norris claims, there is a crucial problem of logic with Rorty's argument. It is one thing to show that philosophical writing often mobilizes covert topological figures and sublimated metaphors, and it is of considerable interest to analyse philosophical texts from this point of view. However, there is simply no good reason to support Rorty's unargued assumption that the presence of 'figural' elements in a piece of argumentative writing necessarily impugns its theoretical adequacy or undercuts its philosophical truth claims. Hence, Norris claims, the importance of respecting the distinctive philosophical valences of Derrida's work, and of not going along with the pseudo-Deconstructive, post-textualist or 'levelling' view of philosophy as 'just another kind of writing'. Norris's point is that Derrida's own mode of argument (in 'White Mythology' (1974) for example) is far from endorsing the vulgar Deconstructionist view that all concepts come down to metaphors in the end, or that philosophy enjoys no distinctive status *vis-à-vis* literature, rhetoric or the human sciences at large. Derrida's purpose, in 'White Mythology', as Norris points out, is precisely to deny that we could simply turn the tables on philosophy (or reason) in the name of literature (as metaphor, rhetoric or style): not least because there is simply no possibility, for example, of discussing 'metaphor' without falling back on some concept of metaphor elaborated in advance by philosophical reason. Norris is rightly concerned to counter the widespread, but erroneous, supposition that due regard for the textual (or 'writely') aspects of our work – in itself a beneficial or rewarding perspective – necessarily 'writes off' (*sic*) the traditional concerns of philosophical discourse and reason.

As Norris argues, Deconstruction, properly understood, involves absolutely no slackening or suspension of the standards (logical consistency, conceptual rigour, modes of truth-conditional entailment, etc.) that properly determine what shall count as a genuine or valid philosophical argument. After all, as Derrida himself put it, in his debate with John Searle:

> the value of truth (and all those values associated with it) is never contested or destroyed in my writings, but only re-inscribed... in more powerful, larger, more stratified contexts... and within those contexts... it should be possible to invoke rules of competence, criteria of discussion and consensus, of good faith, lucidity, rigour, criticism and pedagogy. (Derrida, quoted in Norris, 1991: 156)

To put the matter more concretely, this is to argue that the epistemological and ethical difficulties raised by Clifford and others should not be allowed to disable our attempts to produce good accounts of 'what is going on' in various instances of media consumption but can, in fact, enrich our attempt to pursue that project. This is to say that we can recognize the importance of issues concerning the context of the encounter of representer and represented and the context of the writing of ethnography, and yet still conclude, with the late Bob Scholte, that 'while we may never know the whole truth, and may not have the literary means to tell all that we think we know of truth . . . shouldn't we nevertheless keep trying to tell it?' (Scholte, 1987: 39). To take this position is by no means to defend any naively 'naturalist' epistemology, but it is to argue that the importation of anthropology's 'literary turn', into cultural studies, for all its potential benefits, is also capable of producing a form of muddled relativism, which can then function to disable empirical research, by fiat.

Massey (1991) refers, in this connection, to Mascia-Lees et al.'s observation that 'when western white males – who traditionally have controlled the production of knowledge – can no longer define the truth . . . their response is to conclude that there is not a truth to be discovered' (Mascia-Lees et al., 1989: 15). The issue, as formulated by Hartsock (1987) is that:

> it seems highly suspicious that it is at this moment in history, when so many groups are engaged in 'nationalisms' which involve redefinitions of the marginalised others, that doubt arises in the academy about the possibilities for a general theory which can describe the world, about historical 'progress'. Why is it, exactly at the moment when so many of us who have been silenced, begin to demand the right to name ourselves, to act as subjects rather than objects of history, that just then, the concept of subjecthood becomes problematic . . . [that] . . . just when we are forming our own theories about the world, uncertainty emerges about whether the world can be adequately theorised? (Quoted in Massey, 1991: 33)

One (extreme) form of such disabling uncertainty (and relativism) is that developed by Hartley (1987) in his 'constructivist' account of the television audience as a 'fictional object'. Hartley argues that audiences may be 'imagined' empirically, theoretically or politically, but in all cases the product is a fiction that serves the needs of the imagining institution. The argument is that we must recognize the 'constructivist' character of the research process and drop any ideas of 'capturing' the television audience 'as it is', in its totality. From this perspective, the television audience does not so much constitute an empirical object as exhibit an imaginary status, a realm in which anxieties and expectations, aspirations and fantasies, as to the predicaments of modern society are condensed. Thus, Hartley argues that 'in no case is the audience "real" or external to its discursive construction. There is no "actual" audience that lies beyond its production as a category . . . audiences are only ever encountered . . . as representations' (Hartley, 1987: 125). This stress on the institutionalized discursive practices through which television audiences are constructed (for example, in Hartley's argument, the 'paedocratic discourse' through which the television audience is constituted by broadcasters) is of considerable value, as a corrective to any simple-minded 'naive realism' in the research process. However, it is possible to recognize the necessarily constructivist dimensions of any research process without claiming that audiences only exist discursively. To argue otherwise is to confuse a problem of epistemology with one of ontology. Naturally, any empirical knowledge which we may generate of television audiences will be constructed through particular discursive practices, and the categories and questions present and absent in those discourses will determine the nature of the knowledge we can generate. However, this is to argue, contra Hartley, that while we can only know audiences through discourses, audiences do in fact exist outside the terms of these discourses.

Both Tompkins (1986) and Fish (1989) have offered trenchant critiques of the over-blown claims often made on behalf of the kind of postmodern, Deconstructionist theories which have now achieved the status of orthodoxy within many areas of cultural studies. Such theories stress the (all) importance of perspectivism ('facts can only be known from some particular perspective') and textualism ('the world is a text capable of infinite interpretation'). The problem, as Tompkins formulates it, is that the effect of bringing 'perspectivism' to bear on a particular area of enquiry (history, in her example; cultural studies in the case I am concerned with) is, effectively, to wipe out its subject matter, and to leave nothing but a single idea: perspectivism itself. Tompkins's argument is that, as long as you think that there are (or could be) some kinds of facts that existed outside of any perspective, then the idea of 'perspectivism' will seem to 'annihilate' any particular fact to which it is applied. However, if one recognizes that there are no facts that are not embedded in some perspective on the world, then the argument that any particular set of facts derives from a perspective (or 'world-view'), no longer constitutes a problem. As she puts it, 'if all facts share this characteristic, to say that any one fact is perspectival doesn't change its factual nature in the slightest' (Tompkins, 1986: 76).

As she goes on to argue, this doesn't therefore mean that one needs to accept any old fact – any 'fact' may, of course, be demonstrated to be false – but it does mean that one is precluded from arguing that what x asserts to be a fact is not 'really' a fact, just because it is 'only' a product of their perspective – since this is, ex hypothesi, true of all facts and thus has no particular bearing on any individual fact. Tompkins thus notes that, while the self-reflexive awareness that all facts are situated within interpretative frameworks is useful when discussing historiography, it has literally no bearing on the facts of any particular case. Her conclusion is heretical, as far as cultural studies' emergent epistemological orthodoxy is concerned: 'what this means is that arguments about "what happened" [in some particular case – D.M.] have to proceed much as they did before post-structuralism broke in, with all its talk about language-based reality and culturally produced knowledge. Reasons must be given, evidence adduced, authorities cited, analogies drawn' (Tompkins, 1986: 76).

For Fish, the key problem facing 'textualist' work in history is how to resolve the logical difficulties that follow from the 'assertion of wall to wall textuality' (Fish, 1989: 303) and the assertion that 'there is no such thing as history in the sense of a referential ground of knowledge' (Hunt, quoted in ibid.: 305). As Fish notes, this (in parallel with Hartley's argument) is to deny that the writing of history could ever 'find its foundation in a substratum of unmediated fact' and the problem is then how to reconcile this radical textualism with the attempt to say anything in particular about a given historical event. As he puts it, 'if you think *that* about history, how can you, without contradiction, make historical assertions?' How can one both 'recognise the provisionality and multiplicity of local knowledge' and yet 'maintain that it is possible to give true accounts of a real world?' (ibid.: 305). How can you at once 'assert the textuality of history and make specific and positive historical arguments?' (ibid.: 307).

Fish's answer to the last of these questions is that it is perfectly possible to square the circle here, as soon as one recognizes that asserting the textuality of history and making specific historical arguments have nothing to do with one another, in so far as they are actions in different practices. As he puts it 'the first is an action in the practice of producing general (i.e. metacritical) accounts of history, the practice of answering such questions as…"what is the nature of historical fact?" The second is an action in the practice of writing historical accounts (as opposed to writing an account of how historical accounts get written), the practice of answering questions such as "what happened?"' (ibid.: 307). In parallel with Tompkins's argument, Fish holds that, as the belief that facts are constructed is a general one and is not held with reference to any facts in particular, 'the conviction of the textuality of fact is logically independent of the firmness with which any particular fact is experienced' (ibid.: 308).

Fish's disarming conclusion is that the long road through discourse theory and textualism, in the end, leaves us 'precisely where we always have been', having to make empirical claims 'with reference to evidence, marshalled in support of hypotheses that will be more or less convincing to a body of professional peers' (ibid.: 309), rather than 'brandish[ing] fancy accounts of how evidence comes to be evidence or invok[ing] theories that declare all evidence suspect and ideological', because, as Fish notes, that would be 'another practice, the practice not of giving historical accounts, but the practice of theorising their possibility' (ibid.: 313). Here Fish comes close to Geertz's position, in the debate with Clifford and Marcus, where Geertz notes that, if the traditional anthropological attitude to these theoretical questions ('Don't think about ethnography, just do it') is a problem, nonetheless, to fall (as many would-be postmodern ethnographers have done) into a paralysing (if vertiginously thrilling) trance of 'epistemological nervousness' ('don't do ethnography, just think about it') is no kind of answer. What is needed in this respect, as Haraway puts it, is 'an account of radical historical contingency for all knowledge claims and knowing subjects, a critical practice for recognising our own "semiotic technologies" for making meanings, *and* a no-nonsense commitment to faithful accounts of a "real" world' (Haraway, 1991: 187) – a recognition that the object of our would-be knowledge, while being really 'made up' is nonetheless 'real' for that.

To recap the argument, by the way of conclusion, my concern in this piece has been with the destabilization of two associated theoretical orthodoxies, one concerning the status of the 'active audience' model of media consumption, the other concerning the methodological and epistemological commitments to self-reflexivity and relativism/constructivism, which have come to be widely influential within the field of cultural studies in recent years. My argument has been, in the former case, that some within cultural studies do seem to me to have moved into an unhelpful romanticization of 'consumer freedoms' which forgets the very question of cultural power with which our investigations (or mine, anyway) began. Conversely, I am equally critical of the born-again political economist/sociologists of culture (as manifested, for example, by some of the recent writings of Nicholas Garnham) who seize upon some of the wilder examples of 'active audience theory' to discredit retrospectively the whole enterprise of cultural studies, on the grounds that they always said it would lead to tears. In relation to the case of the methodological/epistemological orthodoxies which I have identified, clustered around the pole of relativism/self-reflexivity, my argument has been that the seeming contemporary 'closure' of these debates in cultural studies around a set of relativist 'certainties' (*sic*), and the widespread presumption of the epistemological correctness (and political effectivity) of these currently fashionable positions is, to say the least, ill advised. As I have argued, these positions themselves display significant epistemological and political deficiencies, to which we must attend. To return, in conclusion, to my earlier arguments, if we need to take care both to avoid some of the unproductive excesses of 'active audience theory', and to reconsider our conception of the relation of micro and macro processes, and if our ethnographic accounts of various forms of media consumption are necessarily themselves texts, which must be looked at (as rhetorical constructions), as well as looked through (to such truths as they can reveal), nonetheless, our ultimate ambition must surely still be to develop ethnographies which will, as Geertz (1973: 3–30) famously put it, sort the winks from the twitches (ibid.: 6).

References

Abercrombie, N. S. and B. S. Turner (1984), *The Dominant Ideology Thesis*, 2nd edition. London: George Allen and Unwin.

Althusser, L. (1971), *Lenin and Philosophy and Other Essays*. London: New Left Books.

Ang, I. (1985), *Watching Dallas*. London: Routledge.

Ang, I. (1990), 'Culture and communication: towards an ethnographic critique of media consumption in the transnational media system', *European Journal of Communication* 5(2): 239–60.

Ang, I. (1991), *Desperately Seeking the Audience*. London: Routledge.

Ang, I and J. Hermes (1991), 'Gender and/in media consumption', pp. 307–29 in J. Curran and M. Gurevitch (eds.), *Mass Media and Society*. London: Edward Arnold.

Barrett, M. (1992), 'Words and things: materialism and method in contemporary feminist analysis', pp. 201–20 (261–79) in M. Barrett and A. Phillips (eds.), *Destabilizing Theory: Contemporary Feminist Debates*. Oxford: Polity Press.

Borges, J. L. (1972), 'Of exactitude in science', p. 141 in J. L. Borges, *Universal of History*. London: Allen Lane.

Budd, B. R. Entman and C. Steinman (1990), 'The affirmation character of American cultural studies', *Critical Studies in Mass Communication* 7(2): 169–84.

Clifford, J. (1986), 'Partial truths', pp. 1–27 in J. Clifford and G. Marcus (eds.), *Writing Culture: The Poetics and Politics of Ethnography*. Berkeley, CA: University of California Press.

Clifford, J. and G. Marcus (eds.) (1986), *Writing Culture: The Poetics and Politics of Ethnography*. Berkeley, CA: University of California Press.

Condit, C. M. (1989), 'The rhetorical limits of polysemy', *Critical Studies in Mass Communication* 6(2): 103–22.

Corner, J. (1991), 'Meaning, genre and context: the problematics of public knowledge in the new audience studies', pp. 267–85 in J. Curran and M. Gurevitch (eds.), *Mass Media and Society*. London: Edward Arnold.

Curran, J. (1990), 'The new revisionism in mass communication research: A reappraisal', *European Journal of Communication* 5(2/3): 135–64.

de Certeau, M. (1984), *The Practice of Everyday Life*. Berkeley, CA: University of California Press.

Derrida, J. (1974), 'White mythology', *New Literary History* 6(1): 7–74.

Derrida, J. (1989), *Limited Inc*, 2nd edition. Evanston, IL: Northwestern University Press.

Durham, J. (1993), *A Certain Lack of Coherence: Writings on Art and Cultural Politics*. London: Kala Press.

Evans, W. (1990), 'The interpretive turn in media research', *Critical Studies in Mass Communication* 7(2): 145–68.

Fabian, J. (1990), 'Presence and representation: the other and anthropological writing', *Critical Inquiry* 19(4): 753–72.

Fish, S. E. (1989), 'The young and the restless', pp. 303–17 in H. A. Veeser (ed.), *The New Historicism*. London: Routledge.

Fiske, J. (1990a), *Introduction to Cultural Studies*, 2nd edition. London: Routledge.

Fiske, J. (1990b), 'Ethnosemiotics', *Cultural Studies* 4(1): 85–100.

Frith, S. (1991), 'The good, the bad and the indifferent: defending popular culture from the populists', *Diacritics* 21(4): 102–15.

Geertz, C. (1973), *The Interpretation of Cultures*. New York: Basic Books.

Geertz, C. (1988), *Works and Lives*. Cambridge: Polity Press.

Gellner, E. (1970), 'Concepts and society', pp. 18–50 in B. Wilson (ed.), *Rationality*. Oxford: Blackwell.

Gellner, E. (1992), *Postmodernism, Reason and Religion*. London: Routledge.

Gewertz, D. and F. Errington (1991), 'We think therefore they are? On occidentalising the world', *Anthropological Quarterly* 64(2): 80–91.

Gray, A. (1992), *Video Play Time: The Gendering of a Leisure Technology*. London: Comedia/Routledge.

Grossberg, L. (1988), 'Wandering audiences, nomadic critics', *Cultural Studies* 2(3): 377–92.

Hall, S. (1977), 'Culture, the media and the ideological effect', pp. 315–48 in J. Curran, M. Gurevitch and J. Woollacott (eds.), *Mass Communication and Society*. London: Edward Arnold.

Hall, S. (1980), 'Encoding/decoding', pp. 128–38 in S. Hall, D. Hobson, A. Lowe and P. Willis (eds.), *Culture, Media, Language*. London: Hutchinson.

Hall, S. (1988), 'Introductory address', International Television Studies Conference, London, July.

Hall, S. (1990), 'Cultural studies: now and in the future', paper presented to conference of that name. University of Illinois, April 1990; repr. in L. Grossberg, C. Nelson and P. A. Treichler (eds.) (1992), *Cultural Studies*. New York: Routledge.

Hamer, M. (1989), 'Review of Clifford Geertz's *Works and Lives*', *Textual Practice* 3(3): 456–9.

Haraway, D. (1991), *Simians, Cyborgs and Women*. London: Free Association Books.

Harris, D. (1992), *From Class Struggle to the Politics of Pleasure: The Effects of Gramscianism on Cultural Studies*. London: Routledge.

Hartsock, N. (1987), cited in Massey, 'Rethinking modernism', *Cultural Critique* 7: 187–206.

Hartley, J. (1987), 'Television audiences, paedocracy and pleasure', *Textual Practice* 1(2): 121–38.

Knorr-Cetina, K. (1981), 'Introduction: the micro-sociological challenge of macro-sociology', pp. 1–47 in K. Knorr-Cetina and A. Cicourel (eds.), *Advances in Social Theory and Methodology*. London: Routledge.

Lacan, J. (1977), *Ecrits*. London: Tavistock.

Liebes, T. and E. Katz (1990), *The Export of Meaning*. New York/Oxford: Oxford University Press.

Lull, J. (1987), 'Audience texts and contexts', *Critical Studies in Mass Communication* 4(3): 318–22.

Marcus, G. (1986), 'Contemporary problems of ethnography in the world system', pp. 165–93 in J. Clifford and G. Marcus (eds.), *Writing Culture: The Poetics and Politics of Ethnography*. Berkeley, CA: University of California Press.

Marcus, G. and M. Fisher (1986), *Anthropology as Cultural Critique*. Chicago: University of Chicago Press.

Martín-Barbero, J. (1988), 'Communication from culture', *Media, Culture and Society* 10(4): 447–65.

Massey, D. (1991), 'Flexible sexism', *Environment and Planning D: Society and Space* 9(1): 31–57.

McGuigan, J. (1992), *Cultural Populism*. London: Routledge.

Miller, D. (1992), '*The Young and the Restless* in Trinidad: a case study of the local and the global in mass consumption', pp. 163–82 in R. Silverstone and E. Hirsch (eds.), *Consuming Technologies*. London: Routledge.

Minh-Ha, T. T. (1989), *Woman, Native, Other*. Bloomington: Indiana University Press.

Morley, D. (1980), *The 'Nationwide' Audience: Structure and Decoding*. London British Film Institute.

Morley, D. (1986), *Family Television: Cultural Power and Domestic Leisure*. London: Comedia.

Morley, D. (1992), *Television Audiences and Cultural Studies*. London: Routledge.

Murdock, G. (1989), 'Cultural studies: missing links', *Critical Studies in Mass Communications* 6(4): 436–40.

Murdock, G. and P. Golding (1974), 'For a political economy of mass communications', pp. 205–34 in R. Milband and J. Saville (eds.), *The Socialist Register 1973*. London: Merlin Press.

Newcomb, H. and P. Hirsch (1987), 'Television as a cultural forum', pp. 455–71 in H. Newcomb (ed.), *Television: The Critical View*, 4th edition. Oxford: Oxford University Press.

Norris, C. (1991), *Deconstruction: Theory and Practice*, rev. edition. London: Routledge.

Pool R. (1991), 'Postmodern ethnography', *Critique of Anthropology* 11(4): 309–31.

Probyn, E. (1993), *Sexing the Self: Gendered Positions in Cultural Studies*. London: Routledge.

Radway, J. (1984), *Reading the Romance: Women, Patriarchy and Popular Literature*. Chapel Hill: University of North Carolina Press.

Richards, I. (1960), 'Variant readings and misreadings', pp. 241–53 in T. Sebeok (ed.), *Style in Language*. Cambridge, MA: MIT Press.

Rorty, R. (1978), 'Philosophy as a kind of writing', *New Literary History* 10: 141–60.

Rorty, R. (1989), *Contingency, Irony and Solidarity*. Cambridge: Cambridge University Press.

Said, E. (1979), *Orientalism*. Harmondsworth: Penguin.

Scholte, R. (1987), 'The literary turn in contemporary anthropology', *Critique of Anthropology* 7(1): 33–47.

Seamann, W. R. (1992), 'Active audience theory: pointless populism', *Media, Culture and Society* 14(2): 301–11.

Silverstone, R. and D. Morley (1990), 'Domestic communication: technologies and meanings', *Media, Culture and Society* 12(1): 31–56.

Tompkins, J. (1986), 'Indians: textualism, morality and the problem of history', pp. 59–78 in H. L. Gates (ed.), *'Race', Writing and Difference*. Chicago: Chicago University Press.

Ullin, R. (1991), 'Critical anthropology twenty years later', *Critique of Anthropology* 11(1): 63–89.

Walby, S. (1992), 'Post-post-modernism? Theorising social complexity', pp. 31–52 in M. Barrett and A. Phillips (eds.), *Destabilising Theory*. Cambridge: Polity Press.

Willis, P. (1977), *Learning to Labor*. Farnborough, UK: Saxon House.

Winch, P. (1958), *The Idea of a Social Science*. London: Routledge and Kegan Paul.

Wright-Mills, C. (1959), *The Sociological Imagination*. London: Oxford University Press.

CHAPTER 12

Disney, Southern Baptists, and Children's Culture: The Magic Kingdom as Sodom and Gomorrah?

Henry A. Giroux

The Southern Baptist Convention in June generated a lot of media attention when it called for a boycott of the Disney Company for promoting "immoral ideologies such as homosexuality." The Southern Baptists were angry because Disney sponsors "Gay Days" at its theme parks, provides health benefits to the domestic partners of gay employees, and publishes books about growing up gay. According to Herb Hilliger, a convention spokesperson, the last straw came in April [1997] when the lead character of the sitcom *Ellen* had the audacity to come out as a lesbian on the Disney-owned ABC.

The Baptists got it right in assuming that something was amiss in Disney's image as an icon of clean childhood fun and healthy family entertainment. Unfortunately, the Southern Baptists got it wrong in attempting to dismantle Disney's pristine image of innocence and good will. The attack on Disney's pro-gay policies suggests not only how widespread gay bashing by the right wing has become in this country but also how gay-friendly policies, in this case, have been appropriated to reinforce Disney's corporate identity as a model of social and civic responsibility. Against the Southern Baptists' retrograde homophobic demands, the land of the Magic Kingdom actually looked progressive – even though Disney was one of the last studios to extend health benefits to same-sex partners. Disney should not be condemned because it refuses to endorse homophobic practices in its labor operations and television programming, but because its pretense to innocence camouflages a powerful cultural force and corporate monolith – in Eric Smoodin's words "a kind of Tennessee Valley Authority of leisure and entertainment" – that commodifies culture, sanitizes historical memory, and constructs children's identities exclusively within the ideology of consumerism.

Far from being a model of moral leadership and social responsibility, Disney monopolizes media power, limits the free flow of information, and undermines substantive public debate. In doing so, it corporatizes public space and limits the avenues of public expression and choice. Disney does not have the power to launch armies, dismantle the welfare state, or eliminate basic social programs for children. On the contrary, Disney's influence

Henry A. Giroux, "Disney, Southern Baptists, and Children's Culture: The Magic Kingdom as Sodom and Gomorrah?" *Z Magazine* (Sept. 1997). Reprinted by permission of the author.

is more subtle and pervasive in its ability to shape public consciousness in its own image through its enormous economic holdings and cultural power. Michael Orvitz, a former Disney executive, was right when he claimed that Disney is not a company but a "nation state" exercising vast influence over global constituencies. Influencing large facets of cultural life, Disney ranks 48th in the Forbes 500 and controls ABC Network News, numerous TV and cable stations, 5 motion picture studios, 429 Disney stores, multimedia companies, and 2 major publishing houses. In 1996, Disney pulled in a record $21 billion in revenues from all of its divisions. Not content to peddle conservative ideologies, it now provides prototypes for developing American culture and civility, including a model town aptly called "Celebration," a prototype school system, and the Disney Institute where it offers the intellectually curious vacations organized around learning educational skills in gardening, radio and television production, cinema studies, and a wide range of fitness programs and cooking classes.

As one of the most powerful media conglomerates in the world, Disney works endlessly to promote cultural homogeneity and political conformity while waging an ongoing battle against those individuals and groups who believe that central to democratic public life is the necessity of democratizing cultural institutions, including those of the mass media. Extravagant feature-length animated films, theme parks, and the Dysnification of West 42nd Street certainly may have entertainment and educational value, but they cannot be used as a defense for Disney's strangulating hold on the message and image business, its stifling of unpopular opinions and dissent, or its relentless corporatizing of civic discourse – all of which undermine cultural and political life in a vibrant democratic society.

Disney's threat to civic life comes from its role as a major communications industry capable of exercising harmful and damaging amounts of corporate power and ideological influence over vast segments of the American cultural landscape. In the Magic Kingdom, choice is about consumption, justice is rarely seen as the outcome of social struggles, and history is framed nostalgically in the benevolent, patriarchal image of Walt Disney. In the animated world of Disney's films, monarchies replace democracy as the preferred forms of government, people of color are cast as either barbarous or stupid, and young Kate Moss-like waifs such as Pocahontas or Megasus in *Hercules* reaffirm the worst kind of gender divisions and stereotypes.

Disney does more than spread its regressive, sanitized, corporate culture across North America and the far corners of the globe. More insidiously, it shamelessly uses its much-touted commitment to wholesome entertainment to market an endless array of toys, clothes, and gadgets to children. Beneath Disney's self-proclaimed role as an icon of American culture lies a powerful educational apparatus that provides ideologically loaded fantasies for children and adults alike. Walt Disney Imagineers have little to do with "dreaming" a better world, or even commenting on the world that today's kids actually inhabit. On the contrary, fantasy for Disney has no basis in reality, no sense of real conflicts, struggles, joys, and social relations. Fantasy becomes a marketing device, a form of hype rooted in the logic of self interest and buying. Disney's view of children as consumers has little to do with innocence and a great deal to do with corporate greed and the realization that behind the vocabulary of family fun and wholesome entertainment is the opportunity for teaching children that critical thinking and civic action in society are far less important for them than assuming the role of passive consumers. Eager to reach children under 12, "who shell out $17 billion a year in gift and allowance income and influence $172 billion more spent by their parents," Disney relies on consultants such as marketing researcher, James McNeal, to tap into such a market. McNeal can barely contain his enthusiasm in targeting children as a fertile market and argues in *Kids as Customers* that the "world is poised on the threshold of a new era in marketing and that ... fairly standardized multinational marketing strategies to children around the globe are viable."

In its search for new markets and greater profits, Disney consistently and inventively finds ways of presenting its films, theme parks, and entertainment offerings as objects of consumption rather than spheres of participation. Art in the Magic Kingdom becomes a spectacle designed to create new markets, commodify children, and provide vehicles for merchandizing its endless array of toys, gadgets, clothes, home accessories and other commodities. Disney's ability to use films and other forms of children's entertainment as launching pads for a vast array of toys can be seen in how films such as *The Lion King*, *Pocahontas*, and more recently, *Hercules*, are used as a pretext to convert J. C. Penny, Toys R Us, McDonald's, and numerous other retailers into Disney merchandising outlets. But the real commercial blitz will be centered in Disney's own marketing and distribution network which includes the Disney Store, the Disney Channel, *Disney* magazine, Disneyland, and Walt Disney World.

Given the recent media attention on the exploitation of children and young adults – over the use of heroin chic in the fashion industry, the sexualization of young girls in the world of high powered models, and the eroticization of 6-year-olds in children's beauty pageants – it is surprising that there is little public outcry over the baleful influence Disney exercises on children. The Southern Baptists and the general public appear indifferent to Disney's role in securing children's desires and needs to the lure of an endless chain of commodities while convincing them that the only viable public space left in which to experience themselves as agents is in the toy sections of Wal-Mart or the local Disney Store.

Disney's role as the arbiter of children's culture may seem abstract when expressed in these terms, but in the aftermath of the promotional blitz for Disney's new animated film, *Hercules*, the mix of educational strategy and greed was brought home to me with great force. My three boys were watching television news clips of the Disney parade in New York City and were in awe that Disney could hold an extravaganza capable of tying up 30 city blocks while pulling out every stop in the glitzy grab bag of pomp and spectacle. Of course, they couldn't wait to see the film, buy the spinoff toys, and be the first on their block to wear a *Hercules* pin. "Pin? What Pin I asked?" I hadn't watched the promotional ad carefully enough. It seems that Disney was providing a special showing of the film, *Hercules*, a few weeks before its general release. But to get a ticket for the special showing, parents had to go to an authorized Disney store to buy a box for $7.00 which contained a ticket, a collector's pin of one of the characters in the film, a brochure, and a tape of a song from the movie, sung by Michael Bolton. Disney made sure that every kid, including my own, knew that with the film came the inevitable flow of stuffed animals, figurines, backpacks, lunchboxes, tapes, videos, and a host of other gadgets soon to be distributed by Mattel, Timex, Golden Books, and other manufacturers of children's culture.

Disney appears ignominious in its attempt to turn the film hero, Hercules, into an advertisement for spin off merchandise. Once Hercules proves himself through a series of brave deeds, Disney turns him into a public relations hero with a marketable trade name for products such as "Air Hercules" sneakers, toy figurines, and action-hero dolls, all of which can be bought in an emporium modeled shamelessly in the film after a Disney Store. Disney executive, Tom Schumacher, claims the film is about building character, pop culture, and what it means to be a celebrity. Character in the land of the Walt Disney Imagineers appears to have nothing to do with integrity. *Hercules* suggests that the Disney dream factory is less a guardian of childhood innocence than a predatory corporation that views children's imaginations as simply another resource for amassing earnings.

What strategies are open to educators, parents, and others who want to challenge the corporate barons shaping children's culture in the United States? First, as a globe-trotting corporation, Disney's economic and political power must be acknowledged for the threat it poses to both children's culture and public life in general. Secondly, battles must be waged to dismantle its control and ownership of large segments of the communications industry. Media critics such as Mark Crispin Miller are right in arguing that such monopolies represent a political and cultural toxin and that their hold must be broken through the creation of broad-based movements dedicated to a wide variety of strategies, including public announcement campaigns, sit-ins, teach ins, and boycotts that would raise public consciousness and promote antitrust legislation aimed at breaking up media monopolies and ownership while promoting economic and cultural democracy. In this instance, Disney must be challenged for the threat it poses in creating the specter of a national entertainment state and for exercising unchecked corporate power within what Eyal Press rightly calls "the injustices of an unregulated global economy."

Thirdly, the time has come to challenge Disney's self-proclaimed role as a medium of "pure entertainment" and take seriously Disney's educational role in producing ideologic-ally loaded fantasies aimed at teaching children selective roles, values, and cultural ideals. Progressive educators and other cultural workers need to pay closer attention to how the pedagogical practices produced and circulated by Disney and other mass media conglom-erates organize and control a circuit of power that extends from producing cultural texts to shaping the contexts in which they will be taken up by children and others. Disney's attempt to control the field of social meanings available to children provides a particular challenge to progressives in making visible the political, economic, and educational apparatuses Disney uses to produce cultural texts as well as the pedagogical practices involved in making such texts meaningful to diverse groups of children and adults. What is at stake here is the necessity for all those concerned about democracy to engage critically how pedagogy becomes central to cultural politics, and how companies such as Disney promote diverse forms of cultural pedagogy as a type of political practice that often works to restrict the capacities of kids to think critically, move beyond the borders of corporate consumerism, and take seriously their roles as critical social agents.

Finally, as a principal producer of popular culture Disney's films, television programs, newscasts, and other forms of entertainment should become serious objects of critical analysis, understanding, and intervention both in and outside of schools. It is almost commonplace to acknowledge that most of what students learn today is not in the classrooms of public schools, or for that matter in the classrooms of higher education, but in the electronically generated media spheres. Consequently, students need to acquire the knowledge and skills to become literate in multiple symbolic forms – so as to be able to read critically the various types of cultural texts to which they are exposed. This is not meant to suggest that we should junk the canon for Disney studies as much as refashion what it is that students learn in relation to how their identities are shaped outside of academic life. Students need to learn multiple literacies and focus on diverse spheres of learning. The issue of what is valuable knowledge is not reducible to the tired either/or culture wars arguments that pervade the academy. Maybe the more interesting questions point in different directions: what is it that students need to learn to live in a substantive democracy, read critically in various spheres of culture, engage those critical traditions of the past that continue to shape how we think about the present and the future, and engage multiple texts for the wisdom they provide and the maps they offer us to live in a world that is more multicultural, diverse, and democratic?

Students also need to learn how to produce their own newspapers, records, television programs, videos, and whatever other technology is necessary to link knowledge and power, pleasure and the demands of public life. Disney got its eye muddied a few years ago when its attempts to create a theme park on an historical Virginia landmark was successfully resisted by active citizens. The Southern Baptists, because of their own prejudice against gays and lesbians, were incapable of seeing that the real threat that Disney poses is not to fulfilling the demands of the gay and lesbian communities, but to the imperatives of democracy and to those children who are essential to carry on its traditions and fulfill its unfinished business. Maybe they should take their kids to a Disney store, reassemble again, and take another vote.

CHAPTER 13

Jennifer David

Seeing Ourselves, Being Ourselves: Broadcasting Aboriginal Television in Canada

Imagine waking up one morning to discover you can no longer understand the world around you. Imagine turning on the radio or the television, only to hear the news reported in a foreign language. Imagine hearing your children suddenly speak a strange tongue. Imagine your friends and colleagues discussing issues and events you know nothing about. Imagine trying to communicate. Imagine how disorienting, frustrating, and isolating this would be. This sense of isolation and disorientation was far from imaginary for aboriginal people in northern Canada who found themselves inundated with Southern, non-aboriginal television programming in the 1970s. New foreign services began to erode languages and cultures that had survived for centuries.

Though the North was geographically isolated, aboriginal people were connected by language and culture. With the introduction of Southern television programming, suddenly they were also culturally and linguistically isolated. To alleviate this isolation, northern aboriginal people joined together and established an aboriginal owned and operated television network called Television Northern Canada (TVNC). TVNC is now expanding into a network by and about aboriginal people across Canada, not just northern Canada. While it is an exciting time for aboriginal broadcasting in Canada, it has been a long uphill struggle.

An idea born of need

Satellite television was introduced to the North in 1974 after the federal government approved an Accelerated Coverage Plan (ACP). The ACP was designed to bring Canada's national broadcaster, the Canadian Broadcasting Corporation (CBC), to underserved and remote regions of Canada. This had an immediate effect on the language and cultures of northern aboriginal people. Debbie Brisebois, in an essay entitled "Whiteout Warning," retells the story of one Inuit woman who described her reaction to watching the TV program 'All in the Family,' and the character Archie Bunker, for the first time:

Jennifer David, "Seeing Ourselves, Being Ourselves: Broadcasting Aboriginal Television in Canada," *Cultural Survival Quarterly* (Summer 1998), pp. 36–9.

There was the father, obviously a stupid man, screaming at his children and his wife. He seemed to hate them. They were lying to him, they were treating him with contempt, they were screaming back at him...and then in the last five minutes everyone kissed and made up...We were always taught to treat our elders with respect. I was embarrassed for those people on TV. I thought, I always knew white people were weird. I wondered if that was really what people were like in the South.

Many aboriginal people protested this 'invasion' of foreign television services. In 1982, the regulatory body for all broadcasting and telecommunications undertakings, the Canadian Radio-Television Telecommunications Commission (CRTC), scheduled a hearing looking into Cable Tiering and Universal Pay TV. Rosemary Kuptana, then a production coordinator for the Inuit Broadcasting Corporation (IBC), likened the foreign programming to an atomic or neutron bomb:

This is the bomb that kills the people but leaves the buildings standing. Neutron-bomb television is the kind of television that destroys the soul of a people, but leaves the shell of a people walking around. This is television in which the traditions, the skills, the culture, the language,-count for nothing. The pressure, especially on our children, to join the invading culture and language and leave behind the language and culture that count for nothing is explosively powerful.

But rather than sit idly by and let foreign television services jeopardize their way of life, a group of concerned Inuit leaders took matters into their own hands. In order to counter the proliferation of Southern, non-aboriginal programming, aboriginal people would have to begin producing their own programs, in their own languages, about their own culture and traditions.

Coordinated by the Inuit Tapirisat of Canada, an umbrella organization for Canadian Inuit, and funded by the federal government, two interactive satellite broadcasting experiments were conducted in the late 1970s. The first was called the INUKSHUK Project. It enabled Inuit in the eastern Arctic (soon to be a new territory named Nunavut), to produce local, Inuktitut-language television programs. These programs were broadcast via satellite for 16.5 hours per day for eight months. It was a huge success. A second project called NAALAKVIK II experienced similar success in both video conference and broadcasting to five Inuit communities in northern Quebec. As stated in a report issued by the Inuit Broadcasting Corporation (IBC), the time had come for aboriginal broadcasting. "INUKSHUK and NAALAKVIK II made clear the need for an Inuit controlled and operated television service and demonstrated...that aboriginal people could adapt sophisticated technology to meet their communication needs."

Following these successful trials and seeking to hear from all Canadians on extending services in the North, the CRTC established a committee. This committee issued the Therrien report in July, 1980 that endorsed the use of broadcasting among aboriginal peoples as a way to preserve and enhance aboriginal language and culture. In 1981, the CRTC granted a broadcast license to IBC and Taqramiut Nipingat Incorporated, two Inuit television programming services.

The next big step for aboriginal communications organizations was the establishment of Northern Native Broadcast Access Program. This Program was a 4-year, $40 million fund dedicated to the development of aboriginal radio and television programming in the North.

The difficulties of ensuring fair access

New aboriginal communications societies began producing quality programming in a number of aboriginal languages across the North. By 1983, there were 13 groups providing valuable cultural programming. But a new difficulty soon arose; although aboriginal broadcasters had production funding, they had no means of ensuring consistent distribution of their programs. At the time, the only available broadcaster was CBC. All programs from the aboriginal producers had to be broadcast during time slots provided by CBC Northern Service. This seriously limited the availability of and access to aboriginal programming within the schedule. IBC programs, including children's programming, were often scheduled after 11 p.m. or were pre-empted if CBC required that time slot. Aboriginal producers knew the only solution was to establish a dedicated satellite television channel. Once again, the aboriginal broadcasters took their concerns to the CRTC and the federal government.

The CRTC responded by setting up an action committee. Aboriginal broadcasters also voiced their concerns with the Federal Task Force on Broadcasting Policy in 1986. This task force made a number of recommendations, including the need for aboriginal broadcasting to be considered an integral part of the Canadian broadcasting system. It also recommended the creation of a separate satellite distribution system to carry aboriginal language programming. The tide was beginning to turn.

With these positive recommendations, six aboriginal communications societies, the CBC, and territorial governments met to begin creating an aboriginal distribution system for northern Canada. This system came to be known as Television Northern Canada. Armed with a detailed study on the need for such a network, the consortium presented their initiative to the federal government. In June, 1988, the government decided to commit $10 million over four years to establish a satellite-delivered, northern, aboriginal, distribution system. It was the beginning of TVNC.

A dream is born – Television Northern Canada

After a number of years of preparation, further studies, and negotiations with the government, private, and public sectors, TVNC went on the air for the first time in January, 1992. It was seen and heard in 96 northern communities, across an area one-third the size of Canada's land mass. There were children's programs, current affairs, documentaries, live phone-in programs, and other special events. TVNC broadcasts programs in English, French, and more than a dozen aboriginal languages. TVNC became an enormous Northern success story.

Moving towards a truly national aboriginal network

Today, TVNC continues to provide a valuable service of northern, aboriginal programming. In June, 1997, however, the TVNC Board of Directors decided to embark on a new path, a path that would lead to the creation of a truly national aboriginal television network seen by all Canadians across the country. At its annual meeting, the TVNC Board of Directors decided it was time to transform from a northern-based network into a national network. There were several reasons for this, the first was that the federal government had been consistently reducing its contribution to TVNC, making it more difficult to continue providing a quality service. In early 1997, the federal government announced it would cut funding to TVNC by 30 percent by 1998. This made it imperative for TVNC to find alternative sources of funding to survive.

The second reason TVNC decided to expand south was to work with southern aboriginal producers. In the 1980s, when TVNC was being formed, the federal government had stated its intention to work with southern aboriginal producers in the same way it was working with northern producers. The government would research the need for funding and distribution of southern aboriginal programs. That research never materialized. By 1997, it was clear that southern aboriginal producers were in the same situation as northern producers were in the late 1980s: they produced valuable programs, but had no consistent distribution system. TVNC began showcasing a number of southern aboriginal productions on the northern network. They have now become a mainstay within the TVNC northern schedule. The unfortunate reality, however, is because TVNC is only broadcast across northern Canada, the programming cannot be seen by the very producers who work so hard to create it.

Since June, 1997, TVNC has been slowly moving towards greater southern distribution of the network. TVNC has negotiated with a number of small, southern cable systems to begin carrying TVNC. TVNC is also negotiating with a number of Direct-to-Home (DTH) satellite distribution undertakings to ensure TVNC is included in packages to DTH viewers.

The most important initiative, however, was TVNC's appearance at a CRTC hearing in November, 1997 to discuss Third National Networks. The CRTC issued a call for comment in June to ask broadcasters, producers, and interested individuals if the CRTC should license a third national network. The CBC and CTV are the only two networks currently recognized as national networks in Canada.

TVNC made its presentation and reminded the Commission of TVNC's unique place in the broadcasting system. It was pointed out that TVNC currently holds a national license, but is not formally recognized as a national network on par with CBC and CTV. TVNC outlined its initiative to transform into a network by and about aboriginal people from across Canada, not just northern Canada. Next, it stated the ways in which it meets the objectives of the Broadcasting Act – a requirement for all national networks. TVNC is a public network, owned and controlled by Canadians, it provides a public service "essential to the enhancement of national identity and cultural sovereignty" by offering a window to the aboriginal world, helps to safeguard and strengthen the fabric of Canada by ensuring aboriginal people have a voice in the media, and fills the need for "programming that reflects the aboriginal cultures of Canada [that] should be provided within the Canadian broadcasting system" as stated by the Broadcasting Act.

During this meeting, TVNC also discussed the positive aspects of a national aboriginal television network which include: jobs for aboriginal people in the communities; role models for aboriginal youth; access to the national media; counteracting negative stereotypes that often exist about aboriginal people; opportunities for aboriginal people to tell their own stories; awards and funds for exceptional aboriginal programming; and strengthening and enhancing aboriginal language and culture. The underlying argument in all the discussions, however, centered on the desire for aboriginal self-determination. TVNC insisted that there can be no self-determination if aboriginal people have no voice with which to communicate their views of the world around them and the issues that affect them. If aboriginal people have control over how their stories are communicated, they are well on their way towards shaping their own futures.

The CRTC issued its report from this hearing in early February, 1998 which contained very good news for TVNC. The CRTC report stated that "TVNC is a unique and significant service . . . and should be widely available throughout Canada." The CRTC also added that it would be willing to accept an application from TVNC that would "reflect the diversity of the needs and interests of aboriginal peoples throughout Canada."

TVNC considered this a very positive sign and a written application will be completed and submitted to the CRTC in June, 1998. If TVNC is successful, a new, national aboriginal television network could be available to all Canadians as early as fall, 1999. TVNC would be the world's first public, national aboriginal network and there would be much to celebrate.

Angus Reid, a well-respected polling firm in Canada, conducted a survey for TVNC in January, 1998, which indicated that two out of three Canadians would support an aboriginal network, even if it replaced an existing service. Further results indicated nearly 50 percent of those surveyed would watch the network at least every few weeks and almost 10 percent would watch every day. There is certainly a desire among non-aboriginal people in Canada that this network could fulfill.

Aboriginal television producers in Canada have come a long way since the early INUKSHUK project and even earlier, when aboriginal people began experimenting with film. Aboriginal people now have the opportunity to take a technology that could have destroyed their centuries-old way of life and transform it into a tool that enhances their language and culture. Canadian aboriginal people may finally have the chance to use their own voices to tell their ancient histories, songs, and dances. Culture and language will be revived. Children will discover and emulate aboriginal superheros. And all aboriginal people will stand tall and take pride in their heritage. We will share with the world our strength, our wisdom, our struggles, our joys.

The day when aborignal people living in Canada will turn on their televisions and see themselves reflected back through the programming on a national aboriginal network may not be far away. When that day comes, sit down and watch, share it with your children and your children's children, and rejoice.

References

January 1995. *Northern Native Broadcasting: A Policy Survey.* Consilium Consulting.

Television Northern Canada. December 1990. Native Television. Network License Application.

1986. *Report of the Task Force on Broadcasting Policy.* Ottawa: Ministry of Supply and Services.

Standefer, Roma L. March 1995. *The Satellite Revolution: The Impact of Television in Canada's Northern Native Communities.* Report prepared for CRTC.

1996. "Gathering Strength." *Royal Commission on Aboriginal Peoples Report* pp. 628–40. Ottawa: Minister of Supply and Services.

Bisebois, Debbie. 1990. *Whiteout Warning.* Ottawa: Inuit Broadcasting Corporation.

CHAPTER 14

Stephen Duncombe

Zines

But what are they? That's the first question I'm usually asked when I start to talk about zines. My initial – and probably correct – impulse is to hand over a stack of zines and let the person asking the question decide, for this is how they were introduced to me.

Some years back I went on a trip to Boston to visit some old friends playing in a band. There I planned to hang out and work as their "roadie," lugging equipment to gigs, setting it up and taking it down. I had played in a couple of punk rock bands in the early 1980s and I suppose part of me wanted to feel again some of the excitement and energy that comes from being in a band and part of a subcultural scene. Fortunately, my descent into nostalgia was nipped in the bud; when I got there the band had broken up. I had little to do except walk around the city, sneak into Widener Library, and hang around my friends' apartment. Scattered around their apartment, piled precariously on the coffee table, buried under old pizza boxes, forgotten in the cracks of the sofa, were scruffy, homemade little pamphlets. Little publications filled with rantings of high weirdness and exploding with chaotic design. *Zines*. Although I knew about zines from my days spent in the punk scene, I had never really given them much time or thought. Now, with plenty of time, I spent hours going through them.

I was awestruck. Somehow these little smudged pamphlets carried within them the honesty, kindness, anger, the beautiful inarticulate articulateness . . . the uncompromising *life* that I had discovered (and lost) in music, then later radical politics, years ago. Against the studied hipness of music and style magazines, the pabulum of mass newsweeklies, and the posturing of academic journals, here was something completely different. In zines, everyday oddballs were speaking plainly about themselves and our society with an honest sincerity, a revealing intimacy, and a healthy "fuck you" to sanctioned authority – for no money and no recognition, writing for an audience of like-minded misfits.

Later I picked up a thick journal crammed with zine reviews called *Factsheet Five*, leafed through their listings, and sent off for hundreds of zines. I discovered tens of thousands more at the zine archive housed in the New York State Library. I even began to publish my own zine and traded mine for others. As I dug through mountains of these piquant publications a whole world that I had known nothing about opened up to me. It was

Stephen Duncombe, "Zines," pp. 1–16 and 199–200 from *Notes from the Underground: Zines and the Politics of Alternative Culture*. New York: Verso, 1997. Reprinted by permission of Verso.

incredibly varied: zines came in more shapes, styles, subjects, and qualities than one would imagine. But there was something remarkable that bound together this new world I had stumbled upon: a radically democratic and participatory ideal of what culture and society might be . . . *ought* to be.

In an era marked by the rapid centralization of corporate media, zines are independent and localized, coming out of cities, suburbs and small towns across the USA, assembled on kitchen tables. They celebrate the everyperson in a world of celebrity, losers in a society that rewards the best and the brightest. Rejecting the corporate dream of an atomized population broken down into discrete and instrumental target markets, zine writers form networks and forge communities around diverse identities and interests. Employed within the grim new economy of service, temporary, and "flexible" work, they redefine work, setting out their creative labor done on zines as a protest against the drudgery of working for another's profit. And defining themselves against a society predicated on consumption, zinesters privilege the ethic of DIY, do-it-yourself: make your own culture and stop consuming that which is made for you. Refusing to believe the pundits and politicians who assure us that the laws of the market are synonymous with the laws of nature, the zine community is busy creating a culture whose value isn't calculated as profit and loss on ruled ledger pages, but is assembled in the margins, using criteria like control, connection, and authenticity.

I came to realize that, considered in their totality, zines weren't the capricious ramblings of isolated cranks (though some certainly were), but the variegated voices of a subterranean world staking out its identity through the cracks of capitalism and in the shadows of the mass media. Zines are speaking to and for an underground culture. And while other groups of individuals come together around the shared creation of their own culture, what distinguishes zinesters from garden-variety hobbyists is their political self-consciousness. Zinesters consider what they do as an alternative to and strike against commercial culture and consumer capitalism. And they write about this openly in their zines.

What was amazing to me, coming from years of sterile academic and political debates on the Left, in which culture was often in the past dismissed as irrelevant to the "real struggle," was that zines seemed to form a true culture of resistance. Their way of seeing and doing was not borrowed from a book, nor was it carefully cross-referenced and cited; rather it was, if you'll forgive the word, organic. It was a vernacular radicalism, an indigenous strain of utopian thought.

I began my study of zines in earnest near the end of the 12-year conservative drive of the Reagan/Bush era. Against this juggernaut the radical political opposition, in which I was an active participant, acted out a tragedy seemingly unchanged for decades. One variant went as follows. Leaders organize a "mass" demonstration. We march. We chant. Fringe groups hawk their ridiculous papers. Speakers are paraded onto the dais to tell us what we already know. We hope the mainstream media puts us on the news for five seconds. Sometimes they do and sometimes they don't. Nothing seems to change. Certainly there were lively and successful models of demonstration and organization – like those of ACT UP in its heyday – but these stand out against the relative failure of the rest. The social movements of the decade that spoke the language and captured the imagination of the public were those not of the Left, but of the Right.

In zines I saw the seeds of a different possibility: a novel form of communication and creation that burst with an angry idealism. A medium that spoke for a marginal, yet vibrant culture, that along with others might invest the tired script of progressive politics with meaning and excitement for a new generation. Perhaps most important, zines were a success story. Throughout the 1980s while the Left was left behind, crumbling and attracting few new converts, zines and underground culture grew by leaps and bounds, resonating deeply with disaffected young people. As a punk rocker, Left politico, and scholar of culture, I was intrigued by their success. Perhaps, I thought to myself, zines were the crack in the seemingly impenetrable wall of the system: a culture spawning the next wave of meaningful resistance.

And so I decided to make the politics of zines and underground culture the focus of my study. By politics in this case I mean simply what zine writers articulate – either explicitly, or as is often the case implicitly – as being the problems of the present cultural, economic, and political system; what they imagine and create as possible solutions to these problems; and what strategies and chances they have for actualizing these ideals on both a small and a large scale.

As I spent more time with zines and zine writers, immersed in this underground world, I realized there was a minor flaw in my theory/fantasy of underground culture as vanguard of world revolution. Witnessing this incredible explosion of radical cultural dissent, I couldn't help but notice that as all this radicalism was happening underground, the world above was moving in the opposite direction. The election of a president who "felt our pain" notwithstanding, politics were becoming more conservative and power was becoming more concentrated. More disturbing was that zines and underground culture didn't seem to be any sort of threat to this above-ground world. Quite the opposite: "alternative" culture was being celebrated in the mainstream media and used to create new styles and profits for the commercial culture industry.

The history of all rebellious cultural and political movements is the history of the unavoidable contradiction of staking out new ground within and through the landscape of the past. But today this laying of claims may be harder than ever. No longer is there a staid bourgeoisie to confront with avant-garde art or a square America to shock with countercultural values; instead there is a sophisticated marketing machine which gobbles up anything novel and recreates it as product for a niche market. When the *New York Times* gushes over zines, when punk feminist Riot Grrls are profiled in *Newsweek*, when "alternative" rock gets its own show on MTV, and when the so-called Generation X becomes an identifiable and lucrative market in the eyes of the editors of *Business Week* and *Advertising Age*, rebelling through culture becomes exceedingly problematic. The underground is discovered and cannibalized almost before it exists.

Alternative culture was discovered not just by the entertainment industry but by the academy as well, particularly by radical scholars – much like myself – looking for the latest historical agent to hang their political hopes, or blame their failures, upon. In the academic world, however, there has been a lot of sloppy thinking about the relationship between culture and politics. Critics have invested capitalist ideology with a totalizing power and reach, arguing that all cultural expressions are inevitably expressions of the logic of the status quo. Or more recently, they do the opposite: make the most outrageous liberatory political claims for the most banal of cultural acts. My purpose here is not to extol or dismiss – for scholarship or social change gains from neither – but to *understand* the politics of zines and underground culture.

The powers that be do not sustain their legitimacy by convincing people that the current system is The Answer. That fiction would be too difficult to sustain in the face of so much evidence to the contrary. What they must do, and what they have done very effectively, is convince the mass of people that *there is no alternative*. What I want to argue in the following pages is that zines and underground culture offer up an alternative, a way of understanding and acting in the world that operates with different rules and upon different values than those of consumer capitalism. It is an alternative fraught with contradictions and limitations... but also possibilities. We can learn from both.

But what are they? Try again: zines are noncommercial, nonprofessional, small-circulation magazines which their creators produce, publish, and distribute by themselves. While shaped by the long history of alternative presses in the United States, zines as a distinct medium were born in the 1930s. It was then that fans of SF, science fiction, often through the clubs they founded, began producing what they called "fanzines" as a way of sharing science fiction stories and critical commentary, and of communicating with one another. Forty years later, in the mid-1970s, the other defining influence on modern-day zines began as fans of punk rock music, ignored by and critical of the mainstream music press, started printing fanzines about their music and cultural scene.

In the early 1980s these two tributaries, joined by smaller streams of publications created by fans of other cultural genres, disgruntled self-publishers, and the remnants of printed political dissent from the sixties and seventies, were brought together and cross-fertilized through listings and reviews in network zines like *Factsheet Five*. As the "fan" was by and large dropped off "zine," and their number increased exponentially, a culture of zines developed. By the early 1990s the two editors of the early *Factsheet Five*, deciding upon a title for a commercially published version of their zine, could honestly and accurately refer to *The World of Zines.*[1]

When I think of the typical citizen of this world, I see in my mind Christine Boarts, the 24-year-old editor of *Slug & Lettuce.* Dressed in black from head to foot, hair multi-hued, rings lining her ears and nose, tattoos circling her wrist and gracing her shoulder, she still thinks of herself as shy and quiet, the weird girl who sat at the back of the class in high school, in a town where "there was nothing goin' down at all." But, as the Velvet Underground song goes, "you know, her life was saved by rock & roll."[2]

It was in the small punk scene in the central Pennsylvania college town where Chris grew up that she found a community (outside her liberal family) where "it was okay that I wasn't like everyone," and it was through her zine that she forged connections to the larger underground scene which gave her the "inspiration and direction" to chart a course for herself outside the mainstream. Surviving on a shoestring, she has just put out her forty-fifth issue of *S&L*, fitting it in someplace between organizing punk shows at New York City's alternative space ABC NO RIO, shooting photos for an upcoming book, crisscrossing the country in a van, and spending the winter in an unheated cabin on a mountain in Virginia. Living on the outskirts of a society that equates success with material acquisition, status, and stability, Chris is poor, marginalized, and perfectly happy.[3]

Like Chris, most zinesters are young and the children of professionals, culturally if not financially middle-class. White and raised in a relatively privileged position within the dominant culture, they have since embarked on "careers" of deviance that have moved them to the edges of this society: embracing downwardly mobile career aspirations, unpopular musical and literary tastes, transgressive ideas about sexuality, unorthodox artistic sensibilities, and a politics resolutely outside the status quo (more often to the left but sometimes to the right). Like Chris, they're simply "not interested" in the "big game" that is the straight world. In short, zine writers and readers, although they'd be horrified to be tagged with such a pat term, are what used to be called bohemians.

It is white, middle-class culture – and its discontents – that informs zines and under-ground culture. But since one of the attributes of zines is their diversity and unpredict-ability, though, the portrait of a young, white, formerly middle-class bohemian looks less and less representative the further one delves into the world of zines. Not all zinesters are young: much older writers like SF fan Don Fitch, who describes his age as "65 going on 17", put out zines like *From Sunday to Saturday*. Some zinesters – like Freedom, a Staten Island NY high-schooler who publishes *Orangutan Balls* – are working-class. And Franetta McMillian, an African-American woman from Delaware, publishes *Sweet Jesus*, while two Los Angeles Chicanos, Lalo Lopez and Estaban Zul, put out *Pocho* – "Kickin' Butt for La Raza" – *Magazine*.[4]

Zine publishers are identified less by who they are, then, and more by what they believe; the best description of one I've come across is actually a composite portrait written in 1946 of a similar genus: the "little magazine" editor or writer of the early twentieth century:

> Such a man is stimulated by some form of discontent – whether with the constraints of his world or the negligence of publishers, at any rate something he considers unjust, boring, or ridiculous. He views the world of publishers and popularizers with disdain, sometimes with despair... [and] he generally insists that publication should not depend upon the whimsy of conventional tastes and choices.[5]

"The whimsy of conventional tastes and choices" certainly plays little part in the subjects picked by these writers, whose zines span almost every field, from the sublime to the ridiculous, making a detour through the unfathomable. But one thing gives coherence to this eclecticism: zinesters' fascination with the margins. These may be the margins of literature or music, explored through a science fiction fanzine like *STET* or the punk rock *Philly Zine*. Or perhaps the perimeter of politics surveyed through the anarchist essays of *instead of A magazine*, the conservative libertarian rants of *Inverted-A HORN*, or *Finster's* feminist-infused stories, opinions, and photo-collages. In the gay safe-sex *Diseased Pariah News* the borders of "acceptable" sexuality are scouted, as they are in the soft-core poetry and pornography of *Ash* and the harder-core *Black Leather Times*. Numerous zines obsessively catalog the ephemera of the past: *Show-Me Blowout* unearths long-dead Missouri garage bands from the fifties and sixties; *8-Track Mind* is devoted to eight-track tape trivia; *Bad Seed* researches JD – juvenile delinquency – pulp novels and lurid teen exploitation films; and *Past Deadline* reprints nineteenth-century newspaper articles. Other writers, turning their attention to the ephemera of the present, celebrate the edges of modern consumer culture through satirical reviews of banal products in zines such as *Meanwhile* and *Beer Frame*. The unaffected drawings, poems, thoughts, and ideas of a young woman in the *Watley-Browne Review*, and the mental meanderings of the residents of an old age home recorded in *Duplex Planet*, chart the boundaries of artistic expression. And even the margins of sense itself are stretched: by an entire zine of pictures of bowling pins in different settings in *Eleventh Pin*, by the nonsensical photo/text collages of *balcony of ignorance*, or by *Your Name Here*, a zine soliciting a new creator, name, and content for each issue.

This hyperspecialization of zines – science fiction, punk rock, eight-track tapes, defunct Missouri garage bands – is a bit misleading, for unlike mainstream "niche market" periodicals, zines don't follow well-laid plans for market penetration or move purpose-fully in a defined direction courting profitable demographics. The majority of zines are specialized, but only to the point that they communicate the range, however wide or narrow, that makes up the personal interests of the publisher. Zines meander and change direction, switching back, then back again, flowing wherever the publisher's interest takes them. The result is less a defined set of discrete topics covered and more an amalgam of the diverse interests of those doing the writing. In fact when Mike Gunderloy, the founding editor of *Factsheet Five*, attempted to make his zine easier to read by ordering zine reviews by category, he says he was flooded by letters in protest.[6] "Yikes! *Factsheet Five* arranged in headings/categories? Urgh!!! When zinedom becomes reduced to 'definitions' it loses its soul," one such letter howls.[7]

A typical zine – although "typical" is a problematic term in this context – might start with a highly personalized editorial, move into a couple of opinionated essays or "rants," criticizing, describing, extolling something or other, and then conclude with reviews of other zines, bands, books, and so forth. Spread throughout this would be poems, a story, reprints from the mass press (some for informational value, others as ironic commentary), and a few hand-drawn illustrations or comix. The editor would produce the content him or herself, solicit it from personal friends or zine acquaintances, or, less commonly, gather it through an open call for submissions.[8] Material is also "borrowed": pirated from other zines and the mainstream press, sometimes without credit, invariably without permission.

The form of the zine lies somewhere between a personal letter and a magazine. Printed on a standard copy machine, fastened together on the side or corner, or folded widthwise to form a folio and stapled in the crease, zines typically run from 10 to 40 pages. They can, however, run over 100 pages as *Maximumrocknroll* does, and range from color reproductions and card stock covers – like those of *Fish Taco* – to what was once sent to me by the editor of *Frederick's Lament*: a seemingly random jumble of smudged copies, mass cultural flotsam and jetsam, and written personal statements stuffed into an envelope.

As zines are put together by hand using common materials and technology – do-it-yourself is the prime directive of the zine world – they consequently look the part, with unruly cut-and-paste layout, barely legible type, and uneven reproduction. There are, however, zines with large circulations, like Chris's *Slug & Lettuce*, that are printed professionally on newsprint (at over 1,000 copies this becomes cheaper). And the decline in the cost of personal computers and the spread of desktop publishing capability to the smallest of offices (where zinester employees can "liberate" computer time) have given more and more people access to equipment to put out professional-looking publications.

Zines cost anywhere from the price of postage to a couple of dollars, but swapping zines through a barter system is common and part of the ethic of participation among equals. Distribution is primarily person-to-person via the mail, though zines are also sold in some book and music stores and traded, sold, or given away at punk rock gigs, SF conventions, and the like. They are advertised via word of mouth, through other zines' review sections, and by zines of zines such as *Factsheet Five*, whose purpose is to review and publicize these media.

The lifespan of a zine ranges from single-issue "one-shots" to volumes spanning years, with their circulation running from 8 copies to *Slug & Lettuce*'s 8,000. But I would estimate 250 as the average circulation, as publishers strive for a scale that allows them to have complete control over production and distribution, while maintaining personal contact with their readers.[9] In line with this ideal of publishing intimacy, zines are almost always one-person operations. A minority are run by small collectives, and a majority accept input from others, but zines for the most part are the expression and the product of an individual.

Enough exceptions exist, however, to break this rule. *Maximumrocknroll*, the long-running punk zine, lists 97 individuals who helped put out the June 1994 issue. True, more than half these people are listed as "shitworkers," a category of contributors you normally do not see credited on the mastheads of established magazines, but nevertheless, *Maximumrocknroll* is known for its large, complex, and reasonably efficient production organization. Unlike any commercial publication, however, large or small, *MRR* is decidedly nonprofit.

To say that zines are not-for-profit is an understatement. Most lose money. It's not that they aim to be in the red; most try to break even, and if money is made, that's fine, it is more money to spend putting out the next issue. And, again, there are exceptions. Mike Gunderloy, former editor of *Factsheet Five*, managed to survive by publishing his zine, albeit with 80-hour work weeks and mercenary forays into computer consulting. R. Seth Friedman, the current editor, is doing the same. But as a rule, and with the exception of free zines and records sent in for reviews, zines are not expected to bring material reward. In fact the very idea of profiting from a zine is anathema to the underground, bringing with it charges of "selling out."[10]

What zines are expected to provide is an outlet for unfettered expression and a connection to a larger underground world of publishers doing the same. But since most zine writers don't send their zines to the Library of Congress to be catalogued, get an ISSN, or list themselves in the *Small Press Review* or *The International Directory of Little Magazines and Small Presses*, it is difficult to determine exactly how large this world is. Such informed sources as Mike Gunderloy estimate that there are currently at least 10,000–20,000 different zine titles circulating, while others such as Seth Friedman have stretched this number up to 50,000.[11] I lean toward the more conservative estimate, but even with 10,000 titles, using the standard magazine readership estimate of three readers per magazine and 250 copies per zine as a safe mean, the estimate of a *possible* total zine readership, and thus primary contact with some facet of the zine world, is as high as 7,500,000. But because zine readers, as part of a whole subculture, tend to read numerous zines, the real number is certainly lower, most likely in the 500,000–750,000 range.

When one thinks of underground culture one's mind naturally turns to big cities, the traditional loci of bohemia, and certainly writers living in San Francisco and New York City produce more zines than any other single locale. But it is more out-of-the-way places like Harvest, Alabama; Freehold, New Jersey; Morganville, Kansas; and Monrovia, California, that, taken together, outstrip the major metropolises as the germination points of zines.[12] Examining the zines reviewed in an issue of *Factsheet Five* – the most complete listing of zines available – I found an almost two-to-one ratio in favor of small-city/suburban/rural origin over large urban areas. Out of the 1,142 zines listed from the USA, 749 originated from outside the major cities in each state.[13] Though surprising, this disparity makes sense: gentrification and the allure of the bohemian life for nonbohemians have sent rents and services in urban areas out of reach for many people, particularly those who eschew stable careers and ideals of materials success. As traditional garrets give way to gentrified lofts and smoky cafés are superseded by the Starbucks coffee chain, creative misfits scattered across the country use the culture that is zines to share, define and hold together a "culture" of discontent: a virtual bohemia.

But what are they? If pushed to come up with a single defining attribute I would have to say this: zines are decidedly *amateur*. While this term has taken on a pejorative cast in a society that honors professionalism and the value of the dollar, the roots of amateurism are far more noble: *amator*, Latin for *lover*. While other media are produced for money or prestige or public approval, zines are done – as *Factsheet Five*'s founding editor Mike Gunderloy is fond of pointing out – for *love*: love of expression, love of sharing, love of communication. And in protest against a culture and society that offers little reward for such acts of love, zines are also created out of *rage*.

Zines are not the only cultural expression of love and rage lurking underground today. Though drawing from a different population – primarily urban, primarily black – and forged out of the distinct crucible of racism and poverty, the hip-hop subculture, through the voice of rap music, addresses issues familiar to the zine underground: "representing" yourself and community, staying true or selling out, and the search for a voice in a society that just doesn't listen. Nor are zinesters the first people painstakingly to construct an alternative culture only to find it gobbled up by the very interests it ostensibly opposes. This is the history of bohemia since the mid-nineteenth century.

Zines are the most recent entry in a long line of media for the misbegotten, a tradition stretching back to Thomas Paine and other radical pamphleteers, up through the underground press of the 1960s, and on towards the internet. The fact that they are not the only underground culture, and that their trajectory is not entirely unique, in my opinion makes this study not less useful, but more so. Although the world of zines operates on the margins of society, its concerns are common to all: how to count as an individual, how to build a supportive community, how to have a meaningful life, how to create something that is yours.

Some readers will no doubt be disappointed – while others, I'm sure, will be thrilled – that in the pages that follow I engage more with the world of zines and less with the words of academics. I did not make this choice because there isn't good scholarship out there – there is. Nor is it out of ignorance of the studies that have been done and the theories presented – you will find them mentioned in my endnotes. But too often the citation of learned authorities is equated with rigorous theoretical analysis. Sometimes it becomes its replacement. Wary of this trap, I privilege the actual material and its interpretation. Focusing my efforts on describing and explaining the phenomenon I'm studying, I then draw the larger theory out of this description and explanation.

Some might also find the structure of this book unorthodox and perhaps unsettling. I struggled mightily with how to organize this seemingly disorganized subject matter, how to discipline undisciplined subjects.[14] In the end I decided to structure the book around major themes in the zine world, with these broken up by subthematic "vignettes." It's not perfect, but I think it works in balancing out the unfolding and chaotic dynamism of the contemporary zine world with the structure necessary to make sense of it. I also think it accurately describes what binds the world of zines together: ideals, actions, and reactions. Finally, it mirrors the structure of zines themselves: at first glance a bit fragmentary, but coming together inevitably to reveal a world, provide an analysis, and make a point.

Still others will be disappointed that I've written a book on zines at all. Isn't this just another exploitation of zines, "selling out" the underground to the above-ground world? Perhaps. But alternative culture has already been discovered – the more important question is who will represent it and how. The ways in which I explore and explain the world of zines certainly bear the mark of my theoretical interests and political concerns, but I'm of the world I write and my concern for the underground runs deeper than its status as this (or last) season's cultural exotica. More important, I'm a conscientious observer and a careful listener. And I believe that what zinesters have to say and what zines represent are too important to stay sequestered within the walls of a subcultural ghetto.

In dealing with such an idiosyncratic subject matter as zines, there exists a distinct temptation just to hand over a stack of them and let readers decide for themselves what they are. But that's impossible here and, in light of the purpose of this book, not even desirable. In recent years I've poured over thousands upon thousands of zines and interviewed scores of zine writers and readers. I've published zines myself and been part of the underground cultural scene. I've read what there is to read and kept a watchful eye on the times in which we live. In the pages that follow I'll apply this experience to act as a guide, mapping out the philosophical and political contours, the twists and turns, the love and rage, that make up this strange subterranean world.

ZINE TAXONOMY

The breadth of zines is vast and any effort to classify and codify them immediately reveals shortcomings. But by looking over the reviews in a number of issues of *Factsheet Five*, I've come up with the following broad categorizations:

Fanzines   These are no doubt the largest and oldest category of zines; one might well argue that all zines are fanzines. Simply, fanzines are publications devoted to discussing the intricacies and nuances of a cultural genre. Within fanzines there are distinct subcategories:

- **science fiction**   Beginning in the 1930s, publications by and for SF fans were the first zines. Now a minority numerically, SF fanzines still make up a solid segment of the zine world.
- **music**   zines, focused on either a particular band or performer or, more commonly, a specific genre, most often punk or "alternative" rock. This category makes up the largest genre of zines in the United States today.
- **sports**   These are not that big in the United States, but very popular in the UK where football (soccer) zines are an integral part of sporting life. Still, in the USA, fans of baseball, wrestling, skateboarding, roller derby, and women's sports all create zines.
- **television and film**   zines, focused on entertainment both popular and patently unpopular; horror and kitsch drama are particularly well represented.
- **etc.**   Fans of household items, mass transit systems, board games, and what-have-you all put out zines – some done seriously, some as satire.

Political Zines   These may be broken down into two subgenres:

- **Politics**   with a big *P*. These may be subdivided again according to more or less traditional categories such as: Anarchist, Socialist, Libertarian, Fascist, and "identity" categories such as Feminist and Queer.
- **politics**   with a small *p*. These do not identify explicitly with traditional categories, but with political/cultural critique as a major focus of the zine.

Personal Zines, or perzines,   are personal diaries open to the public; shared notes on the day-to-day life, thoughts and experiences of the writer.
    Scene Zines   These contain news and views on the local music and underground cultural "scene" in the writer's area.
    Network Zines   Like *Factsheet Five*, these zines concentrate on reviewing and publicizing other zines, music, art, computer BBSs (bulletin board systems), and other underground culture. They serve as nodal points for the bohemian diaspora.

Fringe Culture Zines cover assassination theories and "proof" of secret nefarious undertakings, UFOs, and serial killers. They deal with the standard fare of supermarket tabloids, but explored in much more depth and with far more intelligence and sometimes humor.

Religious Zines Witches, paganists, and born-again Christians, as well as "joke" religions like the Church of the SubGenius and Moorish Science, all put out zines for the faithful and wayward.

Vocational Zines tell the stories of life on the job, whether that job be washing dishes, doing temp work, writing for a newspaper, working as a librarian, or practicing fractal geometry.

Health Zines contain recipes for healthy food, information about diseases and medicine, advice on coping with AIDS and dealing with death, and other health-related issues.

Sex Zines deal with straight, queer, bondage, black leather stories, pictures – a zine for probably every sexual proclivity.

Travel Zines Very often in the form of "road trip" diaries, these zines are travelogues of bumming around on the cheap.

Comix These are underground comic books on themes humorous, serious, and nonsensical.

Literary Zines showcase original short fiction and poetry.

Art Zines contain print media collages, photographs, drawings, and mail art which create a network of artists and a floating virtual gallery.

The Rest – a large category.

Notes

1   Mike Gunderloy and Cari Goldberg Janice, *The World of Zines* (New York: Penguin Books, 1992).
2   Velvet Underground, "Rock & Roll," *Loaded*, Atlantic Records, 1970.
3   Christine Boarts, personal interview, May 29, 1996, New York City.
4   Don Fitch, personal correspondence, April 22, 1994.
5   Frederick J. Hoffman, Charles Allen, and Carolyn F. Ulrich, *The Little Magazine in America* (Princeton: Princeton University Press, 1946), pp. 3–4.
6   Mike Gunderloy's response, "Letters," *Factsheet Five*, 22, 1987, Rensselaer, NY, p. 66.
7   Bob McGlynn, in "Letters," *Factsheet Five*, 31, 1989, Rensselaer, NY, p. 113.
8   The criteria for the zine editor's selection of material from others are not too different from what operates in many journals or magazines: nepotism. Editors ask friends or zine acquaintances whom they like and trust to submit material to their zine. The difference between the zine "old boy network" and that of the mainstream publishing industry is that zine networks are made up of people who are kept – or have opted – out of the halls of cultural power.
9   This small circulation is one of the things that distinguishes zines from other periodicals; as a rule zines have small runs, of under 1,000, while magazines have runs of over 10,000. But this isn't always the case. A zine like the *I Hate Brenda Newsletter*, devoted to slagging the actress who plays Brenda in the TV series *Beverly Hills 90210* and put out by the editors of *Ben Is Dead*, has a circulation of over 25,000; on the other hand, many academic or literary journals are lucky to break 1,000.
10   Most magazines try to deliver a profit, even though some, including substantial ones such as the *New Yorker*, operate at a loss. It is not the actual profit that is the issue, but the intent of the producer that differentiates zines from magazines. I'll stay with the example of the *New Yorker*. It was never published to make money in a purely mercenary sense; it was and is a prestige publication. However, when its losses became too great for the parent company to bear, a new editor was brought in to change its content and layout to make it more popular and profitable. This sort of change would be heresy to most zine writers, who would rather burn at the stake than alter their publication to please anybody but themselves.

11 Gunderloy and Goldberg Janice, *The World of Zines*; Seth Friedman cited in J. Peder Zane, "Now the Magazines of 'Me'," *New York Times*, May 14, 1995, p. E4.

12 These are the birthplaces of *Frederick's Lament, The Holy Experiment*, 10, *The Kansas Intelligencer*, vol. 5, no. 5, and *Moonshines*, vol. 1, nos. 1–2.

13 A breakdown of the geographical origin of zines listed in the Spring 1991 issue of *Factsheet Five* (no. 44) turned up the following results. Out of 1,301 zines listed and reviewed, 49 states were represented, with South Dakota being the lone exclusion. Of the 1,142 US zines listed, California produced the most with 226, New York the second with 135, while Ohio, Texas, and Washington state churned out 47, 46, and 42 respectively. None of these figures are that astonishing when one takes into account the population of these states. In the 1990 census California was ranked first, New York second, Texas third and Ohio seventh. Washington, a state with a relatively small population, makes up for this deficiency with the importance of Seattle and Olympia as cultural centers for music and young people throughout the late 1980s and early 1990s.

Of the 24 foreign countries represented, the major English-speaking nations led the pack, ordered by geographical distance from the USA. Canada was first with 58 zines, followed by the UK with 37 and Australia with 13. Following these, in order, were France, Germany, Finland, the Netherlands, Japan, New Zealand, Sweden, Belgium, Greece, Italy, Spain, Singapore, Poland, Hungary, South Africa, Portugal, Lithuania, Argentina, Brazil, Iceland, and what was then Yugoslavia.

Again, none of this is too surprising: big states, and countries which have large English-speaking and/or well-educated populations, are well represented. The one eye-opener came when I broke down the states according to the categories "major urban" and "suburban/rural." Here, contrary to expectations about the urbanity of underground cultures, I found that the majority of zines did not originate from large metropolitan areas. Only 393 of the zines from the United States originated from the major cities in each state, whereas the remainder – 749 – did not.

It should be noted that doing this sort of sampling from *Factsheet Five* has its strengths and its weaknesses. The main strength is that, up until very recent times, the producers of *Factsheet Five* reviewed every zine that was sent to them. Thus the population was self-selected and not edited. The weaknesses stem from the same source: those individuals who produce publications who don't feel the need to be reviewed by FS_5, or are ignorant of its existence, are not included in my sample. However, my study is of the *culture* of zines, and FS_5 was and may still be the locus of that culture. In addition, those who submit to FS_5 are aware of this culture and have chosen to participate in it. Thus, while this sample may not be representative of all zines in the world, it is representative of a self-conscious world of zines. It also happens to be the only such large-scale listing of a zine universe available.

14 "Disciplining undisciplined subjects" is how friend and anthropologist Ara Wilson once described my project.

CHAPTER 15

The Ho'okele Netwarriors in the Liquid Continent

Kekula P. Bray-Crawford

Access and integration

Access to information and facilitation of communication provide new and enhanced opportunities for expression and perpetuation of the cultural life of communities and peoples, with the potential to accelerate political, economic, social, educational and cultural advancement beyond the scope of traditional institutions and forms of communication. Regional and global information networks expand the voices of cultures and peoples via electronic fora to raise awareness and focus international attention and support on specific cultural issues and efforts. The ability to transcend present boundaries and create what would be an even finer web of information systems is the key to taking cyberculture to its next level.

This chapter assesses the current trends and resources in the area of communications infrastructure and content during a crisis of culture, with examples of successful utilization of communications models and technologies for direct peaceful empowerment of cultures, particularly indigenous peoples.

Envisioning alternative systems through indigenous wisdom and cyberculture

My work as a human rights activist focuses on self-determination for indigenous peoples and the ability to transcend the typical boundaries of political conflict through a cyberculture. I envisage this cyberculture as one in which creativity and intellect could challenge neocolonial initiatives of the twenty-first century and reduce the sufferings endured by indigenous peoples living with Fourth World aggressions.

The course of my own culture in this information age was set by the evolution of an ancient Hawaiian heritage, on one hand, and a deep desire for the integration of knowledge within the expanding field of computer technology, on the other. This is the edge that I use

Kekula P. Bray-Crawford, "The Ho'okele Netwarriors in the Liquid Continent," pp. 162–72 from Wendy Harcourt (ed.), *Women Internet: Creating New Cultures in Cyberspace*. London: Zed Books, 1999. Reprinted by permission of Zed Books.

to navigate and develop what I call 'the Netwarriors' and 'indiginal mapping' (see below). This creativity is now finding an empowering future as it continues to define and establish culturally sensitive uses of technology within the framework of traditional intellectual cultural knowledge and political alternatives. The work has begun to build a bridge of culture, environment and technology for global change.

My path supports a grassroots alternative development agenda, in which indigenous wisdom once again might achieve a greater recognition through articulate technological architecture. Indigenous wisdom could be a vehicle enabling communities to merge together and move towards a restorative system away from a predatory industrial system.

Working for indigenous groups

As an indigenous woman in cyberculture I have had the incredible opportunity to assist in the pioneering stages of establishing a foundation for indigenous rights to be explored and experienced on-line.

This began with the native Hawaiian independence movement in 1992. We were taking greater strides by 1995, when along with my husband Scott Paul Crawford I delivered the first paper on indigenous rights through technology at the Internet Society 1995 International Networking Conference entitled 'Self-Determination in the Information Age', focusing on indigenous initiatives in on-line communications technologies for self-determination.

That summer I received an invitation from Andree Nicola McLaughlin, of the Medgar Evers City University, Brooklyn, New York, to present the first on-line empowerment workshop to the Seventh Annual World Conference of the International Cross-Cultural Black Women's Studies Institute (ICCBWSI), attended by women from over 40 countries and focusing on women's development in Third World countries and Third World conditions in Fourth World circumstances. The presentation received a high degree of resistance, which is indicative of the oppressed conditions experienced by women in Third World countries and mirrors the responses in other fora.

We organized another workshop for the Eighth Annual World Conference for the ICCBWSI in Johannesburg, South Africa in August, 1998. This time we are setting up a computer communications centre, where women in attendance and delegates will have the opportunity daily to sit at a computer, experience the Internet, explore the potentials and possibly create their own web pages for their communities as an economic development initiative, focusing on women of the region, their current situations, needs and solutions. Our goal is to leave at least one community empowered with computers, access, and the ability and commitment to assist others.

In the autumn/winter of 1996, while working as a communications consultant for the International Indian Treaty Council, an indigenous ECOSOC NGO (Category 2), I took a United Nations formal session to the world in real time. This benchmark of opening new space on the Internet set in motion the work of integrating political action with on-line networking in a mobilizing manner, and we founded the Netwarriors.

The Netwarriors movement focuses on UN dynamics and agendas in respect to indigenous peoples' rights. It also reaches beyond this arena for crisis calls affecting indigenous peoples. This particular formal session was the second UN Commission on Human Rights Inter-sessional Working Group on the draft Declaration on the Rights of Indigenous Peoples at Geneva, Switzerland – and we are very proud to say that we completed a successful second year at the UNCHR-IWG in 1997.[1]

In 1998 the Netwarriors have focused on assisting the National Commission for Democracy in Mexico and the EZLN to mobilize world public opinion throughout the holidays. We have become an International On-line Political Observer through this initiative and are receiving when in direct action over 20,000 hits per day. We also took the Netwarriors to the CBD8 (j) in Madrid on 24–9 November 1997 to report on another international standard-setting forum, and the network keeps building.

Indiginal mapping

My professional work also involves the creation of a multimedia, multi-relational database system set within a framework of indigenous cultural knowledge, time and its relationship to land. This is indiginal mapping. SeaSeer, a local software development company, proposes to support the initiative through their expertise in the integration of tools and applications. Artistic creativity, Geographic Information Systems (GIS) and Global Positioning Systems (GPS) provide the other general elements necessary to produce my first indiginal map.

This particular project aims directly at the cultural restoration of traditional knowledge and indigenous wisdom as it relates to site-specific land bases. The core objective is to ensure that indigenous culture survives its transition into a new millennium with a restorative call to the world community.

My regional 1997/8 focus on the Internet is aimed at enabling and access in remote and rural areas of the Pacific. I spent one month in French Polynesia earlier this year training the women of Tuahine (whose members were from Tahiti, Moorea, Huahine, Marqueses and Tahaa) in e-mail communications. They have established a women's cooperative and are working to develop export and trade industries based on traditional goods.

While there I was able to work with the French-owned telephone company to configure Hiti Tau's laptop computers which were donated to them by other networks. Owing to the challenges of language differences, the tools used in my training were paper and a digital camera: pointing and making clicking sounds with my mouth, I attempted to translate between French, English, Maohi, and 'Olelo Hawai'i. Through this intimidating bridging experience, I found comprehension, amazement and a strong desire to learn more. The Maohi (indigenous people of French Polynesia) can only afford a few hours of Internet access per month – an unlimited account in French Polynesia is US$2,000 per month, provided by the government-owned phone company. In December 1996 there were only 10 Internet accounts in the region of French Polynesia; in March 1997 there were 150.

Infrastructure, content and a crisis of culture

As I and other writers on the subject have shown, the swiftly evolving information and communication technologies and networking infrastructures play an expanding role in supporting the cultural expression and perpetuation of the rights and knowledge of indigenous peoples. There are those who feel that the technologies are a detriment to indigenous peoples' rights, but I counter that position, proposing instead that indigenous people are not only fully capable of utilizing this resource but must empower ourselves by it in order to preserve our culture for the next seven generations.

In her paper 'Cultural and Intellectual Property Rights of Indigenous Peoples of the Pacific', Aroha Te Pareake Mead explains:

It is important to note that Western law distinguishes cultural property from that of intellectual property, in that it regards cultural property as being tangible physical expressions of culture, such as music, dance and art forms, whereas intellectual property is seen as the outcomes, both tangible and intangible of ideas or processes that have been the result of human intervention ...

But there is a *terra nullius* – a Latin legal term meaning 'territory belonging to no one'. The general rule of English common law system was that ownership could not be acquired by occupying land already occupied by another, hence settler governments evoked *terra nullius* in the new colonies thereby refusing to acknowledge existent indigenous habitants ...

Intellectual property rights laws do not acknowledge existent customary indigenous knowledge or indigenous ownership. Nor do they agree that indigenous knowledge processes are scientific and technological. Nor do they accommodate a connection between indigenous peoples and their lands and heritage. In short, they do not regard existent indigenous knowledge as being an intellectual property and deserving of protection ... (Suva, Fiji 4 September 1996)

In order to counter the logic of *terra nullius* and to restore indigenous wisdom as a source of cultural and intellectual knowledge, indiginal mapping can be used. Indiginal mapping provides a system of information on different localities that ensures that indigenous children remain in touch with ancestral knowledge and ways through cyberculture.

The politics of cyberculture

As indiginal mapping shows, cyberculture has to be useful for indigenous and other marginalized peoples, and has to be part of a conscious political strategy for change. The information age is so fully upon us that those of us who work within the world of cyberculture speak what is almost another language. As we begin to converse with people from every possible point on the planet to discuss the role of information technologies in our lives and the lives of our people, we must keep central in our minds the purpose and reason for their use.

Interactive media such as the World Wide Web (WWW) are so engaging as to seem almost worthwhile just for their own sake. Almost, but not really. The technology is only a tool, and only as useful as the information it carries. Thus we must continually be aware of the need for content. We cannot become so entranced by the magic of how we put information into cyberspace as to forget that what we put there is actually delivering an impact. The medium is not the message.

While it is possible to dwell on the potential benefits of electronic communications for cultural protection and expression, we must also temper enthusiasm for these technologies with a realistic view of their limitations, particularly regarding access in less developed regions of the world.

David Ronfeldt, in *Cyberocracy is Coming*, warns of the need for equitable distribution of these technologies and freedom of access.

A new distinction is emerging between the information haves and have-nots. Some actors may become global information powers, but others, notably in the Third World, fear 'electronic colonization' and 'information imperialism'. (Ronfeldt, 1992)

If this is true of Third World countries in relation to the First World, then Fourth World nations are at an even greater disadvantage, and in greater need of assistance to gain access to and make positive use of the technologies, which give rise to another main focus of Ho'okele Netwarriors.

Reversing the hierarchy of knowledge

Indigenous peoples of the Fourth World are seeking to assert and perpetuate their cultural identities, along with the integrity of their political voices and rightful political status, as well as their economic and social development. As the world increasingly recognizes that these voices must be heard, for them to be heard in the electronic realm is essential. The voices of the indigenous peoples of the world can help provide the content that makes the use of the technology meaningful in a real way.

A hierarchy of information exists, which runs as follows, from bottom to top: data, information, knowledge, intelligence, wisdom. The indigenous people of the world already hold the ancient wisdom. The question is: can wisdom be translated into data and information in a way that preserves its essence, while allowing us to take advantage of the modern technologies that are available to distribute and share this wisdom in the form of data and information, in an effort to make really knowledgeable and intelligent choices for the future of humanity?

Virtual cultures

Cultures and peoples may benefit from the ability to form 'virtual communities' and to share forms of cultural expression unique to the virtual world. Indigenous peoples who are involved with struggles for cultural survival are very often dispersed, displaced and relocated, having been forced away from their homeland by military, political or economic foreign interests, and those of First World countries.

Communications technologies make possible new kinds of communities, or at least provide possibilities of a certain level of cohesion among a dispersed community which may aid in the expression and perpetuation of cultural identities. Dispersed communities can form and remain cohesive much more easily with the advent of telephones, faxes, e-mail, the Internet and WWW, communications satellites, etc. Territoriality, in one sense, is no longer essentially important in the creation of feelings of community. Thus the body of people capable of participating in the cultural life of the community may be expanded through access to communications technology.

As a direct illustration of this, in 1995 a participant in the creation of the Free Tibet Home Page reported that:

> There is an effort under way now to improve the on-line services in Dharamsala, the home of the Tibetan Government-in-Exile. This will enable a more direct link between Tibet supporters and the officials and organizations where the bulk of Tibetans reside. Tibetan writers are grouping together to inform and educate people on modern Tibetan culture and are looking to disseminate information across countries and oceans. There is a lot of work under way to preserve Tibetan religious texts in electronic form and on CD-ROMs. Most of that is being done in monasteries transplanted to India. (Delisio, 1995)

Tibet is a clear example of a situation where both political and technical access from within the territory itself is extremely limited, yet a government-in-exile, working in partnership with its people and various supporters around the world, is establishing a vital cyberspace community to further the purposes of the people and culture of Tibet. Today you will find 19 references on Yahoo of information and sites related to Free Tibet. Progress?

Resources for integration and solutions

Each indigenous people and Fourth World nation has its own distinct history and current political situation, yet all have much in common in their struggles for cultural and political identity, voice and recognition, and sovereignty over their land and natural resources. Each group may feel isolated and disempowered if unable to see itself in the larger picture. But the establishment of relations between various Fourth World peoples can provide benefits in a number of ways, by sharing experiences, resources and insights so that those who have learned in one way or another can share their knowledge and coordinate actions for solidarity, enhanced effectiveness and the prevention of (or, as in Peng Wan-Ru's case, mourning for) the loss of life.

The electronic media provide vast opportunities for such networking. As new organizational networks are built, cutting across national borders and interests, influential sub- and supranational actors increasingly compete for influence with national actors. As political and economic interests grow in protecting and expanding the networks, the networks themselves may increasingly take precedence over nation-states as the driving factor in domestic and foreign affairs. The setting of standards in the virtual world is paramount in our collective technical manifestations.

Native communities have been actively engaged in creating and utilizing such networks with increasing participation and sophistication.[2] A prime example of indigenous on-line resources can be found at NativeWeb[3] which contains extensive information about a range of native subjects, geographic regions and cultural groups, along with material on native literature, languages, newsletters and journals, organizations and bibliographies. Native-Web also provides pointers to other native information resources, including WWW sites, Gopher and FTP Sites, UseNet newsgroups, and list serves. There are scores of newsgroups and list serve lists related to indigenous issues, including education, health, language, law, spirituality and ecology.

As indigenous peoples seek to protect and perpetuate their cultural rights and assert control over their land and natural resources, access to international legal tools is essential, and being able to access relevant documents instantaneously can provide significant advantages. For example, advocates can access the United Nations directly for related resolutions[4] – though information in certain areas, such as decolonization, is noticeably unobtainable from the United Nations' website, as pointed out by the Special Committee on Decolonization at the 1997 annual seminar in Antigua–Barbuda.

Numerous other sources also exist for accessing valuable international information. Microstate Resources is a virtual library on the WWW developed by Microstate Ltd.,

> for the purpose of fostering public and private sector development in very small states, autonomous territories, colonies, islands and similar domains where problems of scale, isolation and dependence impede balanced development. Utilizing the most advanced information technologies, particularly the Internet and the WWW, Microstate Ltd. has developed linkages to the most critical resources needed by small countries and others interested in their affairs (Leventhal, n.d.).

Documents specifically related to indigenous issues can be found at the Fourth World Documentation Project, organized by John Burrows at the Center for World Indigenous Studies (CWIS) Washington State, in 1992. Its goal is to present the on-line community with the greatest possible access to Fourth World documents and resources. The Fourth World Documentation Project is an on-line library of texts which record and preserve our peoples' struggles to regain their rightful place in the international community. (Burrows, n.d.)

Human rights information is available electronically from a wide range of sources to help people understand their rights and combat abuses of those rights by having the proper information. The Human Rights Web provides a good starting place for research in this area, with links to Web sites with a bearing on human rights, Gopher sites, e-mail lists, list serves, and newsgroups.[5]

A vast range of resources regarding sustainable development can be accessed electronically, to assist cultural groups at the tangible level of providing sustenance to the people in a sustainable manner. One outstanding resource is EnviroLink.[6]

Finally, resources which can be accessed via the Net include not only the files which reside in cyberspace, but also the contacts with the people who put them there, and the growing number of experts, scholars, attorneys, and others who also have access to cyberspace.

Partnerships for access

One solution to the issue of access, which depends more on personal relations and less on institutional actions by First World entities, is to develop effective partnerships between those with the technical ability and the access, and those with the issues and the content. Karen Strom, for instance, has provided Web presences for a wide range of Native American tribes, organizations, museums, and projects, which are hosted on her server at the University of Massachusetts.[7]

Partnerships are a good first step in obtaining access to information remotely. A range of services could be provided, in various combinations, depending on the resources and needs, including providing the physical site and/or the HTML design work or other systems design.

The long-term goal is to provide assistance aimed at each entity having its own server or at least access to a local server. Seeing the material on-line, receiving the positive feedback and experiencing the direct results of this presence can provide the incentive to move into a more active participation with the Internet. Further technical and financial support systems can then be employed, utilizing and expanding on the partnerships that are already in place.

Bridging indigenous culture, the environment and technology

Self-determination in the information age of technology has proved successful on several counts but still not enough. Networking is key to the survival of indigenous culture and indigenous peoples' rights under Fourth World conditions. The ability to support others who continue to be deprived of access is crucial. As Kristin Nauth and Laurie Timmermann point out,

the gap between information haves and have-nots is perilously wide. Connectivity is no simple feat in countries that lack reliable telephone and electrical systems. There are also political hurdles...In the rear guard are nations like Mozambique, which is just emerging from a two decade civil war and has only three telephone lines per 1,000 citizens. (Nauth and Timmermann, 1997)

Protecting and securing an identity through the explosive electronic age is a responsibility indigenous peoples are now embracing. Traditionally removed from the cutting edge of progress, they can join international initiatives to recognize that culture is the basis of knowledge and intellect, and so ensure their identity and achievements in the twenty-first century.

On-line resources provide one level of access to information that may be helpful in mobilizing world public opinion and knowledge to oppose war and crimes against nature and humankind. We need network facilitation, however, to support those incapable either financially or technically of developing or accessing communication infrastructures. Globally, we must act by sharing information in more lucrative and meaningful ways within the new communication infrastructures.

The objectives of military technology are reaching far beyond our imaginations. The satellite pollution surrounding our planet is devastating. The solution to mitigating the disastrous effects of nuclear contamination and waste is not within our grasp or understanding. The compounded waste dump beneath our islands in the South Pacific is far greater than Chernobyl, contained only by 'lava-bubbles' which rest upon an ever-shifting Pacific plate. The ice caps, the ozone, the mass loss of life due to pestilence and the continued genocidal activities of governments – all these shock the mind through the heart if ever truly looked at in the face. Yet we hope, we envision and we struggle in the integrity of our truths to explore and creatively experience a virtual world where these things can be resolved. And, as an indigenous woman, the protection of cultural and intellectual property rights are paramount to my own survival and my work.

Notes

1   http://hookele.com/netwarriors.
2   This includes both the valuable efforts to perpetuate native languages electronically through special fonts, sound files, software applications, etc., as demonstrated by the Hawaiian Language Programme at the University of Hawaii at Hilo on the island of Hawai'i (http://www.olelo.hawaii.edu) and the mirroring of sites in different languages (parts of NativeWeb, for example, are also provided in Spanish).
3   http://www. maxwell.syr.edu/native.
4   http://www.un.org.
5   http://www.hrweb.org/.
6   http://www.envirolink.org.
7   http://hanksville.phast.umass.edu/misc/NAresources.html.

References

Burrows, John (n.d.). *Fourth World Documentation Project.* Centre for World Indigenous Studies, Washington, DC, USA (http://www.halcyon.com/FWDP/fwdp.html).
Delisio, J. (1995). E-mail correspondence, 26 April.
Leventhal, M. (n.d.). *Microstate Resources Home Page* (http://www.microstate.com/).
Nauth, Kristin and Laurie Timmermann (1997). 'Bringing the Web to the Developing World', *New Media,* September 1997.
Ronfeldt David (1992). *Cyberocracy is Coming.* New York: Taylor and Francis.

CHAPTER 16

Richard Kahn and Douglas Kellner

Internet Subcultures and Political Activism

Subcultures traditionally represent alternative cultures and practices to the dominant culture of the established society. While they often construct themselves within and against the governing culture from which they are born, their comparatively smaller population size, their associations with emergent youth culture and the manifold novelties of the day, and their occasionally politically resistant and activist temperaments all serve to ensure that subcultures are constructed so as to be more than mere reproductions of the grander cultural forms, themes, and practices. If the dominant culture provides the semantic codes by which groups attempt to transmit and reproduce themselves, then subcultures represent a challenge to this symbolic order in their attempt to institute new grammars and meanings through which they interpret the world, and new practices through which they transform it.

In this sense, Dick Hebdige has spoken of subcultures as a form of "noise" capable of jamming dominant media transmissions. Of course, as Hebdige also notes, the eventual reality of oppositional culture-jamming is not that it replaces dominant media representations with its own. Rather, alternative subcultures strive to capture media attention, and in so doing become involved in the Janus-faced process of attempting to transform dominant codes even as they become appropriated, commodified, and re-defined by the hegemonic culture which they contest (Hebdige 1979: 90–2).

Our present moment, however, is highly turbulent and complex, and can be characterized as a "postmodern adventure" in which traditional forms of culture and politics are being resurrected, imploded into, and combined with entirely new cultural and political modes in a global media culture that is becoming increasingly dominated by the corporate forces of science, technology, and capital (see Best and Kellner 2001). To speak of postsubcultures, then, is to recognize that the emerging subcultures are taking place in a world that is saturated with proliferating technologies, media, and cultural awareness. Postsubcultures are constructed in new cultural spaces and with innovative forms, entering into novel global configurations by technological advances such as the internet and multimedia which help produce alternative forms of culture and political activism.

Richard Kahn and Douglas Kellner, "Internet Subcultures and Political Activism" (2003). Reprinted by permission of the authors.

Thus, whereas many traditional subcultures, like the Beat Generation, could aspire to the spirituality of "immediate" experience and intimate face-to-face communal relations, this is increasingly difficult for the postsubculture generation. Instead, the new subcultures that are arising around the evolving internet and wireless technologies appear as wholly mediated and committed to the medium of network communication that they correctly recognize as their foundation, while reaching out to help shape the broader culture and polity of which they are a part.

However, as with previous generations of subcultures, internet subcultures seek a certain immediacy of experience that strives to circumvent dominant codes in the attempt to access a wealth of global information quickly and directly, and then to appropriate and disseminate material further. The new subcultural immediacy, then, centers around flows of information and multimedia, and postsubcultures can be seen to be using the internet as an environment that supports their attempts to gain and provide access to information and culture that exists beyond the means of control of the dominant order. In this fashion, subcultures associated with the internet are involved in the revolutionary circulation and democratization of information and culture. In as much as this material is also part of the media-process by which people come to identify and define themselves, the emergent mediated postsubcultures are also involved in the attempt to allow people the freedom to redefine and construct themselves around the kind of alternative cultural forms, experiences, and practices which radical deployments of the internet afford (see Dyer-Witheford 2001; Best and Kellner 2001).

The evolving postsubcultures of the online global network

While there are a plethora of alternative cultures at work on the internet today, it would of course be a mistake to categorize them all as concerned strictly with either democracy or progressive politics. Rather, akin to the complexity of the postmodern era at hand, the subcultures of the internet would be better represented as multiplicitous, with the Net being used for both progressive and reactionary causes by an abundance of groups whose politics range from the far left to the extreme right.

Indeed, while the overall tenor of the revolution that is being brought about by the internet is toward the proliferation of alternative information and forms of culture and subjectivity, many voices affiliated with both hate and violence have also found ready homes amidst its cultural forum. The internet allows a myriad of groups to propagate and propagandize for their cause outside the media and norms traditionally instituted by pre-internet society. Our point here is certainly not to valorize the gains made by such subcultural groups, but rather to note that the use of the internet as a media tool has allowed for the construction of a wide variety of nonmainstream identities and communicative practices. Much like the hypertextual nature of the Web itself, the identities of internet subcultures are often hybridic and complex themselves, revealing a tendency to evolve through constant reorganization and affiliation with other internet subcultural groups. In this sense, many postsubcultures of the internet can be seen as dissolving classical cultural and political boundaries that appear too rigid and ideological for Net life. Still, groups also exist that have clearly defined political orientations.

At work within all of these Net subcultures is also the question of how they stand in relation to the dominant culture. During the late 1980s, major internet subcultures such as BBS (bulletin board systems) hubs represented the leading edge of the technology fringe. Populated mostly by an underground network of technically sophisticated professional users and computer-literate youth, the bulletin boards proffered a veritable "gift economy" of pictures, simple games, and message boards over extremely slow networks. There was little or no discussion of service charges and most BBSs relied upon users to develop online reputations through which proven community service would garnish greater access from friendly SYSOPs (system operators). With the advent of the 1990s, many successful bulletin boards, such as The Well, transferred protocols onto the emerging World Wide Web of hypertext. Within only a few years, corporate and government culture would begin colonizing the web too, and by the time of the dot-bomb tech crash of 2000, early web pioneers such as Yahoo, Amazon, and NCSA (National Center for Supercomputing Applications), would be joined by a huge influx of companies selling everything from advertising to zoo animals.

As the internet went corporate and online service providers like America On-line (AOL), Compuserve, Prodigy, and Earthlink sought to brand and sell the internet experience, many subcultures formed around the new online corporate behaviors with service providers becoming a key to one's on- and offline identity. Historically, similar subcultures had formed around hardware computer manufacturers like Apple, Kaypro, and IBM, but during the 1990s factions erupted within computers as well over software domains such as web browsers (Microsoft vs. Netscape) and search engines (Yahoo vs. Alta Vista). Still, the strongest user bonds seem to have solidified around service providers, with AOL providing a sort of cultural benchmark for the movement. During this time of relative infancy for the internet, AOL helped to bring millions of new internet users online with its graphical user interface (GUI), "You've got mail" aesthetic, and limitless user chatrooms wherein people could find love, local gossip, transsexual vampires, and anything else available to users's imagination!

However, behind the corporate branding and growing of the internet during the 1990s, noncorporate subcultures thrived too. Multi-user Dungeons (MUDs) and their object-oriented relatives, the MOOs, sprang up alongside the WWW, allowing people to explore basic virtual environments and interact with one another in real time. Newsgroups became a rage and an important source of information, debate, and file sharing, as people freely formed topical groups on the internet's Usenet platform. Then, as emailing grew readily popular, an equally large number of list-serves became housed upon the web and available for free user subscription. Large, popular list-serves like Nettime-L, or the Spoon lists housed at University of Virginia, allowed a variety of diverse subcultures to form themselves through group email discussions and opinion postings. And eventually, the WWW itself, though rapidly transforming under the "tech revolution's" pay-to-pay capitalist ideology into a mainstream cultural movement, continued to support a veritable carnival of alternative voices and cultures as well. Far beyond the provocative web antics of Church of the Subgenius or Terence McKenna, the late 1990s revealed a web that people were actively helping to create and not simply experience.[1]

The rise of the internet, then, as cultural and subcultural force, has been multifaceted, and socially and politically complex. While corporate forces rapidly built a bigger and speedier internet for the new millennium, subcultural forces equally rapidly sought to borrow the new online environment for their own sociopolitical intentions. Thus was the case, infamously, with the peer-to-peer (P2P) client Napster, which allowed approximately 60 million users at one point to share and trade a variety of files directly with one another freely. However, when users began sharing huge volumes of copyrighted audio material, because the newly formed broadband networks made such files easily accessible, corporate forces intervened and fractured the movement. Yet a movement had been started that publicized the utopian potential of the Net as subcultural community and bearer of a gift economy. Hence, despite Napster's fall, many continued to believe that the idea of the P2P network signaled a form of cultural revolution, and a number of new P2P communities arose within the internet space previously dominated by Napster.[2]

The music industry, however, has made every attempt to block P2P trading of music online, and there is now intense interest in Hollywood's response to circulating videos and films. Less maliciously, but equally exemplary of how mainstream corporate culture has resituated subcultural movements on the net, is the case of early online zines like *Suck*, *Feed*, and *Salon*. As these online cultural spaces grew in popularity, corporate culture was quick to import and copy elements of their style and reinterpret and reposition them. Suddenly, the trendy use of neon colors like *Feed*'s orange became an industry standard, which as tech became "cool," lent itself equally as well to sneakers, clothing, and record posters as it had to websites. Further elements of zine style such as written and visual language became equally replicated and repositioned as advertising norms. Under such intense corporate pressure many of the successful online zines of the past decade have folded, unable to demonstrate or innovate a particular cultural niche in the face of countless impostors. Even the widely read and discussed *Salon* was rumored to face the possibility of insolvency in 2002, and only Microsoft's online journal *Slate* appears financially secure.

Globalization and Net politics

The present internet moment remains a complex assemblage of a variety of groups and movements, both mainstream and oppositional. However, following the massive hi-tech sector bust at the start of the new millennium, and with economic sectors generally down across the board with the global economic recession, the Terror War erupting in 2001, and the disasterous effects of Bushonomics, much of the corporate colonization of the new media has also waned. Following "9/11," however, the politicization of the internet again emerged as a major cultural issue, and new oppositions are forming around the online rights to freedom of use and information, as well as user privacy, that groups like the Electronic Frontier Foundation (EFF), Computer Professionals for Social Responsibility (CPSR), and the Center for Democracy and Technology (CDT) have long touted. For instance, it emerged in late 2002 that the Bush administration was developing a Total Information Awareness project that would compile a government database on every individual with material collected from a diversity of sources. Intense debate has erupted and the Bush administration is being forced to make concessions to critics concerned about privacy and Big Brother surveillance. Such online political oppositions directly pit post-subcultural groups, many who did not previously have an obvious political agenda, against the security policies of government. In this scenario, internet corporations are often left "in the middle" with the choice to either side with the users who they would court as consumers or with the political administrations. The latter are capable of making business either easy or difficult depending upon which laws are enacted and prosecuted (e.g. Microsoft's antitrust battle under the Clinton administration and then again under Bush).

Still, as the culture of the internet becomes more highly politicized, it is becoming harder for corporations to portray themselves simply as "neutral" cultural forces. Using the very online means that these corporations helped to popularize against them, users are globally beginning to portray for each other a maturing political awareness that perceives corporate and governmental behavior as intertwined in the name of "globalization."[3] As part of the backlash against globalization over the past years, a wide range of theorists have argued that the proliferation of difference and the shift to more local discourses and practices define significant alternatives to corporate globalization. In this view, theory and politics should shift from the level of globalization and its accompanying often totalizing and macro dimensions in order to focus on the local, the specific, the particular, the heterogeneous, and the micro level of everyday experience. An array of discourses associated with poststructuralism, postmodernism, feminism, and multiculturalism focus on difference, otherness, marginality, the personal, the particular, and the concrete over more general theory and politics that aim at more global or universal conditions.[4] Likewise, a broad spectrum of internet subcultures of resistance have focused their attention on the local level, organizing struggles around a seemingly endless variety of identity issues.

However, it can be argued that such dichotomies as those between the global and the local express contradictions and tensions between crucial constitutive forces of the present moment, and that it is therefore a mistake to reject a focus on one side in favor of an exclusive concern with the other (Cvetkovich and Kellner 1997). Hence, an important challenge for the emerging critical theory of globalization is to think through the relationships between the global and the local by observing how global forces influence and even structure an increasing number of local situations. This requires analysis as well of how local forces mediate the global, inflecting global forces to diverse ends and conditions, and producing unique configurations of the local and the global as the matrix for thought and action in the contemporary world (see Luke and Luke 2000).

Globalization is thus necessarily complex and challenging to both critical theories and radical democratic politics. But many people these days operate with binary concepts of the global and the local, and promote one or the other side of the equation as the solution to the world's problems. For globalists, globalization is the solution, and underdevelopment, backwardness, and provincialism are the problem. For localists, globalization is the problem and localization is the solution. But, less simplistically, it is the mix that matters, and whether global or local solutions are most fitting depends on the conditions in the distinctive context that one is addressing and the particular solutions and policies being proposed.

Specific locations and practices of a plurality of postsubcultures constitute perhaps what is most interesting now about oppositional subcultural activities at work within the internet. Much more than other subcultures like boarders, punks, mods, or followers of the New Age, internet subcultures have taken up the questions of local and global politics and are attempting to construct answers both locally and globally as a response. Importantly, this can be done due to the very nature of the medium in which they exist. Therefore, while the internet can and has been used to promote capitalist globalization, the current configuration of online subcultures are interested in the number of ways in which the global network can be diverted and used in the struggle against it.

Technopolitics and the antiglobalization movements

Successful use by the EZLN Zapatista movement in Mexico of the internet dramatized its importance for progressive politics (Best and Kellner, 2001). Beyond deploying the internet as a technology for plotting political organization and for furthering communication, activists quickly drew upon the Zapatista's imaginative use of the internet to begin broadcasting their new messages to a potential global audience. In the late 1990s, activists throughout the world began employing the internet to foster movements against the excesses of corporate capitalism, most dramatically occurring in the protests in Seattle and elsewhere against the World Trade Organization (WTO) meeting in December 1999. A global protest movement surfaced that utilized the internet to organize resistance to the WTO and capitalist globalization, while championing democratization and social justice. Many websites contained anti-WTO material and numerous mailing lists used the internet to distribute critical material and to organize the protest. The result was the mobilization of caravans from throughout the United States to take protestors to Seattle, many of whom had never met and were recruited through the internet. There were also significant numbers of international participants in Seattle which exhibited labor, environmentalist, feminist, anticapitalist, animal rights, anarchist, and other groups organized to protest aspects of globalization and form new solidarities for future struggles. In addition, protests occurred throughout the world, and a proliferation of anti-WTO material against the extremely secret group spread throughout the internet.

Furthermore, the internet provided critical coverage of the event, documentation of the various groups' protests, and debate over the WTO and globalization. Whereas the mainstream media presented the protests as "antitrade," featured the incidents of anarchist violence against property, while minimizing police violence against demonstrators, the internet provided pictures, eyewitness accounts, and reports of police brutality and the generally peaceful and nonviolent nature of the protests. While the mainstream media framed the protests negatively and privileged suspect spokespeople like Patrick Buchanan as critics of globalization, the internet provided multiple representations of the demonstrations, advanced reflective discussion of the WTO and globalization, and presented a diversity of critical perspectives.

The Seattle protests had some immediate consequences. The day after the demonstrators made good on their promise to shut down the WTO negotiations, Bill Clinton gave a speech endorsing the concept of labor rights enforceable by trade sanctions, thus effectively making impossible any agreement and consensus during the Seattle meetings. In addition, at the World Economic Forum in Davos a month later there was much discussion of how concessions were necessary on labor and the environment if consensus over globalization and free trade were to be possible. Importantly, the issue of overcoming divisions between the information rich and poor, and improving the lot of the disenfranchised and oppressed, bringing these groups the benefits of globalization, were also seriously discussed at the meeting and in the media.

More importantly, many activists were energized by the new alliances, solidarities, and militancy, and continued to cultivate an antiglobalization movement. The Seattle demonstrations were followed by April 2000 struggles in Washington, DC, to protest against the World Bank and IMF, and later in the year against capitalist globalization in Prague and Melbourne; in April 2001, an extremely large and militant protest erupted against the Free Trade Area of the Americas summit in Quebec City, and in summer 2001 a sizeable demonstration took place in Genoa.

In May 2002, a surprisingly big demonstration took place in Washington against capitalist globalization and for peace and justice, and it was apparent that a new worldwide movement was in the making that was uniting diverse opponents of capitalist globalization throughout the world. The anticorporate globalization movement favored globalization-from-below, which would protect the environment, labor rights, national cultures, democratization, and other goods from the ravages of an uncontrolled capitalist globalization (see Brecher, Costello, and Smith 2000; Steger 2002). Similar demonstrations had taken place in Monterrey, Mexico, two months earlier and, more recently, two more occurred during June 2002 at Calgary and Ottawa to protest against the G8 Summit meeting in Canada. Each of these demonstrations was comprised of people hailing from many locations and intent on using the venue as an opportunity to promote their voice, and fight in common cause against what is perceived to be the oppression of a dominant monoculture.

Initially, the incipient antiglobalization movement was precisely that: antiglobalization. The movement itself, however, was increasingly global, linking together a diversity of movements into global solidarity networks and using the internet and instruments of globalization to advance its struggles. Following the Battle for Seattle, the internet witnessed the rise of independent media outlets like the Indymedia network (http://www.indymedia.org), with major global cities receiving web portals in which to document, organize, and proliferate information that would not otherwise be readily available through the major media. Countless other organizations and sites have developed similar websites and networks since, like Alternet (http://www.alternet.org), turning the internet from a valuable tool in the antiglobalization struggle into the driving engine for a new global cultural vision for democracy.

Through the practice of the type of large-scale organization and assimilation of information afforded by the internet, many opponents of capitalist globalization evolved from a simple subcultural nihilism to recognize the need for a global movement with a positive vision. Such alternative and oppositional globalizations stand for such things as social justice, equality, labor, civil liberties, universal human rights, and a healthy planet on which to live. Accordingly, the anticapitalist globalization movements began advocating common values and visions, and started defining themselves in positive terms such as the global justice movement.

Thus, technopolitics became part and parcel of the involvement of internet subcultures, a mushrooming global movement for peace, justice, democracy, rights, and other positive values. In particular, the subcultural movements against capitalist globalization exploited the internet to organize mass demonstrations and to disseminate information to the world concerning the policies of the institutions of capitalist globalization. The events made clear that protestors were not against globalization *per se*, but were against neoliberal and capitalist globalization, opposing specific policies and institutions that produce intensified exploitation of labor, environmental devastation, growing divisions among the social classes, and the undermining of democracy. The emerging globalization-from-below movements are contextualizing these problems in the framework of a restructuring of capitalism on a worldwide basis for maximum profit with zero accountability, and have made clear the need for democratization, regulation, rules, and globalization in the interests of people and not profit.

The new movements against capitalist globalization have thus placed the issues of global justice and environmental destruction squarely in the center of important political concerns of our time. Hence, whereas the mainstream media had failed to vigorously debate or even report on globalization until the eruption of a vigorous antiglobalization movement, and rarely, if ever, critically discussed the activities of the WTO, World Bank, and IMF, there is now a widely circulating critical discourse and controversy over these institutions. Stung by criticisms, representatives of the World Bank, in particular, are pledging reform and pressures are mounting concerning proper and improper roles for the major global institutions, highlighting their limitations and deficiencies, and the need for reforms like debt relief from overburdened developing countries to solve some of their fiscal and social problems. Nonetheless, others like the world leaders involved in the G8 and related summits are resorting to holding their meetings in ever more remote regions, their inaccessibility thereby conveying a political reality that new subcultures are eager to reveal to ever-wider audiences.

Indeed, in late 2002 and early 2003, global antiwar movements began to emerge against Bush administration policies against Iraq and the growing threats of war. Reaching out to broad audiences, political groups like MoveOn (www.moveon.org) used the internet to circulate antiwar information, organize demonstrations, and promote a wide diversity of antiwar activities. Thus, after using the internet to successfully organize a wide range of antiglobalization demonstrations, activists, including many young people, are organizing massive demonstrations against the Bush and Blair administrations' threats against Iraq. The global internet, then, is creating the base and the basis for an unprecedented worldwide antiwar/pro-peace movement during a time of terrorism, war, and intense political struggle.

From hackers to terrorists: militant internet culture

To capital's globalization-from-above, the subcultures of cyberactivists have thus been attempting to carry out globalization-from-below, developing networks of solidarity and propagating oppositional ideas and movements throughout the planet. To the capitalist international of transnational corporate-led globalization, a Fifth International, to use Waterman's phrase (1992), of computer-mediated activism is emerging, that is qualitatively different from the party-based socialist and communist Internationals. As the virtual community theorist Howard Rheingold notes (2002), advances in personal, mobile informational technology are rapidly providing the structural elements for the existence of fresh kinds of highly informed, autonomous communities that coalesce around local lifestyle choices, global political demands, and everything in between. These multiple networks of connected citizens and activists transform the so-called "dumb mobs" of totalitarian and polyarchical states into "smart mobs" of socially active personages linked by notebook computers, PDA devices, internet cellphones, pagers, and global GPS positioning systems. Thus, while new mobile technology provides yet another impetus towards experimental identity construction and identity politics, such networking also links diverse communities like labor, feminist, ecological, peace, and various anticapitalist groups, providing the basis for a new politics of alliance and solidarity to overcome the limitations of postmodern identity politics (see Dyer-Witheford 1999; Best and Kellner 2001; Burbach 2001).

Of course, as noted previously, right-wing and reactionary forces can and have used the internet to promote their political agendas as well. In a short time, one can easily access an exotic witch's brew of websites maintained by the Ku Klux Klan, and myriad neo-Nazi assemblages, including the Aryan Nation and various militia groups. Internet discussion lists also disperse these views and right-wing extremists are aggressively active on many computer forums, as well as radio programs and stations, public access television programs, fax campaigns, video, and even rock music productions. These organizations are hardly harmless, having carried out terrorism of various sorts extending from church burnings to the bombings of public buildings. Adopting quasi-Leninist discourse and tactics for ultra-right causes, these groups have been successful in recruiting working-class members devastated by the developments of global capitalism, which has resulted in widespread unemployment for traditional forms of industrial, agricultural, and unskilled labor. Moreover, extremist websites have influenced alienated middle-class youth as well. (A 1999 HBO documentary on "Hate on the Internet" provides a disturbing number of examples of how extremist websites influenced disaffected youth to commit hate crimes.)

A recent twist in the saga of technopolitics, in fact, seems to be that allegedly "terrorist" groups are now increasingly using the internet and websites to promote their causes. An article in the *Los Angeles Times* (Feb. 8, 2001: A1, A14) reported that groups like Hamas use their website to post reports of acts of terror against Israel, rather than calling newspapers or broadcasting outlets. A wide range of groups labeled as "terrorist" reportedly use email, list-serves, and websites to further their struggles, causes including Hezbollah and Hamas, the Maoist group Shining Path in Peru, and a variety of other groups throughout Asia and elsewhere. The Tamil Tigers, for instance, a liberation movement in Sri Lanka, offer position papers, daily news, and free email service. According to the *Los Angeles Times*, experts are still unclear "whether the ability to communicate on-line worldwide is prompting an increase or a decrease in terrorist acts."

Since September 11, 2001, there have been widespread discussions of how the bin Laden Al Qaeda network used the internet to plan the 9/11 terrorist attacks on the US, how the group communicated with each other, got funds and purchased airline tickets via the internet, and used flight simulations to practice their hijacking (see Kellner 2003). Since "Operation Enduring Freedom," news stories have documented how many pro-Al Qaeda websites continue to appear and disappear, serving as propaganda conduits and potential organization channels for remaining terrorist cell members. By encrypting messages within what appear to be simple web pictures, Al Qaeda (or any group or person) can transfer sensitive information that only requires the receiving party to download the picture and then decrypt it in order to reveal the secret message. The sheer volume of video and still picture information on the internet helps to ensure that the information can be circulated even when perused by such powerful governmental surveillance systems as Echelon and Carnivore. But, apparently in response to the threat posed to US "war on terror" interests, the Bush administration has begun the attempt to discontinue websites which it suspects terror cells are frequenting to gain information that could be used in terrorist attacks.

In fact, despite the expectation that any governmental administration would target the information channels of its enemy, it is exactly the mammoth reaction by the Bush administration and the Pentagon to the perceived threats posed by the internet that have the subcultural forces associated with the battle against globalization-from-above fighting in opposition to US security policies. Drawing upon the expertise of a subculture of politically minded computer hackers to inform oppositional groups of security threats and to help defend against them, a technical wing has become allied to those fighting for globalization-from-below. Groups like Cult of the Dead Cow (http://www.cultdeadcow. org) and Cryptome (http://www.cryptome.org) and the hacker journal *2600* (http:// www.2600.org) are figureheads for a broad movement of exceptionally computer-literate individuals who group together under the banner of HOPE (Hackers On Planet Earth) and who practice a politics called "hacktivism" (on hacker culture, see Taylor 1999 and Himanen 2001). The hacktivists have been widely responsible for allowing oppositional subcultures to understand how they may maintain online privacy and how their privacy may be easily jeopardized by anyone seeking to do so.

Additionally, hacktivists have been especially influential in educating the public about governmental and corporate protocols that have been developed in order to survey the habits and attitudes of those active online. Perhaps most importantly, some of the hacktivists are involved in creating open source software programs that can be used freely to circumvent the intervention of government and corporate control into internet experience. Notably, and somewhat scandalously, the hacktivists have released programs like Six/Four (after Tiananmen Square), that combines the peer-to-peer capabilities of Napster with a virtual private networking protocol that makes user identity anonymous, and Camera/Shy, a powerful web-browser stenography application that allows anyone to engage in the type of secret information storage and retrieval that Al Qaeda allegedly uses to combat the Pentagon. Moreover, associated with the hacktivist cause are the "crackers" who create "warez," pirated versions of commercial software or passwords. While anathema to Bill Gates, there is no software beyond the reach of the pirate-crackers, and to the delight of the alternative internet subculture, their often otherwise expensive programs are freely traded and shared over the web and peer-to-peer networks across the globe. Hackers also support the Open Source movement, in which noncorporate softwares are freely and legally traded, improved upon at large, and available for general use by a public which agrees not to sell them in the future. Such free Microsoft competitors, like the operating system Linux (http://www.linux.org) and the word-processing suite OpenOffice (http://www.openoffice.org), provide powerful and economically palatable alternatives to the PC hegemon.

Another hacker ploy is the monitoring and exploitation for social gain of the booming wireless, wide-area internet market (i.e. wi-fi, WAN, or WLAN). Wi-fi, besides offering institutions, corporations, and homes the luxury of internet connectivity and organizational access for any and all users within the area covered by the local network, also potentially offers such freedoms to nearby neighbors and wireless pedestrians if such networks are not made secure. In fact, as the US cybersecurity czar Richard Clarke noted in December, 2002, an astounding number of wi-fi networks are unprotected and available for hacking. This led the Office of Homeland Security to label wireless networking a terrorist threat (http://wired.com/news/wireless/0,1382,56742,00.html). Part of what the government is reacting to is the activist technique of "war-driving," in which a hacker drives through a community equipped with a basic wireless antenna and computer searching for network access nodes (see http://www.wardriving.com). Many hackers had been war-driving around Washington DC, thereby gaining valuable federal information and server access, prompting the government contractor Science Applications International Corporation (SAIC) to begin monitoring drive-by hacks in the summer of 2002 (http://www. securityfocus.com/news/552).

But not all war-drivers are interested in sensitive information, and many more are simply interested in proliferating information about what amounts to free broadband internet access points – a form of internet connectivity that otherwise comes at a premium cost (see http://www.freenetworks.org). Thus, wireless network hackers are often deploying their skills towards developing a database of "free networks," which if not always free of costs, represent opportunities for local communities to knowingly share connections and corporate fees. Needless to say, corporate internet service providers are outraged by this anticapitalist development, and are seeking government legislation favoring prosecution of this mode of "gift economy" activism.

Hacktivists are also directly involved in the immediate political battles being played out around the dynamically globalized world. Hacktivists like the German "The Mixter," who authored the "Tribe Floodnet" program that shut down the website for the World Economic Forum in January 2002, routinely use their hacking skills to cause disruption of governmental and corporate presences online. On July 12, 2002, the homepage for the *USA Today* news site was hacked and altered content was presented to the public, leaving *USA Today* to join such other media magnets as the *New York Times* and Yahoo as the corporate victims of a media hack. In February 2003, immediately following the destruction of the Space Shuttle Columbia, a group calling themselves "Trippin Smurfs" hacked NASA's servers for the third time in three months. In each case, security was compromised and the web servers were defaced with antiwar political messages. Another repeated victim of hacks is the Recording Industry Association of America (RIAA), which, because of its attempt to legislate P2P music trading, has become anathema to internet hacktivists. A sixth attack upon the RIAA website in January, 2003, posted bogus press releases and even provided music files for free downloading!

But while a revolutionary subculture of hackers has formed online, those involved in the fight for an alternative globalization are far from comprising the totality of the hacker population. The US government and Al Qaeda, as well as an increasing number of different political groups, are all engaging in cyberwar as an important adjunct of their political battles. Indeed, Israeli hackers have repeatedly attacked the websites of Hezbollah, while pro-Palestine hackers have reportedly placed militant demands and slogans on the websites of Israel's army, foreign ministry, and parliament. Likewise, in the bloody struggle over Kashmir, Pakistani and Indian computer hackers have waged similar cyberbattles against opposing forces' websites, while rebel forces in the Philippines taunt government troops with cellphone calls and messages and attack government websites as well.

Blogging: a vision of the democratic future of the Net?

On an entirely different note, but equally political and contested in nature, a vibrant new internet subculture has erupted around the phenomenon of "blogging." A blog, tech slang for "web log," is an extension of the World Wide Web of hypertext pages. A blog differs from other webpages, however, in certain key ways. Firstly, most blogs are created using a relatively easy-to-use automated software interface, provided freely (or for a small fee) by companies like Google's Blogger (http://www.blogger.com) or Radio Userland (http://radio.userland.com). Some blog subcultures like the more tech-oriented users of Moveable Type (http://www.movabletype.org), however, disdaining any tinge of capitalism, provide their own interface freely as open source. Whichever is chosen, the interfaces load like any other web page in a user's web browser, but provide a template for users to fill in with their blog's name, style, and features. Additionally, spaces for blog entries exist which incorporate all of the standard features associated with hypertext. When users fill in the information that they would like to post to their web log and hit "publish," the blog interface automatically formats and posts the user's information to their desired blog. This ease of use has made blogging a popular sensation over the last year, with giants like Salon and AOL joining the blogging craze, and with hundreds of thousands of new bloggers constructing blogs and net journals in an increasing trend.[6] Indeed, the highly successful search engine corporation Google scooped up the small company that makes Blogger, providing the potential for a major blogging explosion.

Another feature relatively unique to blogs is their ability to integrate a variety of internet features into their pages. Thus, a typical blog will not only provide postings from a blogger (or a team of bloggers), but it will also provide readers the opportunity to reply to postings and begin discussions with each other and the blog author(s) as would a messageboard. Blogs will also often permit users to subscribe to them, like a list-serve, thereby allowing readers to receive new blog postings directly to their email address. Blogs, and bloggers, are also doing interesting things with the hyperlinks that link webpages together. From the first, blogging has been about community, with bloggers eager to read one another's entries, post comments about them on their own blogs, and provide lists of links to the blog cartels that identify who particular bloggers think is "who" in their blog world.

This has led to interesting networks of links, with dynamic maps of the most popular blogs and the news stories that these blogs discuss being provided in real-time by such sites as Blogdex (http://blogdex.media.mit.edu), Daypop (http://www.daypop.com) and Technorati (http://www.technorati.com). Another result of bloggers' fascination with networks of links has been the subcultural phenomenon known as "Google Bombing." Documented in early 2002, it was revealed that the popular search engine Google had a special affinity for blogs because of its tendency to favor recently updated web content in its site ranking system. With this in mind, bloggers began campaigns to get large numbers of fellow bloggers to post links to specific postings designed around desirable keywords that Google users would normally use to search. A successful Google Bomb would then rocket the initial blog that began the campaign up Google's rankings to No. 1!

Thus, while those in the blog culture often abused this trick for personal gain (e.g. to get their own name and blog placed at the top of Google's most popular search terms), many in the blog subculture began using the Google Bomb as a tool for political subversion. Known as a "justice bomb," this use of blogs serves to link a particularly distasteful corporation or entity to a series of keywords that either spoofs or criticizes the same. Hence, thanks to a Google Bomb, Google users typing in "McDonald's" might very well get a blog link entitled "Lies About Their Fries" as the top entry.

Blogs have not always been political, but post 9/11 the phenomenon of War-blogging appears to be trumping the simple diary format. More blogs than ever are being created to deal with specific political positions and alternative media sources than ever before, and group-style blogs like Fark (http://www.fark.com), Metafilter (http://www.metafilter. com), and BoingBoing (http://boingboing.net), wherein community users post and discuss information of the day, have become extremely popular. But, it is perhaps the new ability to syndicate one's blog that truly marks the blog subculture as a democratic and oppositional culture with which the mainstream must reckon. News blogs like Google (http://news.google.com), NewsIsFree (http://www.newsisfree.com), and Syndic8 (http://www.syndic8.com) daily log syndicated content and broadcast it globally to a diverse audience. This has resulted in a revolution in journalism in which subcultures of bloggers are continually posting and commenting upon news stories of particular interest to them, which are in turn found, read, and republished by the global media.

The examples in this section suggest how technoculture makes possible a reconfiguring of politics, a refocusing of politics on everyday life, and the use of the tools and techniques of emergent computer and communication technologies to expand the field of politics and culture. In this conjuncture, the ideas of Guy Debord and the Situationist International are especially relevant with their stress on the construction of situations, the use of technology, media of communication, and cultural forms to promote a revolution of everyday life, and to increase the realm of freedom, community, and empowerment.[7] To a meaningful extent, then, the new information and communication technologies *are* revolutionary, they *do* constitute a revolution of everyday life being presently enacted by internet subcultures. Yet, it has often been a revolution that also promotes and disseminates the capitalist consumer society, individual and competition, and that has involved new modes of fetishism, enslavement, and domination yet to be clearly perceived and theorized.

The internet is thus a contested terrain, used by Left, Right, and Center of both dominant cultures and subcultures to promote their own agendas and interests. The political battles of the future may well be fought in the streets, factories, parliaments, and other sites of past struggle, but politics is already mediated by broadcast, computer, and information technologies and will increasingly be so in the future. Those interested in the politics and culture of the future should therefore be clear on the important role of the new public spheres and intervene accordingly, while critical cultural theorists have the responsibility of educating students around the cultural and subcultural literacies that ultimately amount to the skills that will enable them to participate in the ongoing struggle inherent in cultural politics.

Subculture activism has thus materialized as a vital new space of politics and culture in which a wide diversity of individuals and groups have used emergent technologies to help produce new subcultures, social relations, and forms of politics. Many of these subcultures may become appropriated into the mainstream, but no doubt ever-new oppositional cultures and novel alternative voices and practices will appear as we navigate the always-receding future.

Notes

1 On MOOs, MUDs, internet chat rooms, and new forms of identity, culture, and community produced by information and communication technologies, see Turkle 1996, 1997.
2 For a solid journalistic account of the Napster and P2P story see Alderman 2001; for an optimistic account of the continuing potential of P2P potentiality, see Barbrook 2002.
3 On globalization, see Cvetkovich and Kellner 1997, Best and Kellner 2001, and Kellner 1998, 2002.
4 Such positions are associated with the postmodern theories of Foucault, Lyotard, Rorty, and have been taken up by a wide range of feminists, multiculturalists, and others. On these theorists and postmodern politics, see Best and Kellner 1991, 1997, 2001, and the valorization and critique of postmodern politics in Hardt and Negri 2000 and Burbach 2001.
5 On technopolitics see Kellner 1997; Armitage 1999; and Best and Kellner 2001.
6 For examples, see our two websites. BlogLeft: Critical Interventions (2002), http://www.gseis.ucla.edu/courses/ed253a/blogger.php (accessed Aug. 2002). Vegan Blog: The (Eco) Logical Weblog (2002), http://getvegan.com/blog/blogger.php (accessed Aug. 2002).
7 On the importance of the ideas of Debord and the Situationist International to make sense of the present conjuncture see Best and Kellner 1997: Ch. 3; and on the new forms of the interactive consumer society, see Best and Kellner 2001.

References

Alderman, J. (2001), *Sonic Boom: P2P and the Battle for the Future of Music*. London: Fourth Estate.
Armitage, J. (ed.) (1999), Special Issue on Machinic Modulations: New Cultural Theory and Technopolitics. *Angelaki: Journal of the Theoretical Humanities* 4(2) (September).
Barbrook, R. (2002), "The Napsterization of Everything." *Science as Culture* 11(2) (June): 277–85.
Best, S. and Kellner, D. (1991), *Postmodern Theory: Critical Interrogations*. London and New York: Macmillan and Guilford Press.

Best, S. and Kellner, D. (1997), *The Postmodern Turn*. New York and London: Guilford Press and Routledge.

Best, S. and Kellner, D. (2001), *The Postmodern Adventure*. New York and London: Guilford Press and Routledge.

Brecher, J., Costello, T., and Smith, B. (2000), *Globalization From Below*. Boston: South End Press.

Burbach, R. (2001), *Globalization and Postmodern Politics: From Zapatistas to High-Tech Robber Barons*. London: Pluto Press.

Burbules, N. and Torres, C. (eds.) (2000), *Globalization and Education*. London, UK, and New York: Routledge.

Cvetkovich, A. and Kellner, D. (1997), *Articulating the Global and the Local: Globalization and Cultural Studies*. Boulder, CO: Westview.

Dyer-Witheford, N. (1999), *Cyber-Marx: Cycles and Circuits of Struggle in High-Technology Capitalism*. Urbana and Chicago, IL: University of Illinois Press.

Hardt, M. and Negri, A. (2000), *Empire*. Cambridge, MA: Harvard University Press.

Hebdige, D. (1979), *Subculture: The Meaning of Style*. London and New York: Routledge.

Himanen, P. (2001), *The Hacker Ethic*. New York: Random House.

Kellner, D. (1997), "Intellectuals, the New Public Spheres, and Technopolitics." *New Political Science* 41–2 (Fall): 169–88.

Kellner, D. (1998), "Globalization and the Postmodern Turn." In R. Axtmann (ed.), *Globalization and Europe*. London: Cassells.

Kellner, D. (2002), "Theorizing Globalization." *Sociological Theory* 20(3) (Nov.): 285–305.

Kellner, D. (2003), *From 9/11 to Terror War: Dangers of the Bush Legacy*. Lanham, MD: Rowman and Littlefield.

Luke, A. and Luke, C. (2000), "A Situated Perspective on Cultural Globalization." In N. Burbules and C. Torres (eds.), *Globalization and Education*. London, UK, and New York: Routledge.

Rheingold, H. (2002), *Smart Mobs: The Next Social Revolution*. Cambridge, MA: Perseus Publishing.

Steger, M. (2002), *Globalism: The New Market Ideology*. Lanham, MD: Rowman and Littlefield.

Taylor, P. (1999), *Hackers*. London and New York: Routledge.

Turkle, S. (1996), "Virtuality and its Discontents." *The American Prospect* 7(24) (Dec.), http://www.prospect.org/print/V7/24/turkle-s.html (accessed Sept. 2002).

Turkle, S. (1997), *Life on the Screen: Identity in the Age of the Internet*. New York: Touchstone Press.

Waterman, P. (1992), *International Labour Communication by Computer: The Fifth International?* Working Paper Series 129. The Hague: Institute of Social Studies.

CHAPTER 17

Staring Back: Self-Representations of Disabled Performance Artists

Rosemarie Garland Thomson

The meaning of the body, thus the meaning of the self, emerges through social relations.[1] We learn who we are by the responses we elicit from others. In social relations, disabled bodies prompt the question, "What happened to you?" The disabled body demands a narrative, requires an apologia that accounts for its difference from unexceptional bodies. In this sense, disability identity is constituted by the story of why my body is different from your body. Disability autobiography is a recently burgeoning form of textual self-representation that centers on answering the urgent question "What happened to you?" through narrative.[2] All forms of self-representation are inherently relational in that they presume that the representation one creates will be apprehended by someone else.

Disability performance art is a genre of self-representation, a form of autobiography, that merges the visual with the narrative. As a fusion of both seeing and telling, disability performance art foregrounds the body as an object both to be viewed and to be explained. The disabled body is not only the medium but the content of performance. The disabled body on view *is* the performance. Rather than only telling the required disability story, then, disability performance acts out that story. In addition to always addressing the question of "What happened to you?" that textual autobiography answers, disability performance at the same time reenacts the primal scene of disability in which the normative viewer encounters the disabled body and demands an explanation. Simply the presence of the visibly disabled performer on stage engenders this dynamic between the performer and her audience.

By presenting her body before a viewer, the visibly disabled performance artist generates the dynamic of staring, the arrested attentiveness that registers difference on the part of the viewer. In the social context of an ablist society, the disabled body summons the stare, and the stare mandates the story. The stare, in other words, evokes the question, "What happened to you?" This stare-and-tell ritual constitutes disability identity in the social realm. This exchange between starer and object registers both the anonymity that

Rosemarie Garland Thomson, "Staring Back: Self-Representations of Disabled Performance Artists," *American Quarterly*, vol. 52, no. 2 (June 2000), pp. 334–8. © The American Studies Association. Reprinted with permission of The Johns Hopkins University Press.

confers agency on the starer and the singularity that stigmatizes the one who is stared at. Staring is thus the ritual social enactment of exclusion from an imagined community of the fully human. This relational model suggests that disability is not simply a natural state of bodily inferiority and inadequacy. Rather, disability is a culturally fabricated narrative of the body, similar to what we understand as the fictions of race and gender.[3]

Why would a person with a visible disability, someone with a body that disrupts the expectations of the complacently normal, deliberately invite the stare-and-tell dynamic that constitutes her otherness? A survey of disability performance art suggests that such performances are platforms for profoundly liberating assertions and representations of the self in which the artist controls the terms of the encounter.[4] In addition to allowing individual expression, this artistic engagement with self-display also provides a medium for positive identity politics and an opportunity to protest cultural images of disabled people. Disabled performance artists manipulate the stare-and-tell dynamic. I would argue, in fact, that disability performance art is a genre of autobiography particularly appropriate to representing the social experience of disability precisely because it allows for creating both visual and narrative self-representations simultaneously and because it traffics in the two realms of representation fundamental to the social construction of disability identity.

One of the most compelling examples of the liberatory potential of disability perform-ance is Mary Duffy, an Irishwoman who appears extensively before US viewers. Duffy, who is armless, with a delicate hand attached directly to one shoulder, always presents herself nude in performances. A "severely disabled" woman by the standards of what disability historian Paul Longmore calls with great irony the "severely able-bodied," Duffy boldly exposes the body that has always been hidden, both shocking and compelling her viewers.[5] Her performances begin with a totally darkened room that wipes away all ocular options, clearing the audience's visual palate. For an almost uncomfortable period of time, the viewers see nothing. Amid the darkness, a series of enigmatic black and white images seem to float up; they are piles of smooth stones that increase in number as each image changes to the next. During this prolegomenon, this critical introduction, the clusters of stones grow and the sound of a chugging train that transforms into a beating heart begins to accompany the images. The suggestion of embryonic development and fetal heartbeat becomes clear. Then out of the darkness the form of Mary Duffy suddenly appears, spotlit from the front and against a black background. The scene dramatically obliterates all visual alternatives except Duffy's ultra-white form, forcing the audience to look at her completely naked body, posed as the classical nude figure of the Venus de Milo, the quintessential icon of female beauty. Young, full-breasted, voluptuous, beautiful, and armless, this living Venus demands with her silent presence that the audience stare at her. This arresting choreography hyperbolically, almost parodically, stages the dynamic of two opposing modes of looking: staring at the freakishly different body and gazing at the female body as a beautiful work of art.

The viewer becomes the starer trained by the social order to see Duffy's body as a pathological lack, a deviation from the norm that has either been hidden away in the asylum or displayed in medical photographs with a black bar over the eyes to obliterate personhood. Hers is the sensationally abnormal body glimpsed furtively in the tabloids and yet proscribed as an object of proper bourgeois looking. Like gawking at a fatal traffic accident or the primal scene, looking at Duffy is at once compelling and illicit. But Duffy's body also evokes the familiar contours of beauty. Duffy's simultaneously starkly disabled and classically beautiful body elicits a confusing combination of the rapt gaze and the intrusive stare. The literally in-your-face white figure against the black background is at once the degraded and the exalted body in the western tradition of looking. The templates culture has supplied her audience are inadequate to make sense of her body. Framed as a work of art, her body is paradox incarnate, leaving her viewers' sense of the order of things in ruins. Hers is the art that transforms consciousness, that grants a new way of seeing the known world.

Having manipulated staring to upset any simple notion of disability identity, Duffy moves into the narrative part of her performance, answering the ritualistic question that her exposed body elicits: "What happened to you?" Shifting the classical allusion from Venus de Milo to Pygmalion, Duffy begins to speak:

> You have words to describe me that I find frightening. Every time I hear them they're whispered or screamed silently, wordlessly through front to middle page spreads of newspapers. Only you dare to speak them out loud. I look for them in my dictionary and I only find some. The words you use to describe me are: "congenital malformation." In my child's dictionary I learn that the first part means "born with." How many times have I answered that question, "Were you born like that or did your mother take them dreadful tablets?" How come I always felt ashamed when answering those big staring eyes and gaping mouths? "Did you have an accident or did your mother take them dreadful tablets?" Those big words those doctors used – they didn't have any that fitted me properly. I felt, even in the face of such opposition, that my body was the way it was supposed to be. It was right for me, as well as being whole, complete and functional.[6]

Unlike Pygmalion, however, Duffy does not affirm the perspective of her creator when she turns from silent object of the stare into a speaking subject. The words she cites are the verbal equivalents of the stare she sets up between herself and the audience. Yet, in this narrative, the words come from her own voice in performance rather than from the array of starers she has faced during her lifetime. By appropriating the words others use to describe her body, she upsets the dynamic of the stare, repeating in a kind of testimony the words of her starers while forcing the audience to look at a classic image of female beauty bearing witness to its own enfreakment by those words.[7] Duffy's telling of her life flings the words, the questions, and the stares back at her lookers, rebuking the aggregate "you" who cast her as pathological specimen, freak of nature, or quintessential lack. She accuses them with their own accusing questions to her about being "born like that." She stares out at them, upbraiding them for their intrusive "staring eyes and gaping mouths" that made her feel "ashamed." Dismissing their perceptions of her body, she insists upon her own self-definition, asserting that "words" such as "congenital malformation" do not accurately describe her experience of herself. Her soliloquy moves from exorcising the oppressive language that defines her to voicing her own version of herself as "being whole, complete and functional."

By manipulating the stare-and-tell ritual so fundamental to disability experience, Duffy mounts a critique of the politics of appearance and an inquiry into what it means to be an embodied person. Her self-representation raises the issue of what is appropriate looking, queries what constitutes beauty, and asks what is the truth of the body. This autobiographical form unsettles cultural assumptions about humanity, femaleness, disability, and self by invoking and juxtaposing all of these categories. By merging the visual and the narrative, body and word signify together in an act of self-making. Unique to disability, this genre manipulates the stare in order to renarrate disability. The body is integral to the word, operating as a material signifier that generates the stare-and-tell dynamic. By appropriating the social practice that constitutes her oppression in order to reimagine her identity, Duffy enacts a kind of communal renunciation of the objectification that she so commandingly rejects in her performances. In creating such an art form, she boldly reimagines disability on behalf of her community: other disabled people for whom the daily business of life is managing, deflecting, resisting, or renouncing that stare.

Notes

1   Erving Goffman, *Stigma: Notes on the Management of Spoiled Identity* (Englewood Cliffs, NJ: Prentice Hall, 1963).
2   G. Thomas Couser, *Recovering Bodies: Illness, Disability and Life Writing* (Madison, WI: Univ. of Wisconsin Press, 1997).
3   This is not to suggest that disability has no lived, corporeal reality. Indeed, disabled subjectivity is determined in part by the experience of impairment and of a disjuncture between an ablist physical environment and the disabled body. Here, however, I want to focus on the social exchange of staring as a cultural context that constitutes disabled identity.
4   Other disabled performance artists include Cheryl Marie Wade, David Roche, Billie Golfus, Carrie Sandoval, and Bob Flanagan; on Flanagan, see Linda Kauffmann, *Bad Girls and Sick Boys* (Berkeley, CA: Univ. of California Press, 1998). Several performers appear in the film *Vital Signs: Crip Culture Talks Back*, directed and produced by David T. Mitchell and Sharon Snyder (Marquette, MI: Northern Michigan Univ. distributor, 1996).
5   Personal conversation with author, 20 June 1997 at Washington, DC.
6   *Vital Signs: Crip Culture Talks Back.*
7   "Enfreakment" is a term coined by David Hevey, *Creatures Time Forgot: Photography and Disability Imagery* (New York: Routledge, 1992).

CHAPTER 18

Johnny Temple

Noise From Underground: Punk Rock's Anarchic Rhythms Spur a New Generation to Political Activism

Over the years you've lied to me
Stolen more than you could ever need
And baffled me with your selfish greed
Your country don't mean much to me.
In fact instead of reverence
And pride in your democracy
You've generated something like
Hate for your dishonesty.
— "Insurrection Chant"

These crude, furious lyrics were choked out by Tomas Squip of the Washington, DC-based punk rock band Beefeater during Ronald Reagan's White House tenure. For many kids at that time, punk music was one of the few vehicles for expressing anger toward what they perceived as the political and cultural bankruptcy around them. But Beefeater's songs and the antiapartheid activism they helped to inspire were destined for obscurity. The music was far too loud and abrasive for most people over the age of 30 and, more significant, inaccessible to the majority of young Americans, whose tastes in music have long been dictated by trends set in the offices of music conglomerates.

"Alternative rock" did enjoy a brief period of mainstream popularity in the early nineties, when it was discovered and disseminated by the major labels, but by mid-1998, it had been declared commercially dead. Today there's only a minimal chance that any music fan – young or old – will encounter through any major media outlet the songs of protest that continue to spring forth from the punk underground; the major record companies have succeeded in erecting a pay-to-play industry that effectively shuts out any band whose label cannot pony up hundreds of thousands of dollars for radio, video, retail and print promotion. When Universal Music and Polygram merged last December to

Johnny Temple, "Noise From Underground: Punk Rock's Anarchic Rhythms Spur a New Generation to Political Activism," *The Nation*, vol. 269, no. 12 (Oct. 18, 1999), pp. 17–22.

form the largest record company in the world – Universal Music Group – the final nail was driven into the coffin of corporate-sponsored punk rock; some 250 bands were dropped to clear the roster for the latest trend, "teen pop," embodied by bands like the Backstreet Boys and Britney Spears.

At the same time, however, the underground remains a well-spring for a wide variety of countercultural currents, with bands ranging from the explicitly political to the nihilistic but aesthetically adventurous. While independent labels can rarely provide the resources musicians need to survive financially, the most influential – Dischord (DC), Touch & Go (Chicago) and Jade Tree (Delaware), to name just a few – offer their bands full creative freedom and access to a vibrant musical community: a true alternative to the bottom-line assault on music. Sometimes musicians and their independent labels forge direct links with organizing efforts – with or without encouragement from the progressive establishment. But perhaps the greatest contribution of today's punks lies in changing minds: spreading an anticorporate message in a culture whose dominant voices are MTV veejays and athletes adorned with the Nike swoosh.

The politically minded underground movement is propelled by bands like Fugazi, which became the crown jewel of the devoutly independent Washington, DC, music scene soon after its first live performance in 1987. Its albums are released by Dischord Records, which has been a cornerstone of the DC music scene since its inception in 1980, and is co-owned by Ian MacKaye, one of Fugazi's two lead singers. The band is revered not only for its distinctive sound but for being one of the few groups to resist the lure of corporate funding when the majors plundered the ranks of independent artists after the Seattle-based underground group Nirvana was signed by Geffen Records in 1991, to huge commercial success. Instead, Fugazi has stayed on course as a pioneer of abrasively poetic, politically charged music. In the process, it has sold nearly 2 million records, primarily through independent distribution channels. This is a tremendous accomplishment – Fugazi has outsold all but a few of its corporate-aligned colleagues, simultaneously eschewing the mainstream media, refusing interviews with MTV and music publications like *Spin* and *Rolling Stone*. "*Spin* is to music what *Cosmopolitan* is to women's issues – it's really just a catalogue with an occasional feature," says MacKaye. "The bands themselves then become products, too. We are not interested in participating in that particular part of rock and roll."

> Merchandise keeps us in line
> Common sense says it's by design
> What could a businessman ever want more
> Than to have us sucking in his store?
> We owe you nothing, you have no control.
> — Fugazi, "Merchandise"

Fugazi continues to call its own shots, musically and commercially. The song "Merchandise" reflects on the ideals driving the band's decision to repudiate the commodity line that accompanies most rock bands (T-shirts, baseball caps, etc.). Through Dischord Records, its CDs are available for $10, as opposed to the industry standard of $16.98. Fugazi's political concerns surface in songs like "Repeater," which explores the growing numbness of Americans in the early nineties toward African-American victims of the violent crack epidemic: "Did you hear something outside/It sounded like a gun/Stay away from that window/It's not anyone/We know. . . ." In the song "Dear Justice Letter," singer

Guy Picciotto rasps, "It's all over... the last fair deal going down," feverishly mourning the loss of Justice William Brennan on the Supreme Court and the ominous ascension of Reagan/Bush appointees.

The nation's capital has been an unlikely hub of underground political and cultural activity since its Revolution Summer in 1985, when members of Beefeater and others in the music community staged "Punk Percussion Protests" in front of the South African Embassy. That year a group of local independent music fans and musicians founded a nonprofit organization, Positive Force, to pursue their political goals. Through Positive Force, Fugazi has donated the proceeds from every live performance in DC since 1989 – more than $100,000 – to grassroots groups ranging from the Community for Creative Nonviolence Homeless Shelter to Washington Inner City Self-Help, a low-income people's organization, to the Tenants and Workers Support Group of Alexandria, Virginia. At the same time, the band maintains a strict policy of low ticket prices – never more than $6, even at benefit concerts – when it could charge what other bands of similar stature do, up to $20 per ticket. "Established fundraisers scratch their heads and think what we're doing is dumb. We could raise so much more money, [but] the low door price is an important part of the band," explains singer/guitarist Ian MacKaye. "If $1,000 is collected at the door, every single dollar goes straight to a group that will use that money directly toward a grassroots operation. It doesn't go through some fundraising organization; there aren't people taking cuts along the way."

These days, much of the energy at Positive Force is channeled into the development of the Arthur S. Flemming Center, which will be owned and operated by DC's Emmaus Services for the Aging. The Flemming Center will house a variety of nonprofit activist and direct-service groups, with special emphasis on local music and art and service to the surrounding low-income community. Also, this past summer Positive Force hosted one of four benefits across the country for Voices in the Wilderness, the humanitarian renegade operation challenging the economic strangulation of Iraqi citizens by the US embargo. Sparked by a feature in the fanzine *Punk Planet* detailing the activities of the organization, underground activists in DC, New York, Philadelphia and Seattle staged events that funded a fact-finding delegation of Congressional aides to Iraq in late August, despite State Department objections and a US travel ban.

The San Francisco Bay Area has similarly been a hotbed of punk activism since the early eighties. As the singer for punk legends the Dead Kennedys, Jello Biafra was dragged through court by the Parents Music Resource Center and lambasted by its talking head, Tipper Gore, for "distribution of harmful matter to minors" after the band released an album with artwork that included a reproduction of a painting by Swiss Surrealist H. R. Giger depicting several rows of copulating male genitalia. Biafra traveled the country raising awareness and money for his First Amendment defense, while underscoring his view that punk rock was a movement of constructive idealism, not of the sullen apathy that the mainstream media have attributed to Generation X. In addition to producing music, Biafra's independent record label, Alternative Tentacles, focuses on spoken-word recordings, including albums featuring lectures by Howard Zinn, Noam Chomsky and death-row inmate Mumia Abu-Jamal.

The mobilization to save the life of Abu-Jamal has been one of the few grassroots movements to unite punks with other artists and activists on a broad scale. On September 11, Mumia 911 – an ad hoc group based in New York – orchestrated more than 100 artist-driven events and actions nationwide for a "national day of art of stop the execution." New York hardcore bands Ricanstruction and Huasipungo hit a Lower East Side nightclub with the same message of resistance that Angela Davis and hip-hop artist Michael Franti propounded in San Francisco's Dolores Park. Maximizing the visceral power and popular appeal of music, theater, spoken word, dance and visual art, Mumia 911 successfully laid the foundation for what the organizers hope will become a sustained movement to "transform the climate of cruelty" that infects American politics.

> *Resistance is everywhere, it always has been and always will be.... Being told you are a worthless piece of shit and not believing it is a form of resistance. One girl calling another girl to warn her about a guy who date raped her is another. And while she may look like a big haired makeup girl who goes out with jocks, she is a soldier along with every other girl, and even though she may not be fighting in the same loud way that some of us can (and do), it is the fact that she is resisting that connects us.*
> — Kathleen Hanna, Bikini Kill, CD liner notes

Though women made inroads toward punk prominence in the early hardcore years, it was not until the nineties that the Riot Grrl movement – championed by some members of the now-defunct Bikini Kill and their peers – ushered Third Wave feminism to the forefront of the punk political agenda. Bikini Kill, whose albums were released by the independent label Kill Rock Stars, based in Olympia, Washington, wrote jarring, confrontational songs that defied the silence surrounding violence against women. Kathleen Hanna, the band's lead singer, found herself counseling young women at concerts who turned to her with their stories of sexual abuse. Hanna helped organize some of the many benefit concerts that Bikini Kill played and, along with several other women, initiated "Girl Talk," a teenage sexual assault support group run out of Olympia's Safe Place Domestic Violence Shelter. After moving to DC, Hanna continued her outreach at such venues as Blair High School in Maryland, where she spoke to student assemblies about rape and the services available to women who have been abused. The response from girls at the public school was overwhelming, and school administrators cleared out the nurse's office to bring Hanna back for private sessions with students.

> *If I love a man, what is it to you?*
> *If my people, my friends, have turned their backs on me, I know why.*
> *But understand one thing: I want to be free, instead of living a lie.*
> — Los Crudos, "A Los Inseguros" (To the Insecure)
> (lyrics translated from the Spanish)

Ideological rifts led to the collapse of the Riot Grrrl movement, but punk feminism remains alive and kicking, and has facilitated the increasing visibility of gay men and lesbians in punk rock through independent bands like Los Crudos, Tribe 8, Pansy Division and The Butchies. Though the band recently dissolved, Los Crudos spent most of the nineties fueling the Latino corner of the punk scene with hardcore songs in Spanish – released on its own label, Lengua Armada – addressing issues ranging from homophobia to California's anti-immigrant ballot propositions. "One of the main reasons for singing in Spanish was to communicate directly with kids in our neighborhood," says the band's Uruguayan singer, Martín Sorrondeguy. Los Crudos worked closely in Pilsen – its Latino neighborhood in Chicago – with community organizations like Project Vida, an AIDS prevention program, and Project Hablo, a support group for Latina victims of domestic violence. Hardcore music played only a small role in the neighborhood events that the band helped to plan. "Punk is important to us, but community is even more important. When we're writing songs with angry lyrics, what's the point if we're not going to extend our hands to try to work with other people?" asks Sorrondeguy. "Punk music has to cross borders; we're all too familiar with borders."

Life after Los Crudos promises more music and political activism for Sorrondeguy, who is now raising money to create a public meeting space in Pilsen. Although it will be used for an occasional punk concert, the space, tentatively titled "Nuestra Casa," will more often be the venue for the activities of community organizers and local artists. Sorrondeguy, however, is digging in his heels for what is likely to be an extended battle to keep Nuestra Casa open: "We have serious issues with the local politicians here, and they will try to close us down." After challenging, at a neighborhood meeting, local alderman Danny Soliz on his favors to outside developers and his support for gentrification-friendly tax codes, Sorrondeguy and his roommates were suddenly evicted from their apartment. In addition to planning Nuestra Casa, an undeterred Sorrondeguy has brought his message to Pilsen's Christo Rey Jesuit High School, where he has twice been invited to speak with students about music, politics and low-income community organizing.

Whereas Los Crudos once represented an anomaly in punk rock, the band has helped to draw young Latinos into the underground through a highly politicized point of entry, and has in turn helped to raise awareness in the predominantly white, middle-class punk subculture. "A lot of new young Latino bands are forming and singing about these issues, singing about how California's propositions have affected them and their families," explains Sorrondeguy. "It brought a whole new voice into punk rock. A lot of kids were not talking about these things, because they weren't directly affecting them. Our experiences were not the same as those of a lot of other punk kids. For us, this became the focal point of what we were doing."

Like Los Crudos, Rage Against the Machine is among the small number of punk groups with nonwhite members; unlike Los Crudos, their music is released by a major label, Epic, and they have sold more than 8 million records. Members of Rage Against the Machine were musically educated in the hardcore scene, and the band continues to take cues from Fugazi and other punk trailblazers. RATM guitarist Tom Morello is dismayed that so few of the band's commercially successful peers on major labels "are willing to take a stance on political issues that go beyond feel-good celebrity causes." The band's overtly political lyrics and the revolutionary visual imagery that it projects in all of its album artwork and music videos are reinforced by RATM's participation in direct actions, including civil disobedience in solidarity with the garment workers' union, UNITE, and the coordination of delegations to Chiapas, Mexico, to help bring an international spotlight to the Zapatista uprising. "I was an angry teenager in a small Midwestern town," says Morello about his own musical upbringing, "and a band like the Clash was giving me a much more accurate portrayal of US foreign policy in Central America than Dan Rather was. It confirmed some of my suspicions and helped fire me up to pursue something bigger than sex, drugs and rock and roll."

Unfortunately, punk rock has not enjoyed the same cachet among older progressives that artists like Country Joe and the Fish and Bob Dylan once did. Punk activism has always existed outside most progressive political channels, and its subversive undercurrents have, for the most part, been unrecognized. Positive Force's co-founder, Mark Andersen, is troubled by this divide. While acknowledging the confrontational – sometimes antisocial

– underpinnings of the musical culture, Andersen has been working for years with his group to build bridges between the underground and like-minded activists. When Positive Force was conceived in the mid-eighties, punk organizers in DC were recovering from an ill-fated partnership with the Revolutionary Communist Party. For the most part, he says, the left has not "reached out to some of the very creative young people who could possibly formulate new ways of approaching political questions, new ways of bridging justice and service, and ultimately building some sort of a movement that could actually put the left in contention for organized power in our society."

Andersen's reflections are echoed by others in the music underground who feel that the traditional left lacks a visible cultural component that could give its causes more populist appeal. Of course, punk rockers must accept some culpability for the chasm that separates them from older generations of political activists. Underground rebellion has too often become more of a vehicle for expressing youthful desires and frustrations than for fighting injustice; for many punks, the prospect of working side by side with older activists who may resemble their parents is decidedly uncool. Fugazi's MacKaye describes his own aversion to activism as a teen: "Straight politics or radical politics – it all seemed boring to me." Having patiently endured the major labels' foray into punk rock, Andersen now sees the development of a broad and inclusive vision as essential to the politics of the underground. "The independent music community needs a political analysis – an anticorporate analysis – to connect it to other common institutions and to a general ethic of fostering healthy, democratic community."

> And now you want to mobilize
> A million misled youth against
> Some enemy that you devised
> Don't trust our loyalty.
> > – Beefeater, "Insurrection Chant"

With independent rock providing many disaffected kids with a portal to political activism, the established left must challenge itself to look beyond the bland feel-goodism being churned out by the major labels. "The great tragedy of the sixties was that there was a whole counterculture that could have been the basis for a transformation," says Positive Force's Andersen. "Somewhere along the line, the politicos and the artists split apart." The organizing efforts of entities like Positive Force and Mumia 911 provide springboards for crossover, but if the left fails to recognize the value of the political and artistic expression that punks have been developing over the past two decades, it will lose one more natural ally in the battle to stem the rightward drift of American politics. Punks, for their part, need to stop romanticizing isolation, or they may find their political endeavors, along with their music, doomed to perpetual obscurity.

Part III

Identity and Ethnicity in the Face of Discrimination and Racism

CHAPTER 19

Nancy Fraser

Rethinking Recognition

In the seventies and eighties, struggles for the 'recognition of difference' seemed charged with emancipatory promise. Many who rallied to the banners of sexuality, gender, ethnicity and 'race' aspired not only to assert hitherto denied identities but to bring a richer, lateral dimension to battles over the redistribution of wealth and power as well. With the turn of the century, issues of recognition and identity have become even more central, yet many now bear a different charge: from Rwanda to the Balkans, questions of 'identity' have fuelled campaigns for ethnic cleansing and even genocide – as well as movements that have mobilized to resist them.

It is not just the character but the scale of these struggles that has changed. Claims for the recognition of difference now drive many of the world's social conflicts, from campaigns for national sovereignty and subnational autonomy, to battles around multi-culturalism, to the newly energized movements for international human rights, which seek to promote both universal respect for shared humanity and esteem for cultural distinctiveness. They have also become predominant within social movements such as feminism, which had previously foregrounded the redistribution of resources. To be sure, such struggles cover a wide range of aspirations, from the patently emancipatory to the downright reprehensible (with most probably falling somewhere in between). Neverthe-less, the recourse to a common grammar is worth considering. Why today, after the demise of Soviet-style communism and the acceleration of globalization, do so many conflicts take this form? Why do so many movements couch their claims in the idiom of recognition?

To pose this question is also to note the relative decline in claims for egalitarian redistribution. Once the hegemonic grammar of political contestation, the language of distribution is less salient today. The movements that not long ago boldly demanded an equitable share of resources and wealth have not, to be sure, wholly disappeared. But thanks to the sustained neoliberal rhetorical assault on egalitarianism, to the absence of any credible model of 'feasible socialism' and to widespread doubts about the viability of state-Keynesian social democracy in the face of globalization, their role has been greatly reduced.

Nancy Fraser, "Rethinking Recognition," *New Left Review*, no. 3 (May–June 2000), pp. 107–20. Reprinted by permission of New Left Review.

We are facing, then, a new constellation in the grammar of political claims-making – and one that is disturbing on two counts. First, this move from redistribution to recognition is occurring despite – or because of – an acceleration of economic globalization, at a time when an aggressively expanding capitalism is radically exacerbating economic inequality. In this context, questions of recognition are serving less to supplement, complicate and enrich redistributive struggles than to marginalize, eclipse and displace them. I shall call this *the problem of displacement*. Second, today's recognition struggles are occurring at a moment of hugely increasing transcultural interaction and communication, when accelerated migration and global media flows are hybridizing and pluralizing cultural forms. Yet the routes such struggles take often serve not to promote respectful interaction within increasingly multicultural contexts, but to drastically simplify and reify group identities. They tend, rather, to encourage separatism, intolerance and chauvinism, patriarchalism and authoritarianism. I shall call this *the problem of reification*.

Both problems – displacement and reification – are extremely serious: insofar as the politics of recognition displaces the politics of redistribution, it may actually promote economic inequality; insofar as it reifies group identities, it risks sanctioning violations of human rights and freezing the very antagonisms it purports to mediate. No wonder, then, that many have simply washed their hands of 'identity politics' – or proposed jettisoning cultural struggles altogether. For some, this may mean reprioritizing class over gender, sexuality, 'race' and ethnicity. For others, it means resurrecting economism. For others still, it may mean rejecting all 'minoritarian' claims out of hand and insisting upon assimilation to majority norms – in the name of secularism, universalism or republicanism.

Such reactions are understandable: they are also deeply misguided. Not all forms of recognition politics are equally pernicious: some represent genuinely emancipatory responses to serious injustices that cannot be remedied by redistribution alone. Culture, moreover, is a legitimate, even necessary, terrain of struggle, a site of injustice in its own right and deeply imbricated with economic inequality. Properly conceived, struggles for recognition can aid the redistribution of power and wealth and can promote interaction and cooperation across gulfs of difference.

Everything depends on how recognition is approached. I want to argue here that we need a way of rethinking the politics of recognition in a way that can help to solve, or at least mitigate, the problems of displacement and reification. This means conceptualizing struggles for recognition so that they can be integrated with struggles for redistribution, rather than displacing and undermining them. It also means developing an account of recognition that can accommodate the full complexity of social identities, instead of one that promotes reification and separatism. Here, I propose such a rethinking of recognition.

The identity model

The usual approach to the politics of recognition – what I shall call the 'identity model' – starts from the Hegelian idea that identity is constructed dialogically, through a process of mutual recognition. According to Hegel, recognition designates an ideal reciprocal relation between subjects, in which each sees the other both as its equal and also as separate from it. This relation is constitutive for subjectivity: one becomes an individual subject only by virtue of recognizing, and being recognized by, another subject. Recognition from others is thus essential to the development of a sense of self. To be denied recognition – or to be 'misrecognized' – is to suffer both a distortion of one's relation to one's self and an injury to one's identity.

Proponents of the identity model transpose the Hegelian recognition schema onto the cultural and political terrain. They contend that to belong to a group that is devalued by the dominant culture is to be misrecognized, to suffer a distortion in one's relation to one's self. As a result of repeated encounters with the stigmatizing gaze of a culturally dominant other, the members of disesteemed groups internalize negative self-images and are prevented from developing a healthy cultural identity of their own. In this perspective, the politics of recognition aims to repair internal self-dislocation by contesting the dominant culture's demeaning picture of the group. It proposes that members of mis-recognized groups reject such images in favour of new self-representations of their own making, jettisoning internalized, negative identities and joining collectively to produce a self-affirming culture of their own – which, publicly asserted, will gain the respect and esteem of society at large. The result, when successful, is 'recognition': an undistorted relation to oneself.

Without doubt, this identity model contains some genuine insights into the psycho-logical effects of racism, sexism, colonization and cultural imperialism. Yet it is theoretic-ally and politically problematic. By equating the politics of recognition with identity politics, it encourages both the reification of group identities and the displacement of redistribution.

Displacing redistribution

Let us consider first the ways in which identity politics tend to displace struggles for redistribution. Largely silent on the subject of economic inequality, the identity model treats misrecognition as a free-standing cultural harm: many of its proponents simply ignore distributive injustice altogether and focus exclusively on efforts to change culture; others, in contrast, appreciate the seriousness of maldistribution and genuinely wish to redress it. Yet both currents end by displacing redistributive claims.

The first current casts misrecognition as a problem of cultural depreciation. The roots of injustice are located in demeaning representations, but these are not seen as socially grounded. For this current, the nub of the problem is free-floating discourses, not *institutionalized* significations and norms. Hypostatizing culture, they both abstract mis-recognition from its institutional matrix and obscure its entwinement with distributive injustice. They may miss, for example, the links (institutionalized in labour markets) between androcentric norms that devalue activities coded as 'feminine', on the one hand, and the low wages of female workers on the other. Likewise, they overlook the links institutionalized within social-welfare systems between heterosexist norms which delegi-timate homosexuality, on the one hand, and the denial of resources and benefits to gays and lesbians on the other. Obfuscating such connexions, they strip misrecognition of its social-structural underpinnings and equate it with distorted identity. With the politics of recognition thus reduced to identity politics, the politics of redistribution is displaced.

A second current of identity politics does not simply ignore maldistribution in this way. It appreciates that cultural injustices are often linked to economic ones, but misunder-stands the character of the links. Subscribing effectively to a 'culturalist' theory of contemporary society, proponents of this perspective suppose that maldistribution is merely a secondary effect of misrecognition. For them, economic inequalities are simple expressions of cultural hierarchies – thus, class oppression is a superstructural effect of the cultural devaluation of proletarian identity (or, as one says in the United States, of 'classism'). It follows from this view that all maldistribution can be remedied indirectly, by a politics of recognition: to revalue unjustly devalued identities is simultaneously to attack the deep sources of economic inequality; no explicit politics of redistribution is needed.

In this way, culturalist proponents of identity politics simply reverse the claims of an earlier form of vulgar Marxist economism: they allow the politics of recognition to displace the politics of redistribution, just as vulgar Marxism once allowed the politics of redistribution to displace the politics of recognition. In fact, vulgar culturalism is no more adequate for understanding contemporary society than vulgar economism was.

Granted, culturalism might make sense if one lived in a society in which there were no relatively autonomous markets, one in which cultural value patterns regulated not only the relations of recognition but those of distribution as well. In such a society, economic inequality and cultural hierarchy would be seamlessly fused; identity depreciation would translate perfectly and immediately into economic injustice, and misrecognition would directly entail maldistribution. Consequently, both forms of injustice could be remedied at a single stroke, and a politics of recognition that successfully redressed misrecognition would counter maldistribution as well. But the idea of a purely 'cultural' society with no economic relations – fascinating to generations of anthropologists – is far removed from the current reality, in which marketization has pervaded all societies to some degree, at least partially decoupling economic mechanisms of distribution from cultural patterns of value and prestige. Partially independent of such patterns, markets follow a logic of their own, neither wholly constrained by culture nor subordinated to it; as a result they generate economic inequalities that are not mere expressions of identity hierarchies. Under these conditions, the idea that one could remedy all maldistribution by means of a politics of recognition is deeply deluded: its net result can only be to displace struggles for economic justice.

Reification of identity

Displacement, however, is not the only problem: the identity politics model of recognition tends also to reify identity. Stressing the need to elaborate and display an authentic, self-affirming and self-generated collective identity, it puts moral pressure on individual members to conform to a given group culture. Cultural dissidence and experimentation are accordingly discouraged, when they are not simply equated with disloyalty. So, too, is cultural criticism, including efforts to explore intragroup divisions, such as those of gender, sexuality and class. Thus, far from welcoming scrutiny of, for example, the patriarchal strands within a subordinated culture, the tendency of the identity model is to brand such critique as 'inauthentic'. The overall effect is to impose a single, drastically simplified group-identity which denies the complexity of people's lives, the multiplicity of their identifications and the cross-pulls of their various affiliations. Ironically, then, the identity model serves as a vehicle for misrecognition: in reifying group identity, it ends by obscuring the politics of cultural identification, the struggles *within* the group for the authority – and the power – to represent it. By shielding such struggles from view, this approach masks the power of dominant factions and reinforces intragroup domination.

The identity model thus lends itself all too easily to repressive forms of communitarianism, promoting conformism, intolerance and patriarchalism.

Paradoxically, moreover, the identity model tends to deny its own Hegelian premises. Having begun by assuming that identity is dialogical, constructed via interaction with another subject, it ends by valorizing monologism – supposing that misrecognized people can and should construct their identity on their own. It supposes, further, that a group has the right to be understood solely in its own terms – that no one is ever justified in viewing another subject from an external perspective or in dissenting from another's self-interpretation. But again, this runs counter to the dialogical view, making cultural identity an auto-generated auto-description, which one presents to others as an obiter dictum. Seeking to exempt 'authentic' collective self-representations from all possible challenges in the public sphere, this sort of identity politics scarcely fosters social interaction across differences: on the contrary, it encourages separatism and group enclaves.

The identity model of recognition, then, is deeply flawed. Both theoretically deficient and politically problematic, it equates the politics of recognition with identity politics and, in doing so, encourages both the reification of group identities and the displacement of the politics of redistribution.

Misrecognition as status subordination

I shall consequently propose an alternative approach: that of treating recognition as a question of social status. From this perspective, what requires recognition is not group-specific identity but the status of individual group members as full partners in social interaction. Misrecognition, accordingly, does not mean the depreciation and deformation of group identity, but social subordination – in the sense of being prevented from participating as a peer in social life. To redress this injustice still requires a politics of recognition, but in the 'status model' this is no longer reduced to a question of identity: rather, it means a politics aimed at overcoming subordination by establishing the misrecognized party as a full member of society, capable of participating on a par with the rest.

Let me explain. To view recognition as a matter of status means examining institutionalized patterns of cultural value for their effects on the relative standing of social actors. If and when such patterns constitute actors as peers, capable of participating on a par with one another in social life, then we can speak of reciprocal recognition and status equality. When, in contrast, they constitute some actors as inferior, excluded, wholly other, or simply invisible – in other words, as less than full partners in social interaction – then we can speak of misrecognition and status subordination. From this perspective, misrecognition is neither a psychic deformation nor a free-standing cultural harm but an institutionalized relation of social subordination. To be misrecognized, accordingly, is not simply to be thought ill of, looked down upon or devalued in others' attitudes, beliefs or representations. It is rather to be denied the status of a full partner in social interaction, as a consequence of institutionalized patterns of cultural value that constitute one as comparatively unworthy of respect or esteem.

On the status model, moreover, misrecognition is not relayed through free-floating cultural representations or discourses. It is perpetrated, as we have seen, through institutionalized patterns – in other words, through the workings of social institutions that regulate interaction according to parity-impeding cultural norms. Examples might include marriage laws that exclude same-sex partnerships as illegitimate and perverse; social-welfare policies that stigmatize single mothers as sexually irresponsible scroungers; and policing practices, such as 'racial profiling', that associate racialized persons with criminality. In each of these cases, interaction is regulated by an institutionalized pattern of cultural value that constitutes some categories of social actors as normative and others as deficient or inferior: 'straight' is normal, 'gay' is perverse; 'male-headed households' are proper, 'female-headed households' are not; 'whites' are law-abiding, 'blacks' are dangerous. In each case, the result is to deny some members of society the status of full partners in interaction, capable of participating on a par with the rest.

As these examples suggest, misrecognition can assume a variety of forms. In today's complex, differentiated societies, parity-impeding values are institutionalized at a plurality of institutional sites, and in qualitatively different modes. In some cases, misrecognition is juridified, expressly codified in formal law; in other cases, it is institutionalized via government policies, administrative codes or professional practice. It can also be institutionalized informally – in associational patterns, long-standing customs or sedimented social practices of civil society. But whatever the differences in form, the core of the injustice remains the same: in each case, an institutionalized pattern of cultural value constitutes some social actors as less than full members of society and prevents them from participating as peers.

On the status model, then, misrecognition constitutes a form of institutionalized subordination, and thus a serious violation of justice. Wherever and however it occurs, a claim for recognition is in order. But note precisely what this means: aimed not at valorizing group identity but rather at overcoming subordination, in this approach claims for recognition seek to establish the subordinated party as a full partner in social life, able to interact with others as a peer. They aim, in other words, to de-institutionalize patterns of cultural value that impede parity of participation and to replace them with patterns that foster it. Redressing misrecognition now means changing social institutions – or, more specifically, changing the interaction-regulating values that impede parity of participation at all relevant institutional sites. Exactly how this should be done depends in each case on the mode in which misrecognition is institutionalized. Juridified forms require legal change, policy-entrenched forms require policy change, associational forms require associational change, and so on: the mode and agency of redress vary, as does the institutional site. But in every case, the goal is the same: redressing misrecognition means replacing institutionalized value patterns that impede parity of participation with ones that enable or foster it.

Consider again the case of marriage laws that deny participatory parity to gays and lesbians. As we saw, the root of the injustice is the institutionalization in law of a heterosexist pattern of cultural value that constitutes heterosexuals as normal and homosexuals as perverse. Redressing the injustice requires de-institutionalizing that value pattern and replacing it with an alternative that promotes parity. This, however, might be done in various ways: one way would be to grant the same recognition to gay and lesbian unions as heterosexual unions currently enjoy, by legalizing same-sex marriage; another would be to de-institutionalize heterosexual marriage, decoupling entitlements such as health insurance from marital status and assigning them on some other basis, such as citizenship. Although there may be good reasons for preferring one of these approaches to the other, in principle both of them would promote sexual parity and redress this instance of misrecognition.

In general, then, the status model is not committed *a priori* to any one type of remedy for misrecognition; rather, it allows for a range of possibilities, depending on what precisely the subordinated parties need in order to be able to participate as peers in social life. In some cases, they may need to be unburdened of excessive ascribed or constructed distinctiveness; in others, to have hitherto underacknowledged distinctiveness taken into account. In still other cases, they may need to shift the focus onto dominant or advantaged groups, outing the latter's distinctiveness, which has been falsely parading as universal; alternatively, they may need to deconstruct the very terms in which attributed differences are currently elaborated. In every case, the status model tailors the remedy to the concrete arrangements that impede parity. Thus, unlike the identity model, it does not accord an *a priori* privilege to approaches that valorize group specificity. Rather, it allows in principle for what we might call universalist recognition, and deconstructive recognition, as well as for the affirmative recognition of difference. The crucial point, once again, is that on the status model the politics of recognition does not stop at identity but seeks institutional remedies for institutionalized harms. Focused on culture in its socially grounded (as opposed to free-floating) forms, *this* politics seeks to overcome status subordination by changing the values that regulate interaction, entrenching new value patterns that will promote parity of participation in social life.

Addressing maldistribution

There is a further important difference between the status and identity models. For the status model, institutionalized patterns of cultural value are not the only obstacles to participatory parity. On the contrary, equal participation is also impeded when some actors lack the necessary resources to interact with others as peers. In such cases, maldistribution constitutes an impediment to parity of participation in social life, and thus a form of social subordination and injustice. Unlike the identity model, then, the status model understands social justice as encompassing two analytically distinct dimensions: a dimension of recognition, which concerns the effects of institutionalized meanings and norms on the relative standing of social actors; and a dimension of distribution, which involves the allocation of disposable resources to social actors.[1]

Thus, each dimension is associated with an analytically distinct aspect of social order. The recognition dimension corresponds to the status order of society, hence to the constitution, by socially entrenched patterns of cultural value, of culturally defined categories of social actors – status groups – each distinguished by the relative honour, prestige and esteem it enjoys *vis-à-vis* the others. The distributive dimension, in contrast, corresponds to the economic structure of society, hence to the constitution, by property regimes and labour markets, of economically defined categories of actors, or classes, distinguished by their differential endowments of resources.[2]

Each dimension, moreover, is associated with an analytically distinct form of injustice. For the recognition dimension, as we saw, the associated injustice is misrecognition. For the distributive dimension, in contrast, the corresponding injustice is maldistribution, in which economic structures, property regimes or labour markets deprive actors of the resources needed for full participation. Each dimension, finally, corresponds to an analytically distinct form of subordination: the recognition dimension corresponds, as we saw, to status subordination, rooted in institutionalized patterns of cultural value; the distributive dimension, in contrast, corresponds to economic subordination, rooted in structural features of the economic system.

In general, then, the status model situates the problem of recognition within a larger social frame. From this perspective, societies appear as complex fields that encompass not only cultural forms of social ordering but economic forms of ordering as well. In all societies, these two forms of ordering are interimbricated. Under capitalist conditions, however, neither is wholly reducible to the other. On the contrary, the economic dimension becomes relatively decoupled from the cultural dimension, as marketized arenas, in which strategic action predominates, are differentiated from non-marketized arenas, in which value-regulated interaction predominates. The result is a partial uncoupling of economic distribution from structures of prestige. In capitalist societies, therefore, cultural value patterns do not strictly dictate economic allocations (*contra* the culturalist theory of society), nor do economic class inequalities simply reflect status hierarchies; rather, maldistribution becomes partially uncoupled from misrecognition. For the status model, therefore, not all distributive injustice can be overcome by recognition alone. A politics of redistribution is also necessary.[3]

Nevertheless, distribution and recognition are not neatly separated from each other in capitalist societies. For the status model, the two dimensions are interimbricated and interact causally with each other. Economic issues such as income distribution have recognition subtexts: value patterns institutionalized in labour markets may privilege activities coded 'masculine', 'white' and so on over those coded 'feminine' and 'black'. Conversely, recognition issues – judgements of aesthetic value, for instance – have distributive subtexts: diminished access to economic resources may impede equal participation in the making of art.[4] The result can be a vicious circle of subordination, as the status order and the economic structure interpenetrate and reinforce each other.

Unlike the identity model, then, the status model views misrecognition in the context of a broader understanding of contemporary society. From this perspective, status subordination cannot be understood in isolation from economic arrangements, nor recognition abstracted from distribution. On the contrary, only by considering both dimensions together can one determine what is impeding participatory parity in any particular instance; only by teasing out the complex imbrications of status with economic class can one determine how best to redress the injustice. The status model thus works against tendencies to displace struggles for redistribution. Rejecting the view that misrecognition is a free-standing cultural harm, it understands that status subordination is often linked to distributive injustice. Unlike the culturalist theory of society, however, it avoids short-circuiting the complexity of these links: appreciating that not all economic injustice can be overcome by recognition alone, it advocates an approach that expressly integrates claims for recognition with claims for redistribution, and thus mitigates the problem of displacement.

The status model also avoids reifying group identities: as we saw, what requires recognition in this account is not group-specific identity but the status of individuals as full partners in social interaction. This orientation offers several advantages. By focusing on the effects of institutionalized norms on capacities for interaction, the model avoids hypostatizing culture and substituting identity-engineering for social change. Likewise, by refusing to privilege remedies for misrecognition that valorize existing group identities, it avoids essentializing current configurations and foreclosing historical change. Finally, by establishing participatory parity as a normative standard, the status model submits claims for recognition to democratic processes of public justification, thus avoiding the authoritarian monologism of the politics of authenticity and valorizing transcultural interaction, as opposed to separatism and group enclaves. Far from encouraging repressive communitarianism, then, the status model militates against it.

To sum up: today's struggles for recognition often assume the guise of identity politics. Aimed at countering demeaning cultural representations of subordinated groups, they abstract misrecognition from its institutional matrix and sever its links with political economy and, insofar as they propound 'authentic' collective identities, serve less to foster interaction across differences than to enforce separatism, conformism and intolerance. The results tend to be doubly unfortunate: in many cases, struggles for recognition simultaneously displace struggles for economic justice and promote repressive forms of communitarianism. The solution, however, is not to reject the politics of recognition *tout court*. That would be to condemn millions of people to suffer grave injustices that can only be redressed through recognition of some kind. What is needed, rather, is an alternative politics of recognition, a *non-identitarian* politics that can remedy misrecognition without encouraging displacement and reification. The status model, I have argued, provides the basis for this. By understanding recognition as a question of status, and by examining its relation to economic class, one can take steps to mitigate, if not fully solve, the displacement of struggles for redistribution; and by avoiding the identity model, one can begin to diminish, if not fully dispel, the dangerous tendency to reify collective identities.

Notes

1   Actually, I should say '*at least* two analytically distinct dimensions' in order to allow for the possibility of more. I have in mind specifically a possible third class of obstacles to participatory parity that could be called *political*, as opposed to economic or cultural. Such obstacles would include decision-making procedures that systematically marginalize some people even in the absence of maldistribution and misrecognition, for example, single-district winner-take-all electoral rules that deny voice to quasi-permanent minorities. (For an insightful account of this example, see Lani Guinier, *The Tyranny of the Majority*, New York 1994.) The possibility of a third class of political obstacles to participatory parity brings out the extent of my debt to Max Weber, especially to his 'Class, Status, Party', in *From Max Weber: Essays in Sociology*, Hans H. Gerth and C. Wright Mills, eds., Oxford 1958. In the present essay, I align a version of Weber's distinction between class and status with the distinction between distribution and recognition. Yet Weber's own distinction was tripartite not bipartite: 'class, status, and party'. Thus, he effectively prepared a place for theorizing a third, political kind of obstacle to participatory parity, which might be called *political marginalization or exclusion*. I do not develop this possibility here, however, but confine myself to maldistribution and misrecognition, while leaving the analysis of political obstacles to participatory parity for another occasion.
2   In this essay, I deliberately use a Weberian conception of class, not a Marxian one. Thus, I understand an actor's class position in terms of her or his relation to the market, not in terms of her or his relation to the means of production. This Weberian conception of class as an *economic* category suits my interest in distribution as a normative dimension of justice better than the Marxian conception of class as a *social* category. Nevertheless, I do not mean to reject the Marxian idea of the 'capitalist mode of production' as a social totality. On the contrary, I find that idea useful as an overarching frame within which one can situate Weberian understandings of both status and class. Thus, I reject the standard view of Marx and Weber as antithetical and irreconcilable thinkers. For the Weberian definition of class, see Max Weber, 'Class, Status, Party'.
3   For fuller discussions of the mutual irreducibility of maldistribution and misrecognition, class and status in contemporary capitalist societies, see Nancy Fraser, 'Heterosexism, Misrecognition, and Capitalism: A Response to Judith Butler', *New Left Review* 1/228, March–April 1998, pp. 140–9; and 'Social Justice in the Age of Identity Politics: Redistribution, Recognition and Participation', in *The Tanner Lectures on Human Values*, volume 19, ed. Grethe B. Peterson, Salt Lake City 1998, pp. 1–67.
4   For a comprehensive, if somewhat reductive, account of this issue, see Pierre Bourdieu, *Distinction: A Social Critique of the Judgment of Taste*, tr. Richard Nice, Cambridge, MA, 1984.

CHAPTER 20

Fidel Castro

The Roots of International Racism

Excellencies:

Delegates and guests:

Racism, racial discrimination, and xenophobia are a social, cultural, and political phenomenon, not a natural instinct of human beings; they arise from wars, military conquests, slavery, and the individual or collective exploitation of the weakest by the most powerful throughout the history of human societies.

No one has the right to sabotage this Conference which tries to mitigate, in some way, the terrible sufferings and the enormous injustice that these experiences have meant, and continue to mean, for the overwhelming majority of humanity. Still less does anyone have the right to set preconditions to this conference, or urge that it not even speak of historical responsibility, fair compensation, or the way we decide to characterize the dreadful genocide being perpetrated, at this very moment, against our Palestinian brothers and sisters by extreme right leaders who, in alliance with the hegemonic superpower, presume to act on behalf of another people which for almost two thousand years was the victim of the fiercest persecution, discrimination and injustice that history has known.

Cuba understands and supports the idea of reparations as an unavoidable moral duty to the victims of racism. It sees a major precedent for this in the indemnification being paid to the descendants of the Jewish people who in the very heart of Europe suffered the odious and brutal racist holocaust. However, Cuba does not think in terms of an impossible search for the direct descendants or countries of origin of the victims of actions that occurred over a period of centuries. What is undeniable is that tens of millions of Africans were captured, sold like a commodity and sent beyond the Atlantic to work in slavery while 70 million indigenous people in that hemisphere perished as a result of the European conquest and colonization.

The inhuman exploitation imposed on the peoples of three continents, including Asia, has marked forever the destiny and lives of over 4.5 billion people living in the Third World today, whose rates of poverty, unemployment, illiteracy, illness, infant mortality,

Fidel Castro, "The Roots of International Racism," *Monthly Review,* vol. 53, no. 7 (Dec. 2001), pp. 24–7.
Copyright © 2001 by M.R. Press. Reprinted by permission of Monthly Review Foundation.

life expectancy, and other calamities – too many to enumerate in the time we have – are certainly awesome and harrowing. They are the current victims of that atrocity which lasted for centuries, and are the ones who clearly deserve compensation for the horrendous crimes perpetrated against their ancestors and peoples.

This brutal exploitation did not end when many countries became independent, not even after the formal abolition of slavery. Right after independence, the main ideologues of the new United States of North America put forward ideas and strategies that were unquestionably expansionist in nature. It was on the basis of such ideas that the original white settlers of European descent, in their march to the west, forcibly occupied the lands on which Native Americans had lived for thousands of years, exterminating millions of them in the process. But they did not stop at the boundaries of the former Spanish possessions; consequently Mexico, a Latin American country that had attained its independence in 1821, was stripped of millions of square kilometers of territory and invaluable natural resources. Meanwhile, in the increasingly powerful and expansionist nation that emerged in North America, the odious and inhuman slavery system stayed in place for almost a century after the famous Declaration of Independence of 1776, in which it was proclaimed that all men are born free and equal.

After the purely formal slave emancipation, African Americans were subjected for another hundred years to the harshest racial discrimination, many of whose features and consequences still persist after almost four more decades of heroic struggles and the achievements of the 1960s, for which Martin Luther King, Jr., Malcolm X, and other outstanding fighters gave their lives. Based on a purely racist rationale, the longest and most severe legal sentences are passed against African Americans, who in the wealthy US society have the highest level of poverty and the most miserable living conditions. Equally terrible, if not even more so, are the disdain and discrimination suffered by the remaining Native American peoples.

Needless to mention the data on the social and economic situation of Africa. Entire countries and even whole regions of Sub-Saharan Africa are at risk of extinction because of a highly complex blend of economic backwardness, extreme poverty and severe diseases, both old and new, that have become a true scourge. And the situation is no less dramatic in numerous Asian countries. On top of all this, there are the huge and unpayable debts, the disparate terms of trade, the ruinous prices of basic commodities, the demographic explosion, neoliberal globalization, and the climate changes that produce long droughts alternating with increasingly violent rains and floods. It can be mathematically proven that such a condition is unsustainable.

The developed countries and their consumer societies, currently responsible for the accelerated and almost unstoppable destruction of the environment, have been the main beneficiaries of conquest and colonization, of slavery, of the ruthless exploitation and the extermination of hundreds of millions of people born in the countries that today constitute the Third World. They have also benefited from the economic order imposed on humanity after two atrocious and devastating wars for a new division of the world and its markets, from the privileges granted to the United States and its allies at Bretton Woods, and from the IMF and the international financial institutions created exclusively by them and for them.

This rich and wasteful world commands the technical and financial resources necessary to pay its debt to humanity. The hegemonic superpower should also pay back its special debt to African Americans, to Native Americans living on reservations, and to the tens of millions of immigrants from Latin America and the Caribbean, as well as from other poor nations, be they mulatto, yellow or black, but victims all of vicious discrimination and scorn.

It is high time to put an end to the dramatic situation of the indigenous communities in our hemisphere. Their own awakening and struggles, and the universal recognition of the monstrous crime committed against them, make this imperative.

There are enough funds to save the world from tragedy.

Let there be an end to the arms race and the weapons trade, which only bring devastation and death.

Allocate to development a good part of the trillion dollars spent annually on marketing, which creates illusions and inaccessible consumer habits while releasing the venom that destroys national cultures and identities.

May the modest 0.7 percent of Gross National Product promised as official development assistance be finally delivered.

Let the tax suggested by Nobel Laureate James Tobin be imposed in a reasonable and effective way on current speculative operations accounting for trillions of dollars every 24 hours. Then the United Nations, which cannot go on depending on meager, inadequate, and belated donations and charities, will have one trillion dollars, yes, one trillion dollars annually to save and develop the world. Given the severity and the urgency of current problems, which threaten the very existence of our species, that is what would really be needed before it is too late.

Put an immediate end to the ongoing genocide against the Palestinian people that is taking place while the world stares in astonishment. May the basic right to life of that people, children and youth, be protected. May their right to peace and independence be respected; then, there will be nothing to fear from UN documents.

I am aware that the need for some relief from the awful situation their countries are facing has led many friends from Africa and other regions to suggest the need for such prudence as would allow them to get something out of this Conference. I sympathize with them but I cannot renounce my conviction that the more candid we are in telling the truth, the more likely we are to be heeded and respected. Centuries of deception are more than enough.

I have only three other short questions based on realities that cannot be ignored.

The rich, developed capitalist countries today participate in the imperialist system and in the global economic order based on the philosophy of egoism and on brutal competition among men, nations, and blocs, to which any feelings of solidarity or any honest international cooperation are completely alien. They live in the deceptive, irresponsible, and hallucinating atmosphere of consumer societies. However sincere might be their blind faith in such a system and the convictions of their most serious statesmen, I ask: Will they be able to understand the severity of the problems of today's world, which in its incoherent and uneven development is ruled by blind laws, by the enormous power and interests of ever-growing and increasingly uncontrollable transnational corporations?

Will they come to understand the impending universal chaos and rebellion? And, even if they wanted to, could they put an end to racism, racial discrimination, xenophobia, and all other related issues?

In my view, we are facing an immense economic, social, and political crisis that is global in scope. Let us become conscious of these realities. Alternatives will emerge. History has shown that only from deep crises have great solutions arisen. The peoples' right to life and justice will prevail in a thousand different ways.

I believe in the mobilization and the struggle of peoples! I believe in ideas that are just! I believe in truth! I believe in man!

Notes

This is the text of a speech delivered by Cuban President Fidel Castro on September 1, 2001, at the World Conference Against Racism, in Durban, South Africa.

The editors thank Victor Wallis for his help with the translation.

CHAPTER 21

Invention, Memory, and Place

Edward W. Said

Over the past decade, there has been a burgeoning interest in two overlapping areas of the humanities and social sciences: memory and geography or, more specifically, the study of human space. Both of them have spawned an extraordinary amount of interesting work, work that has in effect created new fields of study and inquiry. The concern with memory, for example, has branched out to include such increasingly prevalent forms of writing as personal memoirs and autobiography, which nearly every fiction writer of note has attempted, to say nothing of the outpourings of academics, scientists, public figures, and so forth. The national fixation on recollection, confession, and witness has run the whole gamut from public confession – as in the Clinton–Lewinsky scandal – to various studies of the meaning of collective memory, extended reflection and analyses of instances of it, plus numerous chronicles embodying it. I shall have more to say about that later. In addition, and somewhat on the margins, has been a serious, sometimes bitter inquiry into the authenticity of certain memories, as well as, at the other, calmer end of the spectrum, a remarkable academic analysis of the role of invention in such matters as tradition and collective historical experience.

Some examples of intense and even anguished controversy are the following: Was Anne Frank's diary really hers, or was it so altered by publishers, members of her family, or others in its published form so as to conceal the disturbances in her domestic life? In Europe there has been a great and often acerbic debate over the meaning of the Holocaust, with a whole range of opinions as to what happened, why it happened, and what it tells us about the nature of Germany, France, and several other involved countries. The celebrated French classicist Pierre Vidal-Naquet wrote a powerful book some years back called *Assassins of Memory* about French deniers of the Holocaust, and more recently the Papon trial in Bordeaux raised uncomfortable questions related not just to memories of the Occupation but the centrality of French collaborators with the Nazis and what it said about French selective memories of the Vichy regime. In Germany of course debate on the testimonials of the death camps and their philosophical as well as political meaning periodically receives new infusions of controversy, fuelled most recently by the publication of the German translation of Daniel Goldhagen's book *Hitler's Willing Executioners*. In the

Edward Said, "Invention, Memory, and Place," *Critical Inquiry* (Winter 2000), pp. 175–92. Reprinted by permission of The University of Chicago Press and The Wylie Agency.

United States consider the anger provoked by representatives of the official culture and members of the government by the Smithsonian Institution – seen correctly as a sort of embodier of official memory in the country – in its unsuccessful attempts to mount exhibitions, one about the *Enola Gay* and another on the African American experience. Earlier there was a furor over an impressive exhibition at the National Gallery of American Art, *America as West*, which set out to contrast representations of the land, the Indian natives, and the conditions of life in the Western US during the 1860s with the way the land was being forcibly settled and the Indians destroyed, and the transformation of a once peaceful rural environment into a predatory urban one. Senator Ted Stevens of Alaska decried the whole thing as an attack on America even though he avowed that he himself had not seen the exhibit. In any event these controversies raise the question not only of what is remembered but how and in what form. It is an issue about the very fraught nature of representation, not just about content.

Memory and its representations touch very significantly upon questions of identity, of nationalism, of power and authority. Far from being a neutral exercise in facts and basic truths, the study of history, which of course is the underpinning of memory, both in school and university, is to some considerable extent a nationalist effort premised on the need to construct a desirable loyalty to and insider's understanding of one's country, tradition, and faith. As is well known, there's been a robust debate in the US on the matter of national standards in history, in which issues such as whether George Washington or Abraham Lincoln should be allowed more time than they have at present in history curricula have generated very angry arguments. Similarly, as Howard Zinn has suggested in his work, there has been skepticism expressed as to why the study of American history should glorify only the big deeds of big people and neglect to mention what happened to the small ones, the people who built railroads, worked the farms, sweated as laborers in the enormous industrial companies that lie at the heart of this country's immense wealth and power. (He redresses this imbalance in his impressive *People's History of the United States*, which has already sold well over half a million copies.)[1] In a recent article he goes even further. Having been asked to participate in a symposium on the Boston Massacre, Zinn reflected to himself that he wanted

> to discuss other massacres because it seemed to me that concentrating attention on the Boston Massacre would be a painless exercise in patriotic fervor. There is no surer way to obscure the deep divisions of race and class in American history than by uniting us in support of the American Revolution and all its symbols (like Paul Revere's stark etching of the soldiers shooting into the crowd).
>
> I suggested to the people assembled at Faneuil Hall (the wall around us crowded with portraits of the Founding Fathers and the nation's military heroes) that there were other massacres, forgotten or dimly remembered, that deserved to be recalled. These ignored episodes could tell us much about racial hysteria and class struggle, about shameful moments in our continental and overseas expansion, so that we can see ourselves more clearly, more honestly.[2]

These remarks immediately transport us to the vexed issue of nationalism and national identity, of how memories of the past are shaped in accordance with a certain notion of what "we" or, for that matter, "they" really are. National identity always involves narratives – of the nation's past, its founding fathers and documents, seminal events, and so on. But these narratives are never undisputed or merely a matter of the neutral recital of facts. In the United States, for example, 1492 was celebrated very differently by people who saw themselves as victims of Columbus's advent – people of color, minorities, members of the working class, people, in a word, who claimed they had a different collective memory of what in most schools was celebrated as a triumph of advancement and the collective march forward of humanity. Because the world has shrunk – for example, communications have been speeded up fantastically – and people find themselves undergoing the most rapid social transformations in history, ours has become an era of a search for roots, of people trying to discover in the collective memory of their race, religion, community, and family a past that is entirely their own, secure from the ravages of history and a turbulent time. But this too has provoked very sharp debate and even bloodshed. In the Islamic world, how one reads the orthodox tradition (*sunnah*) is being debated, as are the questions of how one interprets stories about the Prophet, which are, basically, memories reconstructed by disciples and friends, and how one can derive an image of contemporary Islamic codes of behavior and law that is consonant and in accordance with those precious, early, in fact aboriginal, memories. Similar questions arise in interpretations of the Christian Gospels, as well as the Judaic prophetic books; these questions have a direct impact on matters of community and politics in the present. Some of this lies behind the much-touted controversy over family values that have been vaunted by political candidates, moral philosophers, and public scolds.

To this whole matter of memory as a social, political, and historical enterprise has been added a complication, to which I referred above, namely, the role of invention. In 1983 two distinguished British historians, Eric Hobsbawm and Terence Ranger, edited a book of essays by various other well-known historians entitled *The Invention of Tradition*.[3] I won't try to summarize the ideas in this subtle and rich collection except to say that what was being studied was the way rulers – social and political authorities in the period since about 1850 – set about creating such supposedly age-old rituals and objects as the Scottish kilt or, in India, the *durbar*, thereby providing a false, that is, invented memory of the past as a way of creating a new sense of identity for ruler and ruled. In India, for example, the *durbar* – whose status as "tradition" was a total fiction – was said to be a great ceremonial pageant designed to be implanted in the Indian memory though it served the British colonial authorities to compel Indians to believe in the age-old history of British imperial rule. "In Africa, too," writes Ranger, "whites drew on invented tradition in order to derive the authority and confidence that allowed them to act as agents of change. Moreover, insofar as they were consciously applied to Africans, the invented traditions [such as compelling Africans to work as laborers on European gentlemen's farms] of nineteenth-century Europe were seen precisely as agents of 'modernization.'"[4] In modern France, according to Hobsbawm, the demise of Napoleon III's empire and the emergence of a politicized working class as evidenced in the Paris Commune convinced the "moderate Republican bourgeoisie" that only it could head off the dangers of revolution by producing a new kind of citizen, "turning peasants into Frenchmen... [and] all Frenchmen into good Republicans." Thus the French revolution was institutionalized in education by developing "a secular equivalent of the church... imbued with revolutionary and republican principles and content." In addition, there was "the invention of public ceremonies. The most important of these, Bastille Day, can be exactly dated in 1880." Thirdly, there "was the mass production of public monuments," of two main kinds – images of the Republic itself such as Marianne – and images of the "bearded civilian figures of whoever local patriotism chose to regard as its notables."[5]

In other words, the invention of tradition was a practice very much used by authorities as an instrument of rule in mass societies when the bonds of small social units like village and family were dissolving and authorities needed to find other ways of connecting a large number of people to each other. The invention of tradition is a method for using collective memory selectively by manipulating certain bits of the national past, suppressing others, elevating still others in an entirely functional way. Thus memory is not necessarily authentic, but rather useful. The Israeli journalist Tom Segev shows in his book *The Seventh Million* that the Holocaust was consciously used by the Israeli government as a way of consolidating Israeli national identity after years of not paying much attention to it.[6] Similarly, historian Peter Novick, in a recently published study of the image of the Holocaust amongst American Jews, shows that before the 1967 war and the Israeli victory against the Arab states, American Jews paid very little attention to that appallingly horrible episode (and in fact tried consciously to deemphasize it as a way of avoiding antiSemitism).[7] It is a long way from those early attitudes to the construction of the Holocaust Museum in Washington. Similarly the controversy surrounding the memories of the Armenian genocide is fuelled by the Turkish government's denial of its role.

My point in citing all these cases is to underline the extent to which the art of memory for the modern world is both for historians as well as ordinary citizens and institutions very much something to be used, misused, and exploited, rather than something that sits inertly there for each person to possess and contain. Thus the study and concern with memory or a specifically desirable and recoverable past is a specially freighted late twentieth-century phenomenon that has arisen at a time of bewildering change, of unimaginably large and diffuse mass societies, competing nationalisms, and, most important perhaps, the decreasing efficacy of religious, familial, and dynastic bonds. People now look to this refashioned memory, especially in its collective forms, to give themselves a coherent identity, a national narrative, a place in the world, though, as I have indicated, the processes of memory are frequently, if not always, manipulated and intervened in for sometimes urgent purposes in the present. It's interesting to contrast this more modern and somehow loosely malleable form of memory with the codified, rigorous art of memory in classical antiquity described by Frances Yates.[8] Memory for Cicero was something organized and structured. If you wanted to remember something for a speech you were about to give, you imagined a building with all sorts of rooms and corners, and in your mind's eye you subdivided the parts of the memory you wished to recall and placed them in various sections of the building; as you spoke you walked through the building in your head, so to speak, noting the places and the objects and phrases as you went along. That way order was maintained in the memory. The modern art of memory is much more subject to inventive reordering and redeploying than that.

As for geography, or geography as I want to use the word, as a socially constructed and maintained sense of place, a great deal of attention has been paid by modern scholars and critics to the extraordinary constitutive role of space in human affairs. Consider, as an easy instance, the word *globalization*, which is an indispensable concept for modern economics. It is a spatial, geographical designation signifying the global reach of a powerful economic system. Think of geographical designations like Auschwitz, think of what power and resonance they have, over and above a particularly specifiable moment in history or a geographical locale like Poland or France. The same applies to Jerusalem, a city, an idea, an entire history, and of course a specifiable geographical locale often typified by a photograph of the Dome of the Rock, the city walls, and the surrounding houses seen from the Mount of Olives; it too is overdetermined when it comes to memory, as well as all sorts of invented histories and traditions, all of them emanating from it, but most of them in conflict with each other. This conflict is intensified by Jerusalem's mythological

– as opposed to actual geographical – location, in which landscape, buildings, streets, and the like are overlain and, I would say, even covered entirely with symbolic associations totally obscuring the existential reality of what as a city and real place Jerusalem is. The same can be said for Palestine, whose landscape functions in the memories of Jews, Muslims, and Christians entirely differently. One of the strangest things for me to grasp is the powerful hold the locale must have had on European crusaders despite their enormous distance from the country. Scenes of the crucifixion and nativity, for instance, appear in European Renaissance paintings as taking place in a sort of denatured Palestine, since none of the artists had ever seen the place. An idealized landscape gradually took shape that sustained the European imagination for hundreds of years. That Bernard of Clairvaux standing in a church in Vezelay, in the heart of Burgundy, could announce a crusade to reclaim Palestine and the holy places from the Muslims never fails to astound me, and that after hundreds of years of living in Europe Zionist Jews could still feel that Palestine had stood still in time and was theirs, again despite millennia of history and the presence of actual inhabitants. This too is also an indication of how geography can be manipulated, invented, characterized quite apart from a site's merely physical reality.

Simon Schama's book *Landscape and Memory* chronicles the to-ing and fro-ing between specific geographical locales and the human imagination. Surely the most compelling aspect of Schama's book is that he shows in dozens of different ways that forests, villages, mountains, and rivers are never coterminous with some stable reality out there that identifies and gives them permanence. On the contrary, as in the example he gives of his family's original village in Lithuania, most of its traces disappeared; he finds instead through the poetry of Adam Mickiewicz how Jews and Poles "were snarled up . . . . in each other's fate" despite his contemporaries' belief that they were "necessarily alien to each other." Geography stimulates not only memory but dreams and fantasies, poetry and painting, philosophy (as in Heidegger's *Holzwege*), fiction (think of Walter Scott's Highland novels), and music (as in Sibelius's *Finlandia* or Copland's *Appalachian Spring*).[9]

But what specially interests me is the hold of both memory and geography on the desire for conquest and domination. Two of my books, *Orientalism* and *Culture and Imperialism*, are based not only on the notion of what I call imaginative geography – the invention and construction of a geographical space called the Orient, for instance, with scant attention paid to the actuality of the geography and its inhabitants – but also on the mapping, conquest, and annexation of territory both in what Conrad called the dark places of the earth and in its most densely inhabited and lived-in places, like India or Palestine. The great voyages of geographical discovery from da Gama to Captain Cook were motivated by curiosity and scientific fervor, but also by a spirit of domination, which becomes immediately evident when white men land in some distant and unknown place and the natives rebel against them. In the modern era Defoe's *Robinson Crusoe* is the essential parable of how geography and conquest go together, providing an almost eerie prefiguration of historical figures like Clive and Hastings in India, or scientific adventurers and explorers like Murchison in Africa decades and decades later. These experiences enable complicated memories for natives and (in the Indian case) Britishers alike; a similar dialectic of memory over territory animates the relationship of French and Algerian accounts of the 130 years of French rule in North Africa. We should never have left or given up India or Algeria, say some, using strange atavistic sentiments like the Raj revival – a spate of TV shows and films like *The Jewel in the Crown*, *A Passage to India*, *Gandhi*, and the fashion of wearing safari suits, helmets, desert boots – as a way of periodically provoking nostalgia for the good old days of British supremacy in Asia and Africa, whereas most Indians and Algerians would likely say that their liberation came as a result of being able after years of nationalist struggle to take hold of their own affairs, reestablish their identity, culture, and language, and, above all, reappropriate their territory from the colonial masters. Hence, to some extent, we witness the remarkable emergence of an Anglo-Indian literature by Anita Desai, Salman Rushdie, Arundhati Roy, and many others, reexcavating and recharting the past from a postcolonial point of view, thereby erecting a new postimperial space.

It is easy to see the fact of displacement in the colonial experience, which at bottom is the replacement of one geographical sovereignty, an imperialist one, by another, native force. More subtle and complex is the unending cultural struggle over territory, which necessarily involves overlapping memories, narratives, and physical structures. No one has studied this more powerfully than the late Raymond Williams in his classic book, *The Country and the City*. What he shows is that literary and cultural forms such as the ode, the political pamphlet, and different kinds of novels derive some of their aesthetic rationale from changes taking place in the geography or landscape as the result of a social contest. Let me explain this more concretely. The mid-seventeenth- to eighteenth-century genre of the country-house poem, with its emphasis on the house's calm stateliness and classical proportions – "Heaven's Centre, Nature's Lap" – is not the same thing in Marvell, Ben Jonson, and, later, in Pope. Jonson draws attention to the way the house was won from disturbing, encroaching peasant populations; Marvell in a more complicated way understands the country house as the result of a union between money, property, and politics; in Pope the house has become a sort of moral center; and later in Jane Austen's *Mansfield Park* it is the very embodiment of all that is benign and actively good in England. Property in all four writers is being consolidated; what we watch is the gradual triumph of a social dialectic celebrating the virtues and necessities of a propertied class, which itself seems to stand for the nation at its best. In each case the writer remembers the past in his or her own way, seeing images that typify that past, preserving one past, sweeping away others. Later writers, say, urban novelists like Dickens and Thackeray, will look back to this period as a sort of rural paradise from which England has fallen; the beauties of the field are replaced by the grimy, dark, sooty, industrial city. Both the retrospective image and the contemporary one, says Williams, are historical constructs, myths of the social geography fashioned in different periods by different classes, different interests, different ideas about the national identity, the polity, the country as a whole, none of it without actual struggle and rhetorical dispute.[10]

All of what I have been discussing here – the interplay between geography, memory, and invention, in the sense that invention must occur if there is recollection – is particularly relevant to a twentieth-century example, that of Palestine, which instances an extraordinarily rich and intense conflict of at least two memories, two sorts of historical invention, two sorts of geographical imagination. I want to argue that we can go behind the headlines and the repetitively reductive media accounts of the Middle East conflict and discern there a much more interesting and subtle conflict than what is customarily talked about. Only by understanding that special mix of geography generally and landscape in particular with historical memory and, as I said, an arresting form of invention can we begin to grasp the persistence of conflict and the difficulty of resolving it, a difficulty that is far too complex and grand than the current peace process could possibly envisage, let alone resolve.

Let us juxtapose some relevant dates and events with each other. For Palestinians 1948 is remembered as the year of the *nakba*, or catastrophe, when 750,000 of us who were living there – two-thirds of the population – were driven out, our property taken, hundreds of villages destroyed, an entire society obliterated. For Israelis and many Jews throughout the world 1998 was the fiftieth anniversary of Israel's independence and establishment, a miraculous story of recovery after the Holocaust, of democracy, of making the desert bloom, and so on. Thus, two totally different characterizations of a recollected event have been constructed. What has long struck me about this radical irreconcilability at the origin of the Palestinian-Israeli conflict is that it is routinely excluded from considerations of related subjects concerning ethnic or collective memory, geographical analysis, and political reflection. This is most evident in studies of the German catastrophe as well as of ethnic conflicts in former Yugoslavia, Rwanda, Ireland, Sri Lanka, South Africa, and elsewhere.

Take Germany first. There is little doubt that it is important to prevent assassins of memory from denying or minimizing the Holocaust; but it is also important not to forget to show the link, well-established in contemporary Jewish consciousness, between the Holocaust and the founding of Israel as a haven for Jews. That this link also meant the disestablishing of the Palestinians from their homes and farms is practically never stated, although for Palestinians it increases the agony of their plight: why, they ask, are we made to pay for what happened to the Jews in Europe by what was in effect a Western Christian genocide? The question never emerges out of the debate in or about Germany, even though it is directly entailed by such facts as the enormous amount of money paid by Germany to Israel in Holocaust reparations and has surfaced again in the claims against Swiss banks. I have no hesitation in saying, yes, Germany and Switzerland ought to pay, but that also means that Palestinians over the past 50 years whose own losses are staggering deserve a hearing, too, especially since to us these payments to Israel go to consolidate Israel's hold not only on what we lost in 1948 but on the territories occupied in 1967. The Palestinians have never received even the slightest official acknowledgement of the massive injustice that was done to them, much less the possibility of staking material claims against Israel for the property taken, the people killed, the houses demolished, the water taken, the prisoners held, and so forth. There is also the complex, almost equally dense and far-reaching matter of Britain's responsibility. What strikes me as more significant is the refusal in the Israeli official narrative to take account of the state's complicity in and responsibility for the Palestinian dispossession. For years and years an assiduous campaign to maintain a frozen version of Israel's heroic narrative of repatriation and justice obliterated any possibility of a Palestinian narrative, in large part because certain key components of the Israeli story stressed certain geographical characteristics of Palestine itself. Take the key notion of liberation: so strong was the story of Jewish independence and reemergence after the Holocaust that it became virtually impossible to ask the question, Liberation and independence from whom? If the question was asked it was always answered as liberation from British imperialism. Or, as the story got elaborated, it was defense against invading Arab armies that wanted to crush the young state. The Palestinians thus faded into the encircling and menacing obscurity of "the Arabs," the fact that they were actual residents occluded and simultaneously denied.

Perhaps the greatest battle Palestinians have waged as a people has been over the right to a remembered presence and, with that presence, the right to possess and reclaim a collective historical reality, at least since the Zionist movement began its encroachments on the land. A similar battle has been fought by all colonized peoples whose past and present were dominated by outside powers who had first conquered the land and then rewrote history so as to appear in that history as the true owners of that land. Every independent state that emerged after the dismantling of the classical empires in the post-World War Two years felt it necessary to narrate its own history, as much as possible free of the biases and misrepresentations of that history by British, French, Portuguese, Dutch, or other colonial historians.

Yet the fate of Palestinian history has been a sad one, since not only was independence not gained, but there was little collective understanding of the importance of constructing a collective history as a part of trying to gain independence. To become a nation in the formal sense of the word, a people must make itself into something more than a collection of tribes, or political organizations of the kind that since the 1967 war Palestinians have created and supported. With a competitor as formidable as the Zionist movement, the effort to rewrite the history of Palestine so as to exclude the land's peoples had a disastrous effect on the quest for Palestinian self-determination. What we never understood was the power of a narrative history to mobilize people around a common goal. In the case of Israel, the narrative's main point was that Zionism's goal was to restore, reestablish, repatriate, and reconnect a people with its original homeland. It was the genius of Herzl and Weizmann to draft thinkers like Einstein and Buber, as well as financiers like Lord Rothschild and Moses Montefiore, into giving their time and effort in support of so important and historically justified a scheme. This narrative of reestablishment and recovery served its purpose not only amongst Jews but also throughout the Western (and even in some parts of the Eastern) world. Because of the power and appeal of the Zionist narrative and idea (which depended on a special reading of the Bible) and because of the collective Palestinian inability as a people to produce a convincing narrative story with a beginning, middle, and end (we were always too disorganized, our leaders were always interested in maintaining their power, most of our intellectuals refused to commit themselves as a group to a common goal, and we too often changed our goals) Palestinians have remained scattered and politically ineffective victims of Zionism, as it continues to take more and more land and history.

Just how deliberate and sustained has been the assault on the history and consequently the dominant public memory of Palestine, and how much attention has been paid over the years to the reconstruction of Jewish history to suit the purposes of Zionism as a political movement, is made stunningly clear by the Scottish historian of the ancient Near East, Keith W. Whitelam, whose book *The Invention of Ancient Israel: The Silencing of Palestinian History* is of paramount importance. Not being myself a scholar of the ancient world generally, nor of ancient Palestine in particular, I cannot make a judgment about every one of the points that Whitelam makes; but I am able to judge what he says about modern scholarship on ancient Israel, and there I was very impressed with his careful, but nevertheless extremely audacious argument. In effect Whitelam is talking about two things: one, the politics of collective memory, and, two, the creation by Zionist scholars and historians of a geographical image of ancient Israel that is shaped by the ideological needs and pressures of the modern Zionist movement.[11]

As I suggested above, collective memory is not an inert and passive thing, but a field of activity in which past events are selected, reconstructed, maintained, modified, and endowed with political meaning. In her 1995 book *Recovered Roots: Collective Memory and the Making of Israeli National Tradition*, the Israeli-American historian Yael Zerubavel shows how before the late nineteenth century the story of Masada was unknown to most Jews. Then in 1862 a Hebrew translation of the Roman sources of Masada in Josephus's *Wars of the Jews* was published, and in a short time the story was transformed by reconstruction into four important things: "a major turning point in Jewish history, a locus of modern pilgrimage, a famous archeological site, and a contemporary political metaphor."[12] When General Yigael Yadin excavated Masada after 1948 the expedition had two complementary aspects: an archeological investigation and "the fulfillment of a national mission."[13] In time the actual place was the site of Israeli army ceremonies, a commemoration of Jewish heroism, as well as a commitment to present and future military skill. Thus was a dim, relatively unknown incident in the past reformulated consciously as a major episode in the nationalist program of a modern state; Masada became a potent symbol of the Israeli national narrative of struggle and survival.

Whitelam presents a remarkably analogous picture of how the history of ancient Palestine was gradually replaced by a largely fabricated image of ancient Israel, a political entity that in reality played only a small role in the area of geographical Palestine. According to Whitelam, ancient Palestine was the home of many diverse peoples and histories; it was the place where Jebusites, Israelites, Canaanites, Moabites, Philistines, and others lived and flourished. Beginning in the late nineteenth century, however, this more complex and rich history was silenced, forced aside, in order that the history of invading Israelite tribes, who for a time suppressed and dispossessed the native peoples, became the only narrative worth considering. Thus the extinction of the indigenous population of Palestine in the late Bronze Age became an acceptable and gradually permanent feature of a sort of triumphalist *Jewish* history for scholars like W. F. Albright, the leading historian of ancient Palestine during the early twentieth century, and made it possible to silence native Palestinian history as it was supplanted by the history of the incoming Israelites. Albright goes so far as retrospectively to condone the destruction of the native inhabitants of ancient Palestine in favor of superior people: "From the impartial standpoint of a philosopher of history," he says, "it often seems necessary that a people of markedly inferior type [that is, the ancient Canaanite Palestinians] should vanish before a people of superior potentialities [the Israelites], since there is a point beyond which racial mixture cannot go without disaster" (quoted in *I*, p. 83).

In its remarkably frank expression of racist attitudes this statement by a supposedly objective scholar, who also happened to be the most influential figure in modern biblical archeology, is chilling. But it suggests how in its desire to overcome obstacles in its path, even to the point of retrospectively condoning dispossession and even genocide, modern Zionism also imposed a sort of teleology retrospectively. Whitelam proceeds to show how scholars like Albright and many others went on in their writing to construct "a large, powerful, sovereign and autonomous ... state [which was] attributed to its founder David" (*I*, p. 124). Whitelam shows how this state was in effect an invention designed to accompany the Zionist attempt in the twentieth century to gain control over the land of Palestine; thus "biblical scholarship, in its construction of an ancient Israeli state, is implicated in contemporary struggles for the land" (*I*, p. 124). Whitelam argues that such a state was far less important than its champions in the present day say it was: The invented ancient Israel "has silenced Palestinian history and obstructed alternative claims to the past" (*I*, p. 124). By inventing an ancient Israeli kingdom that displaced Canaanite Palestinian history, modern scholars have made it nearly impossible for present-day Palestinians to say that their claims to Palestine have any long-term historical validity. Indeed such pro-Zionist scholars have gone on to assert that ancient Israel was qualitatively different from all other forms of government in Palestine, just as modern-day Zionists said that their coming to Palestine turned an "empty" desert land into a garden. The idea in both ancient and modern cases is identical and of course violently contradicts the far more complex, pluricultural identity of the place.

Whitelam is quite right to criticize my own work on the modern struggle for Palestine for not paying any attention to the discourse of biblical studies. This discourse, he says, was really a part of Orientalism, by which Europeans imagined and represented the timeless Orient as they wished to see it, not as it was, or as its natives believed. Thus biblical studies, which created an Israel that was set apart from its environment, and supposedly brought civilization and progress to the region, was reinforced by Zionist ideology and by Europe's interest in the roots of its own past. Yet, he concludes, "this discourse has excluded the vast majority of the population of the region." It is a discourse of power "which has dispossessed Palestinians of a land and a past" (*I*, p. 235).

Whitelam's subject is ancient history and how a purposeful political movement could invent a serviceable past that became a crucial aspect of Israel's modern collective memory. When the mayor of Jerusalem a few years ago proclaimed that the city represented 3,000 years of unbroken Jewish dominance, he was mobilizing an invented story for the political purposes of a modern state still trying to dispossess native Palestinians who are now seen only as barely tolerated aliens.

Along with the idea of Israel as liberation and independence couched in terms of a reestablishment of Jewish sovereignty went an equally basic motif, that of making the desert bloom, the inference being that Palestine was either empty (as in the Zionist slogan, "a land without people for a people without land") or neglected by the nomads and peasants who facelessly lived on it. The main idea was to not only deny the Palestinians a historical presence as a collectivity but also to imply that they were not a people who had a long-standing peoplehood. As late as 1984 a book by a relative unknown called Joan Peters appeared from a major commercial publishing house (Harper and Row) purporting to show that the Palestinians as a people were an ideological, propagandistic fiction; her book *From Time Immemorial* won all sorts of prizes and accolades from well-known personalities like Saul Bellow and Barbara Tuchman, who admired Peters's "success" in proving that Palestinians were "a fairy tale." Slowly, however, the book lost credibility despite its eight or nine printings, as various critics, Norman Finkelstein principal among them, methodically revealed that the book was a patchwork of lies, distortions, and fabrications, amounting to colossal fraud. The book's brief currency (it has since practically disappeared and is no longer cited) is an indication of how overwhelmingly the Zionist memory had succeeded in emptying Palestine of its inhabitants and history, turning its landscape instead into an empty space that, Peters alleged, was flooded in the middle 1940s with Arab refugees from neighboring countries attracted to the place by the hope of prosperity under Jewish settlers.[14] I remember my rage at reading a book that had the effrontery to tell me that my house and birth in Jerusalem in 1935 (before Peters's flood of "Arab" refugees) to say nothing of the actual existence of my parents, uncles, aunts, grandparents, and my entire extended family in Palestine were in fact not there, had not lived there for generations, had therefore no title to the specific landscape of orange and olive groves that I remembered from my earliest glimmerings of consciousness. I recall also that in 1986 I purposefully published a book of photographs by Jean Mohr, *After the Last Sky: Palestinian Lives* for which I wrote an elaborate text whose effect with the interconnected pictures I hoped would be to dispel the myth of an empty landscape and an anonymous, nonexistent people.[15]

All along then the Israeli story, buttressed both subliminally and explicitly with memories of the horrors of an anti-Semitism that ironically took place in an entirely different landscape, crowded out the Palestinian history taking place in Palestine and out of it because of Israeli geographical and physical displacement of the people. The justified feeling of "never again," which became the watchword of Jewish consciousness as, for instance, the massively publicized Eichmann trial revealed the scope of the awfulness of the Holocaust, pushed away the deepening sense of the need for Palestinian assertion that was developing in that community. There is something almost tragically ironic about the way in which the 1967 war on the one hand intensified the assertiveness of a triumphal Israeli identity and, on the other, sharpened the need among Palestinians for organized resistance and counterassertion. Only this time Israel had occupied the rest of Palestine and acquired a population of almost two million people that it ruled as a military power (20 percent of Israel's citizens are Palestinians). Newly excavated memories from the Jewish past emerged – the Jew as warrior, militant, vigorous fighter – and replaced the image of the Jew as scholarly, wise, and slightly withdrawn. The change in iconography is brilliantly chronicled by Paul Breines in his book *Tough Jews*.[16]

With the rise of the PLO, first in Jordan, then after September 1970 in Beirut, a new Palestinian interest arose in the past, as embodied in such disparate activities as organized historical research and the production of poetry and fiction based upon a sense of recovered history, formerly blotted out but now reclaimed in the poetry of Zayyat, Darwish, Hussein, and al-Qassem, in the fiction of Kanafani and Jabra, as well as in painting, sculpture, and historical writing such as Abu Lughod's collection *The Transformation of Palestine*. Later work such as the compilations of Walid Khalidi – *Before Their Diaspora* and *All That Remains* – Rashid Khalidi's study *Palestinian Identity*, Sabry Jiryis's *The Arabs in Israel*, Bayan al Hout's study of the Palestinian elites, Elia Zureik's *The Palestinians in Israel*, and many others, all by Palestinian scholars, gradually established a line of dynastic descent, between the events of 1948 and before and after the catastrophe, that gave substance to the national memory of a Palestinian collective life that persisted, despite the ravages of physical dispossession, military occupation, and Israeli official denials.[17] By the middle of the 1980s, a new direction had begun to appear in Israeli critical histories of the canonized official memories. In my opinion their genesis lay to some considerable extent in the aggravated, but close colonial encounter between Israelis and Palestinians in the occupied territories. Consider that with the accession to power of the right-wing Likud in 1977 these territories were renamed Judea and Samaria; they were onomastically transformed from "Palestinian" to "Jewish" territory, and settlements – whose object from the beginning had been nothing less than the transformation of the landscape by the forcible introduction of European-style mass housing with neither precedent nor basis in the local topography – gradually spread all over the Palestinian areas, starkly challenging the natural and human setting with rude Jewish-only segregations. In my opinion, these settlements, whose number included a huge ring of fortresslike housing projects around the city of Jerusalem, were intended visibly to illustrate Israeli power, additions to the gentle landscape that signified aggression, not accommodation and acculturation.

The new trend in Israeli critical history was inaugurated by the late Simha Flaphan, but then continued in controversial scholarly monographs and books by Bennie Morris, Avi Shlaim, Tom Segev, Ilan Pappe, and Beni Beit Halahmi. Much of this work I believe was fuelled by the Palestinian *intifada*, which laid to rest the idea of Palestinian silence and absence. For the first time a systematic critique of the official version programmatically revealed the crucial role played by invention in a collective memory that had ossified into unyielding, almost sacralized, and, with regard to Palestinians, dehumanized representation. Far from Palestinians having left or run away because they were told to do so by their leaders (this had been the prevalent argument for the suddenly depopulated landscape in

1948), these historians showed that according to Zionist military archives there had been a cold-blooded plan to disperse and exclude the native population, spiriting them away so that Palestinians would not clutter Israel with their non-Jewish presence. Far from the Jewish forces having been a small, outnumbered, and truly threatened population, it was shown that these forces were greater in number than the combined Arab armies, they were better armed, and they had a common set of objectives entirely lacking among their opponents. As for the Palestinians, they were effectively leaderless, unarmed, and in places like Jerusalem – which I recall vividly myself, since I was 12 at the time – completely at the mercy of the Hagganah and the Irgun, whose undeflected purpose was to clear them out unequivocally, as we were indeed. And far from there being a policy of "purity of arms," the stock-in-trade phrase for Israeli military policy, there was a series of massacres and atrocities designed specifically to terrorize the greatly disadvantaged Palestinians into flight and/or nonresistance.

More recently, the distinguished Israeli social historian Zeev Sternhell has revisited the official state archives to show with extraordinary force that what was presented to the world as a socialist democracy was not in fact that at all, but what he himself calls a nationalist socialism designed above all to create a new community of blood, to redeem the land by conquest, and to submit the Jewish individual to a collectivity of almost messianic fervency.[18] Thus in fact Israel was profoundly antisocialist and, rather than encouraging individual rights and an egalitarian concept of citizenship, in fact created a theocracy with a rigorous limit to what the individual was and could expect from the state. The Kibbutzim – long heralded as a unique social experiment in egalitarianism and innovative sharing – were, says Sternhell, window-dressing, extremely limited and circumscribed in their membership (no Arabs were ever allowed to be members). Israel is now the only state in the world that is not the state of its citizens but of the whole Jewish people wherever they may be. Not only has it never had until the present any international boundaries, Israel also has no constitution, but a set of Basic Laws, one of which, the Law of Return, entitles any Jew anywhere the right to immediate Israeli citizenship, whereas Palestinians whose families were driven out in 1948 are allowed no such right at all. Ninety-two percent of the land is held in trust by an agency for the Jewish people; this means that non-Jews, especially Palestinian citizens of Israel who constitute a population of one million people and are almost 20 percent of the state, are simply forbidden to buy, lease, or sell land. One can imagine the outcry in the United States if land was only permitted to Christian whites, for example, and not to Jews or nonwhites.

Thus the dominant pattern in thought about the geography of Palestine, for a millennium and a half inhabited by an overwhelming majority of non-Jews, has been the idea of return: to return to Israel for Jews who have never been there was to return to Zion and an earlier state from which Jews had been exiled. Carol Bardenstein notes in a sensitive study the way the same images of prickly pears, oranges, and trees, thread their way into discourses of memory for both Jews and Palestinians. But the Jewish discourse eliminates from the landscape the former Palestinian presence:

> I had the opportunity to visit a number of sites of former Palestinian villages that have been variously reshaped through tree-planting and related JNF projects, in ways that would appear to promote "collective," if selective, forgetting. If one visits the site of the destroyed village of Ghabsiyah in the Galilee, for example, upon closer scrutiny the trees and landscape themselves yield two very different and contesting narratives converging on the same site. One has to rely on landscape readings, because little else remains. What is most readily visible to the

first-time visitor are the JNF trees planted on the site – the recognizable combination of pine and other trees that have grown over the past four decades in a manner that makes it seem as if perhaps that is all that was ever there.[19]

Let me note in a very brief conclusion what the interplay among memory, place, and invention can do if it is not to be used for the purposes of exclusion, that is, if it is to be used for liberation and coexistence between societies whose adjacency requires a tolerable form of sustained reconciliation. Again I want to use the Palestinian issue as my concrete example. Israelis and Palestinians are now so intertwined through history, geography, and political actuality that it seems to me absolute folly to try and plan the *future* of one without that of the other. The problem with the American-sponsored Oslo process was that it was premised on a notion of partition and separation, whereas everywhere one looks in the territory of historical Palestine, Jews and Palestinians live together. This notion of separation has also closed these two unequal communities of suffering to each other. Most Palestinians are indifferent to and often angered by stories of Jewish suffering since it seems to them that as subjects of Israeli military power anti-Semitism seems remote and irrelevant while their land is taken and homes are being bulldozed. Conversely most Israelis refuse to concede that Israel is built on the ruins of Palestinian society, and that for them the catastrophe of 1948 continues until the present. Yet there can be no possible reconciliation, no possible solution unless these two communities confront each's experience in the light of the other. It seems to me essential that there can be no hope of peace unless the stronger community, the Israeli Jews, acknowledges the most powerful memory for Palestinians, namely, the dispossession of an entire people. As the weaker party Palestinians must also face the fact that Israeli Jews see themselves as survivors of the Holocaust, even though that tragedy cannot be allowed to justify Palestinian dispossession. Perhaps in today's inflamed atmosphere of military occupation and injustice it is perhaps too much to expect these acknowledgements and recognitions to take place. But, as I have argued elsewhere, at some point they must.

Notes

1   See Howard Zinn, *A People's History of the United States* (New York, 1980).
2   Zinn, "The Massacres of History," *The Progressive* 62 (Aug. 1998): 17.
3   See *The Invention of Tradition*, ed. Eric Hobsbawm and Terence Ranger (Cambridge, 1983).
4   Ranger, "The Invention of Tradition in Colonial Africa," in ibid., p. 220.
5   Hobsbawm, "Mass-Producing Traditions: Europe, 1870–1914," pp. 271, 272.
6   See Tom Segev, *The Seventh Million: The Israelis and the Holocaust*, trans. Haim Watzman (New York, 1993).
7   See Peter Novick, *The Holocaust in American Life* (New York, 1999), pp. 146–203.
8   See Frances A. Yates, *The Art of Memory* (Chicago, 1966).
9   Simon Schama, *Landscape and Memory* (New York, 1995), p. 30.
10 See Raymond Williams, *The Country and the City* (London, 1973).
11 See Keith W. Whitelam, *The Invention of Ancient Israel: The Silencing of Palestinian History* (New York, 1996); hereafter abbreviated *I*.
12 Yael Zerubavel, *Recovered Roots: Collective Memory and the Making of Israeli National Tradition* (Chicago, 1995), p. 63.
13 Ibid.
14 See Edward W. Said, "Conspiracy of Praise" and Norman G. Finkelstein, "Disinformation and the Palestine Question: The Not-So-Strange Case of Joan Peters's *From Time Immemorial*," in *Blaming the Victims: Spurious Scholarship and the Palestinian Question*, eds. Said and Christopher Hitchens (New York, 1988), pp. 23–31, 33–69.

15 See Said and Jean Mohr, *After the Last Sky: Palestinian Lives* (New York, 1986).

16 See Paul Breines, *Tough Jews: Political Fantasies and the Moral Dilemma of American Jewry* (New York, 1990).

17 See *The Transformation of Palestine: Essays on the Origin and Development of the Arab–Israeli Conflict*, ed. Abu Lughod (Evanston, IL, 1971); Walid Khalidi, *Before Their Diaspora: A Photographic History of the Palestinians* (Washington, DC, 1984), *All That Remains: The Palestinian Villages Occupied and Depopulated by Israel in 1948*, ed. Walid Khalidi (Washington, DC, 1992); Rashid Khalidi, *Palestinian Identity: The Construction of Modern National Consciousness* (New York, 1997); Sabri Jiryis, *The Arabs in Israel*, trans. Inca Bushnag (New York, 1976); Bayan al Hout, *Political Leadership and Institutions in Palestine, 1917–48* [Arabic] (Beirut, 1984); and Elia Zureik, *The Palestinians in Israel; A Study in Internal Colonialism* (London, 1979).

18 See Zeev Sternhell, *The Founding Myths of Israel: Nationalism, Socialism, and the Making of the Jewish State*, trans. David Maisel (Princeton, NJ, 1998).

19 Carol Bardenstein, "Threads of Memory and Discourses of Rootedness: Of Trees, Oranges, and the Prickly Pear Cactus in Israel/Palestine," *Edebiyât* 8, no. 1 (1998): 9.

CHAPTER 22

Pepi Leistyna

White Ethnic Unconsciousness

I was having a beer down at the local pub in Boston last Saint Patrick's Day when the inevitable conversation broke out about who was Irish. Making the rounds, the bartender inquired about my "ethnic background." Thinking that perhaps he had found some solidarity in the reddish blonde, white guy in front of him, he looked somewhat perplexed when I didn't instantly and eagerly raise my mug to celebrate the holiday at hand.

In the past, I would have simply replied that I was Austrian on my father's side, and French-Canadian on my mother's – leaving out the details of what has historically been a mish-mash of who knows how many relationships. It wasn't that not being Irish (at least not that I know of) resulted in any reluctance to speak up, but rather, I wondered what all of this really meant. Here we were, a bunch of White, third, and fourth generation immigrants who were momentarily, and in some ambiguous and seemingly insignificant way, declaring our ethnic identities: "Italian," "Irish," and another "French-Canadian."

Tony assured us that his mother made the best tomato sauce in the world, Donny claimed that he could drink anyone under the table, and Philip raged about the superiority of Canadian hockey players. What was so ironic about this scene was that these three working-class guys, who were raising their family's coat of arms, are the same ones that readily yell at the television that "America is for Americans!", and for "those people" (which always implies Latino/as, Asians, and Blacks) to "go back home!" At their most accommodating they shout, "Learn English and get a job!", "If our immigrant grandparents made it, then why can't you!" The blatant contradiction between celebrating and denouncing ethnic roots has always gone unmentioned, and thus uncontested. Since I have known these guys for years, it is obvious to me that any authentic connection that each of us have with our ancestors is superficial at best, a connection that comes to life around such holidays. In fact, there is virtually no trace of my grandparents in my life – no religious affiliation, no common language, values, or social practices, nothing but a name. But then what's in a name?

I looked over at Philip and asked him if he knew the meaning of his family name, to which he immediately responded, "of the wood!" – admittingly the only two words in French that he knew. I then inquired if he was aware of the fact that he had the same last

Pepi Leistyna, "White Ethnic Unconsciousness," *Cultural Circles*, vol. 2 (Spring 1998), pp. 33–51. Reprinted by permission of Elementary Education and Specialized Studies, Boise State University.

name as one of the most famous African American intellectuals in US history. With a look of utter disgust, and in blatantly racist overtones, his earlier cries for American patriotism turned into a fervent denial of any affiliation with a Black man.

In Philip's mind, do differences in skin color preclude individuals from any form of ethnic connection, and if so, does being "'American" exclude racial groups other than Whites from membership?[2] What historical and sociopolitical mechanisms have shaped these White men's ethnic identities and perceptions? And, what in fact are the defining characteristics of being "American?"[3] I would like to explore these questions by examining what I refer to as "racenicity," the process through which the sociohistorical and ideological construction of race ("whiteness" in particular) has had a significant impact on defining national identity, ethnicity, and the perception of ethnic differences in the United States. I fully recognize that there are other factors, such as gender, capitalism, class, health, age, locality, religion, and sexual orientation, that play an important role in the construction of ethnicity/culture, as well as in the multiple social identities, discourses, and struggles that we all individually embody. While the discussion of this paper focuses on the effects of the ideological construction of race, the analytic distinction "racenicity" should not be abstracted from these and other important defining factors – in fact we need to develop a more dialectical understanding of the multiple and interconnecting relationships that speak to a more profound understanding of the politics of difference.[4]

The fragmentation of race and ethnicity

Far too often, mainstream scholars and the general public have differentiated between racial and ethnic lines. While there is a plethora of publications that list the two terms side by side, such literature fails to adequately articulate their connection. Consider the following definition of "ethnicity" taken from *Sources: Notable Selections in Race and Ethnicity* (1995):

> Ethnicity refers to an affiliation of people who share similar cultural characteristics. Members of ethnic groups share common languages, religious beliefs, cultural traditions and customs, value systems, and normative orientations. They also share a similar world-view, an ethnic consciousness – a peoplehood. Ethnicity is a sociopolitical construct that emerges from collective experiences in a society. That is, ethnic consciousness is a consequence of or a response to the social conditions minority populations encounter once they migrate to a foreign country. (Aguirre & Baker, p. 24)

While Aquirre and Baker's (1995) definition recognizes ethnicity as a sociopolitical construct, and the fact that social conditions shape experience, it neglects to adequately point out how the sociohistorical and ideological construction of "race" greatly contributes to those "social conditions" – that is, how the racialization of identities, and the racism therein, has played a significant and inextricable role in shaping ethnic identities and perceptions in the United States. As we shall see throughout this paper, understanding the inextricable relationship between the two categories entails dissecting how racialization/racism affects the patterns of everyday living: language, traditions and customs, values and normative orientations, worldviews, etc. In this sense, race and ethnicity should not be observed as entirely separate entities, thus the concept "racenicity" – a point of analysis which embodies, without conflating, a fusion of these two terms.

What is racenicity?

As J. Milton Yinger (1990) points out, "Many recent studies of ethnicity have focused much attention on cultural differences and the value of pluralism, and less attention on how ethnic differences are implicated in the distribution of power and privilege" (p. 22). Ethnicity needs to be understood as being shaped by the lived experiences and institutional forms organized around diverse elements of struggle and domination. In other words, beyond the limits of traditional anthropological/sociological definitions, ethnicity/culture also embodies the experiences and behaviors that are the result of the asymmetrical distribution of power across such social markers as race, gender, class, health, and sexual orientation; i.e., forms of oppression that are lived out (Foucault, 1972; Freire, 1970; Giroux, 1983). Culture does not take place in a social vacuum, but rather, as people interact with existing groups and institutions, and participate in social practices in which the values, beliefs, bodies of knowledge, representations, and styles of communication of the dominant culture are imposed, intergroup tensions inevitably emerge. Within these volatile social relations, groups "may mobilize or invent the rudiments of ethnicity in an effort to oppose discrimination" (Yinger, 1994, p. 22). At the same time, they may also reproduce ethnic patterns that reinforce the status quo.

Racenicity is thus the result of the antagonistic social relations caused by the unequal distribution of power throughout society along racial lines. It is the product and driving force of an ideology in which "whiteness," which I will show has been a sociopolitically and institutionally sanctioned marker of status in the United States, plays a significant role in shaping ethnic identities. As Peter McLaren (1994) contends, "Whiteness does not exist outside of culture but constitutes the prevailing social texts in which social norms are made and remade" (p. 59). As ethnic/cultural differences are purged and social practices are reshaped around this racial identity, a hierarchy emerges that subcategorizes while devaluing groups of people that are designated "racial others," and/or "ethnics." This racist hierarchy has resulted in three general patterns of ethnic/racialized behavior:

1) Groups that are racially subordinated, such as Blacks, Latino/as, Asians, and Native Americans, develop ethnic/cultural artifacts and practices that function to resist social injustice.
2) Some members of racially subordinated populations come to believe in their imposed "inferior status," and consequently buy into the dominant paradigm by attempting to change their ethnic and physical beings in order to "fit in."
3) Most Whites uncritically assimilate the cultural criteria of dominant racist values and practices and as a result are unable to historically situate themselves, that is, they are unable to identify the cultural mechanisms that have shaped their ethnic identities.

It is this last category that I will explore in this essay.

It is important to note here that there is an infinite number of ways in which "racenicity" manifests itself, and that these categories only represent three examples. It is also crucial to recognize that such categories are not fixed in the sense that people either belong to one or the other. Individuals, with their multiple and contingent social identities, may simultaneously participate in liberatory and oppressive social practices.

The point of creating this new analytic category [racenicity] is by no means meant to essentialize race (to imply that racial groups are fixed and exclusive), to assume that all racially subordinated groups/individuals think about is their oppression, or to argue that resistant/oppositional behavior or assimilation manifests itself in deterministic or monolithic ways. Contemporary African-American culture, for example, "is radically complex and diverse, marked by an intriguing variety of intellectual reflections, artistic creations, and social practices" (Dyson, 1993, p. xiii) – it is also cut across by such issues of class, gender, and sexuality. In addition, the concept of racenicity does not imply that racism is monolithic and unchanging. As Paul Gilroy (1987) argues, "Different patterns of 'racial' activity and political struggle will appear in determinate historical conditions" (p. 27).

It is also important to note that this new point of analysis does not imply that the category of "race" is simply a synonym for "ethnicity." Conservative social and educational theorists have historically attempted to obfuscate the realities of racism by hiding behind so-called "ethnic differences" – what they have perceived to be "deficiencies." However, this "cultural deprivation model" has merely served the purpose of strategically disguising, while maintaining, the fabricated legacy of genetic inferiority.

Before I discuss the third previously mentioned manifestation of racenicity, and illustrate how race, beyond mere skin color, is an important source of meaning, (dis)advantage, and identity, it is crucial to first depict whose perspectives and interests have been defining the national standards of racial/ethnic character.

The social construction of whiteness: the yardstick of ethnicity

It is only in a race conscious society that skin color takes on historical, sociocultural, ideological, and political significance. In the seventeenth century the colonial planter class, in what was to become the United States, brought the first enslaved Africans and indentured White servants to the colonies. Facing the realities of labor unrest, interracial marriages, and uprising, this Anglo elite strategically made use of the idea of a "White race" in order to create racial solidarity among the White classes (Allen, 1994). Providing the disenfranchised and propertyless White workers with racial privileges proved successful in ensuring their disassociation with enslaved Blacks, and their servitude to the dominant classes.

Laws were passed to maintain this racial hierarchy in which "White" would come to define "American." In 1790, the first Congress demanded that any naturalized citizen of the United States had to be "White." Adhering to such an ambiguous discriminatory category, this racial marker proved to be extremely difficult to interpret. As David Roediger (1994) states, "the legal and social history of immigration often turned on the question 'Who was White?'" (p. 181). Such groups as the Irish, Italians, Hungarians, Jews, and Greeks, through struggle, would eventually become "White," the Asians and Latino/as were relegated to non-White status.[5]

By the late 1850s, Sir Francis Galton, who spearheaded the "Eugenics Movement," and Herbert Spencer, the father of "Social Darwinism," set forth what they considered to be "historical" and "scientific" evidence for the superiority of Anglo-Saxons. Attributing the dominance of Anglo-Saxons to the purity of their race and culture, Galton and his followers advocated for the sterilization and segregation of racially subordinated groups and poor immigrants (Menchaca & Valencia, 1990).

In the 1870s the Teutonic origins' theory, used to explain the genetic legacy and superiority of Anglos, rapidly spread through US social, religious, labor, media, educational, and political institutions and practices. For most "Whites," this ideological stronghold instilled strong feelings of allegiance to their "race," nationalism, and a firm belief in separate but equal legislation. Needless to say, it was also used to justify the "necessity and right" of Anglo rule.

This ideological stronghold based on whiteness – a pure race and culture, which has fanned the flames of White supremacy in this country, would function to shape percep- tions of racial difference and social relations, and significantly influence the formation of ethnic/cultural identities throughout the United States. In fact this racialized ideology set the infernal standards of ethnicity. "They were standards that accepted Anglo-Saxons as the norm, placed all other Whites on what may be called ethnic probation, and excluded from serious consideration the Japanese, Chinese, Mexicans, and Blacks" (Franklin, 1995, p. 27). Ethnic became associated with racial "otherness," "difference," and "deviance." Cornel West (1993) clearly articulates this dynamic:

> European immigrants arrived on American shores perceiving themselves as "Irish," "Sicilian," "Lithuanian," and so forth. They had to learn that they were "white" principally by adopting American discourse of positively valued whiteness and negatively charged blackness. This process by which people define themselves physically, socially, sexually, and even politically in terms of whiteness or blackness has much bearing not only on constructed notions of race and ethnicity but also on how we understand the changing character of U.S. nationalities. (p. 31)

In their struggle to become "White" – a process that was shrouded in the romanticized guise of "becoming American" – many immigrants, similar to the indentured servants of the past, identified less with their real roots and further disassociated themselves from any threat of "Otherness." Consequently, many poor Whites, such as Italians and Irish, who had been known to readily mix with Blacks and other racially subordinated groups, cut virtually all ties after the Civil War – once again, the infused social logic being that "White," regardless of the level of poverty and oppression that they experienced in society, was at least a step up from being "Black" / "racially other" (Allen, 1994; Feagin & Vera, 1995; Roediger, 1994). As Howard Winant (1995) points out, even during the Civil War, despite Northern white workers' "occasionally enthusiastic support for emancipation," they were nonetheless "determined to maintain the separate and elevated status the designation 'white' bestowed upon them" (p. 33). W. E. B. Du Bois (1935) observed how white workers were willing to sell their labor for less money in order to gain what he referred to as, "a sort of public and psychological wage. They were given deference because they were white. They were admitted freely with all classes of white people to public functions, public parks ..." (p. 700). He also noted that the racial privileges bestowed upon them did little if anything to improve their socioeconomic status, pointing out the reality that they were getting used by the powers that be.

Even some of the more progressive social movements, such as the early struggles to form labor unions, gave way to such an ideology in which whiteness split class conscious- ness, rendering Blacks and other "non-White" groups unprotected outcasts (Goldfield, 1992; Roediger, 1991). As unions adopted racially exclusive forms of organization, the concept of

> race was already present in the way white workers recognized themselves in the 19th century. Why else would they have been more threatened by emancipated black labor (or conquered Mexican labor or immigrant Asian labor) than by the flood of European immigrants in the later 19th century. (Winant, 1995, p. 33)

Drawing this historical portrait of the racialization of identities clearly reveals how racism has historically been an important mechanism of cultural production and repro-duction in the United States, that is, how 400 years of Anglo domination have been a fundamental part (as opposed to an external or separate feature) of most institutional and everyday cultural practices in this society. From this perspective, it is obvious that when we talk about race in this country, it has nothing to do with the biology of skin pigmentation, but rather everything to do with how we see and act in the world based on the sociohistorical/ideological implications of what it means to be associated with a certain color. Thus, the complex and contradicting values and beliefs about race should be considered influential factors in defining "ethnicity." That is, racist ideologies, like any other values and beliefs, inevitably belong to any group's ethos. With that in mind, the two terms, "race" and "ethnicity" should not be dealt with in separation, but rather in conjunction with each other.

The more things change, the more they remain the same: contemporary ramifications of this racial hierarchy

An essential part of the everyday in the United States remains prisoner to the colonial construction of the "White race." Cultural racism, and the resultant racialized ethnic/cultural identities (values, beliefs, norms, traditions, language, worldviews, etc.), continue to be advanced intergenerationally through a predominantly White government, Supreme Court, and media, as well as White schools, business communities, and public opinion (Hill, 1997; Novick, 1995). As Jessie Daniels (1997) documents in her study *White Lies*, the legacy of White supremacy and the current themes and stereotypes of extremist, White supremacist discourse are very much a part of our actual mainstream society. John Ogbu's (1987) research points out, "feelings of aversion, revulsion, and disgust they [negative images of other racial groups] evoke come to be incorporated into the culture of the dominant group and children learn them "naturally" as they learn other aspects of their culture" (p. 260). A. W. Smith's research (1981) illustrates that even today, a person's/group's position on the racial hierarchy in the United States continues to determined how tolerant Whites will be towards "other" people. In fact, except for a few superficial and usually exotic aspects such as food, most ethnic differences continue to be looked upon with disdain – as "anti-American."

Educational institutions continue to perpetuate cultural racism through their curricu-lum (e.g., what/who's values, beliefs, voices, and representations of history, identity, and difference are included?) (Castenell & Pinar, 1993; McCarthy & Crinchlow, 1993), teacher assumptions and teaching styles (Delpit, 1993; McIntyre, 1997), and de facto segregation of racially subordinated students via tracking (Oakes, 1985).

The White corporate owned media is deeply implicated in the current perpetuation of cultural racism. Popular texts, which constitute a wide range of aural, visual, and printed signifiers, are not simply expressive or reflective of social reality, but also formative in that they can influence how we see ourselves, others, and the world around us. The struggle over identity and representation (that is, over who has the power to articulate experience, fashion identities, define the nature of problems, and legitimate solutions) greatly con-tributes to shaping the social relations and ethnic patterns of everyday life – how we look at, feel about, fear, and interact with one another (Kluegel, 1990; Kluegel & Smith 1982, 1983).

Social institutions such as schools, and dominant ethnic values and beliefs in this country not only maintain racist practices, but they also continue to serve to exploit economically underprivileged Whites who are intentionally set up to be, but usually unknowingly, preoccupied with issues of race rather than social class. As epitomized by the opening story of the bar room, Whites continue to buy into images that degrade and demonize Blacks, Latino/as, and so-called "Others." Scapegoats/social outcasts are created and targeted in order to draw the attention away from the very real abuses of power that produce and sustain sociocultural and economic inequality, as well as intergroup conflict in the US. Wallace Lambert and Donald Taylor's study (1990) on "*coping with cultural and racial diversity in urban America*," which examined the attitudes of a diverse sample of people towards multiculturalism, concluded that White Americans, especially the working-class, are the least supportive.

Racenicity: the myth of ethnic identity among assimilated whites

The majority of Whites in the United States believe that all ethnic immigrant groups have had common histories upon entering this country (Alba, 1990). Richard Alba's data revealed that Whites generally view ethnic identification as an individual choice, a private matter and otherwise not very important. Many participants in his sample equated it with their private family history, rather than viewing it as a group's collective experience. As with the men in the barroom, the most frequently identified markers were the superficial elements of food, festivals, and holidays – what Alba refers to as "symbolic characteristics." Some social theorists have argued that assimilation and the retention of symbolic ethnicity is a conscious choice, an option, for ethnic groups in their efforts to become authentic members of the host society (Gans, 1979; Roberts & Clifton, 1982). Roberts and Clifton (1982) claim that:

> Those who possess a "symbolic ethnicity" command the flexibility necessary to participate and benefit as members of a complex industrialized society while also feeling that they belong to a smaller community. This flexibility exists because symbolic ethnicity is a psychological rather than a social construct; it services individual rather than community needs, and, as such, is less subject to forces beyond an individual's control. (p. 19)

However, after dissecting the historical struggle to survive within the United State's racial hierarchy, the idea that "ethnicity is a psychological rather than a social construct," and that one has "individual control and choice" to assimilate, constitutes nothing more than a euphemistic and deceitful portrayal of the harsh sociopolitical realities that have in fact significantly structured cultural identities and contemporary social relations. The irony in this process of racialization, is that by uncritically buying into symbolic ethnicity and the myth of choice, Whites, in general, have actually actively participated in becoming more distanced from themselves.

Racenicity: white ethnic unconsciousness

"The key to understanding White racism is to be found not only in what Whites think of people of color but also in what Whites think of themselves" (Feagin & Vera, 1995, p. xi).

As argued, racialized ethnic patterns are embedded in the cultures and institutions of the United States, but few Whites recognize the impact that such racism has had on shaping our own values, beliefs, personal and social interests, and actions. Nor do we question how such identities are passed down from generation to generation. Unfortunately, the United States is plagued by historical amnesia. Or, at best, the sense of the past that we receive is limited, often distorted, and uncritically assimilated as fact. As Winant (1995) warns, "Forces at play in the construction of contemporary racial identity are descended from a past that we ignore or misinterpret at our peril" (p. 32). Most Whites, even those whose ancestors experienced a great deal of social, cultural, and economic injustice (such as the Irish), have little if any critical recollection of the history of the racialization of identities in this country.

The product of the ideological construction of whiteness, assimilated/indoctrinated Whites, having run the racial gauntlet, have virtually lost their ethnic heritage. Tomato sauce, drinking, sports, and calling oneself Irish, Italian, or French-Canadian certainly don't do justice to a family's history (as argued vociferously by the bar patrons mentioned earlier), nor do baseball, hot dogs, apple pie, and Chevrolet define the complexities of what it means to be "American." Many of us Whites have few if any signposts to help excavate, so as to develop, our cultural identities to transcend race and as such we have become ignorant of who we are. As Stanley Lieberson and Mary Waters' (1986) studies reveal, "There are a substantial number of people who recognize that they are White, but lack any clear-cut identification with, and/or knowledge of, a specific European origin" (p. 264).

Without an understanding of who we are as historical and cultural beings, unable to make linkages to the social and political realities that have shaped our world, we have become vulnerable to ideological manipulation (the cultural criteria that is characteristic of this racist society) which reproduces racist sentiments and thus renders us complicit in the injustices inflicted upon "Others," as well as upon ourselves. The working-class bar patrons, victims of such a disarticulation, were unable to see their own location as an emergent construct of the relation between race and ethnicity such that they couldn't make the connection between what happened to their ancestors as well as to them. Although virtually powerless socioeconomically, they nonetheless buy into the illusion of being part of the norm (the model of national identity) with the self-determining power to do as they please with their ethnic heritage. In fact, many believe that they are "making it," even when, in many cases they are worse off in terms of material struggle and self-actualization than those that they so readily castigate. Most Whites are imprisoned by an assimilationist ideology that paradoxically has claimed to support us while undermining our very beings. Any group's uncritical loyalty to this paradigm is especially disconcerting when such allegiance draws attention away from that powerful center – those that are truly profiting from the present sociocultural and economic conditions.

Racenicity doesn't imply that Whites are without ethnicity – that is, without values, beliefs, a world-view, cultural practices and traditions, etc. It simply argues that we are, for the most part, not only unconscious of the ideologies and power relations that shape and reproduce racialized ethnic patterns, but we are also unable to clearly and profoundly define what those patterns are and why exactly it is that we hold so tightly to them – that is, to articulate the racial categories that "form part of the social blueprint Whites use to orient their actions" (Feagin & Vera, 1995, p. x).[6] It is also important to note that "racenicity" does not imply that racial attitudes are one dimensional, but it does argue that they are not completely separate from other beliefs and values.

The analytic category of racenicity is also not meant to infer that all Whites are ethnically the same, or that pockets of White resistance against racial supremacy are nonexistent. It simply points out the fact that those "Whites," (across differences of gender, class, sexual orientation, local, religion, etc.) or any other group for that matter, who have assimilated the dominant ideology of whiteness (consciously or not) are complicit in the perpetuation of such a racial hierarchy and its concomitant ethnic realities and injustices.

By not recognizing whiteness as a racial identity, most Whites see themselves as race-free and less ethnic than "Others," and consequently take for granted the privileges they secure by such an ideologically charged racial marker (Frankenberg, 1997; MacCannel, 1989; Macintosh, 1990; McIntyre, 1997; Hill, 1997). Frances FitzGerald's (1986) data reveals that White, upper-middle-class professionals don't identify themselves as "ethnic, cultural, or powerful" (p. 218). Ruth Frankenburg's research (1993), which consisted of interviews with White women, showed that whiteness is "difficult for White people to name – those that are securely housed within its borders usually do not examine it" (pp. 228–9). As Peggy McIntosh (1990) asserts, "I think that Whites are carefully taught not to recognize White privilege – My schooling gave me no training in seeing myself as an oppressor, as an unfairly advantaged person, or as a participant in a damaged culture" (p. 31).

The absence of whiteness in mainstream multicultural education

Under the rubric "multicultural education," a great deal of research, literature, curricula, and classroom practices presently attempts to address issues of cultural diversity, as well as racial and economic inequalities. However, the majority of this work, which endeavors simply to "affirm diversity" and identities through positive images of subordinated groups, does so in a limited fashion, focusing on color coordination, food festivals, cut-and-paste add-ons to the existing canon, and group-based methodologies. These efforts, by abstracting particular groups' similarities from an understanding of their various complexities (such as differences among them in terms of gender, class, language, locality, age, health, sexual orientation, etc.), often fall into the trap of essentializing, objectifying, or even romanticizing the lives of those on the margins. Within such limited models that focus exclusively on the "Other," the concept of "difference" is often not taken up in terms of recognizing and critically engaging the dominant referent group – the norm of White, upper-middle class, heterosexual male by which all others are measured. Even the very realities of White supremacy disappear behind such terms as "multiculturalism," "anti-racism," etc. Educators and citizens need to interrogate the unspoken centrality of whiteness in shaping ethnic identities. As McLaren (1994) insists:

> Unless we give white students a sense of their own identity as an emergent ethnicity – we naturalize whiteness as a cultural marker against which Otherness is defined – White groups need to examine their own ethnic histories so that they are less likely to judge their own cultural norms as neutral and universal. (p. 59)

Unfortunately, within existing models of multicultural education, categories such as race and ethnicity remain fragmented (which disregards their interrelationship), and thus, so do the possibilities for excavating, understanding, and transforming our cultural identities. Depoliticized and ahistorical approaches to multicultural education fail to adequately examine the ideologies that inform unequal power relations and social stratification along such lines as race, as well as neglect to name White supremacy as a cultural/ethnic foundation in the United States. Proper exploration of the social construction of "whiteness" as an ideological category and shaper of ethnic identity demands that we as educators reconceptualize our inadequate notions of education, especially multicultural education.[7] Coco Fusco (1988) warns, "To ignore white ethnicity is to redouble its hegemony by naturalizing it. Without specifically addressing white ethnicity, there can be no critical evaluation of the construction of the other" (p. 9).

Schools should embrace critical pedagogy as a point of departure from the confines of the dominant social and educational paradigms. Emphasizing the need for political awareness, critical work is enormously important for developing a theoretical framework that historically and socially situates the deeply embedded roots of racism, discrimination, violence, and disempowerment in this country. Instead of perpetuating the assumption that such realities are inevitable, critical pedagogy compels the participant to explore the relationship between these larger historic, economic, and social constructs and their inextricable connection to ideology, power, the media, and identity. In the critical spirit, Frankenburg (1994) contends,

> Rehistoricizing whiteness and Americanness as locations of cultural practice entails learning more about the multiple histories of assimilation, appropriation, and exclusion that shape the cultural field(s) that White Americans now inhabit. Rehistorizing also requires engagement with whiteness and Americanness as culturally specific spaces rather than as cultureless, culturally neutral, or culturally generic terrain – whiteness and Americanness are like other cultural assemblages ... that generate norms, ways of understanding history, ways of thinking about self and other.... (p. 75)

Theory and practice in this sense work actively through and not on students (as opposed to an ideological imposition) by helping both teachers and students to reflect on how domination works. In becoming aware of both the positions they inhabit and the locations from which they speak, students and teachers are better able to take responsibility for, and transform, their beliefs and actions.

As White educators, students, and citizens, we need to seriously interrogate our collective whiteness, our racenicity, by challenging the narratives of national culture/identity and ethnic character. As James Baldwin (1985) eloquently states, "a price is demanded to liberate all those white children – some of them near forty – who have never grown up, and who never will grow up, because they have no sense of their identity" (p. 320).

Tragically, so many of us Whites buy into the illusion that "our" turf is being invaded by immigrants, "aliens," and "illegals." Such propaganda, which works toward an uncritical allegiance to whiteness, draws attention away from the powerful center – those that are truly profiting from the present social and economic paradigm. Instead, the media, politicians, and other cultural workers create a trumped up nostalgia to go back to some "golden age" when supposedly "things were good." These illusions of a "golden age" need to be ruptured because that very past was when most of us were the ones being exploited, lost our roots, and became imprisoned by assimilationist ideologies that paradoxically have claimed to support us while, in the form of ignorance, fear, and support of an unjust and undemocratic society, have actually undermined our very

beings. This anesthetizing racial consciousness – whiteness, which subdues and consequently subverts any chance of a cultural democracy, urgently needs to be confronted and
transformed. For, it is in fact democracy (which thrives on difference, participation, and
dissent) and not race, that is supposed to unite us as a nation.

Notes

1 While I often use the analytic distinction, "working class" to emphasize my points throughout this paper, by
   no means am I implying that they are the core source of White supremacy in this country. As my argument
   unravels, my intention is to show how the White working class, to a great extent, has been diverted away from
   the sources of power that instill racism and shape their everyday realities. This point of analysis is also not
   meant to essentialize "working class" into some mythical homogenous group. My hope is that schools (and
   other public spheres) can embrace political consciousness as a fundamental part of the educational process so
   that the great many people who are socially and economically disenfranchised, can work to challenge and
   change, rather than participate in the reproduction of the present social order.
2 This also begs the question of whether or not there is an "American" ethnicity.
3 The use of the term "American" is problematic. Its appropriation by the United States is a symbolic example
   of US imperialism in North, South, and Central America.
4 For a discussion of these other issues, see P. Leistyna, A. Woodrum, & S. Sherblom (1996). *Breaking Free: The
   Transformative Power of Critical Pedagogy.* Cambridge, MA: Harvard Educational Review Press.
5 The use of "non-White" is also problematic in that it situates "white" as the referent. While this is important
   for naming racism, it symbolically limits the process of decentering its hold as the norm.
6 By no means do I intend here to act as an apologist for White racism by placing our current problems on
   institutions alone – people breathe life into such bodies which function to reproduce oppressive social
   practices. My goal is to analyze how this cultural production and reproduction occurs.
7 This discussion of the educational implications of racenicity does not imply that schools alone can eradicate
   racism. Society as a whole must work toward the kinds of social agency that can transform any and all unjust
   and undemocratic practices and institutions.

References

Aguirre, A. & Baker, D. (1995) *Sources: Notable Selections in Race and Ethnicity.* Guilford, CT: Dushkin Publishing Group.

Alba, R. D. (1990). *Ethnic Identity: The Transformation of White America.* New Haven: Yale University Press.

Allen, T. (1994). *The Invention of the White Race.* London: Verso.

Baldwin, J. (1985). *The Price of the Ticket: Collected Nonfiction 1948–1985.* New York: St. Martin's.

Castenell, L. & Pinar, W. (1993). *Understanding Curriculum as Racial Text: Representation of Identity and Difference in Education.* New York: SUNY.

Daniels, J. (1997). *White Lies: Race, Class, Gender, and Sexuality in White Supremacist Discourse.* New York: Routledge.

Delpit, L. (1993). The silenced dialogue: Power and pedagogy in educating other people's children. In L. Weis & M. Fine (eds.), *Beyond Silenced Voices: Class, Race, and Gender.* New York: SUNY.

Du Bois, W. E. B. (1935). *Black Reconstruction in America, 1860–1880.* New York: Atheneum.

Dyson, M. (1993). *Reflecting Black: African-American Cultural Criticism.* Minneapolis: University of Minnesota Press.

Feagin, J. & Vera, H. (1995). *White Racism.* New York: Routledge.

FitzGerald, F. (1986). *Cities on a Hill: A Journey Through Contemporary American Cultures.* New York: Simon and Schuster.

Frankenburg, R. (1993). *White Women, Race Matters.* Minneapolis: University of Minnesota Press.

Frankenburg, R. (1994). Whiteness and Americanness: examining Constructions of race, culture, and nation in White women's narratives. In S. Gregory & R. Sanjek (eds.), *Race*. New Brunswick, NJ: Rutgers University Press.

Frankenburg, R. (1997). *Displacing Whiteness: Essays in Social and Cultural Criticism*. London: Duke University Press.

Franklin, J. H. (1995). Ethnicity in American life: The historical perspective. In A. Aguirre, & D. Baker (eds.), *Sources: Notable Selections in Race and Ethnicity*. Guilford, CT: Dushkin Publishing Group.

Freire, P. (1970). *Pedagogy of the Oppressed*. New York: Seabury Press.

Foucault, M. (1972). *Power/Knowledge: Selected Interviews & Other Writings, 1972–1977*. New York: Pantheon.

Fusco, C. (1988). Fantasies of oppositionality, *Afterimage Magazine*. December, 1988.

Gans, H. (1979). Symbolic ethnicity: The future of ethnic groups and cultures in America. *Ethnic and Racial Studies*, 2, 1–20.

Gilroy, P. (1987). *'There aint't no Black in the union jack': The Cultural Politics of Race and Nation*. Chicago: University of Chicago Press.

Giroux, H. (1983). *Theory and Resistance in Education: A Pedagogy for the Opposition*. South Hadley, MA: Bergin & Garvey.

Goldfield, M. (1992). The color of politics in the United States: White supremacy as the main explanation for the peculiarities of American politics from colonial times to the present. In D. LaCapra (ed.), *The Bounds of Race*. Ithica, NY: Cornell University Press.

Hill, M. (1997). *Whiteness: A Critical Reader*. New York: New York University Press.

Kluegel, J. R. (1990). Trends in Whites' explanation of the Black–White gap in socioeconomic status, 1977–1989. *American Sociological Review*, 55, 512–25.

Kluegel, J. R., & Smith, E. R. (1982). Whites' beliefs about Black opportunity. *American Sociological Review*, 47(4), 518–32.

Kluegel, J. R., & Smith, E. R. (1983). Affirmative action attitudes: effects of self-interest, racial affect, and stratification beliefs on Whites' views. *Social Forces*, 61(3), 797–824.

Lambert, W. & Taylor, D.(1990). *Coping with Cultural and Racial Diversity in Urban America*. New York: Praeger.

Lieberson, S. & Waters, M. (1986). Ethnic groups in flux: the changing ethnic responses of American whites. In *Annals of the American Academy of Political and Social Science*, 487 (Sept.).

MacCannell, D. (1989) *The Tourist: A Theory of the Leisure Class*. New York: Schocken Books.

Macintosh, P. (1990). White privilege: unpacking the invisible knapsack. *Independent School* (Winter).

McCarthy, C. & Crinchlow, W. (1993). *Race, Identity, and Representation in Education*. New York: Routledge.

McIntyre, A. (1997). *Making Meaning of Whiteness: Exploring Racial Identity with White Teachers*. New York: SUNY.

McLaren, P. (1994). White terror and oppositional agency. In D. Goldberg (ed.), *Multiculturalism: A Critical Reader*. Cambridge: Blackwell.

Menchaca, M. & Valencia, R. (1990). Anglo-Saxon ideologies in the 1920s–1930s: their impact on the segregation of Mexican students in California. *Anthropology & Education Quarterly*, 21, 222–45.

Novick, M. (1995). *White Lies, White Power*. Monroe, ME: Common Courage Press.

Oakes, J. (1985). *Keeping Track: How Schools Structure Inequality*. New Haven, CT: Yale University Press.

Ogbu, J. (1987). Variability in minority responses to schooling: nonimmigrants vs. immigrants. In G. Spindler & L. Spindler (eds.), *Interpretive Ethnography of Education* (pp. 255–75). Hillsdale, NJ: Lawrence Erlbaum Associates.

Roberts, L. W. & Clifton, R. A. (1982). Exploring the ideology of Canadian multiculturalism. *Canadian Public Policy*, VII:1, 88–94.

Roediger, D. (1991). *The Wages of Whiteness: Race and the Making of the American Working Class.* London: Verso.

Roediger, D. (1994). *Towards the Abolition of Whiteness.* New York: Verso.

Smith, A. W. (1981). Racial tolerance as a function of group position. *American Sociological Review,* 46(5), 558–73.

West, C. (1993). The new cultural politics of difference. In *Beyond a Dream Deferred: Multicultural Education and the Politics of Excellence.* Minneapolis: University of Minnesota Press.

Winant, H. (1995). Dictatorship, democracy, and difference: the historical construction of racial identity. In M. P. Smith & J. R. Feagin (eds.), *The Bubbling Cauldron: Race, Ethnicity, and the Urban Crisis.* London: University of Minnesota Press.

Yinger, J. M. (1994). *Ethnicity: Source of Strength? Source of Conflict?* New York: SUNY.

CHAPTER 23

Bhikhu Parekh

Racial Justice in a Multi-Ethnic Society

When the report on the Future of Multi-Ethnic Britain was published last October [2000] it created a bit of a stir which took many of us by surprise, including those with some experience of public life.[1] The report was much misunderstood, grossly misrepresented, and often deliberately distorted. Even the home office, which had warmly welcomed the report after a careful reading of its final draft, gave in to the pressure of the right-wing media and sought to distance itself from parts of it. The home secretary criticised the Left for its alleged lack of patriotism, implying that all of us on the Commission belonged to the Left and that any attempt to question the narrow right-wing view of patriotism implied a lack of loyalty and affection for Britain.

Now that the controversy has died down and the report is being read and appreciated for its intellectual and moral seriousness, so much so that the ministries involved are willing to discuss how best to implement some of its major recommendations, it would be useful to explore what the report really said, how and why it was read in a particular manner in certain circles, and what the whole episode tells us about the inescapable tensions between a rigorous academic inquiry and the partisan rhetoric of the political marketplace.

Background to the Commission

For those who are not familiar with its background, the Commission on the Future of Multi-Ethnic Britain was made up of 25 individuals, including 7 well-known academics, 3 distinguished journalists, 2 senior police officers, representatives of different communities, one senior and recently retired civil servant, several distinguished public figures including the president of the Liberal Democratic Party, and 2 retired chairs of the Commission for Racial Equality. It had 8 women members and 10 members from the ethnic minorities. The Commission was a microcosm of British society and covered all points of view except rabid racists at one end and peddlers of revolutionary utopias at the other. The published report was unanimous – the unanimity being consensual and not a

Bhikhu Parekh, "Racial Justice in a Multi-Ethnic Society," *Economic and Political Weekly* (Sept. 15, 2001).

product of arm-twisting or subtle moral blackmail that can easily shadow such a multi-ethnic commission.

Our immediate concern was narrow and practical, namely, how to deal with the discrimination and disadvantages to which ethnic minorities are subject in British society. Britain has fairly powerful laws to deal with discrimination, and there is no shortage of decent men and women either. And it has pursued policies designed to tackle racial disadvantage. Yet the problem persists. Racial violence is high, nearly 200 racially motivated murders in the last three years, racial discrimination and disadvantage blight many lives, ethnic minorities are conspicuous by their absence in positions of power, and the way of talking about them does not usually manage to steer clear of either thinly disguised racism or patronising condescension.

The Commission therefore felt that it needed to think afresh about the problem and explore new ways of looking at it. Although legislation and public policies are crucial, they have their limits and cannot by themselves change people's deepest attitudes. Furthermore since laws and policies derive their legitimacy and popular support from a particular way of looking at British society and the place of ethnic minorities within it, new ones cannot be arrived at without radically reconsidering the latter. The Commission therefore was led to ask large questions about the nature of British society, the best way to read its history, how to deepen its collective self-understanding so as to make it hospitable to the presence of ethnic minorities, the appropriate language to describe the contemporary state of race relations, the nature of racism, how to balance the demands of social cohesion with those of cultural differences, the limits of permissible diversity, and so on. And it used answers to these and related questions to generate proposals for appropriate policies and legislation.

Report's central theses

Rather than summarise the report's detailed findings, I would like to highlight its three central theses.

1) Reconceptualising ethnicity

First, the way in which the term ethnic minority has long been used in British political discourse is problematic. The term is generally used to refer to Asians and Afro-Caribbeans and is a substitute for the earlier term 'coloured people'. In other words ethnicity is racialised, which is why the terms ethnic and 'racial' are used interchangeably as in the Race Relations Act 1976 and the Commission for Racial Equality. Racialisation of ethnicity has several disadvantages. It conceptually and politically ghettoises blacks and Asians, implies that white people are free from ethnicity, and concentrates only on colour-based racism. It also makes it difficult to conceptualise and cope with the discrimination that the English might experience in Scotland and Wales, and vice versa. And it prevents us from focusing on such discrimination and disadvantage as the Irish and the Jews might experience and relating their problems to those of Asians and Afro-Caribbeans.

In the report we therefore defined the term 'ethnic group' in non-racial terms, and took it to refer to a group of people who share common historical experiences, a cluster of cultural beliefs and practices, a broad collective consciousness of belonging together, and see themselves and are seen by others as more or less distinct. In this sense of the term we all belong to an ethnic group, irrespective of whether we are English, Scots, Irish, Afro-Caribbeans or Indians. Insofar as Britain consists of different ethnic groups, it is a multi-ethnic society. It would be so even if it had no Asians and Afro-Caribbeans.

Each of these groups is capable of harbouring hostility and discriminating against other groups. Racism is not the monopoly of whites, for Asians and black can also be guilty of it in their relations with each other and with white people, as the recent events in Bradford, Old-ham and even Leeds bear out. While we might legitimately focus on white racism because of the numerical superiority and greater political and economic power of white people in British society, we must remain alert to and struggle against minority racism as well.

That is why the report defines racism widely to refer to all attempts to homogenise, stereotype and take demeaning views of other groups and in so doing to racialise or attribute race-like properties to them. Racism creates races by turning open overlapping, loosely structured and internally differentiated groups into closed and rigid natural or quasi-natural types, and hierarchically grading them on the basis of what are mistakenly believed to be neutral and universal criteria.

The concept of ethnic group is itself not free from difficulties. People marry outside their ethnic groups, they leave their ethnic group or develop only a tenuous relationship with it, and the identity and cultural content of ethnic groups are also subject to constant change. For these and other reasons ethnic groups are more or less loose and open communities bound by real but relatively vague ties of affection, collective memory and common interests. Although they are therefore best seen and described as communities, they are communities of a particular kind, one that is perhaps best captured by calling them ethnic as distinct from religious or political communities. Wherever possible, the report therefore prefers to use the generic term community, and to talk of ethnic community only when it needs to stress the ethnic dimension.

2) Beyond liberal individualist and communitarian dimensions

The second thesis of our report has to do with the best way to conceptualise the British polity. England has its own legal system, an established church, and so on. Scotland too has its own legal and education systems, a different kind of jury system, different standards of evidence and proof, and so on, and has long enjoyed considerable autonomy whose range and depth have been increased by the recent devolution of power. This is also true, albeit to a lesser extent, of Northern Ireland and Wales. With the development of regional consciousness in England, it too is becoming a home of different regional communities, and it is not at all unlikely that they might over time throw up their own distinct educational and administrative systems.

Britain also has different religious and ethnic communities, some of them no doubt more internally united than others. These national, regional, ethnic and other communities are all part of a larger political community, which provides them with both a common framework of interaction and a broadly shared body of values and common purposes. In short, Britain is a community of communities, a community with a collective sense of identity most certainly, but also including within it many communities with a more or less developed sense of their own identity. For those tender-hearted liberals who panic at the mention of communities, the report makes it clear that communities come in different forms, that they are not transcendental entities but made up of individuals, that they refer to nothing more than shared bonds ranging from common interests to the deepest sense of common belonging, and that they are porous and in constant flux.

Even as Britain is a community of communities, it is also a community of individuals, a liberal society whose citizens cherish their individuality and delight in their freedom of self-determination and self-disclosure. They like to make their own choices and jealously guard their freedom against unwanted and unwarranted interference. Obviously they are and cannot avoid becoming members of different regional, civil, religious, cultural and other communities. They are born into a particular religion and most of them retain at least some ties with it. And they all live within rural or urban areas and inescapably share ties of common interest with those around them. They are not, however, imprisoned within or defined by these communities, and remain free to leave and criticise them. Communities do not exist independently of individuals; nor, equally, do individuals exist independently of communities.

Britain is therefore best described as a community of individuals and communities, a community of individuals in their individuality as well as their membership of overlapping communities. To call it only a community of communities would be to ignore the crucial fact that individuals are not defined by or exhausted in their respective communities. And to say that it is only a community of individuals is to ignore the equally crucial fact that the individuals are not isolated and asocial atoms but are members of, and speak and act from within, various communities.

Since both individuals and communities are equally central to Britain's identity and constitute its mutually reinforcing and regulating building blocks, the report on the Future of Multi-Ethnic Britain conceptualises the country as a community of both individuals and communities. As a political community, Britain is based on common interests, affections and mutual belonging, a description that captures the truth of communitarianism. It is a community of individuals, a description that captures the truth of liberalism. And it is a community of communities, a description that goes beyond both individualist liberalism and holistic communitarianism and highlights the countless small and large communities that mediate between and vitalise both the individual and the wider political community.

Once we see Britain as a community of individuals and communities, several important conclusions follow. Its citizens sometimes speak and act as individuals, and sometimes as members of particular communities, and hence its political discourse has both a liberal individualist and a communitarian dimension. Its citizens, again, make some demands as individuals, and others as member of or on behalf of particular communities. The two demands sometimes have conflicting logics and we need to find ways of reconciling them. On strictly liberal individualist grounds, for example, we might need to reduce the currently disproportionate Scottish representation in the House of Commons. However if we saw Britain as a community of communities and Scotland as a major community seeking and needing an adequate political voice, we might view the extent of its representation differently and conclude that, while Scots as individuals are overrepresented, Scotland as a national community is not.

Conceptualising Britain as a community of individuals and communities also has the great advantage of bypassing the dubious language of nationhood and the moral and psychological obsessions created by it. Nations are supposed to be homogeneous, self-contained, closed, based on substantive agreements on the good life, possessing unsharable and inalienable sovereignty, entitled to privilege their collective interests over those of other countries, and constantly on their guard against the dilution of their culture and identity. In the open and globalised modern world, no country can be a nation in this sense, and the seductive but unrealistic dream of making it one invariably ends in a nightmare. No country today shares a single common culture, controls its economy, protects its environment or ensures the physical security of its citizens. Furthermore, the language of nationhood makes it exceedingly difficult for a country to become a member of a wider unit lest that should dilute its identity and compromise its sovereignty.

When we see Britain as a community of individuals and communities rather than as a nation or nation state, we bypass these and other related problems. We appreciate its internal plurality as well as the need to base its unity and cohesion, not on a common substantive vision of the good life but on an acceptance of its cultural and moral diversity within the framework of a shared structure of authority. We also recognise that just as Britain includes several communities, it can itself be part of a wider community, be it the European Union or the larger global community. Contrary to the nationalist rhetoric, political communities are porous, open, loosely structured, and capable of both containing and joining an ever-widening circle of communities. They need to be autonomous and self-governing but not sovereign, and may share their political powers with other such communities when their common interests so require.

3) Cohesion, rights and values

The third thesis of our report has to do with how Britain can become a cohesive political community and foster a common sense of belonging among its diverse regional, national, religious, ethnic and other communities.

Societies are highly fragile structures and can easily fall apart, as we saw in the cases of the Soviet Union, Yugoslavia, Rwanda and elsewhere. Furthermore, their cohesion cannot be secured once and for all, but has to be constantly nurtured by the willing allegiance of its members. Basically the cohesion of any society, including Britain, requires a commonly agreed structure of authority whose decisions are accepted as collectively binding, equal citizenship rights, and a broadly agreed and constantly evolving body of values in terms of which its members structure their relations and debate and resolve their differences. We need common values to structure our collective life and to help us decide which differences to disallow and which ones to tolerate, welcome, cherish, and even officially support. These values are part of our political life, and while we begin by accepting them, we might also revise them if we find them discriminatory, biased, narrow, or unacceptable.

Common values and equal citizenship rights are a necessary but not a sufficient condition of social cohesion and common belonging. Individuals might enjoy all the rights of citizenship, and yet feel that they do not quite belong to the community if the latter's self-definition were to exclude them, or if its dominant culture took a demeaning view of them, or if the rest of their fellow-citizens would not accept them as full fellow-members. British national identity therefore needs to be so defined that all British citizens, whatever their colour, religion, or ethnic origins, feel included in it and can enthusiastically identify with it.

Britain cannot be a cohesive society confident enough to cherish and provide a hospitable framework for its diversities, unless its members share a basic commitment to its continuance and well-being. This is a commitment to live together, to share a common future, to resolve differences in a manner that does not undermine its integrity, and to help preserve a collective culture of civility and mutual concern. Such a commitment lies at the basis of every organised society, and constitutes its vital moral and political capital. The political commitment required to sustain a society is too complex to be captured by such tired concepts as nationalism and even patriotism. It has nothing to do with patre or fatherland or motherland, and has no familial and ethnic overtones. And unlike patriotism which is tied to a particular country and is exclusive in nature, the political commitment I am talking about is open and capable of expansion. There is no obvious moral or psychological reason why one cannot have a deep sense of commitment, belonging and loyalty to both Britain and India, or to Britain and Europe and even towards humankind at large.

A determined intellectual commitment

The three theses of the report on the Future of Multi-Ethnic Britain that I have so far discussed, and several others that I have not, constitute its underlying theoretical structure or political theory. According to it, Britain is made up of both individuals and communities of different kinds, and is both a liberal and a multi-communal society. These communities, including the ethnic communities, are fluid, overlapping, internally diverse and subject to constant reconstitution. Britain needs to hold these individuals and communities together and evolve a sense of unity out of their differences.

It therefore requires common values, which are both procedural and substantive in nature, and a common sense of belonging or political commitment. The values are not and cannot be fixed forever and are subject to contestation and change; and the sense of common belonging must be open, expansive, non-ethnic and hospitable to ethnic minorities. Britain, further, is not and never has been a nation state in the traditional sense. It has long been, and is more so now, a multi-communal state, what Habermas calls a post-nation state.

The political theory as tentatively sketched above is used in the report on the Future of Multi-Ethnic Britain to explore various areas of social life such as education, criminal justice, immigration, asylum, welfare services, employment and political representation, and to make appropriate recommendations concerning how best to eliminate the discrimination and disadvantage suffered by the ethnic minorities in these areas. The report devotes over 200 pages to these recommendations. At a purely practical level, the recommendations can be discussed and accepted or rejected in their own terms. However, if a critic demanded to see their theoretical basis, the implicit political theory would have to be invoked and defended.

The report was the result of a determined intellectual effort on the part of the Commission to think afresh about the question of racial discrimination and disadvantage. The commissioners had several long discussions among themselves, and also with some of the finest minds in the country in the various national seminars organised by it. We on the Commission knew that our report was a complex document. Unlike others of its kind, it was a large volume of 417 pages, and was not just concerned to make practical recommendations but also to explore large theoretical issues to which it devoted over 100 pages, or 8 out of 21 chapters.

So far as its theoretical structure was concerned, it cut across the familiar liberal, conservative, Marxist, communitarian and other approaches, borrowing their insights but also going beyond them and offering a different and richer perspective of its own. Unlike the usual discussions of race, again, the report refused to ghettoise race and see it as a marginal question of eliminating discrimination and disadvantage. Instead it used race to prise open the history, culture and inner structure of British society and to locate its discussion within a wider debate on British national identity and historical self-understanding.

Since the report did not fall within a single philosophical tradition and broke with the conventional discourse on race, it needed to be read in its own terms and without preconceptions. We knew that some would disagree with it. In fact we expected criticism from four quarters:

1) We expected conservative writers to criticise us for rejecting assimilationism in favour of respect for cultural diversity, underplaying the alleged virtues of a strong sense of nationhood, for challenging the traditional nationalist and eulogistic reading of British history, and for relying on law and well-considered government policies rather than the market to eliminate racial discrimination and disadvantage.

2) We thought liberals would welcome the report but criticise us for valuing communities rather than individuals alone, seeking to temper the logic of individualist liberalism with that of multiculturalism, and for giving cultural diversity a public presence rather than confining it to the private sphere. We also expected them to criticise us for diluting the relatively narrow and simplistic language of human rights by stressing the need to develop a pluralistic culture of human rights, and for linking the question of removing discrimination and disadvantage to the larger issue of redefining British identity and reinterpreting British history.

3) We expected socialists and social democrats to criticise us for not fully appreciating that the modern welfare state and the strong sense of social justice, which our proposals presupposed, required a strong sense of social cohesion and national solidarity that our multicultural vision of Britain might seem to weaken. And we also expected them to say, wrongly in our view, that we had privileged diversity over the far more important value of equality.

4) Finally we expected some groups of Marxists and anti-racists to attack us for failing to appreciate that racism was an epiphenomenal product of capitalism or a transient residual legacy of colonialism. We also expected them to criticise us for promoting 'shallow multiculturalism' and diverting attention away from the more important anti-capitalist and/or anti-racist struggles.

In our report we went some way towards anticipating and answering some of these criticisms, often obliquely and implicitly. We could not answer them explicitly and in great detail because that would have made the report ever bulkier, but we did indicate how they could be answered. When some of these criticisms were made after the publication of the report, we either refuted them or admitted honest differences of opinion.[2]

Misrepresentation in media

While we were prepared for serious disagreements, we were wholly unprepared for the kind of denunciation the report provoked from the right-wing media. The report was attacked as irresponsible, anti-British, unpatriotic, anti-white, subversive, illiberal, and so on. I was declared the most dangerous academic in Britain! My fellow commissioners were pilloried and ridiculed, and some even subjected to personal abuse. These denunciations were based on a grotesque misunderstanding and in some cases deliberate distortions of the report, especially parts of chapters 2 and 3 dealing respectively with rethinking the national story and the meaning of Britishness.

The report had said that insofar as the term 'British' was associated with whiteness, it had racial overtones. The media took it to say that the term 'British' was itself racist and should be avoided! The report had said that although Britain should be a cohesive society, it could not be a nation in its conventional ethnocultural sense. The press took this to mean that Britain should not be a united country and should become instead a loose collection of communities! The report had said that although communities were important to their members and deserved public recognition, they were inherently fluid, plural, and overlapping and should not be allowed to oppress their members. The media interpreted this as saying that the report believed in freezing communities and stifling individuality![3] Some of these were cases of simple misunderstanding, others acts of deliberate distortion. How does one explain them? I think several interrelated factors played a part.

Factor 1: Lack of time and accuracy

Since journalists work under what Bourdieu calls 'tyranny of time', they either read relevant parts of the report hurriedly or they lazily reproduced misleading accounts by other newspapers. Once the right-wing *Daily Telegraph* started some of these misunderstandings, other newspapers keep repeating them. Representatives of some of the latter privately admitted to me and my fellow-commissioners that although they were highly suspicious of the *Telegraph*'s story, they did not check its accuracy for lack of time or in order not to lose the 'fun of the frenzy'.

Factor 2: Limited knowledge of the debate

Since race tends to be a ghettoised subject in the British media, few mainstream journalists were or are familiar with the ongoing debates in this area. And with a few honourable exceptions, even those who report on race are largely concerned with day-to-day events and have little interest in and knowledge of the wider debates. It was therefore hardly surprising that the complex arguments of the report were poorly understood or thoroughly misconstrued. We must ourselves accept part of the blame for not expressing ourselves more clearly. None of us, including three of our distinguished journalist commissioners, expected the relevant paragraphs to arouse so much interest and concern, and naturally took no precautions against it.

Factor 3: A proxy target

There was and still is considerable anger at the Macpherson, or more accurately, the Stephen Lawrence Inquiry Report for introducing or rather reviving and legitimising the concept of institutional racism, and providing conceptual and political tools to prise open the inner structure and practices of large organisations. Since that report was accepted by the government and is associated with the senseless murder of a promising young black man, attacking it is not easy, though that has not prevented disguised attempts at discrediting it. Our report shared some of the assumptions and vocabulary of the Macpherson report and provided an obvious proxy target. It was striking that some of the things criticised or misrepresented in our report were precisely those that the Macpherson report too had recommended. Since many of us were associated with the

Labour Party, and I was a Labour Peer, we were also a proxy target for the Labour government.

Factor 4: False assumptions

Since our report was associated with me as its chairman (and unwisely and against my wishes even subtitled The Parekh Report), the impression was created that it was some kind of 'black manifesto' that was bound to say some of the things wrongly attributed to it. The twofold fact that the Commission included such leading left-wing intellectuals as Stuart Hall, and that most of its members, such as Trevor Phillips, Bob Hepple, Yasmin Alibhai-Brown, Herman Ouseley, Judith Hunt, Anne Owers and Sarah Spencer, were prominent champions of progressive causes, seemed to many to reinforce that impression. Many in the media seem to have thought that given the composition of the Commission, they could predict the direction and content of its report, and did not need to bother with a detailed and sympathetic study of the text.

Factor 5: Awakening deep anxieties

Britain, especially England, is currently passing through a difficult period. Thanks to internal devolution, increasing European military and economic integration, the growing diversification of its cultural life, globalisation, and so on, there are deep fears about the integrity of Britain as we have known it for the past three centuries. There is therefore an unconscious censorship, a tendency not to raise certain issues lest they should get out of control. Our report broke this taboo and triggered deep anxieties. The fact that we were acutely aware of these anxieties and had suggested what we thought was a sensible way to assuage them did not matter. The very act of raising questions about British nationhood, the best way to read its history, the nature and sources of its unity, the contestability of what are assumed to be its shared values, and so on, especially from an ethnic minority perspective, was subversive.

Absorbing the important lessons

As I reflect on the hostility in some quarters that followed the publication of the report, I draw several important lessons, of which I will mention three by way of illustration.

First, reports dealing with political subjects should not stray too far from the language of day-to-day politics. Words such as 'post-nation state' and 'racial coding' that we used in the report are fine in academic discourse, but can become sources of confusion and fear in political life. There is an obvious tension between academic and political discourse. The former is playful, inventive, unconcerned with practical consequences; the latter is rhetorical, multivocal, and tied up with deepest passions and fears. For the former, words are primarily tools of analysis; for the latter, weapons of struggle. A report that aims to be both academic and practical, detached and engaged, needs to find ways of resolving this tension. It must be easily intelligible to ordinary citizens, and yet retain the power to challenge their common sense and get them to see familiar things in a radically novel way.

Second, in politics, 'who says' is just as important as 'what' he or she says. Andrew Marr, Tom Nairn and others had written books with such titles as The Day Britain Died and *The Breakup of Britain*. They could get away with things we could not. Black and Asian intellectuals are subject to more stringent tests, and are expected to stay within certain limits. Although the majority of our commissioners were white and of impeccable liberal credentials, the fact that there were so many high-profile black and Asian intellectuals gave the impression that the Commission and its report had a distinctly minority orientation. This imposed intangible and subtle limits on what the report should and should not say, limits which it could transgress, as indeed it did, only at its peril.

Finally, no society is perfect. Each has its inescapable inequalities and injustices which need to be redressed. The question is how to get its members to see this and how to mobilise their moral energies. Uncompromising condemnation of it for its blemishes does not generally help, because the society then becomes unduly defensive and the critics appear to be ungrateful whingers, especially if they happen to belong to minorities. The effective rhetorical and persuasive strategy is to make the society feel good about itself, to put it at ease by highlighting its good practices and values, and then to argue that such a basically good society ought not to tolerate the evils in question. Praising it both establishes one's status as an insider and gives one the right to criticise it.

Although our report is balanced and gives full credit to successive British governments, especially the current Labour government, for its excellent work in reducing racial discrimination and disadvantage, our appreciation is buried in the text and not stated at the very beginning. And as befits an analytical and academic inquiry, its tone is relatively restrained and not effusively generous. This led some, including the [then] home secretary Jack Straw, to complain that the report had been 'grudging' and even somewhat mean in not acknowledging the good work that he and the British society in general had done. It is quite likely that even if the tone of the report had been less detached and more effusive, it would not have made the slightest difference to the right-wing hostility directed at it. It is, however, conceivable that it would have given less excuse to those otherwise well disposed to the report to distance themselves from it.[4]

Notes

This article is based on my keynote address to the annual conference of the UK Political Studies Association held in Manchester in April this year.

1 *The Future of Multi-Ethnic Britain*, Profile Books, Longman, 2000.
2 See, for example, my *Integrating Minorities* (2001, pp. 27 ff) for a response to the criticisms of Alan Wolfe, Jytte Klausen and Amartya Sen. See also the response by Stuart Hall, Tariq Modood and myself to the sympathetic criticisms of Michael Banton, Will Kymlicka and Charles Westin in *The Journal of Ethnic and Migration Studies* 26(4), Oct. 2000: 719–38.
3 Farukh Dhondy wrote a clumsy and ill-informed piece in *The Times of India*. It came to my attention too late to receive a timely reply.
4 Given its current predicament, India too might benefit from a similar commission to ours. It could be composed of leading thinkers drawn from different disciplines and regions, and asked to produce a comprehensive report analysing different areas of our national life and outlining a well-considered agenda of action.

References

Barry, Brian (2001). 'The Muddles of Multiculturalism', *New Left Review*, 8: 49–71.
Banton, Michael (2000). 'Review Symposium. Report of the Commission on The Future of Multi-Ethnic Britain: UK Perspective', *The Journal of Ethnic and Migration Studies*, 26(4): 720–3.

Cross, Malcolm (2000). 'Review Symposium. Report on the Commission on the Future of Multi-Ethnic Britain: UK North American and Continental European Perspectives', *The Journal of Ethnic and Migration Studies*, 26(4): 719–20.

Free Press (2000). Issue no. 119 (Nov.–Dec.), articles by Robin Richardson and Tim Copsill on the Report.

Hall, Stuart, Tariq, Modood and Bhikhu Parekh (2000). 'Response to Banton, Kymlica and Westin', *The Journal of Ethnic and Migration Studies*, 26(4): 734–8.

Kymlicka, Will (2000). 'Review Symposium. Report on the Commission on the Future of Multi-Ethnic Britain: North American View', *The Journal of Ethnic and Migration Studies*, 26(4): 723–31.

Parekh, Bhikhu (2001). 'Integrating Minorities', Annual Diversity Lecture, Institute of Contemporary Arts, London.

Sen, Amartya (2000). 'Other People'. British Academy Lecture given on Nov. 7, published in *Proceedings of the British Academy 2001*.

Westin, Charles (2000). 'Review Symposium. Report on the Commission on the Future of Multi-Ethnic Britain: A View from Continental Europe', *The Journal of Ethnic and Migration Studies*. 26(4): 731–4.

Wolfe, Alan and Klausen, Jytte (2000). 'Celebrating Diversity Is Now Central to Progressive Politics', *Prospect Magazine*, Dec.

Younge, Gary (2000). 'Celebrate, Don't Tolerate Minorities', *The Guardian*, Wednesday, Oct. 11, pp. 7–8.

CHAPTER 24

Elizabeth "Betita" Martinez

Where Was the Color in Seattle?: *Looking for Reasons Why the Great Battle Was So White*

"I was at the jail where a lot of protesters were being held and a big crowd of people was chanting 'This Is What Democracy Looks Like!' At first it sounded kind of nice. But then I thought: is this really what democracy looks like? Nobody here looks like me."
– Jinee Kim, Bay Area youth organizer

In the vast acreage of published analysis about the splendid victory over the World Trade Organization last November 29–December 3, it is almost impossible to find anyone wondering why the 40,000–50,000 demonstrators were overwhelmingly Anglo. How can that be, when the WTO's main victims around the world are people of color? Understanding the reasons for the low level of color, and what can be learned from it, is absolutely crucial if we are to make Seattle's promise of a new, international movement against imperialist globalization come true.

Among those who did come for the WTO meeting were some highly informative third world panelists who spoke Monday, November 29 about the effects of WTO on health care and on the environment. They included activist-experts from Mexico, Malaysia, the Philippines, Ghana, and Pakistan. On Tuesday, at the huge rally on November 30 before the march, labor leaders from Mexico, the Caribbean, South Africa, Malaysia, India, and China spoke along with every major US union leader (all white).

Rank-and-file US workers of color also attended, from certain unions and locals in certain geographic areas. There were young African Americans in the building trades; blacks from Local 10 of the ILWU in San Francisco and Latinos from its Los Angeles local; Asian Americans from SEIU; Teamsters of color from eastern Washington state; members of the painters' union and the union of Hotel Employees and Restaurant Employees (HERE). Latino/a farmworkers from the UFW and PCUN (Pineros and Campesinos del Noroeste) of Oregon also attended. At one point a miner from the South Africa Labor

Elizabeth "Betita" Martinez, "Where Was the Color in Seattle? Looking for Reasons Why the Great Battle Was So White," *ColorLines*, vol. 3, no. 1 (Spring 2000). Reprinted by permission of ColorLines.

Network cried, "In the words of Karl Marx, 'Workers of the world, unite!'" The crowd of some 25,000 people cheered.

Among community activists of color, the Indigenous Environmental Network (IEN) delegation led by Tom Goldtooth conducted an impressive program of events with Native peoples from all over the US and the world. A 15-member multi-state delegation represented the Southwest Network for Environmental and Economic Justice based in Albuquerque, which embraces 84 organizations primarily of color in the US and Mexico; their activities in Seattle were binational.

Many activist youth groups of color came from California, especially the Bay Area, where they have been working on such issues as Free Mumia, affirmative action, ethnic studies, and rightwing laws like the current Proposition 21 "youth crime" initiative. Seattle-based forces of color that participated actively included the Filipino Community Center and the international People's Assembly, which led a march on Tuesday despite being the only one denied a permit. The predominantly white Direct Action Network (DAN), a huge coalition, brought thousands to the protest. But Jia Ching Chen of the Bay Area's Third Eye Movement was the only young person of color involved in DAN's central planning.

Seattle's 27-year-old Centro de la Raza organized a Latino contingent in the labor march and local university groups, including MEChA (Movimiento Estudiantil Chicano de Aztlan), hooked up with visiting activists of color. Black activists who have been fighting for an African American Heritage Museum and Cultural Center in Seattle were there. Hop Hopkins, an AIDS activist in Seattle, also black, made constant personal efforts to draw in people of color.

Still, the overall turnout of color from the US remained around 5 percent of the total. In personal interviews, activists from the Bay Area and the Southwest gave me several reasons for this. Some mentioned concern about the likelihood of brutal police repression. Other obstacles: lack of funds for the trip, inability to be absent from work during the week, and problems in finding child care.

Yet several experienced activists of color in the Bay Area who had even been offered full scholarships chose not to go. A major reason for not participating, and the reason given by many others, was lack of knowledge about the WTO. As one Filipina said, "I didn't see the political significance of it how the protest would be anti-imperialist. We didn't know anything about the WTO except that lots of people were going to the meeting." One of the few groups that did feel informed, and did participate, was the hip-hop group Company of Prophets. According to African American member Rashidi Omari of Oakland, this happened as a result of their attending teach-ins by predominantly white groups like Art and Revolution. Company of Prophets, rapping from a big white van, was in the front ranks of the 6 a.m. march that closed down the WTO on November 30.

The problem of unfamiliarity with the WTO was aggravated by the fact that black and Latino communities across the US lack internet access compared to many white communities. A July 1999 federal survey showed that among Americans earning $15,000–$35,000 a year, more than 32 percent of white families owned computers but only 19 percent of black and Latino families. In that same income range, only 9 percent of African American and Latino homes had Internet access compared to 27 percent of white families. So information about WTO and all the plans for Seattle did not reach many people of color.

Limited knowledge meant a failure to see how the WTO affected the daily lives of US communities of color. "Activists of color felt they had more immediate issues," said Rashidi. "Also, when we returned people told me of being worried that family and peers would say they were neglecting their own communities, if they went to Seattle. They would be asked, 'Why are you going? You should stay here and help your people.'"

Along with such concerns about linkage came the assumption that the protest would be overwhelmingly white as it was. Coumba Toure, a Bay Area activist originally from Mali, West Africa, said she had originally thought, "the whites will take care of the WTO, I don't need to go." Others were more openly apprehensive. For example, Carlos ("Los" for short) Windham of Company of Prophets told me, "I think even Bay Area activists of color who understood the linkage didn't want to go to a protest dominated by 50,000 white hippies."

People of color had reason to expect the protest to be white-dominated. Roberto Maestas, director of Seattle's Centro de la Raza, told me that in the massive local press coverage before the WTO meeting, not a single person of color appeared as a spokesperson for the opposition. "Day after day, you saw only white faces in the news. The publicity was a real deterrent to people of color. I think some of the unions or church groups should have had representatives of color, to encourage people of color to participate."

Four protesters of color from different Bay Area organizations talked about the "culture shock" they experienced when they first visited the "Convergence," the protest center set up by the Direct Action Network, a coalition of many organizations. Said one, "When we walked in, the room was filled with young whites calling themselves anarchists. There was a pungent smell, many had not showered. We just couldn't relate to the scene so our whole group left right away." Another told me, "They sounded dogmatic and paranoid." "I just freaked and left," said another. "It wasn't just race, it was also culture, although race was key."

In retrospect, observed Van Jones of STORM (Standing Together to Organize a Revolutionary Movement) in the Bay Area, "We should have stayed. We didn't see that we had a lot to learn from them. And they had a lot of materials for making banners, signs, puppets." "Later I went back and talked to people," recalled Rashidi, "and they were discussing tactics, very smart. Those folks were really ready for action. It was limiting for people of color to let that one experience affect their whole picture of white activists." Jinee Kim, a Korean American with the Third Eye Movement in the Bay Area, also thought it was a mistake. "We realized we didn't know how to do a blockade. We had no gas masks. They made sure everybody had food and water, they took care of people. We could have learned from them."

Reflecting the more positive evaluation of white protesters in general, Richard Moore, coordinator of the Southwest Network for Environmental and Economic Justice, told me "the white activists were very disciplined." "We sat down with whites, we didn't take the attitude that 'we can't work with white folks,'" concluded Rashidi. "It was a liberating experience."

Few predominantly white groups in the Bay Area made a serious effort to get people of color to Seattle. Juliette Beck of Global Exchange worked hard with others to help people from developing (third world) countries to come. But for US people of color, the main organizations that made a serious effort to do so were Just Act (Youth ACTion for Global JUSTice), formerly the Overseas Development Network, and Art and Revolution, which mostly helped artists. Many activists of color have mentioned Alli Chaggi-Starr of Art and Revolution, who not only helped people come but for the big march in Seattle she obtained a van with a sound system that was used by musicians and rappers.

In Just Act, Coumba Toure and two other members of color – Raj Jayadev and Malachi Larabee – pushed hard for support from the group. As a result, about 40 people of color were enabled to go thanks to special fundraising and whites staying at people's homes in Seattle so their hotel money could be used instead on plane tickets for people of color.

Reflecting on the whole issue of working with whites, Coumba talked not only about pushing Just Act but also pushing people of color to apply for the help that became available.

One of the problems Coumba said she encountered in doing this was "a legacy of distrust of middle-class white activists that has emerged from experiences of 'being used.' Or not having our issues taken seriously. Involving people of color must be done in a way that gives them real space. Whites must understand a whole new approach is needed that includes respect (if you go to people of color thinking you know more, it creates a barrier). Also, you cannot approach people simply in terms of numbers, like 'let's give 2 scholarships.' People of color must be central to the project."

Jia Ching Chen recalled that once during the week of protest, in a jail holding cell, he was one of only two people of color among many Anglos. He tried to discuss with some of them the need to involve more activists of color and the importance of white support in this. "Some would say, 'We want to diversify,' but didn't understand the dynamics of this." In other words, they didn't understand the kinds of problems described by Coumba Toure. "Other personal conversations were more productive," he said, "and some white people started to recognize why people of color could view the process of developing working relations with whites as oppressive."

Unfortunately the heritage of distrust was intensified by some of the AFL-CIO leadership of labor on the November 30 march. They chose to take a different route through downtown rather than marching with others to the Convention Center and helping to block the WTO. Also, on the march to downtown they reportedly had a conflict with the Third World People's Assembly contingent when they rudely told the people of color to move aside so they could be in the lead.

Yet if only a small number of people of color went to Seattle, all those with whom I spoke found the experience extraordinary. They spoke of being changed forever. "I saw the future." "I saw the possibility of people working together." They called the giant mobilization "a shot in the arm," if you had been feeling stagnant. "Being there was an incredible awakening." Naomi, a Filipina dancer and musician, recalled how "at first a lot of my group were tired, grumpy, wanting to go home. That really changed. One of the artists with us, who never considered herself a political activist, now wants to get involved back in Oakland. Seattle created a lot of strong bonds in my small community of coworkers and friends."

They seem to feel they had seen why, as the chant popularized by the Chicano/a students of MEChA goes, "Ain't no power like the power of the people, 'Cause the power of the people don't stop!"

There must be effective follow-up and increased communication between people of color across the nation: grassroots organizers, activists, cultural workers, and educators. We need to build on the contacts made (or that need to be made) from Seattle. Even within the Bay Area, activists who could form working alliances still do not know of each other's existence.

With mass protests planned for April 16–17 in Washington DC at the meeting of the World Bank and the International Monetary Fund (IMF), the opportunity to build on the WTO victory shines brightly. More than ever, we need to work on our ignorance about global issues with study groups, youth workshops, conferences. We need to draw specific links between WTO and our close-to-home struggles in communities of color, as has been emphasized by Raj Jayadev and Lisa Juachon in *The Silicon Valley Reader: Localizing the Effects of the Global Economy*, 1999, which they edited.

Many examples of how WTO has hurt poor people in third world countries were given during the protest. For example, a Pakistani told one panel how, for years, South Africans grew medicinal herbs to treat AIDS at very little cost. The WTO ruled that this was "unfair" competition with pharmaceutical companies seeking to sell their expensive AIDS medications. "People are dying because they cannot afford those products," he said. A Filipino reported on indigenous farmers being compelled to use fertilizers containing poisonous chemicals in order to compete with cheap, imported potatoes. Ruined, they often left the land seeking survival elsewhere.

But there are many powerful examples right here in the US. For starters, consider:

- WTO policies encourage sub-livable wages for youth of color everywhere including right here.
- WTO policies encourage privatization of health care, education, welfare, and other crucial public services, as well as cutbacks in those services, so private industry can take them over and run them at a profit. This, along with sub-livable wages, leads to jeopardizing the lives of working-class people and criminalizing youth in particular.
- Workers in Silicon Valley are being chemically poisoned by the chips they work on that make such wealth for others. WTO doesn't want to limit those profits with protection for workers.
- WTO has said it is "unfair trade" to ban the import of gasoline in which certain cancer-causing chemicals have been used. This could have a devastating effect on people in the US, including those of color, who buy that gas.
- Overall, WTO is controlled by US corporations. It is secretly run by a few advanced industrialized countries for the benefit of the rich and aspiring rich. WTO serves to further impoverish the poor of all countries.

Armed with such knowledge, we can educate and organize people of color.

As Jinee Kim said at a San Francisco report-back by youth of color, "We have to work with people who may not know the word 'globalization' but they live globalization."

CHAPTER 26

A. S. Narang

World Conference Against Racism: Prospects and Challenges

The World Conference against Racism, Racial Discrimination, Xenophobia and Related Intolerance (WCAR) will be held in Durban, South Africa, from August 31 to September 2001. This will be the third UN World Conference on this issue. The previous conferences were held in Geneva in 1978 and in 1983. They focused mainly on ending apartheid in South Africa, but also highlighted other critical issues, including the rights of minorities, indigenous people and migrant workers, and importance of education in preventing racism and discrimination. The upcoming world conference will focus on developing practical, action-oriented measures and strategies to combat contemporary forms of racism and intolerance. It is being suggested that the conference will motivate a critical process, through which a global consensus can be built for the articulation and implementation of new and effective approaches to eliminate racism. There are also voices of pessimism suggesting that there are lots of world conferences organised by the UN, most of them have passed good-intentioned resolutions but have not changed the situation substantially. It is pointed out that after 30 years of the adoption of the UN International Convention on the Elimination of All Forms of Racial Discrimination, and despite other conventions and designation of three decades for the action to combat racism and racial discrimination the incidence of racism, racial discrimination, religious intolerance and ethnic violence are on the increase at a national, regional and global level. Gross violations of human rights such as slavery and discrimination on the basis of country of origin, gender and choice of religion continue unabated in many countries. The world is witness to discrimination against minorities, indigenous peoples and migrant workers; the accusation of institutionalised racism in police forces; harsh immigration and asylum policies; hate sites on the internet and youth groups promoting intolerance and xenophobia. It is in this context that the holding of Third World Conference against Racism has to be seen and prospects it offers analysed.

In one form or another racism is to be found in every society on earth. It is associated with certain forms of entrenched poverty and certain kinds of extreme violence. It is a

A. S. Narang, "World Conference Against Racism: Prospects and Challenges," *Economic and Political Weekly* (July 7, 2001).

denial of human relationship. Yet, for many people it remains almost invisible, unnoticed except when violence is involved. Those who do not experience it often fail to understand how profoundly offensive it is. There always had been protests and movements against this inhuman practice. The modern movement against racism came into being to oppose 'white against black'. Its historical roots are to be found in campaigns against the slave trade and colonialism. In more recent times, it was inspired by the civil rights movement in the US and by resistance to apartheid in South Africa, where racism took a particularly explicit and institutionalised form.

When the international community adopted the United Nations Charter in 1945, it accepted the obligation to pursue the realisation of human rights and fundamental freedom for all, without distinction as to race, sex, language or religion. The Universal Declaration on Human Rights declared that all human beings are born free and equal in dignity and rights. The UN General Assembly on November 20, 1963, adopted the UN Declaration on the Elimination of All Forms of Racial Discrimination. The Declaration reaffirms the principles of the UN Charter and the Universal Declaration of Human Rights, and their fundamental importance to good international relations. It says:

> Discrimination between human beings on the ground of race, colour, or ethnic origin is an offence to human dignity and shall be condemned as a denial of the principles of the Charter of the United Nations, as a violation of the human rights and fundamental freedoms proclaimed in the Universal Declaration of Human Rights as an obstacle to friendly and peaceful relations among nations and a fact capable of disturbing peace and security among nations. (Article 1)

This declaration, though important, is not binding. The UN General Assembly, therefore, on December 21, 1965, adopted the International Convention on the Elimination of All Forms of Racial Discrimination. This Convention, which is a legally binding instrument has been signed by 155 states. Signatory countries agree to condemn racism and to undertake measures to eliminate it in all forms. The Convention also established the Committee on the Elimination of Racial Discrimination, the first such human rights treaty body. It oversees implementation of the Convention by reviewing reports of the States Parties to the Convention.

In 1968, shortly before the Convention entered into force, the first International Conference on Human Rights, meeting in Tehran called for the criminalisation of racist organisations. On December 11, 1969, the General Assembly designated the year 1971 as the International Year for Action to Combat Racism and Racial Discrimination and on November 2, 1972, the General Assembly designated the 10-year period beginning on December 10, 1973 as the Decade for Action to Combat Racism and Racial Discrimination. The programme for the decade was structured around a worldwide education campaign and measures to be taken to implement United Nations instruments promoting the elimination of racial discrimination.

Between 1973 and 2003, the General Assembly designated three decades for action to combat racism and racial discrimination to ensure support for people struggling for racial equality. The programme of Action for the Third Decade, which ends in 2003, underlines the pivotal role of human rights education in securing respect for human rights. It has been marked by a broadening of the problem of racism and the realisation that every society in the world is affected and hindered by discrimination.

The First World Conference to Combat Racism and Racial Discrimination was held in Geneva in 1978, at the mid-point of the first decade. Its declaration and programme of action reaffirmed the inherent falsity of racism and the threat it posed to friendly relations among peoples and nations. It specifically condemned apartheid, "the extreme form of institutionalised racism," as a crime against humanity, an affront to the dignity of mankind and a threat to peace and security in the world. In addition, it recommended that, because of the severe economic inequalities that resulted from racial discrimination, efforts to combat racism should include measures aimed at improving the living conditions of men and women.

The Second World Conference to Combat Racism and Racial Discrimination, held in Geneva, August 1–12, 1983, reviewed and assessed the activities undertaken during the first decade and formulated specific measures to ensure the implementation of United Nations instruments to eliminate racism, racial discrimination and apartheid. Apart from reaffirming its condemnation of racism the declaration adopted by the Conference stated, "Racism and racial discrimination are continuing scourges which must be eradicated throughout the world."

It declared apartheid totally abhorrent to the conscience and dignity of mankind, a crime against humanity, and a threat to international peace and security. Additionally it noted the double discrimination often encountered by women; it stated the urgent need to protect the rights of refugees, immigrants and migrant workers, and it welcomed the establishment of the United Nations Working Group on Indigenous Populations. It also recommended the launch of second decade to combat racism and racial discrimination.

The second decade to combat racism was launched on December 10, 1983. A portion of the programme of action for the second decade focused on the elimination of apartheid, and requested that the Security Council consider the imposition of mandatory sanctions against the government of South Africa. An important result of this was that in 1990, the South African government released Nelson Mandela and began to dismantle the system of apartheid.

Limited success

At the Second World Conference on Human Rights at Vienna in 1993, the declaration welcomed the end of apartheid, but took note of the sombre reality of the increase of intolerance, xenophobia, racism and racial discrimination in many countries, and highlighted the rights of minorities, women and indigenous people. On December 20, 1993, the General Assembly proclaimed the third decade to combat racism and racial discrimination (1994–2005). Also in 1993, the Commission on Human Rights appointed a special Rapporteur on contemporary forms of racism, racial discrimination, xenophobia and related intolerance. He has reported on institutionalised and indirect forms of racism and racial discrimination against national, racial, ethnic, linguistic and religious minorities and migrant workers throughout the world. His mandate has also emphasised new manifestations of racism and xenophobia in developed countries in particular.

Thus, during the last 50 years since the adoption of the Universal Declaration of Human Rights, the international community has made some important advances in the fight against racism. Recent decades have witnessed the end of apartheid in South Africa and its adoption of a new multiracial constitution. In many South African countries, racial discrimination has been and continues to be combated through the abolishment of discriminatory laws. In several countries there has been an increased recognition of indigenous peoples and their rights, particularly through constitutional and legislative changes. Also, science has definitely put to rest any biological or physiological justification for unequal treatment of individuals. Yet, according to the UN's own documents the dream remains only half fulfilled. In the three decades of its existence, the committee on the Elimination of Racial Discrimination, the monitoring body established under the convention, had reached the conclusion that no state was immune to racial discriminatory practices, which often emerged as a reflection of traditions or age-old prejudices or as a result of the introduction of policies or ideologies based on chauvinistic nationalism. Other factors, however, also contributed to racial discrimination in the exercise of economic, social and cultural life, including socio-economic underdevelopment, segregation experienced by indigenous populations, racial conflicts giving rise to violence, and xenophobia against minorities, minority groups, undocumented immigrants, refugees and displaced persons [UN 2000].

As technology brings the peoples of the world closer together and political barriers tumble, racial discrimination, xenophobia and other forms of intolerance continue to ravage our societies. Racist theories are still widespread. Legally, particularly in the US, but also in Europe, numerous racist internet websites spread propaganda cheaply and globally. Most proponents of such theories – whether they are white super-racists in the US, Hindu conservatives in India, Hutu extremists in Rwanda or Tutsi extremists in Burundi, or supporters of policies that discriminate against the Roma in Hungary or against Haitians in the Dominican Republic – tend to construct a pseudo-scientific vision of history that justifies their claim to superiority. At the same time, they dehumanise those they believe are less equal. The group that is discriminated against is said to have genetic predispositions towards criminal tendencies, to be feckless sexually or financially, to be less successful academically, to be unemployed by choice and so on. In extreme cases, the victims are described as more animal-like than human. Because racial discrimination directly or indirectly prevents groups that are discriminated against from getting equal access to essential services – housing, education, employment, health facilities, marriage across the line of discrimination – these claims in time become partially fulfilled wherever the group that discriminates achieves a measure of power. At the extreme, such systems can produce systemic discrimination that covers every aspect of life, including religion, as in the Hindu caste system, which has socially isolated and impoverished – dalits for over one thousand years. Once such systems are established, they are complete worlds and it is exceptionally difficult to change them consensually [ICHRP 2000].

Of course, the existence of racism is widely denied across cultures, countries and regions. This phenomenon of denial makes recognising, identifying and effectively addressing racism particularly difficult. Denial operates on many levels, including even the language that is used to describe certain situations. Terms like, 'ethnic minority', 'ethnic conflict', 'immigration restrictions', 'new immigrants', 'illegal alien', 'urban poor' and 'colour blindness' are used to deny or obscure the racist aspects of certain social behaviours or government policies. In addition to blatant and covert acts and denials, racism can be manifested in attitudes, opinions and stereotypes, ideologies; interpersonal relationships; social practices and institutions. Institutional racism, in which patterns of discrimination, marginalisation and disadvantage become systematic and self-sustaining, is particularly problematic in that it is often considered simply "the way the system works – which is at once the truth and an obfuscation of both the underlying problem and the possible solutions" [IHRLG 2000].

This is what has been happening in recent decades. According to the UN High Commissioner for Human Rights during the last decade alone, racial and ethnic tensions have led to political conflicts and even resulted in genocide, war crimes and crimes against humanity being committed against certain groups. Despite the defeat of apartheid, racially discriminatory laws and policies continue to exist in some states, affecting the civil, cultural, economic, political and social rights available to some groups in their own country. The last decade has been characterised by paradoxical developments. On the one hand, new and efficient ways of deepening cooperation and reducing the centrifugal forces of sovereignty and nationalism are on the rise, and the integrity of nation states is increasingly being challenged by forces of ethnic, cultural, religious or linguistic separation. As a consequence, internal conflicts are destabilising many countries. Religious, ethnic and racial minorities as well as indigenous populations particularly suffer. In many countries they have often been the main victims of prejudice; they are the subject of violence and stigma and their civil, cultural, economic, political and social rights have been systematically violated [CHR 2000].

It is in this context that issues related to racism have been raised at various fora during the last decade of the twentieth century. The Vienna Declaration and Programme of Action resulting from the World Conference on Human Rights in 1993 identified the elimination of racism and racial discrimination as a primary objective for the international community and for the United Nations human rights programme. The International Conference on Population and Development in 1994, the World Summit for Social Development in 1995, the Fourth World Conference on Women, and the follow-up processes of these conferences, all helped to deepen the understanding of how racism persists in the real world and to identify ways and means to combat it. The culmination of growing international concern for the rise in the incidents of racism, racial discrimination, xenophobia and related intolerance, and recognition of the challenges and opportunities in combating these phenomena in an increasingly globalised world was the decision of the UN General Assembly in December 1997 to convene a World Conference against Racism, Racial Discrimination, Xenophobia and Related Intolerance no later than 2001.

The title and objectives of the world conference make it clear that its scope is extended to the many forms of racism and bigotry in our modern world, to xenophobia in all its manifestations, anti-semitism, negrophobia, discrimination against indigenous peoples, migrants, refugees, displaced persons and the minority communities. The definition of racial discrimination for the purpose of the conference is that provided by the International Convention on the Elimination of Racial Discrimination. It says, "any distinction, exclusion, restriction or preference based on race, colour, descent, or national or ethnic origin which has the purpose or effect of nullifying or impairing the recognition, enjoyment or exercise, on an equal footing, of human rights and fundamental freedoms in the political, economic, social, cultural or any other field of public life." This definition of social discrimination, Ion Diaconu, member of the UN Committee on the Elimination of Racial Discrimination, points out is based on objective elements; it involves any distinction, exclusion, restriction or preference; that means one has to identify an appropriate comparator, as they are based on race, colour, descent, or national or ethnic origin. By this enumeration the definition is suitable to protect all persons, as well as racial or ethnic groups.

In view of these, the preparatory committee for the conference has identified the following five themes for the agenda of the Conference:

1) Sources, causes, forms and contemporary manifestations of racism, racial discrimination, xenophobia and related intolerance.
2) Victims of racism, racial discrimination, xenophobia and related intolerance.
3) Measures of prevention, education and protection aimed at the eradication of racism, racial discrimination, xenophobia and related intolerance, at the national, regional and international levels.
4) Provision of effective remedies, recourse, redress, [compensatory] and other measures, at the national, regional and international levels.
5) Strategies to achieve full and effective equality, including international cooperation and enhancement of the UN and other international mechanisms in combating racism, racial discrimination, xenophobia and related intolerance, and follow-up.

Within the framework of above themes and in addition suggestions have been made and are being made by experts, seminars, groups and states for consideration of various aspects of the issues involved. The UN sub-commission on Promotion and Protection of Human Rights points out that following are serious manifestations of racism in the past decade, and will probably continue affecting the next decade. Therefore, they need serious attention. They are:

- The explosion of ethnic conflicts and widespread violence related thereto, which go hand in hand with the return of notions and practices of national or ethnic exclusivity, in total contravention of the principles of the charter of the United Nations and major instruments in the field of human rights;
- The widespread phenomenon of xenophobia, which is alive in various continents, especially in Europe, the principal victims of this situation are immigrants and refugees from developing countries.
- The double discrimination victimisation of persons who suffer from accumulated discrimination, for example on the grounds of race and gender, race and sexual orientation, race and handicap, or race and age [UN 2000].

The sub-commission accordingly suggests for discussion the topics (a) the current realities in the aftermath of slavery and colonialism, including the legal implications of the slave trade and conditions of persons of African descent in the Americas; (b) the impact of economic globalisation on racial equality, including globalisation in the context of the increase in incidents of racism, and the economic basis of racism; (c) the treatment of migrants, refugees, asylum seekers, other non-citizens and displaced persons, as well the related phenomenon of xenophobia; (d) the prevention of racial discrimination, including early warning and urgent procedures, as well as the accountability of non-state actors; (e) the prevention of racial discrimination, through education and labour regulation; (f) remedies, redress mechanisms and reparations for racial discrimination, including affirmative action, and compensation for victims and descendants of victims of racism; (g) international mechanisms for the implementation of the International Convention on the Elimination of All Forms of Racial Discrimination and their progressive development, as well as reservations to the Convention; (h) combating hate speech and promoting tolerance in the digital age; (i) the implications of multiple identities (race, colour, descent, minority, national or ethnic origin, gender); (j) means to be applied to protect the rights of indigenous peoples.

In addition to these various international bodies and NGOs have also highlighted certain important issues. These include

a) Globalisation, racism and discrimination against minorities: This stems from the fact that globalisation and the activities of transnational corporations have an impact on racial discrimination practices and on relationship between ethnic groups. In the discussion of the links between racism and globalisation, the public/private dimensions of the issue assume particular importance, given that the most prominent actors involved in the process of globalisation are private, non-state entities.

b) Ethnic conflicts: This has become a global phenomena that threatens the human right to peace. Though a number of ethnic conflicts are between people of the same colour, there is need to understand the underlying causes.

c) Racism and citizenship: In many cases there is exclusion coinciding with racial and ethnic lines. It is particularly so with migrants who many a times are harassed, intimidated, threatened, subjected to intolerable work conditions, arrested, detained and deported.

d) *De facto* segregation: It is necessary to look at both *de jure* and *de facto* segregation. For instance, whereas *de jure* discrimination has disappeared in South Africa, *de facto* segregation remains and expands.

e) Gender issues: Women may face double discrimination, with their concerns marginalised under the banner of vulnerable groups. Their issues need reflection in their own right often with cross-cutting issues of poverty and ethnic discrimination.

f) Religion: In many countries the question of racism or ethnic discrimination revolves around the concepts of religion versus secularism.

g) Trafficking in human persons: Each year, millions of individuals, the vast majority of them women and children, are tricked, sold, coerced or otherwise become involved in situations of exploitation from which they cannot escape. The conditions of trafficking persons often amount to a contemporary form of slavery.

h) Displacement: In recent years, individuals and groups have fled systematic persecution on the basis of their race, ethnicity, religion or descent, in almost all regions of the world. They face problems also in the states where they seek asylum or refuge.

i) The right of the African peoples to just and fair compensatory measures which include reparation, apologies and pledges of non-repetition of outrages suffered by Africans.

j) Issue of discrimination based on descent: The situation of perennial and persistent forms of discrimination such as discrimination based on caste in Asia, Burakumin in Japan and Roma in Europe, needs affirmation that discrimination based on descent is one form of racial discrimination.

All the above and other suggestions made for inclusion in the agenda of WCAR are based on the hope that the conference will provide a timely opportunity not only to confront the past, but also to shape the present, and the future. While all concerned are expressing that the WCAR will focus on developing practical, action-oriented measures and strategies to combat contemporary forms of racism and intolerance, the preparatory process of the Conference suggests that there are going to be challenges. During the last two years various governments have been expressing their serious reservations on proposed and suggested issues for the agenda. For example, America and the European states are opposed to the compensatory measures, and India does not favour any mention of caste (under the rubric of descent).

Caste issues

The African group has been insisting for inclusion in the agenda and declaration demands of the African people for reparation and compensation for the African Holocaust and other crimes committed against them in the past. In this they are supported by many Asian countries and a number of International NGOs. According to them, foundations of a new, equal and just relationship between all the different races and people of the world cannot be laid without first taking stock of the present situation while keeping the past in mind. Without properly evaluating the wrong inflicted upon the victims of racism and racial discrimination, rectifying them and taking new pragmatic measures against their perpetrators. It is pointed out that the first step in the right direction is the recognition of the Slave Trade as a crime against humanity. Apology and reparation by the former slave-holding nations for all the wrongs done to peoples of Africa are indispensable. Remedy, redress and compensation for Africa's expropriated labour and wealth are the legitimate demands of the African peoples. Heading these demands is the only way to ensure that equality, justice and dignity of the African peoples are preserved and respected, according to this view.

The US, countries of Europe and some others are opposed to inclusion of compensatory measures. Their argument is that while the historical antecedents to contemporary racial issues are acknowledged, too much emphasis on discussion and analysis of history could divert attention and energy from current solutions and remedies for the future. They, therefore, lay emphasis on concrete action for effective remedial measures for the present situation and future rather than harping on the past all the time.

Another controversial suggestion is that of inclusion of discrimination based on descent. According to dalit activists in India and many International NGOs descent-based abuses which can be found in many countries in Asia, such as in India against dalits and in Japan against Burakumin, have so far remained unattended though they are forms of racial discrimination. Caste is discrimination on the basis of work and descent. The definition of racial discrimination given in Article 1(i) of the International Convention on the Elimination of Racial Discrimination does include descent. Interestingly the term 'descent', which is not found in any other international document was suggested by India during the elaboration of the Convention. Of course, it does not indicate in what way it is different from national or ethnic origin. Some experts, however, comment that it would include the notion of caste. The UN Committee on the Elimination of Racial Discrimination in its forty-ninth session in 1996 observed that the term 'descent' mentioned in Article 1 does not solely refer to race. The committee affirms that the situation of the scheduled castes and scheduled tribes falls within the scope of convention. Government of India's stand is that the caste and race are different and therefore it falls beyond the domain of the conference. Also it is a local and social phenomenon and cannot be treated as official, or legally constituted discrimination. In addition in India individual cases of societal discrimination against the scheduled castes are recognised as crimes under the law, forbidden under the constitution and are being appropriately dealt with. Whatever that be, the caste discrimination may or may not come on the official agenda of the conference, it has received the considerable attention particularly of the UN committee on the Elimination of Racial Discrimination and a large number of International NGOs.

In spite of challenges, reservations and difficulties the conference is facing in arriving at consensus for adoption of a declaration and programme of action, it is being felt that the conference is more than a forum for political negotiations. It should be viewed as a time to review the commitment to respect the equality, dignity and rights of all members of the human family; to take stock of what has already been done to combat racial discrimination; and to take resolute action to eradicate racism in all its forms now. Activists feel that the results and impact of the WCAR will extend beyond the final declaration and programme of action that is produced.

These documents will specify mechanisms for follow up, monitoring and accountability – providing a basis upon which long-term actions and strategies can be formulated and implemented [IHRLG 2000b]. However, there is need to be cautious. As is known most UN resolutions and decisions are not legally binding. Signing or endorsing the declaration and programme of action resulting from the World Conference is not the equivalent of passing national legislation or ratifying an international convention or treaty. A programme of action is effective when it is used as a guide for reviewing and adopting national laws and policies. In this context experiences of earlier world conferences like those on Environment and Development (1992), Human Rights (1993), Population and Development (1994), Social Development (1995), Women (1995), Human Settlements (1996) and World Food Summit (1996) are mixed. In spite of these conferences, cases of Human Rights abuses, ethnic cleansing, violence against women, religious intolerance, discrimination, ethnic cleansing, trafficking in human beings, including women and children, etc., continue unabated. Therefore there is a heavy moral responsibility on all participants of the WCAR to make it a success. The conference must state with precision and insistence that the rights of persons of African descent, indigenous peoples, lower castes and national minorities are human rights. It is not sufficient repeatedly to affirm the value of equality, as several generations of politicians, lawmakers and lawyers have done.

References

CHR (2001). *Report of the United Nations High Commissioner for Human Rights and Follow-up to the World Conference on Human Rights*, Commission on Human Rights, UN Economic and Social Council, CE/CN 4/2001, 16, p. 3.

ICHRP (2000). *The Persistence and Mutation of Racism, Versoix*, International Council on Human Rights Policy, pp. 3–4.

IHRLG (2000a). *Bellagio Consultation on the UN World Conference against Racism*, International Human Rights Law Group, Jan., pp. 3–4.

IHRLG (2000b). *Combating Racism Together*, International Human Rights Law Group, Washington, p. 48.

UN (2000a). *Note for the Preparatory Meetings and Activities at the International Regional and National Levels*, General Assembly, Secretary General UN, A/Conf 189/PC 1/8, April, p. 6.

UN (2000b). *Reports, Studies and Other Documentation for the Preparatory Committee and the World Conference*, UN General Assembly, A/Conf 189/PC 1/13/Add 1, pp. 4–5.

Part IV

Gendered Identities in the Realm of Patriarchy

CHAPTER 27

Chandra Talpade Mohanty

Women Workers and Capitalist Scripts: Ideologies of Domination, Common Interests, and the Politics of Solidarity

We dream that when we work hard, we'll be able to clothe our children decently, and still have a little time and money left for ourselves. And we dream that when we do as good as other people, we get treated the same, and that nobody puts us down because we are not like them. . . . Then we ask ourselves, "How could we make these things come true?" And so far we've come up with only two possible answers: win the lottery, or organize. What can I say, except I have never been lucky with numbers. So tell this in your book: tell them it may take time that people think they don't have, but they have to organize! . . . Because the only way to get a little measure of power over your own life is to do it collectively, with the support of other people who share your needs.

Irma, a Filipina worker in the Silicon Valley, California[1]

Irma's dreams of a decent life for her children and herself, her desire for equal treatment and dignity on the basis of the quality and merit of her work, her conviction that collective struggle is the means to "get a little measure of power over your own life," succinctly capture the struggles of poor women workers in the global capitalist arena. In this essay I want to focus on the exploitation of poor Third-World women, on their agency as workers, on the common interests of women workers based on an understanding of shared location and needs, and on the strategies/practices of organizing that are anchored in and lead to the transformation of the daily lives of women workers.

This has been an especially difficult essay to write – perhaps because the almost-total saturation of the processes of capitalist domination makes it hard to envision forms of feminist resistance which would make a real difference in the daily lives of poor women workers. However, as I began to sort through the actions, reflections, and analyses by and about women workers (or wage laborers) in the capitalist economy, I discovered the dignity of women workers' struggles in the face of overwhelming odds. From these struggles we can learn a great deal about processes of exploitation and domination as well as about autonomy and liberation.

A recent study tour to Tijuana, Mexico, organized by Mary Tong of the San Diego-based Support Committee for Maquiladora Workers, confirmed my belief in the radical possibilities of cross-border organizing, especially in the wake of NAFTA. Exchanging ideas, experiences, and strategies with Veronica Vasquez, a 21-year-old Maquila worker fighting for her job, for better working conditions, and against sexual harassment, was as much of an inspiration as any in writing this essay. Veronica Vasquez, along with 99 former employees of the Tijuana factory Exportadora Mano de Obra, SA de CV, has filed an unprecedented lawsuit in Los Angeles, California, against the US owner of Exporta-dora, National O-Ring of Downey, demanding that it be forced to follow Mexican labor laws and provide workers with three months' back pay after shutting down company operations in Tijuana in November 1994. The courage, determination, and analytical clarity of these young Mexican women workers in launching the first case to test the legality of NAFTA suggest that in spite of the global saturation of processes of capitalist domination, 1995 was a moment of great possibility for building cross-border feminist solidarity.[2]

Over the years, I have been preoccupied with the limits as well as the possibilities of constructing feminist solidarities across national, racial, sexual, and class divides. Women's lives as workers, consumers, and citizens have changed radically with the triumphal rise of capitalism in the global arena. The common interests of capital (e.g., profit, accumulation, exploitation, etc.) are somewhat clear at this point. But how do we talk about poor Third-World women workers' interests, their agency, and their (in)visibility in so-called democratic processes? What are the possibilities for democratic citizenship for Third-World women workers in the contemporary capitalist economy? These are some of the questions driving this essay. I hope to clarify and analyze the location of Third-World women workers and their collective struggles in an attempt to generate ways to think about mobilization, organizing, and conscientization transnationally.

This essay extends the arguments I have made elsewhere regarding the location of Third-World women as workers in a global economy.[3] I write now, as I did then, from my own discontinuous locations: as a South Asian anticapitalist feminist in the US committed to working on a truly liberatory feminist practice which theorizes and enacts the potential for a cross-cultural, international politics of solidarity; as a Third-World feminist teacher and activist for whom the psychic economy of "home" and of "work" has always been the space of contradiction and struggle; and as a woman whose middle-class struggles for self-definition and autonomy outside the definitions of daughter, wife, and mother mark an intellectual and political genealogy that led me to this particular analysis of Third-World women's work.

Here, I want to examine the analytical category of "women's work," and to look at the historically specific *naturalization* of gender and race hierarchies through this category. An international division of labor is central to the establishment, consolidation, and mainten-ance of the current world order: global assembly lines are as much about the production of people as they are about "providing jobs" or making profit. Thus, naturalized assumptions about *work* and *the worker* are crucial to understanding the sexual politics of global capitalism. I believe that the relation of local to global processes of colonization and exploitation, and the specification of a process of cultural and ideological homogenization across national borders, in part through the creation of the consumer as "the" citizen under advanced capitalism, must be crucial aspects of any comparative feminist project. This definition of the citizen-consumer depends to a large degree on the definition and disciplining of producers/workers on whose backs the citizen-consumer gains legitimacy. It is the worker/producer side of this equation that I will address. Who are the workers that make the citizen-consumer possible? What role do sexual politics play in the ideological creation of this worker? How does global capitalism, in search of ever-increasing profits, utilize gender and racialized ideologies in crafting forms of women's work? And, does the social location of particular women as workers suggest the basis for common interests and potential solidarities across national borders?

As global capitalism develops and wage labor becomes the hegemonic form of organizing production and reproduction, class relations within and across national borders have become more complex and less transparent.[4] Thus, issues of spatial economy – the manner by which capital utilizes particular spaces for differential production and the accumulation of capital and, in the process, transforms these spaces (and peoples) – gain fundamental importance for feminist analysis.[5] In the aftermath of feminist struggles around the right to work and the demand for equal pay, the boundaries between home/family and work are no longer seen as inviolable (of course these boundaries were always fluid for poor and working-class women). Women are (and have always been) in the workforce, and we are here to stay. In this essay, I offer an analysis of certain historical and ideological transformations of gender, capital, and work across the borders of nation-states,[6] and, in the process, develop a way of thinking about the common interests of Third-World women workers, and in particular about questions of agency and the transformation of consciousness.

Drawing specifically on case studies of the incorporation of Third-World women into a global division of labor at different geographical ends of the new world order, I argue for a historically delineated category of "women's work" as an example of a productive and necessary basis for feminist cross-cultural analysis.[7] The idea I am interested in invoking here is not "the work that women do" or even the occupations that they/we happen to be concentrated in, but rather the ideological construction of jobs and tasks in terms of notions of appropriate femininity, domesticity, (hetero)sexuality, and racial and cultural stereotypes. I am interested in mapping these operations of capitalism across different divides, in tracing the naturalization of capitalist processes, ideologies, and values through the way women's work is *constitutively* defined – in this case, in terms of gender and racial parameters. One of the questions I explore pertains to the way gender identity (defined in domestic, heterosexual, familial terms) structures the nature of the work women are allowed to perform or precludes women from being "workers" altogether.

While I base the details of my analysis in geographically anchored case studies, I am suggesting a comparative methodology which moves beyond the case-study approach and illuminates global processes which inflect and draw upon indigenous hierachies, ideologies, and forms of exploitation to consolidate new modes of colonization (what we refer to in the introductory chapter as "recolonization"). The local and the global are indeed connected through parallel, contradictory, and sometimes converging relations of rule which position women in different and similar locations as workers.[8] I agree with feminists who argue that class struggle, narrowly defined, can no longer be the only basis for solidarity among women workers. The fact of being women with particular racial, ethnic, cultural, sexual, and geographical histories has everything to do with our definitions and identities as workers. A number of feminists have analyzed the division between production and reproduction, and the construction of ideologies of womanhood in terms of public/private spheres. Here, I want to highlight a) the persistence of patriarchal definitions of womanhood in the arena of wage labor; b) the versatility and specificity of capitalist exploitative processes providing the basis for thinking about potential common interests and solidarity between Third-World women workers; and c) the challenges for collective organizing in a context where traditional union methods (based on the idea of the class interests of the male worker) are inadequate as strategies for empowerment.

If, as I suggest, the logic of a world order characterized by a transnational economy involves the active construction and dissemination of an image of the "Third World/ racialized, or marginalized woman worker" that draws on indigenous histories of gender and race inequalities, and if this worker's identity is coded in patriarchal terms which define her in relation to men and the heterosexual, conjugal family unit, then the model of class conflict between capitalists and workers needs to be recrafted in terms of the interests (and perhaps identities) of Third-World women workers. Patriarchal ideologies, which sometimes pit women against men within and outside the home, infuse the material realities of the lives of Third-World women workers, making it imperative to reconceptualize the way we think about working-class interests and strategies for organizing. Thus, while this is not an argument for just recognizing the "common experiences" of Third-World women workers, it *is* an argument for recognizing (concrete, not abstract) "common interests" and the potential bases of cross-national solidarity – a common context of struggle. In addition, while I choose to focus on the "Third World" woman worker, my argument holds for white women workers who are also racialized in similar ways. The argument then is about a *process* of gender and race domination, rather than about the *content* of "Third World." Making Third-World women workers visible in this gender, race, class formation involves engaging a capitalist script of subordination and exploitation. But it also leads to thinking about the possibilities of emancipatory action on the basis of the reconceptualization of Third-World women as agents rather than victims.

But why even use "Third World," a somewhat problematic term which many now consider outdated? And why make an argument which privileges the social location, experiences, and identities of Third-World women workers, as opposed to any other group of workers, male or female? Certainly, there are problems with the term "Third World." It is inadequate in comprehensively characterizing the economic, political, racial, and cultural differences *within* the borders of Third-World nations. But in comparison with other similar formulations like "North/South" and "advanced/underdeveloped nations," "Third World" retains a certain heuristic value and explanatory specificity in relation to the inheritance of colonialism and contemporary neocolonial economic and geopolitical processes that the other formulations lack.[9]

In response to the second question, I would argue that at this time in the development and operation of a "new" world order, Third-World women workers (defined in this context as both women from the geographical Third World and immigrant and indigenous women of color in the US and Western Europe) occupy a specific social location in the international division of labor which *illuminates* and *explains* crucial features of the capitalist processes of exploitation and domination. These are features of the social world that are usually obfuscated or mystified in discourses about the "progress" and "development" (e.g., the creation of jobs for poor, Third-World women as the marker of economic and social advancement) that is assumed to "naturally" accompany the triumphal rise of global capitalism. I do not claim to explain *all* the relevant features of the social world or to offer a *comprehensive* analysis of capitalist processes of recolonization. However, I am suggesting that Third-World women workers have a potential identity in common, an identity as *workers* in a particular division of labor at this historical moment. And I believe that exploring and analyzing this potential commonality across geographical and cultural divides provides both a way of reading and understanding the world and an explanation of the consolidation of inequities of gender, race, class, and (hetero)sexuality, which are necessary to envision and enact transnational feminist solidarity.[10]

The argument that multinationals position and exploit women workers in certain ways does not originate with me. I want to suggest, however, that in interconnecting and comparing some of these case studies, a larger theoretical argument can be made about the category of women's work, specifically about the Third-World woman as worker, at this particular historical moment. I think this intersection of gender and work, where the very definition of work draws upon and reconstructs notions of masculinity, femininity, and sexuality, offers a basis of cross-cultural comparison and analysis which is grounded in the concrete realities of women's lives. I am not suggesting that this basis for comparison exhausts the *totality* of women's experience cross-culturally. In other words, because similar ideological constructions of "women's work" make cross-cultural analysis possible, this does not automatically mean women's lives are the *same*, but rather that they are *comparable*. I argue for a notion of political solidarity and common interests, defined as a community or collectivity among women workers across class, race, and national boundaries which is based on shared material interests and identity and common ways of reading the world. This idea of political solidarity in the context of the incorporation of Third-World women into a global economy offers a basis for cross-cultural comparison and analysis which is grounded in history and social location rather than in an ahistorical notion of culture or experience. I am making a choice here to focus on and analyze the *continuities* in the experiences, histories, and strategies of survival of these particular workers. But this does not mean that differences and discontinuities in experience do not exist or that they are insignificant. The focus on continuities is a *strategic* one – it makes possible a way of reading the operation of capital from a location (that of Third-World women workers) which, while forming the bedrock of a certain kind of global exploitation of labor, remains somewhat invisible and undertheorized.

Gender and work: historical and ideological transformations

"Work makes life sweet," says Lola Weixel, a working-class Jewish woman in Connie Field's film "The Life and Times of Rosie the Riveter." Weixel is reflecting on her experience of working in a welding factory during World War II, at a time when large numbers of US women were incorporated into the labor force to replace men who were fighting the war. In one of the most moving moments in the film, she draws attention to what it meant to her and to other women to work side by side, to learn skills and craft products, and to be paid for the work they did, only to be told at the end of the war that they were no longer needed and should go back to being girlfriends, housewives, and mothers. While the US state propaganda machine was especially explicit on matters of work for men and women, and the corresponding expectations of masculinity/femininity and domesticity in the late 1940s and 1950s, this is no longer the case in the 1990s. Shifting definitions of public and private, and of workers, consumers and citizens no longer define wage-work in visibly masculine terms. However, the dynamics of job competition, loss, and profit-making in the 1990s are still part of the dynamic process that spelled the decline of the mill towns of New England in the early 1900s and that now pits "American" against "immigrant" and "Third-World" workers along the US/Mexico border or in the Silicon Valley in California. Similarly, there are continuities between the women-led New York garment-workers strike of 1909, the Bread and Roses (Lawrence textile) strike of 1912, Lola Weixel's role in union organizing during WW II, and the frequent strikes in the 1980s and 1990s of Korean textile and electronic workers, most of whom are young, single women.[11] While the global division of labor in 1995 looks quite different from what it was in the 1950s, ideologies of women's work, the meaning and value of work for women, and women workers' struggles against exploitation remain central issues for feminists around the world. After all, women's labor has always been central to the development, consolidation, and reproduction of capitalism in the USA and elsewhere.

In the United States, histories of slavery, indentured servitude, contract labor, self-employment, and wage-work are also simultaneously histories of gender, race, and (hetero)sexuality, nested within the context of the development of capitalism. Thus, women of different races, ethnicities, and social classes had profoundly different, though interconnected, experiences of work in the economic development from nineteenth-century economic and social practices (slave agriculture in the South, emergent industrial capitalism in the Northeast, the hacienda system in the Southwest, independent family farms in the rural Midwest, Native American hunting/gathering and agriculture) to wage-labor and self-employment (including family businesses) in the late-twentieth century. In 1995, almost a century after the Lowell girls lost their jobs when textile mills moved South to attract non-unionized labor, feminists are faced with a number of profound analytical and organizational challenges in different regions of the world. The material, cultural, and political effects of the processes of domination and exploitation which sustain what is called the New World Order (NWO)[12] are devasting for the vast majority of people in the world – and most especially for impoverished and Third-World women. Maria Mies argues that the increasing division of the world into consumers and producers has a profound effect on Third-World women workers, who are drawn into the international division of labor as workers in agriculture; in large-scale manufacturing industries like textiles, electronics, garments, and toys; in small-scale manufacturing of consumer goods like handicrafts and food processing (the informal sector); and as workers in the sex and tourist industries.[13]

The values, power, and meanings attached to being either a consumer or a producer/worker vary enormously depending on where and who we happen to be in an unequal global system. In the 1990s, it is, after all, multinational corporations that are the hallmark of global capitalism. In an analysis of the effects of these corporations on the new world order, Richard Barnet and John Cavanagh characterize the global commercial arena in terms of four intersecting webs: the Global Cultural Bazaar (which creates and disseminates images and dreams through films, television, radio, music, and other media), the Global Shopping Mall (a planetary supermarket which sells things to eat, drink, wear, and enjoy through advertising, distribution, and marketing networks), the Global Workplace (a network of factories and workplaces where goods are produced, information processed, and services rendered), and, finally, the Global Financial Network (the international traffic in currency transactions, global securities, etc.).[14] In each of these webs, racialized ideologies of masculinity, femininity, and sexuality play a role in constructing the legitimate consumer, worker, and manager. Meanwhile, the psychic and social disenfranchisement and impoverishment of women continues. Women's bodies and labor are used to consolidate global dreams, desires, and ideologies of success and the good life in unprecedented ways.

Feminists have responded directly to the challenges of globalization and capitalist modes of recolonization by addressing the sexual politics and effects on women of a) religious fundamentalist movements within and across the boundaries of the nation-state; b) structural adjustment policies (SAPs); c) militarism, demilitarization, and violence against women; d) environmental degradation and land/sovereignty struggles of indigenous and native peoples; and e) population control, health, and reproductive policies and practices.[15] In each of these cases, feminists have analyzed the effects on women as workers, sexual partners, mothers and caretakers, consumers, and transmitters and transformers of culture and tradition. Analysis of the ideologies of masculinity and femininity, of motherhood and (hetero)sexuality and the understanding and mapping of agency, access, and choice are central to this analysis and organizing. Thus, while my characterization of capitalist processes of domination and recolonization may appear somewhat overwhelming, I want to draw attention to the numerous forms of resistance and struggle that have also always been constitutive of the script of colonialism/capitalism. Capitalist patriarchies and racialized, class/caste-specific hierarchies are a key part of the long history of domination and exploitation of women, but struggles against these practices and vibrant, creative, collective forms of mobilization and organizing have also always been a part of our histories. In fact, like Jacqui Alexander and a number of other authors in this collection, I attempt to articulate an emancipatory discourse and knowledge, one that furthers the cause of feminist liberatory practice. After all, part of what needs to change within racialized capitalist patriarchies is the very concept of work/labor, as well as the naturalization of heterosexual masculinity in the definition of "the worker."

Teresa Amott and Julie Matthaei, in analyzing the US labor market, argue that the intersection of gender, class, and racial-ethnic hierarchies of power has had two major effects:

> First, disempowered groups have been concentrated in jobs with lower pay, less job security, and more difficult working conditions. Second, workplaces have been places of extreme segregation, in which workers have worked in jobs only with members of their same racial-ethnic, gender, and class group, even though the particular racial-ethnic group and gender assigned to a job may have varied across firms and regions.[16]

While Amott and Matthaei draw attention to the sex-and-race typing of jobs, they do not *theorize* the relationship between this job typing and the social identity of the workers concentrated in these low-paying, segregated, often unsafe sectors of the labor market. While the economic history they chart is crucial to any understanding of the race-and-gender basis of US capitalist processes, their analysis begs the question of whether there is a connection (other than the common history of domination of people of color) between *how* these jobs are defined and *who* is sought after for the jobs.

By examining two instances of the incorporation of women into the global economy (women lacemakers in Narsapur, India, and women in the electronics industry in the Silicon Valley) I want to delineate the interconnections between gender, race, and ethnicity, and the ideologies of work which locate women in particular exploitative contexts.

The contradictory positioning of women along class, race, and ethnic lines in these two cases suggests that, in spite of the obvious geographical and sociocultural differences between the two contexts, the organization of the global economy by contemporary capital positions these workers in very similar ways, effectively reproducing and transforming locally specific hierarchies. There are also some significant continuities between homework and factory work in these contexts, in terms of both the inherent ideologies of work as well as the experiences and social identities of women as workers. This tendency can also be seen in the case studies of black women workers (of Afro-Caribbean, Asian, and African origin) in Britain, especially women engaged in homework, factory work, and family businesses.

Housewives and homework: the lacemakers of Narsapur

Maria Mies's 1982 study of the lacemakers of Narsapur, India, is a graphic illustration of how women bear the impact of development processes in countries where poor peasant and tribal societies are being "integrated" into an international division of labor under the dictates of capital accumulation. Mies's study illustrates how capitalist production relations are built upon the backs of women workers defined as *housewives*. Ideologies of gender and work and their historical transformation provide the necessary ground for the exploitation of the lacemakers. But the definition of women as housewives also suggests the heterosexualization of women's work – women are always defined in relation to men and conjugal marriage. Mies's account of the development of the lace industry and the corresponding relations of production illustrates fundamental transformations of gender, caste, and ethnic relations. The original caste distinctions between the feudal warrior castes (the landowners) and the Narsapur (poor Christians) and Serepalam (poor Kapus/Hindu agriculturalists) women are totally transformed through the development of the lace industry, and a new caste hierarchy is effected.

At the time of Mies's study, there were 60 lace manufacturers, with some 200,000 women in Narsapur and Serepalam constituting the work force. Lacemaking women worked 6 to 8 hours a day, and ranged in age from 6 to 80. Mies argues that the expansion of the lace industry between 1970 and 1978 and its integration into the world market led to class/caste differentiation within particular communities, with a masculinization of all nonproduction jobs (trade) and a total feminization of the production process. Thus, men sold women's products and lived on profits from women's labor. The polarization between men and women's work, where men actually defined themselves as exporters and businessmen who invested in women's labor, bolstered the social and ideological definition of women as housewives and their work as "leisure time activity." In other words, work, in this context, was grounded in sexual identity, in concrete definitions of femininity, masculinity, and heterosexuality.

Two particular indigenous hierarchies, those of caste and gender, interacted to produce normative definitions of "women's work." Where, at the onset of the lace industry, Kapu men and women were agricultural laborers and it was the lower-caste Harijan women who were lacemakers, with the development of capitalist relations of production and the possibility of caste/class mobility, it was the Harijan women who were agricultural laborers while the Kapu women undertook the "leisure time" activity of lacemaking. The caste-based ideology of seclusion and purdah was essential to the extraction of surplus value. Since purdah and the seclusion of women is a sign of higher caste status, the domestication of Kapu laborer women – where their (lacemaking) activity was tied to the concept of the "women sitting in the house" was entirely within the logic of capital accumulation and profit. Now, Kapu women, not just the women of feudal, landowning castes, are in purdah as housewives producing for the world market.

Ideologies of seclusion and the domestication of women are clearly sexual, drawing as they do on masculine and feminine notions of protectionism and property. They are also heterosexual ideologies, based on the normative definition of women as wives, sisters, and mothers – always in relation to conjugal marriage and the "family." Thus, the caste transformation and separation of women along lines of domestication and nondomestica-tion (Kapu housewives vs. Harijan laborers) effectively links the work that women do with their sexual and caste/class identities. Domestication works, in this case, because of the persistence and legitimacy of the ideology of the housewife, which defines women in terms of their place within the home, conjugal marriage, and heterosexuality. The opposition between definitions of the "laborer" and of the "housewife" anchors the invisibility (and caste-related status) of work; in effect, it defines women as *nonworkers*. By definition, housewives cannot be workers or laborers; housewives make male breadwinners and consumers possible. Clearly, ideologies of "women's place and work" have real material force in this instance, where spatial parameters construct and maintain gendered and caste-specific hierarchies. Thus, Mies's study illustrates the concrete effects of the social definition of women as housewives. Not only are the lacemakers invisible in census figures (after all, their work is leisure), but their definition as housewives makes possible the definition of men as "breadwinners." Here, class and gender proletarianization through the development of capitalist relations of production, and the integration of women into the world market is possible because of the history and transformation of indigenous caste and sexual ideologies.

Reading the operation of capitalist processes from the position of the housewife/worker who produces for the world market makes the specifically gendered and caste/class oppos-ition between laborer and the nonworker (housewife) visible. Moreover, it makes it possible to acknowledge and account for the hidden costs of women's labor. And finally, it illumin-ates the fundamentally *masculine* definition of laborer/worker in a context where, as Mies says, men live off women who are the producers. Analyzing and transforming this mascu-line definition of labor, which is the mainstay of capitalist patriarchal cultures, is one of the most significant challenges we face. The effect of this definition of labor is not only that it makes women's labor and its costs invisible, but that it undercuts women's agency by defining them as victims of a process of pauperization or of "tradition" or "patriarchy," rather than as agents capable of making their own choices.

In fact, the contradictions raised by these choices are evident in the lacemakers' responses to characterizations of their own work as "leisure activity." While the fact that they did "work" was clear to them and while they had a sense of the history of their own pauperization (with a rise in prices for goods but no corresponding rise in wages), they were unable to explain how they came to be in the situation they found themselves. Thus, while some of the contradications between their work and their roles as housewives and mothers were evident to them, they did not have access to an analysis of these contradic-tions which could lead to a) seeing the complete picture in terms of their exploitation; b) strategizing and organizing to transform their material situations; or c) recognizing their common interests as women workers across caste/class lines. As a matter of fact, the Serepelam women defined their lacemaking in terms of "housework" rather than wage-work, and women who had managed to establish themselves as petty commodity producers saw what they did as entrepreneurial: they saw themselves as selling *products* rather than *labor*. Thus, in both cases, women internalized the ideologies that defined them as nonworkers. The isolation of the work context (work done in the house rather than in a public setting) as well as the internalization of caste and patriarchal ideologies thus militated against organizing as *workers*, or as *women*. However, Mies suggests that there were cracks in this ideology: the women expressed some envy toward agricultural laborers, whom the lacemakers saw as enjoying working together in the fields. What seems necessary in such a context, in terms of feminist mobilization, is a recognition of the fact that the identity of the housewife needs to be transformed into the identity of a "woman worker or working woman." Recognition of common interests as housewives is very different from recognition of common interests as women and as workers.

Immigrant wives, mothers, and factory work: electronics workers in the Silicon Valley

My discussion of the US end of the global assembly line is based on studies by Naomi Katz and David Kemnitzer (1983) and Karen Hossfeld (1990) of electronics workers in the so-called Silicon Valley in California. An analysis of production strategies and processes indicates a significant ideological redefinition of normative ideas of factory work in terms of the Third-World, immigrant women who constitute the primary workforce. While the lacemakers of Narsapur were located as *housewives* and their work defined as *leisure time activity* in a very complex international world market, Third-World women in the electronics industry in the Silicon Valley are located as *mothers, wives*, and *supplementary* workers. Unlike the search for the "single" woman assembly worker in Third-World countries, it is in part the ideology of the "married woman" which defines job parameters in the Valley, according to Katz and Kemnitzer's data.

Hossfeld also documents how existing ideologies of femininity cement the exploitation of the immigrant women workers in the Valley, and how the women often use this patriarchal logic against management. Assumptions of "single" and "married" women as the ideal workforce at the two geographical ends of the electronics global assembly line (which includes South Korea, Hong Kong, China, Taiwan, Thailand, Malaysia, Japan, India, Pakistan, the Philippines, and the United States, Scotland, and Italy)[17] are anchored in normative understandings of femininity, womanhood, and sexual identity. The labels are predicated on sexual difference and the institution of heterosexual marriage and carry connotations of a "manageable" (docile?) labor force.[18]

Katz and Kemnitzer's data indicates a definition and transformation of women's work which relies on gender, race, and ethnic hierarchies already historically anchored in the US. Further, their data illustrates that the construction of "job labels" pertaining to Third-World women's work is closely allied with their sexual and racial identities. While Hossfeld's more recent study reinforces some of Katz and Kemnitzer's conclusions, she focuses more specifically on how "contradictory ideologies about sex, race, class, and nationality are used as forms of both labor control and labor resistance in the capitalist workplace today."[19] Her contribution lies in charting the operation of gendered ideologies in the structuring of the industry and in analyzing what she calls "refeminization strategies" in the workplace.

Although the primary workforce in the Valley consists of Third-World and newly immigrant women, substantial numbers of Third-World and immigrant men are also employed by the electronics industry. In the early 1980s, 70,000 women held 80 to 90 percent of the operative or laborer jobs on the shop floor. Of these, 45 to 50 percent were Third-World, especially Asian, immigrants. White men held either technican or supervisory jobs. Hossfeld's study was conducted between 1983 and 1986, at which time she estimates that up to 80 percent of the operative jobs were held by people of color, with women constituting up to 90 percent of the assembly workers. Katz and Kemnitzer maintain that the industry actively seeks sources of cheap labor by deskilling production and by using race, gender, and ethnic stereotypes to "attract" groups of workers who are "more suited" to perform tedious, unrewarding, poorly paid work. When interviewed, management personnel described the jobs as a) unskilled (as easy as a recipe); b) requiring tolerance for tedious work (Asian women are therefore more suited); and c) supplementary activity for women whose main tasks were mothering and housework.

It may be instructive to unpack these job labels in relation to the immigrant and Third-World (married) women who perform these jobs. The job labels recorded by Katz and Kemnitzer need to be analyzed as definitions of *women's work*, specifically as definitions of *Third-World/immigrant women's work*. First, the notion of "unskilled" as easy (like following a recipe) and the idea of tolerance for tedious work both have racial and gendered dimensions. Both draw upon stereotypes which infantalize Third-World women and initiate a nativist discourse of "tedium" and "tolerance" as characteristics of non-Western, primarily agricultural, premodern (Asian) cultures. Secondly, defining jobs as supplementary activity for *mothers* and *housewives* adds a further dimension: sexual identity and appropriate notions of heterosexual femininity as marital domesticity. These are not part-time jobs, but they are defined as supplementary. Thus, in this particular context, (Third-World) women's work needs are defined as temporary.

While Hossfeld's analysis of management logic follows similar lines, she offers a much more nuanced understanding of how the gender and racial stereotypes prevalent in the larger culture infuse worker consciousness and resistance. For instance, she draws attention to the ways in which factory jobs are seen by the workers as "unfeminine" or not "ladylike." Management exploits and reinforces these ideologies by encouraging women to view femininity as contradictory to factory work, by defining their jobs as secondary and temporary, and by asking women to choose between defining themselves as women or as workers. Womanhood and femininity are thus defined along a domestic, familial model, with work seen as supplemental to this primary identity. Significantly, although 80 percent of the immigrant women in Hossfeld's study were the largest annual income producers in their families, they still considered men to be the breadwinners.

Thus, as with the exploitation of Indian lacemakers as "housewives," Third-World/immigrant women in the Silicon Valley are located as "mothers and homemakers" and only secondarily as workers. In both cases, men are seen as the real breadwinners. While (women's) work is usually defined as something that takes place in the "public" or production sphere, these ideologies clearly draw on stereotypes of women as homebound. In addition, the *invisibility* of work in the Indian context can be compared to the *temporary/secondary* nature of work in the Valley. Like the Mies study, the data compiled by Hossfeld and Katz and Kemnitzer indicates the presence of local ideologies and hierarchies of gender and race as the basis for the exploitation of the electronics workers. The question that arises is: How do women understand their own positions and construct meanings in an exploitative job situation?

Interviews with electronics workers indicate that, contrary to the views of management, women do not see their jobs as temporary but as part of a life-time strategy of upward mobility. Conscious of their racial, class, and gender status, they combat their devaluation as workers by increasing their income: by job-hopping, overtime, and moonlighting as pieceworkers. Note that, in effect, the "homework" that Silicon Valley workers do is performed under conditions very similar to the lacemaking of Narsapur women. Both kinds of work are done in the home, in isolation, with the worker paying her own overhead costs (like electricity and cleaning), with no legally mandated protections (such as a minimum wage, paid leave, health benefits, etc.). However, clearly the meanings attached to the work differ in both contexts, as does the way we understand them.

For Katz and Kemnitzer the commitment of electronics workers to class mobility is an important assertion of self. Thus, unlike in Narsapur, in the Silicon Valley, homework has an entrepreneurial aspect for the women themselves. In fact, in Narsapur, women's work turns the men into entrepreneurs! In the Valley, women take advantage of the contradictions of the situations they face as *individual workers*. While in Narsapur, it is purdah and caste/class mobility which provides the necessary self-definition required to anchor women's work in the home as leisure activity, in the Silicon Valley, it is a specifically *American* notion of individual ambition and entrepreneurship which provides the necessary ideological anchor for Third-World women.

Katz and Kemnitzer maintain that this underground economy produces an *ideological* redefinition of jobs, allowing them to be defined as *other than* the basis of support of the historically stable, "comfortable," white, metropolitan working class. In other words, there is a clear connection between low wages and the definition of the job as supplementary, and the fact that the lifestyles of people of color are defined as different and cheaper. Thus, according to Katz and Kemnitzer, *women* and *people of color* continue to be "defined out" of the old industrial system and become targets and/or instruments of the ideological shift away from class towards national/ethnic/gender lines.[20] In this context, ideology and popular culture emphasize the *individual maximization* of options for personal success. Individual success is thus severed from union activity, political struggle, and collective relations. Similarly, Hossfeld suggests that it is the racist and sexist management logic of the needs of "immigrants" that allows the kind of exploitative labor processes that she documents.[21] However, in spite of Katz and Kemnitzer's complex analysis of the relationship of modes of production, social relations of production, culture, and ideology in the context of the Silicon Valley workers, they do not specify why it is *Third-World women* who constitute the primary labor force. Similarly, while Hossfeld provides a nuanced analysis of the gendering of the workplace and the use of racial and gendered logic to consolidate capitalist accumulation, she also sometimes separates "women" and "minority workers" (Hossfeld, p. 176), and does not specify why it is women of color who constitute the major labor force on the assembly lines in the Valley. In distinguishing between women and people of color, Katz and Kemnitzer tend to reproduce the old conceptual divisions of gender and race, where women are defined primarily in terms of their gender and people of color in terms of race. What is excluded is an *interactive* notion of gender and race, whereby women's gendered identity is grounded in race and people of color's racial identities are gendered.

I would argue that the data compiled by Katz and Kemnitzer and Hossfeld does, in fact, explain why Third-World women are targeted for jobs in electronics factories. The explanation lies in the redefinition of work as temporary, supplementary, and unskilled, in the construction of women as mothers and homemakers, and in the positioning of femininity as contradictory to factory work. In addition, the explanation also lies in the specific definition of Third-World, immigrant women as docile, tolerant, and satisfied with substandard wages. It is the ideological redefinition of women's work that provides the necessary understanding of this phenomenon. Hossfeld describes some strategies of resistance in which the workers utilize against management the very gendered and racialized logic that management uses against them. However, while these tactics may provide some temporary relief on the job, they build on racial and gender stereotypes which, in the long run, can be and are used against Third-World women.

Daughters, wives, and mothers: migrant women workers in Britain

> Family businesses have been able to access minority women's labor power through mediations of kinship and an appeal to ideologies which emphasize the role of women in the home as wives and mothers and as keepers of family honor.[22]

In a collection of essays exploring the working lives of black and minority women inside and outside the home, Sallie Westwood and Parminder Bhachu focus on the benefits afforded the British capitalist state by the racial and gendered aspects of migrant women's labor. They point to the fact that what has been called the "ethnic economy" (the way migrants draw on resources to survive in situations where the combined effects of a hostile, racist environment and economic decline serve to oppress them) is also fundamentally a gendered economy. Statistics indicate that Afro-Caribbean and non-Muslim Asian women have a higher full-time labor participation rate than white women in the UK. Thus, while the perception that black women (defined, in this case, as women of Afro-Caribbean, Asian, and African origin) are mostly concentrated in part-time jobs is untrue, the *forms* and *patterns* of their work lives within the context of homework and family firms, businesses where the entire family is involved in earning a living, either inside or outside the home bears examination. Work by British feminist scholars (Phizacklea 1983, Westwood 1984, 1988, Josephides 1988, and others) suggests that familial ideologies of domesticity and heterosexual marriage cement the economic and social exploitation of black women's labor within family firms. Repressive patriarchal ideologies, which fix the woman's role in the family are grounded in inherited systems of inequality and oppression in Black women's cultures of origin. And these very ideologies are reproduced and consolidated in order to provide the glue for profit-making in the context of the racialized British capitalist state.

For instance, Annie Phizacklea's work on Bangladeshi homeworkers in the clothing industry in the English West Midlands illuminates the extent to which family and community ties, maintained by women, are crucial in allowing this domestic subcontracting in the clothing industry to undercut the competition in terms of wages and long work-days and its cost to women workers. In addition, Sallie Westwood's work on Gujarati women factory workers in the East Midlands hosiery industry suggests that the power and creativity of the shopfloor culture – which draws on cultural norms of femininity, masculinity and domesticity, while simultaneously generating resistance and solidarity among the Indian and white women workers – is, in fact, anchored in Gujarati cultural inheritances. Discussing the contradictions in the lives of Gujarati women within the home and the perception that male family members have of their work as an extension of their family roles (not as a path to financial independence), Westwood elaborates on the continuities between the ideologies of domesticity within the household, which are the result of (often repressive) indigenous cultural values and practices, and the culture of the shopfloor. Celebrating each other as daughters, wives, and mothers is one form of generating solidarity on the shopfloor – but it is also a powerful refeminization strategy, in Hossfeld's terms.

Finally, family business, which depend on the cultural and ideological resources and loyalties within the family to transform ethnic "minority" women into workers committed to common familial goals, are also anchored in women's roles as daughters, wives, mothers, and keepers of family honor (Josephides 1988, Bhachu 1998). Women's work in family business is unpaid and produces dependencies that are similar to those of home-workers whose labor, although paid, is invisible. Both are predicated on ideologies of domesticity and womanhood which infuse the spheres of production and reproduction. In discussing Cypriot women in family firms, Sasha Josephides cites the use of familial ideologies of "honor" and the construction of a "safe" environment outside the public sphere as the bases for a definition of femininity and womanhood (the perfect corollary to a paternal, protective definition of masculinity) that allows Cypriot women to see themselves as workers for their family, rather than as workers for themselves. All conflict around the question of work is thus accommodated within the context of the family. This is an important instance of the privatization of work, and of the redefinition of the identity of women workers in family firms as doing work that is a "natural extension" of their familial duties (not unlike the lacemakers). It is their identity as mothers, wives, and family members that stands in for their identity as workers. Parminder Bhachu's work with Punjabi Sikhs also illustrates this fact. Citing the growth of small-scale entrepreneurship among South Asians as a relatively new trend in the British economy, Bhachu states that women workers in family businesses often end up losing autonomy and reenter more traditional forms of patriarchal dominance where men control all or most of the economic resources within the family: "By giving up work, these women not only lose an independent source of income, and a large network of often female colleagues, but they also find themselves sucked back into the kinship system which emphasizes patrilaterality."[23] Women thus lose a "direct relationship with the productive process," thus raising the issue of the invisibility (even to themselves) of their identity as workers.

This analysis of migrant women's work in Britain illustrates the parallel trajectory of their exploitation as workers within a different metropolitan context than the US. To summarize, all these case studies indicate ways in which ideologies of domesticity, femininity, and race form the basis of the construction of the notion of "women's work" for Third-World women in the contemporary economy. In the case of the lacemakers, this is done through the definition of homework as leisure time activity and of the workers themselves as housewives. As discussed earlier, indigenous hierarchies of gender and caste/class make this definition possible. In the case of the electronics workers, women's work is defined as unskilled, tedious, and supplementary activity for mothers and homemakers. It is a specifically American ideology of individual success, as well as local histories of race and ethnicity that constitute this definition. We can thus contrast the *invisibility* of the lacemakers as workers to the *temporary* nature of the work of Third-World women in the Silicon Valley. In the case of migrant women workers in family firms in Britain, work becomes an extension of familial roles and loyalties, and draws upon cultural and ethnic/racial ideologies of womanhood, domesticity, and entrepreneurship to consolidate patriarchal dependencies. In all these cases, ideas of *flexibility, temporality, invisibility,* and *domesticity* in the naturalization of categories of work are crucial in the construction of Third-World women as an appropriate and cheap labor force. All of the above ideas rest on stereotypes about gender, race, and poverty, which, in turn, characterize Third-World women as workers in the contemporary global arena.

Eileen Boris and Cynthia Daniels claim that "homework belongs to the decentralization of production that seems to be a central strategy of some sectors and firms for coping with the international restructuring of production, consumption, and capital accumulation."[24] Homework assumes a significant role in the contemporary capitalist global economy. The discussion of homework performed by Third-World women in the three geographical spaces discussed above – India, USA, and Britain – suggests something specific about capitalist strategies of recolonization at this historical juncture. Homework emerged at the same time as factory work in the early nineteenth century in the US, and, as a system, it has always reinforced the conjoining of capitalism and patriarchy. Analyzing the homeworker as a wage laborer (rather than an entrepreneur who controls both her labor and the market for it) dependent on the employer for work which is carried out usually in the "home" or domestic premises, makes it possible to understand the *systematic* invisibility of this form of work. What allows this work to be so fundamentally exploitative as to be invisible as a form of work are ideologies of domesticity, dependency, and (hetero)sexuality, which designate women – in this case, Third-World women – as primarily housewives/mothers and men as economic supporters/breadwinners. Homework capitalizes on the equation of home, family, and patriarchial and racial/cultural ideologies of femininity/masculinity with work. This is work done at home, in the midst of doing housework, childcare, and other tasks related to "homemaking," often work that never ceases. Characterizations of "housewives," "mothers," and "homemakers" make it impossible to see homeworkers as workers earning regular wages and entitled to the rights of workers. Thus, not just their *production*, but homeworkers' *exploitation* as workers, can, in fact, also remain invisible, contained within domestic, patriarchal relations in the family. This is a form of work that often falls outside accounts of wage labor, as well as accounts of household dynamics.[25]

Family firms in Britain represent a similar ideological pattern, within a different class dynamic. Black women imagine themselves as entrepreneurs (rather than as wage laborers) working for the prosperity of their families in a racist society. However, the work they do is still seen as an extension of their familial roles and often creates economic and social dependencies. This does not mean that women in family firms never attain a sense of autonomy, but that, as a system, the operation of family business exploits Third-World women's labor by drawing on and reinforcing indigenous hierarchies in the search for upward mobility in the (racist) British capitalist economy. What makes this form of work in the contemporary global capitalist arena so profoundly exploitative is that its invisibility (both to the market, and sometimes to the workers themselves) is premised on deeply ingrained sexist and racist relationships within and outside heterosexual kinship systems. This is also the reason why changing the gendered relationships that anchor homework, and organizing homeworkers becomes such a challenge for feminists.

The analysis of factory work and family business in Britain and of homework in all three geographical locations raises the question of whether homework and factory work would be defined in these particular ways if the workers were single women. In this case, the construct of the *worker* is dependent on gender ideologies. In fact, the idea of work or labor as necessary for the psychic, material, and spiritual survival and development of women workers is absent. Instead, it is the identity of women as housewives, wives, and mothers (identities also defined outside the parameters of work) that is assumed to provide the basis for women's survival and growth. These Third-World women are defined out of the labor/capital process as if work in their case isn't necessary for economic, social, psychic autonomy, independence, and self-determination – a nonalienated relation to work is a conceptual and practical impossibility in this situation.

Thus far, this essay has charted the ideological commonalities of the exploitation of (mostly) poor Third-World women workers by global capitalist economic processes in different geographical locations. The analysis of the continuities between factory work and homework in objectifying and domesticating Third-World women workers such that their very identity as *workers* is secondary to familial roles and identities, and predicated on patriarchal and racial/ethnic hierarchies anchored in local/indigenous *and* transnational processes of exploitation exposes the profound challenges posed in organizing women workers on the basis of common interests. Clearly, these women are not merely victims of colonizing, exploitative processes – the analysis of the case studies indicates different levels of consciousness of their own exploitation, different modes of resistance, and different understandings of the contradictions they face, and of their own agency as workers. While the essay thus far lays the groundwork for conceptualizing the common interests of women workers based on an understanding of shared location and needs, the analysis foregrounds processes of *repression* rather than forms of *opposition*. How have poor Third-World women organized as workers? How do we conceptualize the question of "common interests" based in a "common context of struggle," such that women are agents who make choices and decisions that lead to the transformation of consciousness and of their daily lives as workers?

As discussed earlier, with the current domination in the global arena of the arbitary interests of the market and of transnational capital, older signposts and definitions of capital/labor or of "the worker" or even of "class struggle" are no longer totally accurate or viable conceptual or organizational categories. It is, in fact, the predicament of poor working women and their experiences of survival and resistance in the creation of new organizational forms to earn a living and improve their daily lives that offers new possibilities for struggle and action.[26] In this instance, then, the experiences of Third-World women workers are relevant for understanding and transforming the work experiences and daily lives of poor women everywhere. The rest of this essay explores these questions by suggesting a working definition of the question of the common interests of Third-World women workers in the contemporary global capitalist economy, drawing on the work of feminist political theorist Anna G. Jonasdottir.

Jonasdottir explores the concept of women's interests in participatory democratic political theory. She emphasizes both the formal and the content aspects of a theory of social and political interests that refers to "different layers of social existence: agency and the needs/desires that give strength and meaning to agency."[27] Adjudicating between political analysts who theorize common interests in formal terms (i.e., the claim to actively "be among," to choose to participate in defining the terms of one's own existence, or acquiring the conditions for choice), and those who reject the concept of interests in favor of the concept of (subjective) individualized, and group-based "needs and desires," (the consequences of choice), Jonasdottir formulates a concept of the common interests of women that emphasizes the former, but is a combination of both perspectives. She argues that the formal aspect of interest (an active "being among") is crucial: "Understood historically, and seen as emerging from people's lived experiences, interests about basic processes of social life are divided systematically between groups of people in so far as their living conditions are systematically different. Thus, historically and socially defined, interests can be characterized as 'objective.'"[28] In other words, there are systematic material and historical bases for claiming Third-World women workers have common interests. However, Jonasdottir suggests that the second aspect of theorizing interest, the satisfaction of needs and desires (she distinguishes between agency and the result of agency) remains a open question. Thus, the *content* of needs and desires from the point of view of interest remains open for subjective interpretation. According to Jonasdottir, feminists can acknowledge and fight on the basis of the (objective) common interests of women in terms of active representation and choices to participate in a democratic polity, while at the same time not reducing women's common interests (based on subjective needs and desires) to this formal "being among" aspect of the question of interest. This theorization allows us to acknowledge common interests and potential agency on the basis of systematic aspects of social location and experience, while keeping open what I see as the deeper, more fundamental question of understanding and organizing around the needs, desires, and choices (the question of critical, transformative consciousness) in order to transform the material and ideological conditions of daily life. The latter has a pedagogical and transformative dimension which the former does not.

How does this theorization relate to conceptualizations of the common interests of Third-World women workers? Jonasdottir's distinction between agency and the result of agency is a very useful one in this instance. The challenges for feminists in this arena are a) understanding Third-World women workers as having objective interests in common as workers (they are thus agents and make choices as workers); and b) recognizing the contradictions and dislocations in women's own consciousness of themselves as workers, and thus of their needs and desires – which sometimes militate *against* organizing on the basis of their common interests (the results of agency). Thus, work has to be done here in analyzing the links between the social location and the historical and current experiences of domination of Third-World women workers on the one hand, and in theorizing and enacting the common *social identity* of Third-World women workers on the other. Reviewing the forms of collective struggle of poor, Third-World women workers in relation to the above theorization of common interests provides a map of where we are in this project.

In the case of women workers in the free-trade zones in a number of countries, trade unions have been the most visible forum for expressing the needs and demands of poor women. The sexism of trade unions, however, has led women to recognize the need for alternative, more democratic organizational structures, and to form women's unions (as in Korea, China, Italy, and Malaysia)[29] or to turn to community groups, church committees, or feminist organizations. In the US, Third-World immigrant women in electronics factories have often been hostile to unions which they recognize as clearly modeled in the image of the white, male, working-class American worker. Thus, church involvement in immigrant women workers' struggles has been a important form of collective struggle in the US.[30]

Women workers have developed innovative strategies of struggle in women's unions. For instance, in 1989, the Korean Women Workers Association staged an occupation of the factory in Masan. They moved into the factory and lived there, cooked meals, guarded the machines and premises, and effectively stopped production.[31] In this form of occupation of the work premises, the processes of daily life become constitutive of resistance (also evident in the welfare rights struggles in the USA) and opposition is anchored in the systematic realities of the lives of poor women. It expresses not only their common interests as workers, but acknowledges their social circumstance as *women* for whom the artificial separation of work and home has little meaning. This "occupation" is a strategy of collective resistance that draws attention to poor women workers' *building community* as a form of survival.

Kumudhini Rosa makes a similar argument in her analysis of the "habits of resistance" of women workers in Free Trade Zones (FTZ) in Sri Lanka, Malaysia, and the Philippines.[32] The fact that women live and work together in these FTZs is crucial in analyzing the ways in which they build community life, share resources and dreams, provide mutual support and aid on the assembly line and in the street, and develop individual and collective habits of resistance. Rosa claims that these forms of resistance and mutual aid are anchored in a "culture of subversion" in which women living in patriarchal, authoritarian households where they are required to be obedient and disciplined, acquire practice in "concealed forms of rebelling" (86). Thus, women workers engage in "spontaneous" strikes in Sri Lanka, "wildcat" strikes in Malaysia, and "sympathy" strikes in the Philippines. They also support each other by systematically lowering the production target, or helping slow workers to meet the production targets on assembly lines. Rosa's analysis illustrates recognition of the common interests of women workers at a formal "being among" level. While women are conscious of the contradictions of their daily lives as women and as workers, and enact their resistance, they have not organized actively to identify their collective needs and to transform the conditions of their daily lives.

While the earlier section on the ideological construction of work in terms of gender and racial/ethnic hierarchies discussed homework as one of the most acute forms of exploitation of poor Third-World women, it is also the area in which some of the most creative and transformative collective organizing has occurred. The two most visibly successful organizational efforts in this arena are the Working Women's Forum (WWF) and SEWA (Self Employed Women's Association) in India, both registered as independent trade unions, and focusing on incorporating homeworkers, as well as petty traders, hawkers, and laborers in the informal economy into their membership.[33]

There has also been a long history of organizing homeworkers in Britain. Discussing the experience of the West Yorkshire Homeworking Group in the late 1980s, Jane Tate states that "a homework campaign has to work at a number of levels, in which the personal interconnects with the political, the family situation with work, lobbying Parliament with small local meetings.... In practical terms, the homeworking campaigns have adopted a way of organising that reflects the practice of many women's groups, as well as being influenced by the theory and practice of community work. It aims to bring out the strength of women, more often in small groups with a less formal structure and organisation than in a body such as a union."[34] Issues of race, ethnicity, and class are central in this effort since most of the homeworkers are of Asian or Third-World origin. Tate identifies a number of simultaneous strategies used by the West Yorkshire Group to organize homeworkers: pinpointing and making visible the "real" employer (or the real enemy), rather than directing organizational efforts only against local subsidiaries; consumer education and pressure, which links the buying of goods to homeworker struggles; fighting for a code of work practice for suppliers by forming alliances between trade unions, women's, and consumer groups; linking campaigns to the development of alternative trade organizations (for instance, SEWA); fighting for visibility in international bodies like the ILO; and, finally, developing transnational links between local grass-roots homeworker organizations – thus, sharing resources, strategies, and working toward empowerment. The common interests of homeworkers are acknowledged in terms of their daily lives as workers and as women – there is no artificial separation of the "worker" and the "homemaker" or the "housewife" in this context. While the West Yorkshire Homeworking

Group has achieved some measure of success in organizing homeworkers, and there is a commitment to literacy, consciousness-raising, and empowerment of workers, this is still a feminist group that organizes women workers (rather than the impetus for organization emerging from the workers themselves – women workers organizing). It is in this regard that SEWA and WWF emerge as important models for poor women workers' organizations.

Swasti Mitter discusses the success of SEWA and WWF in terms of: a) their representing the potential for organizing powerful women workers' organizations (the membership of WWF is 85,000 and that of SEWA is 46,000 workers) when effective strategies are used; and b) making these "hidden" workers visible as *workers* to national and international policy makers. Both WWF and SEWA address the demands of poor women workers, and both include a development plan for women which includes leadership training, child care, women's banks, and producer's cooperatives which offer alternative trading opportunities. Renana Jhabvala, SEWA's secretary, explains that, while SEWA was born in 1972 in the Indian labor movement and drew inspiration from the women's movement, it always saw itself as a part of the cooperative movement, as well. Thus, struggling for poor women workers' rights always went hand-in-hand with strategies to develop alternative economic systems. Jhabvala states, "SEWA accepts the co-operative principles and sees itself as part of the co-operative movement attempting to extend these principles to the poorest women.... SEWA sees the need to bring poor women into workers' co-operatives. The co-operative structure has to be revitalised if they are to become truly workers' organisations, and thereby mobilise the strength of the co-operative movement in the task of organising and strengthening poor women."[35] This emphasis on the extension of cooperative (or democratic) principles to poor women, the focus on political and legal literacy, education for critical and collective consciousness, and developing strategies for collective (and sometimes militant) struggle *and* for economic, social, and psychic development makes SEWA's project a deeply feminist, democratic, and transformative one. Self-employed women are some of the most disenfranchised in Indian society – they are vulnerable economically, in caste terms, physically, sexually, and in terms of their health, and, of course, they are socially and politically invisible. Thus, they are also one of the most difficult constituencies to organize. The simultaneous focus on collective struggle for equal rights and justice (struggle against) coupled with economic development on the basis of cooperative, democratic principles of sharing, education, self-reliance, and autonomy (struggle for) is what is responsible for SEWA's success at organizing poor, home-based, women workers. Jhabvala summarizes this when she says, "The combination of trade union and co-operative power makes it possible not only to defend members but to present an ideological alternative. Poor women's co-operatives are a new phenomenon. SEWA has a vision of the co-operative as a form of society which will bring about more equal relationships and lead to a new type of society."[36]

SEWA appears to come closest to articulating the common interests and needs of Third-World women workers in the terms that Jonasdottir elaborates. SEWA organizes on the basis of the objective interests of poor women workers – both the trade union and cooperative development aspect of the organizational strategies illustrate this. The status of poor women workers as workers and as citizens entitled to rights and justice is primary. But SEWA also approaches the deeper level of the articulation of needs and desires based on recognition of subjective, collective interests. As discussed earlier, it is this level of the recognition and articulation of common interest that is the challenge for women workers globally. While the common interests of women workers as *workers* have been variously articulated in the forms of struggles and organization reviewed above, the transition to identifying common needs and desires (the *content* aspect of interest) of Third-World women workers, which leads potentially to the construction of the *identity* of Third-World women workers, is what remains a challenge – a challenge that perhaps SEWA comes closest to identifying and addressing.

I have argued that the particular location of Third-World women workers at this moment in the development of global capitalism provides a vantage point from which to a) make particular practices of domination and recolonization visible and transparent, thus illuminating the minute and global processes of capitalist recolonization of women workers, and b) understand the commonalities of experiences, histories, and identity as the basis for solidarity and in organizing Third-World women workers transnationally. My claim, here, is that the definition of the social identity of women as workers is not only class-based, but, in fact, in this case, must be grounded in understandings of race, gender, and caste histories and experiences of work. In effect, I suggest that homework is one of the most significant, and repressive forms of "women's work" in contemporary global capitalism. In pointing to the ideology of the "Third-World woman worker" created in the context of a global division of labor, I am articulating differences located in specific histories of inequality, i.e., histories of gender and caste/class in the Narsapur context, and histories of gender, race, and liberal individualism in the Silicon Valley and in Britain.

However, my argument does not suggest that these are *discrete* and *separate* histories. In focusing on women's work as a particular form of Third-World women's exploitation in the contemporary economy, I also want to foreground a particular history that Third- and First-World women seem to have in common: the logic and operation of capital in the contemporary global arena. I maintain that the interests of contemporary transnational capital and the strategies employed enable it to draw upon indigenous social hierarchies and to construct, reproduce, and maintain ideologies of masculinity/femininity, techno-logical superiority, appropriate development, skilled/unskilled labor, etc. Here I have argued this in terms of the category of "women's work," which I have shown to be grounded in an ideology of the Third-World women worker. Thus, analysis of the location of Third-World women in the new international division of labor must draw upon the histories of colonialism and race, class and capitalism, gender and patriarchy, and sexual and familial figurations. The analysis of the ideological definition and redefinition of women's work thus indicates a political basis for common struggles and it is this particular forging of the political unity of Third-World women workers that I would like to endorse. This is in opposition to ahistorical notions of the common experience, exploitation, or strength of Third-World women or between Third- and First-World women, which serve to naturalize normative Western feminist categories of self and other. If Third-World women are to be seen as the *subjects of theory and of struggle*, we must pay attention to the specificities of their/our common *and* different histories.

In summary, this essay highlights the following analytic and political issues pertaining to Third-World women workers in the global arena: 1) it writes a particular group of women workers into history and into the operation of contemporary capitalist hegemony; 2) it charts the links and potential for solidarity between women workers across the borders of nation-states, based on demystifying the ideology of the masculinized worker; 3) it exposes a domesticated definition of Third-World women's work to be in actuality a strategy of global capitalist recolonization; 4) it suggests that women have common interests as workers, not just in transforming their work lives and environments, but in redefining home spaces so that homework is recognized as work to earn a living rather than as leisure or supplemental activity; 5) it foregrounds the need for feminist liberatory knowledge as the basis of feminist organizing and collective struggles for economic and political justice; 6) it provides a working definition of the common interests of Third-World women workers based on theorizing the common social identity of Third-World women as women/workers; and finally, 7) it reviews the habits of resistance, forms of collective struggle, and strategies of organizing of poor, Third-World women workers. Irma is right when she says that "the only way to get a little measure of power over your own life is to do it collectively, with the support of other people who share your needs." The question of defining common interests and needs such that the identity of Third-World women workers forms a potentially revolutionary basis for struggles against capitalist recolonization, and for feminist self-determination and autonomy, is a complex one. However, as maquiladora worker Veronica Vasquez and the women in SEWA demonstrate, women are already waging such struggles. The end of the twentieth century may be characterized by the exacerbation of the sexual politics of global capitalist domination and exploitation, but it is also suggestive of the dawning of a renewed politics of hope and solidarity.

Notes

Even after a number of new beginnings and revisions, this essay remains work in progress. I have come to the conclusion that this is indicative of both my own level of thinking about these issues as well as the current material and ideological conditions which position Third-World women wage-laborers in contradictory ways. I would like to thank Jacqui Alexander for careful, systematic, and patient feedback on this essay. The essay would not have been possible without Satya Mohanty's pertinent and incisive critique, and his unstinting emotional and intellectual support. My students at Hamilton College and colleagues at various institutions where I have presented sections of this argument are responsible for whatever clarity and lucidity the essay offers – thanks for keeping me on my toes. It is my involvement with the staff and board members of Grassroots Leadership of North Carolina that has sharpened my thinking about the struggles of poor and working people, and about the politics of solidarity and hope it engenders. Finally, it was Lisa Lowe, and then Mary Tong of the Support Committee for Maquiladora Workers, who brought the cross-border organizing of Veronica Vasquez and other workers to my attention. I thank all these organizers for teaching me and for the grass-roots organizing work they continue to do in the face of great odds.

1 See Karen Hossfeld, "United States: Why Aren't High-Tech Workers Organised?" in Women Working Worldwide, eds., *Common Interests: Women Organising in Global Electronics* (London: Tavistock), pp. 33–52, esp. pp. 50–1.

2 See "Tijuanans Sue in LA after Their Maquiladora Is Closed," by Sandra Dribble, in *The San Diego Union-Tribune*, Friday, Dec. 16, 1994. The Support Committee for Maquiladora Workers promotes cross-border organizing against corporate impunity. This is a San Diego-based volunteer effort of unionists, community activists, and others to assist workers in building autonomous organizations and facilitating ties between Mexican and US workers. The Committee, which is coordinated by Mary Tong, also sees its task as educating US citizens about the realities of life, work, and efforts for change among maquiladora workers. For more information write the Support Committee at 3909 Centre St., #210, San Diego, CA 92103.

3 See my essay, "Cartographies of Struggle: Third World Women and the Politics of Feminism," in Mohanty, Russo, and Torres, eds. *Third World Women and The Politics of Feminism*, (Bloomington: Indiana University Press, 1991), especially p. 39, where I identified five provisional historical, political, and discursive junctures for understanding Third-World feminist politics: "decolonization and national liberation movements in the third world, the consolidation of white, liberal capitalist patriarchies in Euro-America, the operation of multinational capital within a global economy, ... anthropology as an example of a discourse of dominance and self-reflexivity, ... (and) storytelling or autobiography (the practice of writing) as a discourse of

oppositional consciousness and agency." This essay represents a continuation of one part of this project: the operation of multinational capital and the location of poor Third-World women workers.

4   See the excellent analysis in Teresa L. Amott and Julie A. Matthaei, *Race, Gender and Work: A Multicultural Economic History of Women in the United States* (Boston: South End Press, 1991), esp. pp. 22–3.

5   See Bagguley, Mark-Lawson, Shapiro, Urry, Walby, and Warde, *Restructuring: Place, Class and Gender* (London: Sage Publications, 1990).

6   Joan Smith has argued, in a similar vein, for the usefulness of a world-systems-theory approach (seeing the various economic and social hierarchies and national divisions around the globe as part of a singular systematic division of labor, with multiple parts, rather than as plural and autonomous national systems) which incorporates the notion of the "household" as integral to understanding the profoundly gendered character of this systemic division of labor. While her analysis is useful in historicizing and analyzing the idea of the household as the constellation of relationships that makes the transfer of wealth possible across age, gender, class, and national lines, the ideologies of masculinity, femininity, and heterosexuality that are internal to the concept of the household are left curiously intact in her analysis – as are differences in understandings of the household in different cultures. In addition, the impact of domesticating ideologies in the sphere of production, in constructions of "women's work" are also not addressed in Smith's analysis. While I find this version of the world-systems approach useful, my own analysis attempts a different series of connections and theorizations. See Joan Smith, "The Creation of the World We Know: The World-Economy and the Re-creation of Gendered Identities," in V. Moghadam, ed., *Identity Politics and Women: Cultural Reassertions in International Perspective* (Boulder: Westview Press, 1994), pp. 27–41.

7   The case studies I analyze are: Maria Mies, *The Lacemakers of Narsapur, Indian Housewives Produce for the World Market* (London: Zed Press, 1982); Naomi Katz and David Kemnitzer, "Fast Forward: the Internationalization of the Silicon Valley," in June Nash and M. P. Fernandez-Kelly, *Women, Men, and the International Division of Labor* (Albany: SUNY Press, 1983), pp. 273–331; Katz and Kemnitzer, "Women and Work in the Silicon Valley," in Karen Brodkin Sacks, *My Troubles Are Going to Have Trouble with Me: Everyday Trials and Triumphs of Women Workers* (New Brunswick, NJ: Rutgers University Press, 1984), pp. 193–208; and Karen J. Hossfeld, " 'Their Logic Against Them:' Contradictions in Sex, Race, and Class in the Silicon Valley," in Kathryn Ward, ed., *Women Workers and Global Restructuring* (Ithaca: Cornell University Press, 1990), pp. 149–78. I also draw on case studies of Black women workers in the British context in Sallie Westwood and Parminder Bhachu, eds., *Enterprising Women* (New York: Routledge, 1988).

8   See my discussion of "relations of rule" in "Cartographies." There has been an immense amount of excellent feminist scholarship on women and work and women and multinationals in the last decade. In fact, it is this scholarship which makes my argument possible. Without the analytic and political insights and analyses of scholars like Aihwa Ong, Maria Patricia Fernandez-Kelly, Lourdes Beneria and Martha Roldan, Maria Mies, Swasti Mitter, and Sallie Westwood, among others, my attempt to understand and stitch together the lives and struggles of women workers in different geographical spaces would be sharply limited. This essay builds on arguments offered by some of these scholars, while attempting to move beyond particular cases to an integrated analysis which is not the same as the world-systems model. See especially Nash and Fernandez-Kelly, *Women, Men and the International Division of Labor*; Ward, ed., *Women Workers and Global Restructuring*; *Review of Radical Political Economics*, vol. 23, no. 3–4, (Fall/Winter 1991) special issue on "Women in the International Economy"; Harriet Bradley, *Men's Work, Women's Work* (Minneapolis: University of Minnesota Press, 1989); Lynne Brydon and Sylvia Chant, *Women in the Third World, Gender Issues in Rural and Urban Areas* (New Brunswick, NJ: Rutgers University Press, 1989).

9   See Ella Shohat and Robert Stam, *Unthinking Eurocentrism: Multiculturalism and the Media* (London and New York: Routledge, 1994), esp. pp. 25–7 In a discussion of the analytic and political problems involved in using terms like "Third World," Shohat and Stam draw attention to the adoption of "third world" at the 1955 Bandung Conference of "non-aligned" African and Asian nations, an adoption which was premised on the solidarity of these nations around the anticolonial struggles in Vietnam and Algeria. This is the genealogy of the term that I choose to invoke here.

10 My understanding and appreciation of the links between location, experience, and social identity in political and intellectual matters grows out of numerous discussions with Satya Mohanty. See especially his essay, "Colonial Legacies, Multicultural Futures: Relativism, Objectivity, and the Challenge of Otherness," in *PMLA*, Jan. 1995, pp. 108–17. See also Paula Moya's essay in this collection for further discussion of these issues.

11 Karen Brodkin Sacks, "Introduction," in Karen Brodkin Sacks and D. Remy, eds., *My Troubles Are Going to Have Trouble with Me*, esp. pp. 10–11.

12 Jeremy Brecher, "The Hierarch's New World Order – and Ours," in Jeremy S. Brecher et al., eds., *Global Visions, Beyond the New World Order* (Boston: South End Press, 1993), pp. 3–12.

13 See Maria Mies, *Patriarchy and Accumulation on a World Scale: Women in the International Division of Labor* (London: Zed Press, 1986), pp. 114–15.

14 Richard J. Barnet and John Cavanagh, *Global Dreams: Imperial Corporations and the New World Order* (New York: Simon and Shuster, 1994), esp. pp. 25–41.

15 For examples of cross-national feminist organizing around these issues, see the following texts: Gita Sahgal and Nira Yuval Davis, eds., *Refusing Holy Orders, Women and Fundamentalism in Britain* (London: Virago, 1992); Valentine M. Moghadam, *Identity Politics and Women, Cultural Reassertions and Feminisms in International Perspective* (Boulder: Westview Press, 1994); *Claiming Our Place, Working the Human Rights System to Women's Advantage* (Washington, DC: Institute for Women, Law and Development, 1993); Sheila Rowbotham and Swasti Mitter, eds., *Dignity and Daily Bread: New Forms of Economic Organizing among Poor Women in the Third World and the First* (New York: Routledge, 1994); and Julie Peters and Andrea Wolper, eds., *Women's Rights, Human Rights: International Feminist Perspectives* (New York: Routledge, 1995).

16 Amott and Matthaei, eds., *Race, Gender and Work*, pp. 316–17.

17 Women Working Worldwide, *Common Interests*, ibid.

18 Aihwa Ong's discussion of the various modes of surveillance of young Malaysian factory women as a way of discursively producing and constructing notions of feminine sexuality is also applicable in this context, where "single" and "married" assume powerful connotations of sexual control. See Aihwa Ong, *Spirits of Resistance and Capitalist Discipline: Factory Women in Malaysia* (Albany: SUNY Press, 1987).

19 Hossfeld, "Their Logic Against Them," p. 149. Hossfeld states that she spoke to workers from at least thirty Third-World nations (including Mexico, Vietnam, the Philippines, Korea, China, Cambodia, Laos, Thailand, Malaysia, Indonesia, India, Pakistan, Iran, Ethiopia, Haiti, Cuba, El Salvador, Nicaragua, Guatemala, Venezuela, as well as southern Europe, especially Portugal and Greece). It may be instructive to pause and reflect on the implications of this level of racial and national diversity on the shop floor in the Silicon Valley. While all these workers are defined as "immigrants," a number of them as recent immigrants, the racial, ethnic, and gender logic of capitalist strategies of recolonization in this situation locate all the workers in similar relationships to the management, as well as to the US state.

20 Assembly lines in the Silicon Valley are often divided along race, ethnic, and gender lines, with workers competing against each other for greater productivity. Individual worker choices, however imaginative or ambitious, do not transform the system. Often they merely undercut the historically won benefits of the metropolitan working class. Thus, while moonlighting, overtime, and job-hopping are indications of individual modes of resistance, and of an overall strategy of class mobility, it is these very aspects of worker's choices which supports an underground domestic economy which evades or circumvents legal, institutionalized, or contractual arrangements that add to the indirect wages of workers.

21 Hossfeld, "Their Logic Against Them," p. 149: "You're paid less because women are different than men" or "Immigrants need less to get by."

22 Westwood and Bhachu, "Introduction," *Enterprising Women*, p. 5. See also, in the same collection, Annie Phizacklea, "Entrepreneurship, Ethnicity and Gender," pp. 20–33; Parminder Bhachu, "Apni Marzi Kardhi, Home and Work: Sikh Women in Britain," pp. 76–102; Sallie Westwood, "Workers and Wives: Continuities and Discontinuities in the Lives of Gujarati Women," pp. 103–31; and Sasha Josephides, "Honor, Family, and Work: Greek Cypriot Women Before and After Migration," pp. 34–57.

23 P. Bhachu, "Apni Marzi Kardhi, Home and Work," p. 85.

24 For a thorough discussion of the history and contemporary configurations of homework in the US, see Eileen Boris and Cynthia R. Daniels, eds., *Homework, Historical and Contemporary Perspectives on Paid Labor at Home* (Urbana: University of Illinois Press, 1989). See especially the "Introduction," pp. 1–12; M. Patricia Fernandez-Kelly and Anna García, "Hispanic Women and Homework: Women in the Informal Economy of Miami Los Angeles," pp. 165–82; and Sheila Allen, "Locating Homework in an Analysis of the Ideological and Material Constraints on Women's Paid Work," pp. 272–91.

25 Allen, "Locating Homework."

26 See Rowbotham and Mitter, "Introduction," in Rowbotham and Mitter, eds., *Dignity and Daily Bread*.

27 Anna G. Jonasdottir, "On the Concept of Interest, Women's Interests, and the Limitations of Interest Theory," in Kathleen Jones and Anna G. Jonasdottir, eds., *The Political Interests of Gender* (London: Sage Publications, 1988), pp. 33–65, esp. p. 57.

28 Ibid., p. 41.

29 See Women Working Worldwide, eds., *Common Interests*.

30 Ibid., p. 38.

31 Ibid., p. 31.

32 Kumudhini Rosa, "The Conditions and Organisational Activities of Women in Free Trade Zones: Malaysia, Philippines and Sri Lanka, 1970–1990," in Rowbotham and Mitter, eds., *Dignity and Daily Bread*, pp. 73–99, esp. p. 86.

33 Swasti Mitter, "On Organising Women in Casualized Work: A Global Overview," in Rowbotham and Mitter, eds., *Dignity and Daily Bread*, pp. 14–52, esp. p. 33.

34 Jane Tate, "Homework in West Yorkshire," in Rowbotham and Mitter, eds., *Dignity and Daily Bread*, pp. 193–217, esp. p. 203.

35 Renana Jhabvala, "Self-Employed Women's Association: Organising Women by Struggle and Development," in Rowbotham and Mitter, eds., *Dignity and Daily Bread*, pp. 114–38, esp. p. 116.

36 Ibid., p. 135.

CHAPTER 28

Joy James

Radicalizing Feminisms from "The Movement" Era

In order for us as poor and oppressed people to become a part of a society that is meaningful, the system under which we now exist has to be radically changed. This means that we are going to have to learn to think in radical terms. I use the term radical in its original meaning – getting down to and understanding the root cause. It means facing a system that does not lend itself to your needs and devising means by which you change that system. That is easier said than done. But one of the things that has to be faced is, in the process of wanting to change that system, how much have we got to do to find out who we are, where we have come from and where we are going.

– Ella Baker

Roots

"The Movement" era largely existed from 1955 to 1975 and includes the black civil rights struggles, the American Indian Movement (AIM), Chicano activism, and Puertorriqueño insurrections, and militant feminism. During the height of the black liberation and black power movements, veteran activist Ella Baker's cogent assessment of the political contradictions of liberalism among black elites advocating civil rights distinguished between attempts to become "a part of the American scene" and "the more radical struggle" to transform society. According to Baker, "In . . . struggling to be accepted, there were certain goals, concepts, and values such as the drive for the 'Talented Tenth.' That, of course, was the concept that proposed that through the process of education black people would be accepted in the American culture and they would be accorded their rights in proportion to the degree to which they qualified as being persons of learning and culture. . . ."[1] For Baker, the common belief, that "those who were trained were not trained to be *part* of the community, but to be *leaders* of the community," implied "another false assumption that being a leader meant that you were separate and apart from the masses, and to a large extent people were to look up to you, and that your responsibility to the people was to

Joy James, "Radicalizing Feminism from 'The Movement' Era," pp. 73–94 and 200–4 from *Shadowboxing: Representations of Black Feminist Politics*. New York: Palgrave, 1999. Copyright © Joy James. Reprinted with permission of Palgrave Macmillan.

represent them." This precluded people from acquiring their own sense of values; but the 1960s, according to Baker, would usher in another view: "the concept of the right of the people to participate in the decisions that affected their lives."[2]

Political agitation and movements historically have increased the scope of black leadership; however, African American participation in political decisions has historically been translated through corporate, state, or philanthropic channels. A century ago the vision and resources of the American Baptist Home Missionary Society (ABHMS) allowed wealthy, white Christian missionaries to support the black elite Talented Tenth as a shadow of themselves as influential, liberal leaders and to organize privileged black Americans to serve as a buffer zone between white America and a restive, disenfranchised black mass. During the Reconstruction era, funding elite black colleges such as Spelman and Morehouse (named after white philanthropists) to produce aspirants suitable for the American ideal, the ABHMS sought to encourage the development of race managers rather than revolutionaries.[3] To the extent that it followed and follows the funders' mandate, the Talented Tenth was and remains antirevolutionary. Supported by white influential liberals, the Talented Tenth historically included women. It therefore liberalized or deradicalized the protofeminism of historical black female elites. Contemporary black feminist politics as pursued by elites imbued with the bourgeois ideology of "race uplift" evince the same antirevolutionary tendency as the early Talented Tenth. Vacillating between race management and revolutionary practice, black feminisms are alternately integrated into or suppressed within contemporary American corporate-consumer culture.

Yet as Baker noted, the 1960s ushered in a more democratic, grass-roots-driven form of leadership. The new "wave" of black feminisms originating from that time invariably connects with historical antiracist struggles in the United States. Black women created and continue to create feminisms out of militant national liberation or antiracist movements in which they often function as unrecognized organizers and leaders. Equally, their contributions to American feminisms are inadequately noted even among those who document the history of contemporary radical feminism. Emerging from black militant groups, African Americans shaped feminist politics. These sites of emergent antiracist feminism influenced the more radical dimensions of black feminisms despite their inherent contradictions. For instance, the Combahee River Collective traces its origins to political formations now generally perceived as uniformly sexist:

> Black feminist politics [has] an obvious connection to movements for Black liberation, particularly those of the 1960s and 1970s. Many of us were active in those movements (Civil Rights, Black nationalism, the Black Panthers), and all of our lives were greatly affected and changed by their ideologies, their goals, and the tactics used to achieve their goals. It was our experience and disillusionment within these liberation movements, as well as experience on the periphery of the white male left, that led to the need to develop to politics that was antiracist, unlike those of white women, and anti-sexist, unlike those of Black and white men.[4]

The Combahee River Collective took its name from the June 2, 1863, guerrilla foray led by the black revolutionary Harriet Tubman in South Carolina's Port Royal region that freed hundreds of enslaved people and became the first and only military campaign in the United States planned and executed by a woman. During the Civil War, Tubman, the first American woman to lead black and white troops in battle, headed the Intelligence Service in the Department of the South. Before making a name for herself as a military strategist and garnering the people's title of "General Tubman," the formerly enslaved African woman had proven herself to be "a compelling and stirring orator in the councils of the abolitionists and the anti-slavers."[5] Tubman's distinct archetype for a black female warrior belies conventional narratives that masculinize black history and resistance. Although males remain the icons for black rebellion embattled with white supremacy and enslavement, women also engaged in radical struggles, including the strategy of armed self-defense. As fugitives with bounties on their heads, they rebelled, survived, or became casualties of state and racial-sexual repression.

Despite being designated "outlaws" and made outcasts because of their militancy, historical or ancestral black women such as Tubman have managed to survive in political memory. A few have been gradually – marginally – accepted into an American society that claims their resistance by incorporating or "forgiving" their past revolutionary tactics for humanitarian goals. Tubman's antebellum criminalized resistance to slavery, like Ida B. Wells's post-Reconstruction antilynching call to arms, typifies a rebellion that later became legitimized through American reclamation acts. The contradiction is that the nation's racial progressivism seeks to reclaim black women who bore arms to defend themselves and other African Americans and females against racial-sexual violence in a culture that continues to condemn black physical resistance to political dominance and violence while it supports at the same time the use of weapons in the defense or expansion of the nation-state, individual and family, home and private property.

Seeking explicitly to foster black female militancy in the 1970s, without the reservations of ambivalence that national culture exhibits toward black insurrectionists, Combahee black feminists selected an Afra-American military strategist and guerrilla fighter as their archetype. Their choice of Tubman over her better-known contemporary, Sojourner Truth, suggests an intent to radicalize feminism. Truth, not Tubman, is closely identified with feminism because of her work as a suffragette and collaboration with prominent white feminists of her day. Tubman is identified with black people – men, women, and children – and military insurrection against the US government. Her associations with white men are better known than those with white women; for instance, she actively planned to participate in John Brown's raid on Harper's Ferry despite the warnings of the prominent abolitionist and profeminist Frederick Douglass. With this African warrior and freedom fighter as their feminist model, the Combahee River Collective emerged in 1977 to contest the liberalism of the National Black Feminist Organization (NBFO) that preceded it.

In its manifesto, the collective expresses its "serious disagreements with NBFO's bourgeois-feminist stance and their lack of a clear political focus" and offers an activist alternative.[6] The collective, which included feminist authors and educators Barbara Smith, Gloria Hull, and Margo Okazawa-Rey, would later organize against a series of murders targeting black girls and women in the Boston area. Combahee's black feminist manifesto emphasizes radical activism rather than liberal politics: "Although we are feminists and Lesbians, we feel solidarity with progressive Black men.... Our situation as Black people necessitates that we have solidarity around the fact of race, which white women of course do not need to have with white men, unless it is their negative solidarity as racial oppressors. We struggle together with Black men against racism, while we also struggle with Black men about sexism."[7]

Given the prevalence of antiradical bias in American society, and despite writer bell hooks's definition of feminism that evokes the collective's ideology, Americans must continue to wade deeply beyond the mainstream to retrieve critiques such as the following issued by the Combahee River Collective:

> We realize that the liberation of all oppressed peoples necessitates the destruction of the political-economic systems of capitalism and imperialism as well as patriarchy. We are socialists because we believe that work must be organized for the collective benefit of those who do the work and create the products, and not for the profit of the bosses. Material resources must be equally distributed among those who create these resources. We are not convinced, however, that a socialist revolution that is not also a feminist and antiracist revolution will guarantee our liberation.[8]

Ideology and feminist identity

Black feminists faced the challenge of how to maintain Combahee's integrative analyses – combining race, gender, sexuality, and class – with more than rhetoric, the challenge, that is, of how to express their critiques in viable political practice amid organizing in nonelite communities. Rhetoric notwithstanding, all antiracist and antisexist politics are not equally ambitious or visionary in their confrontations with state dominance and in their demands and strategies for transforming society by rechanneling economic and political power. Conservative attempts to bring "closure" to or contain the black revolutionary struggles that fueled radical black feminism such as Combahee altered the transformative potential of black feminist ideology.[9] "Closure" itself is likely an illusory pursuit, given the continuance of repressive conditions – impoverishment, abrogation of rights, racial and sexual denigration – that engendered revolutionary struggle.

Although the greatest opponent to antiracist and feminist revolutionary struggles has been the counterrevolutionary state (arguably, in the twentieth century, embodied by the United States),[10] black feminist writings often pay insufficient attention to state repression and the conflictual ideologies and divergent practices (from liberal to revolutionary) found within black feminisms. This may be partly due to the considerable energy that some focus upon the marginalization of black feminisms in European American and African American culture (as well as in African and Latin American cultures) and partly due to the often-obscured antiradical tendencies found within black feminisms.

Liberal, radical, and revolutionary black feminisms may be presented as ideologically unified and uniformly "progressive" while simultaneously being viewed as having little impact beyond black women. Sorting out progressive politics within black feminisms, we may distinguish between ideological trajectories that reveal the at times compliant, often ambiguous, and sometimes oppositional relationships of black feminisms to state hegemony. Delineating ideology works to place in context black feminist attitudes toward institutional and political power. In the blurred political spectrum of progressives that broadly includes "liberal," "radical," "neoradical," and "revolutionary" politics and their overlap, all of these camps change character or shape-shift to varying degrees with the political context and era. For instance, no metanarrative can map radical or "revolutionary" black feminism, although the analyses of activist-intellectuals such as Ella Baker serve as outlines. Some reject while others embrace the self-proclaimed "revolutionary" that manifests through rhetorical, literary, cultural, or conference productions. "Revolutionary" denotes dynamic movement rather than fixed stasis within a political practice relevant to change material conditions and social consciousness. As the revolutionary has a fluid rather than a fixed appearance, its emergence remains episodic. As conditions change, what it means to be a "revolutionary" changes. "Revolutionaries" or "radicals" are not disembodied; rather they are understood (and so definable) only within context. (As a result, the articulation of a final destination for radical or revolutionary black feminisms remains more of a motivational ideal; and the pronouncement of an arrival at the final destination is a depoliticizing mirage.)

Despite ideological fluidity and border crossings, some useful generalizations can be made. Black feminisms that accept the political legitimacy of corporate-state institutional and police power but posit the need for humanistic reform are considered *liberal.* Black feminisms that view female and black oppression as stemming from capitalism, neocolonialism, and the corporate state are generally understood to be *radical.* Some black feminisms explicitly challenge state and corporate dominance and critique the privileged status of bourgeois elites among the "left"; those that do so by connecting political theory for radical transformation with political acts to abolish corporate-state and elite dominance are *revolutionary.*

Differentiating between liberalism and radicalism – or even more so between "radical" and "revolutionary" – to theorize about black feminist liberation politics is extremely difficult but essential for understanding some limitations of "left" politics and black feminisms. Part of the difficulty in delineating the "left" of black feminisms stems from the resurgence of the right and its modification of liberal and progressive thought.

New terminology denotes the pervasive influence of conservatism, as "neo" becomes a standard political prefix for the post-civil-rights and postfeminist movements era. The efficacy of a rightist conservatism has led to the coupling of reactionary with conservative politics to construct the rightist hybrid "neoconservative"; the merger of the conservative with liberal politics to create the right-leaning "neoliberalism"; and the marriage of liberalism with radicalism to produce "neoradicalism" as a more corporate form of radical politics. Alongside "neoconservatism" and "neoliberalism" can be found "neoradicalism." All denote a drift toward conservatism. This drift has led to deradicalizing trends that include the hegemony of bourgeois intellectuals within neoradicalism and the commodification of the "revolutionary" as performer who captures the attention and imagination of preradicalized masses while serving as storyteller for apolitical consumers. Responding to revolutionary struggles, the counterrevolutionary, antirevolutionary, and neoradical surface to confront and displace activism, inspired and sustained by vibrant rebellions.

Neoradicalism, like liberalism, denounces draconian measures against women, poor, and racialized peoples; and, like liberalism, it also positions itself as "loyal" opposition to the state. Therefore, what it denounces is not the state itself but its excesses – prison exploitation and torture, punitive measures toward the poor, environmental degradation, counterrevolutionary violence, and contra wars. Abolition movements, directed by neoradicals, rarely extend their rhetoric consistently to call for the abolition of capitalism and the corporate state. Movements led or advocated by those representing the disenfranchised are marked by the appearance of the symbolic radical.

All black feminists, including those who follow conventional ideology to some degree, share an outsider status in a commercial culture. That marginalization is not indicative of – but often confused with – an intrinsic or inherent radicalism. Ideological differences among African Americans belie the construction of black women or, even more significantly, black feminists as a "class." Refusing to essentialize black women or feminism, writers such as bell hooks have noted the conflictual political ideologies found among black women. In 1991 hooks's "Must We Call All Women 'Sister'?" questioned feminist championing of Anita Hill that made little mention of the fact that the then Reagan-Republican had promoted antifeminist, antigay/lesbian, antidisabled, and anti-civil-rights policies at the Equal Employment Opportunity Commission (EEOC) under the supervision of Clarence Thomas.[11] The gender solidarity that surrounded Hill obscured her support for ultra-conservative policies. Prior to her courageous testimony at the Senate Judiciary Committee hearings – hearings that eventually confirmed Thomas as a Supreme Court justice – Hill had implemented reactionary attacks on the gains of the civil rights and women's movements – movements that had enabled nonactivists such as Hill and her former supervisor to attend Yale Law School.

Legal theorist Kimberlé Crenshaw has noted the consequences of African Americans' failure to distinguish and discuss political ideologies among black public figures. Crenshaw criticizes a racial uniformity in black solidarity that includes reactionaries. At a July 1998 gathering of black lawyers critical of the American Bar Association's invitation to Thomas to keynote its annual meeting, Crenshaw gave a scintillating critique of black support for Thomas. She contended that because of his race, African Americans paid little attention to his right-wing politics and so failed to distinguish between "conservative" and "reactionary" ideologies. (The endorsement by neo-Nazi David Duke of Thomas's appointment to the Court underscores the affinity right-wing ideologues felt for the Republican replacement to Justice Thurgood Marshall.[12]) According to Crenshaw, ideological distinctions eroded black opposition to former President George Bush's Supreme Court nominee, but if black Americans had maintained and sharpened the distinction between conservative and reactionary positions, more would have actively opposed Thomas's appointment.

Crenshaw's argument has merit. Conservatism has some respectability among black women and men immured in the "race uplift" of Booker T. Washington's black capitalism (even though they are not fully compliant with his prohibitions against competing with whites). Reactionary politics, however, hold no respectable public place among African Americans. Historically viewed as extensions of white supremacy and racial dominance, reactionaries have been considered anathema for black and female lives. Yet African Americans seem unwilling to publicly, critically discuss black reactionaries in service to the state and to distinguish their *counter*revolutionary service from the *anti*revolutionary disavowals of black liberals and neoradicals. (In similar fashion, maintaining distinctions between revolutionaries and radicals appears to be equally problematic.)

Just as blurring the lines between black reactionaries and conservatives politically accommodates reactionaries by reclassifying them as respectable "conservatives," some black feminisms have erased distinctions between liberalism and the radicalism that incited dynamic, militant formations (like the Combahee River Collective). Given that liberalism has accrued the greatest material resources and social legitimacy among progressives, the coalition of liberals and radicals to foment neoradicalism means that respectability has been designated to dual beneficiaries. Liberal black feminism garners the image of being on the "cutting edge" by appending itself to symbols of radicalism and hence increases its popularity as "transformative." Radicals are able to maximize their visibility and the market for their rhetoric via legitimization through association with liberalism. The terms for merger may be weighted toward the more privileged liberalism, and its offshoot neoliberalism, than radicalism or neoradicalism. Liberalism also allows black feminisms to increase their compatibility with mainstream American politics and with mainstream African American political culture.

From their strong fidelity to the Democratic Party (which under the Clinton administration increased police powers and punitive measures against the poor), it may be inferred that African Americans generally do not favor political "extremism."[13] Shunning reactionary or revolutionary politics, most black Americans support a progressive liberalism (left of center) that has a greater social conscience, and therefore moral content, than that of the general society. Yet this – and their sometimes outraged, and at times outrageous, condemnations of white supremacy – consequently places most African Americans outside narrowly construed conventional politics and allows them to be portrayed as political "extremists."

With centrism the conventional political stance, some black feminisms have reconfigured radicalism to fit within liberal paradigms.[14] Doing so enables a black feminist erasure of revolutionary politics and a rhetorical embrace of radicalism without material support for challenges to transform or abolish, rather than modify, state-corporate authority. An analogy for black feminist erasures can be made with the framing of a painting. The mat establishes the official borders for viewers. Often matting crops off the original borders of the picture. If incorrectly done, the mat encroaches upon the image itself and the signature of the image-maker. In framing black feminisms for public discourse and display, the extreme peripheries of the initial creation are often covered over. Placing a mat over the political vision of black feminisms establishes newer (visually coordinated) borders that frequently blot out the fringes – revolutionaries and radical activists – and allow professional or bourgeois intellectuals and radicals to appear within borders as the only "insurgents." With layered or overlapping mats that position rhetoric as representative of revolutionary struggle, the resulting portrait will leave liberals or neoradicals in the position of gender and race "rebels."

Reshaping radicalism

Although a great impetus for the development of black feminisms came from black liberation movements, antiradicalism within American feminism (as well as masculinism among American radicals) obscured black female militancy. Antiradical sentiment, which has led some black feminist writers to dismiss black women's ideological critiques of black feminist politics as "sectarian," raises the issue of the place of revolutionary and anti-revolutionary thought within progressive black feminism.

Black feminist liberation ideology challenges state power by addressing class exploitation, racism, nationalism, and sexual violence with critiques of and activist confrontations with corporate-state policies. The "radicalism" of feminism recognizes racism, sexism, homophobia, and patriarchy but refuses to make "men" or "whites" or "heterosexuals" the *problem* in lieu of confronting corporate power, state authority, and policing. One reason to focus on the state rather than on an essentialized male entity is that the state wields considerable dominance over the lives of nonelite women. The government intrudes upon and regulates the lives of poor and incarcerated females more than it does bourgeois and nonimprisoned ones, determining their material well-being and physical mobility and affecting their psychological and emotional health. Never the primary economic providers for black females, given the history and legacy of slavery, un- and underemployment, and racialized incarceration, the majority of black men exert little economic control over female life, although they retain considerable physical, sexual, and psychological dominance.

Radical black feminists' liberation theories address their nemeses: political violence, in both its private and public manifestations; counter-revolutionary state-police repression;

and liberal antirevolutionary discourse that portrays radical black feminism as an idealistic maverick in order to contain radical feminism. Radicalizing potential based on incisive analyses, autonomy from mainstream and bourgeois feminism, independence from masculinist or patriarchal antiracism, a self-critique of neoradicalism, and most important, activism (beyond "speech acts") that connects with "grass-roots" and nonelite objectives and leadership all mark a transformative black feminism.

Revolutionary action or radical sentiments of "The Movement" era were not discarded by progressives solely because they became "anachronistic." These actions proved to be dangerous and costly in the face of state and corporate opposition and co-optation. The attacks launched against militancy had to do with its effectiveness or its potential to effect radical change.

Today in American politics in general and in black feminisms in particular there occurs the "mainstreaming" of radicalism as a form of resistance to radical politics. Formerly radical means – such as protest marches and demonstrations disrupting civic and economic affairs – are increasingly deployed for nonradical or liberal ends such as the maintenance of affirmative action. Likewise, formerly radical causes – such as prisoners rights' activism and advocacy to abolish the "prison industrial complex" – are increasingly administered through conferences, research, and social service centers financed by corporate philanthropy seeking to influence policy objectives.

In corporate culture, gender and race are filtered through class to juxtapose and contrast "workers" and "professionals." To the extent that corporate culture has infiltrated US progressive movements, the polarities of worker/manager resurface to foster a resistance to or reshaping of radicalism embodied in a "corporate left." Those able to raise large sums of money through corporate largess to institutionalize their political formations and identities as astute "organizers," maintaining a political leadership that reflects the style of chief executive officers and mirrors state-corporate sites (among which academia is included), would qualify as members of the corporate left. Their status as sophisticated politicos often goes unchallenged because of the material resources they garner. Sites of the corporate left and their corresponding political styles are not known for being accountable to disenfranchised communities or democratic processes. Rather they are known for funding alternative entities to diffuse radical movements viewed as irrelevant by some progressives. Socialist Joan Roelofs argues that "One reason capitalism doesn't collapse despite its many weaknesses and valiant opposition movements is because of the 'nonprofit sector.' Yet philanthropic capital, its investment and its distribution, are generally neglected by the critics of capitalism. . . . Some may see a galaxy of organizations doing good works – a million points of light – but the nonprofit world is also a system of power which is exercised in the interest of the corporate world."[15] Whether through the academy, government agencies, or private foundations, an emergent "corporate left" has helped to deradicalize feminism and antiracism and thus antiracist feminism or feminist antiracism. Distinguishing between the "revolutionary" and the postmovement hybrid "neoradical" places a finer point on analyses of progressive black feminist politics and their contradictions.

Questions of co-optation and integrity are audible to those who listen attentively for sounds of political independence from corporate-state influence. The din can be confusing given that conflictual allegiances abound in American politics and culture. For instance, the oxymoronic wit of PBS "public service announcements" that validates corporate-state funders while broadcasting acquiescence to business elites reappears in progressive projects funded by state or corporate entities and severed from nonelite, community leadership. Searching for political independents, we find that liberalism competes with and censures radicalism while radicalism competes with and censures revolutionary action. Both forms of censorship seem to be guided by an amorphous framework of what constitutes responsible "left" politics delineated within a rapacious corporate world that funds the political integration of "radicals" on terms that follow, as a prime directive, the maintenance of stability and the accumulation of capital.

Corporate culture oils radicalism's slide into neoradicalism. According to consumer advocate Ralph Nader, being raised in American culture often means "growing up corporate." (For those raised "black," growing up corporate in America means training for the Talented Tenth.) A person need not be affluent to grow up corporate; he or she need only adopt a managerial style. When merged with radicalism, the managerial ethos produces a "neoradicalism" that as a form of commercial "left" politics emulates corporate structures and behavior. As corporate funders finance "radical" conferences and "lecture movements," democratic power-sharing diminishes. Radical rhetoricians supplant grass-roots organizers and political managers replace vanguard activists. Within this context, feminist "radicals" are discouraged from effective oppositional politics to social and state dominance and organic links to nonelite communities. Instead, they are encouraged as progressives to produce "ludic feminism" that, according to feminist theorist Teresa Ebert, "substitutes a politics of representation for radical social transformation."[16] Ludic feminism has a curious relationship to black feminisms because the latter has been shaped and contextualized by radical movements.

in the politics of "sisterhood"

In the late 1960s, liberal bourgeois feminism among white women gradually expanded to include black women. This emergent multiracial "sisterhood" transferred the nineteenth-century white missionary mandate – promote elite leadership to serve as interpreters of and representatives for racialized and marginalized nonelites – to white bourgeois feminists. The result was a political paradox. Black feminisms pushed white feminisms (in their various ideologies) to repudiate ethnocentrism and racism and so to some degree "radicalized" America's dominant feminisms. The more financially endowed white cultural feminism supported and "mainstreamed" black feminisms by rewarding liberal politics within it; thus, to some degree, black feminist politics was deradicalized by normalizing its liberalism. This logically follows the historical trajectory of white radical feminism in contemporary American politics.

Amid the political battles waged by white middle-class women in "The Movement" era, Alice Echols's *Daring to Be Bad: Radical Feminism in America, 1967–1975* notes three forms of activism.[17] First, there emerged the "politicos" who worked in civil rights organizations such as the Student Nonviolent Coordinating Committee (SNCC), antiwar and radical youth groups such as Students for a Democratic Society (SDS), and revolutionary or underground spinoffs such as the Weathermen. Out of these formations emerged radical women who became disaffected because of the sexism of male-dominated organizations and who, as "radical feminists," subsequently developed organizations, such as Redstockings, opposed to the state's dehumanizing domestic and foreign policies.

"Cultural feminists" accrued gains from the concessions that radical feminists were able to wrest in the 1960s; according to Echols, cultural feminists, as liberal feminists, benefited from the militancy of radical feminists whom they later excised in order to consolidate an image of respectability and to garner corporate support for mainstream feminism. Women such as Gloria Steinem, Robyn Morgan, and other founders of *Ms.* magazine came to represent the cultural feminism that, unlike its radical rivals, defined men, not the state, as the primary "enemy" of women. *Radical* feminists acknowledged that men needed to change sexist attitudes and behavior, writes Echols, but emphasized structural critiques of capitalism and the state. Radical feminists became increasingly marginalized and eventually supplanted by cultural feminists who expressed politics less critical of, and so more compatible with, the state and its financial centers. In fact, *Ms.*'s early funders were white corporate males who – while categorized as women's "oppressors" – nevertheless became the financiers of mainstream feminisms.[18] (Given their accommodationist politics and access to state and corporate resources, such feminisms, whether conservative or liberal in ideology, might be considered "state feminism.")

Echols's depiction of cultural feminism, supplanting radical feminism because of its complementarity with state hegemony, resonates with the black liberation struggles of the period she analyzes.[19] This analysis raises important questions about the aspirations and dimensions of today's black cultural feminism and its relationship to black radical feminism. For instance, we might ask if a cultural form of black feminism (one that essentializes or generalizes African women or women of color) functions as a buffer against revolutionary feminist critiques that cite capitalism and the state as primary obstacles to black and therefore female advancement? Can cultural black feminism exist as a hybrid heavily invested in political appearances of revolutionary symbolism and representations shaped by ludic feminism rather than political organizing with nonelites for revolutionary action?

If the answer to either or all of these questions is "yes" or even "perhaps," then race, gender, or class is not the radicalizing impetus or deradicalizing tendency influencing black feminisms. Political ideologies shape feminist assimilation. As it is more assimilable, liberal black feminism remains more likely to be promoted into the political mainstream as normative among gender-progressive African Americans. Like the general society, mainstream feminism allows scant political space for revolutionary antiracists, even if they are white feminists, whose militant critiques of state power contest the assumptions (and funding) of liberal feminism. Cultural or liberal black feminism wields more influence in bourgeois, European American feminism than revolutionary white antiracist feminism does. Compatible ideologies allow white liberal feminist politics transracial privileges that mask its alienation from or antipathy toward radical antiracism. New forms of multiracial feminism allow dominant white feminists such as Gloria Steinem to "privilege" black female political celebrities like Alice Walker over white female political prisoners like Marilyn Buck. Revolutionary, antiracist white women, rarely referred to by feminists (or by black militants and white antiracists), are even more isolated than the white radical feminists and groups described by Echols.

The low visibility granted antiracist revolutionary white women in mainstream feminism coexists with their marginalization in discursive "critical white studies" and "abolition of whiteness" and "race traitor" movements, where whites challenge the existential if not always material benefits of white supremacy. Often in feminist and political discourse there is little mention of whites who viewed racism, patriarchy, and economic exploitation as embedded in state power and so who as revolutionaries resisted the state. Few liberal feminists or antiracists know much about Sylvia Baraldini, an Italian national convicted of aiding black revolutionary Assata Shakur to escape from prison. She and white female revolutionaries Susan Rosenberg and Marilyn Buck (and black male revolutionaries), who were also convicted of assisting Shakur, are serving sentences of between thirty and seventy years. (Baraldini received an additional three years for refusing to testify before a grand jury investigating the Puerto Rican Independentista movement.)[20] Likewise, the case of Judy Bari, the white feminist EarthFirster!, garners little attention in liberal feminism, black or white or multicultural, perhaps because it points to the continuance of COINTELPRO (under the guidance of FBI veteran Richard Wallace Held) in policing white female radical environmentalists.[21] Bari, a nonviolent activist who died from breast cancer in March 1997, survived a May 1990 car bombing, which, according to her attorneys was never seriously investigated by the police and FBI. She offered analyses that connected FBI repression of the Black Panther Party and the American Indian Movement with the repression of environmental radicals. The meeting and embrace between Bari and Ramona Africa, who survived the Philadelphia police's 1985 bombing of the African organization MOVE in which 11 African Americans (including 4 children) died, reflect radical forms of transracial "sisterhood" and political solidarity.

Revolutionary feminist politics are more likely than liberal feminist politics to note the political ramifications of radical alliances for "sisterhood" and antiracist feminisms. Such politics are also more inclined to scrutinize coalitions between radical and liberal black feminisms and white radical and bourgeois feminisms. While there has been considerable discussion of the interracial conflict between black and white women, some focusing on collaboration between the two groups, there has been little analysis of the ramifications of cross-ideological coalitions between African and European American women.

For instance, initially US white feminists refused to participate in the Free Angela Davis campaign, one of the most publicized political trials in "The Movement" era, stating that Davis's case was not a "woman's issue."[22] The 1970 to 1972 campaign, co-led by black communist activist Charlene Mitchell, however, received an incredible opportunity to broaden its appeal and expand its base when Gloria Steinem agreed to chair the fund-raising committee of the National United Committee to Free Angela Davis. Steinem had by then emerged as an influential powerbroker and fund-raiser for institutional or state feminism. This made her a valued asset to some radical campaigns. On one level, this coalition between Steinem's and Davis's organizations appears as an act of solidarity in a sisterhood that transcends racial and ideological barriers. On another level, the association is problematic and politically confusing. That Steinem had previously headed an organization that received funding from the Central Intelligence Agency was public knowledge among progressives and Americans in general; according to Echols, Steinem responded to the disclosure of this information by *Ramparts* magazine by granting a *New York Times* interview to explain that she only worked indirectly with "liberal" elements within the agency. (Steinem's perception of what gains might accrue from such a relationship is of less interest for this discussion than what state police viewed as its potential benefits from alliances with liberal feminists).[23] The Free Angela Davis campaign was led by the Communist Party USA and supported by the Black Panther Party, nonrevolutionary organizations by 1971 whose "radical" politics mutated under state disruption of their internal operations and infiltration of organizational leadership and rank and file.[24] Both organizations advocated a militancy (and at times a patriarchy) seemingly incompatible with cultural or liberal feminism. Their curious alliance with anticommunist, bourgeois white feminisms may reflect either attempts to embrace feminism or a developing antirevolutionary sentiment.

The emergence of the "neoradical" persona as the symbolic rebel projects a form of cultural feminism that "radicalizes" conventional politics at the same time that it deradicalizes revolutionary politics. The "antirevolutionary" politics of liberals or neoradicals is not synonymous with "counterrevolutionary" state destabilization policies that include police repression, infiltration, and co-optation. Whereas the antirevolutionary also can be the antireactionary or antiright, seeking a centrist or center-left politics, the counterrevolutionary is pro-right or reactionary. Antirevolutionaries, though, may be incorporated into state or corporate counterrevolutionary initiatives. Within US feminism and civil rights advocacy, anticommunism is such a cultural pillar that progressives who embrace this ideology find expedient alliances with corporate-state power and funds tenable. White feminists such as Steinem (who with hundreds of other prominent people signed a 1998 *New York Times* ad calling for a new trial for death-row intellectual and black activist Mumia Abu-Jamal; and who with the *Ms.* Foundation raised funds for "anti-prison-industrial-complex conferences") have no monopoly on conflictual political personas that offer contradictory images of resistance and allegiance to the state. For example, after the death of former Supreme Court Justice Thurgood Marshall in the 1990s, media reported that while serving as chief litigator for the National Association for the Advancement of Colored People during the 1960s civil rights movement, he had supplied names of young SNCC radicals suspected of "communist sympathies" to the FBI. Marshall's anticommunism and antirevolutionary views rooted him in the mainstream with other progressives.

Conclusion

The legacies of black female radicals and revolutionaries contest arguments that state repression and resistance to it are not "black women's issues" or are too "politicized" for "feminism." Such legacies also contradict contentions that feminism is inherently "bourgeois" and therefore incapable of an organic revolutionary politics. Yet even the "revolutionary" is marked in a corporate culture (where commercials at one time proclaimed that Revlon Corporation made "revolutionary cosmetics for revolutionary women"). Revolutionary black feminism transgresses corporate culture by focusing on female independence; community building/caretaking; and resistance to state dominance, corporate exploitation, racism, and sexism. Emphasizing economic and political power rather than social service programs for the disenfranchised, it challenges basic social tenets expressed in "law and order" campaigns. It does not restrict itself to political dissent channeled through lobbying and electoral politics or accept the corporate state as a viable vehicle to redress disenfranchisement.

In the United States, the blurred lines among revolutionary, antirevolutionary, and counterrevolutionary politics allow for the normative political and discursive "sisterhood" that embraces conservative and liberal women of various ethnic backgrounds yet rarely extends itself to radical or revolutionary women. Adherence to mainstream political ideology appears key to any movement's general acceptance. Political marginalization generally follows challenges to repressive state policies (and critiques of female or feminist complicity in those practices). The revolutionary remains on the margin, more so than any other form of (black) feminism.

The symbiotic relationship between subordinate black feminists and the "white" masculinist state contests any presumption of a unified politics. Seeking a viable community and society, antiracist feminisms can serve as either sedative or stimulant. Conflicting messages about the nature of political struggle and leadership can be found within black feminisms, which function as "shadows" – both in the negative aspects attributed to them and in their subordinate status on the American scene. Ever present, often ignored but completely inescapable, their plurality is seen as monolithic and depicted as the antithesis of the "robust American" body. Fending their shadows as American alter political egos, black women paint varied portraits of the shadow boxer as radical: as lone warrior, successful corporate fund-raiser for and beneficiary of progressive issues, individual survivalist, and community worker receptive to the leadership of nonelites in opposing state-corporate dominance.

Progressive black feminisms face the predicament of struggling to maintain radical politics despite their inner conflicts. Yet this, after all, is the shadow boxer's dilemma: to fight the authoritative body casting the boxer off while simultaneously battling with internal contradictions.

Notes

1   Ella Baker, "The Black Woman in the Civil Rights Struggle," quoted in Joanne Grant, *Ella Baker* (New York: Jack Wiley & Sons, 1998), 230. Baker presented this speech in 1969 at the Institute for the Black World in Atlanta, Georgia.

2   Ibid. Harvard historian Evelyn Brooks Higginbotham documents that white Christian philanthropists such as Henry Morehouse and other leaders within the American Baptist Home Missionary Society (ABHMS) in 1896 promoted the concept of the "Talented Tenth" as black elite race leaders. ABHMS funded the emergence of this elite to serve a population facing severe discrimination and persecution following the aborted Reconstruction. ABHMS explicitly created the Talented Tenth with a dual purpose: to function as a model showcase for whites (and blacks) as a living demonstration that black intellectual and moral inferiority were myths and to counter revolutionary and anarchistic tendencies among an increasingly disenfranchised black populace. See Evelyn Brooks Higginbotham, *Righteous Discontent: The Women's Movement in the Black Baptist Church, 1880–1920* (Cambridge, MA: Harvard University Press, 1993).

In 1903 W. E. B. Du Bois popularized the term in *The Souls of Black Folk* with his essay "The Talented Tenth." A century after white liberal missionaries coined the phrase, the idea of the Talented Tenth is being revitalized by Harvard's black intellectual elites Henry Louis Gates Jr., whose *The Future of the Race* (New York: Knopf, 1996), co-authored with fellow Harvard professor Cornel West, and 1998 PBS/Frontline documentary *The Two Nations of Black America*, promote the formation of the Talented Tenth.

3   See Higginbotham, *Righteous Discontent*. Today, for US-based revolutionaries and political prisoners to exist as more than a cult of martyrs like the Gnostic Christians, the Talented Tenth, as "buffer zone," would grant the preferential option to the poor, imprisoned, and militant.

4   Combahee River Collective, "The Combahee River Collective Statement," in Barbara Smith, ed., *Home Girls* (New York: Kitchen Table: Women of Color Press, 1983), 273.

5   Earl Conrad, "I Bring You General Tubman," *The Black Scholar*, vol. 1, no. 3–4 (Jan.–Feb. 1970), 4.

6   Combahee River Collective, "The Combahee River Collective Statement," 279.

7   Ibid., 275–6.

8   Ibid.

9   For an example, see Patricia Hill Collins's discussion of organizing in *Black Feminist Thought* (Cambridge, Mass: Unwin Hyman, 1990).

10   US counterrevolutionary initiatives have been extensive and costly in terms of human rights abuses. See Noam Chomsky, *The Culture of Terrorism* (Boston: South End Press, 1988).

11   bell hooks, "Must We Call All Women 'Sister'?" *Z Magazine* (Feb. 1992), 19–22.

12   At a 1997 New York University forum on black women writers, on a panel shared with Angela Davis, Elaine Brown referred to former Us leader Maulana Karenga as an American "Buthelezi"; Kimberlé Crenshaw makes the same reference to Clarence Thomas in her July 1998 presentation. Karenga's Us was involved in the 1969 shooting at UCLA that killed Black Panthers Alprentice "Bunchy" Carter and John Huggins. Buthelezi is the South African Chief who was a formidable opponent to the African National Congress and the antiracist freedom movement, leading the "Inkata Freedom Fighters" in a murderous alliance with the apartheid police and military.

13 Accounts of the increased powers of state and federal police and the dismantling of welfare and economic support for impoverished peoples during the 1990s regularly appeared in progressive publications such as *The Nation, Emerge* magazine, *The Progressive*, and *Mother Jones*.

14 In *Black Feminist Thought*, Patricia Hill Collins erases black women's associations with radical groups. Citing the literary and political achievements of Angela Davis, Bernice Johnson Reagon, and Ella Baker, she fails to mention the *radical* organizations with which they worked (and for which they are largely known): the Soledad Brothers Defense Committee, the Communist Party USA, and the Black Panther Party for Davis; and the Student Nonviolent Coordinating Committee for Reagon and Baker.

15 Joan Roelofs, "The Third Sector as a Protective Layer for Capitalism," *Monthly Review*, vol. 47 (Sept. 1995), 16–17.

16 Teresa L. Ebert, *Ludic Feminism* (Ann Arbor: The University of Michigan Press, 1996), 3.

17 Alice Echols, *Daring to Be Bad: Radical Feminism in America 1967–1975* (Minneapolis: University of Minnesota Press, 1989). Echols's insightful text is somewhat limited by her failure to fully research and analyze the contributions of black feminist radicals such as Frances Beale, a founder of the Student Nonviolent Coordinating Committee's Black Women's Alliance, and Barbara Smith, a founder of The Combahee River Collective.

18 See Echols, *Daring to be Bad*, for documentation of initial funding for *Ms*. In 1998, *Ms*. magazine, with black feminist Marcia Ann Gillespie as Editor in Chief, became completely owned by women.

19 Echols's descriptions of the strife between radical and liberal feminists parallel to some degree the black liberation movement's conflictual relationship between revolutionary nationalism found in the Black Panther Party (which advocated an end to imperialism, capitalism, and racism, and "power to the people," not the police) and the cultural nationalism of Us and its emphasis on an "African" lifestyle. There was overlap between the two "camps"; for instance, the New York chapter of the Black Panther Party synthesized an African (American) aesthetic with critiques of capitalism, government corruption, and police violence.

20 Imprisoned since the mid-1980s (the United States has denied the Italian government's request for extradition or leniency), Sylvia Baraldini has spoken out, from her jail cell in Danbury, Connecticut, on behalf of African American death-row inmate and political prisoner Mumia Abu-Jamal. An internationalist and student radical in the 1960s and 1970s, Baraldini protested the Vietnam war, demonstrated for women's rights, and campaigned against apartheid and colonialism in Africa. Organizing to expose COINTELPRO, she was a member of the Committee to Free the Panther 21 (21 defendants who were acquitted of all charges after years of harassment and incarceration in New York). Parole guidelines specify 40 to 52 months incarceration for the crimes for which Baraldini was convicted; she has served over four times that.

During the 1980s, Susan Rosenberg and Sylvia Baraldini were housed at the Women's High Security Unit at Lexington, Kentucky. The unit was closed in 1988 because of an international human rights campaign that opposed its use of torture against female political prisoners. Both women were subjected to years of isolation in all-white subterranean cells, daily strip-searches, sleep deprivation, sexual abuse, and a complete denial of privacy, including male guards watching them shower.

Syliva Baraldini, Susan Rosenberg, and Marilyn Buck fall within the category of "political prisoner" as defined by Amnesty International, which documents over 100 political prisoners or prisoners of conscience within the United States. Amnesty International has also declared US citizen Lori Berenson a Peruvian political prisoner. The reporter, a former MIT student, went to Peru in 1994 to write about the Peruvian poor and the government's violations of their rights and welfare and was sentenced to life imprisonment by a hooded-military tribunal. Like Berenson, hundreds of Peruvians falsely convicted by Peru's military secret tribunal were never given written notice of the charges or evidence, adequate access to a competent lawyer; or allowed to cross-examine witnesses testifying against them. See Rhoda Berenson's Mother's Day article about her daughter, "A Mother's Story," *Vogue* (May 1997), 310–13.

The US government has condemned Berenson's incarceration. In August 1996, 87 members of the House and 20 members of the Senate sent letters to President Alberto Fujimori noting Peru's violations of international standards and urging its government to grant Berenson "a fair trial." Clinton met with Fujimori in May 1997, formally requesting that Berenson be granted a civilian trial. Despite the rhetoric of diplomacy, US military aid to Peru has continued. Currently there are no indications of a possible new trial for Berenson.

21 See Judi Bari, *Timber Wars* (Monroe, ME: Common Courage Press, 1994). Notorious for its anti-Panther violence, today COINTELPRO largely focuses on white radical peace or environmental activists and members of the Puerto Rican Independence Movement. Currently, the majority of US political arrests stem from antinuclear weapons or anti-School of the Americas demonstrations, while grand juries are used to derail Puerto Rican Independence activism. For evaluations of the political use of grand juries and the

policing of the environmental and Puerto Rican Independence movements, see Joy James, ed., *States of Confinement: Policing, Detention & Prisons* (New York: St. Martin's Press, 2000).

22 For more information, see Angela Davis and Bettina Aptheker, eds. *If They Come in the Morning* (New Rochelle, NY: The Third Press, 1971); Angela Davis, *Angela Davis: An Autobiography* (New York: Random House, 1974); and, Joy James, ed., *The Angela Y. Davis Reader* (Oxford: Blackwell, 1998).

23 Echols's summary of this "incident" bears quoting at length: In 1967,

> *Ramparts* magazine revealed that the CIA had subsidized a number of domestic groups including the National Student Association (NSA) and the Independent Research Service (IRS), an organization which Steinem had helped found. The IRS had been established in 1959 to encourage American students to participate in the communist-dominated World Festivals of Youth and Students for Peace and Freedom. Steinem had been the director of the IRS from 1959 through 1960 and had continued to work for the organization through 1962. Redstockings alleged that the CIA established the IRS to organize an anti-communist delegation of Americans to disrupt the festival. They also claimed that Steinem and the IRS had been involved in gathering information on foreign nationals attending the festivals. However, Steinem's own account of the IRS's involvement in the festival differed dramatically from the Redstockings' version. Shortly after the *Ramparts* article appeared, the *New York Times* published an interview with Steinem in which she admitted that she had known about the CIA funding, but claimed that she had never been asked to gather information on Americans or foreigners who participated in the festivals. According to Steinem, the IRS had encouraged Americans to attend the festivals in order to open up the lines of communication between the East and the West. In fact, Steinem maintained that the CIA's involvement was benign, if not enlightened: "Far from being shocked by this involvement I was happy to find some liberals in government in those days who were far-sighted and cared enough to get Americans of all political views to the festival. (Echols, *Daring to be Bad*, 265–6.)

In 1975, based on the *Ramparts* article, women activists in Redstockings published an exposé, hoping to stay the erosion of radical feminist politics before the more financially endowed cultural or liberal feminist politics represented by *Ms.* and Steinem. Echols's critique of the Redstockings "exposé" notes that throughout the 1950s and 1960s, "liberalism and anti-communism were coterminous" and that "Redstockings presented no evidence to support their insinuation that Steinem and *Ms.* were currently in league with the CIA" (268). Also see Barbara Leon, "Gloria Steinem and the CIA," in Kathie Sarachild, ed., *Redstockings: Feminist Revolution* (New York: Redstockings, 1975); and "CIA Subsidized Festival Trips," *New York Times*, Feb. 21, 1967, L33.

24 The Communist Party USA had been heavily infiltrated by government agents and decimated by the McCarthy era of the 1950s. At the time of the trial, it could not be termed a "revolutionary" organization nor could the Black Panther Party, although it began as a revolutionary community-based effort to counter police brutality only to be later crippled by infiltration, police violence, and a murderous factionalism (partly instigated by the FBI's COINTELPRO). See Ward Churchill and Jim Vander Wall, *Agents of Repression: The FBI's Secret Wars Against the Black Panther Party and the American Indian Movement* (Boston: South End Press, 1990).

CHAPTER 29

Leonie Pihama

Mana Wahine Theory:
Creating Space for Māori Women's Theories

Just by being Māori and a woman, who thinks about her life and her people – one is on the cutting edge. That is where Māori women live – on the cutting edge.[1]

Introduction

Aotearoa (New Zealand) is a colonized space. The colonial invasion of this country has, as is the case with Indigenous Peoples across the world, disrupted many of the fundamental values that underpin Māori epistemologies. As we are well aware, the strategies of colonizers to undermine Indigenous Peoples' language and cultural practices have been deliberate and calculated. This is without doubt the case in Aotearoa for Māori people.

The notion of collaboration for change is not one that has a high priority in many radical Māori circles. Where it is acknowledged that as a minority population in our own land the support from *tauiwi*[2] is important, it has been the experience of many Māori involved in movements for reclamation of our rights that those movements must and can only be led by Māori. This position is also taken by many Māori women who are seeking change regarding issues of gender oppression. Such a notion is inherent within Te Tiriti o Waitangi, signed in this country between Māori and the Crown on February 6, 1840. Te Tiriti o Waitangi is a crucial document in the articulation of Māori sovereignty within this country.[3] It also affirms and guarantees the maintenance of fundamental rights of Māori as the Indigenous people of this country. These rights are encapsulated in Article 2, which notes:

> Ko te Kuini o Ingarangi ka wakarite ka wakaae ki nga Rangatira ki nga hapū ki nga tangata katoa o Nu Tirani te tino rangatiratanga o o ratou wenua o ratou kainga me o ratou taonga katoa. Otiia ko nga Rangatira o te Wakaminenga me nga Rangatira katoa atu ka tuku ki te

Leonie Pihama, "Mana Wahine Theory: Creating Space for Māori Women's Theories" (2002). Reprinted by permission of the author.

Kuini te hokonga o era wahi wenua e pai ai te tangata nona te Wenua ki te ritenga o te utu e wakaritea ai e ratou ko te kai hoko e meatia nei e te Kuini hei kai hoko mona.[4]

The struggle for *tino rangatiratanga* as noted within Te Tiriti o Waitangi, is a struggle for Māori sovereignty, and as is the case for many Indigenous Peoples around the world, that struggle has been a part of the experience of this country since colonization. *Tino rangatiratanga* is an expression of Māori aspirations for self-determination, Māori autonomy, Māori sovereignty. As such it is expressed as a key objective in many Māori movements. For Māori women there has been an increasing movement towards validation and affirmation of our positions, understandings and theorizing from a distinctively Māori foundation. This chapter asserts that Western feminist analyses are inadequate in providing in-depth analysis of Māori women's experiences, and that there is a growing focus on the development of what is termed 'Mana Wahine Theory'. Mana Wahine Theory is a theoretical framework that provides analysis drawing upon Māori knowledge and in particular with a decolonizing intention in regard to the position and voice of Māori women. Theory is important for Māori women; however, it is emphasized that theory must be developed from our own place.

Western feminisms have been dominant in the explanation and analysis of gender relations in this country. The history of Black and Indigenous women's attempt to be 'included' within those explanations has, on the whole, been unsuccessful. In many instances this has meant a retreat by Black and Indigenous women from 'white women's' movements, and a reformulation as black women's groups. For Māori women, there has been a movement away from Pākehā/Western feminisms to a reclamation of Māori women's theories. An exploration of this movement is critical to this thesis. The development of Māori women's theories is not however contingent on the existence of Western feminisms. It is my argument that Māori women's theories are not dependent on Western theories. Mana Wāhine stands irrespective, and often in spite of, the existence of Western feminist frameworks. On the whole, Western feminisms have denied the existence of 'others' and have tended to serve the interests of white women. It is argued that there is a growing need for Māori women to be active in the development and articulation of theoretical frameworks that are more able to engage issues pertaining to Māori women, with all our diversity. It is my opinion that there is a need for Māori women to speak to and for ourselves; to focus our work on engaging the issues that are important to us.

It is my contention that given the current context of colonization within which we find ourselves, theories are needed that are able to engage the complexities of Māori women's experience and the discourses that have been presented. To date there has been limited discussion in regard to how those theories may be developed. Much of what has been advanced has come directly from Māori women. It is my view that this is not only appropriate but is essential to the articulation of Māori women's analyses. I do not argue for a singular theory. I do not argue that Western theories are totally irrelevant to Māori women's analysis. Nor do I seek to impose a framework on all Māori women. What I am arguing is that it is critical that Māori women take control of spaces where our stories can be told. This includes theoretical space. Our voices have been silenced for too long. The silencing of Māori women's voices has meant the silencing of our theories, worldviews. It has meant that Māori women's stories are able to then be defined as 'myths', and therefore some figment of the cultural imagination. The marginalization of Māori women's theories is such that we are constantly having to try and 'find' ourselves within the texts of the dominant group. We are forever trying to see ourselves in the images created by the colonizers. This has been the case in regard to the dominance of Western feminist analyses in Aotearoa and has led to an active debate by Māori women in regard to the usefulness, or otherwise, of Western feminist frameworks.

Debate over usefulness of Western Feminisms'

The label Māori Feminism is problematic for many Māori women. This problematic is located within an analysis that identifies a fundamental contradiction in the use of the label in relation to Māori women's analyses and theories of the world. Much of the criticism is based in an idea that the terms Māori and Feminism do not sit comfortably together, and that for some Māori women their experiences of Feminism and/or what is often termed the 'Women's Movement' has not been a healthy one but has mirrored their experiences of wider Pākehā society, where Māori ideas and concepts have been marginalized and denied and Māori women's voices been silenced.

> I've been involved in civil rights issues, socialism and feminism. Being a black woman requires you to have a split personality. The Women's Liberation Movement is racist, the anti-racist movement is sexist and the socialist movement is both racist and sexist. This leaves black women out on a limb.[5]

> The question of 'what is feminism?' took up a great deal of discussion. Feminism to me is a many splendoured thing. Its analysis covers all forms of oppression, not just sexism but racism and capitalism. It's not reformist like the Women's Liberation movement of the 60's and 70's, which sought equality and the 'laundry list' through the system. Being 'given' your freedom is hardly freedom; the power to give is also the power to take away. Feminism is a revolutionary concept that seeks to destroy that power, that questions the foundations that cause oppression – not ask for handouts! 'Feminism' in the white woman's movement touches only on sexism. Racism and capitalism aren't seen as relevant issues.[6]

> We are in fundamental tension with the project of white women. Where western feminism may have provided some useful analyses of patriarchy there continues the imposition of white matriarchy.[7]

Māori women, like indigenous women, black women and women of color worldwide, have consistently voiced outrage at being constantly located as 'Other' within dominant discourses, raising issues of difference and marginalization. Representations and definitions of Māori women have been, in many instances, historically constituted through the voices of the colonizer. We have been defined, painted, filmed, researched, imaged within dominant Pākehā frameworks and assumptions. The voices of Māori women have been marginalized or made invisible within the power relations that exist in our colonial experience. It is understandable then that feminism as a concept is viewed as problematic, particularly for Māori women who have historically been on the margins of what has been seen as a predominantly white women's movement. This does not mean that all Māori women have thrown out the term feminism. Ngahuia Te Awekotuku and Kathie Irwin argue that the fundamentals which underpin the notion of feminism are not unknown to Māori, and therefore to negate the term in its entirety would not be useful to Māori women.

Ngahuia Te Awekotuku notes that Māori women's work preceded feminism as Māori women. As is shown in the discussion of Māori women's movements, our *tūpuna wāhine* have consistently worked to shift the effects of colonization. For many this meant that their work was focused in the Māori community and therefore few joined the feminist movement. She raises the point that some Māori women find the term feminist a contradiction, and view feminism as an imported idea that is Pākehā and therefore has no relevance to Māori. Feminism, some argue, *imposes a foreign way of seeing, and of being*.[8] The strength of the antifeminist position for some Māori is noted in a prevailing belief that Māori women's involvement in feminism is 'un-Māori'.[9] Ngahuia disagrees with such a position, arguing instead that the term feminism can be defined by Māori women to be what Māori women want it to be, that our definitions are related to our own experiences and definitions of how we describe and analyze our oppression as Indigenous women in the world. Māori women have been oppressed, denied of economic, political, social power, and a feminist analysis can be used to view and explain what has happened. Like the need to redefine the term theory, it is therefore necessary to redefine the concept of feminism, drawing from the potential that exists within the term. In Ngahuia's terms feminism constitutes 'Woman-initiated political action – at its ripest and most elemental.'[10]

Similarly Kathie Irwin argues that there is no one single theory of feminism but that there are many.[11] She maintains that in order to understand more fully the positioning and needs of Māori girls and women it is essential to develop Māori feminist theories even when groups of Māori do not perceive this as necessary.

> The development of theories of Māori feminisms is an urgent task facing both the women's and Māori movements if the life chances and life styles of Māori women are to be improved. This assertion is likely to be denied by some traditionalists, to be debated but not seen as a priority by some activists, to be laughed at by some chauvinists and patriarchs, to be taken up by increasing numbers of Māori feminists. However it is received, it will remain permanently on the agenda of both movements.[12]

Ripeka Evans also argues for the effectiveness of Māori feminism in making change for Māori women. Again, as with Kathie and Ngahuia, she states that there are real differences between Māori feminism and Pākehā feminism. Māori feminism, she argues, is distinctive in that it is founded in Māori philosophies and values and because the outcomes for Māori women are not solely located in gender but lie in much wider political change.[13] However, Linda Tuhiwai Smith and Donna Awatere are more cautious in regard to feminism. White feminisms, Linda notes, while useful at one level, can perpetuate 'otherness' at another. Linda argues that existing feminist analyses fail to recognize the cultural and historical realities of Māori women.[14] She asserts that race and class may mean that Māori women's alliances with Pākehā women may at best be tenuous, reminding us that cultural institutions are sites of struggle, and therefore it is not surprising that some Māori women view Pākehā feminism with suspicion. She notes that in the building of a *wharenui* in a mainstream Pākehā girls school, 'issues of race and class differences tended to struggle against any potentially common interests of gender.'[15]

A similar theme was outlined in Donna Awatere's book *Māori Sovereignty*, where she explored the possible alliances available to Māori in the struggle for sovereignty. She writes:

> The first loyalty of white women is always to the White Culture and the White Way. This is true as much for those who define themselves as feminists as for any other white woman.[16]

Further to which, Donna Awatere raises a number of other criticisms of the ways in which Päkehä women position themselves as the voice for all women. Firstly, she argues white feminists assume a position of defining feminism for all women, while denying the struggles of Mäori women. The ability to control definitions is, she argues, a consequence of white power and privilege.[17] Secondly, in assuming a right to speak for all, individual Päkehä women are able to then view themselves as 'spearheading' a challenge to patriarchy that all will benefit from. The flaw in such an assumption is the underestimation of the strength of patriarchal institutions and the liberal belief that individual success necessarily means real change for all.[18] Statements such as this are not limited to Mäori women. Indigenous women, Black women, women of color have raised major concerns about the inability of white women to engage through feminism with the multiple experiences of women who are not white, heterosexual, or middle class.

Lee Maracle, a member of the Stoh:lo Nation, challenges the inadequacy of white women's theories to engage the issues for Native women.[19] She reminds us that the idea that white women are racist should not be a surprise, nor is the idea that white people create definitions that serve their own interests. The white women's movement is no different in this regard in that it is created and defined in ways that serve the interests of dominant group women. However, like Ngahuia, she argues that Indigenous women are a part of the struggle for emancipation of women and that we must define that movement on our own terms. It is a movement that is about the liberation of all from domination and therefore must be a struggle against all forms of oppression.[20] This is also indicated by Devon A. Mihesuah, who argues that the focus of white women on gender oppression and their overlooking of racial and cultural considerations is often alienating to Indian women.[21] What is also crucial for Indigenous women is that locating of gender issues clearly within the gambit of wider social, cultural, and political issues. Winona Stevenson of the Cree nation notes,

> I believe that while feminists and Indigenous women have a lot in common, they are in separate movements. Feminism defines sexual oppression as the Big Ugly. The Indigenous Women's movement sees colonization and racial oppression as the Big Uglies. Issues of sexual oppression are seldom articulated separately because they are part of the Bigger Uglies. Sexual oppression was, and is, one part of the colonization of Indigenous Peoples.[22]

Hawaiian academic and activist Haunani Kay Trask has been a consistent voice in the Indigenous women's networks bringing forward challenges to the limitations of Western feminisms and the need for Indigenous women to articulate our own theories and practices.[23] A key to the relationship of Indigenous women to feminism is the need to recognize that Indigenous women seeking to achieve self-determination or sovereignty work towards this goal as a people. For Haunani this means that Haole[24] women need to position themselves alongside Hawaiian people in the struggle to overthrow an oppressive regime; however, she points out that this is a rare and difficult alliance. The centrality of gender in white feminism and the limited definition of what constitutes struggle for women means that few Haole women are active in alliance with Hawaiian women in the wider struggles of self-determination. Haunani argues that in Hawaii Haole feminists have refused to support sovereignty movements and have defined feminism in their own interests – interests which fail to include the positioning of Indigenous women.

> In Hawaii, they see the oppression of women but they refuse to see the oppression of Hawaiian women as a product of colonialism. To grasp the nature of our oppression requires an understanding that haole – feminist, marxist, etc. – are part of the colonial forces.[25]

As with Māori women's critique of Western feminism, Haunani argues that the univeralizing of feminist issues as being the same for all women does not serve the interests of Indigenous women where issues of race and culture are critical. She argues that Indigeous women are exploited by both white men and white women, and that exploitation by our colonizers cannot be separated from sexual oppression.[26] Haunani emphasizes that the universalizing tendencies of Western feminism have reduced oppression for all women to a common denominator of gender, when this is not the reality of many Indigenous women. Nor is it the reality for many Black women and Women of Color. The publications *This Bridge Called My Back*[27] and *Making Face, Making Soul: Haciendo Caras*[28] provide article after article of analysis and critique by Women of Color, Indigenous women, and Black women. In her preface to *This Bridge Called My Back*, Cherrie Moraga discusses the analogy of 'the bridge' for women of color. A bridge is walked over, and walked upon, as are the backs of Black/Indigenous women and Women of Color. The symbolism of such an analysis is not lost on Māori women. We too know the state of being walked upon, of being walked over, of being trampled upon. Since the theft and desecration of Papatuanuku, the Earth Mother, by the colonial invaders of this land, Māori women have experienced 'this bridge called my back'.

In an open letter to white feminist writer Mary Daly, Audre Lorde highlights the invisibility of Black women in white women's writings and calls into question processes of selective marginalization of Black women by white feminist authors. In a challenging statement she questions Daly's use of Black women's writings:

> So the question arises in my mind, Mary, do you ever really read the work of black women? Did you ever read my words, or did you merely finger through them for quotations which you thought might valuably support an already-conceived idea concerning some old and distorted connection between us? This is not a rhetorical question. To me this feels like another instance of the knowledge, crone-logy and work of women of color being ghettoized by a white woman dealing only out of a patriarchal western-european frame of reference.[29]

What is most evident in the anthology *This Bridge Called My Back* is the fundamental agreement that Women of Color must of necessity engage the complex interrelationship of race, gender, class, and heterosexism in their analysis. This means that there is a clear place for feminist analyses that incorporate the intersections of all forms of oppression, and therefore all forms of struggles. For many of the writers there is a need to develop alliances with those groups that are able to engage those oppressive structures. The Combahee River Collective's 'Black Feminist Statement' outlines clearly a desire for analysis that is complex and which actively engages all forms of oppression. In providing background to the formation of the Collective it is noted that this group of Black women were drawn together by analysis that was antiracist and antisexist and grew to include analysis of heterosexism and economic oppression.[30] A key concern is also that of the need to actively address the racism of the white women's movement. This is a common theme through the writings of many Black women, Indigenous women, and Women of Color. Such challenges to racism in the white women's movement are heard internationally, just as is the call for Black women, Indigenous women, and Women of Color to focus upon our analysis from our own cultural, social, and political identities.

As the Combahee River Collective asserts, it is for Black women to realize the liberation of Black women. This must also be said for Māori women. An area of particular interest for Māori is that of *tino rangatiratanga* and sovereignty, therefore an analysis of the relationship of feminism to sovereignty movements is a critical one. It is also one that is fraught with complexities in regard to the positioning of gender, race, and Indigenous rights. This is highlighted by Devon A. Mihesuah:

> Indian women who participated in the takeover at Wounded Knee in 1973 washed clothes, prepared food, and stayed in the background while the flamboyant males spoke to the media. Deb Lamb's research on the takeover reveals that some Indian women could not have cared less about the opinion white feminists held about what appeared to be their subservient roles. Many Indian women concede that male American Indian Movement leaders were and are sexist, having learned misogynist ways of thinking from white society. Nevertheless, the women agree that combating racism against their tribes is more important than personal gain.[31]

Here Devon asserts the need for Indian women to define themselves in their own terms. That is necessary for Indigenous women if we are to represent ourselves from a position in our own context. However, articulating the need to focus energies solely on racism maintains an assumption that racism and sexism can exist separate from each other. For Māori women this is not an assumption that can be made, and to do so is to repeat the mistakes that we so fervently critique in regard to white feminism, that is the nonrecognition of the intersection of oppressive ideologies and practices. What this means is that many Māori women, while rejecting the singular focus on gender of Pākehā feminism, do attempt to engage the wider issues for Māori within a framework that is inclusive of race, gender, and class.

Māori women's involvement in the so-called 'second wave' of feminism through the seventies corresponded with Māori women's activeness in Māori sovereignty movements. Māori women's groups were clearly a feature of Māori nationalist movements through the 1970s and 1980s.[32] Powerful statements were made by Māori women in the movement, and these appeared in feminist magazines such as *Broadsheet*. It may be stated, however, that Māori women's involvement in both past and present expressions for *tino rangatiratanga* have often been overlooked by the mainstream media, and in fact Māori women's leadership in Māori communities more generally has often been denied. These issues are engaged by Geraldine Heng[33] in relation to Third-World struggles, where Third-World feminisms are described as having had a tenuous and often contradictory relationship with nationalism. She notes that Third-World feminism rose in tandem with Third-World nationalist movements, and that female emancipation is a 'powerful political symbol'.[34] In this discussion, Third-World feminism has aligned with nationalism and expresses a feminism that is directly relevant to its own context. Nationalist movements can, however, be equally antifeminist, and feminism can be presented by antifeminist nationalism as being: 'of foreign origin, and influence, and therefore implicitly or explicitly antinational'.[35]

The analysis from Geraldine Heng raises the contradictory nature that feminism may be constructed as within nationalist movements. Similar discussion is given by bell hooks,[36] Cheryl Clarke,[37] and the Combahee River Collective.[38] These issues remind us of the necessary complexities of Indigenous women's analyses, in that we are seeking to provide forms of analysis that are able to express issues of sovereignty, race, class, and gender in ways that recognize the interconnection.

bell hooks, a prolific Black woman writer in this area, challenges Western feminism to be more expansive in analysis. She asserts that feminist analysis must be open to the wider possibilities that are a part of engaging gender alongside analyses of race, culture, class, and sexuality. In a groundbreaking analysis of feminism, *Feminist Theory: From Margin to Center*,[39] bell hooks reminds us that feminism in America did not emerge from those who are most victimized and that feminist writers themselves wrote as if those women did not exist. The invisibilization of black women, women of color, Indigenous women existed both through sexist oppression and through the development of white feminism that centered on the 'plight' of the white middle-class woman. As such, feminism in America was constructed within what hooks refers to as a 'one-dimensional perspective on womens reality'.[40] Racism is inherent in such a positioning, and the failure to recognize that leads to the refusal to recognize and acknowledge the experiences of Indigenous women, Black women, and Women of Color. As hooks so powerfully writes;

> The idea of 'common oppression' was a false and corrupt platform disguising and mystifying the true nature of women's varied and complex social reality. Women are divided by sexist attitudes, racism, class privilege, and a host of other prejudices. Sustained woman bonding can occur only when these divisions are confronted and the necessary steps are taken to eliminate them. Divisions will not be eliminated by wishful thinking or romantic reverie about common oppression despite the value of highlighting experiences all women share.[41]

Angela Davis provides cutting-edge analysis in her writings related to gender, race, and class.[42] Her writing is strongly influenced by involvement in radical Black movements and therefore is theorized from a location where race, class, and gender are viewed in their interrelationship to each other. Angela Davis notes that from as early as 1895 Black women were organizing after having been 'shunned' by a 'racially homogenous women's rights movement'.[43] The contemporary women's movement continues its racially homogenous character through the ongoing assumption that Black women's experiences are marginal to a gendercentric analysis. As Angela Davis states:

> They have falsely presumed that women's issues can be articulated in isolation from issues associated with the Black movement and the labor movement. Their theories and practice have frequently implied that the purest and most direct challenge to sexism is one exorcised of elements related to racial and economic oppression – as if there were such a phenomenon as abstract womanhood abstractly suffering sexism and fighting back in an abstract historical context.[44]

For feminism to be useful for those women who have been rendered invisible there must be a serious commitment to the inclusion of wider issues that impact on Black women, Indigenous women, and Women of Color. Trinh T. Minh-ha[45] provides a discussion about the ways in which selected Women of Color become constructed in the position of 'specialness'. In such a position a white First-World women audience expects Women of Color to express their differences. Specialness and difference is affirmed only if one is able to paint oneself as authentic as defined by white First-World women.[46] The notion of specialness as the chosen 'Other' is one that is not uncommon to Māori women, particularly in regard to the white women's movement. Māori women continue to be published as 'special editions' and to appear on the fringe of women's conferences. Only select Māori women are viewed as acceptable speakers, and others, even when deemed appropriate speakers by Māori women, are often rejected by Pākehā women academics.

Few Māori women have published books either as sole authors or editors. Most literature published in Aotearoa regarding Māori women, and likewise women of the Pacific more widely, is edited by Pākehā women. As Linda Tuhiwai Smith has noted, Māori women have tended to be anthologized by others.[47]

The women referred to in this discussion have been instrumental in my own thinking about how Māori women engage feminism. They have each provided analysis of not only the ways in which Western feminisms have rendered nonwhite women invisible, but have done so in a context of recognizing the need for analysis that is incorporative of gender in ways that are connected to wider social, economic, political, and cultural realities. None of these women dismiss the need for focus on women's experiences; rather they promote analyses that position gender as interrelated to issues of colonization, capitalism, heterosexism, classism, and racism. For Māori women, such an analysis is absolutely essential as we live within a context of colonialism that has been both driven and justified by acts of racism and capitalist exploitation.

While it is important, as Ngahuia Te Awekotuku, Kathie Irwin, and Linda Tuhiwai Smith have reminded us, to utilize what is useful within Western feminism, it is also important to know more intimately the aspects of Western feminism and its development that have not been so good for us as Māori women. The critique of Western feminism is not solely located in notions of who controls the definition but also in engaging some fundamental tenets of the various forms of Western feminisms that exist from liberal to poststructural. In order to do that, however, it is important to outline the theoretical analysis that will provide the foundation from which the critique emerges. Lee Maracle, on the relationship of Western feminism to Indigenous women's developments, affirms the desire of Māori women to voice our own theories. She writes,

> The women of the world are re-writing history with their bodies. White women of Can-America are a footnote to it all. I am not in the habit of concerning myself with footnotes. I am concerned about us, though. White women figure too largely in our minds. Let us stop chasing them and challenging their humanity at every turn. Let us begin by talking to each other about ourselves. Let us cleanse the dirty shack that racism left us. Let us deal with our men-folk and the refuse of patriarchy they borrowed from white men.[48]

The movements towards Māori women's theories are an extension of what our *tūpuna wāhine* have laid down for us since the time of Te Kore. It is from this understanding that the relationship to Western feminism is engaged. It is not necessary to totally dismiss Western feminism. The concepts underpinning feminism do not belong solely to white women. Indigenous women, black women, and women of color have all voiced some degree of distrust in white women's movements. The distrust has often been in regard to the inability of white women to see and engage the racism within their own movements. There has also been strong critique of how white women, feminist or not, are benefited by acts of colonization and therefore are resistant to the need for an examination of colonialism and racism. There are Māori women who see the term 'Māori feminism' and recognize that the underpinning notions of affirming women's worldviews and struggling against oppression are not owned by Pākehā women. Māori feminism names a form of feminist approach that affirms Māori women naming our own realities and solutions. The critique of Western feminists' tendency to universalize all women's experiences within their own framework is one that is voiced by a range of Māori and Indigenous women. Women's experiences are socially, culturally, and politically bound, and must be engaged in that way. The notion of gender oppression as culturally bound raises issues in regard to the role of Māori men in challenging white patriarchal and internalized sexism. It is argued that Māori men have a role in challenging all forms of colonial oppression including those forms that may serve the interests of Māori men. There are few Māori men that actively analyze the gendered nature of colonization; however, it is argued that challenge to colonial patriarchy benefits not only Māori women but all Māori people in that it is a challenge to an unjust social form that has been imported to Aotearoa and therefore has no place here. Māori men must be called into account in regard to challenging not only racism, classism, and colonization, but also sexism. The challenge is clear; however, Māori women can't wait for Māori men to catch up, we need to continue with the struggle, and the affirmation of Mana Wāhine as theory is one part of that movement. Before looking any further I need to signal the many ways in which Māori women name their theorizing. Mana Wāhine, Kaupapa Wāhine, Māori Feminism are all concepts drawn on by Māori women. The naming of the analysis is an important part of the theorizing process.

Mana Wāhine

There are two key components of the term 'Mana Wāhine': the concepts 'Mana' and 'Wāhine'. Rangimarie Turuki Pere maintains that *mana* is fundamentally beyond translation. It is multidimensional and relates to notions that she describes as psychic influence, control, prestige, power, vested and acquired authority and influence, being influential or binding over others, and that quality of the person that others know she or he has![49]

The multidimensional nature is also highlighted by Manuka Henare.[50] According to Manuka, in order to understand Māori worldviews there must be an understanding of *mana* and its related concepts. As with Rangimarie Pere's description, Manuka highlights that *mana* cannot be translated as a singular English concept. Mana Māori is noted as being 'Māori wellbeing and integrity, and emphasises the wholeness of social relationships, it expresses continuity through time and space'. Mana is also referred to as 'generative power'; 'linked to powers of the spiritual ancestors', and implies 'purity as a potency'.[51] *Mana*, Henare writes, is connected to every form of activity within Māori society and is generated through collective relationships.

> Mana is a quality which cannot be generated for oneself; neither can it be possessed for oneself, rather mana is generated by others and is bestowed upon both individuals and groups. In the Māori world, virtually every activity, ceremonial or otherwise, has a link with the maintenance of and enhancement of mana. It is central to the integrity of the person and the group.[52]

Māori Marsden also notes the social relations that are central to *mana*, noting that *mana* is a 'divine authority' that is bestowed upon a person to fulfill particular functions. It is bestowed by the people and enhances a person's prestige to undertake obligations in social and political matters.[53]

The concept 'Wāhine' is translated in general terms as meaning 'woman'. Conceptually we can see Wāhine as being the intersection of the two words *wā* and *hine*. Wā relates to notions of time and space, *hine* relates to a female essence. The term Wāhine designates a certain time and space for Māori women, but is by no means a universal term like 'woman' in English. There are many times and spaces that Māori women move through in our lives; Wāhine is one of those. There are others. There are varying terms that relate to times in our lives and relationships. From birth we begin a journey through those many spaces. As such, the term Wāhine should not be seen as a dualism with the term *tane*, as we see in the constructed binaries of female and male that exist in the West and which are defined in biological terms. To acknowledge the many ways in which Māori talk about various stages of life is to recognize the complex ways that our people have always viewed roles and relationships. There are a range of terms within *te reo Māori* which all relate to differing stages of life and to the various relationships that exist.[54] Some relate specifically to female essences, others to the interrelationships between people. The point I am making here is that there is not, as we are often presented with, a simplistic dualistic or oppositional relationship between Māori women and Māori men, but there are varying ways in which roles and relationships are negotiated. This means that analysis that relates to Māori women cannot be simplistic, but needs to recognize that relationships within Māori society are multiple.

Mana Wāhine theory: reclaiming Māori women's theoretical space

Theory is identified as a tool that Māori women can use actively to explain and debate with the world. In my view it is crucial that Māori women define and control theory, while simultaneously providing critique of those non-Māori theorists that have defined theory within which we are supposed to 'fit'. We need to control our own theories of the world and construct theories that embrace the experiences and realities of all Māori women and not just a selected few. Mana Wāhine is identified as a framework through which we can develop theories that will support the projects of Māori women.[55] Kathie Irwin argues strongly for the development of Māori women's theories. She asserts a need to take from Western feminism what may be useful for Māori women, while simultaneously framing Māori women's theories within Māori epistemologies, *te reo me ōna Tikanga*. She argues the need to develop theoretical frameworks which allow for Māori women to position themselves within Te Ao Māori while providing for critical analysis and much-needed research into what is happening for Māori women now and what Māori women themselves determine to be important aspects of Māori feminist theories.[56]

This is a view that has been expressed by many Māori women. It is a call to recognize and acknowledge that Indigenous Peoples have been debating issues of oppression for many generations and therefore we as Māori women have a history of analysis that can be drawn upon in terms of understanding, analyzing, and explaining our position and context.[57] This is expressed powerfully by Kathie Irwin, who notes theory is

> a powerful intangible tool which harnesses the powers of the mind, heart and soul. It has the power to make sense of a mass of ideas, observations, facts, hunches, experiences. With the right theory as a tool we can take the right to our into rangatiratanga, our sovereignty as Māori women, to be in control of making sense of our world and our future ourselves. We can and must design new tools – Māori feminist theories, to ensure that we have control over making sense of our world and our future. This is a feminist position in which the artificial creation, inflation, and maintenance of male power over women is unacceptable.[58]

Māori people have a wariness of theory. This wariness, and at times disdain, is well deserved. However, as Kathie Irwin so clearly states, if we are able to define, develop, and control our own theoretical base as Māori women, then theory is a tool that we can use for our own interests. For the interests of Māori women to be catered for in theoretical discourse we need to ensure that our theoretical developments take a wide view of what is happening for Māori women. That then requires a framework that is able to place *te reo Māori me ōna tikanga* at the center alongside issues of gender, class, race, and sexuality. For Mana Wāhine theory there needs to be an ability to engage the wider contextual issues for Māori while also ensuring that there is a strong analysis of the specific ways in which Māori women are positioned in the world. This is crucial, as we are located within a societal context where Māori women often bear the brunt of government policies although, I would argue, they are holding up Māori society.

Ngahuia Te Awekotuku states that Māori women are making 'fresh inroads' in a range of areas. In the tertiary sector, new developments are occurring as Māori women create and teach courses specific to Māori women's knowledges, *tikanga*, and issues. This is happening in two languages, *te reo Māori* and English, and in terms of practice, research, theoretical developments, and presentations. As such Ngahuia has argued that Māori women 'are reaching a critical milestone in our own political growth, with the writing and discussion of our own theory and analysis'.[59]

I agree with these sentiments and argue further that the development and articulation of Māori women's theories is essential to the ongoing struggle of not only Māori women but for the well-being of Māori more generally. This assertion is made in light of the developments of Mana Wāhine that assert the need for analyses that are able to engage the multiple realities of our lives and therefore move beyond simplistic definitions or analysis. A key role for Mana Wāhine theory is to undertake the challenge referred to by Ani Mikaere of making sense of the contradictions that face Māori women daily. Ani has laid significant groundwork in her writing, drawing on a specifically Māori women's analysis to identify key problematics in the ways in which Māori women are represented.[60]

The assertion of Māori women's theories is not new. Mana Wāhine Theory has its foundation and origins in Maori knowledge, much of which is itself ancient. What we as Māori women are having to do in our present context is reassert our positions and status within our own communities as well as wider society. The status of Māori women has been seriously misrepresented. Mana Wāhine as a theoretical framework asserts that Māori women must be recognized in the many roles that are ours, and that includes our leadership, *rangatira* positions. Mana Wāhine is an assertion of our intrinsic *mana* as descendants of our ancestors, as holders and maintainers of knowledge. An underlying tenet of Mana Wāhine is that Māori women have always had critical roles in Māori society. With this as a fundamental understanding we can then undertake a process of examining how and why such an understanding is not presented in day-to-day, common-sense discourse about Māori women, and most importantly, whose interests are served in the denial of such an understanding.

For the Māori woman academic Kathie Irwin, the experiences of Māori women and the theorizing of those experiences need to be undertaken with both a focus on being female and being Māori, and those can be analyzed through Māori frameworks that incorporate at the center of analysis Māori concepts of the world. In promoting these ideas Kathie identifies that there is a need for Māori women to struggle against any beliefs that attempt to deny Māori women access to the necessary knowledge and tools that will enable us to take control of our own definitions and knowledge bases. In her article 'Towards Theories of Māori Feminisms', she argues that the tools of analysis need to be developed by Māori women:

We don't need anyone else developing the tools which will help us to come to terms with who we are. We can and will do this work. Real power lies with those who design the tools – it always has. The power is ours. Through the process of developing such theories we will contribute to our empowerment as Māori women, moving forward in our struggles for our people, our lands, our world, ourselves.[61]

The message is clear. It is for Māori women to determine our own theories. However, this cannot be done in isolation but within the context of what it means to struggle against patriarchal institutions and also against colonial oppression, for they are inseparable. The struggles for our people, our lands, our worlds, ourselves are struggles that are a part of our daily lives as Māori women, they are never about just being Māori or just being women but are about a combination of what those things mean. What this then opens is an idea that race, gender, and class are interacting in complex ways, and that any form of analysis needs to incorporate these considerations. The term Mana Wāhine Theory is seen as an umbrella term under which Māori women's theories can be located. I agree with Linda Tuhiwai Smith in her assertion that Mana Wāhine is an appropriate notion as any form of Māori feminism draws from *te reo Māori me ōna tikanga*.[62] Ngahuia Te Aweko-tuku explains that Mana Wāhine is not reactionary, it is not a response or reaction to male violence against us, but a process whereby Māori women are able to be pro-active in determining our future. It is also a process of rediscovering the strength of Māori relationships.[63] Mana Wāhine is a framework that enables us to engage in the rediscovery and pro-active work that Ngahuia contends is necessary for Māori. Mana Wāhine Theory refers to Māori women's analyses that encompass the complex realities of Māori women's lives. It is defined within cultural terms and in a context that affirms fundamental Māori values and the ways in which they are negotiated. As such, Mana Wāhine brings to the fore a need for analysis that will reclaim Māori worldviews in terms of gender and gender relationships. As Linda Tuhiwai Smith writes,

It is a strong cultural concept which situates Maori women in relation to each other and upholds their mana as women of particular genealogical groupings. It also situates Maori women in relation to the outside world and reaffirms their mana as Maori, indigenous women. Mana Wāhine Maori is the preferred Maori label for what counts as Maori feminism. It is a term which addresses both the issues of race and gender as well as locates the struggle for Maori women within two distinct societies.[64]

Notes

1   L. T. Smith cited in Ngahuia Te Awekotuku, 'He Whiriwhiri Wahine: Framing Women's Studies for Aotearoa', in L. T. Smith (ed.), *Te Pua 1* (Auckland: Te Puawaitanga, 1992).

2   *Tauiwi* refers to those peoples that have settled on our lands but are not *tangata whenua* or people of the land, therefore are not Indigenous Peoples.

3   E. T. J. Durie, 'The Treaty in Māori History', in William Renwick (ed.), *Sovereignty and Indigenous Rights: The Treaty of Waitangi in International Contexts* (Wellington: Victoria University Press, 1991), pp. 156–69.

4   A translation provided by Hugh Kawharu of this article is as follows:

The Queen of England agrees to protect the Chiefs, the Subtribes, and all the people of New Zealand in the unqualified exercise of their chieftainship over their lands, villages, and all their treasures. But on the other hand the Chiefs of the Confederation and all the Chiefs will sell land to the Queen at a price agreed to by the person owning it and by the person buying it [the latter being] appointed by the Queen as her purchase agent. (Ibid., 319)

5   Jan, cited in *Broadsheet* (Auckland: Broadsheet Collective, Nov. 1980).

6   Mona, cited in ibid.

7   Smith, 1992.

8   Ibid., 10.

9   Ibid., 11.

10 Ibid.

11 K. Irwin, 'Towards Theories of Maori Feminisms', in Rosemary Du Plessis et al. (eds.), *Feminist Voices: Women's Studies Texts for Aotearoa/New Zealand* (Auckland: Oxford University Press, 1992), pp. 1–21.

12 Ibid., 4.

13 Ripeka Evans, 'The Negation of Powerlessness: Maori Feminism, a Perspective', *Hecate* 20(2) (1994): 53–65.

14 Smith, 1992.

15 L. T. Smith, 'Getting Out From Down Under: Māori Women, Education and the Struggles for Mana Wahine', in M. Arnot and K. Weiler (eds.), *Feminism and Social Justice in Education* (London: Falmer Press, 1993), p. 73.

16 Donna Awatere, *Māori Sovereignty* (Auckland: Broadsheet, 1984), p. 42.

17 Ibid.

18 Ibid.

19 Lee Maracle, *I Am Woman: A Native Perspective on Sociology and Feminism* (Vancouver: Press Gang Publishers, 1996).

20 Ibid.

21 Devon A. Mihesuah, 'Commonality of Difference: American Indian Women and History', in *Natives and Academics: Researching and Writing about American Indians* (Lincoln, NB: University of Nebraska Press, 1998).

22 R. Jonson, W. Stevenson, and D. Greschener, 'Peekiskwetan' 1993 6 CJWL 153, at 159, cited in Ani Mikaere, 'The Balance Destroyed: The Consequences for Māori Women of the Colonisation of Tikanga Māori', unpublished dissertation, Master of Jurisprudence, University of Waikato, Hamilton, 1995.

23 Haunani K. Trask, *Eros and Power: The Promise of Feminist Theory* (Philadelphia: University of Pennsylvania Press, 1986).

24 *Haole* refers to the white American colonizers of the Hawaiian lands.

25 Haunani Kay Trask, *From a Native Daughter: Colonialism and Sovereignty in Hawaii* (Monroe, ME: Common Courage Press, 1993).

26 Trask, 1986, p. 177.

27 C. Moraga and G. Anzaldua (eds.), *This Bridge Called My Back* (New York: Kitchen Table Women of Color Press, 1983).

28 G. Anzaldua, *Making Face, Making Soul: Haciendo Caras* (San Francisco: Aunt Lute Foundation, 1990).

29 Moraga and Anzaldua, 1983, pp. 95–6.

30 Combahee River Collective, 'A Black Feminist Statement', in Moraga and Anzaldua, 1983, p. 212.

31 Ibid., 41.

32 Recently at a dinner held by one of the few remaining Māori women's groups from that time, Amorangi, it was noted that at least 10 Māori women's groups were formed through this time period.

33 Geraldine Heng, ' "A Great Way to Fly": Nationalism, the State, and the Varieties of Third-World Feminism', in M. J. Alexander and C. T. Mohanty (eds.), *Feminist Genealogies, Colonial Legacies, Democratic Futures* (New York: Routledge, 1997).

34 Ibid., 31.

35 Ibid., 34.

36 b. hooks, *Yearning: Race, Gender and Cultural Politics* (Boston: South End Press, 1990).

37 Cheryl Clarke, 'Lesbianism: An Act of Resistance', in Moraga and Anzaldua, 1983, pp. 128–37.

38 Combahee River Collective, 1983.

39 b. hooks, *Feminist Theory: From Margin to Center* (Boston: South End Press, 1984).

40 Ibid., 2.

41 Ibid., 44.

42 Angela Y. Davis, *Women, Culture and Politics* (New York: The Women's Press, 1984).

43 Māori women also sought involvement in the women's movement in Aotearoa through the late nineteenth century.

44 Davis, 1984, p. 18.

45 Trinh T. Minh-ha, *Woman, Native, Other: Writing Postcoloniality and Feminism* (Bloomington: Indiana University Press, 1989). This is perhaps an example of who defines what is 'appropriate' writing in terms of

feminist publications: Minh-ha attempted 33 times to have her book published before being successful (personal communication).

46   Ibid.

47   Smith, 1993.

48   Maracle, 1996, p. 139.

49   Rangimarie Turuki Pere, *Te Wheke: A Celebration of Infinite Wisdom* (Gisborne: Ao Ako Global Learning New Zealand Ltd., 1991).

50   Manuka Henare, *Ngä Tikanga me ngä Ritenga o te ao Mäori: Standards and Foundations of Mäori Society,* Report of the Royal Commission on Social Policy, vol. III, part 1 (Wellington: Government Printer, 1988).

51   Ibid., 16.

52   Ibid., 18.

53   Mäori Marsden, *The Natural World and Natural Resources: Mäori Value Systems and Perspectives* (Wellington: Ministry of the Environment, 1988).

54   *Kotiro, hine, tamawähine, tuakana, teina, tamahine, tuahine, Wähine, whaea, ruahine, juia, kaumätua,* are all terms that relate to different phases of the life of a Mäori girl or woman.

55   Te Awekotuku, 1992; Smith, 1992; Irwin, 1992. R. Evans, 'Mäori Women as Agents of Change', paper presented to Winter Lecture Series, University of Auckland, reprinted in *Te Pua,* vol. 3, no. 1 (Auckland: Te Puawaitanga, 1993). L. Pihama and D. Mara, 'Gender Relations in Education', in E. Coxon, K. Jenkins, J. Marshall, and L. Massey (eds.), *The Politics of Learning and Teaching in Aotearoa – New Zealand* (Palmerston North: Dunmore Press, 1994), pp. 215–50. Toni-Kristin Liddell, 'Mahuika: He Ahi Komau: The Post-Colonial Invisibilisation of Mana Wahine in Maori Mythology', unpublished Master of Arts dissertation, University of Auckland, Auckland.

56   Irwin, 1992.

57   Smith, 1992.

58   Irwin, 1992, p. 5.

59   Te Awekotuku, 1992, p. 12.

60   Mikaere, 1995.

61   Irwin, 1992, p. 5.

62   Ibid., 58.

63   Te Awekotuku, 1992.

64   Ibid., 62.

CHAPTER 30

Tahmeena Faryal

Revolutionary Association of Women in Afghanistan (RAWA): Women Working for Freedom

On behalf of RAWA, I am really grateful to the *News & Letters* Committee, the Chicago Foundation for Women and all the other co-sponsoring groups. I can't name each and every one of them, but I hope they all accept most heartfelt thanks for all their efforts.

By now I assume everyone knows about Afghanistan and what's going on in that country. But still people may not know how all this tragedy began in Afghanistan. Because of what they get from the media, many here might think that the tragedies in Afghanistan, especially for women, begin with Taliban.

Usually there are questions: Why don't the people of Afghanistan rise up? Are these atrocities accepted by the people, do they represent their culture and tradition or religion?

I hope to address some of these issues this evening. I will have to go a bit into the history of Afghanistan, which is important in relation to what has been happening since the fundamentalists took power, and to what is happening now and after the September 11 events.

The Afghan tragedy

The tragedy of Afghanistan began with the Soviet invasion in 1979. Had they not invaded Afghanistan, we would not have had the fundamentalists, the *jihadi* bands now in the Northern Alliance. We would not have had the Taliban and Osama bin Laden and the September 11 incidents.

As you know, Afghanistan has a very key position as a crossroads between central Asia, south Asia and the Middle East. Because of its importance in that region of the world, it has been invaded by different countries and powers throughout its more than 5,000 years of history.

The people of Afghanistan always rose against these invasions, fought and defeated them with their bare hands. Unfortunately, Russia had not learned from that history and

Tahmeena Faryal (2002), "Revolutionary Association of Women in Afghanistan (RAWA): Women Working for Freedom," *Against the Current*, vol. XVI, no. 6 (Jan.–Feb. 2002), pp. 5–8. Reprinted by permission of Against the Current.

thought they would be able to occupy Afghanistan easily and achieve their other goals in the world.

From the very first day, the people of Afghanistan rose against the Soviets in different parts of the country. The war against the Soviets lasted ten years. As a result, we lost more than two million people. More than five million people became refugees in different countries, mainly the two neighboring countries of Iran and Pakistan; and around five million people were disabled.

While the Russians came to Afghanistan with direct military invasion, other countries such as Pakistan, Iran, Saudi Arabia, the United States, France and other countries had their hands indirectly in the situation.

They supported the fundamentalists with a sole purpose: to enable them to fight against Russia and make Afghanistan a Vietnam for Russia. Obviously, that was without any attention to the fact that one day these fundamentalists would take power in Afghanistan, and given their nature, what would happen to the people of that country.

These fundamentalists then and now are all misogynists, anti-civilization, anti-democracy, terrorists, and dependent on foreign countries. As RAWA had predicted, all the tragedies happened when the fundamentalists took power in 1992.

Unfortunately, in the beginning people thought they would be better than the Soviets and their puppet regime, as they came in the name of Islamic revolution. The people of Afghanistan made the same mistake as the people of Iran when Khomeini also came under the name of Islamic revolution.

But soon, because of the crimes they committed against humanity, people realized they were worse than the Soviets and their puppet regime. From 1992 to 1996, the criminals were known more as *jihadis*. (During the Cold War they were known as *mujahadeen*, which means about the same thing, those who fight for god.)

They committed crimes that we had never before witnessed in Afghanistan and as a result of the internal fighting – there were eight parties all of which wanted to keep the power and control the country – 70 to 80% of the capital city of Kabul was totally destroyed.

That destruction also occurred in other main cities where they had their strongholds and were fighting against each other like cats and dogs. The hospitals, schools and museums – and Afghanistan had some of the best museums in the world because of its very ancient history – were looted and destroyed by them.

Their first and easiest victims were the innocent women of Afghanistan. There were many cases of rape, forced marriages, and abduction of women. Many women killed themselves because they did not want to be married by force to one of those fundamentalist commanders. Fathers killed their own daughters because they didn't want them to be married to those fundamentalists.

But what makes that time even more tragic was that it never got media coverage, and that the regime was recognized by the international community. I don't think the Afghan people will forgive the international community for that. And RAWA, as representative of half the population, asks why the most brutal, misogynist and criminal regime was recognized by the international community.

Unfortunately, it was only RAWA that covered the atrocities and crimes through its publications, and held many demonstrations in order to expose and condemn these atrocities, from a place that was and is obviously still not safe for us, Pakistan, because we wanted people to know.

The different countries involved in Afghanistan, mainly because of building the pipeline there, realized that they were not able to achieve their objectives. So they looked for another force to work with. And that force (or movement as they call themselves) was the Taliban.

Taliban means religious students who are trained and supported in Pakistani religious schools called *madrassas*. This began during the Cold War. Most of them were orphans of the resistance war. But at a very young age they were taken to those religious schools and brainwashed, and especially brainwashed about women.

During their many years of religious education, they lived with other boys and all their teachers were men. They never had the experience of living in a normal family environment. And that was the main reason that when they took power they imposed all the restrictions on women with such impunity.

At first, the Taliban emerged in some southern parts of Afghanistan in 1994. Then in 1996 they seized control of the capital city and advanced from there to take many parts of the country away from the other fundamentalists, because the people of Afghanistan were so tired and fed up with the other groups and thought the Taliban would be better.

The Taliban came under the banner of establishing peace and security and stability, which was what people needed. But instead they imposed a list of restrictions, not only against women but also many general restrictions.

Women and men imprisoned

Half of the population under the Taliban do not have the right to an education. The educational institutions were called gateways to hell.

Women do not have the right to work. Before the fundamentalists, women in urban areas used to take part actively in the society. We had 40% women doctors, 60% female teachers, including university teachers. More than half of the university students were women. Overnight, they were ordered to stay at home and not work any more.

In the capital city of Kabul alone, there are more than 70,000 widows. Those who had lost their husbands and other family members could lead a decent life when they had jobs. After they were ordered not to work, they had to go to beggary or prostitution in order to survive and feed their children, or just experience a gradual death or see their children dying before their very eyes.

They are all ordered to be fully covered with the veil, the *burqa*. I brought one here, and you are welcome to try it on later if you wish. They are even ordered to paint their windows dark so they can't be seen by men from outside the house. They are not allowed to wear shoes that make noise or colorful clothing as, according to the Taliban, they would attract male attention to themselves.

As I mentioned, there are many restrictions on men. They have to have long beards if they go outside. They also have to be dressed in traditional clothing. If the Taliban finds any man dressed in Western-style clothing, he can be beaten or put into prison.

They have ordered the entire male population to pray five times a day in the mosque. In that prescribed time of praying, if any man is found walking on the street he can be beaten or imprisoned, or insulted in public.

It doesn't matter if he is ill or very old. We got an interesting report that the Taliban had beaten up a 70-year-old father because at the time of prayer he wasn't in the mosque because he was sick. He was beaten by a 17- or 18-year-old Iranian Talib, the age of his grandson.

Obviously, he could not bear that humiliation. He couldn't do anything back. But when he came home he said, I will shave my beard with wine – the beard shows the force of an Afghan man and wine is forbidden in Islam – so in order to show his anger, he did that.

They even go to people's homes searching for tapes and TVs and VCRs. If they find any, they hang them on the trees in the streets to show people that those are instruments of Satan, as they call them.

After more than two decades of war and with all these restrictions on people, especially women, the majority of the population today in Afghanistan suffers from mental and psychological problems.

According to a study by Physicians for Human Rights, 90% of Afghan women suffer from mental and psychological problems – and that study was done in 1997. So by now in this environment, if it isn't 100% it is 99% of women suffering this way. It will take a very, very long time to bring these people to a normal life and revive them and their minds.

The roots of September 11

From the very beginning, RAWA had warned the many different countries creating and supporting the fundamentalists. We warned that the Taliban regime wouldn't just be a danger to that region, but to the world, and to the countries that once created and supported them. Unfortunately, on September 11 that's what happened.

With the loss of thousands of innocent lives, attention was drawn to Afghanistan, a country which for years Amnesty International called the largest forgotten tragedy. If September 11 hadn't happened, it would still be the largest forgotten tragedy today.

It is always our question: Why? Is it because the people of Afghanistan did not deserve freedom, did not deserve lives, do not deserve democracy? Is it because they are not human beings? If we believe in equal rights for people, and we beat the drum of democracy and human rights, there should have been some practical steps years ago toward ending the human rights violations in Afghanistan.

Unfortunately, all the United Nations did was to express concern about the situation and try to bring the warring factions together and ask them to form a unified government. We knew that would never happen; they are too hostile toward each other and would never form a unified government. Even if they did, it would be yet another catastrophe for the people of Afghanistan.

Against terrorism and bombing

RAWA said that the combat against terrorism should have started many years ago. But we don't think the bombing is the solution . . . If today they get rid of Osama bin Laden and some terrorist camps in Afghanistan, tomorrow there will be hundreds more of them. There is always the danger and possibility that the Pakistan government will be toppled by fundamentalists.

Another issue that is very scary – and people in Afghanistan are already terrified – is the Northern Alliance. It is well-documented by Amnesty International and Human Rights Watch, the State Department itself, and organizations such as RAWA that crimes and atrocities occurred when the groups now in the Northern Alliance had power from 1992 to 1996.

Again, there is no concern for the people of Afghanistan, especially the women in our country. If once again they take the power, the same crimes and atrocities will happen. The different groups in the Northern Alliance have come together because they have a common enemy, the Taliban. But if tomorrow they take power, these different groups will again start fighting with each other. And again the people of Afghanistan will be the victims.

RAWA's struggle

But there has also been resistance. Women under the Taliban are not allowed to go on the streets alone; they have to be accompanied by a male relative. But if you go to Afghanistan you will find many women on the streets alone.

This is resistance begun by women who took the risk of going out alone because they didn't have any other option. They had lost all the male breadwinners who could accompany them. There are cases where women were beaten in public, put into prison, but still they didn't give up.

There are thousands of home-based classes run by women as individuals in different parts of Afghanistan. Since they banned education for women, this is the only option for many people to educate their children, and for many women to earn a decent living rather than beggary.

Some of these classes have been discovered by the Taliban. The teachers were put in prison or beaten up in front of the students. But again they wouldn't give up.

The main visible and mobilized form of resistance that I am happy to talk about is the work and the struggle of RAWA. It's actually the oldest women's group in Afghanistan.

It was established in 1977; its founding leader, Mina, was assassinated in 1987 by KGB agents with the help of an Afghan fundamentalist group in Pakistan. They thought with her assassination they would stop RAWA and the women's movement in Afghanistan.

In the beginning, RAWA was not a political organization. It was an organization of women struggling for women's rights in Afghanistan, even before the Soviet invasion or the fundamentalists. Particularly in the rural areas, women did not enjoy some of their basic rights. There was a need for such an independent organization to be established to struggle for those rights.

We do not have national emancipation. We cannot demand simply women's emancipation. RAWA took part in the war of resistance from Pakistan, along with the people of Afghanistan, mainly by establishing schools, a hospital, and some other projects for women and children.

We had to transfer the bulk of our activities to Pakistan because the situation in Afghanistan was too risky to operate there, although some members did remain in Afghanistan. Some are there now, in the present situation.

Through various activities, such as demonstrations or our publications and later our web site (www.rawa.org), we tried to expose and condemn the criminal nature of the Taliban. Unfortunately, RAWA was the only women's organization in Afghanistan which took this responsibility. It has always been alone in exposing the crimes and the nature of the different fundamentalist groups.

Obviously, that's taking a great risk. Since its inception, RAWA has been an underground organization, not only in Afghanistan but also in Pakistan, since Pakistan has been supportive toward the fundamentalists.

RAWA has a number of humanitarian projects. Mainly in the educational field, income-generating projects, and mobile health clinics. RAWA had a hospital in one of the cities of Pakistan, which served 300–400 women and children a day.

We ran that hospital for many years, especially during the Soviet war. But after some of the NGOs that supported the hospital stopped their support, RAWA couldn't run it anymore and we had to close it down. We are hopeful now that we can soon reopen the hospital thanks to our supporters, mainly in this country, who are trying to raise the money to enable RAWA to reopen this hospital.

RAWA has many secret home-based classes for girls, as well as literacy classes for women, inside Afghanistan. And we run schools for refugee children in Pakistan, mainly in the refugee camps. It has income-generating projects mainly for widows who, as I mentioned, have no other means to survive except beggary and prostitution.

These income-generating projects are usually carpet weaving or embroidery and other handicrafts. RAWA provides them with raw materials and helps them find a market and sell their products.

The mobile health teams are in different areas in Afghanistan and refugee camps. The health team is usually composed of one or two doctors, sometimes more than that, and a few nurses. The team spends a day in a remote village in Afghanistan or in a refugee camp where people have no access to a hospital, doctors or medicine. They treat as many people as possible. Obviously everything is free, including the medicine.

Lack of health care facilities is one of the main problems for the people in Afghanistan. People die from very treatable diseases. Fifteen percent of Afghan children die before reaching the age of five.

Another important activity of RAWA is to document the human rights violations in Afghanistan by filming and making reports. This is the riskiest part of RAWA's work.

A team of RAWA members documented the execution scene of women that happened in the public sports stadium in 1999. That was the first public execution of women, and RAWA members managed to document it, under the *burqa*.

That was a big risk. The team knew that if they were arrested with that tape they could have been executed like the women who were executed in the stadium. It has always been important for RAWA not only to condemn the crimes and to tell the Afghan people that we're with them, that we know their real miseries and tragedies, but also to alert the outside world of these real tragedies.

As you can imagine, our website made RAWA known to people in other countries. We always say we should be the most thankful people to the internet.

RAWA's website is the most complete website dealing with the plight of Afghan women. There are thousands of records, not only about the crimes of the Taliban but also about the crimes of other groups, *jihadis* of the Northern Alliance, and about RAWA and its work.

It also has RAWA's viewpoints, including our two statements on the September 11 incident and the US bombing. There are many photos of the atrocities in Afghanistan, as well as photos of RAWA's work and activities.

RAWA began its website in 1997. It was only after that our message was heard and seen by many thousands, maybe millions of people, especially women, all over the world. Today RAWA and its website has hundreds of very committed supporters, in this country and many other countries.

We are very privileged to have their support and sympathy for our work. Even at the level of individuals, they have made a great difference in the lives of thousands of people, especially women and children, in Afghanistan. Usually they build awareness campaigns through whatever means they can – at the level of universities or colleges, or speaking at women's conferences.

These supporters have raised awareness about the situation of women in Afghanistan and the work of RAWA. And obviously raising that awareness is very helpful to funding and supporting RAWA's projects.

As a political organization, RAWA does not enjoy vigorous support from governments or NGOs. Whenever we approach them for support, they say you have these political viewpoints, or just sometimes the word revolution in our name is a problem. But thanks to the website, we have managed to receive financial support from some women's organizations, especially in this country, as well as many individual contributions, through which we are able to run our projects and activities.

Mainly through the website and the support we got, we were led to understand that we should not confuse the governments with the people. We want people in this country and around the world not to confuse the innocent, ordinary Afghans with the Taliban and terrorists.

Innocent Afghans hate the Taliban and other fundamentalists and terrorists as much as people in this country and throughout the world do. And they also want to see the end of their domination as soon as it can happen.

And we carry this message to our people: They should not confuse the governments with the people. If the government of Pakistan has always been supportive of the fundamentalists, the people of Pakistan have always been very respectful and hospitable to the Afghan refugees.

If the US government has always played a negative role toward Afghanistan, the people of this country have been very supportive to our cause. In fact, maybe due to the language, or access to the internet, or the population of this country, we have most of our support and supporters in this country.

As the title for this evening says: The other America welcomes the other Afghanistan.

CHAPTER 31

Miriam Ching Yoon Louie

Minjung *Feminism: Korean Women's Movement for Gender and Class Liberation*

South Korea stands as a major example of a nation that has gained a modern industrial base because of globalization; its women appear a prime instance of those who have been victims first of colonialism and then of globalization of the economy. For the first half of the twentieth century, Japan subjected Korea to harsh and racist colonial rule. As Japanese militarism grew in the 1930s, thousands of Korean women were enslaved as prostitutes for the army and for a time continued as such for the US forces who defeated Japan in 1945. During the Cold War Korea was divided into a communist North Korea and a South Korea, which was allied with the United States. As a US ally, South Korea prospered from global investment of capital and from huge quantities of foreign aid, even though its government was a repressive dictatorship.

Oddly enough, the story of a postwar South Korean feminism begins here: in the labor movement, being crushed by squads of police in the 1970s. In fact, for almost two centuries women's common work experience has led to unionization and other organizations that build political unity. Women artisans in nineteenth-century Europe could be found agitating in front of city halls, parliaments, and factories for better working conditions. Many suffrage movements had large contingents of factory workers, and even after suffrage was obtained women workers lobbied for any number of causes to help their sex. Can meaningful movements for rights and social justice take shape when the trend of the past few decades has been the growth of global economic forces setting policies for small towns and entire nations alike? Since the postwar period, such globalization has brought large multinational corporations to set up plants in East Asia and other 'emerging' nations like South Korea. Governments in these countries have drawn the multinationals to install these factories by promising a docile female workforce that can be paid very low wages. As women flock to industries and sweatshops working for multinational firms, they suffer exploitation, putting in incredibly long hours for miniscule wages in addition to the tasks they have to perform as housewives and mothers. Sexual harassment and political surveillance are also regular features of this work experience.

Miriam Ching Yoon Louie, "*Minjung* Feminism: Korean Women's Movement for Gender and Class Liberation," *Women's Studies International Forum*, vol. 18, no. 4 (2000), pp. 417–30. Copyright © 1995, reprinted with permission from Elsevier.

Studies show that women in emerging economies not only benefit from improved education and access to birth control, they find in factory work a source of solidarity and thus an avenue to political activism. This chapter hypothesizes that in the case of South Korea sexual harassment and the bad working conditions associated with the global economy shaped workers into feminists in the 1970s and 1980s. Workers, not the middle classes, built the road to South Korean feminism. This activism grew out of the mass movement of ordinary people seeking better work conditions and political democracy. However, women's agitation grew within an environment that was full of paradoxes.

Bad koju chang [pepper bean paste] is a grievance for 1 year; a bad wife is a grievance for 100 years.

You can only get the real taste of dried fish and women if you beat them once every 3 days.

(Korean proverbs; Tieszen, 1977)

These two samples from the stockpile of misogynist folk sayings reveal centuries of socially sanctioned oppression of women. Yet from the rocky soil of sexism, a mass-based women's movement has sprouted. The feminist movement weds together the *minjung undong* (mass people's movement) with the struggle for *vo'song haebang* (women's liberation). The character of the Korean women's movement stems from two specific features: its intimate relation to the *minjung* movement, and the way the movement organizes around issues of gender and class.

First, the Korean women's movement developed in tandem with the broader *minjung* movement. *Minjung* movement origins are deeply rooted in the suffering of young women factory workers, whose super-exploited labor in export-oriented industries produced the precious start-up capital for South Korea's much touted 'economic miracle.' Their struggles riveted the attention and support of the budding democratic movement. As the movement grew, activists fleshed out feminist analysis and launched distinct women's organizations and coalitions.

Second, in terms of the intersection between gender and class, the movement brings its *minjung* orientation to organizing among women, focusing on the most oppressed women of the urban and rural poor. At the same time, within the broader masses, women are seen as 'the oppressed of the oppressed,' the core of the *minjung*. Subtle differences between socialist and Marxist feminists revolve around how to interpret the precise interpenetration of gender and class oppression.

Here a brief explanation of the concept of *minjung* is in order. The democratic movement reclaimed the term from the earlier anti-Japanese colonial movement, investing it with deep strategic, political, cultural, and spiritual meaning while fighting successive military dictatorships (1961–1992). *Minjung* ideology posits that the central thread running through Korean history is the oppression of the laboring masses and that the true national identity of Korea can be discovered in the lives, culture, and struggles of the *minjung* – the locked out, the exploited, the downtrodden, the have-nots. Populist in character, the *minjung* movement includes students, intellectuals, workers, peasants, church activists, writers, cultural workers, and other democratic forces (Koo, 1987).

This chapter will provide background on *minjung* feminism's origins and the tensions it is managing. Also included are specific examples of organizing work among workers and against sexual violence. The primary sources used are interviews with movement organizers and the materials they provided. Many movement leaders served time in prison and endured government repression. They bring years of experience, commitment, and sacrifice to their work. As a third-generation Korean Chinese working in support of Asian immigrant women workers and women of color in the United States, I thoroughly enjoyed listening to my Korean *ja mael* sisters share stories.

Women's movement roots

Minjung feminism's beginning includes two sub-stages. The first encompasses the struggles of women factory workers for democratic unions, battles which deeply influenced the beginning of the *minjung* movement. The second occurs when the women's movement takes distinct theoretical, practical, and organizational forms.

Yo'kong undong: *factory girls' movement*

Drawn from the countryside, *yo'kong*, or factory girls, toiled day and night in export-oriented industries, such as textiles, garments, electronics, plastics, wig and food processing (Koo, 1987, p. 105) under General Pak Chung Hee's regime (1961–1979). Their sweated labor financed South Korean economic development, providing seed capital for the later development of heavy industry, for example, chemicals, steel, autos, machinery, and shipbuilding. They endured the lowest wages, sexual harassment, exhaustion, and heartbreaking abuse to support parents and siblings and pay tuition for their brothers' education (Spencer, 1988). Some shop owners split single floors into two levels to house twice the production, stunting the women's physical and intellectual health by forcing them to crouch over their machines for long shifts. They often lived jammed together in company dormitory barracks, called 'chicken coops,' with mattresses rotated between shifts of workers. During this period South Korea gained international notoriety for the world's longest work week and highest rate of industrial accidents (Bello and Rosenfeld, 1990, p. 25).

These women spearheaded the democratic union movement throughout the 1970s when labor rights were completely suspended under martial law. They had to take on the interlocking repressive structures of foreign and domestic capital sponsored by the state, including the Korean CIA (KCIA), draconian national security and labor laws, *baekgo'ldan* (White Skull Squadron) police tactical squads, sell-out government-controlled unions, and ex-military male *kusadae* (Save the Company) thugs. For example, police beat striking women workers at the Dongil Textile Company in Inchon, dragging them by their hair, forcing human feces down their throats and across their breasts before throwing them into jail. Yet these workers went on to win their strike and elect a woman as union president in 1972, marking the first time in South Korean history for a woman to be elected to such a position (Committee for Asian Women [CAW], 1990, p. 38). The women managed to hold on to leadership and keep the union democratic for six years until they were finally overcome by the government and management.

The *Chunggye Pibok* Union (Garment Makers Union) headed by Lee So Sun, mother of martyred worker Chun Tae Il, also managed to keep their democratic union alive until General Chun Doo Hwan's regime finally crushed it in the early 1980s. The union gave voice to the 20,000 young women who worked at Seoul's Peace Market in a one-block long, four-storey high maze of tiny cubicles for less than $30 a month (Ogle, 1990, pp. 72–5).

Liberation theologists such as Reverend Cho Wha Soon, religious organizations such as the Urban Industrial Mission, the Catholic Church's Young Christian Workers, and student-turned-worker organizers encouraged women workers using popular literacy, transformation, and consciencization methods. They urged workers to right injustices by examining their own lives and taking collective action for justice – to 'see, judge, act' (Ogle, 1990, p. 88). The *minjung* movement fused with women workers' struggles in a synthesis process which simultaneously politicized women workers' struggles while giving the cross-class *minjung* movement its working-class base and orientation.

Similar to many of the veteran activists in today's women's movement, Maria Chol Soon Rhie came to consciousness because of the struggles of women factory workers in the 1970s (Rhie, 1991). Now an organizer of the Committee for Asian Women, a pan-Asian workers' leadership development network, she explains the intersection of her feminist and class consciousness:

> I did not start out as a feminist. When I came into contact with the movement I was most concerned about my country and about workers' lives. The suicide of Chun Tae II really affected me and made me question what I was doing with my life. A Chonggye Garment Workers' Union organizer, Chun set himself on fire to protest the inhumane conditions of workers, shouting: 'We are not machines! Improve working conditions! Do not waste my death!' I felt compelled to understand the conditions that drove him to his death. College could not give me the answer. For 3 years I worked in a factory to learn about workers' lives. After 2 years I organized a small group of workers. (Rhie, 1991, p. 7)

> I began to learn more about women's lives. When you are born into a family and culture and grow up with inequality it is difficult to be aware of it. In some ways it is easier for workers to recognize their condition after joining the workforce than it is for women who have grown up oppressed. Destroying old conceptions about women is difficult. Discussion of women's issues get [sic] squeezed because workers are busy fighting to change yellow [company] unions into democratic unions.... True democratic changes will come through the women's movement. Democracy must include women's democracy. Even now men ask why women need to struggle separately. Why not just fight for democracy? Have you heard of *yo'song haebang* [women's liberation]? Women have to come together autonomously to form their own voice so they can stand up. (Maria Chol Soon Rhie, personal communication, 25 June 1991)

Throughout the 1970s women workers stood up for their rights, laying the foundation for the democratic union and *minjung* movements with pitched battles at companies like Dongil, Sygnetics, Bando, Songsa, Pangrim, Hankook Mobang, Dongsu, Yanghaing, Y. H. Trading and others. In fact, when women workers protested the Y. H. plant closure in Seoul, police bludgeoned them, killing one woman and provoking riots in the industrial zones of Masan and Pusan. As dictator Pak Chung Hee argued with his friend and head of the KCIA Kim Jae Kyu about how to handle the riots, Kim shot Pak to death in 1979 (Ogle, 1990, pp. 86–92).

Minjung *movement arises from ashes of Kwangju*

The dictator's death provided a potential democratic opening, and students and workers around the country demonstrated for change, taking over the city of Kwangju in the oppressed region of Cholla-do. But soon South Korean troops with the tacit consent of the US Military Command in Korea drowned the Kwangju rebellion in a sea of blood, leaving over 2,000 people dead (CAW and Korean Women Workers Association [KWWA], 1992, p. 6).

The Kwangju uprising catalyzed, radicalized, and cross-fertilized the student, labor, religious, and women's *minjung* movements. The massacre exposed the intractable dictatorial nature of the new regime and US complicity with its occupational army of 40,000 troops. Newly elected US President Reagan greeted General Chun Doo Hwan as the first foreign head of state received at the White House, further fanning the flames of anti-Americanism. Direct involvement in the Kwangju massacre hobbled Chun's regime (1980–1987) with a credibility crisis.

Spurred on by women's activism in the expanding student and labor movements, the women's movement assumed distinct theoretical, political, and organizational forms by the mid-1980s. Women students and organizers from the labor movement of the 1970s, together with a group of professors from Ewha University (the first institution to provide formal education for women and girls in Korea), organized study groups, put together the first women's studies courses, and developed the Institute of Women's Research. Discussion groups and seminars revolved around such topics as the history of Korean women's organizations since the end of the nineteenth century; work and family from a feminist viewpoint; women's literature; the relation between Korea's division, the denial of human rights, and women's oppression; and the connection between martial law and male domination (Cho Ailee and Nam Yunju, personal communication, 23 May 1992; Cho Haejoang, personal communication, 15 July 1991).

The pace of development of the women's movement escalated in tandem with the broader battle against the dictatorship. In 1985 organizers convened a giant women's rally with the theme 'Women's Movement in Unity with National Democratic *Minjung* Movement.' A cultural night co-sponsored by the Women for Equality and Peace and the government-controlled Federation of Korean Trade Unions drew 50,000 women workers and acted as the basis for a subsequent solidarity strike in Kuro, the main industrial area of Seoul. In 1986, women rallied in support of Kwon In Suk, a woman labor organizer who was raped and tortured by police at the Buchon police station. The fury unleashed by this incident and other sex torture cases sparked the formation of Korean Women's Associations United (KWAU), a national coalition of thirty-three worker, peasant, religious, research, environmental, housewife, and anti-violence organizations in 1987. KWAU was born amidst the explosion of tear gas canisters as protesters battled with riot police. The movement forced Chun to announce that he would step down at the end of his term, and led General Roh Tae Woo, Chun's hand-picked successor, to announce that direct presidential elections would be allowed (CAW and KWWA, 1992, p. 7).

Thus, the beginnings of the feminist and *minjung* movements are closely intertwined, from the struggles of young women factory workers to the full flowering of the women's movement during the pitched street battles to bring down the dictatorship during the late 1980s. The next sections on organizing among women workers and against sexual violence offer examples of how the women's movement tackles the intersection of gender and class.

Fighting for democracy in the union and the family

Women shoulder double burden

Gender discrimination intensifies the exploitation of women workers. Even the government-controlled Korean Federation of Trade Unions admits that women's wages are still only 53 percent of men's. Women must often work longer hours to compensate for low wages. Women work an average of 53.2 hours per week, not counting their unpaid work in the home.

Today's *yo'kong* (factory girls) are second and third generation urban dwellers. By 1987, women were 55 percent of the paid workforce, including 60 percent of service, 47 percent of commercial, 40 percent of manufacturing, and 38 percent of all office workers. Some one million women work in the service sector in restaurants, cabarets, room salons, saunas, public baths, tea houses, hotels, massage parlors, and barber shops. Women's movement activists say that almost 30 percent of these jobs are sex industry-related (Chung, 1991).

Women are punished for their marital status. The myth persists that a good wife and mother does not work outside the home. Meanwhile, growing numbers of women work and raise children without social or spousal support. Married women forced out of their jobs upon marriage do piecework at home to make ends meet. As their children grow older they return to work in factories at the worst jobs for the lowest pay, often as temporary workers. Some 45 percent of married women work, and married women now constitute 30 percent of all women workers. Due to the lack of childcare in Korea, many leave their children at home alone, resulting in stress for the mothers and tragic accidents among the children. Yet no matter how many hours women put in at work, most Korean men expect their wives to wait on them when they get home (CAW and KWWA, 1992, pp. 18–20).

According to Kim Eun Shil, a medical anthropology doctoral candidate at the University of California researching views of sexuality and reproduction among women workers, many working-class marriages are common law. She explains,

> Among the working class, consensual unions are common (i.e., living together without a marriage ceremony). With the increase in urbanization more young girls live separate from their family, often in factory dormitory, with little money. They feel lonely. Marriage is important to get parental recognition and exchange goods and gifts. But working class women's family networks are too poor to come up with the goods. A lot of working women have kids but have not gone through a marriage ceremony. Some get married after they have a couple of kids. They confided to me that they feel abnormal and ashamed, but that they could not afford to get married in a traditional way. . . . Sex outside of marriage for men is supposed to be a customary practice, not morally correct, but allowable given men's supposedly 'lusty nature.' For women the standard is chastity. (Kim Eun Shil, personal communication, 12 July 1991)

History professor and editor of *Women & Society* magazine, Chung Hyun Back explains why women turned to the labor movement:

> Korean women workers used to have a little fantasy about marriage. In biographies written during the 1970s, women laborers voiced their dreams of marrying a 'man with a necktie,' that is a white collar worker who would help them escape from poverty. But they could never find this guy with the necktie. They began to realize that they would have to accept a manual laborer as their partner. When their fantasies of social mobility evaporated, they began to search for other solutions. That's when they turned to the labor movement as a means of improving their conditions. (Chung, 1991)

Organizing along the global assembly line

The Korean Women Workers Association (KWWA) organizes against gender discrimination at work and in the union movement, and presses for shared responsibility between women and men in the home. The formation of the KWWA in 1987 proved key in overcoming the fragmentation and break in the continuity of women workers' struggles caused by state repression and forced retirement upon marriage and childbirth.

The KWWA office sits in the middle of Kuro, the main industrial district of Seoul. Walls are plastered with leaflets. A doorway jammed with well-worn pairs of shoes leads into a room with a low table encircled by women workers sitting on the floor. Organizer Yoon Hae Ryun is gratified that KWWA allows blacklisted *son bae* (senior classmate) veterans such as herself to connect with their *hu bae* (junior classmate) workers to show them the ropes and bridge the gap between the generations of women workers fighting for their rights. Sitting in the tiny front room, she explains how she got involved in labor organizing:

> I started working in a factory when I was 14 when there were no democratic unions. I worked in a coat factory sewing from 8 a.m. to 2 a.m. every day. Our lives were really hard. We began to say that we should not have to work like this. I decided to get involved in the 1985 cooperative strike in Kuro launched by democratic unions. Chun Doo Hwan did his best to destroy the unions. When we started this strike, I told my family about it in order to prepare them for what might happen. They were shocked and cried and cried. I was the only wage earner in the family because the kids were in school and my father was too old to continue his job as a laborer lifting materials. I got arrested and spent 6 months in jail with workers and students. All of my friends from work were there. It was so crowded that there was no place to sleep. You had to sleep like a knife. (She tautly presses her arms against her body to resemble a knife.) When I got out of jail I went back to the factory to work, but I kept getting dismissed from jobs. It got to the stage where I was blacklisted and could not get work. So together with other displaced women workers, I began to work with the KWWA to support women workers in their struggle. (Yoon Hae Ryun, personal communication, 28 May 1992)

KWWA advocates higher wages and an eight-hour work day; ending sexual discrimination in the workplace; maternity protection, including menstruation leave, maternity leave, breast-feeding, and daycare facilities; halting sexual harassment and violence; solidarity among women inside and outside of the labor movement; and women's leadership training. Since 1989, KWWA has run a childcare center for workers as well as '*nolli bang*/playroom,' an after school study program for older children. KWWA has chapters in the industrialized zones of Seoul, Pusan, Buchon, Inchon, Changwon-Masan, and Kwangju. KWWA discussion groups, educational materials, and comic books feature struggles to form women's sections within unions to build 'democratic unions' and 'democratic families' supportive of women workers (CAW and KWWA, 1992; KWWA, 1993).

Clerical and bank workers' unions are female dominated. Women office workers who have no hope of getting promoted and who, until recently, were forced to retire when they married, are more active in labor-organizing drives than men and often have a strong feminist consciousness. The Korean Women's Association for Democracy and Sisterhood was founded to support the struggle of the women office workers against discriminatory pay, petty errands, and having to deliver the 'three Cs' – coffee, copy, and cigarettes – to their male bosses. The membership of the highly progressive democratic teachers' union is also majority female.

Korean women workers' organizations also build links with other groups in Asia through participation in the Committee for Asian Women (CAW). Korea was one of the earliest outposts along the global assembly line. Now Korean women are fighting lay-offs and the replacement of permanent workers with contingency workers hired through a third agency and from other countries. Because these women are not protected by unions, they can be fired at will. Korean workers are also hard hit by factory flight to newer regions of transnational corporate penetration where workers are less organized and lower paid (CAW, 1993, p. 12). Korean women workers launched courageous campaigns against plant closures by Pico Products, Tandy Corporation, and Control Data Electronics of the United States and Sumida Corporation of Japan. Despite beatings and arrests, Pico Korea unionists who had produced cable TV parts chased the runaway company to corporate headquarters in Liverpool, New York with pickets, a hunger strike, a lawsuit, and national tour supported by the Korean American community and US labor unions (Liem and Kim, 1992).

CAW organizes exchanges between women workers' groups in Korea, the Philippines, Malaysia, Japan, Sri Lanka, Thailand, Indonesia, India, Taiwan, and Hong Kong so women workers can better confront class and gender abuse up and down the global assembly line (CAW, 1993).

Breaking the silence: organizing against sexual violence

Korea has a long history of subjugation and violence against women. But this legacy reached new lows under colonialism and imperialist domination when occupiers systematically raped the women of the raped nation. Division of the country into two antagonistic halves by foreign powers during the Cold War necessitated a huge military apparatus whose waste products were the sex industry and increased levels of male violence against women. South Korea has the world's third highest rate of sexual assault according to a 1989 study by the Korea Criminal Policy Institute (Korea Sexual Violence Relief Center (KSVRC), 1992, p. 11).

Confucianism, militarism, violence, and the sex industry

Jun Yeonny, a Korean Sexual Violence Relief Center volunteer, graduate of Ewha Women's Studies Department and now a Women's Studies professor at Kun San College in Seoul, explains how Confucian ideology subordinates and silences women:

> To understand why Korean women face such a high degree of sexual harassment and assault, you have to understand Korean social structure, especially the patriarchal system with its strong tradition of Confucianism. Under Confucianism women are subordinate to father, then husband, then son. Furthermore, Confucianism emphasizes the ideology of virginity and chastity for women as well as the supremacy of family. So if a women is the victim of an attack she does not want to publicize it. In Korea, incest rape is a big problem. But under Confucian ideology, if there are problems in the family they should be settled in private or suffered in silence, not brought out into the open. (Jun Yeonny, personal communication, 24 April 1992)

Sexual violence also stems from foreign domination, military occupation, and repression in Korean modern history, including Japan's forty-year colonization of Korea (1905–1945), the Korean War (1950–1953), the introduction of foreign troops including continued occupation by 37,000 US troops, military governments (1961–1987), the growth of the Korean military to 600,000 troops in the south and one million in the north, and compulsory military service and training in use of deadly force for all men in Korea. English literature professor Cho Ailee, member of the Research Center for Women's Studies explains:

You have to understand that Korea is a very violent society. We have lived directly under military governments for 30 years. Even though the sixth Republic of Roh Tae Woo [(1988–1992) was] ostensibly civilian, in reality the military still wields power. For Roh Tae Woo to reach the position of general, a lot of people had to die. The military and police have killed people demonstrating for democracy. *Kusadae* thugs beat up workers. In this violent military climate, men's violence against women is sanctioned. (Cho Alice, personal communication, 23 May 1992)

Militarism exacerbates the growth of prostitution and the sex industry as well as other forms of sexual violence against women. In addition to numerous Korean bases and posts, some forty US bases remain on Korean soil. An average of 2,000 altercations between local Koreans and US military personnel occur each year. In 1991, out of 1,373 reported cases of crimes committed by US soldiers, only eighteen were prosecuted (Lee Yeung Hee, personal communication, 27 May 1992). Many of these incidents are crimes against women, like the case of Kenneth Markel, a GI stationed at Tongduchon, who bashed the head of Yoon Geum Yi, a poor factory worker turned prostitute. He then stuck a Pepsi bottle into her vagina, an umbrella up her anus, a match between her teeth, and left her to die in a pool of blood (Lee, 1993a, pp. 16–17).

During the 1970s the Pak Chung Hee regime encouraged the development of the sex industry to entice foreign exchange out of Japanese businessmen. Korea also served as an 'R & R' (rest and recreation) center for US GIs during the Vietnam War. Thus, women factory and sex industry workers were called up to sacrifice themselves 'for the sake of the nation.' Sex tours included not only air travel, hotel, and transportation, but also the sexual services of Korean women (Haruhi, 1985; Lie, 1991; Louie, 1989). The women's movement educated the public about these problems, but the sex industry only went underground. The pornography industry, prostitution, massage parlors, hostess bars, and sex barber shops still abound in Korea. Although the sex industry's initial impetus was serving foreign soldiers and businessmen, these days its main customers are Korean men.

'Comfort women' caught in crossfire of militarism, colonialism, and sexism

Professor Jun Yeonny (1992) reflects, 'Perhaps the comfort women were the first victims of the sex industry' (Jon Yeonny, personal communication interview, 24 April 1992). Japan forced women to sexually service its Imperial Army and work its war industries during World War II, an act the Pak Chung Hee regime was to imitate three decades later. Euphemistically called *Chong Shin Dae* or 'Comfort Girl Corp,' this episode stands as one of the most humiliating reminders of the forty years Korea suffered as Japan's colony. Of the estimated 100,000 to 200,000 women drafted, more than 80 percent were Korean, with other women 'recruited' from China, Taiwan, the Philippines, Malaysia, Indonesia, and Thailand ('Presumed drafted,' 1992). Survivor Shim Mi Ja, of the Korean Council for Women Drafted under Japanese Rule, remembers her ordeal:

When I was 16 years old [a] policeman tried to rape me so I punched him in the ear. Then they beat me so hard that I passed out. When I woke up I was in Fukuoka, Japan. They made me serve as a *Chong Shin Dae* prostitute for 6 years, between 1939 and 1945. . . . After I was kidnapped and sent to Japan I never saw my family again because my home town is in North Korea. (Shim Mi Ja, personal communication, 15 July 1992)

The hijacking and rape of Korean women embodied the ultimate subjugation of the colonized. Given its proximity to Japan, China, and the Soviet Union, Korea served as Japan's geostrategic bridgehead to take over the Asian continent and pilot Japan's plans for a 'Greater Asian Co-Prosperity Sphere' (Eckert et al., 1990, p. 316). Korea acted as Japan's rice basket and source of raw materials and captive labor when the Japanese Imperial Army thrust into Asia and the Pacific after the declaration of war with China in 1937. Korean girls between the ages of 11 and 18 were gang raped almost every day after they arrived in the military camps. Japanese officers enjoyed the perk of sex with the teenage virgins, after which regular soldiers took their turn. The girls serviced between thirty and sixty men a day. They lived in dread of Saturday night when the numbers of men would increase (Chai, 1993a).

For these survivors of rape, bombings, murder, and suicide, deep scars remain. Dr Yun Chung-Ok, the first researcher to discover documents proving Japanese government complicity in 'recruiting' Korean schoolgirls, says that many women did not come home after the war because they were afraid of shaming their families. Others who did talk about what happened to them were shunned in a classic case of victim blaming (Neuberger, 1993).

Survivors break decades of silence with women's movement support

The *minjung* feminist movement provided shelter and support needed for comfort troop survivors to speak out after nearly half a century of silence and shame. Working together with the survivors in the Korean Council for Women Drafted under Japanese Rule are feminist professors, young women's movement activists, as well as the broader coalition of Korean women's groups, Japanese feminists, progressive lawyers, and Korean church and community groups in Japan. *Chong Shin Dae* became a hot issue in 1991 when survivors Kim Han Sun and Mun Ok Ju came forward and told their stories and Korean and Japanese journalists and lawyers began investigating. During June 1991 Korean reporters tracked down almost 200 survivors (Cho Nyeran, personal interview, 5 May 1992).

The Korean Council is also lobbying the Korean government to take a more active role in pressuring the Japanese government to pay reparations to survivors before they die. The Korean government had been silent, supposedly having settled the issue of reparations – not including *Chong Shin Dae* survivors' claims – with the Japanese government back in 1965. Apparently, the pay-off for government silence was a massive infusion of Japanese loan and investment capital.

The Korean Council, which is publishing a book of survivor interviews, has issued the following demands: Japanese government admission that Korean women were drafted as *Chong Shin Dae*, a government apology and full investigation, a monument dedicated to the victims, reparations for the survivors, full rights for Koreans in Japan, an independent position on the issue from the Korean government, a commitment that Japanese school-children be taught the true history about this and other war crimes, and a commitment that Japanese people of conscience help Koreans reveal crimes committed during World War II.

Survivors' support groups

In addition to the comfort women's survivors group, activists have organized a number of support mechanisms for victims of sexual violence. The Women's Hot Line in Seoul was founded in the mid-1980s and belongs to the Korean Women's Associations United, the national *minjung* women's umbrella coalition. The group recently conducted a survey which revealed that one in ten married women are beaten by their husbands almost daily. Activists are now waging a campaign to save the life of Lee Sun Shim, recently charged with the murder of her husband who beat her constantly for twenty years ('One in ten,' 1994). Another women's center called 'My Sister's Place' assists Korean women involved with servicemen at the US base in Tongduchon (Moon and Yu, 1987). Ewha Women's Studies Department graduates also founded the Korean Sexual Violence Relief Center to assist victims of rape and domestic violence and supported a Seoul National University teaching assistant who won a sexual harassment case against a professor, the first landmark decision of its kind.

Members of the Korean Council, Korean Sexual Violence Relief Center, and the Korean Women's Associations United, together with comfort troop survivors from other Asian countries, delivered their testimony and demands to the Human Rights Commission of the United Nations at its meeting in June 1993 in Vienna (Chai, 1993b; Lee, 1993b, pp. 16–19). Similar to mass rape victims of the war in Bosnia, Asian women demand an end to foreign domination, war, militarism, sexual slavery, and violence against women.

Minjung feminism in transition

Although radical *minjung* feminism exercises majority influence among feminist intellectuals and organizers, the movement is not monolithic. Differences exist over how to interpret the intersection between gender and class oppression. Another area of concern is how the collapse of socialism and the crisis of Marxism impact the South Korean movement. Still another challenge facing the movement is how to make the transition from organizing under a military dictatorship to organizing under a civilian government.

Transitioning from military to civilian rule

In order to survive blacklisting, imprisonment, torture, and decimation of leadership over decades of military dictatorship, the movement matured its political consciousness, ideological commitment, forms of organization, and breadth of alliances. Now Korean Women's Associations United, like the giant national worker and student federations, is shifting gear to the new political climate with a civilian president in the face of continued economic restructuring and recession. Although President Kim Young Sam's administration purged the military from key government positions and is waging a campaign against corruption, the basic structure of the army and police remains intact. The government has neither repealed the notorious National Security Law nor democratized labor laws, and has opened the rice market, threatening to further impoverish peasants. Kim has called on workers to make sacrifices 'for the sake of the nation' (KWWA, 1993).

At the same time the electoral process and expansion of civil society allows the citizenry to become more active, legitimizing Kim's government. Groups such as the Korean Women's Associations United have begun to register as legal organizations with the government, which both broadens the groups' appeal to women and also allows them to receive government and other sources of funding for their projects. Additionally, *minjung* women leaders from the labor and slum dwellers movements such as Choi Soon Young and Hong Mi Young ran for regional legislative positions and won. The

Minister of Women's Affairs, Kwon Young Ja, journalist who lost her job because of her opposition to the former regime, is also working hard with a number of community women leaders to bring about reforms (Chung Hyung Back, personal communication, 13 May 1994).

Na Young Hee, who serves as KWAU's General Secretary and heads up daily operations surrounded by a staff of energetic young women out of the coalition's headquarters in Chung-dong, Seoul, describes the decision-making process:

> Debates and arguments arise about the political direction and focus of the movement. We have to organize a lot of open and participatory discussions before reaching a final conclusion. Because we target the mass of grassroots people we do not take extreme positions but try to act as a broad umbrella organization. (Na Young Hee, personal communication, 2 June 1992)

Forty-nine-year-old Han Myeong Suk, the current president of KWAU, works with the Christian Academy. A veteran of the democratic rights movement, she was incarcerated in the women's prison close to the army barracks during the Kwangju massacre in 1980, where she witnessed many violent acts committed against Kwangju citizens that she will never forget. Speaking to a group of Korean American women in Oakland, California about KWAU's work, Han Myeong Suk describes current challenges:

> Traditionally, the government tried to coopt our demands for reform while suppressing the leadership. But now is the time for our groups to dig in and work on the diverse issues that impact women. The people's movement is at another crossroads. In March there was a big conference summit of all the movements where it was decided that we would respond to government reform gestures in a positive manner. How many people were jailed and tortured, how many people died, how many people sacrificed so much to bring about the changes we have today? (Han, 1993)

Activists from the women's movement of the 1980s worry about the alienation of young women in the 1990s who are turning away from social movements and feminism. Yonsei University sociology professor Cho Haejoang, who comments on culture and the media, suggests that feminists critically re-examine 'compulsory motherhood' within the South Korean context and pay more attention to differences in experience, especially differences between generations:

> It seemed that the women's movement was going to pick up its tide on a large scale. However, in the 1990s, we find ourselves at a loss. Women of the younger generation who are eager to separate themselves from their mothers (the embodiments of colonial modernization) and who are free from the Utopian ideologies of the 1980s, find a way out in the 'Global postmodern culture.'... The roles and images of women were transformed without accompanying change in the deep structure of sexism. Women exist for men's everyday living and to cater to the male ego. Modernity, understood as the birth of the individual, is only for the male gender. (Cho, 1995, p. 29)

KWAU details how women are 'the primary victims of the "development dictatorship"' (KWAU, 1995, p. 16) in a report analyzing the impact of structural adjustment policies on women for the UN World Summit on Social Development in Copenhagen in March 1995. KWAU chronicles how women remain vulnerable to exploitation as cheap labor and contingency workers, lay-offs during periods of structural adjustment, poverty as the heads of households, as well as state reinforced patriarchy, sexual discrimination, and violence, both within and outside of the family.

Women are the *minjung* of the *minjung*. They were the bottom of a Confucian hierarchy that exploited and spurned the peasant, the laborer, the female. Under Japanese colonial domination they embodied the analogy of Korea as the raped nation, forced to submit to the lust of the occupier's war machine. After the war their slave-like labor in export-oriented factories and the sex industry yielded the capital accumulation necessary to sky-rocket South Korea into coveted Four Little Dragons status. They continue to enrich foreign and domestic capitalists and act as modern-day comfort women soothing soldiers and businessmen.

When Korean women stood up for even the most basic rights, they immediately confronted the interlocking structures of male privilege, foreign domination, state-supported capitalism, and a repressive military apparatus, which, though supposedly erected to protect them against the communist enemy from without, increasingly turned inward to slaughter the *minjung* within. If the goal of the *minjung* movement is to empower the oppressed masses to realize democracy, human rights, workers liberation, national independence, and peaceful reunification, then women are the movement's primary constituency core, the oppressed of the oppressed.

In fact, the *minjung* movement has developed hand-in-hand with the struggles of poor women for class and gender liberation. The international women's movement can learn much from the advanced experiences of our Korean sisters. First, we can learn from the movement's *minjung* orientation of focusing analytical and practical organizing energies on the struggles of grassroots women, utilizing the methodologies of popular literacy, transforming and giving witness to enable poor women to release their voices, and then flanking them in their struggles for justice. Second, we can learn from their combination of theoretical and practical organizing work; from their careful process of building unity through constant discussion, debate, compromise, and evaluation; and from their experiences in organization and coalition building to break isolation and fragmentation between regions, sectors, and generations. The Korean women's movement has begun to share its experiences within international forums and networks of women workers and survivors of sexual violence.

Today the movement faces new challenges, including the global economic restructuring process which continues to abuse and discard workers similar to worn-out shoes, the diversification of Korea's class and occupational structure, the collapse of alternative left ideologies and solutions, and a government whose rhetoric about change does not match its conservative actions. But, whatever the future brings, Korean women have begun their search for liberation. Whereas desperate women once turned to shamans to exorcise evil spirits and change their luck, today's vibrant *minjung* feminists use shamanistic rituals (*kut*) to purge foreign domination, militarism, capitalism, and sexism; to release the *han*, the accumulated suffering and grief of tortured political prisoners, *Chong Shin Dae* comfort women, and rape victims so their souls can find peace. The past suffering, sacrifice, dedication, experience, and leadership of Korean women gives the movement every basis to chart a new course where feminism will be at the core of *minjung* liberation.

Acknowledgments

Special thanks to Korean women's movement activists who took time from hectic organizing schedules to swap stories. Many thanks also to Linda Burnham and Elizabeth Martinez of the Women of Color Resource Center and Max Elbaum of *Crossroads* Magazine for their helpful editorial comments.

References

Bello, Walden, and Rosenfeld, Stephanie (1990) *Dragons in Distress: Asia's Miracle Economies in Crisis*, San Francisco: Institute for Food and Development Policy.

Chai, Alice Yun (1993a) Presentation about comfort women at Asian Resource Center, Oakland Chinatown, California, 3 June.

Chai, Alice Yun (1993b) Violated women: why, everywhere, a 'wall of silence?' *Honolulu Advertiser*, p. B3, 25 July.

Cho Haejoang (1986) *Male Dominance and Mother Power: The Two Sides of Confucian Patriarchy in Korea*. Paper presented at workshop of the International Cultural Society of Korea, Seoul, Korea.

Chao Haejoang (1995) *Living with Conflicting Femininity of Mother, Motherly Wife and Sexy Woman – A Transition from Colonial-Modern to Postmodern*. Paper presented at the Workshop on 'Gender and Social Change in Late Twentieth Century Korea,' Columbia University, New York, 10–11 March.

Chung Hyung Back (1991) *Women in Korea*. Paper presented at meeting of Korea Reunification Symposium Committee and the Department of Asian American Studies, University of California, Berkeley, CA, 14 March.

Committee for Asian Women (CAW) (1990) *Moving On: Education in Organizing*. Hong Kong: Author.

Committee for Asian Women (CAW) (1993) *Asian Women Workers Newsletter*, 12(3).

Committee for Asian Women (CAW) and Korean Women Workers Association (KWWA) (1992) *When the hen crows... Korean Women Workers Educational Programs*. Hong Kong: CAW.

Eckert, Carter, J., Lee, Ki-baik, Lew, Young Ick, Robinson, Michael and Wagner, Edward (1990) *Korea Old and New: A History*. Seoul, Korea: Ilchokak Publishers for the Korea Institute of Harvard University.

Han Mycong Suk (1993) Presentation on Korean women at Asian Resource Center, Oakland, California, 18 April.

Haruhi, Tono (1985) Military occupation and prostitution tourism. In *Female Sexual Slavery and Economic Exploitation: Making Local and Global Connection*. UN Non-Governmental Liaison Service Consolidation held in San Francisco. 25 October 1984.

Koo, Hagen (1987) Women factory workers in Korea. In Eui-Young Yu and Earl Philips (eds), *Korean Women in Transition: At Home and Abroad* (pp. 103, 112). Los Angeles: California State University.

Korea Sexual Violence Relief Center (KSVRC) (1991) *Korea Sexual Violence Relief Center Pamphlet*. Seoul: KSVRC.

Korean Women's Associations United (1995) The effects on women of the Korean economic development model. In *Effects of Economic Development in South Korean Society* (pp. 16–22). Seoul: Korea NGO Forum for Social Development.

Korean Women Workers Association (KWWA) (1993) Working women. *KWWA Journal*, 1.

Lee, Jin Sook (1993a) The murder of Yoon Geum Yi. *Korea Report*, 16: 16–17.

Lee, Jin Sook (1993b) Korean NGOs raise human rights issue at the UN world conference on human rights in Vienna, *Korea Report*, 18, 16–19.

Lie, John (1991) *From Kisaeng to Maech'un: The Transformation of Sexual Work in Twentieth-century Korea.* Unpublished manuscript.

Liem, Ramsey, and Kim, Jinsoo (1992) The Pico Korea workers' struggle., Korean Americans, and the lessons of solidarity, *Amerasia Journal*, 18(1): 49–68.

Louie, Miriam Ching (1989) Third world prostitutes. *Off Our Backs*, 6(10): 14–15.

Moon, Fay II., and Yu, Bok Nim (1987) My sister's place reports. Eijungboo, Korea, Home of 8th US Army: My Sister's Place.

Neuberger, Mary Jo (1993) Violence is global. *Village Voice*, 20 April, p. 20.

Ogle, George 1: (1990) *South Korea: Dissent Within the Economic Miracle*, London: Zed Books.

One in Ten Korean Wives Beaten Every Day (1994) *San Francisco Examiner*, 10 April, p. A17.

200,000 Presumed Drafted as 'Comfort Girls' (1992) *Korea Times*, 17 January, p. 1.

Rhie, Maria Chol Soon (1991) Korea: starting small, growing strong. In Committee for Asian Women (eds). *Many Paths, One Goal: Organising Women Workers in Asia* (pp. 6–19). Hong Kong: CAW.

Spencer, Robert F. (1988) *Yokong: Factory Girl*. Seoul: Royal Asiatic Society.

Tieszen, Helen Rose (1977) Korean proverbs about women. In Sandra Mattielli (ed.), *Virtues in Conflict: Tradition and the Korean Woman Today* (pp. 49–66). Seoul: Royal Asiatic Society.

CHAPTER 32

Jackson Katz

Reconstructing Masculinity in the Locker Room: The Mentors in Violence Prevention Project

Few violence prevention programs of any kind foreground discussions of masculinity. In his work with college athletes, Jackson Katz positions the sociocultural construction of manhood as central to the problem of men's violence against women, as well as the basis of potential sources of prevention. Through the Mentors in Violence Prevention (MVP) Project at North-eastern University in Boston, Katz and his colleagues seek to reduce men's violence against women by inspiring athletes and other models of traditional masculine success to challenge and reconstruct predominant male norms that equate strength in men with dominance over women. The Project specifically encourages participants to use their stature among their peers on campus to promote healthier attitudes and behaviors towards women.

Thirty college football players sit apprehensively in a cramped locker room, waiting to hear what we will say to them about rape, battering, and sexual harassment. Some recount to their younger teammates unpleasant experiences they've had with "date rape" sem-inars. They're clearly not here voluntarily. Their coach, who attended an orientation session about our program with the entire athletic staff several weeks earlier, has required his players' attendance. He introduces the session and then leaves the room because, as an authority figure, his presence could inhibit the young men's honesty.

I tell the student-athletes that my co-presenter and I are here because the level of men's violence against women in our society is out of control. I tell them it is time we stopped avoiding or denying the problem, and instead started talking about violence against women as a *men's* issue. Calling this violence a "women's issue," I say, is in fact part of the problem. Why? It sends a signal to guys that it is not our concern: Why would a man concern himself with *women's* issues? And besides, I continue, don't issues that affect the women and girls that we care about affect us, too?

Jackson Katz, "Reconstructing Masculinity in the Locker Room: The Mentors in Violence Prevention Project," *The Harvard Educational Review*, vol. 65, no. 2 (Summer 1995), pp. 163–74. Copyright © 1995 by the President and Fellows of Harvard College. All rights reserved.

I ask the young men to raise their hands if they have a sister, girlfriend, mother, grandmother, or female friend. This usually prompts laughter, and some grumbling, but eventually they all put up their hands. The message is clear: it is simplistic and divisive to reduce gender-based violence to a "battle between the sexes" where one side wins at the expense of the other. Men's and women's lives are too interconnected. I remind them that during the course of this presentation, every woman we talk about who has been raped, or abused by her boyfriend, or assaulted by a man in some other way, is somebody's sister, somebody's mother, somebody's daughter. This violence doesn't happen to some abstract category of "women." It happens to women we know and love.

Then I introduce my partner in the Mentors in Violence Prevention (MVP) Project, Byron Hurt, who is in his mid-twenties and a former football quarterback who went through college on a full athletic scholarship. Our different backgrounds – I am Jewish, White, of European descent, and Byron is African American – underscore the fact that sexual harassment of women is a pervasive societal problem that cuts across social distinctions. Byron asks the athletes to close their eyes. "Imagine," he says, "that the woman closest to you – your mother, your girlfriend, your sister – is being assaulted by a man. It's happening at a party, in a residence hall, on the street. Now imagine," he continues, "that there's a man in a position to stop the assault. But he doesn't. He just ignores the situation, or watches."

When the guys open their eyes, Byron asks them how they felt about the assault, and then about the man who stood idly by. They reply that they're upset by the assault, and disgusted that the male bystander didn't intervene. "He's a punk," they offer, a "coward," a "wimp." During the meeting, Byron and I often remind them of how they felt about men who were in a position to prevent or interrupt sexist abuse, but did nothing. This interactive exercise reinforces our point about the need for male leadership on these issues because, of course, no one wants to think of himself as a coward or a wimp.

The exercise also highlights the role of bystanders in reducing incidents of men's violence against women. MVP doesn't address male student-athletes as potential perpetrators; we address them as brothers, friends, teammates; popular students, and, very importantly, as potential mentors for younger kids. We help them see that they are in a position to provide the male leadership necessary to prevent a lot of pain and suffering.

I tell them that's the reason Northeastern University's Center for the Study of Sport in Society created the MVP Project: to inspire male leadership in reducing men's violence against women, an area where up to now there has been precious little male initiative.[1]

MVP: changing masculine norms

Few violence prevention programs of any kind foreground discussions of masculinity. This is unfortunate, because whether the victim is female or male, males commit more than 90 percent of violent crimes (FBI, 1993). When many of these crimes are examined, we can see that attitudes about manhood are often among the critical variables leading to the assault. This is especially obvious in extreme cases of men's violence against women (e.g., rape, battering). Considering this reality, discussing issues of gender, as we do in MVP, should be regarded as a basic component of *any* violence prevention program.

For men who choose to confront these issues, sexual assault and abuse can involve intensely personal feelings and experiences. Some men are themselves survivors of such abuse. Others have women and girls close to them who have been assaulted. Due to the pervasiveness of these problems in college and high school populations, it is inevitable that some men who participate in anti-rape programs have themselves raped or otherwise abused women.

These factors, in part, explain why all-male workshops help many men "open up." Alan Berkowitz, counseling center director and assistant professor of psychology at Hobart and William Smith College, was an early advocate of focusing on cultural constructions of masculinity in anti-rape work. He has pioneered an all-male anti-rape workshop model. According to Berkowitz (1994), all-male workshops have a number of advantages:

> They allow men to speak openly without fear of judgment or criticism by women, make it less likely that men will be passive or quiet, and avoid the gender-based polarization that may reinforce men's rape-prone attitudes. In addition, a diversity of opinions and viewpoints can be expressed, reflecting men's variety of attitudes and beliefs about appropriate sexual relationships and allowing participants to deconstruct the monolithic image of masculinity the media have presented to them. (p. 36)

This is not to denigrate women's leadership or ability to teach men. However, properly trained men can connect with peers and younger males in a way that is not available even to the best female trainers and teachers. Of course, this is also true in the reverse: male educators, no matter how sensitive or skilled, cannot presume to relate to their female students' experience in the same way as could a woman.[2]

Providing a structured opportunity for men to talk with each other about masculinity – particularly as it relates to men's violence against women – is perhaps the single most important characteristic of the Mentors in Violence Prevention Project. We hold no illusions that a few discussions, however meaningful, will by themselves change deep-seated behaviors. But the sessions accomplish the critical first step of breaking men's silence around these issues.

Many theorists have argued that the socialization of men in the United States encourages a constellation of attitudes and behaviors that predispose them to dominate and abuse women and other men in a variety of ways (Berkowitz, 1992). Because formation of a gendered and sexual identity is one of the important developmental tasks for young adults (Chickering, 1969), adolescent and late-adolescent males and females are particularly susceptible to culturally dominant sex-role assignments.

Severe antisocial aggression, including men's violence against women and gay-bashing, is primarily a learned behavior (Eron, 1987). Eron and others have argued that while genetic and hormonal factors undoubtedly play a role, the learning environment in which the child develops has been viewed as more important. According to Eron, continual and repeated images of violent masculinity in the broadcast media (including sports) reinforce sociocultural norms, which in turn provide standards and values children can use to evaluate the appropriateness of their own behavior and the behavior of others.

One aim of the MVP project is to contribute to a change in the sociocultural construction of masculinity that equates strength in men with dominance over women. Because male athletes, particularly those who are successful in what Mariah Burton Nelson (1994) refers to as the "manly sports" of football, basket-ball, and hockey, are important masculine role models for many young males, others' perceptions of these athletes' attitudes toward women help to shape the norms of male behavior.

As Berkowitz (1992) reports, recent research suggests that rape is best understood as an extreme on a continuum of sexually assaultive behaviors, and that sexual assault is engaged in by many men and may be somewhat normative. Many studies have examined the frequency of sexual assaults committed by college men. In one study by Rapaport and Burkhart (1984), only 39 percent of males sampled denied coercive involvement, while 28 percent admitted having used a coercive method at least once, and 15 percent admitted to forcing a woman to have intercourse at least once. Koss and others, using data from a large, nationally representative sample of college and university students, found that 25 percent of male respondents had committed some form of sexual assault since age fourteen (Koss, Gidycz, & Wisniewski, 1987, and Koss, 1988, cited in Berkowitz, 1994).

This research also suggests that sexual assault is best understood as occurring in a sociocultural environment that promotes rape-supportive attitudes and socializes men to adhere to them. A key premise of MVP is that the male student-athletes can help to delegitimize "rape-supportive" and "battering-supportive" attitudes by publicly repudiating the sexist, domination-oriented definitions of masculinity that reinforce them.

In more recent work, Berkowitz (1994) also states that there is evidence that many men are uncomfortable with other men's bragging about sexual exploits, dislike men's preoccupation with commenting on women's bodies, and misperceive the extent of other men's sexual activity. These men may belong to a "silent majority" who keep their discomfort to themselves rather than express disagreement or intervene in an environment which they perceive as unsympathetic.

Because of their privileged place within the social hierarchy, successful male athletes have an enhanced level of credibility with their male peers and with younger males. In particular, because these men are seen in many ways as exemplars of traditional masculine success, their attitudes about gender carry weight.[3] With proper guidance and training, they are in a unique position to break the silence of the silent majority.

The MVP playbook

The MVP model involves holding three 90-minute sessions each year with each participating college team. A fourth session is scheduled for those student-athletes who wish to be trained further for work with younger students in middle and high schools. The sessions, about half of which are held in locker rooms, usually take place either before or after the team's season, at the rate of roughly once a month. College student-athletes are busy people; one of the biggest challenges we have faced is scheduling.

Before we are ready to schedule any sessions at a college, the MVP team gives a presentation to the entire coaching staff, male and female, at a meeting organized by the athletic director. At this meeting, we introduce the Project much in the same way we do with the student-athletes, and then take the coaches through a typical session, including a demonstration of how we use the MVP Playbook. At the end of the meeting, we begin to schedule individual sessions with various coaches. We usually try to work with the high-profile teams, including football, basketball, hockey, baseball, and lacrosse. Time and resource constraints on our part prevent us from working with every team at a college.

At the first session with the student-athletes, after we have introduced ourselves and conducted the preliminary exercises, we distribute our key teaching tool, the MVP Playbook, which is the focus of the first three sessions. This Playbook, which MVP staff created and designed, consists of a series of party and residence hall scenarios portraying 13 actual and potential sexual assaults. The scenarios range from sexist comments overheard in the locker room to verbal threats of physical harm, date rape, and gang rape. We make it clear that we see all of these manifestations of sexism as interconnected. We also discuss the relationship between sexism and heterosexism. Playbook scenarios include the harassment of gays and lesbians.

Most of the scenarios focus on bystander behavior, while a few deal with the young men as potential perpetrators. The three MVP sessions facilitated by Byron and myself are highly interactive, as the student-athletes are asked to share experiences they've had in high school or college that are similar to the ones included in the Playbook.

The Playbook scenarios are designed to be as realistic as possible. For example, one called "Slapshot" sets this scene:

> At a party, a teammate pushes and then slaps his girlfriend. People are upset but don't do anything. He's not your close friend, but he is your teammate.

After having someone read the scenario, we have someone else read the "train of thought," which is a type of mental checklist that we suggest men in these situations go through: "If nobody else is stepping in, why should I? ... It could get ugly.... He could turn on me.... Am I ready to get into a fight, if it comes to that? ... What if he has a weapon? ..." The train of thought is followed on each page by a list of practical and realistic options for intervention: "Nothing – it's none of my business.... Get a bunch of people to contain the boyfriend.... Talk to the woman and let her know you are willing to help.... Report the incident to the coach."

The train of thought concept is adapted from the Habits of Thought model developed by Ronald Slaby of the Harvard Graduate School of Education, who was also an early advisor to the MVP Project. Slaby's model (1994) provides a basis for understanding the behavior of victims, perpetrators, and bystanders. He suggests that behavior is the outcome of social experiences, including personal experiences with violence and those transmitted by the media, interacting with habits of thought (i.e., beliefs, impulsive and reflective tendencies, and problem-solving skills).

The great benefit of implementing this model in working with male student-athletes on the issue of men's violence against women is that rather than focus on the men as actual or potential *perpetrators*, we focus on them in their role as potential *bystanders*. This shift in emphasis greatly reduces the participants' defensiveness. It also allows us to emphasize one of our key points: that when men don't speak up or take action in the face of other men's abusive behavior toward women, that constitutes implicit consent of such behavior. When we discuss with the young men their options for intervention in the various scanarios; we are careful not to choose for them the "best" option: that choice is for each person to make based on a unique set of circumstances. The options we provide are meant to serve as a guide. The list is not comprehensive, but the one option we always include – and strongly discourage – is to do nothing.

Many of the men with whom we work, and men in our society in general, have been socialized to be passive bystanders in the face of sexist abuse and violence. This conditioning is reflected in the oft-heard statement that a situation "between a man and his woman" is "none of my business." When we hear this sentiment articulated in our MVP sessions, we frequently refer back to the initial exercise in which we asked the men how they felt about a fictional man who did nothing when he was in a position to stop violence against a woman they cared about. We remind the men that they all agreed that the bystander was a punk and a coward. In other words, we've positioned the response "it's none of my business" in a new light. It's no longer an acceptable and reasonable attitude held by "one of the guys," but is instead seen as a poor excuse to hide feelings of fear or moral cowardice.

The Playbook and its various scenarios lead to highly interactive discussions about real-life situations that most men have experienced, or at least known about, in their families, circles of friends, teams, home or campus communities. Byron and I share stories from our own lives, and we encourage the young men to do the same. The discussions are typically animated and fast-moving. The discussions can also be intense – with one team, for example, we spent an entire 90-minute session discussing the "Slapshot" scenario.

We then use the personal anecdotes and accounts to raise a number of different issues: Why do men hit women? Does a man establish his manhood by physically controlling a woman? What, then, does it mean to be a man? The specifics vary, but the message advanced in these discussions is consistent: that men have a critical role to play in reducing men's violence against women. We emphasize, furthermore, that violence against women is located on a continuum. It includes not just overt acts of physical abuse, but encompasses the full range of behaviors including sexist comments and jokes, and sexual harassment. We make it clear that we need men to provide leadership to change behavior in all of these areas.

The fourth session is reserved for selected student-athletes who have attended the first three sessions and have expressed an interest in talking to middle and high school boys and girls about men's violence against women. The selection process itself is a key to the success of this stage of the program because we need to be sure that the "mentors" we're training are credible on these issues. Though no fool-proof method exists to ensure selection of effective mentors, we have developed a set of guidelines that the athletic department, in consultation with the counseling center, the health education department, and/or the women's center can use in evaluating potential candidates. We don't necessarily look for young men who have advanced levels of feminist consciousness. The most important requirement is that their reputation and record be consistent with their public commitment to work against sexism.

Our model for preparing college male student-athletes to become mentors for youth does not require extensive knowledge on the part of participants, and at every level we have tried to streamline our message so that we can involve as many student-athletes as possible. We assign several articles for them to read, including the introduction to *Stopping Rape: A Challenge for Men*, by Rus Funk; the introduction to *Power at Play: Sports and the Problem of Masculinity* by Michael Messner; "Men Changing Men," by Robert Allen and Paul Kivel; "What Men Need to Know About Date Rape" by Marybeth Roden; "Male Athletes and Sexual Assault" by Merrill Melnick; "On Becoming Anti-Rapist," by Haki Madhubuti; "Beyond BS and the Drumbeating: Staggering Through Life as a Man" by Frank Pittman; and "The Myth of the Sexual Athlete" by Don Sabo. We also discuss at some length the process of talking both to boys and girls about violence against women, including issues such as what to expect, how to answer difficult questions, and the difference between being a role model and being an expert in the eyes of the adolescents.

We send at least one staff member from the MVP Project out with these student-athletes to meet with both classes and teams of middle and high school students. Our current high school model consists of both male and female college student-athlete mentors and MVP staff meeting in single-sex groups with male and female teams or team captains. After these sessions, we schedule a mixed gender meeting and facilitate a joint discussion. The MVP staff then keeps in touch with the student-athlete mentors over the course of the year, and tries to involve them in speaking engagements as often as their schedules permit. We also put student-athlete mentors in touch with local battered women's and rape crisis shelters for possible participation in their youth outreach or other educational programs.

Practical origins of the MVP project

The Mentors in Violence Prevention Project has its roots in my previous area of study, the social construction of violent masculinity through sports and media imagery. My focus was in the area of sports sociology, specifically male sports culture. Both personal experience and my review of the sports literature confirmed my assumption that there was not a lot being done in the sports culture itself to address the issue of violence, particularly male violence against girls and women. In the past few years, numerous articles in the mainstream media have detailed the involvement of high school, college, and professional athletes in the battering, rape, and gang rape of women. However, few effective college or high school-based prevention programs have specifically targeted the male athlete population. Athletes for Sexual Responsibility, started by Sandra Caron, is a pioneering and successful program at the University of Maine. Dr. Andrea Parrot, Nina Cummings, and Tim Marchell have developed a comprehensive curriculum to work with male athletes at Cornell University, and Tom Jackson has developed a successful program working with student-athletes at the University of Arkansas. But these and a few others were the rare exceptions. This was clearly an area ripe for educational innovation.[4]

During the spring of 1992, I approached administrators at the Center for the Study of Sport in Society at Northeastern University in Boston, Massachusetts, and presented them with an idea for a new program. The Center already sponsored both a degree-completion program for former Division One college athletes and Project Teamwork, which placed a multiracial and gender-mixed team of former collegiate, Olympic, and professional athletes into middle and high schools to discuss violence prevention as it relates to issues of racial, ethnic, and gender sensitivity. Why not try a similar approach on the issue of men's violence against women? My recent experiences as an educator-activist suggested that this was a promising endeavor. In 1988 I had founded Real Men, an antisexist men's organization based in Boston. Since 1990 I had been travelling around the country on the high school and college lecture circuit talking about my activist work with Real Men, using my background as a former all-star football player and as the first man to earn a minor in Women's Studies at the University of Massachusetts at Amherst to reach men with the message that sexism was *our* issue. While these types of programs are typically mandatory at the high school or middle school level, programming committees at colleges across the country have historically found it difficult to attract men to programs about men's violence against women, or any programs that foreground a discussion of masculinity.[5]

My proposal to create a program that would inspire other male athletes to provide leadership in the effort to prevent men's violence against women was greeted enthusiastically by executive director Richard Lapchick and associate director and head of programs Art Taylor at the Center for the Sport in Society at Northeastern. Over the next several months, the three of us worked together in developing grant proposals, which culminated in our being awarded a three-year grant from the United States Department of Education's Fund for the Improvement of Postsecondary Education (FIPSE). I was subsequently hired to run the MVP Project, which officially commenced in September 1993.

The FIPSE grant funded the creation of a campus-based program that would use male student-athletes as role models, peer leaders, and mentors to high school students on the issues of battering, rape, and sexual harassment. We also initiated plans to develop a complementary project that was aimed at college female student-athletes. Our commitment was to develop the program at four schools during the first year, two more in the second, and an additional three in the third year. Our goal was to create a model that was replicable and transferable to virtually every college and high school in the country.

We are still in the first couple of years of our project, so it is difficult to measure its potential for long-term success. One evaluative tool we have used is a pre- and post-test survey, which measures attitudes about intervening in incidents involving gender violence. Initial results indicate, not surprisingly, that the most powerful idea we have to counteract in order to be successful is the idea that matters between men and women, including violence, are "private." We also have received a great deal of written and verbal feedback from participating team members suggesting that the MVP sessions are popular with and considered useful by the student-athletes. Many of the men have told us that this was the first time they had ever talked about these issues with other men in a safe space.

We have also developed a three-day training of trainers model that allows MVP staff to travel to colleges and introduce selected male professional staff to the Project's goals and teaching methods. The local staff trainers are typically selected by the Dean of Students and Athletic Departments and may work in residence life, counseling, health education, athletics, or Greek [i.e. fraternity] affairs. We strongly recommend that they have some experience with gender issues and good group facilitation skills. Several meetings with teams are included in these training sessions, so the prospective trainers can observe actual MVP sessions.

We plan to develop a comprehensive package of materials, including Playbooks and training manuals and a training video, in order to facilitate the national dissemination of the MVP model. In the spring of 1995 we will pilot a version of the Playbook for female college student-athletes in which women consider a number of alternative bystander responses to scenarios of gender-related violence. In addition, we plan to produce Playbooks for high school boys and girls.

Conclusion: moving beyond silence in sports culture

A great deal of defensiveness has long existed in the sports culture about men's violence against women. Even before the O. J. Simpson case, for example, few people in sport wanted to talk about the rape or abuse of women by male athletes, and how the sexist subculture of the major male team sports (i.e., football, basketball, hockey, baseball) might contribute to the problem. However, recent media attention given to incidents of abusive behavior toward women by high-profile athletes has launched the issue into the national spotlight.

High school and college athletic departments have been particularly sensitive to this heightened focus on athletes' roles in violence against women. Until recently, many athletic administrators in the United States have been wary of initiating workshops on violence against women, in part due to the belief that offering this type of program acted as a tacit acknowledgement of wrongdoing by athletes within their institution. Such an impression might hurt the public image and the recruiting potential of the athletic department or the school.

Institutional myopia was also responsible for the reluctance of the sports community to confront the issue of men's violence against women. Most high school and college athletic programs are concerned with winning games and building programs, not with "changing the world," as some characterize any form of social awareness education. Some athletic administrators and coaches can see the value in providing alcohol and substance abuse education to their student-athletes; the need for this is self-evident and essentially non-controversial. But the mention of male athletes and rape in the same sentence is often met with stony silence by defensive athletic staffs, if not with angry denials.

A widespread perception exists in our society that male athletes, especially football, basketball, hockey, and baseball players, are disproportionately responsible for sexually assaulting women. This perception has been fed actively since the mid-1980s by a series of newspaper and magazine stories and a handful of surveys that purport to show a link between male team sports and the abuse of women. A recent study of ten Division One schools, completed by researchers at the University of Massachusetts at Amherst and Northeastern University, found that male student-athletes were six times as likely as their non-athlete peers to be reported for sexual assault to campus judicial affairs (Crossett, Benedict, & McDonald, 1995). An ever-growing list of publicized incidents of rape and abuse involving high school, collegiate, and professional athletes has also emerged. There have been enough of these incidents to confirm in the minds of many what the formal statistics have been unable to determine conclusively: that the male team sports culture somehow *encourages* this sort of behavior.

The MVP Project does not deal directly with whether or not dynamics of the male team sport culture promote sexism and the abuse of women, although we do talk about the public perception of athletes as disproportionately abusive. We focus instead on the social status of male student-athletes and the ways their leadership can make a critical difference in reducing all men's violence toward women. This approach avoids the accusatory rhetoric that often accompanies discussions about whether athletes are more or equally likely as other men to assault women. This strategy is partially born of necessity: if you want to work on violence prevention successfully with athletic departments and student-athletes, it makes sense not to alienate and offend them.

Finally, it is not critical to the success of our project to determine whether or not athletes assault women more often than do non-athletes. While one of our goals is to educate athletes in order to prevent them from committing violence, the overarching objective of our project is to reduce men's violence against women – particularly on college and high school campuses – by inspiring male student-athletes to use their stature among their male peers in the larger student body to promote healthier attitudes and behavior towards women. The rationale is straightforward. If we can convince popular athletes and other exemplars of traditional "masculine" success to model nonsexist behavior, we believe they can contribute to a dramatic shift in male behavior toward women. At the very least, they will help to catalyze a growing intolerance by all men for the abuse of women.

Notes

1   The initial rationale for founding the MVP Project was to inspire male leadership on issues that had been historically been considered "women's issues." MVP's next phase involves inspiring female leadership. Unlike many anti-rape or anti-abuse programs for women, which typically teach women how to prevent or avoid

assaults by men, the MVP Female Student-Athlete Project addresses women in the role of bystanders. This project, which is being piloted in the spring of 1995, seeks to empower female student-athletes and other female student leaders to interrupt and confront sexist behaviors and attitudes, and to use their status and position to mentor female high school and middle school students involved in sports and leadership activities.

2   The MVP Female Student Athlete Project features all-female sessions.

3   A similar dynamic applies in other areas. In an article entitled "Psychological Factors Inhibiting Arms Control Activism," Gilbert (1988) argues that the identity of the person advocating arms control can influence how the message is received by Americans concerned with patriotism and national loyalty. Thus, the peace movement's support from liberal actors and musicians, who have become identified with a relatively narrow band of liberal politics, does not enhance the prospect that arms control will become a broader movement.

    On the other hand, when conservative former government officials like McGeorge Bundy and George Kennan advocate a change in official nuclear arms policy, it is very difficult to dismiss their comments as mere anti-establishment rhetoric (Gilbert, 1988). In much the same way, it is difficult for young men to dismiss the words of star college football, basketball, and hockey players who tell them they're not impressed with guys who abuse women or try to prove how tough they are by dominating them. Hence the leadership of trained MVP mentors can broaden support among men for a shift in attitudes toward women, especially with respect to physical aggression and sexual coercion.

4   Dr. Tom Jackson, Department of Psychology, 216 Memorial Hall, University of Arkansas, Fayetteville, AR 72701 (501) 575-4256; Dr. Andrea Parrot, Nina Cummings, and Tim Marchell, Health Education Office, Gannett Health Center, Cornell University, Ithaca, NY 14853 (607) 255-4782; Dr. Sandra Caron, Athletes for Sexual Responsibility, University of Maine, Room 12, 5749 Merrill Hall, Orono, ME 04469 (207) 581-3138.

5   My speech entitled "Football, Feminism, and Other Contemporary Contradictions," however, often attracted audiences of 150–500 people, with a higher percentage of men in the audience than typically attended a gender issues program. The speech combined insights about the cultural factors contributing to men's violence against women with a pep talk to men about our need to take an active antisexist stance. Many times the campus groups who sponsored my speeches would invite the various men's athletic teams. Frequently I would meet with athletic team captains, coaches, and athletic administrators for dinner, or for a brief presentation prior to my public speech.

References

Allen, R., & Kivel, P. (1994, Sept.–Oct.). Men changing men. *Ms.*, pp. 50–3.

Berkowitz, A. (1992). College men as perpetrators of acquaintance rape and sexual assault: A review of recent research. *Journal of American College Health*, 40, 175–81.

Berkowitz, A. (1994). A model acquaintance rape prevention program for men. *New Directions for Student Services*, 65, 35–42.

Chickering, A. (1969). *Education and Identity*. San Francisco: Jossey-Bass.

Crosset, T., Benedict, J., & McDonald, M. (1995). Male student athletes reported for sexual assault: A survey of campus police departments and judicial affairs offices. *Journal of Sports and Social Issues*.

Eron, L. (1987). The development of aggressive behavior from the perspective of a developing behaviorism. *American Psychologist*, 5, 435–42.

Federal Bureau of Investigation. (1993). *Uniform Crime Reports*. Washington, DC: Author.

Funk, R. E. (1993). *Stopping Rape: A Challenge for Men*. Philadelphia: New Society.

Gilbert, R. (1988). The dynamics of inaction: Psychological factors inhibiting arms control activism. *American Psychologist*, 10, 755–64.

Madhubuti, H. (1993). On becoming anti-rapist. In E. Buchwald, P. R. Fletcher, & M. Roth (eds.), *Transforming a Rape Culture*. Minneapolis: Milkweed Editions.

Melnick, M. (1992). Male athletes and sexual assault. *Journal of Physical Education, Recreation, and Dance*, 63(5), 32–5.

Messner, M. (1992). *Power at Play: Sports and the Problem of Masculinity*. Boston: Beacon Press.

Nelson, M. B. (1994). *The Stronger Women Get, the More Men Love Football*. New York: Harcourt Brace.

Rapaport, K., & Burkhart, B. (1984). Personality and attitudinal characteristics of sexually coercive college males. *Journal of Abnormal Psychology*, 93, 216–21.

Roden, M. (1990). *What Men Need to Know about Date Rape*. Santa Monica, CA: Rape Treatment Center.

Pittman, F. (1992, Jan.–Feb.). Beyond BS and the drumbeating: Staggering through life as a man. *Psychology Today*, pp. 78–84.

Sabo, D. (1989). The myth of the sexual athlete. *Changing Men*, 1(20), 38–9.

Slaby, R. (1994). Development of psychological mediators of violence in urban youth. In J. McCord (ed.), *Growing up Violent: Contributions of Inner-City Life*. New York: Oxford University Press.

Part V

Heterosexism and Homophobia:
Critical Interventions

CHAPTER 33

Dennis Altman

The Globalization of Sexual Identities

Most of the literature about globalization and identity is concerned with the rebirth of nationalist, ethnic, and religious fundamentalism, or the decline of the labor movement.[1] (I am using "identity" to suggest a socially constructed myth about shared characteristics, culture, and history which comes to have real meaning for those who espouse it.)[2] Here I concentrate on the identity politics born of sexuality and gender, and the new social movements which arise from these, already foreshadowed in the previous chapter. These new identities are closely related to the larger changes of globalization: consider the globalization of "youth," and the role of international capitalism in creating a teenage identity in almost every country, with specific music, language, fashion, and mores.[3] In recent years this is expressed in terms of "boy" and "girl" cultures, as in references to "boy bands" or "a booming girl culture worldwide,"[4] which suggests the invention of an intermediate generational identity between "children" and "youth."

Over the past decade I've been researching and thinking about the diffusion of certain sorts of "gay/lesbian" identities, trying to trace the connections between globalization and the preconditions for certain sexual subjectivities.[5] My examples are drawn predominantly from Southeast Asia because this is the part of the "developing" world I know best, but they could even more easily be drawn from Latin America, which has a particularly rich literature exploring these questions.[6] The question is not whether homosexuality exists – it does in almost every society of which we know – but how people incorporate homosexual behavior into their sense of self. Globalization has helped create an international gay/lesbian identity, which is by no means confined to the western world: there are many signs of what we think of as "modern" homosexuality in countries such as Brazil, Costa Rica, Poland, and Taiwan. Indeed the gay world – less obviously the lesbian, largely due to marked differences in women's social and economic status – is a key example of emerging global "subcultures," where members of particular groups have more in common across national and continental boundaries than they do with others in their own geographically defined societies.

It is worth noting that even within the "first world" there is a range of attitudes toward the assertion of gay/lesbian identities. While they have flourished in the English-speaking

Dennis Altman, "The Globalization of Sexual Identities," pp. 86–105 and 188–93 from *Global Sex*. Chicago: University of Chicago Press, 2001. Reprinted by permission of University of Chicago Press and Dennis Altman.

countries and in parts of northern Europe, there is more resistance to the idea in Italy and France, where ideas of communal rights – expressed through the language of multiculturalism in Australia and Canada, and through a somewhat different tradition of religious pluralism in the Netherlands and Switzerland – seem to run counter to a universalist rhetoric of rights, which are not equated with the recognition of separate group identities.[7] The United States shares both traditions, so that its gay and lesbian movement argues for recognition of "civil rights" on the basis of being just like everyone else, and in some cases deserving of special protection along the lines developed around racial and gender discrimination.

At the same time the United States has gone farthest in the development of geographically based gay and lesbian communities, with defined areas of its large cities – the Castro in San Francisco, West Hollywood, Halsted in Chicago, the West Village in New York – becoming urban "ghettos," often providing a base to develop the political clout of the community. (In almost all large American cities politicians now recognize the importance of the gay vote.) This model has been replicated in a number of western countries, whether it is the Marais in Paris or Darlinghurst in Sydney. There is some irony in the fact that, while homosexual rights have progressed much further in the countries of northern Europe, the United States remains the dominant cultural model for the rest of the world.

This dominance was symbolized in accounts in Europe of "gay pride" events in the summer of 1999, which often ignored national histories and attributed the origins of gay political activism to the Stonewall riots of 1969, ignoring the existence of earlier groups in countries such as Germany, the Netherlands, Switzerland, and France, and the radical gay groups which grew out of the 1968 student movements in both France and Italy. (Stonewall was a gay bar in New York City which was raided by the police, leading to riots by angry homosexuals and the birth of the New York Gay Liberation Front.) In cities as diverse as Paris, Hamburg, and Warsaw the anniversary of Stonewall was celebrated with Christopher Street Day, and the dominance of American culture is summed up by the press release from the Lisbon Gay, Lesbian, Bisexual, and Transgender Pride committee boasting of the performances of a "renowned DJ from New York City" and "Celeda – the Diva Queen from Chicago."

Thinking and writing about these questions, it became clear to me that observers, indigenous and foreign alike, bring strong personal investments to how they understand what is going on, in particular whether (in words suggested to me by Michael Tan) we are speaking of "ruptures" or "continuities." For some there is a strong desire to trace a continuity between precolonial forms of homosexual desire and its contemporary emergence, even where the latter might draw on the language of (West) Hollywood rather than indigenous culture. Such views are argued strenuously by those who cling to an identity based on traditional assumptions about the links between gender performance and sexuality, and deny the relevance of an imported "gay" or "lesbian" identity for themselves. Thus the effeminate *bakkla* in the Philippines or the *kathoey* in Thailand might see those who call themselves "gay" as hypocrites, in part because they insist on their right to behave as men, and to desire others like them.[8] For others there is a perception that contemporary middle-class self-proclaimed gay men and lesbians in, say, New Delhi, Lima, or Jakarta have less in common with "traditional" homosexuality than they do with their counterparts in western countries. As Sri Lankan author Shaym Selvadurai said of his novel *Funny Boy*, which is in part about "coming out" as gay: "The people in the novel are in a place that has been colonized by Western powers for 400 years. A lot of

Western ideas – bourgeois respectability, Victorian morality – have become incorporated into the society, and are very much part of the Sri Lankan society."[9]

"Modern" ways of being homosexual threaten not only the custodians of "traditional" morality, they also threaten the position of "traditional" forms of homosexuality, those which are centered around gender nonconformity and transvestism. The title of the Indonesian gay/lesbian journal *Gaya Nusantara*, which literally means "Indonesian style," captures this ambivalence nicely with its echoes of both "traditional" and "modern" concepts of nation and sexuality, but at the same time it is clearly aimed at "modern" homosexuals rather than the "traditional" transvestite *waria*.[10]

It is often assumed that homosexuals are defined in most "traditional" societies as a third sex, but that too is too schematic to be universally useful. As Peter Jackson points out, the same terms in Thailand can be gender *and* sexual categories.[11] Here, again, we are confronted by considerable confusion, where similar phenomena can be viewed as either culturally specific or as universal. Insofar as there is a confusion between sexuality and gender in the "traditional" view that the "real" homosexual is the man who behaves like a woman (or, more rarely, vice versa) this is consistent with the dominant understanding of homosexuality in western countries during the hundred years or so before the birth of the contemporary gay movement. The idea of a "third sex" was adopted by people like Ulrichs and Krafft-Ebing as part of an apologia for homosexuality (giving rise to Carpenter's "intermediate sex").[12] In the 1918 novel *Despised and Rejected* the hero laments: "What had nature been about, in giving him the soul of a woman in the body of a man?"[13] Similar views can be found in Radclyffe Hall's novel *The Well of Loneliness* (1928), whose female hero calls herself Stephen. Today many people who experience homosexual desires in societies which do not allow space for them will see themselves as "men trapped in women's bodies" or vice versa.

In popular perceptions something of this confusion remains today – and persists in much popular humor, such as the remarkably successful play/film *La cage aux folles* (*The Birdcage*) or the film *Priscilla, Queen of the Desert*. George Chauncey argues that the very idea of a homosexual/heterosexual divide became dominant in the United States only in the mid-twentieth century: "The most striking difference between the dominant sexual culture of the early twentieth century and that of our own era is the degree to which the earlier culture permitted men to engage in sexual relations with other men, often on a regular basis, without requiring them to regard themselves – or be regarded by others – as gay...Many men...neither understood nor organised their sexual practices along a hetero-homosexual axis."[14] John Rechy's landmark novel *City of Night* (1963) captures the transition to "modern" concepts: his world is full of "hustlers," "queens," "masculine" or "butch" homosexuals, whom he sometimes calls "gay."[15]

If one reads or views contemporary accounts of homosexual life in, say, Central America, Thailand, and Côte d'Ivoire,[16] one is immediately struck by the parallels. It is of course possible that the observers, all of whom are trained in particular ethnographic and sociological methods, even where, as in the case of Schifter, they are indigenous to the country of study, are bringing similar – and one assumes unconscious – preconceptions with them. Even so, it is unlikely that this itself would explain the degree of similarity they identify. In the same way, the Dutch anthropologist Saskia Wieringa has pointed to the similarities of butch–femme role-playing in Jakarta and Lima, and how they echo that of preliberation western lesbian worlds.[17] In many "traditional" societies there were complex variations across gender and sex lines, with "transgender" people (Indonesian *waria*, Thai *kathoey*, Moroccan *hassas*, Turkish *kocek*, Filipino *bayot*, Luban *kitesha* in parts of Congo) characterized by both transvestite and homosexual behavior. These terms are usually – not always – applied to men, but there are other terms sometimes used of women, such as *mati* in Suriname, which also disrupt simplistic assumptions about sex and gender.[18] As Gilbert Herdt says: "Sexual orientation and identity are not the keys to conceptualizing a third sex and gender across time and space."[19] In many societies there is confusion around the terms – for example the *hijras* of India, who were literally castrated, are sometimes considered equivalent to homosexuals even though the reality is more complex.[20]

Different people use terms such as *bayot* or *waria* in different ways, depending on whether the emphasis is on gender – these are men who wish in some way to be women – or on sexuality – these are men attracted to other men. Anthropology teaches us the need to be cautious about any sort of binary system of sex/gender; Niko Besnier uses the term "gender liminality" to avoid this trap[21] and it should also alert us against the sort of romanticized assumptions that some Americans have brought to understanding the Native American *berdache*.[22] Besnier also stresses that such "liminality" is not the same as homosexuality: "Sexual relations with men are seen as an optional consequence of gender liminality, rather than its determiner, prerequisite or primary attribute."[23] The other side of this distinction is that there are strong pressures to define *fa'afafine* (the Samoan term) or other such groups in Pacific countries as asexual, thus leading to a particular denial in which both Samoans and outsiders are complicit.[24]

Certainly most of the literature about Latin America stresses that a homosexual *identity* (as distinct from homosexual practices) is related to rejection of dominant gender expectations, so that "a real man" can have sex with other men and not risk his heterosexual identity. As Roger Lancaster put it: "Whatever else a *cochon* might or might not do, he is tacitly understood as one who assumes the receptive role in anal intercourse. His partner, defined as 'active' in the terms of their engagement, is not stigmatized, nor does he acquire a special identity of any sort."[25] Thus the *nature* rather than the *object* of the sexual act becomes the key factor. However, there is also evidence that this is changing, and a more western concept of homosexual identity is establishing itself, especially among the middle classes.

Sexuality becomes an important arena for the production of modernity, with "gay" and "lesbian" identities acting as markers for modernity.[26] There is an ironic echo of this in the Singapore government's bulldozing of Bugis Street, once the center of transvestite prostitution in the city – and its replacement by a Disneyland-like simulacrum where a few years ago I was taken to see a rather sanitized drag show presented to a distinctly yuppie audience.[27] There is an equal irony in seeing the decline of a homosexuality defined by gender nonconformity as a "modern" trend just when transsexuals and some theorists in western countries are increasingly attracted by concepts of the malleability of gender.[28] From one perspective the fashionable replica of the stylized "lipstick lesbian" or "macho" gay man is less "post-modern" than the *waria* or the Tongan *fakaleiti*.[29]

Perhaps the reality is that androgyny is postmodern when it is understood as performance, not when it represents the only available way of acting out certain deep-seated beliefs about one's sexual and gender identity. Even so, I remain unsure just why "drag," and its female equivalents, remains a strong part of the contemporary homosexual world, even where there is increasing space for open homosexuality and a range of acceptable ways of "being" male or female. Indeed there is evidence that in some places there is a simultaneous increase in both gay/lesbian identities *and* in transgender performance, as in recent developments in Taiwan where drag shows have become very fashionable, and some of the performers, known as "third sex public relations officers," insist that they are not homosexual even when their behavior would seem to contradict this.[30] Similar comments could probably be made about *onnabe*, Japanese women who dress as men and act as the equivalent of geishas for apparently heterosexual women, and Jennifer Robertson describes the incorporation of androgyny into the "'libidinal' economy of the capitalist market" as "gender-bending" performers are turned into marketable commodities.[31] In the west it has become increasingly fashionable to depict transvestism in unmistakably heterosexual terms; what was daring (and possibly ambiguous) in the 1959 film *Some Like It Hot* becomes farce in the 1993 film *Mrs. Doubtfire*.[32] But at the same time there is, particularly in the United States, the emergence of a somewhat new form of transgender politics, in which the concern of an older generation to be accepted as the woman or man they "really" are is replaced by an assertion of a transgender identity and the malleability of gender.[33] (Western writers tend to be reasonably careful to distinguish between *transsexual* and *transvestite*. However, this distinction is often not made in parts of Asia and, I assume, other parts of the world.)

Speaking openly of homosexuality and transvestism, which is often the consequence of western influence, can unsettle what is accepted but not acknowledged. Indeed there is some evidence in a number of societies that those who proclaim themselves "gay" or "lesbian," that is, seek a public identity based on their sexuality, encounter a hostility which may not have been previously apparent. But there is a great deal of mythology around the acceptance of gender/sexual nonconformity outside the west, a mythology to which for different reasons both westerners and nonwesterners contribute. Romanticized views about homoeroticism in many nonwestern cultures, often based on travel experiences, disguise the reality of persecution, discrimination, and violence, sometimes in unfamiliar forms. Firsthand accounts make it clear that homosexuality is far from being universally accepted – or even tolerated – in such apparent "paradises" as Morocco, the Philippines, Thailand, or Brazil: "Lurking behind the Brazilians' pride of their flamboyant drag queens, their recent adulation of a transvestite chosen as a model of Brazilian beauty, their acceptance of gays and lesbians as leaders of the country's most widely practised religion and the constitutional protection of homosexuality, lies a different truth. Gay men, lesbians and transvestites face widespread discrimination, oppression and extreme violence."[34]

Just as the most interesting postmodern architecture is found in cities like Shanghai or Bangkok, so too the emphasis of postmodern theory on pastiche, parody, hybridity, and so forth is played out in a real way by women and men who move, often with considerable comfort, from apparent obedience to official norms to their own sense of gay community. The dutiful Confucian or Islamic Malaysian son one weekend might appear in drag at Blueboy, Kuala Lumpur's gay bar, the next – and who is to say which is "the real" person? Just as many Malaysians can move easily from one language to another, so most urban homosexuals can move from one style to another, from camping it up with full awareness of the latest fashion trends from Castro Street to playing the dutiful son at a family celebration.

To western gay liberationists these strategies might seem hypocritical, even cowardly (and some westerners expressed surprise at the apparent silence from Malaysian gay men after the arrest of Anwar on sodomy charges). But even the most politically aware Malaysians may insist that there is no need to "come out" to their family, while explaining that in any case their lover is accepted as one of the family – though not so identified. (The Malaysian situation is further complicated by the fact that Muslims are subject to both civil and *sharia* laws, and the latter have been used quite severely, against transvestites in particular.) Some people have suggested that everything is possible *as long as it is not stated*, but it is probably more complex than that. For many men I have met in Southeast Asia being gay does mean a sense of communal identity, and even a sense of "gay pride," but this is not necessarily experienced in the vocabulary of the west.

Middle-class English-speaking homosexuals in places like Mexico City, Istanbul, and Mumbai will speak of themselves as part of a gay (sometimes "gay and lesbian") community, but the institutions of such a community will vary considerably depending on both economic resources and political space. Thus in Kuala Lumpur, one of the richer cities of the "developing" world, there are no gay or lesbian bookstores, restaurants, newspapers, or businesses – at least not in the open way we would expect them in comparable American or European cities. There is, however, a strong sense of gay identity around the AIDS organization Pink Triangle – its name is emblematic – and sufficient networks for a gay sauna to open and attract customers. Yet when a couple of years ago I gave some copies of the Australian gay magazine *Outrage* to the manager of the Kuala Lumpur sauna, I was told firmly there could be no display of something as overtly homosexual as these magazines – which are routinely sold by most Australian newsagents. In the same way there is also a strong lesbian network in the city, and many women use office faxes and email to arrange meetings and parties.

At that same sauna I met one man who told me he had heard of the place through a friend now living in Sydney. In conversations I have had with middle-class gay men in Southeast Asia there are frequent references to bars in Paris and San Francisco, to Sydney's Gay and Lesbian Mardi Gras, to American gay writers. Those who take on gay identities often aspire to be part of global culture in all its forms, as suggested by this quote from a Filipino anthology of gay writing: "I met someone in a bar last Saturday... He's a bank executive. He's mestizo (your type) and... loves Barbra Streisand, Gabriel Garcia Marquez, Dame Margot Fonteyn, Pat Conroy, Isabel Allende, John Williams, Meryl Streep, Armistead Maupin, k. d. lang, Jim Chappell, Margaret Atwood and Luciano Pavarotti."[35]

Similarly magazines like *G & L* in Taiwan – a "lifestyle" magazine launched in 1996 – mixes local news and features with stories on international, largely American, gay and lesbian icons. As mobility increases, more and more people are traveling abroad and meeting foreigners at home. It is as impossible to prevent new identities and categories traveling as it is to prevent pornography traveling across the Internet.

As part of the economic growth of south and east Asia the possibilities of computer-based communications have been grasped with enormous enthusiasm, and have created a new set of possibilities for the diffusion of information and the creation of (virtual) communities. Whereas the gay movements of the 1970s in the west depended heavily on the creation of a gay/lesbian press, in countries such as Malaysia, Thailand, and Japan the Internet offers the same possibilities, with the added attraction of anonymity and instant contact with overseas, thus fostering the links with the diaspora already discussed. Work by Chris Berry and Fran Martin suggests that the Internet has become a crucial way for young homosexuals to meet each other in Taiwan and Korea – and in the process to develop a certain, if privatized, form of community.[36] In Japan the Internet has become a central aid to homosexual cruising.

It is precisely this constant dissemination of images and ways of being, moving disproportionately from north to south, which leads some to savagely criticize the spread of sexual identities as a new step in neocolonialism: "The very constitution of a subject entitled to rights involves the violent capture of the disenfranchised by an institutional discourse which inseparably weaves them into the textile of global capitalism."[37] This position is argued with splendid hyperbole by Pedro Bustos-Aguilar, who attacks both "the gay ethnographer... [who] kills a native with the charm of his camera" and "the union of the New World Order and Transnational Feminism" which asserts neocolonialism and western hegemony in the name of supposed universalisms.[38]

Bustos-Aguilar's argument is supported by the universalist rhetoric which surrounded the celebration of the twenty-fifth anniversary of Stonewall, but he could have had great fun with a 1993 brochure from San Francisco which offered "your chance to make history... [at] the first ever gay & lesbian film festival in India & parallel queer tour" – and even more with the reporter from the *Washington Blade* who wrote of Anwar's "ostensibly being gay."[39] It finds a troubling echo in the story of an American, Tim Wright, who founded a gay movement in Bolivia, and after four years was found badly beaten and amnesiac: "And things have gone back to being what they were."[40]

A more measured critique comes from Ann Ferguson, who has warned that the very concept of an international lesbian *culture* is politically problematic, because it would almost certainly be based upon western assumptions, even though she is somewhat more optimistic about the creation of an international *movement*, which would allow for self-determination of local lesbian communities.[41] While western influences were clearly present, it is as true to see the emergence of groups in much of Latin America, in Southeast Asia, and among South African blacks as driven primarily by local forces.

It is certainly true that the assertion of gay/lesbian identity can have neocolonial implications, but given that many anti/postcolonial movements and governments deny existing homosexual traditions it becomes difficult to know exactly whose values are being imposed on whom. Both the western outsider and the local custodians of national culture are likely to ignore existing realities in the interest of ideological certainty. Those outside the west tend to be more aware of the difference between traditional homosexualities and contemporary gay identity politics, a distinction sometimes lost by the international gay/lesbian movement in its eagerness to claim universality.[42] New sexual identities mean a loss of certain traditional cultural comforts while offering new possibilities to those who adopt them, and activists in non-western countries will consciously draw on both traditions. In this they may be inconsistent, but no more than western gay activists who simultaneously deploy the language of universal rights and special group status.

In practice most people hold contradictory opinions at the same time, reminding us of Freud's dictum that "it is only in logic that contradictions cannot exist." There are large numbers of men and fewer women in non-western countries who will describe themselves as "gay" or "lesbian" in certain circumstances, while sometimes claiming these labels are inappropriate to their situation. It is hardly surprising that people want both to identify with and to distinguish themselves from a particular western form of homosexuality, or that they will call upon their own historical traditions to do so. This ambivalence is caught in this account by a Chinese-Australian: "[Chinese] gays were determined to advance their cause but in an evolutionary rather than revolutionary way. They seized on issues such as gayness, gay culture, gay lifestyle, equal rights for gays and so on. In romantic poems the gay dreams of our ancestors were represented by two boys sharing a peach and the emperor who cut his sleeves of his gown rather than disturb his lover sleeping in his arms. To revive this dream, and enable millions of Chinese-born gays to choose their lifestyle, is a huge task. But it has happened in Taiwan, as it did in Hong Kong, and so it will in China."[43]

There are of course examples of Asian gay groups engaging in political activity of the sort associated with their counterparts in the west. Indonesia has a number of gay and lesbian groups, which have now held three national meetings. The best-known openly gay figure in Indonesia, Dede Oetomo, was a candidate of the fledgling Democratic People's Party in the 1999 elections, which followed the overthrow of Suharto. There have been several small radical gay political groups established in the Philippines in recent years, and gay demonstrations have taken place in Manila. ProGay (the Progressive Organization of Gays in the Philippines), as its name suggests, is concerned to draw links between specifically gay issues and larger questions of social justice.[44] The first lesbian conference was held in Japan in 1985,[45] and there have been lesbian organizations in Taiwan since 1990 and the Philippines since 1992.[46] The international lesbigay press carried reports of a national conference of lesbians in Beijing in late 1998 and in Sri Lanka the following year. There have been several *tongzhi* gatherings in Hong Kong (a term adopted to cover "lesbians, bisexuals, gays and transgendered people"), and a manifesto adopted by the 1996 meeting argued that "[c]ertain characteristics of confrontational politics, such as through coming out and mass protests and parades may not be the best way of achieving *tongzhi* liberation in the family-centred, community-oriented Chinese societies which stress the importance of social harmony."[47] (An odd myth, given the revolutionary upheavals in twentieth-century China.) None of these groups have the history or the reach of gay/lesbian movements in Latin America, where Brazil, Argentina, Chile, and Mexico all have significant histories of a politicized homosexuality.

In many cases homosexual identities are asserted without an apparent gay/lesbian movement. In 1998 there was a move by bar owners in Kuala Lumpur to organize a gay-pride party which was canceled after a protest by the Malaysian Youth Council. The best example of a nonpolitical gay world can probably be found in Thailand, where there is a growing middle-class gay world, based neither on prostitution nor on traditional forms of gender nonconformity (as in the person of the *kathoey*), but only a small lesbian group, Anjaree, and no gay male groups at all since the collapse of a couple of attempts to organize around HIV in the late 1980s.[48] In late 1996 controversy erupted in Thailand after the governing body of the country's teacher-training colleges decreed that "sexual deviants" would be barred from entering the colleges. While there was considerable opposition to the ban (subsequently dropped), other than Anjaree most of this came from nongay sources. In the ensuing public debate one could see contradictory outside influences at work – both an imported fear of homosexuals and a more modern emphasis on how such a ban infringed human rights. As Peter Jackson concluded: "A dynamic gay scene has emerged . . . in the complete absence of a gay rights movement."[49]

Indeed it may be that a political movement is the least likely part of western concepts of homosexual identity to be adopted in many parts of the world, even as some activists enthusiastically embrace the mores and imagery of western queerdom. The particular form of identity politics which allowed for the mobilization of a gay/lesbian electoral pressure in countries like the United States, the Netherlands, and even France may not be appropriate elsewhere, even if western-style liberal democracy triumphs. The need of western lesbian/gays to engage in identity politics as a means of enhancing self-esteem may not be felt in other societies. Even so, one should read Jackson's comment about Thailand with some caution. Already when he wrote it there was an embryonic group in Bangkok around an American-owned and -run gay bookstore. At the end of 1999 one of the country's gay papers organized a gay festival and twilight parade in the heart of Bangkok, announcing it as "the first and biggest gay parade in Asia where Asian gay men have a basic human right to be who they want to be and love who they want to love."[50] Similarly, accounts of homosexual life in Japan alternate between assuming a high degree of acceptance – and therefore no reason for a political movement – and severe restrictions on the space to assert homosexual identity, though the gay group OCCUR has recently gained a certain degree of visibility.

The western gay/lesbian movement emerged in conditions of affluence and liberal democracy, where despite other large social issues it was possible to develop a politics around sexuality, which is more difficult in countries where the basic structures of political life are constantly contested.[51] Writing of contemporary South Africa Mark Gevisser notes: "Race-identification overpowers everything else – class, gender and sexuality."[52] In the same way basic questions of political economy and democratization will impact the future development of gay/lesbian movements in much of Asia and Africa. Yet in Latin America and eastern Europe gay/lesbian movements have grown considerably in the past decade, and there are signs of their emergence in some parts of Africa, for example in Botswana and in Zimbabwe, where President Mugabe has consistently attacked homosexuality as the product of colonialism.[53] Similar rhetoric has come from the leaders of Kenya,[54] Namibia, and Uganda, whose President Museveni has denounced homosexuality as "western" – using the rhetoric of the Christian right to do so.[55] Anglican bishops from Africa – though not South Africa – were crucial in defeating moves to change the Church of England's attitudes toward homosexuality at the 1998 decennial Lambeth Conference. South Africa is a crucial exception, perhaps because apartheid's denunciation of homosexuality made it easier for the African National Congress to develop a policy of acceptance as part of their general support for "a rainbow nation." Even so, some elements of the ANC are strongly homophobic, revealed in the rhetoric of many of Winnie Mandela's supporters.[56]

While many African officials and clergy maintain that homosexuality is not part of precolonial African culture, the evidence for its existence – and the slow acknowledgment of its role in African life – is emerging across the continent. One might speculate that the strong hostility from some African political and religious leaders toward homosexuality as a "western import" is an example of psychoanalytic displacement, whereby anxieties about sexuality are redirected to continuing resentment against colonialism and the subordinate position of Africa within the global economy. Western-derived identities can easily become markers of those aspects of globalization which are feared and opposed. Similarly, a 1994 conference for gay/MSMs (men who have sex with men) in Bombay was opposed by the National Federation of Indian Women, an affiliate of the Communist part of India, as "an invasion of India by decadent western cultures and a direct fall-out of our signing the GATT agreement."[57] Whether the federation was aware of how close its rhetoric was to right-wing Americans such as Patrick Buchanan is unknown.

Part of the appearance of modernity is the use of western languages. Rodney Jones has noted the importance of English as part of the cultural capital of Hong Kong homosexuals,[58] and when I attended an AIDS conference in Morocco in 1996 participants complained that despite an attempt to ensure equal use of Arabic it was "easier" to talk about sexuality in French. A similar emphasis on English is noted by James Farrar in presumably heterosexual discos in Shanghai, where ironically the Village People song "YMCA" has now become "a globalized dance ritual in which the dancers are encouraged to use their hands to make shapes of the English letters, identifying themselves momentarily with a boundless global ecumene of sexy happy youth 'at the YMCA.'"[59] One assumes the Shanghai dancers are unaware of the clearly gay overtones to both the song and the group. I admit to particular pleasure in reading this piece; an early proposal for my book *The Homosexualization of America* was rejected by an editor who complained (this was in 1982) that in a year no one would remember the Village People, the image with which I began that book.

A common language is essential for networking, and the past 20 years have seen a rapid expansion of networks among lesbian and gay groups across the world. In 1978 the

International Lesbian and Gay Association (ILGA) was formed at a conference in Coventry, England.[60] While ILGA has largely been driven by northern Europeans, it now has member groups in more than 70 countries and has organized international meetings in several southern cities. Other networks, often linked to feminist and AIDS organizing, have been created in the past two decades, and emerging lesbian and gay movements are increasingly likely to be in constant contact with groups across the world. The inspiration from meeting with other lesbians at international women's conferences has been a powerful factor in the creation of lesbian groups in a number of countries. Thus the Asian Lesbian Network, which now includes women from 12 or 13 countries, began at an International Lesbian Information Service conference in Geneva in 1986.[61]

In recent years there has been some attempt to promote international networking among transgendered people – or, as Americans now call them, transfolk – with both the British-based International Gender Transient Affinity and the US-based Gender Freedom International lobbying to protect transgendered people across the world from what seems to be routine harassment and persecution. The paradox of globalization is played out in constructions of sex/gender which combine the premodern with the modern, so that people identifying with "traditional" forms of transgender identity will employ modern techniques of surgery and hormone therapy to alter their bodies.

The two largest international gay/lesbian institutions are probably those based around the Metropolitan Community Church and the Gay Games. The MCC is a Protestant sect founded by the Reverend Troy Perry in Los Angeles in 1968, whose congregations and ministers are largely homosexual, with an estimated congregation of more than 40,000 in some 16 countries. Similar gay churches have emerged somewhat independently in several other societies such as South Africa and Mexico.[62] The Gay Games, modeled on the Olympics, which refused the use of its name, were first held in San Francisco in 1982, and have since become a major international event every four years, for which cities contend very bitterly. They also generate considerable international publicity, much of it of a somewhat voyeuristic nature.[63] Both of these "networks," it is worth stressing, originated in the United States.

Homosexuality becomes a particularly obvious measure of globalization, for the transformation of local regimes of sexuality and gender is often most apparent in the emergence of new sorts of apparently "gay" and "lesbian," even "queer," identities. Yet we must beware reading too much into these scripts. What is happening in Bangkok, Rio, and Nairobi is the creation of new forms of understanding and regulating the sexual self, but it is unlikely that they will merely repeat those forms which were developed in the Atlantic world. Walking through the "gay" area of Tokyo's Shinjuku you will see large numbers of young men in sneakers and baseball caps (or whatever happens to be the current "gay" look) but this does not mean they will behave or view themselves in the same way as equivalent young men in North America or northern Europe.

Prostitute versus sex worker

A growing globalization of both identities and human rights is reflected in the growth of sex-worker groups and the regulation of prostitution. In recent years there have been legislative attempts in a number of first-world countries to decriminalize prostitution and at the same time to control certain forms of sex work, especially that involving enforced prostitution or children.[64] There is a bitter division between those who argue that human rights should mean the end of prostitution (understood as "sex-slavery" to use Kathleen Barry's phrase)[65] and those who argue that adults should have the right to use their bodies to make money, and should be protected from exploitation and danger in making use of that right. Indeed the use of the term "sex worker" is a deliberate ploy to demystify the category of "prostitute," and the terms "sex work" and "sex worker" "have been coined by sex workers themselves to redefine commercial sex, not as the social or psychological characteristic of a class of women, but as an income-generating activity or form of employment for women and men."[66] One of the most eloquent statements comes from the Indian group Durbar Mahila Samanwaya Committee, even if the language clearly reflects western academic discourse.

> The "prostitute" is rarely used to refer to an occupational group of women earning their livelihood through providing sexual services, rather it is deployed as a descriptive term denoting a homogenised category, usually of women, which poses threats to public health, sexual morality, social stability and civic order. Within this discursive boundary we system-atically find ourselves to be targets of moralising impulses of dominant social groups through missions of cleansing and sanitising both materially and symbolically. If and when we figure in political or development agenda we are enmeshed in discursive practices and practical projects which aim to rescue, rehabilitate, improve, discipline, control or police us.[67]

The first sex-worker organization seems to have been COYOTE (standing for Call Off Your Old Tired Ethics), which was established by Margo St. James in San Francisco in 1973 with support from the Glide Memorial Church and the Playboy Foundation.[68] Apparently unconnected to this a group emerged in France in the mid-1970s, following the murder of several prostitutes in Lyons in which the police showed little interest. Out of this group, and the subsequent English Collective of Prostitutes, came the formation of the International Committee for Prostitutes' Rights. COYOTE organized the First World Meeting of Prostitutes in Washington in 1976, following which other groups emerged, such as Red Thread in the Netherlands. At the Second World Whores' Congress in Brussels in 1986 delegates demanded that "[p]rostitution should be redefined as legitim-ate work and the prostitutes should be redefined as legitimate citizens."[69]

This shift toward seeing prostitution as work is reflected in the development of "sex-work" organizations in some developing countries, the first of which seems to have been in Ecuador, followed by groups in a number of other Latin American countries[70] and a couple in Southeast Asia such as Talikala in Davao City, the Philippines. The women who founded Talikala were concerned from the outset to empower sex workers, and were attacked by conservative Catholics for "promoting prostitution," ironic as the initial funding for the project came from the Maryknoll Fathers. In 1995 sex workers in the Sonagachi area of Calcutta organized the Durbar Mahila Samanwaya Committee, which claims to be the registered organization of more than 40,000 female, male, and transsexual sex workers of West Bengal[71] and with the Usha Co-operative runs its own STI clinics, a cooperative credit union, literacy classes, and a crèche. One report suggested 3,000 people attended the first national prostitution conference in India in 1997.[72] Even if this sort of organizing was in part inspired by western ideas, does that make it less significant? One might remember that the Indian independence movement was also influenced by western concepts of nation and democracy – and itself became a major inspiration for the American and South African civil rights movements. In the same way the Durbar Mahila Samanwaya Committee has taken the mobilization of sex workers to a scale beyond that reached in any western country.

During the 1990s an international network of sex-work projects (NSWP) has sought to link sex-worker groups in both rich and poor countries, often organizing around international HIV/AIDS conferences. By the end of the decade the network linked groups in forty countries, but was limited by huge difficulty in getting resources, and the dependence on a handful of dedicated volunteers.[73] Gaining acceptance for sex-worker groups has been a tough ongoing struggle, with only a few governments being willing to accord any recognition at all. In both Australia and New Zealand the national organizations have at times played a role in national AIDS advisory bodies, but this is rare, nor have better-established community AIDS organizations always been particularly supportive. Guenter Frankenberg's comment about Germany applies elsewhere: "The gay dominated AIDS-Hilfen have effectively colonized junkies, prostitutes and prisoners, speaking for them instead of enabling them to be their own advocates."[74] The recognition of representatives of both sex workers and lesbians in the 1998 Indonesian Women's Congress which followed the downfall of Suharto was therefore particularly significant,[75] as was the inclusion of lesbianism on the official agenda of the 1998 All National Women's Conference in India.

Most people who engage in sex for money have no sense of this comprising their central identity, and they may well be repelled by attempts to organize around an identity they would strongly reject. It is a fact that money will be involved in a great many sexual encounters in almost any cash economy, and that the great majority of such transactions will not involve people who identify themselves as professional sex workers, but see it rather as one among a number of strategies to survive.[76] This is true of young African girls who find "sugar daddies" (sometimes known as "spare tyres") to help with their school fees, as it is of American beach bums who accept hospitality and gifts in exchange for sexual favors. We should be skeptical of those studies which claim to tell us that 36% of sex workers are positive/negative/use condoms or whatever: this assumes a fixed population, which is a dangerous fiction. It seems useful to think of prostitution not as a fixed state or identity, but rather as a continuum ranging from organized prostitution, through brothels, escort agencies, and so forth, to unpremeditated transactions resulting from chance encounters.

This does not mean that organization around conditions of employment and protection from abuse may not be successful. Speaking of drug users, Chris Jones suggested the idea of a "pragmatic community...a community in action affected by various forces producing potentially pro-active responses to various situations."[77] We need to know more about organizations which may well include sex workers without making this a central definition, as in the example of the Ghana Widows' Association, which according to at least one account includes large numbers of women in Accra working in commercial sex.[78] In early 1998 a group known as the Henao Sisters was established in Port Moresby (Papua New Guinea) for women known as *raun-raun* girls, those who move in and out of prostitution. While the group grew out of a peer-education program established by a government-supported program for HIV-prevention education, the initiative for its development appears to have come from the women themselves who are faced with ongoing issues of survival, violence, and police harassment.

As both the examples of gay/lesbian and sex-worker identities show, socioeconomic change will produce new ways of understanding ourselves and our place in the world. The breakdown of the extended family household as both an economic and social unit was one of the most important consequences of industrialization in the western world. In turn the growth of affluence, and the shifting emphasis from production to consumption, has meant a steady shrinking in households as even the nuclear family is replaced by large numbers of unmarried couples, of single-parent families, of people living large parts of their lives alone or in shared households. With this has come a new range of identities, as people seek to make sense of their lives as divorced, single, unmarried, or sole parents. Both commercial pressures to target specific "demographics" and the personal need to define one's identity in psychological terms means the growth of new sorts of support and social groups for, say, divorcées, single fathers, people living in multiple relationships (for which the word "polyandry" has been revived).

Unlike identities based on sexuality such as "lesbian" or "transvestite," these are identities based on relationship status and can in fact cross over definitions of sexuality. In Harvey Fierstein's play *Torch Song Trilogy* there is an angry argument where Arnold tries to make his mother accept that the loss of his lover is equivalent to her loss of her husband. There are small signs that this emphasis on relationship identities is spreading beyond the rich world, such as a report of an attempt to found "the Divorced Women's Tea-house" in Beijing in 1995. The association foundered on Chinese government restrictions on the creation of nongovernmental organizations.[79]

Underlying all these developments is an increasing stress on ideas of individual identity and satisfaction, and the linking of these concepts to sexuality. One of the dominant themes in post-Freudian western thinking about sex has been to explain why sexuality is so central to our sense of self, and thus the basis of both psychological and political identity. These assumptions about sexuality are far from universal; as Heather Montgomery warned, speaking of children in the sex industry in Thailand: "Sexuality was never identified with personal fulfilment or individual pleasure . . . Prostitution was an incidental way of constructing their identities."[80] Similarly Lenore Manderson wrote, also of Thailand: "For women, commercial sex is the mechanism by which many women today fulfill their obligations as mothers and daughters. For them, the body and its sexual expression in work are a means of production rather than a mirror to the self."[81]

That last phrase is crucial, for it sums up the dominant script by which westerners have interpreted sexuality for the past century, whether they have sought genetic and biological explanations or, like the radical Freudian school derived from thinkers like Wilhelm Reich and Herbert Marcuse, have sought to develop concepts of repression and sublimation to explain political attitudes and behavior.[82] In some ways Frantz Fanon also belongs to this tradition, and the fact that he wrote from the position of a colonized Algerian has made him particularly attractive to postcolonial theorists, who tend to ignore his strong homophobia.[83] This attempt to link sexuality with the political is far less fashionable today, where sexuality is more commonly linked with contemporary capitalism, and we increasingly think of ourselves as consumers rather than citizens. Indeed it is the Right who seem to set the agenda for sexual politics, through attacks on abortion, contraception, and homosexuality, which they link clearly to dissatisfaction with the whole tenor of modern life, yet refusing, except for a small group of religious thinkers, to see the connection between contemporary capitalism and the changes in the sex/gender order they so abhor.

Notes

1   E.g., Frances Fox Piven, "Globalizing Capitalism and the Rise of Identity Politics," in L. Panitch, ed., *Socialist Register* (London: Merlin, 1995), 102–16; Leslie Sklair, "Social Movements and Global Capitalism," in F. Jameson and M. Miyoshi, eds., *The Cultures of Globalization* (Durham: Duke University Press, 1998), 291–311.

2 For a clear exposition of this view of social constructionism see Jeffrey Weeks, *Sexuality and Its Discontents* (London: Routledge & Kegan Paul, 1985).

3 E.g., Beverley Hooper, "Chinese Youth: The Nineties Generation," *Current History* 90:557 (1991): 264–69.

4 See Sherrie Inness, ed., *Millennium Girls* (Lanham, MD: Rowman & Littlefield, 1999); Marion Leonard, "Paper Planes: Travelling the New Grrrl Geographies," in T. Skelton and G. Valentine, eds., *Cool Places: Geographies of Youth Cultures* (London: Routledge, 1998), 101–18.

5 Much of this section draws on work originally published in the mid-1990s. See especially Dennis Altman, "Rupture or Continuity? The Internationalization of Gay Identities," *Social Text* 14:3 (1996): 77–94; Altman, "On Global Queering," *Australian Humanities Review*, no. 2, July 1996 (electronic journal, www.lib.latrobe.edu.au); Altman, "Global Gaze/Global Gays," *GLQ* 3 (1997): 417–36.

6 See the bibliography in Balderston and Guy, *Sex and Sexuality in Latin America*, 259–77; the chapters on Brazil and Argentina in B. Adam, J. W. Duyvendak, and A. Krouwel, eds., *The Global Emergence of Gay and Lesbian Politics* (Philadelphia: Temple University Press, 1999); and the special issue of *Culture, Health, and Society* (1:3 [1999]) on "alternative sexualities and changing identities among Latin American men," edited by Richard Parker and Carlos Carceres.

7 For a discussion of the French position see David Caron, "Liberté, Egalité, Sero-positivité: AIDS, the French Republic, and the Question of Community," in Boule and Pratt, "AIDS in France," 281–93. On the Netherlands see Judith Schuyf and Andre Krouwel, "The Dutch Lesbian and Gay Movement: The Politics of Accommodation," in Adam, Duyvendak, and Krouwel, *Global Emergence of Gay and Lesbian Politics*, 158–83. On Australia see Dennis Altman, "Multiculturalism and the Emergence of Lesbian/Gay Worlds," in R. Nile, ed., *Australian Civilisation* (Melbourne: Oxford University Press, 1994), 110–24.

8 I owe thanks to a long list of people who over the years have discussed these issues with me, including Ben Anderson, Eufracio Abaya, Hisham Hussein, Lawrence Leong, Shivananda Khan, Peter Jackson, Julian Jayaseelan, Ted Nierras, Dede Oetomo, and Michael Tan.

9 Jim Marks, "The Personal Is Political: An Interview with Shaym Selvadurai," *Lambda Book Report* (Washington) 5:2 (1996): 7.

10 The original Indonesian term was *banci*. The term *waria* was coined in the late 1970s by combining the words for "woman" and "man." See Dede Oetomo, "Masculinity in Indonesia," in R. Parker, R. Barbosa, and P. Aggleton, eds., *Framing the Sexual Subject* (Berkeley: University of California Press, 2000), 58–9 n. 2.

11 See Peter Jackson, "Kathoey><Gay><Man: The Historical Emergence of Gay Male Identity in Thailand," in Manderson and Jolly, *Sites of Desire*, 166–90.

12 See Jeffrey Weeks, *Coming Out* (London: Quartet, 1977); John Lauritsen and David Thorstad, *The Early Homosexual Rights Movement* (New York: Times Change Press, 1974).

13 A. T. Fitzroy, *Despised and Rejected* (London: Gay Men's Press, 1988; originally published 1918), 223.

14 George Chauncey, *Gay New York* (New York: Basic Books, 1994), 65.

15 John Rechy, *City of Night* (New York: Grove, 1963).

16 E.g., Annick Prieur, *Mema's House, Mexico City* (Chicago: University of Chicago Press, 1998); Jacobo Schifter, *From Toads to Queens* (New York: Haworth, 1999); Peter Jackson and Gerard Sullivan, eds., *Lady Boys, Tom Boys, Rent Boys* (New York: Haworth, 1999); *Woubi Cheri* (1998), directed by Philip Brooks and Laurent Bocahut.

17 Saskia Wieringa, "Desiring Bodies or Defiant Cultures: Butch-Femme Lesbians in Jakarta and Lima," in E. Blackwood and S. Wieringa, eds., *Female Desires: Same-Sex Relations and Transgender Practices across Cultures* (New York: Columbia University Press, 1999), 206–29.

18 Gloria Wekker, "What's Identity Got to Do with It? Rethinking Identity in Light of the Mati Work in Suriname," in Blackwood and Wieringa, *Female Desires*, 119–38.
    Compare the very complex typologies of "same-sex" groups in Will Roscoe and Stephen Murray, eds., *Boy-Wives and Female Husbands: Studies in African-American Homosexualities* (New York: Palgrave Macmillan, 2001), 279–82; and in the same volume, Rudolf Gaudio, "Male Lesbians and Other Queer Notions in Hausa," 115–28.

19 Gilbert Herdt, *Third Sex, Third Gender: Beyond Sexual Dimorphism in Culture and History* (New York: Zone Books, 1996), 47.

20 See Serena Nanda, "The Hijras of India: Cultural and Individual Dimensions of an Institutionalized Third Gender Role," in E. Blackwood, ed., *The Many Faces of Homosexuality* (New York: Harrington Park Press, 1986), 35–54. And read her comments in light of Shivananda Khan, "Under the Blanket: Bisexualities and AIDS in India," in Aggleton, *Bisexualities and AIDS*, 161–77.

21 See Niko Besnier, "Polynesian Gender Liminality through Time and Space," in Herdt, *Third Sex, Third Gender*, 285–328. Note that the subtitle of Herdt's book is "Beyond Sexual Dimorphism in Culture and History."

22 See Ramon Gutierrez, "Must We Deracinate Indians to Find Gay Roots?" *Outlook* (San Francisco), winter 1989, 61–7.

23 Besnier, "Polynesian Gender Liminality," 300.

24 See Lee Wallace, "*Fa'afafine: Queens of Samoa* and the Elision of Homosexuality," *GLQ* 5:1 (1999): 25–39.

25 Roger Lancaster, "'That We Should All Turn Queer?': Homosexual Stigma in the Making of Manhood and the Breaking of a Revolution in Nicaragua," in Richard G. Parker and John H. Gagnon, *Conceiving Sexuality: Approaches to Sex Research in a Postmodern World* (New York and London: Routledge, 1995), 150.

26 See Henning Bech, *When Men Meet: Homosexuality and Modernity* (Chicago: University of Chicago Press, 1997); Kenneth Plummer, *The Making of the Modern Homosexual* (London: Hutchinson, 1981).

27 See Laurence Wai-teng, "Singapore," in Donald J. West and Richard Green, eds., *Sociolegal Control of Homosexuality: A Multi-Nation Comparison* (New York: Kluwer, 1997), 134; and the remarkable Singapore film *Bugis Street* (1995), directed by Yon Fan – remarkable for having been made at all.

28 E.g., Sandy Stone, "The Empire Strikes Back: A Posttranssexual Manifesto," in P. Treichler, L. Cartwright, and C. Penley, eds., *The Visible Woman* (New York: New York University Press, 1998), 285–309.

29 See Niko Besnier, "Sluts and Superwomen: The Politics of Gender Liminality in Urban Tonga," *Ethnos* 62:1–2 (1997): 5–31.

30 Thanks to Arthur Chen of the AIDS Prevention and Research Center, Taipei, for this information.

31 Jennifer Robertson, *Takarazuka: Sexual Politics and Popular Culture in Modern Japan* (Berkeley: University of California Press, 1998), 207.

32 For some of the complications in reading cinematic versions of cross-dressing see Marjorie Garber, *Vested Interests* (New York: Routledge, 1992).

33 See Leslie Feinberg, *Transgender Warriors* (Boston: Beacon, 1996); Kate Bornstein, *Gender Outlaw* (New York: Routledge, 1993).

34 Sereine Steakley, "Brazil Can Be Tough and Deadly for Gays," *Bay Windows* (Boston), June 16, 1994.

35 Jerry Z. Torres, "Coming Out," in N. Garcia and D. Remoto, eds., *Ladlad: An Anthology of Philippine Gay Writing* (Manila: Anvil, 1994), 128.

36 Chris Berry and Fran Martin, "Queer'n'Asian on the Net: Syncretic Sexualities in Taiwan and Korean Cyberspaces," *Inqueeries* (Melbourne), June 1998, 67–93.

37 Pheng Cheah, "Posit(ion)ing Human Rights in the Current Global Conjuncture," *Public Culture* 9 (1997): 261.

38 Pedro Bustos-Aguilar, "Mister Don't Touch the Banana," *Critique of Anthropology* 15:2 (1995): 149–70.

39 Kai Wright, "Industrializing Nations Confront Budding Movement," *Washington Blade*, Oct. 23, 1998.

40 Pedro Albornoz, "Landlocked State," *Harvard Gay and Lesbian Review* 6:1 (1999): 17.

41 Ann Ferguson, "Is There a Lesbian Culture?" In J. Allen, ed., *Lesbian Philosophies and Cultures* (Albany: State University of New York Press, 1990), 63–88.

42 See, e.g., the interview by William Hoffman with Mumbai activist Ashok Row Kavi, *Poz*, July 1998, which proclaims him "the Larry Kramer of India."

43 Bing Yu, "Tide of Freedom," *Capital Gay* (Sydney), May 1, 1998.

44 In July 1999 the paper *ManilaOUT* listed over twenty gay, lesbian, and "gay and lesbian-friendly" organizations in Manila.

45 Naeko, "Lesbian = Woman," in B. Summerhawk et al., eds., *Queer Japan* (Norwich, VT: New Victoria Publishers, 1998), 184–7.

46 Malu Marin, "Going beyond the Personal," *Women in Action* (ISIS International Manila) 1 (1996): 58–62.

47 Manifesto of Chinese Tongzhi Conference, Hong Kong, Dec. 1996. Thanks to Graham Smith for providing this source.

48 See Andrew Matzner, "Paradise Not," *Harvard Gay and Lesbian Review* 6:1 (winter 1999): 42–4.

49 Peter Jackson, "Beyond Bars and Boys: Life in Gay Bangkok," *Outrage* (Melbourne), July 1997, 61–3.

50 Statement from *Male* magazine, quoted in *Brother/Sister* (Melbourne), Sept. 16, 1999, 51.

51 There is a similar argument in Barry Adam, Jan Willem Duyvendak, and Andre Krouwel, "Gay and Lesbian Movements beyond Borders?" in Adam, Duyvendak, and Krouwel, *Global Emergence of Gay and Lesbian Politics*, 344–71.

52 Mark Gevisser, "Gay Life in South Africa," in Peter Drucker, *Different Rainbows* (London: Millivres, 2001), 116.

53 Dean Murphy, "Zimbabwe's Gays Go 'Out' at Great Risk," *Los Angeles Times*, July 27, 1998.

54 For one view of the situation in Kenya see Wanjira Kiama, "Men Who Have Sex with Men in Kenya," in Martin Foreman, ed., *AIDS and Men: Taking Risks or Taking Responsibility*? (London: Zed Books), 115–26.

55 Chris McGreal, "Gays Are Main Evil, Say African Leaders," *Guardian Weekly*, Oct. 7–13, 1999, 4.

56 See Carl Stychin, *A Nation by Rights* (Philadelphia: Temple University Press, 1998), chap. 3.

57 *Times of India*, Nov. 9, 1994, quoted by Sherry Joseph and Pawan Dhall, "No Silence Please, We're Indians!" in Drucker, *Different Rainbows*, 164.

58 Rodney Jones, "'Potato Seeking Rice': Language, Culture, and Identity in Gay Personal Ads in Hong Kong," *International Journal of the Sociology of Language* 143 (2000): 31–59.

59 James Farrar, "Disco 'Super-Culture': Consuming Foreign Sex in the Chinese Disco," *Sexualities* 2:2 (1999): 156.

60 John Clark, "The Global Lesbian and Gay Movement," in A. Hendriks, R. Tielman, and E. van der Veen, eds., *The Third Pink Book* (Buffalo: Prometheus Books, 1993), 54–61.

61 "The Asian Lesbian Network," *Breakout* (newsletter of Can't Live in the Closet, Manila) 4:3–4 (1998): 13.

62 On South Africa see Graeme Reid, "'Going Back to God, Just as We Are': Contesting Identities in the Hope and Unity Metropolitan Community Church," *Development Update* (Johannesburg) 2:2 (1998): 57–65. For a discussion of a gay church in Azcapotzalco, on the outskirts of Mexico City, see "Living la Vida Local," *Economist*, Dec. 18, 1999, 85–7.

63 Coverage of the 1994 games in New York by the Brazilian press is discussed in Charles Klein, "'The Ghetto Is Over, Darling': Emerging Gay Communities and Gender and Sexual Politics in Contemporary Brazil," *Culture, Health, and Society* 1:3 (1999): 239–41.

64 This legislation, it might be argued, is another form of western discourse being deployed to counter a largely western-generated phenomenon. See Eliza Noh, "'Amazing Grace, Come Sit on My Face,' or Christian Ecumenical Representations of the Asian Sex Tour Industry," *Positions* 5:2 (1997): 439–65.

65 Kathleen Barry, *Female Sexual Slavery* (New York: New York University Press, 1984). This should be read alongside the very different views of G. Phetersen, ed., *A Vindication of the Rights of Whores* (Seattle: Seal Press, 1989). A more contemporary statement drawing on Barry's work is Sheila Jeffreys, *The Idea of Prostitution* (Melbourne: Spinifex, 1997). For an overview of some of the relevant literature see Lynn Sharon Chancer, "Prostitution, Feminist Theory, and Ambivalence," *Social Text*, no. 37 (1993): 143–71; Wendy Chapkis, *Live Sex Acts* (London: Cassell, 1997).

66 Jo Bindman with Jo Doezema, *Redefining Prostitution as Sex Work on the International Agenda* (London: Anti-Slavery International, 1997), 1. See also Cheryl Overs and Paulo Longo, *Making Sex Work Safe* (London: Network of Sex Work Projects, 1997).

67 *See Workers' Manifesto*, theme paper of the First National Conference of Sex Workers organized by Durbar Mahila Samanwaya Committee, Calcutta, Nov. 14–16, 1997. Compare Wendy Chapkis's statement that "[t]here is no such thing as The Prostitute; there are only competing versions of prostitution" (*Live Sex Acts*, 211).

68 See Valerie Jenness, *Making It Work: The Prostitutes' Rights Movement in Perspective* (New York: Aldine de Gruyter, 1993).

69 Cecilie Hoigard and Liv Finstad, *Backstreets: Prostitution, Money, and Love*, translated by K. Hanson, N. Sipe, and B. Wilson (Cambridge: Polity, 1992), 181.

70 See Kemala Kempadoo, "Introduction: Globalizing Sex Workers' Rights," and Angelita Abad et al., "The Association of Autonomous Women Workers, Ecuador," in K. Kempadoo and J. Doezema, eds., *Global Sex Workers* (New York: Routledge, 1998), 1–28, 172–7.

71 "The 'Fallen' Learn to Rise," and "Sex Worker's Co-operative," publications of Durbar Mahila Samanwaya Committee, Calcutta, 1998–9.

72 "Prostitutes Seek Workmen Status," *Statesman Weekly*, Nov. 22, 1997.

73 There is an interview with the central figure in the development of NSWP, Cheryl Overs, in Kempadoo and Doezema, *Global Sex Workers*, 204–9. Overs here pays tribute both to her "mates in the global village" and to her Australian background.

74 Guenter Frankenberg, "Germany: The Uneasy Triumph of Pragmatism," in D. Kirp and R. Bayer, eds., *AIDS in the Industrialized Democracies* (New Brunswick: Rutgers University Press, 1992), 121.

75 "Sex Appeal," *Far Eastern Economic Review*, Feb. 4, 1999, 29–31.

76 This sort of "transactional sex" is discussed in Lori Heise and Chris Elias, "Transforming AIDS Prevention to Meet Women's Needs," *Social Science and Medicine* 40 (1995): 931–43.

77 Chris Jones, "Making a Users Voice," paper presented at the Fifth International Conference on Drug-Related Harm, Toronto, March 1994, 7.

78 See Alfred Neequaye, "Prostitution in Accra," in M. Plant, ed., *AIDS, Drugs, and Prostitution* (London: Routledge, 1993), 178–9.

79 Matt Forney, "Voice of the People," *Far Eastern Economic Review*, May 7, 1998, 10.

80 Heather Montgomery, "Children, Prostitution, and Identity," in Kempadoo and Doezema, *Global Sex Workers*, 147.

81 Lenore Manderson, "Public Sex Performances in Patpong and Explorations of the Edges of Imagination," *Journal of Sex Research* 29:4 (1992): 473. See also Barbara Zalduondo, "Prostitution Viewed Cross-Culturally: Toward Recontextualizing Sex Work in AIDS Intervention Research," *Journal of Sex Research* 28:2 (1991): 232–48.

82 On the sexual radicals see Paul Robinson, *The Freudian Left* (New York: Harper & Row, 1969).

83 See Frantz Fanon, *Black Skin, White Masks* (London: Pluto, 1986), and the introduction to that volume by Homi Bhabha, vii–xxvi.

Black Lesbians: Passing, Stereotypes, and Transformation

When I piece together the snippets of images and ideas that help form the picture of myself that I carry in my head it's as if I'm wrestling with a tornado. Imagine the special effect that experts conjure up in the movies: houses, cars, cows, books, kitchen table conversations all swirl around whole, until, released by the gale, they smash to the ground and I have to reassemble them. It's a cataclysmic process experienced, I think, by many people of color, especially of my generation. Growing up with television news coverage of the civil rights and black power movements, the newly recovered history of black Americans, my father's tales of life as a black man, and the pieces of grandmother's youth on an Indian reservation mingled with all the mainstream books, movies and television shows. These were the competing elements I wrangled into manageable reference points for grounding.

Because I knew, even as an adolescent, that I wanted to be a writer, it's not surprising that I absorbed many aspects of the arts almost as fully as I did personal experience. Released in 1959, *Imitation of Life* raised my first real questions about how we decide who we are – even before I was consciously aware of political movements, analyzing family history or embracing the quest for identity. This remake of an earlier adaptation of the Fannie Hurst novel had a powerful impact on me partly because I was such a media baby and because it featured the young stars who appeared in all the banal teen movies I also watched – Troy Donahue, Sandra Dee, Susan Kohner. But most important was its unexpected emotional impact – it threw me into confusion about race, identity, and loyalty.

The story is of a black girl, Peola, who chooses to pass for white, denying her community and humiliating her dark-skinned mother. For me, as an adolescent child in a mixed-race family (before the term was in vogue), some of whose members were also light-skinned, watching the film evoked dread and sorrow. At the moment when the daughter (played by a black actress in the 1934 film and by a white actress in this later version) denies her heritage my stomach clenched in fear as if I were watching her step out of a 20 story window, a decision that could never be rescinded. The presumed advantages of faux whiteness didn't seem worth the loss of family to me; and the deep shame of

Jewelle Gomez, "Black Lesbians: Passing, Stereotypes, and Transformation," pp. 161–77 from *Dangerous Liaisons: Blacks, Gays, and the Struggle for Equality*. New York: The New Press, 1999.

disavowing one's heritage shook me to the core. But the allure of masquerading as "the other" was also a compelling mystery.

I didn't know then how common stories about blacks passing as white were, even in my own family. Later, in college, when I read work from the writers of the 1920s I realized that "passing" had a long and complicated history in African American society, and, I imagine in all oppressed communities.

The "passing" novel of the early 1900s was a popular genre written by black writers as well as white. In Nella Larson's classic novel, *Quicksand*, her light-skinned protagonist, Helga, is a schoolteacher who scurries out of the sun to avoid becoming darker. Yet she chafes under the self-hatred of the black middle class which is manifested in their proscriptions: "Dark complected people shouldn't wear yellow, or red or green."[1] She escapes to Chicago where she lives in ambivalence and bitterness. In another novel, *Passing*, Larson's protagonist, Claire, marries a white professional and lives as a white woman and like Helga, cuts herself off from her history and the community that had been her support.

"Passing" novels were thought to help invest white readers in the lives of the light-skinned, educated black protagonists and thereby gain sympathy for the plight of black people in general. That strategy – convincing white people that black people were exactly like them – had some success for the civil rights movement but at the same time its usefulness was limited in an evolving political arena. Its focus on external effects served to short-circuit black exploration of our identities as unique individuals with variations within the group of class, gender, sexual orientation. We formed our own personal mythology of who black people were, which was almost as narrow and misleading as the stereotypes that white people clung to.

During the 1960s, I managed to never mention my sexual desire in any personal conversation with friends. I could feel the expectations pressing in on me. Oblique references made it clear that no contemporary African queen was ever queer. But even a decade earlier, Fanon had written: "If one wants to understand the racial situation psycho-analytically, not from a universal viewpoint but as it is experienced from individual consciousnesses, considerable importance must be given to sexual phenomenon."[2]

Today, the "passing" novel has been gone for more than half a century and the "passing" strategy has lost currency in the black political arena. It is almost that long since Fanon suggested the examination of "sexual phenomenon" within the context of race. Yet African Americans are still walking around the edge of the room, trying to ignore the elephant sitting in the middle. I think many would prefer me to "pass" in the black community. For some African Americans, I can be a lesbian in what they imagine as my "dark, secret world," but when I'm in "the community," the message to me is: don't bring "that mess." Asking me to pass as a heterosexual, to not call myself a dyke is a demand for self-hatred and delusion equal to saying black people shouldn't wear "yellow or red or green." It is a demand for a lie I was able to tell by not telling in my youth. Today, the question of a lie feels more significant. Adrienne Rich wrote some years ago that "Truthfulness has never been considered import-ant for women, as long as we have remained faithful to men, or chaste."[3] I think both women and people of color have been rewarded for lying too long. By pretending to be less than we are we've avoided punitive notice, unfair restrictions, and overt aggression. Girls pretend not to be as smart as boys so they can be dating material; black people pretend not to know "nuthin' 'bout birthing babies." Each pose a lie and a protection; each lie a brick shoring up the status quo, blocking my view to myself. My ongoing engagement with eliminating the layers of illusion and to coalesce the parts that are me is too important to ever concede to such a demand. And each word that some consider a label, I see as a door – a door which opens onto more aspects of me. As Mary Helen Washington says in discussing Nella Larson's classic novel *Quicksand*, "Passing is an obscene form of salvation."[4] Just as a black woman passing for white is required to "deny everything about her past," a black lesbian who passes for heterosexual is required to deny everything about her present.

Recently, I had an experience in a black-owned bookstore in the Bay Area that I'm sure is repeated regularly across the country in all types of establishments. I was browsing the shelves with the comforting camaraderie and laughter of the black cashier and two black patrons in the background. The discussion roamed freely then turned to the topic of the "rights" that gay people were "demanding." The three were united in their disdain for gay peoples' very basic civic concerns. Without thinking, the people I'd thought of as "family" only moments before were repeating the same bigotry I'd heard from radical conservatives. They were refusing to recognize any validity in another's desire to be equal before the law, even though that had been the cornerstone of the civil rights movement. It was as if the previous 50 years had never happened and the idea of struggle for civil recognition was anti-American.

I stood among the shelves, stock-still, feeling like the proverbial deer in headlights. If I moved, or indicated I was listening, they would know I was a lesbian! They would do something ugly. I was the elephant in the room – invisible, passing, lying – until the conversation turned to another topic. Then I reshelved the book I was holding and didn't return to the store for many months. As I slipped out of the store, I understood that I'd missed an opportunity to challenge their misinformation, but there was something disturbing about hearing such callous dismissal from black people in a bookstore who only moments before had felt so close. I wanted to shout at them, words Barbara Smith had written: "The oppression that affects Black gay people, female and male, is pervasive, constant, and not abstract. Some of us die from it."[5]

As I walked away I tried to calm my anger and humiliation. But the reality of how easily they erased who I was kept cutting into me. It was a reminder to me that in my 20 years of writing and presenting my work in the United States, Canada, and Europe, I've only been invited to read in a black-owned bookstore once. If I knew it intellectually before, that day I knew in my heart that it's true: those closest to you can cause the most hurt.

I didn't know what to say to the people in the bookstore, maybe because the work it would have taken to make them see me was more than I could handle in one visit. But the encounter made it clearer still that my image of who I am has no substance without all the elements swirling around inside me. Even if black people would so easily reject me, I would never cast them out of my blood. It is for me alone to decide which face I see in the mirror.

In the mid-1970s, a white woman interviewing me for a job asked me who I would choose to play me if Hollywood was making a movie. She couldn't know how complex a question that was. Finding an image to represent me is a trip back into the maelstrom. Although I'd been an avid fan of popular culture, growing up I knew that I wasn't reflected in the movies or on television. Peola, who'd settled for an "imitation of life," certainly wasn't me. But who could be? The question was both intriguing and frustrating.

I'd always liked Ernestine Wade, the actress who played the much-maligned Sapphire on television's "Amos and Andy." Even then I knew that for a black woman to be independent she would have to risk having her name become synonymous with being a bitch. But I didn't think I'd be mentioning Sapphire to a prospective white employer.

I was a major fan of movie queen Dorothy Dandridge, but the tragedy that remained part of her mystique didn't really fit me. And I never could quite see myself as a sarong-wearing siren.

I finally chose Diana Sands, who'd played the sister in the film version of "Raisin in the Sun." She easily embodied the character's outspoken intelligence and determination, qualities I wanted to believe were mine. Searching for the suitable personality to fit my idea of myself was a great exercise for me but turned out to be useless as an interview tool: my future employer had no idea who Diana Sands was.

Twenty years later if I were asked to make a casting choice I have a wider field to examine, but again who would I pick? Angela Bassett? Too thin and buffed. Vanessa Williams? Too ethereal. Alfre Woodard? Interesting possibility. But I doubted any of them would ever allow themselves to be filmed with their hair natural, not straightened, much less play a lesbian.

In almost every case, when I encountered the images of black women, the subtleties of who we might be were almost completely unexamined – in the media, in the public consciousness, and in the black community. And the particulars of who black lesbians might be are not even a question in the larger world.

Lesbians, usually white in movies and books, are generally presented as a bundle of tics and quirks that reflect the heterosexual world's fear and ambivalence. As a teenager, I looked for myself in all of them. The icy Lakey of Mary McCarthy's novel, *The Group* (produced as a film in 1966), the pathetic Martha of *The Children's Hour* (1962), the predatory Jo in the film version of *Walk on the Wild Side* (1962) were all one dimensional concoctions designed to intrigue and repulse. For years the stereotypical lesbian was the only image I could find with which to identify.

It wasn't until much later that I understood that one way to maintain lesbian invisibility is, paradoxically, to create exaggerations or stereotypes that obliterate the reality. The same had been done with African Americans and most other ethnic Americans over the years: Steppin Fetchit, Aunt Jemima, Charlie Chan, the Frito Bandito helped more than one generation of Americans overlook the real people behind the laugh. When we say that something frightening gives us the "willies" most of us don't remember that the term is derived from the actor Willie Best who perfected a comic character who embodied fear, especially of ghosts. His eye-rolling, stuttering, lazy character was featured in Hollywood movies during the 1930s and in them was often the butt of racial jokes from stars like Bob Hope. But Best's brilliant parody became the stereotype that, lacking solid alternative images, came to stand for all black men. The same can be said for every mammy/maid stock character since *Gone with the Wind*. The reality of who we are as black people is subsumed under the one-dimensional distortions that are standard in mass culture. It has been much the same for lesbians although they haven't been such a standard part of the core consciousness.

In 1968, I saw a film, *The Killing of Sister George*, with which I identified as a lesbian for the first time even though it featured no black women. Unlike the infamous, *The Well of Loneliness*, which I read in the mid-1960s, this was not a romantic plea for acceptance. The Radclyffe Hall novel, published in 1927, was a lesbian "passing" novel of sorts, which issued a call for tolerance because the "invert" supposedly had no choice and so desperately wanted to be just like everyone else. Except for the tragic flaw of desire we might fit into society just fine. *The Killing of Sister George*, based on the British play by Frank Marcus, was no such plea. It featured the first fully developed (not to be confused with saintly) lesbian character I'd ever seen on the screen. Some critics and lesbians condemned it as stereotypical, but it actually worked for me because it took the archetype of a harddrinking, butch lesbian and gave it dimension, emotion, vulnerability.

In the film, Sister George is the kindly village nurse character of a popular British soap opera. The actress who plays George is her hedonistic opposite. The center of her own dynamic social world, she has an edgy, sexual relationship with a lover, and close supportive friends. George, as she is known off camera too, is successful in her life and her work until her downfall is engineered by a jealous, fashionable television executive who seduces her lover. It's not a pretty picture of lesbians, but it's a gritty, compelling close-up of people.

In the film I found several elements for the first time. First, a real portrayal of the complexity of sexuality between women. George and her girlfriend (who dresses perpetually in baby-doll pajamas) are not the vanilla couple usually depicted, if depicted at all. They are not platonic lesbians or peck-on-the-cheek-lesbians. Their sexual game playing has a guttural quality drawn from a very deep place of desire and need.

The friendship women show each other in the film is also significant to the story, it is as important an element as the lover's betrayal. George's confidant is a sympathetic prostitute who takes their bond seriously. This rendering of a specifically working-class acceptance transcends liberal tolerance.

Additionally, contrasts between the working-class and upper-class women of the story frame the conflicts perfectly. The prostitute, the working-class bit players in the soap opera, and George are clearly at the mercy of the wealthy upper echelons who barely notice the complications of the lives of their "inferiors."

Most importantly for me, I saw lesbians within the context of a community, a possibility that was always being denied by the larger culture. In the passing stories Peola, Helga and Claire sacrifice their family and community connections to achieve their goals. In passing as white they become lonely, isolated women. Literature and media often cast lesbians in the same isolating spotlight. In the other portrayals I'd seen, lesbians were anomalies, the only one of their "kind," doomed because of their desire. George has lesbian friends and places to go. Her best friend is a willing listener; George and her coworkers are regulars in a pub and the gay folk have a club of their own. George is sexually aggressive, with an acerbic wit and a hard-edged, sometimes overwhelming presence; but she's part of a world of people who love and appreciate her. She does not live alone in the woods, she is not the lone one in her class reunion, she is not on the verge of suicide. She's a woman who goes to work every day, drinks in her favorite bar every day, and goes home to a lover every night. Her doom is sealed not by the fact that she's a lesbian but by her stubborn innocence in the face of a wealthy, manipulative rival.

Through much of my twenties, the patching together of ideas about black women and about lesbians became a giant game of hopscotch. I was always balanced precariously on one foot or the other. Shortly after I discovered Sister George, I saw a play which fed into the established stereotypes I'd expected. But, like the encounter in the black bookstore, this experience was more disturbing because the play was by a black playwright. Ed Bullins' short drama *Clara's Ole Man* was originally written and performed in San Francisco in 1965 and I saw it in New York City in 1969. In it, Clara invites a young, educated man home to visit with her while her "ole man" is at work. But her "ole man" is actually a woman called Big Girl, who happens to take the day off. After continuous consumption of cheap wine and much verbal sparring between the two rivals, Big Girl reveals her relationship with Clara to the young man and has him beaten up by friends who are street thugs. Bullins was one of the few black playwrights of the black arts movement of the 1960s to use lesbian or gay characters in his work. It seems his focus was less on queerness itself than it was on exploring "seedy" aspects of the black community, of which homosexuality happened to be one.

Bullins used the very characterizations found in Sister George but to much less effect. Big Girl drinks incessantly, is controlling and rude, she even humiliated her lover, Clara, by revealing an abortion which she aided. Big Girl's bad behavior might be a defensive reaction to an interloper but, as written by Bullins, she has no other side to her character, no tenderness or love. The play leaves you with the impression that Clara could only have stayed with Big Girl because she's grateful for her help with the abortion and so browbeaten she can't make a life on her own. Unwittingly, perhaps, Bullins trotted out the very antilesbian rhetoric that has pervaded middle-class black life.

In the late 1960s, Huey Newton was able to recognize the importance of the gay rights movement and the need for coalition between the Black Panthers and gay activists. It's a recognition that black working-class people have had for generations, always keeping a place for queer people in their communities. When black anthropologist John Langston Gwaltney interviewed a cross-section of black America for a book he was preparing he concluded: "In black culture there is a durable, general tolerance, which is amazingly free of condescension, for the individual's right to follow the truth where it leads."[6] This is the general attitude I'd grown up with living with my great grandmother and with other relatives. My father, Duke, worked in several bars in the South End of Boston in the 1950s and '60s. Wherever he worked it was comfortable ground for straight and gay patrons who crossed class boundaries – railroad workers, prostitutes, and store owners sat side by side.

But as the black middle class grew in the 1960s, class territory became more delineated and the black middle class, who might be said to be "passing" in their emulation of white values and culture, didn't want anyone around who would call attention to difference. Maybe, fearful of the demonization of black sexuality during slavery and the Jim Crow era, sex became a taboo subject. And nothing calls attention to sex more than a black choir queen or a dapper black butch. They both were welcome in Duke's bar but they better not show up in Estelle's Cocktail Lounge. The importance of assimilation for many in the black middle-class made being openly queer increasingly difficult in the black community. As a young woman I was taught to respect the different patrons in my father's bar. Today the black community seems to have only the voice given it by the middle-class or wealthy sports figures and other entertainers who have access to the media and prefer an image of self-righteous rectitude to one of communal inclusivity.

Despite the transcendent nature of the movements of the 1960s, I've come to learn that I cannot depend on the black community to embrace me as long as I refuse to chop off the part of me that's a black lesbian. The narrow focus of both the Million Man March (1997) and the Million Woman March (1998) confirmed that sexuality, gender oppression, and class issues will remain the elephant in the room. But it seemed after I was finally able to find a lesbian community, I couldn't rely on them to embrace me either. My experiences with white lesbians were rarely reflected in the literature. Books with titles such as *Twilight Girl* seemed designed for the titillation of the larger world and served neither black nor white lesbians well.

Through the 1970s most fiction was usually in the same vein featuring hapless, victimized white lesbians and victimizing black lesbians. Their characteristics and behavior (haughty, disturbed, unstable, hysterical, violent, greedy, manipulative, to name a few from several books) seem attributable to their being black. No further social context was ever provided. So in the end, as with Willie Best, the reader experiences a pathology not a person.

Ann Allen Shockley broadened that universe in 1974 with *Loving Her*, the first novel by a black woman about black lesbians. It tells the story of a young black singer who finds the courage to escape an abusive husband and accept the love of a white woman. Written in the wake of the wave of pulp fiction, it relies on some of the same conventions and drew some criticism because of the interracial relationship. But Shockley continued to write best-selling stories featuring black lesbians, many of which had something every other story had failed to include: a sense of humor. Her hysterically funny novel *Say Jesus and Come to Me* (1982) has some issues and ideas I have examined more critically in other essays. But the most engaging aspect of the work is its ability to capture the cultural substance of black women – the language, physicality, and the humor. The story of a black lesbian minister who ends her slippery seductive ways when she falls in love with a singer allowed black lesbians to recognize ourselves within a black context for the first time on the page.

Although purely popular literature, Shockley's books raise more ideas about black lesbians than any fiction written before it. They introduce the issue of the isolation of the black professional woman in her own community, racism within the recording industry and in the women's movement, and the layers of fear of black lesbians in and out of the closet. Shockley also places her black lesbian characters within the realms of many economic classes of the black community. The black lesbians Shockley presents are workers, mothers, ministers, and all the possibilities one should expect. They, like Sister George, are part of a large community that recognizes their existence.

Published in the same year as Shockley's novel, Alice Walker's *The Color Purple* and Audre Lorde's *Zami* were for the first time literature in which I saw credible and indelible images of black lesbians that related to me. By then I was no longer scanning pages and screens looking for the idea of a lesbian. I had made my own life working in New York, and had developed a circle of friends, many of them black lesbians and gays. The distorted images offered by pulp novels and B movies no longer meant much to me except as historical markers. But I understood that they formed the basis for many others' ideas about who I was.

In the black community I was/am still a peculiar individual; a black lesbian is more often seen through than seen. I understood the need to not speak of sexuality in the black community. The enduring effects of the distortion and exploitation of black sexuality during slavery were still like solid chains around our thoughts. We dared not draw attention to our desire.

But Walker's and Lorde's books smashed that enforced black silence in ways that no other work had done and few books have done since. The effect of these books was felt so strongly, to some extent, because they both were set in our historical past. The idea that lesbianism was a white, modern thing was challenged when we read about the loving between Shug and Celie in the era of juke joints and moonshine. Shug Avery's reputation as a lively lusty woman gives her choice of Celie considerable weight. It implies the power and validity of black women's desire as no heterosexual love story has ever done. Reading about Audre Lorde making her way through the lesbian life of New York's West Village in the 1950s makes that sexual self-determination a heroic goal akin to the other struggles for human rights she's experienced. And just as had been true with the recovery of black history in the 1960s, it was no longer easy to dismiss black lesbians once we were identified as part of black history.

Audre Lorde's *Zami* was the first autobiographically based, full-length work from the perspective of a black lesbian. Previous to that only individual articles by Anita Cornwell in *The Ladder* and some pieces in the short-lived black lesbian publication *Azalea* were available. Audre's development of the term "biomythography" helped her to create the cultural context that previous writers either didn't know, didn't care about, or didn't understand were crucial. When she wrote about the magical yet ordinary event of a party of black lesbians in Queens, New York, she's offering a recognizable setting that allows for the complexity of black lesbian life. The party revealed the possibility of fulfilled working-class and middle-class black lesbians – there is the implication that the world is larger than simply their rejection from mainstream society.

Today, in an era in which the white gay sidekick has become *de riguer* in films and on television; in a decade when the publishing arms of corporations have invested millions in writers of queer fiction, autobiography, and queer studies; the black lesbian is still rarely represented on film or in print. And if she is, it is never as fully realized as the characters created by Alice Walker or Audre Lorde. When a black lesbian does make an appearance, she's still tragic (television adaptation *The Women of Brewster Place*), peripheral (the teacher, Blue, in the mainstream novel *Push*), or a caricature (Cleo, played by Queen Latifah in the film *Set It Off*).

There is a surface similarity to Sister George in Queen Latifah's Cleo in *Set It Off* that almost engaged me. She's loud, overbearing, sexually aggressive, intriguing breaks from the traditional passive roles, even though it represents a simplistic heterosexual reading of lesbian. The script's focus on only those characteristics leaves Cleo with little else to define her. The film portrayal is also something of an artifact – in the alternative meaning of that word – that is something observed in a scientific experiment, something that doesn't exist naturally. Other than Cleo's lover, the lesbian community is completely invisible. Once again the lesbian is alone in an island of heterosexuality. Cleo is dropped down into the working-class black life of Los Angeles with no history or antecedents, either socially or in cinema.

To see Queen Latifah's posturing, violent, immature character in 1998, one would never imagine the previous existence of any film portrayal of black lesbians. Although there may be no mainstream, popular culture reference points, two films from the mid-1980s had already opened up the territory with more insight and complexity. Sheila McLaughlin's *She Must Be Seeing Things* and Lizzie Borden's *Born in Flames* each featured black lesbian characters in central roles. In one case the black woman is a jealous lover, comically obsessed with her fantasies of betrayal, and in the other the black character leads a contemporary lesbian feminist revolution. More recently, other film-makers have created better realized black lesbian characters. Julie Dash's film *Daughters of the Dust* subtly presents two women in the early part of the century who are clearly partners. In Cheryl Dunye's comedy, *Watermelon Woman*, a young lesbian researches the life of a fictionalized black character actress who was a lesbian in order to help find herself. These depictions are spread widely along the spectrum of lesbian representation and postulate the possibilities of so much in between, it's difficult to accept the single dimension offered by *Set it Off*.

In Cleo I hear echoes of Willie Best and Butterfly McQueen – character actors whose marvelous eccentricities (parodied so sweetly in *Watermelon Woman*) came to stand for being black in the general culture and ultimately obscured the possibility of taking them seriously as actors or as black people.

When the three people in that black bookstore dismissed equal rights for gays, they didn't picture me or any of the characters created by Audre Lorde or Cheryl Dunye. They imagined the caricature of lesbians that is repeatedly reinforced by popular culture in films like *Set It Off*. I wouldn't argue against the artistic freedom that results in such archaic portrayals. I can only be grateful that there are alternative places for young lesbians of color to now look for their reflection and at the same time feel very sad that mainstream culture – black and white – still needs the comfort of such distorted information.

In retrospect, what made me flee from my brothers and sisters in that store was more than anger and humiliation, it was exhaustion. After a lifetime commitment to human rights, I feel almost the same about educating black people about their heterosexism as I do about educating white people about their racism. It's time for them to check themselves.

In an essay written by Cheryl Clarke in 1983, she says: "It is ironic that the Black Power movement could transform the consciousness of an entire generation of black people regarding black self-determination and, at the same time, fail so miserably in understanding the sexual politics of the movement and of black people across the board." The underlying tone of Clarke's essay reveals a similar weariness with confronting the lagging black community that I feel continually. It is also a sentiment sadly echoed more than a decade later by the editors of *Afrekete*, the first anthology with the words "black lesbian" on its cover. Published in 1995, it takes its name from a mythic character in Audre Lorde's *Zami*. In the introduction, the editors comment: "We did not contemplate too long the specter of political debate that the writing would meet. We take on these debates every day in everything we do. It is tiring. It mutes our passion."[7] There always comes a turning point in a struggle, when the focus shifts, the power dynamic changes. I feel that happening in my pursuit of approval from the black community. The energy I've put into recognizing myself as a whole person has come to mean more than my disappointment at their failure to transform themselves.

For years I had hoped for growth and change in the black community so that the one-dimensional, male-dominated mythology of who we are did not continue to represent all that we could be. But the discourse of black politics and culture flows through the generations with the same male voice – from Baraka and Bullins to Gates, Lee and Als. Even when it is queer or queer friendly, it's a voice comfortable with leaving black women in the background or speaking for black women and letting black lesbians remain invisible.

Maybe in moving from the East to the West Coast in mid-life I got to see things from a different perspective. Unlike in New York, African Americans are not the primary voice for progressive social change in California. The larger Asian American and Spanish-speaking communities have varying strategies and philosophies they employ – not to mention thier different histories. Because we are a part of the Pacific Rim, there is a more global orientation to the activism. Discussions about ethnic concerns are presumed to be connected to the environment, gender parity, and economic class.

But, whatever the reasons, in the struggle for social change it is I, in fact, who have been transformed. I see a larger picture of human rights than the civil rights or black power movements showed me. Those movements were only the first door I walked through. Learning the extent and complexity of oppression on a global as well as local level has necessitated walking through many more doors than I ever would have suspected in the 1960s.

When I work with my writing students or relate to my young cousins and nieces and nephews, I insist that they see these doors, I could be the "unmarried aunt" but I prefer to be "the dyke aunt" – much more interesting and more accurate. And if it causes a storm, better the maelstrom I know than the one caused by unspoken secrets. One of my greatest joys was telling my 10-year-old niece that I was a lesbian and seeing the understanding fill her eyes. Whatever she'd heard in her school or with her friends was forever changed by my ability to be that image she had been unable to find for herself. Her affection for me and my partner, because my family made room for that experience, is the radical social change I've been looking for. She is the community I need for my context, my support.

When I talk to her and other young people I want them to be willing to go out into the storm, no matter how uncertain the outcome. I pass on to them Audre Lorde's words: "I speak without concern for the accusations/that I am too much or too little woman/that I am too black or too white/or too much myself..."[8]

Notes

1 Nella Larson, *Quicksand* (New York: A. A. Knopf, 1928), 191.
2 Frantz Fanon, *Black Skin, White Masks* (New York: Grove Press, 1967), 160.
3 Adrienne Rich, *On Lies, Secrets, and Silence* (New York: W. W. Norton, 1979), 188.
4 Mary Helen Washington, ed., *Invented Lives* (New York: Doubleday, 1987), 164.
5 Barbara Smith, ed., *Home Girls* (New York: Kitchen Table Women of Color Press, 1983), xlvii.
6 John Langston Gwaltney, *Drylongso* (New York: Random House, 1980), xxvii.
7 Audre Lorde, *Zami: A New Spelling of My Name* (Watsonville, CA: The Crossing Press, 1982), xi.
8 Audre Lorde, *Undersong: Chosen Poems Old and New* (New York: W. W. Norton & Co., 1992), 110.

CHAPTER 35

Pat Califia

Trashing the Clinic and Burning Down the Beauty Parlor: *Activism Transmutes Pitiable Patients into Feisty Gender Radicals*

Since the late 1960s, a growing number of cross-dressers and transsexuals have turned to the political arena to improve conditions for themselves and their communities. The original style of transgender activism focused on such things as laws against female impersonation, policies that made it difficult for transsexuals to obtain identification papers and change other official records so they conformed with their gender of preference, lobbying for greater availability of sex reassignment, forming social groups for cross-dressers and their significant others, educating the general public about transvestism and transsexuality, and doing outreach so that people troubled by gender dysphoria would find it easier to locate the resources they needed to cope with their distress.

This style of transgender activism is still going strong. Today it is exemplified by Virginia "Charles" Prince's Tri-Ess Sorority (which has drawn fire for excluding homosexual men), the International Foundation for Gender Education, Renaissance Education Association, and an annual conference on transsexuality and the law, organized by Houston activist and attorney Phyllis Randolph Frye and sponsored by the International Conference on Transgender Law and Employment Policy, Inc. (ICTLEP). This conference has been held annually since 1992 and typically deals with such issues as insurance law, employment rights, medical law, and international law.

Through ICTLEP, Stephen Whittle, Lecturer in Law at Manchester University in Manchester, England, has provided American activists and lawyers with the latest international case-law statistics and civil-rights strategies that are being used in other countries, particularly the United Kingdom and Western Europe. But the conference has historically suffered from a lack of full participation by the female-to-male community. ICTLEP organizers have recently taken steps to boost FTM participation by featuring FTM keynote speaker Michael Hernandez in 1994. Writer/activist and president of FTM

Pat Califia, "Trashing the Clinic and Burning Down the Beauty Parlor: Activism Transmutes Pitiable Patients into Feisty Gender Radicals," pp. 221–4 from *Sex Changes: The Politics of Transgenderism*. San Francisco: Cleis Press, 1997. Reprinted by permission of Cleis Press.

International Jamison Green received ICTLEP's Transgender Pioneer Award in 1995, and the honor went to Whittle in 1996. The 1996 conference broke new ground by specifically addressing FTMs, transgendered youth, members of the gender community who have not had full sex reassignment, and transgendered people of color.

Like any change, this one will apparently take time. Panelist Jamison Green commented, "It's depressing to think that after five years of transgender community activism, this three-hour session is the first block of time Transgen has devoted to FTM issues. Even sadder is the fact that we could barely scratch the surface of topics pertaining to law – we had to spend the majority of the time explaining the basic reality of FTM existence, so ignorant were the majority of attendees."[1] This state of affairs will hopefully improve with the recent appointment of FTM attorneys Spencer Bergstedt and Shannon Minter as ICTLEP directors. Minter is currently employed as the Staff Attorney for the National Center for Lesbian Rights (NCLR).[2]

ICTLEP founder Frye was instrumental in getting Houston's laws against cross-dressing repealed in the eighties. With Karen Kerin of It's Time America and Riki Wilchins of the Transexual Menace, she coordinated a largely successful effort to have each and every one of over 500 Senate and House officeholders lobbied by transgender activists on October 4, 1995, National Gender Lobbying Day. Kerry Lobel of the National Gay and Lesbian Task Force (NGLTF) and Nancy Buermeyer of the Human Rights Campaign were on hand to give practical lobbying pointers and encouragement.

One of the organizers of that event recalls her experience:

> I remember getting on the underground subway that runs between the House and Senate, and just as we start off toward the House, coming back at us from the other way is an entire carload of cross-dressers, just returning from lobbying the Senate. And of course their driver is trying to keep this totally bored expression like, "Hey, no big deal. I see this every day."
>
> I went into the Rayburn Building cafeteria, which is this block-long thing where many of the Capital Hill staff go to lunch. And I look around, and suddenly notice there are fifty – maybe sixty – transpeople filling about a third of the tables. And then I notice staffers coming in are doing the same thing. They walk in, start to look around, then really look around, and suddenly notice ohmyfuckinggawd the Rayburn Building cafeteria is filled with men in dresses and transsexuals and who only knows what other kinds of gender-perverts and all of a sudden they're hearing another chorus of "Welcome to Gender Hell!"
>
> The First National Gender Lobbying Day marked a definitive turning point for transpeople. It was the first time genderqueers came in from the shadows of passing and assimilation to the brightest of national lights and said, "No! I'm not going away. I'm not going to hide. I'm not going to be ashamed anymore. I work and pay taxes and vote, and I'm going to live with the same dignity and rights accorded every other US citizen. It was incredibly moving to see one hundred transpeople and friends standing together on the Capital Hill steps with this *visible* determination and pride in all their faces.[3]

The older type of transgender activism closely resembles the "civil rights" approach which characterized the lesbian and gay movement through much of the seventies and eighties. Gay activists in those decades focused on the repeal of sodomy laws; securing First Amendment protection for lesbian and gay male media; passage of local, state, and federal laws banning antigay discrimination; demands that local police departments recognize and take steps to address gay bashing; outreach to young men and women who were "coming out" to make it easier for them to find the gay community; lobbying to remove homosexuality as a diagnostic category from the *Diagnostic and Statistical Manual* of the American Psychiatric Association; and attempts to educate the general public about homosexuality.

Several factors combined in the mid-nineties to produce a change in the tone of transgender activism and its agenda. One was the emergence of a stronger, larger, and more visible FTM community. Another factor was a shift in survival strategies for transsexuals. Rather than attempting to blend in and remain closeted about being transsexual, more and more transgendered people, especially women, began to speak out, write, and work as out transsexual activists. This was a direct result of several nasty transsexual purges committed by many lesbian organizations during the eighties. Transgendered women who attempted to join lesbian organizations were for the most part already politicized by feminism and by confronting antigay discrimination in their daily lives. These vicious purges made it clear that being closeted simply would not work. Transgendered lesbians had few alternatives to becoming radicalized. It was either that, or a retreat to the heterosexual world, a life of complete isolation and silence, or suicide. Lesbian feminists who refused to accept transgendered women as women and tried to drive them away ironically created a generation of determined transgendered women who will do anything but disappear.

The process of sex reassignment itself has also spawned transgender activists. Gender clinics have been operating long enough now in this country to create a significant number of people who are angry about the way these programs are run. Rather than being grateful for any help they are given, transsexuals today are questioning the authority of the medical and mental-health professionals who function as gatekeepers of sex reassignment. While many of them still want access to hormones and surgery, gender dysphoric men and women are uneasy about being labeled as mentally-ill people in need of treatment. The gender community has at this point accumulated a lot of folk wisdom about what you need to tell the doctors to get admitted to a gender-reassignment program. The dangerous side effects of hormones and the shortcomings of surgery are well-known. Transsexuals are becoming informed consumers of medical service, and they want more control over what they receive from their healthcare providers, and more accountability.

Some of this attitude is connected with the growing visibility of the S/M community, particularly the component of sadomasochism that has to do with body modification. One of the basic tenets of S/M is the individual's right to own his or her own body, and make whatever temporary or permanent changes to that body the individual pleases either for sexual gratification or for purposes of adornment. A new sort of transgendered person has emerged, one who approaches sex reassignment with the same mindset that they would obtaining a piercing or a tattoo. This is very different from the old attitude toward hormone therapy and surgery – that it was necessary to receive this treatment because one was a woman trapped in a man's body or vice versa.

There is a growing number of people who are diagnosed as gender dysphoric, but for one reason or another are not deemed to be good candidates for sex reassignment. Gender identity programs can turn down applicants for many reasons – age, a history of psychiatric illnesses, homosexuality, fetishism, sadomasochism, a criminal record, inability to tolerate hormones, a medical history of cancer, possessing a face or body that the surgeon believes will never pass muster as a member of the gender of preference ("somatically inappropriate"), poverty, employment in the sex industry, a refusal to aspire to be a feminine woman or a masculine man, or uppitiness.

Until the mid-nineties, these people had few options. They could try to pay for sex reassignment themselves – an expensive proposition, complicated by the difficulty of finding a doctor in private practice who was knowledgeable enough or willing to supervise such treatment. They could attempt to find a place for themselves on the margins of the cross-dressing community or the gay community. They could try to resign themselves to living in the gender they had been assigned at birth. They could attempt to drown their pain with drug addiction or alcohol, or they could stop living in some more final way.

Today, the growing visibility of the transsexual community has created an alternative: to identify as transgendered rather than female or male, and question the binary gender system that generates these labels. People who cannot "pass" as men or women have little to lose by becoming outspoken gender activists. It feels better to fight oppression, even though it is hard work, than it does to run away from it and try to hide. There's no shame in losing a battle from time to time. All warriors sometimes lose. But it's better to be a warrior, even a defeated one, than a civilian casualty. One can obtain enough pride and dignity from that stance in life to live, even if the conditions of life are frightening and precarious.

Of course, there are also many actively-involved transgender activists who could quite easily turn their backs on their own community and fade into the woodwork. Green comments, "I find that my passability works as a great educational tool in my own activist work. There are quite a few transactivists who...could pass perfectly well. We could do other things with our lives. But we feel strongly about trans oppression and the people whose lives are affected by it, and we want to see it stopped. Instead of 'woodworking,' or disappearing into the mainstream – as we are capable of and qualified to do – we have chosen not to do so."[4]

Outside of the transsexual community, other changes were taking place that made it possible for the new transgender activist to emerge. One was a parallel shift in the strategy of gay activists outraged by lack of effective government intervention and pharmaceutical industry indifference or outright profiteering in dealing with the AIDS pandemic. The rise of a bisexual community that attempted, with mixed results, to affiliate itself with lesbian and gay political goals and social institutions also created a new paradigm for transgender activists.

The increasing visibility of prosex feminism, with its opposition to censorship and emphasis on the value of pleasure and its affirmation of a woman's right to take control over her own body, also had a role to play in the development of a new phase of transgender activism. Prosex feminism's recognition of the contributions communities of sexual-minority women had made to the women's movement created an atmosphere that was much less hostile to transgendered women than the classic radical lesbian feminism of the late seventies and the eighties. This is not to say that prosex feminists have been wholehearted allies of transgendered people; but this more open attitude has created the possibility of more dialogue, and opened a little more space within which "gennies" and transgendered women can encounter one another as something other than enemies.

In fact, however, it would be hard to say which one of these factors "caused" any of the others. Rather than claiming there was a chronological chain of events that led to the formation of groups like the Transexual Menace, it would be more realistic to view all these historical changes as synergistic events, each of which affected and triggered the others, much the same as the breaking shot that opens a game of pool.

In order to give the reader a sense of the flavor of transgender activism in the last few years, it is necessary to describe some of the specific cases or causes around which the gender community has recently rallied, protested, organized, and generally kicked ass. The pathetic, deluded, and self-destructive people portrayed by Harry Benjamin and Richard Green as being in desperate need of rescue by enlightened doctors and therapists could never have created the ruckus that resulted from each of the events outlined below. Nor could these results have been achieved by quiet, well-mannered, closeted transsexuals who politely waited for liberal judges or medical professionals to give them the charitable treatment they needed to eke out a life in the shadows of normal society. Even old-fashioned civil-rights-style transsexual activists are learning that it pays to be rowdy.

Anne Ogborn should be credited as a forerunner of transgender direct action groups. Ogborn's life experiences included a period of living with the hijra in India.[5] Wilchins recalls her surfacing in the summer of 1992 in New York, selling T-shirts that said, "Sex Change: Ask Me How." Ogborn tried to form chapters of a group called Transgender Nation in San Francisco, Washington, DC, and other cities. Wilchins says it took her a whole year to admit that the concept was a good idea, and that it was possible to get enough transpeople together for an effective picket or demonstration. Wilchins modified Ogborn's concept slightly and formed the Transexual Menace to protest the fact that transsexuals had been left out of the title of Stonewall 25, a New York gay/lesbian/bisexual march that was to commemorate the twenty-fifth anniversary of the Stonewall rebellion in June of 1994. The group's slogan is, "Why should a transsexual be a menace to you?"

The ejection of a transgendered woman from the Michigan Womyn's Music Festival (MWMF) in 1991 is an event that some observers credit with touching off an in-your-face, rabble-rousing style of gender activism that has more in common with Queer Nation and ACT-UP than it has with the Human Rights Campaign Fund. Nancy Jean Burkholder, an electrical engineer from New Hampshire, had attended the Michigan festival in 1990 without a problem. But for some reason, in 1991, another festival-goer asked Burkholder if she was a transsexual, and she told her the truth. Despite the fact that she had yet to enjoy a lesbian relationship, the postoperative Burkholder defined herself as a lesbian feminist. In what must have been a frightening display of force, security guards ejected her from the festival grounds at midnight, without allowing her to contact any of her friends or collect her belongings.[6]

Burkholder did not go away quietly. She and her supporters, including the ubiquitous Wilchins, organized to inform the larger lesbian community and other transgendered women about the shoddy and abusive treatment she had received. But it wasn't until 1994 that enough collective anger had accumulated to result in a visible political action: Camp Trans. Wilchins, one of the key organizers, recalls:

> To my knowledge, Camp Trans was the first time transpeople ever coordinated and pulled off a national event. Not only that, it was the first time that significant numbers of the hard-core lesbian-feminist community backed us. In a sense it was an echo of the Sex Wars in a distant place – off a dirt road in the middle of Michigan – and between our tents and the front gate thirty yards away was as clear a division around issues of hierarchy and legitimacy, diversity and tolerance, as you're likely to find anywhere.
>
> The first year, we had only four or five people (it wasn't even called Camp Trans) and folks were so afraid of being hassled inside that they wouldn't even wear our pro-Nancy buttons back through MWMF's main gate. But at Camp Trans, there were thirty people there continuously. And we drew hundreds of folks from inside the festival. We knew something

was up. But when (in the first two days) I sold every one of the three dozen Transexual Menace T-shirts I'd brought, including the one I was wearing on my back, and these women were wearing them back *inside* the main gate and around the festival – then we knew the prevailing winds had definitely shifted.[7]

Camp Trans consisted of about two dozen transgendered women and their supporters, who simply rented a campsite across the road from the Michigan Womyn's Music Festival, and made their presence known. About one hundred festival-goers left MWMF's grounds to hear a reading by Leslie Feinberg and Minnie Bruce Pratt.

James Green describes his participation at Camp Trans:

I conducted two workshops at Camp Trans on FTM issues – of course these were not so well-attended as Leslie and Minnie Bruce's reading, but a couple dozen people walked out of the festival.... The next day, Leslie, an intersexed person named Cody, Jessica Xavier, Nancy Burkholder, Riki Anne Wilchins, and I had a meeting with the festival security team. The trans women were very quiet and let Leslie, Cody and me do most of the talking. Leslie started by introducing hermself and getting into a bit of an argument about the "womyn-born-womyn" policy. S/he threatened to denounce the festival at all public-speaking events heesh ever did in the future. Next, Cody, who looked like your basic butch dyke but said she had genitals that were indeterminate, asked if she would be welcome in the festival and expressed her reservations about being welcome based on her identity as an intersexed person.

Then I introduced myself and told them first that I did not want to go into the festival. They were visibly relieved at this news. "But," I said, "I'm here in support of my transsexual sisters and there's something I don't understand about your policy. If in fact your policy of exclusion is based on your belief that once a man, always a man, then you must also believe once a woman, always a woman. [pause] And I don't think you want me in your festival." They were shocked. They looked like I had just slapped them in the face. They excused themselves and said they would report back to Lisa and Boo and would return in twenty minutes. They were back much sooner than that with their capitulation that a measure of self-definition was appropriate. At that point, Leslie and Riki led the entire contingent of Camp Trans (minus myself, a nontranssexual male journalist ... and a nontranssexual woman who did not want to go) on a victory march through the festival grounds, accompanied by the Lesbian Avengers.[8]

Lisa Vogel and "Boo" Price, the women who own the for-profit festival, had announced that they would not change their admission policy, which stated that the festival was for "womyn-born-womyn" only. However, they added the somewhat contradictory and chickenshit statement that they would allow festival attendees to decide for themselves whether or not they were "womyn-born-womyn." There was a split among the transactivists at this point, with Davina Anne Gabriel, who is postoperative, reportedly saying that preoperative women should not enter the festival. Wilchins argued against that, using the slogan "passing is privilege. We should not be ashamed of our genitals." So the small contingent she led through the gates of Michigan included pre-, post-, and non-operative transsexual women.[9]

A large contingent of separatist campers reportedly left the event when they heard that transsexuals had been allowed on the land. Their viewpoint was articulated by lesbian-separatist musician and singer Alix Dobkin, who said, "Every lesbian I know supports transsexuals' rights to live their lives. But I support our right to define our own space. I'm very disappointed to learn that they have chosen to support sex-role stereotypes – to be women, which they are not. They're not being who they are. They're trying to be who we are. To me it feels like a male invasion of my sacred space." Dobkin had signed a statement with Wilchins calling for respectful dialogue and "mutually acceptable common ground," but apparently that ground could not be the Michigan Womyn's Music Festival.[10]

Camp Trans was held again in 1995. Three transsexual women led by Davina Anne Gabriel of Kansas City, Missouri reportedly entered the festival and outed themselves. They did not encounter any problems with festival security or staff.[11]

The plight of transsexual lesbians highlights an ideological double-bind. Feminists cannot have it both ways. If we are going to claim that biology is not destiny and present a political analysis of gender as something that is socially constructed, we have to make room in our world view for women who were not born with XX chromosomes. To do otherwise is to subscribe to biological determinism, the regressive belief that our genetic structures determine our potential as human beings, and the notion that biological sex can be used as a justification for placing limits upon the freedom, intellectual abilities, and creative talents of women.

The tragic case of Brandon Teena galvanized transactivists who were energized by their partial victory at Michigan. The brutal and bigoted murder of this young, transgendered man stirred indignation in the heart of any decent or compassionate person. But the way Teena's case was handled by gay organizations, which labeled it antilesbian violence, and written about by lesbian journalist Donna Minkowitz, who insisted on calling Teena a woman and referring to him by female pronouns, created a great deal of anger in the gender community, especially among FTMs who recognized Brandon Teena as one of their own. In Donna Minkowitz's 1994 *Village Voice* article about the case, the headline on the first page says, "Brandon Teena Was a Woman Who Lived and Loved as a Man. She Was Killed for Carrying It Off."[12] Yet in her own article, Minkowitz says that, although Teena hung out with gay men, "she" frequently made negative comments about lesbians. Teena repeatedly told anyone he was intimate with that he was a man. The inability of gay media or organizations to process this case as a violation of transsexuals' human rights encouraged many transgendered people to become more outspoken, since it became very clear that the older, larger, and more well-established gay institutions were deeply insensitive to the implications of Teena's murder.

In 1994, Brandon Teena (whose birth name was Teena Brandon) moved to Falls City, Nebraska to live as a man. He may have been planning on eventually seeking out sex-change surgery. He was originally from nearby Lincoln, Nebraska. By all accounts, Teena passed easily as a man, and quickly became something of a local Don Juan. He was discovered to have a female body when cops arrested him on a misdemeanor check-forgery charge two weeks prior to his slaying. The police then outed him by telling the local newspaper, the *Falls City Journal*, about the discrepancy between Teena's gender at birth and his public identity. Teena seems to have been quite a scam artist. By the time he died, he had nearly a score of charges pending for petty crimes like check forgery, credit-card fraud, and auto theft. But what happened to him was way out of proportion to any crime he might have committed. By New Year's Eve, he had been raped and brutally murdered by Tom Nissen and John Lotter, two former friends. Teena was 21 when he died.

John Lotter was a former boyfriend of Teena's date for the Christmas party. At that party, Lotter and Nissen held Teena down, forcibly removed his trousers, and insisted that his girlfriend Lana Tisdale look at his crotch. Afterward, Lotter and Nissen employed a ruse to get Teena alone, and raped him twice. They also beat him severely. Teena escaped when his assailants locked him in a bathroom and ordered him to take a shower to remove forensic evidence. He got out of the house through the bathroom window. Teena reported the attack to police, who refused to make an arrest. Richardson County Sheriff Charles Laux allowed his department to conduct an investigation, which involved interviewing dozens of people and preparing an extensive report, but forbade the arrest of the two men the cops themselves believed to be the culprits. One week later on New Year's Eve of 1993, Teena was shot to death. Two companions, Lisa Lambert and a young black man, Phillip DeVine, were also killed. Lambert's infant son survived the attack on the farmhouse.

Laux seems to be quite a piece of work, the prototype of a redneck lawman who doesn't think the law should protect everyone. He is reported to have told Teena's mother, when she called to ask why no one had been arrested for the rape, "You can call it, 'it' as far as I am concerned."[13] Fortunately, when he ran for reelection shortly after the murders occurred, he was voted out of office. But he has since been elected to the Richardson County Commission.[14] Local law-enforcement people seem to have been a callous and bigoted bunch of bullies who had little regard for the safety of anyone who might be regarded as different. Brandon's mother JoAnn has considered a civil suit against County Attorney Douglas Merz, who told Minkowitz, "I don't know what a hate crime is. I don't know if we have laws against hate crimes in Nebraska."[15] The fact that anyone was ever arrested or tried for this murder seems to be a miracle.

After two days of deliberation, a jury found Marvin Thomas Nissen, 22, guilty of the December 30, 1993 first-degree murder of Brandon Teena and second-degree murder of Teena's two roommates, Lisa Lambert and Phillip DeVine.[16] Nissen agreed to testify against Lotter, who was claiming that he slept in the car outside the farmhouse while Nissen went inside and did the killings. His claims to nonviolence were somewhat strained by the fact that he reportedly ripped the sink off the wall of his jail cell twice while he was in custody awaiting trial. Lotter was found guilty of murder in May 1995. On February 21, 1996, Nissen received a life sentence, and Lotter was given the death penalty.[17] Nissen has since filed an appeal with the Supreme Court, arguing that authorities lacked probable cause to arrest him without a warrant shortly after the bodies were discovered.[18]

In a demonstration called by Wilchins, the Transexual Menace protested the *Village Voice* coverage of Teena's murder, specifically objecting to the use of female pronouns in Minkowitz's article. In fact, they upped the gender ante by referring to Teena as an M2M (male-to-male), a new term that disputes the idea that transgendered men were ever women.[19] Despite the outrage expressed by the transgender community about Minkowitz's use of female pronouns to describe Teena, in October of 1995, a sidebar in an *Out* magazine article about the Sean O'Neill case still referred to Teena as "she."[20]

But gender activists did not stop with attacking defamation in the alternative press. Forty or so gender activists and friends showed up in Falls City, Nebraska for the opening day of Lotter's murder trial, May 15, 1995. A silent vigil was held outside the Richardson County Courthouse. Leslie Feinberg, Minnie Bruce Pratt, and Kate Bornstein were present, among others. Another participant places this event in context:

> In retrospect, there's no doubt this was a turning point for transactivism. It was the first really visible national demonstration we ever pulled off. And it started our practice of doing memorial vigils whenever a transperson is killed in a gender hate crime. After Brandon, we did Tyra Hunter, Chanel Picket, Deborah Forte, and Christian Paige. I got a call from a national news magazine about covering the stories, and they asked, "What is with all the trans-violence lately? Why is it on the increase?" I responded, "Gender activism is very reliable work. About every four or five months, like clockwork, another transperson is killed

in a fairly unambiguous hate crime. It's not that there's an increase. It's just that before the vigils, no one was paying attention."

I had called Nancy Nangeroni and said, "Let's call this off. What's the point of going to a town of two thousand people in the middle of nowhere? We'd do more good simply by sending the air fare to his mother." Nancy kept repeating that someone *had* to show up when transpeople were killed. So we kept to our commitment. In the end, forty people flew to the middle of Nebraska to stand that vigil. Almost all were strangers to one another, and almost all of them said the same thing to me when they called to sign up: "I don't know why I'm going. I just know I have to be there."

As Tony [*nota bene*: Barreto-Neto] has pointed out, Brandon died essentially because the sheriff refused to protect him, because he couldn't see him as a person. And so after he's murdered, just – what? A year and a half later? – into that same station walks another transsexual man who says to the same cops, "Look, I'm a transsexual man, just like Brandon, and I also carry a badge and a gun, just like you. I'm a brother officer; we *are* you. We are everywhere."[21]

Ending violence against the differently-gendered continues to be one of the most poignant and crucial items on the agenda for the Transexual Menace and similar organizations. During National Gender Lobbying Day in 1995, 35 activists from across the United States picketed outside Mayor Marion Barry's office to express their anger over the death of transgendered woman Tyra Hunter, and the ensuing cover-up by District of Columbia Fire Department Chief Otis J. Latin.

On August 7, 1995, Hunter was badly hurt in a hit-and-run automobile accident. An Emergency Medical Service (EMS) technician is reported to have jumped back from her body when he cut her pants off, to enable him to treat one of her injuries, and saw her penis. This EMS technician, whose identity is being protected by the Fire Department, is said to have shouted, "That ain't no bitch!" Treatment of Hunter's injuries came to a halt while other technicians gawked at and ridiculed her. The outraged and frightened cries of bystanders, who are quoted as saying, "It don't make any difference, he's [*sic*] a human being," finally alerted an EMS supervisor, who treated her. She died in a local hospital shortly after being transported there. Over 2,000 people attended her funeral on August 12, a clear sign that, unlike far too many incidents of official abuse of transgendered people, this case was not going to be swept under the rug.

Friends told transgendered activists that Hunter was 24, had lived full-time as a women since she was 14, and worked as a hairdresser. She was well-liked in her neighborhood, a gentle person who had never imagined she would die prematurely while suffering the humiliation of being reviled by the same people who were supposed to rescue and care for her.

An organization called Together in Tyra's Memory (TTM) was formed to protest this terrible incident of neglect. Among the supporters of TTM were Gay Men and Lesbians Opposing Violence; DC Coalition of Black Gay Men, Lesbians and Bisexuals; Gay and Lesbian Alliance Against Defamation of the National Capital Area; Capital City National Organization of Women; Log Cabin Republicans, DC Chapter; Gay and Lesbian Activists Alliance; Queer Nation; Transgender Nation of Washington, DC, and several other groups.

Despite pressure from TTM, the fire department insisted on its right to conduct an "internal inquiry," and issued nothing more than a one-page press release, which said they could not determine what had occurred despite the availability of at least 8 known eye witnesses.[22]

The sad death of Deborah Forte of Haverhill, Massachusetts should also be mentioned here. Ironically, the same day activists were packing up to leave their vigil at John Lotter's trial for murdering Brandon Teena, Forte died. She was found with three very deep stab wounds in her chest, other knife wounds, a smashed nose, multiple severe blows to her head and face, and the marks of partial strangulation. The man who was arrested in connection with her death, Michael J. Thompson, allegedly confessed to a coworker that he killed Forte after he went home with her, began "messing around," and discovered that she had a penis.[23]

Gender ambiguity makes many, if not most, people uncomfortable. But differently-gendered people are no longer taking violence for granted. And they are asking the rest of society to take a stand with them, to acknowledge that this discomfort is the result of ignorance and prejudice, and can no longer be used as a justification for harassment, assault, or murder.

The case of *The People of the State of Colorado vs. Sharon Clark, a.k.a. Sean O'Neill*, a female-bodied person who was charged with several crimes as a result of having sex with teenage girls who believed he was a young man, fortunately had a much happier ending than the Brandon Teena tragedy.

El Paso County prosecutors got four girls to confess that Sharon Clark (living as Sean O'Neill) had had consensual sex with them for months while posing as a boy. Twenty-year-old Clark was charged with one to 8 years for each of 11 felony counts (sexual assault, criminal impersonation, and sexual assault on a child). If convicted on all counts, he could have spent 32 years in prison. Two of the four complainants were 14 and O'Neill had been 18 when some of the sex occurred. The district attorney claimed O'Neill had raped the girls by withholding a crucial piece of sexual information from them.

This situation came to the attention of law enforcement personnel when one of O'Neill's girlfriends filed a harassment complaint against him. O'Neill had told her he was in love with someone else, they quarreled, and he threatened her. Police arrested O'Neill in a shopping mall and found a Colorado ID card in the name of Sharon Clark on his person. O'Neill admitted that he was, legally speaking, Sharon Clark. That night, a pair of policewomen reportedly decided to bring him up on charges of criminal impersonation and sexual assault. The girlfriend who had filed the harassment complaint was so upset by this news that she is said to have thrown her keys in a cop's face.

Gender activists were frightened about the potential consequences of this case in part because of the location where it was being tried. Colorado Springs is the home of over 53 Religious Right groups, 2 Christian colleges, and 10 evangelical bookstores. The homophobic Amendment 2 passed here in 1992 by the greatest margin in the state. In 1990, Charles Daugherty, a 26-year-old man, was found guilty of criminal impersonation for enrolling in a local high school as a girl named Cheyen. Daugherty's punishment set a scary precedent for O'Neill. Some of them also recalled the 1991 case of Jennifer Saunders in England. Saunders was given a 6 year prison term (which was later reduced, but only after she had spent 9 months in custody) for allegedly deceiving another young girl about her true sex. The difference in that case was that Saunders was very emphatic about her lesbian identity, although she admitted to sometimes passing as male to deceive the homophobic friends and families of her girlfriends.[24]

Much of the gay and lesbian community's information about O'Neill's case came from Minkowitz. Once again, she downplayed the male gender identity of the key figure in this tale. Minkowitz says, "To me, he [*nota bene*: Sean O'Neill] looks like a cute dyke, the sort of semibutch woman you can meet on hiking trails all over Colorado Springs."[25] O'Neill reportedly did not use the term *transsexual* or *transgendered* to describe himself, but neither did he call himself a lesbian. Certainly the negative public attitude toward lesbian sex had a bearing on the case. O'Neill was reportedly dyke-bashed frequently in high school, and he was beaten up by a group of teenagers after he appeared on the *Jerry Springer* show. It's possible, because of this, to wonder if O'Neill's cross-dressing and passing as a man was not at least partly motivated by a desire to escape antigay violence, as well as gender dysphoria. It seems pretty clear that some of O'Neill's girlfriends kept dating him even after they became aware of his female anatomy. But this is not what they told their parents or the district attorney's office. And it seems improbable that this case would have gone to court if O'Neill had been a genetic male.

Still, it is puzzling to find Minkowitz balking again and again at using the same male pronouns to describe O'Neill that he uses to describe himself. The reader is left with the impression that even if O'Neill had been taking testosterone and was scheduled for chest surgery, Minkowitz might not have been able to bring herself to see him or write about him as a man.

As Minkowitz pointed out, under Colorado law, one is guilty of first-degree sexual assault if one "causes submission of the victim" by violence or threats, and guilty of second-degree sexual assault if one causes submission by "any other means." Sean's lawyer Bill Martinez told Minkowitz that theoretically you could be found guilty under this statute if you falsely told a sex partner, "No, I'm not married" or "Yes, I am independently wealthy."

The other cause for concern was the possible consequences, not just for O'Neill, but for gay men, lesbians, and transgendered people (especially those who were preoperative or non-operative) if O'Neill was convicted. Wilchins commented, "If you look androgynous and someone wants to claim that you're passing yourself off as the other gender, you've just committed a felony." Wilchins wonders why it is the transsexual person's obligation to reveal their gender. "Did Sean's lovers tell him what their gender is?" she asked Minkowitz. Minkowitz connects this to debates about whether HIV-positive people must inform their partners. "Does everyone have an obligation to reveal their gender – or to know it?" she wonders. Robin Kane of NGLTF added, "As we learn more and more about transgendered people, we learn that there is a continuum of gender identification, and that it might actually be impossible for some people to disclose their gender fully."[26]

One of the transactivists who met O'Neill during the course of organizing events to draw attention to the case disputes the characterization of him as a "sexual predator."

> To give you a sense of what a crock the prosecution was, we took Sean to lunch after the sentencing, and while we're all trying to eat lunch his beeper keeps going off with one of the girls who is supposed to be his "victim" calling him. The district attorney kept referring to him as a dangerous and predatory "pedophile." And here's Sean, who weighs about ninety pounds soaking wet. One of his public defenders is a petite woman of about five-four and Sean just about reaches her shoulder.[27]

O'Neill wound up pleading guilty to one count of second degree sexual assault, and all other charges were dropped. On February 16, 1996, a judge gave O'Neill 6 years of supervised probation, therapy with Dr. Muller (a psychiatrist from Denver who gave testimony on Sean's behalf) or some other doctor who understood gender disorder, all sexual contact to be reported to a therapist, no unsupervised contact with anybody under 18, sex offender counseling, possibly some alcohol issues that needed to be dealt with, and

90 days in El Paso County Jail. The judge stressed that he would find a place for O'Neill to serve his sentence where he would not be harmed. The nervous young man, who had appeared in court with his girlfriend, was visibly relieved.

Gender activists took a large portion of the credit for ameliorating the effects of the criminal case against O'Neill. Their visibility helped to shift the public and judicial view of O'Neill, from predatory lesbian to immature teenage boy burdened by a confused gender identity. In statements before sentencing, District Attorney Schwartz reportedly said, "Sean O'Neill is a predator. She should be removed from the community."[28] Defense attorney Bill Martinez countered, "Sean O'Neill is a troubled young person doing his best to find his way, and to find affection in this world, without role models or appropriate guidance."[29]

While it seems clear that sending O'Neill to prison would have been a great injustice, it is disturbing to see the entire issue of lesbian sex side-stepped here. If O'Neill had been butch- rather than male-identified, it is doubtful that the gay or lesbian community would have sprung into action to provide assistance to the defense attorneys, largely because age-of-consent issues and cross-generational sex are involved.

Transexual Menace had scheduled a press conference and demonstration in support of O'Neill on the courthouse steps preceding the hearing. About 750 flyers were distributed that read, "Free Sean O'Neill – Don't Let Colorado Springs Make Gender Non-Conformity a Crime! . . . The Cops & DA want to waste tens of thousands of dollars of your tax money regulating sex & gender."[30] FTM activists Green and Tony Barreto-Neto, a deputy sheriff from Hillsborough County, Florida, and founder of Transgendered Officers Protect and Serve (TOPS), had testified on his behalf. About 20 people came from all over the country to attend the trial, which then had to be moved to a larger courtroom. One observer reported that transgendered people and their friends made up over half the audience. Wilchins comments, "The Sean O'Neill demonstration was the first time trans-men really came into their own in gender activism. We not only had a great turnout by them, but we also got to see Jamison [*nota bene*: Green] and Tony [*nota bene*: Barreto-Neto] testifying on Sean's behalf. A whole new segment of the community was starting to come out, get visible, and be political."[31]

The new, more public and outrageous style of gender activism has not superseded work on more traditional issues, which has proceeded according to the temperate pace of governments and courtrooms. Attempts to gain the same protection for their civil rights that racial minorities and (in some municipalities and states) gay men and lesbians have won have been ongoing among gender activists. In Minnesota, a transsexual World War II veteran lobbied the state legislature to include "gender difference" as a protected civil-rights category. In 1974, Diana Slyter co-wrote the Minneapolis ordinance that was this country's first prohibition of discrimination against transpeople.[32] Early in 1993, Minnesota passed a law that forbids discrimination againstpeople "having or being perceived as having a self-image or identity not traditionally associated with one's biological maleness or femaleness."[33] And in December of 1994, the San Francisco Board of Supervisors outlawed discrimination against transsexuals in schools, housing, public accommodations, and the workplace.

This came only after a careful foundation of hearings and other research had been laid. In 1994, the San Francisco Human Rights Commission organized its first forum on discrimination against transgendered people. On May 12, a four-and-a-half hour hearing took place before the Commission. More than fifty transgendered speakers testified about discrimination. Kiki Whitlock, chair of the Transgender Task Force and a member of the

Commission's Gay, Lesbian, Bisexual, and Transgender Advisory Committee, said, "It was a very historic hearing. It's a necessary first step toward legislation so that transgendered people will be a protected class." Among those who testified were Green, photographer Loren Cameron, and San Francisco Police Department Sergeant Stephan Thorn.[34]

In September of 1994, the commission published a groundbreaking paper, "Investigation into Discrimination Against Transgendered People." The principal author was Green, as a contractor to the city, under the supervision of Human Rights Commission staff member Larry Brinkin, who had done much to gain official recognition of the institutionalized oppression transpeople face and to generate moral indignation against that oppression. Out of all these actions, later that year came unanimous passage by the San Francisco Board of Supervisors of an amendment to Article 33 of the Police Code and Chapter 12 of the city's Administrative Code, which add "gender identity" to the list of attributes for which a person may not be discriminated against.

As the author of this report, Green encountered "FTM invisibility" during news coverage of the extension of civil-rights protection to transgendered people.

> The press was all about men in dresses. Mention of FTM presence or issues was absolutely minuscule. Several times at the courthouse, when the press was doing interviews, I stood by and listened as reporters inquired who wrote the report, and when I was pointed out to them as the author I could see them looking right through me, looking past me to find the man in a dress who must have written the report and whom they would want to interview. More than once a reporter asked me incredulously, "You wrote this report?" They assumed because of my "normal" appearance that I wouldn't be newsworthy.... Does it matter that the world doesn't know we exist, or doesn't take us seriously? You bet it does.... Invisibility does not equate with acceptance.[35]

When the law was passed, supervisor Tom Ammiano, a gay man, joked, "A guy can't get a pink slip just for wearing one."[36] Ammiano's relatively benign humor took a malignant turn on a national level. Satirical articles in the *Wall Street Journal* and other prominent daily newspapers lambasted San Francisco for what was perceived as a ridiculous and frivolous action. Some of these articles were published in newspapers that no longer feel free to publish similar diatribes against the concept of lesbian and gay rights. Unfortunately, it seems, progress in one area of sexual prejudice does not seem to guarantee progress in another. Transphobia is a separate entity from, although it is related to, homophobia, and activism is the only way to counter its harmful effects.

The Human Welfare and Community Action Commission in Berkeley cast a near-unanimous vote to include transgendered people as a protected group under its anti-discrimination policy on September 20, 1995.[37] But progressive policies on transgender rights still does not sit well in many quarters. Additional backlash against the San Francisco ordinance recently appeared in local media. Transactivists had to picket the *San Francisco Chronicle* after the newspaper ran a story that implied that taxpayers would have to pay thousands of dollars for sex-change surgeries because of the law protecting transsexuals from discrimination. This story was picked up by the Associated Press wire service, which alleged there were 6,000 people in San Francisco who might apply for sex-change surgery. It then appeared all over the country. What actually happened was that members of the San Francisco Transgender Community Task Force and the Human Rights Commission approached Supervisor Tom Ammiano and asked him why transexually-related medical services were excluded from the insurance coverage of city employees. They were asking for the removal of an exclusion from existing insurance coverage, not attempting to impose an additional tax on citizens. And there were only approximately 7 transsexual city employees, not 6,000. The later, larger figure may have come from an estimate of the total number of transgendered people in all of San Francisco.[38]

Transsexual activists have won important victories not only in this country, but abroad. On April 30, 1996, the European Court of Justice confirmed the recommendation of Advocate General Tesauro and said that it is against European law to discriminate against a transsexual person in employment. This ruling affects an estimated 40 to 50 thousand European transgendered people and 4,000 to 5,000 in the United Kingdom. This matter began in an unfair-dismissal case brought by a Press for Change activist known only as "P" against her former employers, the Cornwall County Council. The British government was thus placed under pressure to amend the Sex Discrimination Act and the Equal Pay Act to close a loophole that had been used by employers who wanted to dismiss FTM or MTF employees. The European Court decision was especially welcome, since earlier in the year "P" had lost a bid to get the sex on her birth certificate changed. British law continues to make it all but impossible for transsexuals to do this, and since this is their only form of legal identification there, they are outed as transgendered any time they must show their papers.[39]

Sadly, the efforts of transgendered activists to gain basic civil liberties protection for themselves and their community have encountered an obstacle where these efforts should have found allies. In June of 1994, HRC, a venerable gay-rights, organization formerly known as the Human Rights Campaign Fund, declined to include transsexual people as a protected class in the Employment Non-Discrimination Act (ENDA), a job discrimination bill it was promoting in Congress to protect lesbians and gay men from being fired for their sexual orientation. ENDA drafter Chai Feldblum was quoted as telling the International Conference on Transgender Law and Employment Policy that HRC "couldn't afford inclusion because it might cost us twenty votes."[40]

Transgender activists were enraged by this news, and quite correctly pointed out that it is often a perceived gender difference that alerts a homophobe to the presence of a gay men or lesbian. A law that did not extend protection to transsexuals and transgendered people might leave effeminate gay men, butch dykes, or anybody who was perceived as violating social sex-role stereotypes vulnerable to unfair termination of employment or other unequal treatment. Transactivists worked to get themselves mentioned in the bill, and succeeded, but HRC insisted on omitting transpeople again when ENDA was reintroduced on June 16, 1995.

After six months of leafleting and picketing by transactivists, HRC agreed to assist transactivists in drafting an amendment to ENDA and helped them to lobby for its inclusion. This tenuous peace was reached only after the gender community had held demonstrations to educate people about HRC's discriminatory policies in at least 18 cities.[41] Green feels that "Chai Feldblum has come to a new understanding of the synergy between gay and trans issues. Recently, in a speech at Harvard University she was reported to say that she now believed transpeople should be included in ENDA, and what changed her mind was meeting Shannon Minter, staff attorney for the National Center for Lesbian Rights in San Francisco, who has recently come out as FTM. She was able to have a personal experience of what transgender means through meeting someone she could respect and identify with, and whose gender difference was perceptible to her."[42]

It is never pretty when one disadvantaged group sells out another in an attempt to promote its own interests. Nor is it usually good political strategy. The roots of prejudice against homosexuals and the hatred and fear of transsexuals are so closely woven together that it is not really all that difficult to educate people simultaneously about both communities. No reasonable person at HRC could credibly claim that a significant portion of the gay and lesbian community is not also part of the gender community. Gay lobbyists in Washington often propose legislation that they know has a snowball's chance in hell of passing, but they continue to introduce these bills as a way of maintaining gay visibility and reminding legislators that some Americans are still waiting to be given the protection we need in order to meet our basic survival needs. It would be so easy to include everyone who ought to be protected in the same bill. Why should every single minority have to fight its own separate struggle for recognition and acceptance? I know that some gay men and lesbians believe that we must separate our community from the even more stigmatized realm of cross-dressers and transsexuals, or we will never achieve our political goals. But it seems very important for us to ask ourselves if we will have achieved anything, if we are recognized as a minority group entitled to full civil rights, and differently-gendered people are not. As the Transexual Menace flyer protesting HRC's discriminatory policies *vis-à-vis* ENDA stated, "A queer movement that's not for ALL of us is good for NONE of us!"[43]

Indeed, it is a lack of an analysis of gender among gay male activists that has created debilitating splits between gay men and lesbians. I believe that we cannot fully understand our own oppression without also understanding the roots of transphobia. If our goal is to create a just society where people are not persecuted for difference in their sexual behavior or personal appearance, among other things, we cannot afford to remain ignorant about every type of sexual prejudice and the ways our society tries to repress and shame us for deviation. As long as the words *sissy* and *bulldagger* remain slurs, gay men and lesbians will have a common cause with the transgendered community. It would be better to acknowledge it and move ahead with a new group of solid allies and supporters than it would be to engage in yet another exhausting and stupid attempt to jettison "undesirables" from the Lavender Freedom Train.

As Riki Wilchins, editrix of *In Your Face*, says:

> The fight against gender oppression has been joined for centuries, perhaps millennia. What's new today, is that it's moving into the arena of open political activism. And nope, this is not just one more civil rights struggle for one more narrowly-defined minority. It's about all of us who are genderqueer: diesel dykes and stone butches, leatherqueens and radical fairies, nelly fags, crossdressers, intersexed, transexuals, transvestites, transgendered, transgressively gendered, intersexed, and those of us whose gender expressions are so complex they haven't even been named yet. More than that, it's about the gender oppression which affects everyone: the college sweetheart who develops life-threatening anorexia nervosa trying to look "feminine," the Joe Sixpack dead at forty-five from cirrhosis of the liver because "real men" are hard drinkers. But maybe we genderqueers feel it most keenly, because it hits us each time we walk out the front door openly and proudly.... We're not invisible anymore. We're not well behaved. And we're not going away. Political activism is here to stay.
>
> So get out. Get active. Picket someone's transphobic ass. Get in someone's genderphobic face. And while you're at it, pass the word: the gendeRevolution has begun, and we're going to win.[44]

In a personal communiqué, she adds:

> I am not personally interested in being a transgender activist – even less a transsexual activist. What I am interested in is fighting a liberatory struggle against gender-based oppression – all the ways in which culture seeks to regulate, confine, and punish bodies, gender, and desire.[45]

Notes

1 Vicky Kolakowski, "Fifth International Transgender Law Conference Held in Houston," *Bay Area Reporter*, July 11, 1996, pp. 25–6.

2 Phyllis Frye, "ICTLEP Appoints Another FTM to Board of Directors," Dec. 12, 1996 press release from ICTLEP.

3 Riki Anne Wilchins, "Quotes, Quotes, Quotes," e-mail to the author, Dec. 13, 1996, p. 1. Unpublished.

4 Jamison Green, "Chapter 7," Dec. 21, 1996 e-mail to the author, p. 2. Unpublished.

5 Anne Ogborn, "Going Home," pp. 2–3, and "Hijras and Intersexuals," p. 3, *Hermaphrodites with Attitudes*, vol. 1, no. 1, Winter 1994.

6 John Taylor, "The Third Sex," *Esquire*, April 1995, pp. 102–14.

7 Wilchins, "Quotes, Quotes, Quotes," op. cit., pp. 2–3.

8 Green, op. cit., pp. 2–3.

9 Interview with Riki Anne Wilchins by the author, Dec. 12, 1996. Unpublished.

10 Fish, "Moshing with Michigan Womyn (& Transsexuals!)," *San Francisco Bay Times*, Aug. 25, 1994, p. 53.

11 Riki Anne Wilchins, "Michigan Womyn's Music Festival Controversy Grinds On," *In Your Face*, Fall 1995, p. 6.

12 Donna Minkowitz, "Love Hurts," *Village Voice*, April 19, 1994, p. 24.

13 Ibid., p. 25.

14 Riki Anne Wilchins, "Brandon Teena Revisited," GenderPAC press release, Dec. 6, 1996.

15 Minkowitz, op. cit.

16 Mindy Ridgway, "Nebraska Man Guilty of Brandon Teena's Murder," *San Francisco Bay Times*, March 23, 1995, p. 4.

17 Green, op. cit., p. 3.

18 Riki Anne Wilchins, "Seeking A New Trial," GenderPAC press release, Dec. 6, 1996.

19 Riki Anne Wilchins, "New York Citaaay," *In Your Face*, Spring, 1995, p. 3.

20 Dorothy Atcheson, "Culture Vultures in Nebraska," *Out*, Oct. 1995, p. 100. Sidebar to Donna Minkowitz, "On Trial: Gay? Straight? Boy? Girl? Sex? Rape?," *Out*, Oct. 1995, pp. 99–101, 140–6.

21 Wilchins, "Quotes, Quotes, Quotes," op. cit., pp. 3–4.

22 Riki Anne Wilchins, "Another One, It Just Doesn't Stop: Tyra Hunter," *In Your Face*, Fall 1995, pp. 2–3.

23 Riki Anne Wilchins, "The Murder of Deborah Forte," *In Your Face*, Fall 1995, p. 2.

24 Anna Marie Smith, "The Regulation of Lesbian Sexuality through Erasure: The Case of Jennifer Saunders," in Karla Jay (ed.), *Lesbian Erotics*, New York: New York University, 1995, pp. 164–79.

25 Donna Minkowitz, "On Trial: Gay? Straight? Boy? Girl? Sex? Rape?," *Out*, Oct. 1995, p. 100.

26 Ibid., p. 146.

27 Wilchins, "Quotes, Quotes, Quotes," op. cit., p. 4.

28 Jamison Green, "Predator?" *San Francisco Bay Times*, vol. 17, no. 9, Feb. 22, 1996, p. 3. Reprinted in *FTM Newsletter*, issue 34, May 1996, pp. 2–6. Page numbers in text refer to the *Bay Times*, original printing.

29 Ibid., p. 29.

30 Ibid., p. 2.

31 Wilchins, "Quotes, Quotes, Quotes," op. cit., pp. 4–5.

32 Margaret Deirdre O'Hartigan, "Stealing Our History," an unpublished review of Leslie Feinberg's *Transgender Warriors*, p. 4.

33 Dan Levy and David Tuller, "Opening Up the World of Drag," *San Francisco Chronicle*, May 28, 1993, pp. A-1 and A-17.

34 Dennis Conkin, "Human Rights Commission Addresses Transgender Issues," *Bay Area Reporter*, May 19, 1994, p. 1.

35 James Green, "Keynote Address for the FTM Conference," Aug. 18, 1995, pp. 11–12. Unpublished.

36 Jeff Stryker, "Bigotry and Ignorance vs. the 'Transgendered'," *San Francisco Examiner*, Dec. 13, 1995, p. A-33.

37 Mary Ann Swissler, "Berkeley Adopts Transgender Rights," *Bay Area Reporter*, Oct. 12, 1995, p. 5.

38 Riki Anne Wilchins, "SF Chronicle Has Transphobia Attack," GenderPAC press release, Oct. 18, 1996. The article "Move to Cover City Worker's Sex Changes" appeared in the *San Francisco Chronicle* on Sept. 23, 1996.

39 Christine Burns, "Victory in the European Court of Justice," April 30, 1996, press release by Press for Change.

40 Transexual Menace flyer headed "HRCF to Transpeople: Drop Dead!", undated.

41 Riki Anne Wilchins, "1995: A Breakout Year in Review," *In Your Face*, Fall 1995, p. 1.

42 Green, "Chapter 7," op. cit., pp. 4–5.

43 Transexual Menace flyer headed "Hey HRCF: Can You Spell I-N-C-L-U-S-I-O-N?," undated.

44 Riki Anne Wilchins, "A Note from Your Editrix," *In Your Face*, Spring 1995, p. 4.

45 Interview with Riki Anne Wilchins by the author, op. cit.

CHAPTER 36

At a Turning Point: Organized Labor, Sexual Diversity, and the New South Africa

Mazibuko K. Jara, Naomi Webster, and Gerald Hunt

Collin Ndaba, the general secretary of a trade union, calls Charity into his office with a very somber expression on his face. He says, "Charity, I have something serious to tell you. Mazibuko has been hiding something from you and Cornelia. Do you know he is gay? He has spoken to me about protecting the rights of gay and lesbian workers, but I am going to ignore him." Charity is thinking: Mazibuko is working for a lesbian and gay rights organization. He does not have to be gay to work for lesbian and gay equality. Why does it matter one way or the other? Anyway, why should a trade union official be thinking this way? Shouldn't unions be supporting equal rights? However, Charity feels she cannot express what she is thinking because the union's policies do not yet include provisions for lesbian and gay equality.

The above story is one example of a continuing but slowly changing attitude toward sexual minorities within post-apartheid South Africa. Although there have been significant legal and constitutional changes in relation to gays and lesbians, many South African individuals, organizations, and institutions have been slow to rethink long-standing prejudicial attitudes and to alter practices toward sexual minorities. So far, organized labor appears not to be a notable exception to this trend. On the one hand, many labor leaders supported the new government when it was enacting change in the legal and constitutional apparatus of the post-apartheid Republic of South Africa, including the incorporation of sexual orientation as a category for nondiscrimination. On the other hand, very few labor federations or trade unions have changed their internal policies, procedures, and collective agreements to reduce or eliminate discrimination on the basis of sexual orientation in areas such as hiring, firing, and benefit coverage. Nevertheless, South Africa continues to be in the midst of enormous change in relation to human rights and equity issues. There are encouraging signs, especially within the judiciary, that

Mazibuko K. Jara, Naomi Webster, and Gerald Hunt, "At a Turning Point: Organized Labor, Sexual Diversity, and the New South Africa," pp. 191–205 from G. Hunt (ed.), *Laboring for Rights: Unions and Sexual Diversity Across Nations*. Princeton: Temple University Press, 1999. Reprinted by permission of Temple University Press. © 1999 by Temple University. All rights reserved.

discriminatory attitudes and practices toward sexual minorities are changing. Moreover, organized labor seems increasingly committed to gender and other equity issues and now might be more amenable to initiatives directed at equality for sexual minorities than at any other point in its history. This chapter undertakes to review, assess, and analyze these developments.[1]

The new South Africa

Collective applause was heard throughout the world in April 1994 when Nelson Mandela's African National Congress Party (ANC) was swept into power through a massive victory in the first-ever democratic, nonracial elections held in South Africa. After years of civil riots, bloodshed, and protest, South Africa finally entered a post-apartheid period. Once the celebrations were over, work began in earnest to restructure the political and social landscape of the country. Expectations were high, especially from the large black majority, many of whom had been living in abject poverty but now had hopes for a much improved life politically, socially, and economically. Equally hopeful about the prospects for change were other groups, not the least of which were gays and lesbians, who had lived under a cloud of oppression, inequality, and intolerance.

Since 1994, human rights issues have been at the forefront of debate and legislative change in South Africa. Soon after coming into power, the ANC government passed the Human Rights Commission Act (1996), which created a central commission and regional offices to hear complaints and undertake educational initiatives. In 1996, a new constitution was enacted, guaranteeing protection and outlawing unfair discrimination by the state or individuals on 13 grounds, including race, gender, sex, and marital status. Also included, after considerable lobbying and pressure, were gays and lesbians, making it the only constitution in the world specifically guaranteeing protection, nondiscrimination, and equality for this minority group.

In tandem with the new constitution and the creation of a Human Rights Commission, the ANC brought forward several important pieces of legislation designed to protect and enhance workers' rights and generally reinforce broader equity initiatives. A new Labor Relations Act (LRA) was enacted in September 1995, and a Basic Conditions of Employment Act (BCEA) and an Employment Equity Act (EEA) were enacted in 1998. The new LRA has been widely seen as a victory for organized labor and reinforces the anti-discrimination clauses of South Africa's constitution. It specifically includes sexual orientation as grounds for nondiscrimination in the workplace. The BCEA includes provisions for such things as "humane" working hours and conditions, maternity leave, and the elimination of child labor. It also includes a clause acknowledging the "life partner" of any employee for the purposes of family responsibility, thus recognizing and potentially accommodating all types of families inside and outside of traditional marriages, including same-sex couples. The LRA provisions were transitional until the passing of the EEA. The EEA outlaws unfair discrimination on 17 grounds including race, gender, sex, sexual orientation, marital status, and HIV/AIDS status. The EEA also requires employers to develop and implement employment equity initiatives to help address and correct apartheid inequities in the workplace. Designated groups under the EEA are black people, women, and people living with disabilities. The EEA defines family to include partners in the same way as the BCEA.

The terms of the EEA were quite controversial and strongly opposed by many white people in positions of power. The provisions in the EEA were only achieved through an employment and equity alliance made up of 22 organizations, including the National Coalition for Gay and Lesbian Equality, the South African Council of Churches, the Southern Africa Catholic Bishops' Conference, and a number of trade unions. Notably, the South African Council of Churches did support the expanded definition of family to include same-sex partners, even though some coalition members were opposed to the idea.

Also contributing to a much more progressive environment has been the creation of a number of investigatory commissions. A Human Rights Commission was established by the Human Rights Commission Act to promote respect for human rights and a culture of human rights, as well as to investigate and to report on the observance of human rights and take steps to secure appropriate redress where human rights have been violated. It also has a research and education role. The Commission of Gender Equality Act, passed in 1996, created a Commission on Gender with the power to monitor, investigate, research, educate, lobby, advise, and report on issues concerning gender inequity. The Truth and Reconciliation Commission, headed by Bishop Desmond Tutu, was created to explore and expose apartheid-era injustices in business, policing, the law, and the church, and to recommend corrective action and compensation plans for victims.

Thus, the ANC set itself a massive agenda with an overarching goal: to unify South Africa as a model of democracy after years of having being ruled by a powerful white-minority regime – all to be achieved within a country in the throws of an economic downturn, very high unemployment and underemployment, enormous income disparities, an extremely serious violent crime problem, and significant emigration of professionals. In spite of the enormity of the task, though, this emerging political order has created the framework for the transformation of South Africa toward a people-centered, democratic state based on equality, respect for human rights, dignity, and justice for all. In so doing, it has offered the lesbian and gay rights movement a unique moment in history to demand full membership and equality in the new South Africa.

The rise of a gay and lesbian rights movement

At a press conference held in Washington, DC, in December 1996, the well-known activist Zackie Achmat indicated that the fight for gay and lesbian rights in South Africa would continue to be "part and parcel" of the larger liberation movement.[2] Early organizing for gay and lesbian rights, however, reflected the racially divided nature of the country; the movement was primarily white and conservative. The rise of gay and lesbian activism in South Africa, as a result, is closely linked to its transition from a uniracial to a multiracial movement, and one much more aligned with broader civil rights goals.[3]

The first wave of political activism emerged in 1968 in response to a law reform movement aimed at making virtually any homosexual activity a serious criminal offence. Up until this period, gay life had focused on underground bars, house parties, and cruising, all within an environment where public, but not private, male homosexual acts were unlawful. However, when a draconian anti-gay bill was introduced by the government in 1968 to amend the Sexual Offences Act, designed to make homosexuality itself statutorily illegal and to bring lesbians within the scope of the law, gays and lesbians started to mobilize. The first "public" meetings aimed at gay rights within South Africa were organized mainly by an urban and professional group of white men and women, with the singular goal of preventing the passage of the proposed bill. These meetings had the effect of bringing together for the first time a group committed to political activism, helping to forge a sense of a community with a common purpose. Their initiatives drew attention to the worse excesses of the bill but did not prevent its passage in a somewhat modified but still outrageous form in March 1969. Among other things, the amendments raised the age of consent for male homosexual activity from 16 to 19, outlawed dildos, and criminalized almost all male sexual activity within the public and private domain. So stern was the new law that it became illegal for a male person to commit any act designed to stimulate sexual passion at a "party"; where a party was defined as any occasion involving more than two people, sexual passion could be something as innocent as dancing. Sodomy became a schedule 1 offense, lumping it together with serious crimes such as murder, rape, and treason. Nevertheless, there was some very slight cause for celebration because the original bill had proposed making it illegal for two women to live together and contained provisions for a mandatory three-year prison term for all homosexual acts.

Ironically, these new and harsh measures ushered in an era in which gay and lesbian life, including a degree of activism, began to flourish. While all public spaces such as parks and washrooms were even more closely monitored for homosexual activity, and house raids on private parties remained common, the police appeared prepared to look the other way when it came to bars and private clubs, as long as minors or liquor were not in evidence. In other words, homosexuality continued to be tolerated in spite of the repressive laws, as long as it took place indoors, especially in ghettoized commercial spaces, and out of sight. This in turn lead to the creation of "meeting spaces" and the beginnings of a community based on a shared sense of isolation and oppression. At the same time, though, the already stratified feature of gay and lesbian life was reinforced. Those without the money to go to bars, and those too frightened to be seen in a gay place, had few other options. Oddly as well, even under apartheid, blacks were allowed to enter bars that did not serve alcohol, and although some of the few that had sufficient funds did try, they were often refused admission by the management.

Within these constraints and contradictions, a gay and lesbian subculture took root during the 1970s. On the one hand, nearly any kind of homosexual activity was illegal; on the other hand, a vibrant urban commercial scene began to emerge, tentative as it was, since it existed at the whim of the authorities. The government, police, and military were increasingly preoccupied with growing tensions and rebellion in the black townships rather than the private diversions of homosexuals. For most of the gays and lesbians enjoying the outlets provided by bars and private clubs, the primary goal was social rather than political, a fact that may also have helped to foster a certain level of tolerance by the police.

Toward the end of the 1970s, however, there was a resurgence of more enthusiastic policing of places where gays and lesbians gathered, fueled in part by a political and media-driven campaign equating gay life with pedophilia. In response to this renewed sense of vulnerability and oppression, a new wave of activism began to take shape in the early 1980s. The Gay Association of South Africa (GASA) formed in 1982, an amalgamation of several other smaller groups, and although largely a socially oriented, white middle-class and conservative mix of people, it provided a forum for political discussions. Although its main publication was banned by the authorities, the group was able to organize social events and meetings and hold an annual convention. In October 1982, GASA organized the largest gay event ever to take place up until that time, a Gay Jamboree held in the Transvaal Country Club attended by over 3,000 people. By May 1985, GASA was holding conventions at a downtown Johannesburg hotel, complete with speeches on gay liberation. Brazenly, given the legal situation, it opened an office in 1983 and subsequently a community center, and by 1984 it had spawned one of the first women's interest groups. For all its advances, however, GASA espoused and tried to foster an apolitical stance. Its manifesto specifically required the organization to be a "moderate, non-political answer to gay needs."

By the mid-1980s, the emerging AIDS crisis, more vigorous policing, the rise of a gay and lesbian presence in the black townships, and a growing mass of anti-apartheid and pro-democracy individuals provided the impetus for more activist-driven and less racially divided gay and lesbian organizations. The Gay and Lesbian Organization of Witwatersrand (GLOW) started in 1983; the Organization of Lesbian and Gay Activists in Cape Town (OLGA) followed in 1987. Partly the result of softening of apartheid rules in 1989 and 1990, these groups were able to organize the first gay and lesbian rights march held in Johannesburg in 1990, drawing a crowd of around 800. These marches became annual events and were expanded to include theater events, film festivals, and sporting activities. During the late 1980s, these groups developed manifestos that were expressly nonracist, nonsexist, nondiscriminatory, and pro-democracy. As a result, blacks became more active participants in the groups, leaders began to forge alliances with the growing anti-apartheid movement, and alliances with the African National Congress were forged. These alliances, however, were not without conflict and difficulties. Winnie Mandela's assertion in 1991 that "Homosex is not in black culture" spoke to a deeply rooted feeling among many black freedom fighters that homosexuality was "un-African," a byproduct of colonial capitalism, something "circumstantial" rather than "organic." Still, in 1991, an ANC Constitutional Committee drafting a bill of rights included a provision to outlaw sexual orientation discrimination, largely the result of lobbying by GLOW and other national and international groups. Subsequently, in 1993, the ANC incorporated protection on the basis of sexual orientation into its draft constitution, albeit in the face of considerable internal dissent and once again under pressure from national and international gay and lesbian rights groups.[4]

A regrouping and amalgamation of organizations in the early 1990s resulted in the birth of the National Coalition for Gay and Lesbian Equality (NCGLE) in December 1994. This umbrella organization, representing over 80 urban and rural gay and lesbian organizations in South Africa, along with one from Zimbabwe and one from Swaziland, was created with a mandate to ensure sexual orientation remained a listed ground of nondiscrimination in the final constitution. Once that goal was achieved in 1996, the coalition set to work on a much broader agenda aimed at the elimination of sexual orientation discrimination in South Africa through education and lobbying efforts, as well as initiating court challenges based on the new constitution. In 1997, the coalition and the statutory Human Rights Commission applied to the High Court to have the sodomy laws declared unconstitutional. In spite of opposition from a variety of groups, in a 1998 decision, they were successful. The 11-judge panel also declared that men who had been convicted of sodomy since 1994 could demand monetary damages and have their criminal records cleared.

From the beginning, one of NCGLE's major objectives was to confront discrimination in the workplace. By 1996, it was ready to focus more attention and resources toward achieving this goal. One of NCGLE's actions was to set up an Equal Rights Project (ERP) with the express purpose of examining all aspects of the lives of gays and lesbians in South Africa, but with a particular focus on the workplace. The ERP led to the formation of a Johannesburg-based gay and lesbian legal advice center in August 1997. The center has since dealt with more than 80 cases of workplace discrimination and harassment.

Most of these cases were resolved within the new statutes and rules set out by the constitution, LRA, EEA, and the BCEA.

Sexual orientation issues in the workplace

As the new millennium approaches, South Africa is similar to many other countries in the issues that remain contested terrain for sexual minorities. Although the 1990s witnessed enormous change in the laws affecting the lives of sexual minorities, prejudicial attitudes, policies, and practices in many facets of life, especially in the workplace, have been much more resistant to change. Here as elsewhere in the world, sexual minorities face discrimination in hiring, firing, and promotion decisions, violence and harassment, and the failure to have same-sex relationships recognized for legal and benefit coverage.

The most obvious form of discrimination takes place when a person applying for a job or promotion does not get it, or is fired or demoted because of his or her sexual orientation. Obviously, an employer can attempt to cover up and disguise the real motives for these decisions, making it difficult to establish a case. Another related area of concern is the threat of harassment and violence, since gays and lesbians are often subject to jokes, taunts, and beatings based purely on their sexuality. Outlawing these forms of discrimination is an important first step, one the government has initiated by provisions in the new constitution, Labor Relations Act, and proposed Code of Employment Practices on Sexual Harassment. However, legal change, important as it is, does not mean the problems disappear, only that legal recourse is available. Many people are reluctant to take legal action. Instead, they look to employers to institute measures aimed at preventing and confronting discrimination within specific work sites. Sexual minorities also look to trade unions for assistance. Unions can engage in collective bargaining with employers for agreements that articulate these issues and provide mechanisms for their resolution. Moreover, unions can provide financial and moral support in mounting legal challenges against employers.

Perhaps the most blatant form of discrimination related to sexual orientation is the failure to recognize same-sex relationships for the purpose of legal and benefit coverage. Most workplaces offer at least some benefits to employees and their families but routinely exclude people who do not fit the heterosexual norm. In South Africa, this is particularly problematic because many people obtain their medical coverage through workplace-based schemes, and because medical aid is enjoyed by a very small minority of South Africans, it is one of the most appealing and crucial benefits offered by employers. Most medical plans allow for the registration of legally married spouses and children but specifically exclude unmarried couples, even though the new constitution and LRA provisions prohibit discrimination on the basis of marital status. As a result, access to medical benefits for same-sex couples and their families is often denied. In addition, especially in unionized settings, a wider range of benefits may be available. These benefits include superior medical aid, pension schemes, housing supplements, and retirement provisions. A few employers also provide benefits related to education and training, as well as various forms of leaves for such things as child care and bereavement. As with medical coverage, these benefits tend to be restricted to employees and their legal spouses and do not provide for same-sex or common-law couples.

Although it is widely believed by gays and lesbians that the above forms of workplace discrimination are everyday occurrences, and there is no evidence to suggest otherwise, little research has documented the extent of the problem. What is perhaps most telling is that employers continue to deny medical, pension, and housing benefits to gay and lesbian employees when requested, forcing workers to appeal to the courts for assistance. Even then, employers contest the legitimacy of the claims and seem prepared to expend considerable sums of money on litigation. One of the few ways to examine the extent of the problem is by considering the issues brought to the Equal Rights Project of NCGLE. Of the 15 cases brought forward between September 1996 and 1997, 7 had to do with refusal to include a same-sex partner for medical aid; 3 had to do with dismissal on the basis of sex orientation; 5 involved harassment. It must be kept in mind, though, that these figures probably represent the tip of an iceberg, since most people would be extremely reluctant to lodge a formal discrimination charge on the basis of sexual orientation. It should also be noted that the majority of cases were brought forward by white gays and lesbians, who are more likely to have access to support and legal advice favoring such actions.

A similar sense of the problem comes from data collected by the Center of Applied Legal Studies at the University of Witwatersrand. The center began in 1980 in an attempt to address human rights violations, and it has been involved in legal issues related to labor, gender, land rights, and AIDS. The center's Gender Research Project (GRP) incorporated issues related to sexual orientation and undertook research in this area. In June 1996, the GRP convened a workshop to look at issues that could best be addressed by unions. The results showed that hiring and firing issues ranked as most important, followed closely by refusal of medical aid for partners, and harassment. If we combine the information from NCGLE and the GRP, the issues that emerge as most critical are medical aid coverage, fear of not being hired or of being dismissed if found out to be gay or lesbian, and harassment. Even though the data arise from very limited sampling, these findings provide a picture of what people believe to problematic, and they help to prioritize concerns that could be addressed by unions.

As we will highlight in the next sections, the labor movement played a direct role in the creation of new human rights legislation and institutions. It is therefore reasonable to expect that labor might lead the way in developing policies and practices designed to ensure that equity initiatives actually are implemented, especially within the workplace. As we will see, however, labor has so far been reluctant to push forward further reforms.

Organized labor in the South African context

Trade unions have existed in South Africa since the 1890s but have paralleled the racially divided history of the country. The first black trade union was the Industrial and Commercial Workers Union (known as the ICU – "I see you white man"). Formed by dock workers in 1919 in Cape Town, the ICU became one of the first major mobilizing tools for black workers against exploitation and national oppression. However, the ICU was short-lived; by 1930, it was dead in all but name. Between 1930 and the banning of the ANC and the Pan African Congress in 1961, there were attempts to build trade unions and federations among black workers, especially in light of the fact that black workers represented the majority of workers in the country. This period also saw the rise of a number of socialist organizations committed to building a stronger labor movement. Unions that emerged during this period included the African Mine Workers Union, the African Federation of Trade Unions, the Council of Non-European Trade Unions, and the

South African Congress of Trade Unions. These organizations remained largely powerless, since white workers continued to organize separately in so-called "sweetheart" unions. Nevertheless, these unions and federations became sites where workplace struggles were articulated and links were made to broader struggles for national liberation.

The upsurge in racial repression during 1960–1992 effectively crushed these unions and moved their political operations underground. White workers' unions, however, continued to grow during this period but tended to offer little resistance to the apartheid state. In spite of these enormous roadblocks, the beginnings of a strong and progressive, nonracial trade union movement was taking place in the 1970s, with organizing activity in the major industrial cities of Durban, Cape Town, and Witwatersrand. These developments led to the birth of several trade unions and federations, some of which continue today.

Since 1992, organized labor in South Africa has been in a much more stable period. It now has the distinction of having the fastest growing trade union membership in the world. The 1997 Annual Report of the International Labor Organization (ILO) reported that, between 1985 and 1995, trade union membership had fallen in 72 of the 92 countries it surveyed, but that membership in South Africa had increased by nearly 127 percent. According to the ILO report, union density in South Africa in 1995 was 41 percent of the economically active population, compared to 37 percent in 1992, giving it the highest unionization rate of any developing country. The largest growth in membership has occurred in the public sector. South Africa now has several trade union confederations, including the Coalition of South African Trade Unions (Cosatu), the Federated Unions of South Africa (Fedusa), and the National Congress of Trade Unions (Nactu).

Cosatu is overwhelmingly the largest, most progressive, and important union confederation.[5] It was founded in 1985, the result of an amalgamation of several other federations at the height of anti-apartheid conflict. Cosatu is now the fastest growing federation of its type in the world, with nearly 2 million members drawn from 19 affiliates covering a wide range of unions in manufacturing, public services, mining, transportation, construction, and the service sector. Although an explicitly nonracial and nonsexist union, historically most of Cosatu's membership has been black males in blue-collar occupations. These demographics, however, have been in a state of accelerated change in the post-apartheid period, mainly the result of large increases in public sector membership (which now accounts for 19 percent of Cosatu's members) and recent affiliations with white-collar bank employee and teachers' unions. One of the most dramatic changes at Cosatu, given its history as a "black" federation committed to the overthrow of the apartheid state, has been the recent addition of prison warders and police to its membership ranks. Female membership has been on the rise, and Cosatu now has a woman vice-president.

In addition to its strategic position within the labor movement, Cosatu is a key player in political and government circles. It is a member of the influential tripartite alliance with the governing ANC and the South African Communist Party, and many former Cosatu leaders now serve as ANC cabinet ministers, members of parliament, provincial premiers, and government officials. The organization has played a significant role in the development of new human rights legislation and helped to draft the new Labor Relations Act.

Thus, after a long history of oppression and struggle, South Africa now has a growing and vibrant trade union movement with very strong links to the ANC government and other centers of political influence. As a result, alliances and links with organized labor in South Africa are an important and necessary component of any social change momentum, no less so for the gay and lesbian rights movement.

Organized labor in South Africa has a mixed history in relation to equity issues. Although long-standing divides and tensions along racial and class lines have been hugely narrowed in the post-apartheid period, they still exist. Cosatu, for example, is grappling with recent influxes of white, professional members, such as teachers, who arrive with somewhat different issues and concerns from the predominately black, working-class membership base. However, Cosatu is formally committed to accommodating these developments in its organizing campaigns, education programs, and collective bargaining strategies.[6] Less open to change has been the heterosexual, male-dominated power base of the labor movement. Struggles to incorporate issues related to gender and sexual orientation have been fraught with tension and conflict.

Although some notable achievements have been made, gender discrimination and issues related to the empowerment of women within labor organizations remain highly contested. As early as 1984, female labor leaders were calling for more priority to be placed on women's issues; women's forums were established to push their unions toward improved harassment and violence policies, maternity leave provisions, pay equity, occupational equity, and union representation.[7] But even in Cosatu, arguably the most progressive federation, the development of policies and practices related to gender issues has been haphazard and slow. Cosatu sponsored a women's conference in April 1988 and has organized several since then. However, as recently as the 1991 Cosatu General Congress, women had to fight to maintain these gender forums as places where women's confidence and skills could be fostered, a struggle that ended with the explicit provision that men could be part of these gatherings. Debate and conflict over these forums continues, and a 1995 report indicated that "women were still taking responsibility for organizing them but that men tended to dominate the discussions in these forums when they attended." More dramatically, in a few instances, women were literally dragged away from meetings by a husband or brother.[8]

Over the years, though, a number of the issues raised by women have been addressed. In areas such as sexual conduct, sexual harassment, organizing campaigns, collective bargaining provisions, and policy interventions, progress has been made. For example, when allegations of serious sexual harassment arose at the 1994 Cosatu conference, a new code of conduct on sexual behavior and harassment for its member unions was quickly drafted and made policy by May 1995. As well, a growing number of unions have successfully negotiated collective agreements with good provisions for maternity leave and child care facilities and allowances. Unions such as Numsa (National Union of Metalworkers of South Africa) and CWIU (Chemical Workers' Industrial Union) have made commitments to fight for such things as pay equity and free pap smears. FAWA (Food and Allied Workers Union) has gone so far as to take the employers of one of its members to court in a sexual discrimination case, and CWIU was able to get a manager fired for sexually harassing a woman worker at a tire factory.

While gains have been made in issues most affecting women, women remain under-represented in positions of power. A 1994 survey found that only one regional union secretary was a woman, and that no general secretary or union president had ever been a woman. At the same time, the survey found that by 1994, 8 percent of national officers of Cosatu and its affiliate unions were women, compared to only 5 percent in 1990. Also as a measure of at least some change, by 1997, Cosatu had a woman in a senior executive role.[9]

Women activists are cautiously optimistic, reporting that gender issues are on labor's agenda and that more and more unions have taken up issues related to child care, parental rights, and sexual conduct. They assert, however, that action has been sporadic and inconsistent, and every advance has been an uphill battle. At the current time, Cosatu is leading the parade on women's issues and has appointed a full-time national gender coordinator to oversee activities in this area.

In contrast, organized labor has not been nearly as open to change on issues related to sexual orientation. As we have already noted, alliances between gay and lesbian rights activists and the labor-infused ANC have been in place since the late 1980s, but they have a history of conflict. Most components of the labor movement supported, or at least did not oppose, the new constitution and several other important pieces of legislation that include sexual orientation as protected grounds. It has, however, been slow to move beyond these initiatives. Overall, organized labor appears at best unresponsive, and at worse antagonistic, in the fight to change prejudicial attitudes and practices related to sexual orientation.

Cosatu is the only federation that has a general policy committing it to equality for gays and lesbians. So far, it has only taken a few steps to act beyond its policy statement. Although Fedusa, with a primarily white constituency, does not have a formal policy statement in this area, the loosely organized Fedusa Equity Forum is aimed at discussing affirmative action and employment equity issues within the union, and this may be a site where sexual orientation issues will emerge in the future. To date, no other federation has shown any activity on issues of concern to sexual minorities. Several indicated when contacted by phone that they expect to develop policies in the near future, but so far there has been no concrete action.

The Transport and General Workers Union (TGWU), a Cosatu affiliate, is the only trade union known to refer specifically to gay and lesbian equality. In an August 1995 revision to its constitution, it states: "we are committed to build and maintain a democratic worker-controlled union based on the principles of non-racism, non-sexism, and non-homophobia." Until recently there had been little action, but in 1998 the union's education department, in conjunction with the NCGLE, decided to run courses for staff and members highlighting sexual diversity issues. TGWU is expected to pass a further resolution at its August 1999 congress affirming its commitment to gay and lesbian rights, placing it at the forefront of unions active in the area of sexual minority rights. As a result, the TGWU stands out, since no other union is known to have adopted a formal policy or program based on the interests or demands of gays and lesbians.

Another union that has recently shown some interest in confronting the discrimination sexual minorities face is the National Education, Health and Allied Workers Union (NEHAWU). This very large union of 250,000 members in the public sector has now adopted a positive position on gay and lesbian rights, and has been the site of courses and presentations run by the NCGLE.

In several cases, workers have been demonstrably "out" within their unions, but without much in the way of formal support or recognition from their union leadership. The mines are a good example. Several historical and contemporary texts document a lengthy tradition of same-sex relationships among mine workers in South Africa.[10] The mining industry has always represented a good job for black men, and the lack of opportunities in general has meant that more gay men found their way into this occupational category than might be expected by people unfamiliar with the indigenous history of the country. Over the years, informal and formal gay social and support groups developed in the major mining regions of South Africa, the best organized in Newcastle (KwaZulu Natal coal mining region) and Welkom (Free State gold fields). These gay miners' support groups were able to create an environment of tolerance and acceptance in what might otherwise have been a fairly hostile situation. There are reports of gay marriages taking place within these mining communities, but most of the activities have been sports-related or purely social. Gay and lesbian support groups in the gold fields, for example, organized soccer tournaments between its members and straight coworkers, an arrangement that appears to have produced considerable goodwill and little conflict. Recently, however, the mandate of these groups appears to be changing; some have started to raise questions and make demands within their union (NUM) related to discriminatory practices by employers. At the mining conglomerate Anglo-American, for instance, a gay group of employees indicated they would file a suit to win medical and other benefits for same-sex partners. This case appears to be proceeding, but so far with little support from the union.

Another interesting case is within union members of the police force. In May 1997, lesbian and gay members of the South African Police Services launched the Gay and Lesbian Police Network with the approval of their management and union. This network was aimed at securing employment equity in the ranks and improving relations between the police and the gay and lesbian community more generally. Supported by this network, Jolande Langemaat, a Johannesburg police officer, filed suit against the South African Police Service when they refused to extend medical coverage under the Police Medical Aid Scheme to her partner of 11 years. In February 1998, the Pretoria High Court ruled in her favor and declared the medical plan regulations unconstitutional. Even though asked to do so, the South African Police Union (SAPU) and the Police, Public, and Civil Rights Union (POPCRU) did not offer any support in the case. Recently, though, the SAPU has become more supportive of sexual minority issues and is now involved in the resolution of the Langmaat case.

In summary, South African unions have done little to take up issues important to gays and lesbians in the period following enactment of the new constitution. Some unions have opposed initiatives and court challenges. For example, between August 1997 and October 1997, several organizations, including labor- and union-affiliated groups, linked the court application for the decriminalization of same-sex activity to child molestation, some going so far as to suggest it might be justifiable to explore the limitation of constitutional rights of lesbians and gays. So far, unions have been an absent voice in supporting specific court challenges arguing for same-sex employment benefits, in some cases denying that discrimination had even occurred. While most unions will not publicly oppose equality for lesbian and gay workers because they do not wish to be seen to oppose the constitution or the LRA, they stop short of any other type of support. Some union leaders have gone on record as not wishing unions to get sidetracked from other priorities. Some have gone so far as to use the argument that "homosexuality is un-African" and that "workers will not understand lesbian and gay issues."

A strategy for change

Why have labor federations and unions been mostly unsupportive in fighting for an end to discrimination based on sexual orientation? Why have so few lesbian and gay workers organized themselves within their unions with the aim of forcing change? In those unions where support groups do exist, such as the police and miners, why have they not been able to bring their unions more directly onside? While there are no single or simple answers to these questions, it is useful to explore some of the factors that may be at play, as a starting point for mapping a strategy for change.

South Africa has traditionally been a society with an overlay of conservative religions and cultures, and until very recently, sexuality issues of any type were not generally a discussion topic. It is also a country only recently released from the horrors of a racially divided system, and one where human rights amendments are relatively new and untested. The racist and colonial past left many attitudes and practices that are hard to change. This is particularly the case in relation to sexual diversity. The labor movement is no different from most other institutions in embodying all of the conflicts and contradictions of the new Republic of South Africa. Although an activist-driven gay and lesbian rights movement has existed for some time, it has been preoccupied with broader reforms and only recently focused more of its attention on workplace issues. In other words, the legal and constitutional architecture for gay and lesbian rights has only recently been put into place, and the identification and analysis of issues affecting this group is a relatively new and controversial phenomenon for labor organizations. That said, the timing is ideal for accelerating the pace of change.

Unions and labor federations in South Africa are growing in size and importance, have well-established links with the political process, and are positioned to be key players in the social transformation of South Africa. Therefore, forging an alliance with organized labor must remain a critical goal for the gay and lesbian rights movement if workplace equity goals are to be achieved, in spite of the fact that labor has until now shown little enthusiasm for the project. Activists must identify the issues that trade unions share with sexual minorities, as well as the opportunities and new approaches that will promote alliances. Achieving these goals will necessitate a multifaceted strategy involving data collection, litigation, education, and coalition building.

The first step toward bringing about change is to better document the extent of the problem. Such information and statistics would help convince organized labor that inequities do exist, in particular that blatant income disparities are created when some workers are denied access to the benefits and perks available to others. The ERP project of the NCGLE has already started to compile this sort of information, and a database of this type is beginning to take shape.

The new legislative environment in South Africa is very amenable to litigation in the area of sexual minority rights. Nevertheless, initiatives are hampered by a judiciary largely from the old political order, some of whom appear to be opposed to progressive change in this area. Of note, though, is the recent appointment of Edwin Cameron, a noted gay activist, to the high courts. Overall, the new Constitutional Court, the highest court in the land, is made up of judges who are likely to support equality on all grounds. Careful selection of cases to go forward at this level will provide the most promising opportunities. However, litigation must be coupled to effective engagement with independent statutory institutions such as the Commission on Gender Equality and the Human Rights Commission, since these institutions have powers to investigate and litigate as well as advise the government.

Litigation requires careful planning and large financial commitments. This is where labor can play a significant role because it has the human and financial resources to undertake such activities. Convincing unions and federations that such commitments are necessary and appropriate must become a strategic goal of the movement for sexual minority rights. Recent policy statements by such key players as Cosatu open the door for further dialogue, and recent successes, such as Jolande Langemaat's suit against the Police Medical Aid Scheme, should help define the necessity and parameters for such discussions. Closely related to litigation is the potential offered by collective bargaining and arbitration. Significant change could occur very quickly if trade unions were persuaded to take sexual orientation issues related to hiring, firing, harassment, and benefits to the bargaining table.

Education is another important area for action. Activists must be instrumental in the development of educational programs designed to ensure their concerns are not avoided or overlooked, within and outside the labor movement. Again, the new human rights and employment legislation opens doors for activists to position their concerns within the broader educational efforts that are taking place.

Finally, coalition building should be part of any overall strategy. Building relationships with women's groups, anti-poverty groups, the disabled, and other minorities would strengthen the potential access to organized labor and draw attention to the common demand for equal and fair treatment in the workplace. Alliances with women's forums in unions could prove to be the single best way to penetrate labor's agenda, since relationships of this type have been so successful in other countries profiled in this book. Lesbian and gay caucuses in some trade unions, such as the miners and police, are also important sites for coalition building. These caucuses have a good chance of being seen as legitimate and not outsiders by trade union members and represent important entry points for action.

Conclusion

The political articulation of issues related to sexual diversity is relatively new in South Africa, and only recently emerging as a workplace concern. Progress has been swift at the level of constitutional and legal change, but so far few individuals, organizations, or institutions seem to have altered their long-standing prejudicial attitudes and practices. Organized labor appears not to be an exception to this trend. Although Cosatu, the largest and most influential labor federation in the country, includes sexual orientation in its nondiscrimination statement, trade unions as a group have been reluctant to take up these issues in any tangible way. As a result, litigation based on the provisions of the new legislation have been the primary mode for activists.

Nevertheless, there is room for optimism. South Africa is in a process of accelerated transformation, and perhaps nowhere else on earth are the opportunities for social change more abundant. Although there are forces who long for a return to the oppressive, racist past, and other forces with a very conservative agenda, the overwhelming momentum is toward change that will establish equality and human rights as the sustaining architecture of the new social order. Given this new era, minorities of all kinds, including sexual minorities, have an unparalleled opportunity to acquire equal rights, and the responsibilities that go with them. It will be increasingly difficult for political, business, judicial, and labor leaders who espouse unequivocally a philosophy of equal rights to turn around and say, "But we didn't mean gays and lesbians." To gain ground, though, activists must act quickly and assertively to forge better alliances with key players such as organized labor, and by using every other resource at their disposal, including but not limited to the judiciary.

Within the new South Africa, equality for gays and lesbians must be positioned as a national reconstruction issue and a trade union issue. As Carl Stychin notes, gay and lesbian rights issues in South Africa cannot be divorced from the problems in housing, jobs, and safety nor from the gender, racial, and sexual oppression that has for so long plagued the country.[11] The trade union movement is sufficiently powerful and mature to discuss sexual minority issues openly, and with sufficient pressure could be transformed from sideline observer to ally.

Notes

1 We have prepared this chapter by drawing on our personal experience within the Equal Rights Project (ERP) of the National Coalition for Gay and Lesbian Equality (NCGLE) based in Johannesburg, as well as our telephone and personal contacts with labor federations, trade unions, and activists.

2 Quoted in the *Washington Blade*, 13 Dec. 1996, p. 24.

3 A comprehensive account of early and recent gay and lesbian life and activism in South Africa can be found in M. Gevisser and E. Cameron, eds., *Defiant Desire: Gay and Lesbian Lives in South Africa* (New York: Routledge, 1996). Much of the information for this section is drawn from this resource, with additional insight taken from B. Adam, *The Rise of a Gay and Lesbian Movement*, rev. ed. (New York: Twayne Publishers, 1995); C. Dunton and M. Palmberg, *Human Rights and Homosexuality in Southern Africa* (Uppsala, Sweden: Nordiska Afrikainstitutet, 1996); C. Stychin, *A Nation by Rights* (Philadelphia: Temple University Press, 1998), chap. 3.

4 See Gevisser and Cameron, *Defiant Desire*, pp. 63–74.

5 See Cosatu website for details at www.cosatu.org.za.

6 See Cosatu website section, "Changing with the Times."

7 See "Women Workers," report prepared by Fosatu (now defunct Federation of South African Trade Unions), 1984; and "No Turning Back," report prepared by the Witwatersrand University Women's Forum, 1992.

8 See Cosatu website section, "No Woman, No Cry, Zabalaza," where there is a report on the Cosatu Gender Winter School held in 1995.

9 "No Woman, No Cry."

10 See N. Miller "Going Underground," in *Defiant Desire*, ed. Gevisser and Cameron; V. Ndatshe "Two Miners," in M. Krouse, ed., *The Invisible Ghetto: Lesbian and Gay Writing from South Africa* (Johannesburg: COSAW Publishing, 1993); M. wa Sibuyi "Tinkoncana Etimayinini: The Wives of the Mines," in M. Krouse, ed., *The Invisible Ghetto.*

11 See Stychin, *A Nation by Rights*, p. 76.

CHAPTER 37

Doug Ireland

Gay Teens Fight Back: A New Generation of Gay Youth Won't Tolerate Harassment in Their Schools

Jared Nayfack was 11 years old and living in the heart of conservative Orange Country, California, when he told his best friend from school that he was gay – "and my friend then came out to me," says Jared. When he turned 15, Jared celebrated his birthday by coming out to his parents and closest friends. By then, he was attending a Catholic high school, and on a school-sponsored overnight field trip, Jared and his schoolmates decided to spend their free evening at the movies seeing *The Rocky Horror Picture Show*. "Some of us had decided to get all costumed up to see it, and when the teacher who was with us saw us she threw a fit: She forced me to get up in front of the other 21 students – many of whom I didn't know – and tell them I was gay. Most of the kids supported me, but later that evening, one of them – a lot bigger than I was; he had a black belt in martial arts – came into my hotel room and beat me up. I was a bloody mess, and he could have killed me if another student hadn't heard my screams and stopped him." Instead of punishing Jared's assailant, the school's dean suspended Jared and put him on "academic and behavioral probation." "The dean told me that even though I was forced to tell the others that I was gay, I was at fault because I'd 'threatened the masculinity' of the kid who'd beat me up," Jared recalls.

In fear, Jared transferred to a public high school, the South Orange County High School of the Arts. "I thought I'd be safe and could be out when I came there – after all, it was an arts program. Boy, was I wrong. Within two weeks people were yelling 'fag' at me in the halls and in class. I was dressed a little glam, if you will – nothing really offensive, just a little makeup. But when I went to the principal to complain, she did nothing about the harassment and told me that I was 'lacking in testosterone,'" Jared explains. To fight back, Jared and some gay and straight friends formed a club called PRIDE, which made a 25-foot-long rainbow banner to put up in school decorated with multicolored hands and the slogan, HANDS FOR EQUALITY (the banner was banned). The club also made beaded rainbow bracelets that many students wore – "even a lot of the football players," according to Jared – but the club was forbidden by the administration "because it didn't have

Doug Ireland, "Gay Teens Fight Back: A New Generation of Gay Youth Won't Tolerate Harassment in Their Schools," *The Nation* (Jan. 31, 2000), pp. 21–3.

anything to do with the curriculum." The harassment got worse – so bad that Jared had to leave school two months before graduation. "I had to fight to *be* before I could study," Jared explains, "but I left there feeling really let down and like a failure – we hadn't gotten anywhere."

When he enrolled as a freshman at the University of California, Santa Cruz, Jared says, "I was embraced by a huge and loving queer community. They told me, 'It's OK to be angry' – that's something I hadn't heard before." Feeling a bit burned out for his first six months at Santa Cruz Jared avoided gay activism – until the day he attended a conference of gay youth. "There were kids pulling together – I just knew I had to help out." He attended a youth training institute run by the Gay, Lesbian and Straight Education Network (GLSEN); began working with Gay/Straight Alliances (GSAs) at two high schools near the university; edited and xerox-published an anthology of adolescent writings about AIDS; created a performance piece, as part of his self-designed major in "theatrical activism," about homophobia with a cast of 7 straight boys to the hit song "Faggot" by the rock group Korn; and now speaks to gay youth groups around the country. Today Jared is only 18.

Jared's story is fairly typical of a whole new generation of lesbian and gay adolescents: brave, tough and resilient, comfortable with their sexual identity and coming out at earlier ages, inventing their own organizations – and victimized by violence and harassment in their schools. Says Rea Carey, executive director of the National Youth Advocacy Coalition (NYAC), an alliance of local and national service agencies working to empower gay youth: "Five or ten years ago, kids would go to a youth service agency and say, 'I need help because I think I'm gay.' Today, more and more they say, 'I'm gay and so what? I want friends and a place to work on the issues I care about.' Being gay is not their problem, it's their strength. These kids are coming out at 13, 14, 15, at the same age that straight people historically begin to experience their sexuality. But they are experiencing more violence because of that."

Quantifying the number of assaults on lesbian and gay youth isn't easy. In most states, gay-run Anti-Violence Projects are woefully underfunded and understaffed (when they have any staff at all), and students are rarely aware of them, according to Jeffrey Montgomery, the director of Detroit's Triangle Foundation and the spokesman for the National Association of Anti-Violence Projects. Teachers and school administrators most often don't report such incidents. After pressure from state governments sympathetic to the Christian right, the Clinton/Gore Administration's Centers for Disease Control removed all questions regarding sexual orientation from its national Youth Risk Behavior Survey. Now the only state to include them is Massachusetts.

There, according to its most recent questioning of nearly 4,000 high school students by the Massachusetts Department of Education, kids who self-identified as gay, lesbian or bisexual were seven times more likely than other kids to have skipped school because they felt unsafe (22.2 percent versus 3.3). A 1997 study by the Vermont Department of Health found that gay kids were threatened or injured with a weapon at school three times more than straight kids (24 percent versus 8). And a 5-year study released in January by Washington State's Safe Schools Coalition – a partnership of 74 public and private agencies – documented 146 incidents in the state's schools, including 8 gang rapes and 39 physical assaults (on average, a single gay kid is attacked by more than two offenders at once).

With the antigay crusades of the religious right and the verbal gay-bashings of politicians like Trent Lott legitimizing the demonization of homosexuals, it is hardly surprising that homophobia is alive and well among gay kids' classmates. In November 1998, a poll of 3,000 top high schoolers by *Who's Who Among American High School Students* – its twenty-ninth annual survey – found that 48 percent admitted they are prejudiced against gays, up 19 percent from the previous year (and these are, as *Who's Who* proclaims, "America's brightest students").

All this means that, as Jon Lasser, an Austin, Texas, school psychologist (and heterosexual parent) who has interviewed scads of gay kids for his PhD thesis, puts it, "Many have a form of post-traumatic stress syndrome that affects their schoolwork – the fear of getting hurt really shakes them up and makes it hard to concentrate."

The mushrooming growth of Gay/Straight Alliances in middle and high schools in just the past few years has been the gay kids' potent response. There is strength in numbers: GSAs break the immobilizing isolation of gay students and raise their visibility, creating a mechanism to pressure school authorities into tackling harassment; educate teachers as well as other students; create the kind of solidarity among straight and gay kids that fosters resistance to bigotry and violence; provide meaningful safe-sex education; and help gay adolescents to speak and fight for themselves. The GLSEN national office has identified at least 400 GSAs, but since the GSA movement has been student-initiated and many self-starting groups are still not in touch with national gay organizations, the figure is undoubtedly much higher. There are 85 GLSEN chapters around the country, and while GLSEN began seven years ago primarily as an organization of teachers and other school personnel, it is making an increasing effort to include students in its organizing.

Another strategy that has frightened reluctant school administrators into steps to protect gay youth has been lawsuits by the kids themselves. The first on record was brought by a 16-year-old Ashland, Wisconsin, student, Jamie Nabozny, who in 1996 won a $900,000 judgment against school authorities who failed to prevent Nabozny's torturous harassment from seventh through eleventh grades, including beatings that put him in the hospital. Currently there are nine similar suits pending, including cases in Illinois, Washington, New Jersey, Minnesota, Missouri and several in California (one brought by the first-ever group of lesbian student plaintiffs, in the San Jose area). But as David Buckel, the Lambda Legal Defense and Education Fund's staff attorney specializing in school matters, points out, "A lot of people call and say 'I can't afford to go to court,' or 'We live in a small town and I can't put my family through that,' or 'If we sue and win it'll raise our neighbors' taxes and we'll get bricks through our window.'" (And in late December, Orange County gay students filed a law-suit against school officials, seeking to lift their ban on a GSA at El Modena High School on the grounds that the interdiction violated their First Amendment rights.)

In a civilized country, one would think, legislation to protect kids from violence and harassment in their schools should be unexceptional. However, despite a loopy *New York Times* editorial praising the Republican Party for a kinder-and-gentler attitude toward gays, the GOP has taken the lead in opposing state-level safe-schools bills protecting gay kids. In Washington last year, for the second year in a row, openly gay State Representative Ed Murray – a progressive Seattle Democrat – led the fight for his bill that would have added lesbian and gay students to a law forbidding sexual and malicious harassment in the schools. "We had the votes to pass it this year in the House, which is split 49 to 49 – we had all 49 Democrats and picked up 16 Republicans. But because of the tie in party membership, all House committees are co-chaired by Democrats and Republicans, and the GOP education committee co-chairman refused to let the bill out of committee. If it had been sent to the Senate, where Democrats have a majority, it would have passed."

The way in which the GOP continues to use same-sexers as a political football to advance its chances could be seen clearly in California, where Assemblywoman Sheila Kuehl (an open lesbian who co-starred in TV's *Dobie Gillis* series in the sixties) saw her Dignity for All Students Act beaten in the Assembly by one vote. GOP front groups "targeted only Democratic Latino legislators from swing districts in an unprecedented campaign-style effort," says Jennifer Richard, Kuehl's top aide. This included prayer vigils at their district offices, very sophisticated phone-banking that switched those called directly into Assembly members' offices to complain, mailings in Spanish to every Hispanic-surnamed household and full-page ads costing $8,000–$12,000 each in local papers. The mailings and ads featured photos of a white man embracing a Latino, a black man kissing a Latino and a Latino kid in a Boy Scout uniform, and called on voters to "stop the homosexual agenda," which "doesn't like the Boy Scout pledge to be morally straight." These ads were reinforced by a $30,000 radio ad blitz by the Rev. Lou Sheldon's Traditional Family Values Coalition in the targeted legislators' districts.

Despite a Youth Lobby Day that brought 700 gay students to Sacramento to support the Kuehl bill, two Latino Democrats caved in to the pressure, ensuring the bill's defeat by one vote. But in a shrewd parliamentary maneuver, its supporters attached a condensed version as an amendment to an unrelated bill in the senate, which passed it – then sent it to the assembly, where it was finally approved by a six-vote margin (making California the first state to codify protections for gender-nonconforming students, who experience the most aggressive forms of harassment). Similar bills died or were defeated last year in Colorado, Delaware, Illinois and Texas (in New York, one introduced by openly gay State Senator Tom Duane is still bottled up in committee).

The difference such bills can make can be seen in Massachusetts, which has had a tough and explicit law barring discrimination against and harassment of gay students since 1993, and where its implementation benefited from strong support by then-Governor William Weld (a Republican) and his advisory council on gay and lesbian issues. Massachusetts is the only state that encourages the formation of gay student support groups as a matter of policy – which is why there are now 180 GSAs in the Bay State alone. There, the state Safe Schools program is run by GLSEN under a contract with the state's Education Department, and it organizes eight regional conferences each year for students who want to start or have just started their own GSA.

There is a skein of service agencies in large cities that operate effective programs for gay youth, including peer counseling, drop-in centers, teacher training, AIDS education and assistance for victims of violence (for listings of and links to groups for gay youth, visit *The Nation*'s website at www.thenation.com). But these programs are all dreadfully underfunded and in many places, like Texas, are denied access to the schools. Also, gay youths themselves often complain that there is a lack of support from the adult gay movement. Says Candice Clark, a 19-year-old lesbian who graduated in 1998 from a suburban Houston high school, "A lot of the older gay community here is fearful of the youth as jailbait, since so many people think that if you're gay you're a pedophile." She also notes that the failure of Congress to pass ENDA – the Employment Non-Discrimination Act for lesbians and gays – means that adults, expecially teachers, can be fired if their sexual orientation is discovered.

Richard Agostinho, 22, who founded the Connecticut youth group Queer and Active after the 1998 murder of Matthew Shepard, and who serves as one of the NYAC national board's youth members, says the local adult-led groups "are not building relationships with young people – they need to go out and recruit them and engage in mentoring of sorts. There are plenty of young people who could add emotion and power to this movement. But if a 17- or 18-year-old goes to a meeting of a local group or community center in a roomful of 30- or 40-somethings, the adults frequently fail to create an atmosphere in which the youth feel comfortable contributing. It's a problem very similar to involving people of color or anyone not traditionally represented at these tables."

The urgency of putting the problems facing gay adolescents on the agenda of every local gay organization is underscored by a study released last September by GLSEN. It showed that of nearly 500 gay students surveyed, almost half said they didn't feel safe in their schools: 90 percent reported verbal harassment, 46.5 percent had experienced sexual harassment, 27.6 percent experienced physical harassment and 13.7 percent were subjected to physical assault.

But this new generation of adolescent activists won't be ignored. For, as Jared Nayfack says, "When you do this work you open up a whole area of your heart and soul, and when you stop, you feel it deeply. Activism is addictive – you don't ever want to stop unless there's nothing left to do . . . and that will be a long time."

Part VI

Getting Informed, Getting Involved:
Places to Turn To

CHAPTER 38

Ien Ang

Who Needs Cultural Research?

The massive lack of public understanding of what contemporary humanities scholarship entails becomes painfully clear to me when I am asked by, say, the hairdresser, what I do. As part of my ongoing fieldwork, I generally decide to tell the truth. "I am a university teacher," I say. "Oh," would be the answer, "what do you teach?" I take a deep breath and say: "Cultural Studies." What follows is usually a big silence. Conversation closed. And the hairdresser is not the only one who is embarrassed. She (or he) probably feels very ignorant because she doesn't know what I'm talking about, while I feel bad about making her feel that way and feel hopelessly cut off from what she stands for: the general public.

Part of the silence is related to a general unawareness of the complex meanings of the term "culture" itself. For most people, "culture" is extraordinary, set apart from daily life. It is either synonymous to art, something elevated and lofty, or refers to "other people" such as migrants or Aborigines. In other words, culture is either aesthetics or anthropology, and has nothing to do with their own lives. In the academic world, what is now called "cultural studies" has revolutionised the study of culture in contemporary society, by doing away with the separation between aesthetics and anthropology. "Culture" in cultural studies relates to the production and negotiation of meaning and value, and this is an ongoing, plural, often conflictive process taking place in all dimensions of social activity, be it at the workplace, in education, the media, in international relations, even in the hairdresser's salon. Culture is neither institutions nor texts nor behaviours, but the complex interactions between all of these. In other words, culture is not only very ordinary, to speak with Raymond Williams, it is also fundamentally practical and pervasive to social life, as it is inherent to how the world is made to mean, and therefore how the world is run. That is, arguments about how the world should be run always involve a politics of representation – the level of politics where meanings and values are struggled over – and therefore necessarily comprise a fundamental cultural dimension. "Culture" is integral to and constitutive of social life, not something outside of or a mere addition to it.

The global growth of "cultural studies" within academia in the past few decades is itself an indication of the increasing significance and contentious nature of the dimension of "culture" in contemporary life and society. In general, a sense of cultural crisis is evident everywhere around the globe despite the apparent economic success of global capitalism: the falling away of a consensus over what counts as "progress" or of universal value, the deepening of cultural divisions along lines of class, race, gender, region, religion, and so on, the real and perceived proliferation of all forms of violence, the wild growth of the Internet, the growing uncertainty about the shape of the new world disorder in the twenty-first century as the authority of the West is challenged by rising non-western nations, and so on. To use cultural studies jargon, "culture" has become an increasingly intense and multidimensional "site of struggle" in this complex, postmodern world.

In this light, "cultural studies" is very much the intellectual discipline (or transdiscipline) of the contemporary moment. To understand itself the world needs cultural studies more than ever. Or does it? As cultural studies has gained a small (and insecure) foothold within universities, especially the newer ones, it has also become very much a disciplinary world of its own, with its own discourses, institutions and networks, not to mention its own internal conceptual quarrels, often quite impenetrable to the wider world of public life. This is not something I want to criticise, as all professional practices, including academic disciplines, need to have a space for the clarification of their own paradigms and procedures. However, the promise of cultural studies was precisely that it would be an intellectual practice firmly located in and concerned with the major issues of the day, and as such would provide a bridge between the academic world and the social world "out there." The origins of cultural studies in adult education rather than the academe is one indication of its fundamental social and political aspirations. In this sense, cultural studies can be seen as a form of "applied humanities," in sentiment at least if not in all of its practice. I think we need to reclaim this background. That is, I do firmly believe that the world needs cultural studies more than ever. But if so, then we will have to find practical ways of convincing others that the intricate knowledges and understandings we are capable of producing have some relevance to them. "Relevance" here is the major issue. When and how can cultural studies knowledge be said to be relevant? Or perhaps, to put it in a more activist register, how can we make it more relevant?

These are not fancy questions designed to prop up cultural studies' utopian radical credentials. On the contrary, what is at stake here are the very pragmatic conditions in which the production of knowledge is organised in contemporary society, and the place of our kind of work within it. We are all experiencing the effects of the increasing commercialization, bureaucratization and corporatization of universities, where socially-sanctioned knowledge production (under the general rubric of "science") has traditionally been concentrated. We are all worried about the dwindling resources for university research provided by government, which especially threatens the future viability of research in the humanities and social sciences. But these changes, which are related to broader changes in the economic and political environment, are structural and not likely to be reversed any time soon, so it is of no use simply to lament and resist them, lest we want to contribute to our own further marginalization. As Bill Readings remarks in his book *The University in Ruins*, "it is not a matter of coming to terms with the market, establishing a ratio of marginal utility that will provide a sanctuary. Such a policy will only produce the persistent shrinking of that sanctuary."[1] Instead, Readings recommends a certain opportunism, an institutional pragmatism that responds creatively to changing circumstances, and does not retreat from them. This would mean, at the very least, taking the notion of "utility" out of the sphere of marginality and seriously addressing it as we continue to think through our own politics of knowledge.

In their recent book *The New Production of Knowledge*, an international team of researchers led by Michael Gibbons, Director of the Science Policy Unit at the University of Sussex, goes so far as suggesting that an entirely new mode of knowledge production is emerging at present.[2] This Mode 2, as they call it, is slowly gaining prominence over an older mode of knowledge production, or Mode 1, which most of us still hold as the ideal model for university research – what is known as basic research – where problems are set, examined, and solved in a context governed by the academic interests and codes of practice of a specific disciplinary community, curiosity-driven and based on individual creativity, often pursued without some practical goal in mind. In Mode 2, by contrast, knowledge production is guided by the imperative that it should be useful to someone, whether industry, government, or society more generally. In other words, the context of application drives the form and content of the knowledge sought after. This context of application involves a heterogeneous set of practitioners and experts, working together on a problem defined in a specific and localized context. Gibbons insists that this mode of knowledge production is more than just "applied research." It does not simply apply already existing knowledge, but is shaped by a diverse set of intellectual and social demands that may give rise to the creation of genuinely new knowledge, characterized by transdisciplinarity, social accountability, and reflexivity.

According to Gibbons, Mode 2 knowledge will not supplant the traditional disciplinary structure of Mode 1 knowledge, but supplement it and interact with it. Indeed, it is important to emphasise that without continued work in Mode 1, Mode 2 would not be able to exist, as the latter depends substantially on key concepts, findings, and insights developed in the former. The rise of Mode 2 knowledge production, especially in the advanced postindustrial world, is deeply embedded in the present socio-economic order, increasingly dependent as it is on the generation and use of specialized forms of information and knowledge for wealth creation and societal governance. Indeed, the very expansion of higher education in the past few decades has greatly increased the number of graduates trained in research skills, many of whom now work as knowledge workers in an increasingly diverse range of institutional contexts in both private and public sectors. Thus, interestingly, to the extent that universities continue to produce quality graduates, they undermine their monopoly as knowledge producers. As a result, the sharp distinction between academic and non-academic players in knowledge production has weakened. Today, knowledge production has become much more widely distributed, taking place in many more types of social settings, and involving many different types of individuals and organizations in a vast array of different relationships. As Gibbons puts it, "the boundaries between the intellectual world and its environment have become blurred."[3]

While the description of Mode 2 knowledge production is clearly biased towards the world of science and technology, Gibbons is adamant that Mode 2 also implicates the humanities and social sciences. Indeed, he talks up the increased demand for the sorts of knowledge the humanities have to offer, especially in their capacity to provide critical reflection on human projects and endeavours. It is the function of the humanities, Gibbons remarks, "to provide an understanding of the world of social experience. And they are valued for the insights and guidance we expect to be able to derive from them."[4] A similar attempt to be inclusive of the humanities and social sciences can be found in the Australian Federal Government's 1999 Green Paper on higher education research and research training, which clearly takes its cues from research policy analysis as carried out by Gibbons.[5] Thus it is stated at the outset that "research in the humanities and social sciences makes a major contribution to our sense of identity and cohesiveness as a nation," promoting "an appreciation of our culture and history," fostering "understanding of different traditions and customs, and of the importance of tolerance and respect," as well as stimulating "debate on the goals, directions and values to which our democratic society aspires."[6]

All well and good, but the paper does not subsequently spell out at all how these kinds of uses of research are to be nurtured in a policy framework preoccupied with the commercialization of research and enhancing the nation's competitive economic advantage. Similarly Gibbons, who in his book devotes a full chapter to the humanities, clearly has difficulties operationalizing the contexts of application for humanities knowledge in the market-driven knowledge society of today. The usefulness of humanities knowledge is diffuse and inferential, and therefore difficult to measure and circumscribe. Interestingly, Gibbons points out that humanities scholarship has always had more Mode 2 characteristics than the natural sciences, as exemplified by the genre of the essay, arguably "one of the oldest forms of Mode 2 production." Essays, according to Gibbons, "roam freely in the territories seemingly held by the specialisms, link together what otherwise would remain fragmented analyses."[7] In this respect, the form of the essay (rather than the scientific research paper) is highly conducive to the construction and dissemination of meaning throughout society.[8] However, how can the "context of application" of the essay, published in the public domain and with an anonymous readership, be concretised? In other words, while the *form* of at least some humanities research may display Mode 2 characteristics, the difficulty to quantify and commodify its uses inhibits its insertion into the emergent *social and economic arrangements* of Mode 2 knowledge production with their emphasis on calculable usefulness in clearly demarcated strategic contexts. The situation is not helped by the fact that the professionalization of humanities scholarship has tended to move it more towards Mode 1 production practices, with its emphasis on disciplinary specialization and relative disconnection from the larger social world, rather than towards Mode 2, with its more problem-focused, multidisciplinary and collaborative orientation. This is the case also for cultural studies, as a brand of "applied humanities."

For those of us who are university researchers in Australia, the growing importance of Mode 2 knowledge production is instantly recognizable in the massively increased funds in the past few years provided by the Australian Research Council for its SPIRT grants scheme.[9] This scheme awards projects in which academics collaborate with "partners in industry," as the jargon has it. Indeed, "partnerships" is the buzzword of the moment: the 1999 Good Universities Guide University of the Year Award, for example, will be based on the notion of "productive knowledge through partnerships." Clearly, the Mode 2 system of knowledge production is being vigorously encouraged and promoted by research policy makers in this country and elsewhere. But what *are* partnerships? How are they formed? And most importantly for the purposes of this paper, how can cultural studies research tap into this new scheme of things?

The upbeat discourse of partnerships is often presented as a way for the university to become more involved and integrated with the wider community and society at large. The University of Western Sydney, for example, describes itself as an "innovative joint-venture university" fully in tune with the emergent knowledge-based society of the twenty-first century, fostering a culture of partnerships primarily with constituencies in its local context, the vast region of Greater Western Sydney – touted as the fastest growing region in Australia. This is fine as an objective, especially for a new university such as UWS which still needs to carve out a distinctive identity for itself within the highly competitive higher education field.

However, the clear subtext of the pursuit of partnerships is a ruthlessly economic rationale: it is a way of getting more external funding for research in a time of diminishing public funds. As a result, only those potential partners tend to be deemed worth pursuing – and yes, polygamy is fully allowed, even looked upon favorably here – who have funds to bring into the partnership, a kind of dowry as it were, as in the widely-used matched funding approach to research resource allocation. Mostly these partners are private or public sector corporate entities from the world of business, industry, or government and not, say, grassroots community groups or members of the general public, who are citizens or consumers and not "stakeholders." Indeed, in a regime where the amount of earned external income is one of the key indicators of a university's supposed performance, the preoccupation with money-drawing partnerships is enormous. Thus, any time a new partner has been signed up, the UWS Research Office proudly announces through the university-wide listserver the amount of funding that has been raked in. The unintended consequence is that the significance of research activities which are not based on the securing of external funding is symbolically diminished, remaining more or less invisible to the university community as a whole. This, as should be clear, is especially disadvantageous for humanities research.

Is it impossible for humanities researchers to enter into partnerships with others? Of course not. Indeed, research in the cultural studies mould would seem to have a lot to offer to external partners from many corners of society, especially, as remarked at the beginning of this paper, in light of the growing prominence of the cultural dimension of society. However, precisely because partners are expected to pay up, there is a danger for the whole notion of research partnerships – and Mode 2 knowledge production in general – to be framed in an instrumentalist, often commercial or merely practical horizon of expectations. This affects the definition of "usefulness" of research, which may be shrunk to rather narrow, short-termist dimensions. Topics that are flavours of the month may easily attract resources, others will not. For example, in Sydney local councils, government departments, the police, community organizations, even small business associations have recently been very keen to fund research on Arab youth and crime. This is not surprising given the moral panic raging in town over so-called "Lebanese gangs." In all likelihood the research is imagined to be able to provide some direct solution to this "problem" of youth crime; this is what the "partners in research" would be willing to spend money on.

This returns me to the issue of "relevance" of cultural studies. It would be the distinctive intellectual contribution of cultural studies research here to highlight the fact that the very demonization of Lebanese boys as potential criminals may be part of the whole problem, exacerbating rather than alleviating divisions and tensions within the community. The research would then have to critique the intimate assumptive connection made between "ethnicity," "youth," and "crime" in dominant public discourses, and its complex, contradictory effects on why the boys act the way they do. *Cultural* research of this kind would be aimed at highlighting the underlying cultural meanings and assumptions which contribute to the construction of the "problem" of "Lebanese youth gangs." It would point to the politics of representation involved in attempts to manage and police these young people, and in doing so, it would induce a conceptual shift in thinking about the issues concerned. In other words, the research would generate a mode of self-reflexivity by explicating the biases implicit in the very way in which the "problem" is named and described. But would the partners be happy with this kind of research? Would they put money in it? Would they find it useful and relevant?

Those partners who are exclusively looking for straightforward problem-solving outcomes are unlikely to be interested in research that makes issues more complex rather than more simple. Yet this is exactly what cultural research, as a mode of applied humanities, can do well, and I would argue, should do. Unfortunately, the instrumentalist framework in which partnerships are currently forged does not easily make space for research whose usefulness lies in opening up new questions rather than providing answers to existing ones. If cultural research is to find an appropriate place in the emerging Mode 2 world of knowledge production, then the definition of the useful or the relevant will have to be stretched beyond the level of immediacy. We will have to demonstrate that keeping questions open is actually useful, that thinking more complexly and reflexively about issues is actually practical, if not here and now then in the longer term, in light of social sustainability, for example.

We live in an increasingly complex world. In a world obsessed with economic growth, the free market, and technological speed and efficiency, what many groups within society need most today are not just material resources, but crucially, intellectual resources that enable them to grasp and interpret the world around them and their own place within it. Anecdotal evidence suggests that there is a great thirst for new ideas, and that there is a great poverty of vision and of fresh ways of thinking about things at the grassroots level. For example, in local governments and other organizations concepts such as "community," "identity," and "multiculturalism," or even "access and equity," to name but a few, have become stale, stuck in closed circuits of meaning devoid of the capacity to inspire creative ways of dealing with the issues at hand. The populism that now pervades Australian public culture in the wake of Pauline Hanson is both a symptom and an effect of the malaise, which is a cultural deadlock in need of specific, cultural interventions – interventions which illuminate the constitutive role of meaning, representation, and value in the diagnosis and management of social environments.[10]

This, I would argue, is why the world needs cultural studies more than ever. As contemporary society has become increasingly opaque to most citizens, what is in shortest supply is the kind of knowledge and skill that enables citizens to "read" their own environments, to understand their own multiple contributions to the shaping of those environments, and to interrogate their own mindsets. What is also desperately needed is the capacity for people to self-reflexively invent common grounds within which situated social futures can be imagined and worked towards together with an increasingly wide range of differently positioned others. In short, the distinctive intellectual currency and social utility of cultural studies research lies in its capacity for inducing conjunctural questioning, rather than in providing positivist answers to set questions. To be sure, this is the kind of knowledge production expertise that is required for the writing of a good essay. The skill and knowledge that cultural researchers channel into more or less obscure essay writing may be transferable to collaborative contexts which would benefit from the illumination and interrogation of the very process of meaning production. The very notion that culture is always contested, that meaning is always negotiated and constructed in concrete contexts, can be mobilized and applied in myriad strategic contexts in partnership with other specialist knowledge producers and users. There's nothing more practical than that.

Notes

1   Bill Readings, *The University in Ruins* (Cambridge: Harvard University Press, 1996), 175.
2   Michael Gibbons et al., *The New Production of Knowledge: The Dynamics of Science and Research in Contemporary Societies* (London: Sage, 1994).
3   Gibbons, 81.
4   Gibbons, 105.

5   The Hon. Dr. David Kemp MP, Minister for Education, Training and Youth Affairs, *New Knowledge, New Opportunities. A Discussion Paper on Higher Education Research and Research Training* (Canberra: DETYA, June 1999).

6   Kemp, 2; web version: http://www.detya.gov.au/highered/otherpub/greenpaper/fullpaper.pdf.

7   Gibbons, 106.

8   The example provided by Gibbons et al. is that of the *Annales* historians.

9   SPIRT = Strategic Partnerships with Industry – Research and Training Scheme.

10 Pauline Hanson is a white, right-wing populist politician who gained a seat in parliament in 1996 on an anti-aboriginal and anti-multicultural agenda, speaking on behalf of the "ordinary Australian." She established the proto-nationalist "one nation party," a political movement comparable to but less militant than that of David Duke or France's Jean-Marie Le Pen. By 2000 her popularity has waned considerably, but her influence still resonates in the more conservative tone pervading dominant public discourse in Australia.

List of Activist Organizations and Web Resources

Readers should note that the web addresses of the following list of organizations and resources are prone to change. If an address does not work, try using the name of the organization or website.

ABANTU for Development
(Kenya) www.abantu.org.

Abya Yala Net
(South and Meso American Indian Rights) http://abyayala.native.org.

Accion Zapatista
www.utexas.edu/students/nave/index.html.

ACME: Action Coalition for Media Education
www.mediacoalition.org.

Act: Advocating Change Together
(disability rights and great links) www.selfadvocacy.com.

Act Up/NY: AIDS Coalition to Unleash Power
www.actupny.org.

Adalah: The Legal Center for Arab Minority Rights in Israel
www.adalah.org.

ADDAMEER: Prisoners Support and Human Rights Association
(Israel) www.addameer.org.

AFL-CIO
www.aflcio.org.

African-American Women: On-Line Archival Collections
http://scriptorium.lib.duke.edu/collections/african-american-women.html.

African Women Global Network
www.osu.edu/org/awognet/.

Africa Policy Information Center
www.africapolicy.org/index.php.

Africa South of the Sahara
(resources and organization links) www.sul.stanford.edu/depts/ssrg/africa/hurights.html.

Alliance for Community Media
(US) www.alliancecm.org.

All Walks of Life
(disability issues) www.awol-texas.org.

Alternative Information and Development Centre (AIDC)
(South Africa) http://aidc.org.za/.

Alternative Press Center
www.altpress.org.

Alternative Radio
(US, great tape collection) www.alternativeradio.org.

Alternative Research
(US, political surveillance and repression) http://sun3.lib.uci.edu/~dtsang/.

AlterNet.Org: Independent News and Information
www.alternet.org.

Amanaka'a: Amazon Network
(human rights) www.amanakaa.org.

Amazon Watch
www.amazonwatch.org.

American-Arab Anti-Discrimination Committee
www.ADC.org.

American Civil Liberties Union
www.aclu.org.

American Indian Movement
www.aimovement.org.

Amnesty International
www.amnesty.org.

Anjaree Group
(lesbian activism, Thailand) www.anjaree.org.

Antagonism: Anti-Capitalist & Anti-State Struggle for World Community
(UK) www.geocities.com/antagonism1/index.html.

Anti-Capital Web
www.webcom.com/maxang/.

Anti-Defamation League
www.adl.org.

Antifascist Web Sites
http://users.westnet.gr/~cgian/antifa.htm.

Antiracist/Antifascist Links
www.le-libertaire.org/Antifas/liens.html.

Anti-Racism Resource Center
www.pocho.com/racism/home.html.

Anti-Slavery London
www.antislavery.org.

Armchair Activist
http://ndavis.bi.org/act/.

Art and Revolution
www.artandrevolution.org.

Art Crimes: Alternative Media Links
www.graffiti.org.

Article 19: International Centre on Censorship
(UK/South Africa) www.article19.org.

Artists against Racism International
www.artistsagainstracism.org.

ASHA for Education
(an action group for basic education in India) www.ashanet.org.

Asia Monitor Resource Center
(Hong Kong, independent labor movements) www.amrc.org.HK/.

Asian Human Rights Commission: Human Rights Solidarity
(Hong Kong) www.ahrchk.net.

Asian Pacific American Labor Alliance
www.apalanet.org.

Asia Pacific Center for Justice and Peace
(US) www.apcjp.org.

ASAP: Action in Solidarity with Asia and the Pacific
www.asia-pacific-action.org.

Asociacion Madres de Plaza de Mayo
(Argentina) www.madres.org.

Association for Progressive Communications
(US) www.apc.org.

Association for Union Democracy
(US) www.uniondemocracy.org.

Association of Alternative Newsweeklies
(US) http://aan.org/gbase/Aan/index.

Astraea Lesbian Action Foundation
(funding agency) www.astraea.org.

Australian Human Rights and Civil Rights
(activist links) http://home.vicnet.net.au/~victorp/vphuman.htm.

Autonomedia
(progressive global news and activism for artists) www.autonomedia.org.

Banabans
(indigenous struggles of this group in the Central Pacific) www.banaban.com.

Baobab's Corporate Power Information Center
http://bapd.org/gbawer-1.html.

BAOBAB for Women's Human Rights
(Nigeria) www.whrnet.org/partners_baobab.htm.

Behind the Mask
(South Africa, information about Gay/Lesbian developments in Africa) www.mask.org.za/index2.html.

Bioengineering Action Network of North America
www.tao.ca/~ban/index.html.

Black Radical Congress: Forging a Black Liberation Agenda for the 21st Century
(US) http://blackradicalcongress.com/index.html.

BLK Homie Pages
(black Lesbian and Gay information) www.blk.com.
Bread and Roses
(art and labor) www.bread-and-roses.com.
British Columbia Civil Liberties Association
www.bccla.org.
California Newsreel
(critical videos) www.newsreel.org.
Campaign against Foreign Control of Aotearoa (CAFCA)
http://canterbury.cyberplace.co.nz/community/CAFCA/.
Campaign against Sanctions on Iraq
www.cam.ac.uk/societies/casi/.
Canadian Association of Media Education Organizations (CAMEO)
http://interact.uoregon.edu/MediaLit/CAMEO/index.html.
Caribbean Association for Feminist Research and Action
www.cafra.org.
Casa Alianza
(global offices, police violence against Latin American children) www.casa-alianza.
org/EN/index-en.shtml.
CEE Bankwatch Network
(monitors activities of international financial institutions) www.bankwatch.org.
Center for Asian-Pacific Women in Politics (CAPWIP)
(Philippines) www.capwip.org.
Center for Campus Organizing (CCO)
http://bapd.org/gcepng-1.html.
Center for Commercial Free Public Education
(US) www.commercialfree.org.
Center for Democratic Renewal
(US, hate crimes) www.publiceye.org/cdr/cdr.html.
Center for Digital Democracy: Preserving and Expanding Democratic Digital Media
www.democraticmedia.org.
Center for Economic Justice
(US) www.econjustice.net.
Center for Economic and Social Rights (CESR)
(US) www.cesr.org.
Center for Media and Democracy: PR Watch
(US) www.prwatch.org.
Center for Media and the Black Experience /Hype: Monitoring the Black Image in the Media
(US) www.ayaed.com/hype/index.htm.
Center for Media Education
(US) www.cme.org.
Center for Media Literacy
(US) www.medialit.org.
Center for Migration Studies
(US) http://cmsny.org.

Center for Popular Economics
  (US) www.populareconomics.org.
Center for Third World Organizing (CTWO)
  (US) www.ctwo.org.
Center for World Indigenous Studies
  www.cwis.org.
Centre for Peace, Non-violence, and Human Rights
  (Croatia) www.centar-za-mir.hr/.
Chiapas Media Project
  (Mexico) www.chiapasmediaproject.org.
Children's Defense Fund
  (US, see especially parent resource network) www.childrensdefense.org.
Child Labor Coalition
  (US) www.natlconsumersleague.org/clc.htm.
Citizens for Independent Public Broadcasting (CIPB)
  (US) www.cipbonline.org.
Citizens for Police Review
  (US) www.korrnet.org/cpr/.
Citizens for Tax Justice (CTJ)
  (US) www.ctj.org.
Clandestine Radio
  (global news) www.clandestineradio.com.
Class War: Class Unity, Class Pride
  (UK) www.geocities.com/CapitolHill/9482/.
Clean Clothes Campaign
  (working conditions in the garment industry) www.cleanclothes.org.
Colours of Resistance
  (Canada, anti-racist & anti-capitalist) www.tao.ca/%7Ecolours/.
Columbia Earthscape: An On-Line Resource on the Global Environment
  www.earthscape.org.
Columbia Human Rights Network/Red de Derechos Humanos en Columbia
  http://colhrnet.igc.org.
Columbia Labor Monitor
  www.prairienet.org/clm/.
Columbia Support Network
  (peace and justice for Columbia) www.columbiasupport.net.
Commercialism in Education Research Unit
  www.schoolcommercialism.org.
Contemporary Philosophy, Critical Theory, and Postmodern Thought
  http://carbon.cudenver.edu/~mryder/itc_data/postmodern.html.
Contemporary Postcolonial and Postimperial Literature in English
  (resource links) www.scholars.nus.edu.sg/landow/post/index.html.
Corporate Accountability Project
  (US) www.corporations.org.
Corporate Watch: Holding Corporations Accountable
  (UK) www.corporatewatch.org.uk.
CODESRIA: Council for the Development of Social Science Research in Africa
  (Senegal) www.sas.upenn.edu/African_Studies/codesria/codes_Menu.html.

Critical Resistance Youth Force/The Campaign to Defeat the Prison Industrial Complex
   (US) www.youthEC.org.
Critical Theory Resource Guide
   www.unl.ac.uk/library/aishums/crithe.shtml.
Crosspoint Anti Racism
   (great links) www.magenta.nl/crosspoint/.
Cultstud-L
   (lists, resources, and links) www.cas.usf.edu/communication/rodman/cultstud/.
Cultural Studies and Critical Theory
   (links to Marxism, sexuality, culture, etc.) http://eserver.org/theory/.
Cultural Studies/Critical Theory
   www.erraticmpact.com/~topics/html/cultural_studies.htm.
Cultural Studies Central
   www.culturalstudies.net.
Cybergrrl Safety Net
   (domestic violence) www.cybergrrl.com.
Cyber Semiotic Institute
   www.chass.utoronto.ca/epc/srb/cyber.html.
DAWN: Development Alternatives with Women for a New Era
   (Fiji) www.dawn.org.fj/.
Death Penalty Information Center
   www.deathpenaltyinfo.org.
Deep Dish Television
   www.igc.org/deepdish/.
Democratic Socialists of America (DSA)
   www.dsausa.org.
Disability Rights Action Coalition for Housing (DRACH)
   (US) www.libertysources.org/housing/nac3.html.
Dyke TV
   (US) www.dyketv.org.
Eactivist.org
   www.eactivist.org.
Earth Action
   (UK) www.earthaction.org.
Earth Watch Institute
   www.earthwatch.org.
East Timor Action Network
   www.etan.org.
Economic Democracy Information Network (EDIN)
   www.nathannewman.org/EDIN/.
Ecoropa
   (European environmental organization) www.gsf.de/UNEP/ukeco.html.
Eldis: The Gateway to Development Information
   (10,000 documents and organizations) www.eldis.org.
Electronic Civil Disobedience/The Electronic Disturbance Theatre
   www.thing.net/~rdom/ecd/ecd.html.

Electronic Frontier Foundation: Protecting and Promoting Freedom in the Electronic Frontier
(US) www.eff.org.

Escape Links
(UK, progressive sites) www.hrc.wmin.ac.uk/guest/radical/LINKS.htm.

Esperanza Peace and Justice Center
(US, civil rights, economic justice, and art) www.esperanzacenter.org.

Essential Information: Encouraging Activism
www.essentialaction.org.

Ethical Junction: Making Ethical Choices Easy
(UK and Ireland, access to ethical organizations and ethical trading) www.ethical-junction.org.

European and North American Women Action
(great links) www.enawa.org.

European Commission against Racism and Intolerance (ECRI)
www.coe.int/t/E/human_rights/ecri/.

EZLN: Ejercito Zapatista de Liberacion Nacional
(Zapatista home page) www.ezln.org.

Factsheet Five
(information on zines) www.factsheet5.com.

FAIR: Fairness and Accuracy in Reporting
(US) www.fair.org.

Feminist.Com
www.feminist.com.

Feminists for Free Expression
www.ffeusa.org.

Feminist Internet Gateway
www.feminist.org/gateway/listnews.html.

50 Years is Enough: US Network for Global Economic Justice
(US) www.50years.org.

Food Not Bombs
http://home.earthlink.net/foodnotbombs/.

Free Burma Coalition
www.freeburmacoalition.org.

Freedom of Information Center
(US) http://web.missouri.edu/~foiwww/.

Free Radio Berkeley/Free Communications Commission
www.freeradio.org.

Friends of Tibetan Women's Association
www.fotwa.org.

Frontline News: The Struggle against Imperialism and Transnational Capital
http://hjem.get2net.dk/graversgaard/.

Gay Asian Pacific Alliance
www.gapa.org.

Gay Media Database
(newspaper, magazine, journal directory publishers, expos, and Web/TV/radio) www.gaydata.com.

Gay Media Resource List
www.northbound-train.com/gaymedia.html.

Gender & Ethnicity Resources
www.usc.edu/isd/archives/ethnicstudies/gender.html.

Gendercide Watch
www.gendercide.org.

Glaad: Gay and Lesbian Alliance against Defamation
(US) www.glaad.org.

GLAS: Gay and Lesbian Arabic Society
www.glas.org.

Global Action: May Our Resistance Be as Transnational as Capital
http://flag.blackened.net/global/.

Global Ecovillage Network
www.gaia.org.

Global Exchange
(human rights) www.globalexchange.org.

Global March against Child Labor
http://globalmarch.org/index.html.

Global Network against Weapons and Nuclear Power in Space
(UK) www.globenet.free-online.co.uk/.

Global Unions
(labor news) www.global-unions.org.

Globalvision New Media/Media Channel.org
(US) http://globalvision.igc.org/index.htm.

Government Accountability Project
(US) www.whistleblower.org.

Grassroots International: A People-to-People Partnership for Social Change
www.grassrootsonline.org.

Green Net
(peace, human rights and the environment, great links) www.gn.apc.org.

Greenpeace
www.greenpeace.org.

Group for the Study of Working Class Life
(US) http://naples.cc.sunysb.edu/CAS/wcm.nsf.

Growl: Grassroots Organizing for Welfare Leadership
(US) www.ctwo.org/growl/.

Guerrillagirls
(feminist activism) www.guerrillagirls.com.

Guerrilla News Network
www.guerrillanews.com.

Haringey Solidarity Group
(UK, political organizing) http://hgs.cupboard.org/agitator/data/h/hsgoo051.html.

Human Rights Campaign: Working for Lesbian and Gay Equal Rights
(US) www.hrc.org.

Human Rights Watch
(US) www.hrw.org.

Humrahi: Forum for Gay Men in New Delhi, India
www.geocities.com/WestHollywood/Heights/7258/.

ICARE: Internet Centre Anti-Racism Europe
  www.icare.to/.
Illuminations: The Critical Theory Web Site
  www.uta.edu/huma/illuminations/.
Independent Media Center
  (grassroots coverage) www.indymedia.org.
Independent Press Association: The Antidote to Monopoly Media
  (US) www.indypress.org.
Index of Native America: Resources on the Internet
  www.hanksville.org/Naresources/.
Indigenous Environmental Network
  (US) www.ienearth.org.
Indigenous Peoples Council on Biocolonialism
  (US) www.ipcb.org.
Indigenous Rights (Aotearoa)
  (New Zealand) www.converge.org.nz/pma/indig.htm.
Indigenous Women of the Americas
  www.ainc-inac.gc.ca/dec/wmn_e.html.
In Fact: Challenging Corporate Abuse, Building Grassroots Power
  (US) www.infact.org.
Information for Socialists
  http://sunsite.unc.edu/spc/.
Institute for Global Communications
  www.igc.org.
Institute for Multiracial Justice
  (US) www.multiracialjustice.org.
Institute for Social and Cultural Change/Z Media Institute
  (US) www.zmag.org.
Instituto Paulo Freire
  (Brazil) www.paulofreire.org.
Interfaith Center on Corporate Responsibility
  (US) www.iccr.org.
Interhemispheric Resource Center (IRC)
  www.irc-online.org.
International Concerned Family and Friends of Mumia Abu-Jamal
  www.mumia.org.
International Criminal Court (CICC)
  www.iccnow.org.
International Gay and Lesbian Human Rights Task Force (IGLHRC)
  www.iglhrc.org.
International Labor Rights Fund
  www.laborrights.org.
International Women's Health Coalition (IWHC)
  www.iwhc.org.
Interreligious Foundation for Community Organization (IFCO) (Pastors for Peace)
  www.ifconews.org.
Iraq Action Coalition
  http://iraqaction.org.

Jabiluka Action Group - Melbourne
(Australian activist events and news) http://vic.jag.org.au/.
Jamming the Media
http://home.earthlink.net/~garethb2/jamming/resources.html.
Jay's Leftist and 'Progressive' Internet Resources Directory
www.neravt.com/left/.
Jews for Radical & Economic Justice (JFREJ)
(US) www.jfrej.org.
Jobs with Justice
(US) www.jwj.org.
JustAct: Youth Action for Global Justice
(US) www.justact.org/home/index.html.
Just Cause Law Collective
(US) www.lawcollective.org.
Kensington Welfare Rights
(US) www.kwru.org.
Kids against Pollution, Poverty & Prejudice
www.kidsagainstpollution.org.
Know Your Rights
www.studentactivism.org.
Kurdish Human Rights Project
(UK) www.khrp.org.
Kurdish Women's Studies Network
www.oise.utoronto.ca/projects/kwnet/.
Labor and Workers Links
http://members.aol.com/_ht_a/yoda348846/labor.html.
LaborNet: Global Online Communication for a Democratic, Independent Labor Movement
www.labornet.org.
Labor Notes: Putting the Movement Back in the Labor Movement
(US) www.labornotes.org.
Labour Start: Where Trade Unionists Start Their Day on the Net
www.labourstart.org/index.shtml.
La Neta
(resources on Mexico) www.laneta.apc.org.
Language Policy Website & Emporium
(working against the English-Only movement)
http://ourworld.compuserve.com/homepages/JWCRAWFORD/.
League of Revolutionaries for a New America
www.lrna.org.
Leftist Links Archives
www.cruznet.net/~marcus/leftist-links.html.
Lesbian Avengers
(US) www.lesbianavengers.org.
Lesbian.Org: Promoting Lesbian Visibility on the Internet
www.lesbian.org.
Links to Labor and Social Websites in Japan
http://oohara.mt.tama.hosei.ac.jp/links/elinks-social.html.

Macronet
(major links) www.macronet.org.

MADRE: Demanding Human Rights for Women and Families around the World
www.madre.org.

Malcolm X: A Research Site
www.brothermalcolm.net.

Manavi
(community-based women's organization for women from Bangladesh, India, Nepal, Pakistan, and Sri Lanka) www.research.att.com/~krishnas/manavi/.

Maori Independence Site
http://aotearoa.wellington.net.nz/.

Mapping Our World/Topos de Vies
(Canada, children's rights) www.mappingourworld.org.

Maquila Solidarity Network
(sweatshop activism) www.maquilasolidarity.org.

Marxists Internet Archive
www.marxist.org.

McSpotlight
(UK, follows the agenda of organizations such as McDonalds) www.mcspotlight.org.

Medecins Sans Frontieres (MSF)/Doctors Without Borders (DWB)
www.doctorswithoutborders.org.

Media Access Project
(US) www.mediaaccess.org.

Media Alliance
(US) www.media-alliance.org.

Media Awareness Network/Reseau Education-Medias
(Canada) www.media-awareness.ca/.

Media Education Foundation
(US, great video selection) www.mediaed.org.

Media Literacy Online Project
http://interact.uoregon.edu/mediaLit/homepage/.

Media Tenor: Institute for Media Analysis
(South Africa) www.media-tenor.co.za/.

Media Watch
(US) www.mediawatch.com.

MIFTAH: The Palestinian Initiative for the Promotion of Global Dialogue and Democracy
(Jerusalem) www.miftah.org.

Milarepa
(overview of the struggles in Tibet) www.milarepa.org.

Mobilization for Global Justice
www.a16.org.

Muckraker: Center for Investigative Reporting
(US) www.muckraker.org.

MuralArt.com
www.muralart.com.

National Alliance of Media Arts and Culture (NAMAC)
  (US) www.namac.org.
National Alliance to End Homelessness
  (US) www.endhomelessness.org.
National and International Gay and Lesbian Organizations and Publications
  http://faculty.washington.edu/alvin/gayorg.htm.
National Association of African Americans for Positive Imagery
  www.naaapi.org.
National Association of Black and White Men Together
  (US) www.NABWMT.com.
National Black United Front
  (US) www.nbufront.org.
National Center for Human Rights Education (CHRE)
  (US) www.nchre.org.
National Coalition against Censorship
  (US) www.ncac.org.
National Gay and Lesbian Task Force
  (US) www.ngltf.org.
National Indian Youth Leadership Project
  (US) www.niylp.org.
National Labor Committee: For Workers & Human Rights
  (US-based, but has international campaigns) www.nlcnet.org.
National Native American AIDS Prevention Center
  (US) www.nnaapc.org.
National Network for Immigrant and Refugee Rights
  (US) www.nnirr.org.
National Organizers Alliance: Fly in the Face of Injustice
  (US) www.noacentral.org.
National Priorities Project: Data for Democracy
  (US) www.natprior.org.
Native American Public Telecommunications: Empowering, Educating, and Entertaining through Native Media
  www.nativetelecom.org.
Native Americans and the Environment
  http://cnie.org/NAE/.
Native Net: Dedicated to Protecting and Defending Mother Earth and the Rights of Indigenous Peoples Worldwide
  http://niikaan.fdl.cc.mn.us/natnet/.
NativeWeb
  (global) www.nativeweb.org.
Natural Resources Defense Council
  (US) www.nrdc.org.
NetAction
  (grassroots internet action) www.netaction.org.
Network in Solidarity with the People of Guatemala/La Red en Solidaridad con el Pueblo de Guatemala (NISGUA)
  www.nisgua.org.

Network of East-West Women (NEWW)
www.neww.org.

New Pages: Alternatives in Print and Media
www.newpages.com.

Nicaragua Solidarity
http://home.earthlink.net/~dbwilson/nsnhome.html.

Nothingness.Org: Situationist International
www.nothingness.org.

October 22nd Coalition: Stop Police Brutality and the Criminalization of a Generation
(US) www.october22.org.

Ontario Coalition against Poverty
(Canada) www.ocap.ca/.

Open Secrets.Org: Your Guide to the Money in American Elections
www.opensecrets.org.

Organisation for Alternative Development and Global Justice
www.odag.org.

Out Proud: Be Yourself
(US, national coalition for Gay, Lesbian, Bisexual, and Transgender youth) www.outproud.org.

Outreach
(Australia, sexuality and youth) www.also.org.au/outreach/.

Outside Anti-Fascist Links
www.geocities.com/CapitolHill/1131/oth_links.html.

Oxfam International
(antipoverty) www.oxfam.org.

Ozgurluk.org
(liberation struggles in Turkey and Kurdistan) www.ozgurluk.org.

Panic Encyclopedia: The Definitive Guide to the Postmodern Scene
www.freedonia.com/panic/.

Paper Tiger Television: Smashing the Myths of the Information Industry
(great links) www.papertiger.org.

PARC: Pacific Asia Resource Center
(movement in Japan to facilitate solidarity links with Asian peoples in struggle) www.parc-jp.org.

Peace Brigades International
www.peacebrigades.org/index.html.

Peace Development Fund's Listening Project
(voices of social change organizers and activists) www.peacefund.org.

Peace Movement Aotearoa
(New Zealand) www.converge.org.nz/pma/.

People for Better TV
(US) www.bettertv.org.

Political Research Associates: The Public Eye
(US, monitors how the political right undermines democracy and diversity) www.publiceye.org.

Popular Education for People's Empowerment
(Philippines) www.pepe.org.

Poverty and Race Research Action Council
  (US) www.prrac.org.
Prison Activist Resource Center
  (US) www.prisonactivist.org.
Prison Moratorium Project
  (US) www.nomoreprisons.org.
Progressive Resource/Action Cooperative
  www.praivienet.org/prc/.
Project Censored.Org
  (US) www.projectcensored.org.
Project South: The Institute for the Elimination of Poverty and Genocide
  www.projectsouth.org.
Project Underground
  (US, against mining and oil exploitation) www.moles.org.
Prometheus Radio Project
  (US) www.Prometheusradio.org.
Protest.net/Front Door
  (up-coming protests) www.protest.net.
Public Citizen Global Trade Watch
  www.citizen.org/trade/.
Pure Food Campaign
  (US) www.purefoods.org.
Queer Resources Directory
  www.qrd.org/qrd/.
Radical Routes: A Network of Little Fishes
  (co-ops) www.radicalroutes.org.uk.
Radikala.com
  (left green movement in Northern Europe) www.radikala.com.
Radio 4 All
  www.radio4all.org.
Radio for Peace International/Radio Paz Internacional
  (Costa Rica) www.rfpi.org.
Radio Free Maine
  (US) www.radiofreemaine.com.
Radio Tower
  (internet radio station directory) www.radiotower.com.
Reading International Solidarity Centre
  www.risc.org.uk/index.html.
Reclaim the Streets
  (UK, social-ecological revolutions) www.reclaimthestreets.net.
Refuse and Resist
  www.refuseandresist.org/altindex.html.
Reference Center for Marxist Studies
  http://marxistlibrary.org/index.html.
Religion and Socialism Commission
  http://dsausa.org/rs/.
Revolutionary Association of the Women of Afghanistan
  http://rawa.false.net/index.html.

Right to Know Network
  http://rtk.net.
Romani Rights
  (Gypsy information) www.geocities.com/~patrin/rights.htm.
Samizdat
  (information on political struggles in France) www.samizdat.net.
San Papiers
  (French refugee resistance) www.bok.net/pajol/.
Sarah Zupko's Cultural Studies Center
  (resources and links) www.popcultures.com.
School of the Americas Watch
  (watch on US army training) www.soaw.org/new/.
Schools not Jails: No Justice No Peace
  www.schoolsnotjails.com.
Schmacher UK
  (sustainable future) www.schumacher.org.uk.
Seeds of Peace Center for Coexistence
  (Jerusalem, empowering children of war to break the cycle of violence) www.seedsofpeace.org.
Semiotics for Beginners
  www.aber.ac.uk/media/Documents/S4B/semiotic.html.
Shundahai Network
  (fight for Shoshone sovereignty) www.shundahai.org.
Simon Wiesenthal Center
  (international Jewish Human Rights Organization) www.wiesenthal.com.
Social Inequality and Classes
  (links) www.pscw.uva.nl/sociosite/topics/inequality.html.
Social Justice and Social Justice Movements
  (links to religious activism) http://philebus.tamu.edu/~cmenzel/justice.html.
Society for Cinema Studies Caucus on Class
  http://terri1.home.mindspring.com.
Solidarity Federation: International Workers Association
  (UK) www.solfed.org.uk.
Solidarity: The Revolutionary, Socialist, Democratic, Feminist, Anti-Racist Organization
  (US) http://solidarity.igc.org.
Soulforce Action Center
  (US, religion and sexuality) www.soulforce.org.
Women's Net at SANGONET
  (South Africa) http://womensnet.org.za.
Speakout: Institute for Democratic Education and Culture
  (US) www.speakersandartists.org.
Stolen Lives: Killed by Law Enforcement
  (US) www.stolenlives.org.
Students for a Free Tibet
  www.tibet.org/sft/.
Subvertising
  (countering ads) www.subvertise.org.

Survival International
(UK, world-wide organization supporting tribal peoples) www.survival-international.org.

Sustain: The Alliance for Better Food and Farming
(UK) www.sustainweb.org/index.asp.

Sweatshop Watch
(US) www.sweatshopwatch.org.

The African Women's Development and Communication Network (FEMNET)
(Kenya) www.africaonline.co.ke/femnet/.

The Alliance for Democracy
(US) www.thealliancefordemocracy.org.

The Alliance for Sustainable Jobs and the Environment
(US) www.asje.org.

The Association for Union Democracy
(US) www.uniondemocracy.org.

The Audre Lorde Project: Center for Lesbian, Gay, Bisexual, Two Spirit, and Transgender People of Color Communities
(US) www.alp.org.

The BADvertising Institute
(US) www.badvertising.org.

The Billboard Liberation Front
www.billboardliberation.com.

The Blue Planet Project
(Canadians protecting fresh water from privatization)
www.canadians.org/blueplanet/index2.html.

The Body: An AIDS and HIV Information Resource
www.thebody.com/govt.html.

The Campaign to Label Genetically Engineered Foods
(US) www.thecampaign.org.

The Center for Public Integrity: Watchdog in the Corridors of Power
(government accountability) www.publicintegrity.org/dtaweb/home.asp.

The Center for Working-Class Studies at Youngstown State University
(US) www.as.ysu.edu/~cwcs.

The Coalition to Abolish Slavery and Trafficking (CAST)
(US) www.trafficked-women.org/index.html.

The Council for Responsible Genetics
www.gene-watch.org.

The Direct Action Media Network
www.tao.ca/earth/damn/.

The Disability Rights Activist
www.disrights.org.

The Durham People's Alliance
(progressive Web sites) www.durhampa.org/progressive.htm.

The Eritrean Political Opposition
www.meskerem.net.

The Free Radio Network
www.frn.net.

The Great Speckled Bird Striker Page
  (labor links and activities) www.thebird.org.
The Institute for Global Communications
  www.igc.org.
The International Lesbian and Gay Association
  www.ilga.org/default.htm.
The International Office of the Leonard Peltier Defense Committee
  www.freepeltier.org.
The Labor Heritage Foundation: Works to Strengthen the Labor Movement through the Use of Music and the Arts
  (US) www.laborheritage.org.
The Loka Institute
  (US, democratizing research, science, and technology) www.loka.org.
The Marxist Page
  http://lists.village.virginia.edu/~spoons/marxism_html/index.html.
The Media Foundation
  (Canada) www.adbusters.org.
The Militia Watchdog
  (resources and information on right-wing extremism in the US) www.militia-watch-dog.org.
The National Lesbian and Gay Journalists Association (NLGJA)
  (US) www.nlgja.org.
The New York City Gay and Lesbian Anti Violence Project
  (US) www.avp.org.
The Noam Chomsky Archive
  www.Zmag.org/chomsky/index.cfm.
The Progressive Media Project: Diversifying America's Opinion Pages
  www.progressive.org/mediaproj.htm.
The Ruckus Society
  (US, civil disobedience) www.ruckus.org.
The South and Meso American Indian Rights Center: Linking Indian Peoples of the Americas (SAIIC)
  http://saiic.nativeweb.org.
The South Asian Women's Network (SAWNET)
  www.umiacs.umd.edu/users/sawweb/sawnet/.
The Women's Environmental Network
  (UK) www.wen.org.uk.
The Video Activist Network
  (US, great links) www.videoactivism.org.
Third World Newsreel
  (alternative media arts organization) www.twn.org.
Undercurrents: Alternative News Videos
  www.undercurrents.org.
UNICEF: United Nation's Children's Fund
  www.unicef.org.
Unions against Corporate Tyranny
  www.asia-pacific-action.org/uact/.

Union for Radical Political Economics
(US) www.urpe.org.

Union Nationale des Femmes Sahraovies
(Saharan Arab Democratic Republic women's struggles and human rights) www.arso.org/NUSW-1.htm.

Union Resource Network
www.unions.org/default2.asp.

Union Ring
(labor resource) www.geocities.com/CapitolHill/5202/unionring.html.

United for a Fair Economy
(US) www.ufenet.org.

United for Intercultural Action
(Netherlands) www.unitedagainstracism.org.

United Students against Sweatshops
www.usasnet.org.

Unite!: Stop Sweatshops Campaign
www.uniteunion.org.

Urban 75
(Web sites featuring activism) www.urban75.com.

Voice of the Shuttle: Cultural Studies Page
(see also media studies page and cyberculture page) http://vos.ucsb.edu/.

Wal-Mart Watch
www.walmartwatch.com/neighbor/.

War Resisters League
(US) www.warresisters.org.

Washington Office on Latin America: Promoting Human Rights, Democracy, and Social and Economic Justice in Latin America
www.wola.org.

Way.Net: Connecting Progressive Activists and Artists
www.way.net/.

WebActive Directory
(progressive groups online) www.webactive.com.

We the People
(progressive links) www.wtp.org.

Witness for Peace
(social justice in the Americas) www.witnessforpeace.org.

Women of Uganda Network
www.wougnet.org.

Women's Crisis Centre, Penang/Pusat Krisis Wanita, Penang (WCC)
(Malaysia) www.wccpenang.org.

Women's Environment & Development Organization
(US) www.wedo.org.

Women's Global Network for Reproductive Rights
(Netherlands) www.wgnrr.org.

Women in Law and Development in Africa (WILDAF)
(Zimbabwe) http://site.mweb.co.zw/wildaf/.

Women's Human Rights Net
(Zagreb) www.babe.hr/.

Women's Human Rights Resources
www.law-lib.utoronto.ca/diana.

Women's International Cross-Cultural Exchange (ISIS-WICCE)
(Uganda) www.isis.or.ug/.

Women's International League for Peace and Freedom
www.wilpf.org.

Working Class Movement Library
www.wcml.org.uk.

Working TV
(Canada, labor) http://workingtv.com.

World's Indigenous Women's Network
www.sixkiller.com.

World Socialist Web Site
www.wsws.org.

WTOACTION.org
(grassroots activism against the WTO, major links) http://wtoaction.org.

Young Democratic Socialists
(US) www.ydsusa.org.

Youth Activism.Org
www.youthactivism.org.

YouthPeace
(US, against militarism and police brutality) www.nonviolence.org.

Zapatistas in Cyberspace: A Guide to Analysis and Resources.
www.eco.utexas.edu/faculty/Cleaver/zapsinvcyber.html.

A List of Journals that Go
Against the Grain

Abafazi (journal of women of African Descent) (US)
Aboriginal Voices (contemporary Native lifestyles and cultural issues) (Canada)
Abya Yala News: Journal of the South and Meso American Indian Rights Center (US)
Accord (international review of peace initiatives) (UK)
Ace: The Association of Clandestine Radio Enthusiasts Newsletter (US)
Ache: A Journal for Black Lesbians (US)
Achilles Heel (radical men's magazine) (UK)
Action for Solidarity (labor) (UK)
Adbusters: A Journal of the Mental Environment (interrogation of advertising, and con-
    sumer activism) (Canada)
Advocate: The National Gay and Lesbian News Magazine (US)
Advertising Age Magazine (what's up in the industry) (US)
Affilia: Journal of Women and Social Work (US)
African American Review (literature and culture) (US)
African Studies Quarterly (electronic) (US)
Afterimage: The Journal of Media Arts and Cultural Criticism (US)
Against the Current (current world events and activism) (US)
Agenda: Empowering Women for Gender Equity (South Africa)
Albion Monitor: The News You're Missing (US)
Al-Raida (social, economic, and legal conditions of women in the Arab world) (Lebanon)
Alternatives: Social Transformation and Humane Government (international relations and
    politics) (Canada)
Alternatives Economique (political economy) (France)
Alternatives Journal: Environmental Thought, Policy, and Action (Canada)
Amerasia (Asian-American issues) (US)
American Dispatches (investigative journalism) (US)
American Ethnologist (US)
American Historical Review (US)
American Imago (psychoanalysis and culture) (US)
American Indian Culture and Research Journal (US)
American Journalism Review (US)

American Prospect: A Journal for the Liberal Imagination (politics, news, and social policy) (US)

American Quarterly (cross-disciplinary approaches to culture) (US)

American Spectator (general news) (US)

Amicus Journal: A Publication of the Natural Resources Defense Council (US)

AMPO: Japan-Asia Quarterly Review (news and politics) (Japan)

Anarchist Studies (theory, history, and culture) (UK)

Anarcho-Syndicalist Review (anarchism and the labor movement) (US)

Angelaki: Journal of the Theoretical Humanities (UK)

Angles (contemporary events, politics, arts, and entertainment from a Translesbigay perspective (Canada)

Antipode: A Radical Journal of Geography (US)

Arab Studies Quarterly (US)

Archipelago: Cuadernos de Critica de la Cultura (cultural criticism) (Spain)

Arena Journal (critical and feminist theory) (Australia)

Arena Magazine: The Australian Magazine of Left Political, Social, and Cultural Commentary (Australia)

Arethusa (literature and cultural studies of the ancient world) (US)

Ariel: A Review of International English Literature (Canada)

Arizona Journal of Hispanic Cultural Studies (US)

Art Forum (US)

Art Journal (US)

Asheville Global Report (electronic) (US)

Asian Ethnicity (UK)

Asian Journal of Women's Studies (Korea)

Asian Labour Update (Hong Kong)

Asian Survey (contemporary Asian affairs) (US)

Assemblage: A Critical Journal of Architecture and Design Culture (US)

Association of Lesbian/Gay and Bisexual Psychologies Newsletter (Germany)

Astrolabe (electronic) (ethical navigation through virtual technologies) (US)

Atlantis: A Women's Study Journal (Canada)

Aufheben: Revolutionary Perspectives (socialist research and activism) (UK)

Australian Bulletin of Labour (Australia)

Australian Feminist Law Journal (Australia)

Australian Feminist Studies (Australia)

Australian Humanities Review (electronic) (interdisciplinary) (Australia)

Australian Journal of Anthropology (Australia)

Australian Journal of Cultural Studies (Australia)

Australian Marxist Review (Australia)

Auto Free Times: Revolutionary Ecology and Economics (US)

Aztlan: A Journal of Chicano Studies (US)

Bad Subjects: Political Education for Everyday Life (electronic) (US)

Bay Windows (Boston Gay and Lesbian newspaper) (US)

Belles Lettres (feminism and cultural studies) (US)

Berkeley Journal for Theoretical Studies in Media and Culture (US)

Berkeley Journal of Sociology: A Critical Review (US)

Berkeley Women's Law Journal (civil rights) (US)

Bill of Rights Journal (civil rights) (US)

Bitch: The Feminist Response to Pop Culture (US)
Black Scholar: Journal of Black Studies and Research (US)
Blu (pop culture, politics, and spirituality) (US)
Body & Society (cultural and political analyses of the body) (UK)
Bogong: The Journal of the Canberra and South-East Region Environment Centre (Australia)
Bombay Dost (news of sexual minorities) (India)
Border Crossings (electronic) (Australia)
Borderlines (political and environmental life on the Mexican/US border) (US)
Border/Lines (art, literature, and cultural criticism) (Canada)
Boston Review: A Political and Literary Forum (US)
Boundary 2 (international literature and culture) (US)
Boycott Action News (environmental justice and labor) (US)
Briarpatch (politics and activism) (Canada)
Bridges: A Journal for Jewish Feminists and Our Friends (US)
Broadsheet (feminist issues) (New Zealand)
Bulletin of Concerned Asian Scholars (US)
Bulletin of the Atomic Scientists (peace activists) (US)
Business Ethics: Corporate Social Responsibility Report (US)
Cahiers Marxiste (Belgium)
Callaloo (African and African-American literary journal) (US)
California Prisoner (prisoner rights) (US)
Camera Obscura: A Journal of Feminism and Film Theory (US)
Canadian Dimension (activists interested in Canadian politics and labor) (Canada)
Canadian Ethnic Studies Journal (Canada)
Canadian Journal of Communication (Canada)
Canadian Journal of Women and the Law (Canada)
Canadian Women Studies/Les Cahiers de la Femme (Canada)
Cantilevers (ideas and resources for peace) (UK)
Capital and Class (research and activism) (UK)
Capital Gay (electronic) (Lesbian and Gay issues) (UK)
Capitalism, Nature, Socialism: A Journal of Socialist Ecology (US)
Car Busters (alternatives to gas operated transportation) (France)
CARF: Campaign Against Racism and Facism (UK)
Caribbean Labour Journal (Jamaica)
Caribbean Quarterly (Jamaica)
Caribbean Studies (US)
Calyx: A Journal of Art and Literature by Women (US)
Censorship News (US)
Center/Fold: Toronto Centre for Lesbian & Gay Studies Newsletter (Canada)
Chartist: For Democratic Socialism (UK)
Chiapas (Mexican cultural politics) (Mexico)
China Rights Forum: The Journal of Human Rights in China (US)
Church & State (people united for the separation in the US) (US)
CineAction (progressive film movements) (Canada)
Cineaste: America's Leading Magazine on the Art and Politics of Cinema (US)
Cinema Journal (from the Society for Cinema Studies) (US)
Citizenship Studies (citizenship and human rights) (US)
City Limits: New York's Urban Affairs News Magazine (US)

City & Society (urban, national, and transnational/global anthropology, presented by SUNTA as part of the American Anthropological Association) (US)

Civic Arts Review: Ideas and Practices for Good Citizenship (US)

Civil Rights Journal (US)

Clamor: New Perspectives on Politics, Culture, Media, and Life (US)

Claridad: El Periodico de la Nacion Puertorriquna (general news in Puerto Rico) (Puerto Rico)

Collective Action News (labor movements) (US)

College Literature (theory, pedagogy, and literary criticism) (US)

Colonial Latin American Review (US)

Colorlines Magazine: Race, Culture, and Action (US)

Colors: Opinion and the Arts in Communities of Color (US)

Columbia Bulletin: A Human Rights Quarterly (US)

Columbia Journalism Review (US)

Columbia Journal of Gender and Law (US)

Comenius: Wetenschappelijk Forum voor Opvoeding, Onderwijs, en Cultuur (feminism, politics, and culture) (Holland)

Common Dreams: Breaking News and Views for the Progressive Community (electronic) (US)

Common Sense: Journal of Edinburgh Conference of Socialist Economists (UK)

Communal/Plural: Journal of Transnational and Crosscultural Studies (UK)

Communication Theory (US)

Communique (biodiversity and intellectual property) (Canada)

Communist and Post-Communist Studies (international communist and postcommunist states and movements) (US)

Community Media Review (US)

Conditions (feminist/Lesbian writers) (US)

Configuration: A Journal of Literature, Science, and Technology (US)

Consortium (electronic) (current events) (US)

Constellations: An International Journal of Critical and Democratic Theory (US)

Consumption, Markets, and Culture (interdisciplinary approaches to national and global consumption) (US)

Continuum: Journal of Media & Cultural Studies (Australia)

Co-op: America's Boycott Action News (US)

Counterpoise: For Social Responsibilities, Liberty, and Dissent (US)

Counterpunch (investigative reporting of politics, big business, and corruption) (US)

Corporate Watch (UK)

Covert Action Quarterly (investigative journalism) (US)

Critical Arts: A Journal of Cultural Studies (South Africa)

Critical Asian Studies (US)

Critical Horizons: A Journal of Social and Critical Theory (Australia)

Critical Inquiry (cultural studies, critical theory, literature) (US)

Critical inQueeries (Australia)

Critical Matrix: The Princeton Journal of Women, Gender, and Culture (US)

Critical Musicology Journal (electronic) (UK)

Critical Public Health (UK)

Critical Quarterly (literary criticism and cultural studies) (UK)

Critical Review: An Interdisciplinary Journal of Politics and Society (US)

Critical Sociology (US)

Critical Social Policy: A Journal of Theory and Practice in Social Welfare (socialist, feminist, and anarchist perspectives) (UK)

Critical Studies in Mass Communication (US)

Critique: A Journal of Socialist Theory (Scotland)

Critique: A Journal for Critical Studies of the Middle East (US)

Critique of Anthropology: A Journal for the Critical Reconstruction of Anthropology (UK)

Crone Chronicles: A Journal for Conscious Aging (US)

Crosscurrents (promoting human rights, democracy, and social and economic justice in Latin America) (US)

Ctheory (electronic) (international journal of theory, technology, and culture) (Canada)

Cuba Update (politics, economics, and art) (US)

Cultronix (electronic) (interdisciplinary journal of art and cultural studies) (US)

Culture and Organization (UK)

Cultural Anthropology (from the Society for Cultural Anthropology) (US)

Cultural Critique (cultural studies, feminism, critical theory, literature) (US)

Cultural Dynamics (sociology, psychology, and philosophy) (UK)

Cultural Logic: An Electronic Journal of Marxist Theory and Practice (US)

Cultural Studies – Critical Methodologies (UK)

Cultural Studies: Theorizing Politics, Politicizing Theory (US)

Cultural Studies from Birmingham (electronic) (UK)

Cultural Survival Quarterly: World Report on the Rights of Indigenous Peoples and Ethnic Minorities (US)

Culture Machine (electronic) (international research and theory in culture) (UK)

Culture, Theory, and Critique (UK)

Curve Magazine: The Nation's Best-Selling Lesbian Magazine (US)

Daedalus: Journal of the American Academy of Arts and Sciences (US)

Dalhousie Review (literary review and critique) (Canada)

Dark Night Field Notes (anthropology and Native peoples) (US)

Dear Habermas: A Journal of Postmodern and Critical Thought Devoted to Academic Discourse on Peace and Justice (electronic) (US)

Debate: Voices from the South African Left (South Africa)

Debate Feminista (feminist research and theory) (Mexico)

Democracy and Nature: The International Journal of Inclusive Democracy (environment and social justice) (UK)

Democratic Left (activists for socialism) (US)

Der Feminist: Beitraege zur Theorie und Praxis (feminist issues) (Germany)

Detours & Delays: An Occasional Journal of Aesthetics and Politics (electronic) (UK)

Developments (fighting against poverty in developing nations) (UK)

Diacritics (literary criticism) (US)

Dialectica: Revista de Filosofia, Ciencias Sociales, Literatura y Cultura Politica de la Bene-merita Universidad Autonoma de Puebla (critical social theory) (Mexico)

Dialectical Anthropology: An Independent International Journal in the Critical Tradition Committed to the Transformation of Our Society and the Humane Union of Theory and Practice (US)

Dialogue & Initiative: Journal of Theory and Practice of the Committees of Correspondence (Marxist thought and action) (US)

Diaspora: A Journal of Transnational Studies (Canada)

di Base (alternative labor unions) (Italy)

Die Philosophin: Forum fuer Feministche Theorie und Philosophie (feminist theory and philosophy) (Germany)

Differences: A Journal of Feminist Cultural Studies (US)

Disability and Society (human rights and discrimination) (UK)

Disability Studies Quarterly (US)

Disclosure: The National Newspaper of Neighborhoods (community organizing) (US)

disClosure: A Journal of Social Theory (US)

Discourse (cultural studies, media, literature, and sexuality) (US)

Discourse: A Journal for Theoretical Studies in Media and Culture (US)

Discourse: Studies in the Cultural Politics of Education (Australia)

Discourse & Society: An International Journal for the Study of Discourse and Communication in their Social, Political, and Cultural Contexts (UK)

Dissent (politics and policy) (US)

Dollars and Sense: What's Left in Economics (US)

Double Take (photography and social issues) (US)

Earth First! Journal: The Radical Environmental Journal (US)

Earth Island Journal: International Environmental News (US)

East Timor Estafeta (voice of the East Timor Action Network) (US)

Eat the State (political news) (US)

Echanges: Bulletin du Reseau "Echanges et Movement" (labor and class analysis) (France)

Ecologist (political economy and the environment) (UK)

Econews (environmental justice) (US)

Economic and Industrial Democracy: An International Journal (Sweden)

Economic and Political Weekly (India)

Economy and Society (political economy and cultural studies) (UK)

Ecumene: A Journal of Cultural Geographies (UK)

El Acratador: Counterinformation Bulletin of the Ateneo Libertario of Zaragoza (Spain)

ELH: A Journal of English Literary History (US)

Emanzipation: Femistiche Zeitschrift fur Kritische Frauen (feminism) (Germany)

Emergences: Journal for the Study of Media and Composite Cultures (US)

Emperor's Clothes: Piercing a Fog of Lies (electronic) (global current events) (US)

Enculturation: A Journal of Rhetoric, Writing, and Culture (US)

Envio (current events in Central America) (Nicaragua)

Environmental Action Magazine (electronic) (Australia)

E: The Environment Magazine (electronic) (US)

Ethnic and Racial Studies (UK)

Ethnicities (interdisciplinary dialogue on issues of nation and identity) (UK)

Ethos: The Journal of the Society for Psychological Anthropology (US)

European Journal of Communication (theory and research) (UK)

European Journal of Cultural Studies (UK)

European Journal of Social Theory (challenges facing the social sciences) (UK)

European Journal of Women's Studies (UK)

European Labor Forum (UK)

Extra! Fairness and Accuracy in Reporting: The Magazine of FAIR (US)

EZLN (electronic) (information on the Zapatistas) (Mexico)

Fem (third world women's issues) (Mexico)

Feminisms (US)

Feminista (electronic) (US)

Feminist Art Journal (US)

Feminist Collections: A Quarterly of Women's Studies Resources (US)

Feminist Economics: Journal of the International Association for Feminist Economics (US)

Feminist Ethics (activism) (US)

Feminist Issues: A Journal of Feminist Social and Political Theory (US)

Feminist Media Studies (US)

Feminist Review (UK)

Feminist Studies (US)

Feminist Studies in Aotearoa Journal (New Zealand)

Feminist Teacher (US)

Feminist Theory: An International Interdisciplinary Journal (UK)

Film Quarterly (US)

Foreign Control Watchdog (New Zealand)

Foreign Policy in Focus (US)

49th Parallel: An Interdisciplinary Journal of North American Studies (UK)

Free Associations: Psychoanalysis, Groups, Politics, Culture (UK)

French Studies (published for the Society for French Studies) (UK)

Frontiers: A Journal of Women's Studies (US)

Fuse Magazine (arts and investigative journalism) (Canada)

Gay & Lesbian Review (literature and culture worldwide) (US)

Gay Times (UK)

GCN: The National Queer Progressive Quarterly (US)

Gender and Education (US)

Gender and History (UK)

Gender and Society (US)

Gender Issues (US)

Gender, Place and Culture: A Journal of Feminist Geography (UK)

Genders: Presenting Innovative Work in the Arts, Humanities, and Social Theories (US)

Gender, Technology, and Development (international explorations of linkages between gender relations and technological development) (India)

Gender, Work, and Organization (UK)

GeneWatch: A Bulletin for the Council for Responsible Genetics (activists in biotechnology) (US)

Global Society: Journal of Interdisciplinary International Relations (UK)

Global Update Seattle Newsletter (US)

GLQ: A Journal of Lesbian and Gay Studies (US)

Granta (literary magazine) (UK)

Grassroots Economic Organizing Newsletter (US)

Grassroots Fundraising Journal (US)

Green Guide (environmental issues) (US)

Green Journal (electronic) (environmental issues) (US)

Green Left Weekly (environment and socialism) (Australia)

Green Teacher (enhancing environmental and global education) (Canada)

Haiti Progress (Haiti)

Haringey Solidarity Group Newsletter (civil rights struggles in North London) (UK)

Hecate: An Interdisciplinary Journal of Women's Liberation (Australia)

Hedgehog Review (interdisciplinary approach to contemporary culture) (US)

Heresies: A Feminist Publication on Art and Politics (US)

Herizons Magazine (political issues for women) (Malaysia)

Historical Materialism: Research in Critical Marxist Theory (UK)

Historical Studies in Industrial Relations (UK)

History Workshop Journal (European labor and feminist concerns) (UK)

Holocaust and Genocide Studies (US)

Homologie Documentatiecentrum Homostudies (Lesbian and Gay studies) (Holland)

Human Rights Monitor (Switzerland)

Human Rights Solidarity (Hong Kong)

Human Rights Tribune/Tribune des Droits Humains (Canada)

Human Rights Watch (US)

Hurricane Alice: A Feminist Quarterly (US)

Hypatia: A Journal of Feminist Philosophy (US)

Idea Central: The Virtual Magazine of the Electronic Network (electronic) (resources) (US)

Identities: Global Studies in Culture and Power (explores racial, ethnic, and national identities) (US)

Il Paese Delle Donne (feminism) (Italy)

Images: A Journal of the Gay and Lesbian Alliance Against Defamation (US)

Impact Press: Covering Issues the Way the Media Should (electronic) US)

In Context/Yes! (covers the sustainability movement) (US)

Index on Censorship: The Magazine for Free Speech (UK)

Indian Journal of Gender Studies (India)

IndiaStar Review of Books (US)

Industrial and Labor Relations Review (US)

Industrial Worker (US)

Indymedia (electronic) (of IMC: Independent Media Center; grassroots, noncorporate coverage of global news) (US)

Infusion: The National Magazine for Progressive Student Activists (US)

Iniciativa Socialista (critical theory) (Spain)

In Motion Magazine (electronic) (multiculturalism and democracy) (US)

Inquiry: An Interdisciplinary Journal of Philosophy (Norway)

Intelligence Report (analysis of political extremism and bias crimes) (US)

Interact (newsletter of Amnesty International USA Women's Human Rights Program) (US)

Inter-Asia Cultural Studies (UK)

International Feminist Journal of Politics (UK)

International Gay and Lesbian Review (US)

International Journal of Cultural Policy (UK)

International Journal of Cultural Studies (Australia)

International Labor and Working-Class History (global labor movements) (US)

International Migration Review (US)

International Socialism: A Quarterly Journal of Socialist Theory (UK)

International Socialist Forum (electronic) (UK)

International Socialist Review: A Quarterly Journal of Revolutionary Marxism (US)

International Viewpoint (international relations and socialism) (UK)

Intersections: Gender, History and Culture in the Asian Context (electronic) (Australia)

Interventions: International Journal of Postcolonial Studies (UK)

In the Family: A Magazine for Lesbians, Gays, Bisexuals and their Relations (US)

In These Times (news and social policy) (US)

Iris: A Journal about Women (US)

JAC: A Journal of Composition Theory (US)

JoSCCI: Journal of Social Change and Critical Inquiry (social, cultural, and political causes and effects of globalization) (Australia)

Journal for Cultural and Religious Theory (US)

Journalism: Theory, Practice, and Criticism (US)

Journal of Aesthetic and Art Criticism (US)

Journal of African Cultural Studies (UK)

Journal of Asian American Studies (US)

Journal of Asian Studies (US)

Journal of Baha'I Studies (Canada)

Journal of Black Studies (US)

Journal of British Studies (US)

Journal of Broadcasting and Electronic Media (US)

Journal of Cinema and Cultural Theory (India)

Journal of Collective Negotiations in the Public Sector (labor) (US)

Journal of Commonwealth Literature (UK)

Journal of Communication (US)

Journal of Communication Inquiry (US)

Journal of Community Practice (research, theory, and practice for community groups and organizing) (US)

Journal of Consumer Culture (UK)

Journal of Criminal Justice and Popular Culture (electronic) (US)

Journal of Culture and Communication (arts, media, pop culture) (US)

Journal of Democracy (theory and practice of democracy) (US)

Journal of Feminist Studies in Religion (US)

Journal of Film & Video (US)

Journal of Gender Studies (UK)

Journal of Homosexuality (US)

Journal of Intercultural Studies (globalization and identity) (Australia)

Journal of International Women's Studies (US)

Journal of Latin American Anthropology (US)

Journal of Latin American Cultural Studies (UK)

Journal of Lesbian Studies (US)

Journal of Material Culture (explores the relationship between artifacts and social relations) (UK)

Journal of Narrative Theory: A Triannual Journal in Culture and Criticism (US)

Journal of Palestine Studies: A Quarterly on Palestinian Affairs and the Arab–Israeli Conflict (US)

Journal of Peace Research (Norway)

Journal of Political Ecology: Case Studies in History and Society (US)

Journal of Political Ideologies (UK)

Journal of Popular Culture (US)

Journal of Popular Film and Television (US)

Journal of Prisoners on Prisons (Canada)

Journal of South Asian Women's Studies (Italy)

Journal of Spanish Cultural Studies (international perspectives on notions of Spanish culture) (US)

Journal of the History of Sexuality (US)

Journal of Urban Affairs (US)

Journal of Visual Culture (UK)

Journal of Women and Religion (US)

Journal of Women's History (US)

Journal X: A Biannual Journal in Culture and Criticism (US)

Jouvert: A Journal of Postcolonial Studies (electronic) (US)

J_Spot: Journal of Social and Political Thought (electronic) (Canada)

Jump Cut: A Review of Contemporary Media (US)

Kalliope: A Journal of Women's Art and Literature (US)

Kaurapuuro (anarchist culture) (Finland)

Kinesis: News about Women that's not in the Dailies (Canada)

Kunapipi: Journal of Post-Colonial Writing (Australia)

Labor, Capital, and Society/Travail, Capital, et Societe: A Journal on the Third World (Canada)

Labor History (US)

Labor Notes: The State of Native America (union movements) (US)

Labor Studies Journal (US)

Labyrinth: International Journal for Philosophy, Feminist Theory, and Cultural Hermeneutics (electronic) (Austria)

Language and Literature (UK)

Lateral: A Journal of Textual and Cultural Studies (electronic) (Australia)

Latin American Literary Review (US)

Latin American Perspectives: A Journal on Capitalism and Socialism (US)

Left Business Observer (economics) (US)

Left Curve (art and cultural critique) (US)

Left History: An Interdisciplinary Journal of Historical Inquiry and Debate (Canada)

Lies of Our Times (US)

Lesbian and Gay Law Notes (publication of the Lesbian and Gay Law Association of greater New York) (US)

Lesbian Herstory Archives Newsletter (US)

Lesbian News (US)

Letras Femeninas (journal of the Asociacion de Literatura Femenina Hispanica; scholarship and literature of Latina women) (US)

Lila: Asia Pacific Women's Studies Journal (from the Institute of Women's Studies) (Philippines)

Lilith: The Jewish Women's Magazine (US)

Limina: A Journal of Historical and Cultural Studies (Australia)

Links: International Journal of Socialist Renewal (Australia)

Lip Magazine (electronic) (US)

Literature/Film Quarterly (US)

Live Culture (art, media, and cultural studies) (electronic) (US)

LM (news and art criticism) (UK)

Lola Press (feminist international and interdisciplinary magazine) (Germany)

Lumpen Magazine (culture, media, and politics) (US)

Manushi: A Journal about Women and Society (Indian political, economic, and social issues) (India)

M/C: A Journal of Media and Culture (electronic) (Australia)

Meanjin Quarterly (literature and the arts) (Australia)

Media, Culture, and Society (UK)

Media, Culture, and Technology (electronic) (Sweden)

MediaFile (media activism and investigative journalism) (US)

Media International Australia: Incorporating Culture and Policy Journal (Australia)

Media Report to Women (US)

Mediations: On-line Publication of the Marxist Literary Group (electronic) (US)

Media Watch (US)

Men and Masculinities (gender research) (US)

Meridians (feminism, race, transnationalism) (US)

Mexican Labor News and Analysis (Mexico)

Middle East Report (political movements) (US)

Minerva: An Internet Journal of Philosophy (electronic) (Ireland)

MLN (critical studies in modern languages and comparative literature) (US)

Modern Asian Studies (UK)

Modern Fiction Studies (US)

Modern Jewish Studies (UK)

Modernism/Modernity (from 1860 to the present, studies in music, architecture, visual art, literature, and social history) (US)

Modern Language Notes (critical studies in language and literature) (US)

Monthly Labor Review (US)

Monthly Review: An Independent Socialist Magazine (political economy and socialist movements) (US)

Mother Earth News (health and nature) (US)

Mother Jones: Exposes and Politics (media, culture, and politics) (US)

Mots Pluriels (Australia)

Mouth: Voice of the Disability Nation (US)

Moving Out: A Feminist Literary and Arts Journal (US)

Ms. (women's issues) (US)

Mujer/Fempress: Red de Communicacion Alternativa de la Mujer (Third World women's issues) (Chile)

Multinational Monitor (labor rights and transnational corporations) (US)

NACLA: Report on the Americas (North American Congress on the Americas, US foreign policy and Latin America) (US)

National Catholic Reporter (US)

Native Americas (US)

Nature, Society and Thought: A Journal of Dialectical and Historical Materialism (Marxist analysis) (US)

NCCWO Bulletin (National Lawyers Guild and the National Committee to Combat Women's Oppression) (US)

Negations: An Interdisciplinary Journal of Social Thought (US)

New Art Examiner (US)

New Formations (interdisciplinary journal of culture, politics, and theory (UK)

New German Critique (critical theory and cultural studies) (US)

New Interventions: A Journal of Socialist Discussion and Opinion (UK)

New Labor Forum: A Journal of Ideas, Analysis, and Debate (US)

New Left Review (critical theory) (UK)

New Literary History (reasons for literary change) (US)

New Party News: A Fair Economy, a Real Democracy, a New Party (US)

New Perspectives Quarterly (current affairs) (UK)

New Political Economy (social policy) (UK)

New Politics: A Journal of Socialist Thought (opposition to all forms of imperialism) (US)

News and Letters (Marxist news) (US)

Newsletter on Intellectual Freedom (censorship issues) (US)

N-Media-C: The Journal of New Media and Culture (electronic) (US)

Nonviolent Activist: The Magazine of the War Resisters League (peace movements) (US)

Nora: Nordic Journal of Women's Studies (Norway)

NWSA Journal (a publication of the National Women's Studies Association) (US)

October (art, history, criticism, and politics) (US)

Off Our Backs: The Feminist Newsjournal (Feminist and Lesbian issues) (US)

On the Issues: The Progressive Women's Quarterly (US)

Other Voices: The (e) Journal of Cultural Criticism (electronic) (US)

Our Times: Canada's Independent Labour Magazine (Canada)

Out Magazine (New Mexico's Gay, Lesbian, and Bisexual news) (US)

Oxford Literary Review (UK)

Pacifica Review: Peace, Security, and Global Change (Australia)

Paideusis: Journal for Interdisciplinary and Cross-cultural Studies (electronic) (Romania)

Pakistan Journal of Women's Studies (Pakistan)

Paragraph (critical theory) (UK)

Parallel: Gallery//Journal (electronic) (postmodernism and poststructuralism) (Australia)

Passages: Journal of Transnational and Transcultural Studies (US)

Peace and Change: A Journal of Peace Research (US)

Peace and Freedom: Magazine of the Women's International League for Peace and Freedom (US)

Peace Magazine (peace movements) (Canada)

Peace News for Nonviolent Revolution (global nonviolent peace movements) (UK)

Peace Review (global) (US)

PeaceWork: Global Thought and Action for Non-Violent Social Change (US)

Perforations (electronic) (art, theory, technology, and community) (US)

Philosophy and Social Criticism: An International, Inter-disciplinary Journal (US)

Political Affairs: Theoretical Journal, Communist Party USA (US)

Political Environments (environmental and feminist issues) (US)

Political Theory: An International Journal of Political Philosophy (US)

Politics and Society (political economy and sociology) (US)

Polygraph: An International Journal of Culture and Politics (US)

Pop Matters: The Magazine of Global Culture (electronic) (US)

Positions: East Asia Cultures Critique (US)

Postcolonial Studies: Culture, Politics, Economy (Australia)

Postmodern Culture (electronic) (US)

Post/Urban Textualities (literacy and technology) (US)

Poverty and Race (US)

PRE/TEXT: A Journal of Rhetorical Theory (US)

Proactivist.Com News (electronic) (US)

Processed World Magazine (electronic) (pop cultural subversive practice) (US)

Progressive (current events) (US)

Progressive Populist (newspaper on labor in the heartland) (US)

Progressive Response (electronic) (US)

Progressive Review (electronic) (news that takes on the Washington establishment) (US)

Public Culture (cultural studies) (US)

Pursuit of Happiness: A Journal of Radical Social Critique (neo-Marxist and postmodern perspectives) (US)

Quarterly Review of Film and Video (US)

Qui Parle (critical work in the humanities) (US)

qvMagazine (Gay Latino issues) (US)

Race & Class: A Journal for Black and Third World Liberation (UK)

Race, Gender & Class: An Interdisciplinary and Multicultural Journal (US)

Race Traitor: Treason to Whiteness is Loyalty to Humanity (US)

Radical America (labor and class analysis) (US)

Radical Chains (Marxism) (UK)

Radical History Review (labor and socialist histories) (US)

Radical Philosophy: A Journal of Socialist and Feminist Philosophy (UK)

Radical Philosophy Review: A Journal of Progressive Thought (US)

Radical Psychology: A Journal of Psychology, Politics, and Radicalism (electronic) (US)

Radical Teacher: A Socialist, Feminist Journal on the Theory and Practice of Teaching (US)

Ragged Edge (disability issues and human rights) (US)

Raritan (literature, history, and criticism) (US)

Realidad Economico: Revista de Economico (Marxism and political economy) (Argentina)

Red Pepper: The Magazine for Free Radicals (European culture and socialism) (UK)

Religious Socialism (publication of the Religion and Socialism Commission of the Democratic Socialists of America) (US)

Representations (art, literature, history, anthropology, and social theory) (US)

Research in African Literatures (US)

Resist Newsletter (global resistance movements) (US)

Resources for Feminist Research/Documentation sur la Recherche Feministe (Canada)

Resurgence Magazine (ecological economics) (UK)

Rethinking Marxism: A Journal of Economics, Culture, and Society (US)

Rethinking Schools (US)

Review of Black Political Economy (Australia)

Review of Education/Pedagogy/Cultural Studies (US)

Review of Political Economy (US)

Review of Radical Political Economics (US)

Review of Social Economy (UK)

Revolutionary Marxism Today (US)

Revolutionary Worker (US)

Rock and Rap Confidential (music and politics newsletter) (US)

SAGE: A Scholarly Journal on Black Women (Canada)

Salem Review (electronic) (peace and justice in the Middle East) (US)

SAMAR: South Asian Magazine for Action and Reflection (South Asians living in the US) (US)

Science as Culture (cultural studies approaches to technology and science) (UK)

Science & Society: An Independent Journal of Marxism (US)
Science, Technology & Human Values (sponsored by the Society for the Social Studies of Science) (US)
Scope: An On-line Journal of Film Studies (electronic) (UK)
Screen (film and television studies) (UK)
Semiotica (journal of the International Association for Semiotic Studies) (Germany)
Sex Roles: A Journal of Research (US)
Sexualities: Studies in Culture and Society (human sexual experience in the late modern world) (UK)
Sexuality and Culture (sociocultural issues in sexuality) (US)
Sierra: Exploring, Enjoying, and Protecting the Planet (US)
Signs: A Journal of Women in Culture and Society (US)
Simile: Studies in Media and Information Literacy (Canada)
Sincronia (electronic) (social sciences and humanities) (Mexico)
Sinister Wisdom: A Journal for Lesbians (writers, poets, and artists) (US)
Sites: A Journal for South Pacific Cultural Studies (New Zealand)
Slovo (inter-disciplinary journal of Russian, Eurasian, and East European affairs) (UK)
Small Axe: Journal of Caribbean Cultural, Political, and Social Culture (UK)
Smoke Signals (electronic) (indigenous women's issues) (US)
Social Alternatives (environment and culture) (Australia)
Social Anthropology: The Journal of the European Association of Social Anthropologists (UK)
Social Criticism Review (alienation between people and nature) (Holland)
Social Identities: Journal for the Study of Race, Nation and Culture (UK)
Social Justice: A Journal of Crime, Conflict, and World Order (US)
Social Semiotics: A Transdisciplinary Journal in Functional Linguistics, Semiotics, and Critical Theory (Australia)
Socialism and Democracy (US)
Socialist Affairs: The Journal of the Socialist International (UK)
Socialist Register (political economy) (UK)
Socialist Renewal (policy initiatives) (UK)
Socialist Review (socialist politics and culture) (US)
Social Policy: The Magazine about Movements (US)
Social Politics: International Studies in Gender, State, and Society (US)
Social Problems Journal (US)
Social Theory and Practice: An International and Interdisciplinary Journal of Social Philosophy (US)
Social Text: A Journal of Cultural and Political Analysis (US)
Sociologie du Travail (labor) (France)
Sojouner: The Women's Forum (progressive politics) (US)
Souls: A Critical Journal of Black Politics, Culture, and Society (US)
South Atlantic Quarterly (social and cultural theory) (US)
Space and Culture (Canada)
SPAN: Journal of the South Pacific Association for Commonwealth Literature and Language Studies (New Zealand)
Spare Change (homeless newspaper) (US)
Standards: The International Journal of Multicultural Studies (US)
Stay Free (commercialism and culture in the US) (US)
Strategies: Journal of Theory, Culture & Politics (US)

Studies in Marxism (UK)

Studies in Political Economy: A Socialist Review (Canada)

Symbolic Interaction (research and theory around interpersonal conduct and experience) (US)

Subaltern Studies (postcolonial theory) (India)

Substance: A Review of Theory and Literature (US)

Surfaces (electronic) (culture) (Canada)

Survival News: AIDS Survival Project (a coalition of people affected by HIV) (US)

Symposium: Journal of the Canadian Society for Hermeneutics and Postmodern Thought (Canada)

Technology and Culture: The Journal of the Society for the History of Technology (US)

Television & New Media (trends in TV and new media studies) (US)

Telos (journal of political thought and critical theory) (US)

Ten (cultural studies) (UK)

Textual Practice (international journal of radical literary studies) (UK)

Thamyris (identity and art) (Holland)

The Activist (peace, ecology, and human rights) (Canada)

The Activist (electronic) (critical analyses of youth) (US)

The Advocate: The National Gay and Lesbian Newsmagazine (US)

The AHFAD Journal: Women and Change (Sudan)

The American Journal of Semiotics (US)

The Bay Area Reporter (San Francisco Gay and Lesbian news) (US)

The Canadian Forum (news on the popular cultural front) (Canada)

The Colombian Labor Monitor (struggle in Colombia) (US)

The Corner House (growth of a democratic, nondiscriminatory, civil society) (UK)

The Corporate Examiner: A Publication Examining Policies and Practices of Major US Corporations (US)

The Ecologist: Rethinking Basic Assumptions (UK)

The Edge: The E-Journal of Intercultural Relations (electronic) (US)

The European Journal for Semiotic Studies (Sweden)

The Evergreen Chronicles (Gay, Lesbian, Bisexual, and Transgendered art issues) (US)

The Freedom Socialist: Voice of Revolutionary Feminism (US)

The Frontal View (electronic) (African-centered thought) (US)

The Futurist: A Magazine of Forecast, Trends, and Ideas about the Future (US)

The Hammer: A Working Class Journal of Cultural Thought and Action (US)

The Humanist: A Magazine of Critical Inquiry and Social Concern (science, religion, politics, and popular culture) (US)

The Laborer (union and labor issues) (US)

The Lesbian Connection Magazine: For, By, and About Lesbians (US)

The Militant (US)

The Nation (current events and political commentary) (US)

The New Internationalist (UK)

Theory and Society: Renewal and Critique in Social Theory (US)

Theory, Culture & Society: Explorations in Critical Social Science (UK)

Theory & Event (electronic) (political theory and current events) (US)

The Public Eye (monitors and analyzes right-wing movements) (US)

Thesis Eleven: Rethinking Social and Political Theory (Australia)

The Southern Review (literature and critical commentary on US Southern culture and history) (US)

The Web Journal of French Media Studies (electronic) (UK)

Third World Quarterly: Journal of Emerging Areas (political economy) (UK)

Third World Resurgence (Philippines)

13th Moon: A Feminist Literary Magazine (US)

Tikkun: A Bimonthly Jewish Critique of Politics, Culture, and Society (US)

Thresholds: Viewing Culture (electronic) (US)

Topia: A Canadian Journal of Cultural Studies (Canada)

Torquere: A Journal of the Canadian Lesbian and Gay Studies Association (Canada)

Toward Freedom: A Progressive Perspective of World Events (electronic) (US)

Tradeswomen (labor and feminism) (US)

Transformations: A Resource for Curriculum Transformation and Scholarship (women's studies) (US)

Transgender Tapestry: Celebrating Our Diversity of Gender Expression (US)

Transition: An International Review (Third World concerns with particular focus on Africa) (US)

Trouble and Strife: A Radical Feminist Magazine (UK)

Turning the Tide: A Journal of Anti-Racist Activism, Research, and Education (US)

Tyoplittinen Aikauskirja (labor) (Finland)

Undercurrent (electronic) (interdisciplinary analysis of pop culture) (US)

Union Democracy Review (US)

Urban Desires: An Interactive Magazine of Metropolitan Passion (electronic) (US)

Urban Ecology: Environment, Equity, Community Design (US)

Urban 75 (electronic) (action news) (UK)

US–Japan Women's Journal: A Journal for the International Exchange of Gender Studies (Japan)

UTNE: The Best of the Alternative Media (US)

Velvet Light Trap (essays on issues in film studies) (US)

Virtual Sisterhood (ezine) (US)

Visual Anthropology Review: Journal of the Society for Visual Anthropology (US)

Visual Studies (UK)

Vmag (cultural issues in Japan) (Japan)

Voices of Thai Women (Bangkok)

Wasafiri: Caribbean, African, Asian and Associated Literatures in English (literature, art, film, and pedagogy) (UK)

Washington Monthly (political journalism) (US)

White Collar (union and labor issues) (US)

Whole Earth Review: Access to Tools, Ideas, and Practices (US)

Why Magazine: Challenging Hunger and Poverty (US)

Wildcat (leftist politics) (Germany)

Windy City Times (Chicago-based Gay and Lesbian newspaper) (US)

Women: A Cultural Review (UK)

Women and Criminal Justice (US)

Women and Language (US)

Women and Performance: A Journal of Feminist Theory (US)

Women and Work: News from the US Department of Labor (US)

Women in Action (Philippines)

Women's Rights Law Reporter (US)

Women's Studies Journal (New Zealand)

Women Studies in Communication (electronic) (Australia)

Women Studies International Forum (UK)

Women's International Network News (US)

Women's Studies Quarterly: An Educational Project of the Feminist Press at the City University of New York (US)

Working-Class Notes Newsletter (US)

Working USA (labor movements) (US)

Workplace: Journal of Academic Labor (electronic) (US)

World Literature Written in English (postcolonial literature) (Singapore)

World Views: A Quarterly Review of Resources for Education and Action (US)

World Watch: Working for a Sustainable Future (US)

Yale Journal of Criticism (US)

Yale Journal of Law and Feminism (US)

Yo! Youth Outlook: The World through Young People's Eyes (US)

Z Magazine (current international affairs and US foreign policy) (US)

Suggested Reading

The following is a list of suggested reading subdivided according to parts of the present volume. Entries marked with an asterisk are of particular interest.

Introduction

Dictionaries

- *Keywords: A Vocabulary of Culture and Society.* Raymond Williams. *
- *Basic Concepts in Sociology.* Max Weber.
- *The Dictionary of Anthropology.* (Ed.) Thomas Barfield.
- *The Penguin Dictionary of Psychology.* Arthur S. Reber.
- *The Concise Oxford Dictionary of Sociology.* (Ed.) Gordan Marshall.
- *The Blackwell Dictionary of Twentieth-Century Social Thought.* (Eds.) William Outhwaite and Tom Bottomore. *
- *The Social Science Encyclopedia.* (Eds.) Adam Kuper and Jesse Kuper.
- *A Dictionary of Modern Critical Terms.* Roger Fowler.
- *Dictionary of Cultural Theorists.* (Eds.) Ellis Cashmore and Chris Rojek. *
- *A Concise Glossary of Cultural Theory.* Peter Brooker.
- *A Dictionary of Cultural and Critical Theory.* (Ed.) Michael Payne. *
- *Cultural Criticism: A Primer of Key Concepts.* Arthur Asa Berger.
- *Key Concepts in Post-Colonial Studies.* (Eds.) Bill Ashcroft, Gareth Griffiths, and Helen Tiffin. *
- *Encyclopedia of Post-Colonial Literatures in English.* (Eds.) Eugene Benson and L. W. Conolly.
- *Key Concepts in Communication and Cultural Studies.* (Eds.) Tim O'Sullivan, John Hartley, Danny Saunders, and Martin Montgomery. *
- *The Routledge Critical Dictionary of Postmodern Thought.* (Ed.) Stuart Sim. *
- *The Development Dictionary: A Guide to Knowledge as Power.* (Ed.) Wolfgang Sachs.
- *Feminism and Psychoanalysis: A Critical Dictionary.* (Ed.) Elizabeth Wright.
- *The Dictionary of Feminist Theory.* Maggie Humm.
- *A Feminist Dictionary.* Cheris Kramarae, Paula A. Trichler, and Ann Russo. *

- *The Routledge Critical Dictionary of Feminism and Postfeminism.* (Ed.) Sarah Gamble. *
- *The Blackwell Dictionary of Political Science.* (Ed.) Frank Bealey.
- *The Concise Oxford Dictionary of Politics.* (Ed.) Iain McLean.
- *Safire's New Political Dictionary: The Definitive Guide to the New Language of Politics.* William Safire.
- *A New Dictionary of Political Analysis.* Geoffrey Roberts and Alistair Edwards.
- *A Dictionary of Political Thought.* Roger Scruton.
- *Black Women in America: An Historical Encyclopedia.* (Eds.) Darlene Clark Hine, Elsa Barkley Brown, and Rosalyn Terborg-Penn.
- *The Dictionary of World Politics: A Guide to Concepts, Ideas, and Institutions.* Graham Evans and Jeffrey Newnham.
- *A Dictionary of Diplomacy.* (Eds.) G. R. Berridge, Alan James, and Sir Brian Barder.
- *Dictionary of the Middle East.* Dilip Hiro.
- *Political Dictionary of Israel.* Bernard Reich and David H. Goldberg.
- *Dictionary of Human Rights Advocacy Organizations in Africa.* Santosh C. Saha.
- *Wall Street Dictionary.* Robert J. Shook.
- *Dictionary of Financial Terms.* Virginia B. Morris.
- *The American Political Dictionary.* Milton Greenberg and Jack C. Plano.
- *The Harper Collins Dictionary of American Government and Politics.* Jay M. Shafritz.
- *The Congress Dictionary: The Ways and Meanings of Capitol Hill.* Paul Dickson, Paul Clancy, and Thomas P. O'Neill.
- *Dictionary of American Legal Usage.* David Mellinkoff.
- *Historical Dictionary of Law Enforcement.* Mitchel P. Roth.

Introductory texts

- *Introducing Hegel.* Lloyd Spencer and Andrzej Krauze.
- *Marx for Beginners: Philosophy, Economic Doctrine, Historical Materialism.* (Eds.) Ruis and Tom Engelhardt. *
- *Kierkegaard for Beginners.* Donald D. Palmer.
- *Introducing Nietzsche.* Laurence Gane and Kitty Chan.
- *Saussure for Beginners.* W. Terrence Gordon. *
- *Freud for Beginners.* Richard Osborne.
- *Introducing Heidegger.* Jeff Colins and Howard Selina.
- *Introducing Walter Benjamin.* Howard Caygill, Alex Coles, and Andrzej Klimowski. *
- *Brecht for Beginners.* Michael Thoss.
- *Introducing Sartre.* Philip Thody.
- *Structuralism and Poststructuralism for Beginners.* Donald Palmer. *
- *Introducing Barthes.* Philip Thody and Ann Course. *
- *Introducing Lacan.* Darian Leader and Judy Groves.
- *Foucault for Beginners.* Lydia Alix Fillingham. *
- *Derrida for Beginners.* Jim Powell. *
- *Introducing Cultural Studies.* Ziauddin Sardar and Borin Van Loon. *
- *Teach Yourself Cultural Studies.* Will Brooker.
- *Introducing Postmodernism.* Richard Appignanesi and Chris Garratt.
- *Anarchism for Beginners.* Colin Ward.
- *Social Movements: An Introduction.* Donatella Della Porta and Mario Diani.

- *Building Bridges: The Emerging Grassroots Coalition of Labor and Community.* (Eds.) Jeremy Brecher and Tim Costello.
- *In the Tiger's Mouth: An Empowerment Guide for Social Action.* Katrina Shields.
- *Self, Identity, and Social Movements.* (Eds.) Sheldon Stryker, Timothy J. Owens, and Robert W. White.
- *Encyclopedia of American Activism: 1960 to the Present.* Margaret B. Dicanio. *
- *Organizing for Power and Empowerment.* Jacqueline B. Mondros and Scott M. Wilson.
- *Left Guide: A Guide to Left-of-Center Organizations.* (Ed.) Derk Arend Wilcox.
- *Let the People Decide: Neighborhood Organizing in America.* Robert Fisher.
- *Reclaiming America: Nike, Clean Air, and the New National Activism.* Randy Shaw. *
- *Power in Movement: Social Movements and Contentious Politics.* Sidney G. Tarrow.
- *Transnational Social Movements and Global Politics: Solidarity Beyond the State.* (Eds.) Jackie Smith, Charles Chatfield, and Ron Pagnucco.
- *Activists Beyond Borders: Advocacy Networks in International Politics.* Margaret E. Keck and Kathryn Sikkink.
- *Community Organizing: Building Social Capital as a Development Strategy.* Ross J. Gittell and Avis Vidal.
- *Organizing for Social Change.* Kim Bobo, Jackie Kendall, and Steve Max. *
- *The Activist's Handbook: A Primer.* Randy Shaw.
- *The Oxford History of the Prison.* Norval Morris.

Taking the next step

- *Contested Knowledge: A Guide to Critical Theory.* John Phillips.
- *Introduction to Critical Theory: Horkheimer to Habermas.* David Held. *
- *The Blackwell Companion to Social Theory.* (Ed.) Bryan S. Turner.
- *Breaking Free: The Transformative Power of Critical Pedagogy.* (Eds.) Pepi Leistyna, Arlie Woodrum, and Steve Sherblom. *
- *The Handbook of Critical Theory.* (Ed.) Davis M. Rassmussen.
- *Culture: Key Ideas.* Christopher Jenks.
- *The Terms of Cultural Criticism: The Frankfurt School, Existentialism, Poststructuralism.* Richard Wolin.
- *Structuralism and Since: From Levi-Strauss to Derrida.* (Ed.) John Sturrock. *
- *An Introductory Guide to Post-Structuralism and Postmodernism.* Madan Sarup.
- *What is Cultural Studies: A Reader.* (Ed.) John Storey. *
- *Studying Culture: An Introductory Reader.* (Eds.) Ann Gray and Jim McGuigan.
- *Introduction to Contemporary Cultural Studies.* David Plunter.
- *Tools for Cultural Studies.* Tony Thwaited, Loyd Davis, and Warick Mules.
- *British Cultural Studies.* Graeme Turner. *
- *Black British Cultural Studies: A Reader.* (Eds.) Houston Baker, Manthia Diawara and Ruth H. Lindeborg. *
- *Australian Cultural Studies: A Reader.* (Eds.) John Frow and Meaghan Morris. *
- *French Cultural Studies.* Jill Forbes and Michael Kelly.
- *Spanish Cultural Studies: An Introduction.* (Eds.) Helen Graham and Jo Labanyi.
- *German Cultural Studies: An Introduction.* (Ed.) Rob Burns.
- *South Asian Cultural Studies.* Vinay Lal.
- *Modern Chinese Literary and Cultural Studies in the Age of Theory: Reimagining a Field.* (Ed.) Rey Chow.

- *Relocating Cultural Studies.* (Eds.) Valda Blundell, John Shepard, and Ian Taylor.
- *Postmodern Theory: Critical Interrogations.* Steven Best and Douglas Kellner. *
- *Postmodernism: A Reader.* Thomas Docherty. *
- *The Concept of the Political.* Carl Schmitt.
- *The Common Courage Reader: Essays for an Informed Democracy.* (Ed.) Kevin Griffith. *
- *Ethics and Activism: The Theory and Practice of Political Morality.* Michael L. Gross.
- *Talking about a Revolution: Interviews with Michael Albert, Noam Chomsky, Barbara Ehrenreich, bell hooks, Peter Kwong, Winona Laduke, and Manning Marable.* South End Press Collective.
- *Civil Society 16.* (Eds.) Stuart Hall, Doreen Massey, Michael Rustin, and Andrea Hess.

Put on your seatbelt

- *Critique of Judgment.* Immanuel Kant.
- *Phenomenology of Spirit.* Georg Wilhelm Friedrich Hegel.
- *Das Capital.* Karl Marx. *
- *Fear and Trembling.* Søren Kierkegaard.
- *The World as Will and Representation.* Arthur Schopenhauer.
- *The Basic Bakunin: Writings 1869–1871.* (Ed.) Robert M. Cutler.
- *The Birth of Tragedy.* Friedrich Nietzsche.
- *Cours de Linguistique Generale (Course in General Linguistics).* Ferdinand de Saussure. *
- *Economy and Society: An Outline of Interpretive Sociology.* Max Weber.
- *Ideas – General Introduction to Pure Phenomenology.* Edmund Husserl.
- *Illuminations.* Walter Benjamin. *
- *The Illusions of Progress.* Georges Sorel.
- *Selections from the Prison Notebooks.* Antonio Gramsci. *
- *The Basic Problems of Phenomenology.* Martin Heidegger.
- *The Principle of Hope.* Ernst Bloch.
- *Mind and Society.* Lev Vygotsky. *
- *Marxism and the Philosophy of Language.* V. N. Voloshinov. *
- *The Dialogical Imagination.* Mikhail Bakhtin. *
- *Ideology and Utopia.* Karl Mannheim.
- *The Bataille Reader.* (Eds.) Fred Botting and Scott Wilson.
- *One-Dimensional Man.* Herbert Marcuse. *
- *The Dialectic of Enlightenment.* Max Horkheimer and Theodore Adorno. *
- *Phenomenology of Perception.* Maurice Merleau-Ponty.
- *The Fear of Freedom.* Erich Fromm.
- *Being and Nothingness.* Jean-Paul Sartre.
- *Everyday Life in the Modern World.* Henri Lefebvre.
- *On Revolution.* Hannah Arendt. *
- *Philosophical Investigations.* Ludwig Wittgenstein. *
- *Ecrit: A Selection.* Jacques Lacan.
- *The Uses of Literacy.* Richard Hoggart.
- *Culture and Society.* Raymond Williams. *
- *The Sociological Imagination.* Charles Wright Mills. *
- *Power/Knowledge: Selected Interviews and Other Writings 1972–1977.* Michel Foucault. *
- *Writings and Difference.* Jacques Derrida. *
- *Interpretation Theory: Discourse and the Surplus of Meaning.* Paul Ricoeur.

- *Toward a Rational Society*. Jürgen Habermas.
- *Habermas and the Public Sphere*. (Ed.) Craig Calhoun. *
- *Beyond Left and Right*. Anthony Giddens.
- *The Imaginary Institution of Society*. Cornelius Castoriadis. *
- *The Stanley Fish Reader*. (Eds.) Stanley Eugene Fish and H. Aram Veeser.
- *Styles of Radical Will*. Susan Sontag.
- *Blindness and Insight: Essays in the Rhetoric of Contemporary Criticism*. Paul de Man.
- *DeSchooling Society*. Ivan Illich.
- *Postmodernism or, the Cultural Logic of Late Capitalism*. Fredric Jameson. *
- *The Postmodern Condition: A Report on Knowledge*. Jean-François Lyotard. *
- *Stuart Hall: Critical Dialogues in Cultural Studies*. (Eds.) David Morley and Kuan-Hsing Chen. *
- *The Anti-Aesthetic: Essays on Postmodern Culture*. (Ed.) Hal Foster.
- *The Practices of Everyday Life*. Michel de Certeau.
- *Hegemony & Socialist Strategy: Towards a Radical Democratic Politics*. Ernesto Laclau and Chantal Mouffe. *
- *Mapping Ideology*. Slavoj Žižek.
- *Deconstruction in Context: Literature and Philosophy*. (Ed.) Mark C. Taylor.
- *The Predicament of Culture: Twentieth-Century Ethnography, Literature, and Art*. James Clifford.
- *The Dialectic of Freedom*. Maxine Greene.
- *The Poetics of Posmodernism*. Linda Hutcheon.
- *Uncommon Cultures*. Jim Collins.
- *The Transparent Society*. Gianni Vattimo.
- *The Mode of Information: Poststructuralism and Context*. Mark Poster. *
- *Ideology: The Politics of a Concept*. Michele Barrett.
- *Domination and the Arts of Resistance: Hidden Transcripts*. James C. Scott.
- *The Condition of Postmodernity*. David Harvey. *
- *Cultural Studies*. (Eds.) Lawrence Grossberg, Cary Nelson, and Paula Treichler. *
- *Out There: Marginalization and Contemporary Cultures*. (Eds.) Russel Ferguson, Martha Gever, Trinh T. Minh-ha, and Cornel West. *
- *Sources of the Self: The Making of the Modern Identity*. Charles Taylor. *
- *A Critical and Cultural Theory Reader*. (Eds.) Anthony Easthope and Kate McGowan.
- *From Modernism to Postmodernism*. (Ed.) Lawrence Cahoone. *
- *The Cultural Studies Reader*. (Ed.) Simon During. *
- *Theory as Resistance*. Mas'ud Zavarzadeh and Donald Morton. *
- *Between Borders: Pedagogy and the Politics of Cultural Studies*. (Eds.) Henry Giroux and Peter McLaren.
- *Postmodernism and Popular Culture*. Angela McRobbie. *
- *Relocating Cultural Studies: Developments in Theory and Research*. Valda Blundell, John Shepard, and Ian Taylor.
- *Geographical Imaginations*. Derek Gregory.
- *Cultural Studies*. Fred Inglis.
- *Cultural Politics: Class, Gender, Race, and the Postmodern World*. Glenn Jordan and Chris Weedon.
- *English Studies/Cultural Studies: Institutionalizing Dissent*. (Eds.) Isaiah Smithson and Nancy Ruff.
- *Multiculturalism: A Critical Reader*. (Ed.) David Theo Goldberg. *

- *Consumption and Identity at Work.* Paul du Gay.
- *Cultural Studies and Cultural Value.* John Frow. *
- *Modernity: An Introduction to Modern Societies.* (Eds.) Stuart Hall, David Held, Don Hubert, and Kenneth Thompson. *
- *Theorizing Culture: An Interdisciplinary Critique after Postmodernism.* (Eds.) Barbara Adam and Stuart Allan.
- *Borders, Boundaries, and Frames: Essays in Cultural Criticism and Cultural Studies.* (Ed.) Mae G. Henderson.
- *Hybrid Cultures: Strategies for Entering and Leaving Modernity.* Nestor Garcia Canclini and Silvia L. Lopez.
- *Legal Studies as Cultural Studies: A Reader in (Post)Modern Critical Theory.* (Ed.) Jerry Leonard.
- *Justice Interruptus: Critical Reflections on the "Postsocialist" Condition.* Nancy Fraser.
- *Democracy and Difference.* (Ed.) Seyla Benhabib. *
- *The Death and Rebirth of American Radicalism.* Stanley Aronowitz. *
- *Questions of Cultural Identity.* (Eds.) Stuart Hall and Paul du Gay. *
- *Disciplinarity and Dissent in Cultural Studies.* (Eds.) Cary Nelson and Dilip Parameshwar Gaonkar. *
- *Culture and Truth: The Remaking of Social Analysis.* Renato Rosaldo. *
- *Field Work: Sites in Literary and Cultural Studies.* (Eds.) Marjorie Garber and Rebecca L. Walkowitz.
- *Cultural Methodologies.* (Ed.) Jim McGuigan.
- *Introduction to Action Research: Social Research for Social Change.* Davydd J. Greenwood and Morten Levin.
- *From Sociology to Cultural Studies.* (Ed.) Elizabeth Long.
- *Bringing it all Back Home: Essays on Cultural Studies.* Lawrence Grossberg.
- *Cultural Studies in Question.* (Eds.) Marjorie Ferguson and Peter Golding. *
- *Border Matters: Remapping American Cultural Studies.* Jose David Saldivar.
- *Belief and Resistance.* Barbara Hernstein Smith.
- *The Eight Technologies of Otherness.* (Ed.) Sue Golding.
- *Chinese Society: Change, Conflict and Resistance.* (Eds.) Elizabeth J. Perry and Mark Selden.
- *The Citizenship Debates.* (Ed.) Gershon Shafir.
- *Too Soon Too Late: History in Popular Culture.* Meaghan Morris. *
- *Visual Culture: The Reader.* (Ed.) Jessica Evans.
- *In Search of Politics.* Zygmunt Bauman. *
- *Without Guarantees: In Honour of Stuart Hall.* (Eds.) Paul Gilroy, Lawrence Grossberg, and Angela McRobbie. *
- *Methodology of the Oppressed.* Chela Sandoval.
- *Contingency, Hegemony, Universality: Contemporary Dialogues on the Left.* Judith Butler.
- *Cultural Resistance Reader.* (Ed.) Stephen Duncombe. *
- *A People's History of the United States.* Howard Zinn. *
- *Literacy: Reading the Word and the World.* Paulo Freire and Donaldo Macedo. *
- *Teaching against the Grain: A Pedagogy of Possibility.* Roger Simon.
- *The Social Mind: Language, Ideology, and Social Practice.* Jim Gee.
- *Culture and Power in the Classroom: A Critical Foundation for Bicultural Education.* Antonia Darder.
- *Presence of Mind: Education and the Politics of Deception.* Pepi Leistyna.

Introductory texts

- *An Introduction to Post-Colonial Theory.* Peter Childs and Patrick Williams.
- *Beginning Postcolonialism.* John McLeod. *
- *Postcolonial Theory: An Introduction.* Leela Gandhi.
- *Fanon for Beginners.* Deborah Wyrick. *
- *Che for Beginners.* Sergio Sinay and Miguel Angel Scenna. *
- *Pan-Africanism for Beginners.* Sid Lemelle.
- *Panic Rules: Everything You Need to Know about the Global Economy.* Robin Hahnel.

Taking the next step

- *Post-Colonial Literatures in English: History, Language, Theory.* Dennis Walder.
- *The Imagination of the New Left: A Global Analysis of 1968.* George Katsiaficas.
- *Workers of the World Undermined: American Labor's Role in U.S. Foreign Policy.* Beth Simms.
- *Poor People's Movements.* Francis Fox Piven and Richard A. Cloward.
- *Freedom Under Fire: U.S. Civil Liberties in Times of War.* Michael Linfield. *
- *Democracy Unbound: Progressive Challenges to the Two Party System.* David Reynolds.
- *Break-ins, Death Threats and the FBI: The Covert War against the Central American Movement.* Ross Gelbspan. *
- *Stop the Killing Train: Radical Visions for Radical Change.* Michael Albert. *
- *The CIA's Greatest Hits.* Mark Zepezaver.
- *Searching for Everada: A Story of Love, War, and the CIA in Guatemala.* Jennifer K. Harbury.
- *Global Village or Global Pillage: Economic Reconstruction from the Bottom Up.* Jeremy Brecher and Tim Costello.
- *East Timor: Genocide in Paradise.* Matthew Jardine.
- *No Trespassing: Squatting, Rent Strikes, and Land Struggles Worldwide.* Anders Corr.
- *Non-Violent Social Movements: A Geographical Perspective.* (Eds.) Stephen Zunes, Lester R. Kurtz, and Sarah Beth Asher.
- *Transnational Social Movements and Global Politics: Solidarity beyond the State.* (Eds.) Jackie Smith, Charles Chatfield, and Ron Pagnucco.
- *Between Resistance and Revolution: Cultural Politics and Social Protest.* (Eds.) Richard Gabriel Fox and Orin Starn.
- *The Paths to Domination, Resistance, and Terror.* (Eds.) Carolyn Nordstrom and Joann Martin.
- *Globalize This: The Battle against the World Trade Organization.* (Eds.) Kevin Danaher and Roger Burbach.
- *Rogue State: A Guide to the World's Only Superpower.* William Blum. *
- *Corporate Predators: The Hunt for Mega-Profits and the Attack on Democracy.* Russell Mokhiber and Robert Weissman.
- *Democratizing the Global Economy: The Battle against the World Bank and the IMF.* (Ed.) Kevin Danaher.
- *Resource Rebels: Native Challenges to Mining and Oil Corporations.* Al Gedicks.

- *Peasants on Plantations: Subaltern Strategies of Labor and Resistance in the Pisco Valley, Peru.* Vincent C. Peloso.
- *Telltale Stories from Central America: Cultural Heritage, Political Systems, and Resistance in Developing Countries.* Samuel Z. Stone.
- *Sweatshop Warriors: Immigrant Women Workers Take on the Global Factory.* Miriam Ching Yoon Louie.
- *Is Oil Thicker than Blood? A Study of Oil Companies' Interests and Western Complicity in Indonesia's Annexation of East Timor.* Geroge Aditjondro.
- *Made in Indonesia: Indonesian Workers Since Suharto.* Dan La Botz.
- *Culturicide, Resistance, and Survivial of the Lakota/"Sioux Nation."* James V. Fenelon.
- *Voices of American Indian Assimilation and Resistance: Helen Hunt Jackson, Sarah Winnemucca and Victoria Howard.* Siobhah Senier.
- *The Search for Political Space: Globalization, Social Movements, and the Urban Political Experience.* Warren Magnusson.
- *Globalization and the Politics of Resistance.* Barry K. Gills.
- *Globalization and Social Movements.* Pierre Hamel.
- *Peasants against Globalization: Rural Social Movements in Costa Rica.* Marc Edelman.
- *Naming the Enemy: Anti-Corporate Movements Confront Globalization.* Amory Starr.
- *The Global Activists Manual: Local Ways to Change the World.* (Ed.) Mike Prokosch.
- *Rethinking the Politics of Globalization: Theory, Concepts, and Strategy.* Iain Watson.
- *Five Days that Shook the World: The Battle for Seattle and Beyond.* Alexander Cockburn.
- *Global Citizen Action.* Michael Edwards.
- *From ACT UP to the WTO: Urban Protest and Community Building in the Era of Globalization.* (Eds.) Benjamin Shepard and Ronald Hayduk.
- *Egalitarian Politics in the Age of Globalization.* (Ed.) Craig Murphy.
- *Fast Food Nation.* Eric Schlosser. *
- *Globalizations and Social Movements: Culture, Power, and the Transnational Public Sphere.* (Eds.) John A. Guidry, Michael D. Kennedy, and Mayer N. Zald.
- *9–11.* Noam Chomsky.
- *Fighting against the Injustice of the State and Globalization: Comparing the African American and Oromo Movements.* Asafa Jalata.
- *Global Capital, Political Institutions, and Policy in Developed Welfare States.* Duane Swank.

Put on your seatbelt

- *Black Skin, White Masks.* Frantz Fanon. *
- *Decolonizing the Mind.* Ngugi Wa Thiong'o. *
- *The Colonizer and the Colonized.* Albert Memmi. *
- *Return to the Source: Selected Speeches by Amilcar Cabral.* Amilcar Cabral.*
- *Discourse on Colonialism.* Aimé Césaire. *
- *American Civilization.* C. L. R. James. (Eds.) Anna Grimshaw and Keith Hart. *
- *George Lamming; Conversations: Essays, Addresses, and Interviews, 1953–1990.* (Ed.) Richard Drayton.*
- *Orientalism.* Edward Said. *
- *The Post-Colonial Critic: Interviews, Strategies, Dialogues.* Gayatri Chakravorty Spivak. *

- *Intifada: Palestinian Uprising against Israeli Occupation.* (Eds.) Zachary Lockman and Joel Beinin.
- *A Small Place.* Jamaica Kincaid.
- *Nation and Narration.* (Ed.) Homi Bhabha. *
- *Borderlands La Frontera: The New Mestiza.* Gloria Anzaldua. *
- *Beyond Postcolonial Theory.* E. San Juan, Jr.
- *Occupied America: A History of Chicanos.* Rodolfo Acuna.
- *The Empire Writes Back: Theory and Practice in Post-Colonial Literatures.* Bill Ashcroft, Gareth Griffiths, and Helen Tiffin.
- *Recasting Women: Essays in Indian Colonial History.* (Eds.) Kumkum Sangari and Sudesh Vaid.
- *When the Moon Waxes Red.* Trinh T. Minh-Ha. *
- *Imperial Eyes: Travel Writing and Transculturation.* Mary Louise Pratt.
- *The State of Native America: Genocide, Colonization, and Resistance.* (Ed.) M. Annette Jaimes.
- *Decolonizing Feminisms: Race, Gender and Empire-Building.* Laura Donaldson.
- *Contesting Power: Resistance and Everyday Social Relations in South Asia.* (Eds.) Douglas Haynes and Gyan Prakash.
- *Writing Diaspora: Tactics of Intervention in Contemporary Cultural Studies.* Rey Chow. *
- *Recasting the World: Writing after Colonialism.* Jonathan White.
- *Year 501: The Conquest Continues.* Noam Chomsky. *
- *The Nation and its Fragments.* Partha Chatterjee.
- *The Rhetoric of English India.* Sara Suleri.
- *Allegories of Empire: The Figure of Woman in the Colonial Text.* Jenny Sharp.
- *The Location of Culture.* Homi Bhabha. *
- *Colonial Discourse and Post-Colonial Theory.* (Eds.) Patrick Williams and Laura Chrisman.
- *Migrancy Culture and Identity.* Iain Chambers.
- *De-Scribing Empire: Post-Colonialism and Textuality.* Chris Tiffin and Alan Lawson.
- *Colonial and Postcolonial Literature: Migrant Metaphors.* Elleke Boehmer.
- *Postcolonial Literatures: Achebe, Ngugi, Desai, Walcott.* (Eds.) Michael Parker and Roger Starkey.
- *Colonial Desire: Hybridity in Theory, Culture, and Race.* Robert J. C. Young.
- *The Post Colonial Studies Reader.* (Eds.) Bill Ashcroft, Gareth Griffiths and Helen Tiffin. *
- *Imperial Leather: Race, Gender, and Sexuality in the Colonial Contest.* Anne McClintock. *
- *Thread of Blood: Colonialism, Revolution, and Gender on Mexico's Northern Frontier.* Ana Maria Alonso.
- *Contemporary Postcolonial Theory: A Reader.* (Ed.) Padmini Mongia. *
- *The Arnold Anthology of Post-Colonial Literatures in English.* (Ed.) John Thieme.
- *Jihad vs. McWorld: How Globalism and Tribalism are Shaping the World.* (Eds.) Benjamin R. Bauber and Andrea Schulz.
- *Colonial Discourse/Postcolonial Theory.* (Eds.) Francis Barker, Peter Hulme, and Margaret Iversen.
- *The Post-Colonial Question: Common Skies, Divided Horizons.* (Eds.) Iain Chambers and Lidia Curti.
- *Subaltern Studies IX: Writings on South Asian History and Society.* (Eds.) Shahid Amin and Dipesh Chakrabarty. *

- *Social Change and Political Discourse in India*, vol. 3: *Structures of Power Movement of Resistance: Region, Religion, Caste, Gender and Culture in Contemporary India*. (Ed.) T. V. Sathyamurthy.
- *Post-Colonial Drama: Theory, Practice, Politics*. Helen Gilbert and Joanne Tompkins.
- *The Postcolonial Aura: Third World Criticism in the Age of Global Capitalism*. Arif Dirlik. *
- *East Timor's Unfinished Struggle: Inside the Timorese Resistance*. Constancio Pinto and Matthew Jardine.
- *Cartographies of Diaspora: Contesting Identities*. Avtar Brah.
- *Postcolonial African Philosophy: A Critical Reader*. Emmanuel Chukwudieze.
- *Dangerous Liaisons: Gender, Nation, & Postcolonial Perspectives*. (Eds.) Anne McClintock, Aamir Mufi, and Ella Shohat. *
- *Geographies of Resistance*. (Eds.) Steve Pile and Michael Keith.
- *Following Christ in a Consumer Society: The Spirituality of Cultural Resistance*. John F. Kavanaugh.
- *Translation and Subjectivity: On Japan and Cultural Nationalism*. Naoki Sakai and Meaghan Morris.
- *Hong Kong: Culture and the Politics of Disappearance*. M. A. Abbas and Ackbar Abbas.
- *Tensions of Empire: Colonial Cultures in a Bourgeois World*. (Eds.) Fredrick Cooper and Ann Laura Stoler.
- *Postcolonial Criticism*. (Eds.) Bart Moore-Gilbert, Gareth Stanton, and Willy Maley.
- *Colonialism/Postcolonialism*. Ania Loomba.
- *Imagined Communities*. Benedict Anderson. *
- *Delusions and Discoveries: India in the British Imagination, 1880s–1930*. Benita Parry and Michael Sprinker.
- *Inventing Western Civilization*. Thomas C. Patterson.
- *People's Rights: Social Movements and the State in the Third World*. (Eds.) Manoranjan Mohanty and Partha N. Mukherji.
- *Fantasies of the Master Race: Literature, Cinema, and the Colonization of American Indians*. Ward Churchill. *
- *African Identities: Race, Nation, and Culture in Ethnography, Pan-Africanism, and Black Literature*. Kadiati Kanneh.
- *Masks of Conquest: Literary Study and British Rule in India*. Gauri Viswanathan.
- *Nationalism and Cultural Practice in the Postcolonial World*. Neil Lazarus.
- *Post-Colonial Literatures: Expanding the Canon*. (Ed.) Deborah L. Madsen.
- *Post-Colonial Translation: Theory and Practice*. (Eds.) Susan Bassnett and Harish Trivedi.
- *Feminisms and Internationalism*. (Eds.) Mrinalini Sinha, Angela Woollacott, and Donna Guy.
- *Postcolonial Theory and English Literature*. (Ed.) Peter Childs.
- *Imperialism: Theoretical Directions/Key Concepts in Critical Theory*. (Ed.) Ronald H. Chilcote.
- *Postcolonialism: Critical Concepts in Literary and Cultural Studies*. (Ed.) Diana Brydon.
- *Postcolonial Discourses: An Anthology*. (Ed.) Gregory Castle.
- *Power Politics*. Arundhati Roy.
- *The Power of Identity*. Manuel Castells. *
- *Lineages of the Present: Ideological and Political Genealogies of Contemporary South Asia*. Aijaz Ahmad. *

■ *Strange Encounters: Embodied Others in Post-Coloniality.* Sara Ahmed.
■ *Eqbal Ahmad: Confronting Empire, David Barsamian Interviews.* Eqbal Ahmad and David Brasamian. *
■ *Nations and Identities: Classic Readings.* (Ed.) Vincent P. Pecora.
■ *Jose Marti Thoughts.* Carlos Ripoll. *
■ *Emiliano Zapata: Revolucionario de Mexico/Zapata the Revolutionary.* Teo Vera. *
■ *Augusto Caesar Sandino.* Pedro A. Vives Azancot. *
■ *Mohandas K. Gandhi: Autobiography.* Mohandas Karamchand Ganghi.
■ *Gandhi on Non-Violence.* (Ed.) Thomas Merton. *
■ *Elementary Aspects of Peasant Insurgency in Colonial India.* Ranajit Guha.
■ *The Revolt of the Masses.* Jose Ortega Y Gasset. *
■ *Guerrilla Warfare.* Che Guevara. *
■ *Pedagogy of the Oppressed.* Paulo Freire. *
■ *The New Libertarian Gospel: Pitfall of the Theology of Liberation.* Father Juan Gutierrez.
■ *Philosophy of Liberation.* Enrique Dussel. *
■ *Voice of the Voiceless: The Four Pastoral Letters and Other Statements.* Archbishop Oscar Romero. *
■ *Frontiers of Theology in Latin America.* (Ed.) R. Gibellini.
■ *Revolutionary Priests: The Complete Writings of Camilo Torres.* Camilo Torres.
■ *The Church at the Grassroots in Latin America: Perspectives on Thirty Years of Activism.* (Eds.) John Burdick and W. E. Hewitt. *
■ *Mujerista Theology: A Theology for the Twenty-First Century.* Ada Maria Isasi-Diaz.
■ *From the Place of the Dead: The Epic Struggles of Bishop Belo of East Timor.* Arnold Kohen.
■ *Domination and Cultural Resistance: Authority and Power among Andean People.* Roger Neil Rasnake.
■ *Long Walk to Freedom: The Autobiography of Nelson Mandela.* Nelson Mandela.
■ *Living in Truth.* Vaclav Havel. *
■ *Untouchable Freedom: A Social History of a Dalit Community.* Vijay Prashad.
■ *I Rigoberta Menchu: An Indian Woman in Guatemala.* Rigoberta Menchu.
■ *The Chiapas Rebellion.* Neil Harvey.
■ *Livelihood and Resistance: Peasants and the Politics of Land in Peru.* Gavin Smith.
■ *Return of Guatemala's Refugees: Reweaving the Torn.* Clark Taylor. *
■ *Cultural Power, Resistance and Pluralism: Colonial Guyana, 1838–1900.* Brian L. Moore.
■ *Cultures of Politics Politics of Cultures: Re-Visioning Latin American Social Movements.* (Eds.) Sonia E. Alvarez, Evelina Dagnino, and Arturo Escobar. *
■ *Our World is Our Weapon: Selected Writings of Subcomandante Marcos.* (Ed.) Juana Ponce De Leon.
■ *The War against Oblivion: Zapatista Chronicles 1994–2000.* John Ross.
■ *Salt of the Mountain: Campa Ashaninka History and Resistance in the Peruvian Jungle.* Stefano Varese.
■ *Ethics for the New Millennium.* Dali Lama. *
■ *Dona Licha's Island: Modern Colonization in Puerto Rico.* Alfredo Lopez.
■ *Cultural Adaptation and Resistance on St. John: Three Centuries of Afro-Caribbean Life.* Karen Fog Olwig.
■ *Colonial Dilemma: Critical Perspectives on Contemporary Puerto Rico.* (Eds.) Edwin Melendez and Edgardo Melendez.

- *Philanthropy and Cultural Imperialism.* Robert Arnove.
- *Globalization Unmasked: Imperialism in the 21st Century.* Henry Veltmeyer and James F. Petras.
- *The Modern/Colonial Capitalist World-System in the Twentieth Century: Global Processes, Antisystemic Movements, and the Geopolitics of Knowledge.* (Ed.) Ramon Grosfoguel.
- *Chilean Voices: Activists Describe Their Experiences of the Popular Unity Period.* (Eds.) Colin Henfrey and Bernardo Sorj.
- *Takeover in Tehran: The Inside Story of the 1979 U.S. Embassy Capture.* Massoumeh Ebtekar and Fred A. Reed.
- *From a Native Daughter: Colonialism and Sovereignty in Hawaii.* Haunani-Kay Trask.
- *Cultivating Workers: Peasants and Capitalism in a Sudanese Village.* Victoria Bernal.
- *Roads to Dominion: Right-Wing Movements and Political Power in the United States.* Sara Diamond.
- *Eyes Right: Challenging the Right Wing Backlash.* (Ed.) Chip Berlet. *
- *Insurgencies: Constituent Power and the Modern State.* Antonio Negri and Maurizia Boscagli.
- *Postmodern Geographies: The Reassertion of Space in Critical Social Theory.* Edward Soja. *
- *Globalization: Public Culture.* (Ed.) Arjun Appadurai.
- *Empire.* Michael Hardt and Antonio Negri. *
- *The Virilio Reader.* (Ed.) James Der Derian. *
- *A Place in the World: Places, Cultures, and Globalization.* (Eds.) Doreen Massey and Pat Jess.
- *Globalization: The Human Consequences.* Zygmunt Bauman. *
- *The Cultures of Globalization.* (Eds.) Fredric Jameson and Masao Miyoshi. *
- *Acts of Resistance: Against the Tyranny of the Market.* Pierre Bourdieu. *
- *The Globalization Reader.* (Eds.) Frank J. Lechner and John Boli.
- *Globalizing Cities: A New Spatial Order?* (Eds.) Peter Marcuse and Ronald Van Kempen.
- *Capitalism in the Age of Globalization: The Management of Contemporary Society.* Samir Amin.
- *Local Histories/Global Designs.* Walter D. Mignolo.
- *Flexible Citizenship: The Cultural Logics of Transnationality.* Aihwa Ong.
- *Places and Politics in an Age of Globalization.* (Eds.) Roxann Praziak and Arif Dirlik. *
- *Civil Society in Yemen: The Political Economy of Activism in Modern Arabia.* Sheila Carapico.
- *Eyes without Country: Searching for a Palestinian Strategy of Liberation.* Souad R. Dajani.
- *The Failure of Political Islam.* Oliver Roy.
- *The Middle East and the United States: A Historical and Political Reassessment.* (Ed.) David W. Lesch.
- *War against the Planet: The Fifth Afghan War, U.S. Imperialism and Other Assorted Fundamentalisms.* Vijay Prashad. *
- *Cultural Resistance: Global and Local Encounters in the Middle East.* Samir Khalaf.
- *Reading & Teaching the Postcolonial: From Baldwin to Basquiat and Beyond.* Greg Dimitriadis and Cameron McCarthy.
- *Development Encounters.* (Ed.) Pauline E. Peters.

- *Rebellion, Repression, Reinvention: Mutiny in Comparative Perspective.* (Ed.) Jane Hathaway.
- *International Encyclopedia of Economics of Education.* (Ed.) Martin Carnoy.
- *Literacies of Power: What Americans are not Allowed to Know.* Donaldo Macedo.
- *Revolutionary Multiculturalism: Pedagogies of Dissent for the New Millennium.* Peter McLaren.
- *Gramsci, Freire and Adult Education: Possibilities for Transformative Action.* Peter Mayo.
- *Collateral Damage: Corporatizing Public Schools – A Threat to Democracy.* Kenneth J. Saltman. *

Insightful books on class struggle / introductory texts

- *Trotsky for Beginners.* Tariq Ali. *
- *Introducing Keynsian Economics.* Peter Pugh and Chris Garratt. *
- *Mao for Beginners.* Ruis and Friends.
- *Chaos or Community: Seeking Solutions, not Scapegoats for Bad Economics.* Holly Sklar. *
- *Let Them Eat Ketchup: The Politics of Poverty and Inequality.* Sheila Collins.
- *Disposable Domestics: Immigrant Women Workers in the Global Economy.* Grace Chang.
- *Coalitions across the Class Divide: Lessons from the Labor, Peace, and Environmental Movements.* Fred Rose. *
- *Bridging the Class Divide and Other Lessons for Grassroots Organizing.* Linda Stout and Howard Zinn.
- *Corporation Nation: How Corporations are Taking over Our Lives and What We Can Do About It.* Charles Derber. *
- *Economic Apartheid in America: A Primer on Economic Inequality and Insecurity.* Chuck Collins and Felice Yeskel.
- *The Ultimate Field Guide to the U.S. Economy: A Compact and Irreverent Guide to Economic Life in America.* James Heintz, Nancy Flobre, the Center for Popular Economics, United for a Fair Economy, and the National Priorities Project. *
- *Behind the Label: Inequality in the Los Angeles Apparel Industry.* Edna Bonacich and Richard Appelbaum. *

Taking the next step

- *Wage-Labour and Capital: Value, Price and Profit.* Karl Marx. *
- *The History of Manners.* Norbert Elias.
- *The Origin of Negative Dialectics: Theodore W. Adorno, Walter Benjamin, and the Frankfurt Institute.* Susan Buck-Morss. *
- *The Dialectical Imagination: A History of the Frankfurt School and the Institute of Social Research, 1923–1950.* Martin Jay.
- *Strike!* Jeremy Brecher.
- *Detroit, I Do My Dying: A Study in Urban Revolution.* Dan Georgakas, Maruin Surkin, and Manning Marable.
- *Hard Pressed in the Heartland: The Hormel Strike and the Future of the Labor Movement.* Peter Rachleff.
- *Controlling the Dangerous Classes: A Critical Introduction to the History of Criminal Justice.* Randall G. Shelden.

- *Streets of Hope: The Fall and Rise of an Urban Neighborhood.* Peter Medoff and Holly Sklar.
- *For Crying Out Loud: Women's Poverty in the United States.* (Eds.) Diane Dujon and Ann Withorn.
- *Consumption (Key Ideas).* Robert Bocock.
- *Development, Crisis, and Class Struggle: Learning from Japan and the East.* Paul Burkett and Martin Hart-Landsberg.
- *Take the Rich off Welfare.* Mark Zepezaver and Arthur Naiman.
- *The Perpetual Prisoner Machine: How America Profits from Crime.* Joel Dyer.

Put on your seatbelt

- *The Marx–Engels Reader.* (Ed.) Robert C. Tucker. *
- *Grundrisse: Foundations of the Critique of Political Economy.* Karl Marx. *
- *The Condition of the Working Class in England.* Friedrich Engels. *
- *The Revolution Betrayed: What is the Soviet Union and Where is it Going.* Leon Trotsky.
- *History and Class Consciousness.* Georg Lukács.
- *Selections from Political Writings.* Antonio Gramsci. *
- *Rosa Luxemburg: Writings and Reflections.* Rosa Luxemburg. *
- *From Max Weber: Essays in Sociology.* Max Weber. *
- *Negative Dialectics.* Theodor Adorno.
- *White Collar: The American Middle Classes.* Charles Wright Mills.
- *Counterrevolution & Revolt.* Herbert Marcuse.
- *Marxism for Our Times: C. L. R. James on Revolutionary Organization.* (Ed.) Martin Glaberman. *
- *Marxism and Freedom: From 1776 Until Today.* Raya Dunayerskaya.
- *The Making of the English Working Class.* E. P. Thompson. *
- *In the Tracks of Historical Materialism.* Perry Anderson.
- *Althusser: A Critical Reader.* (Ed.) Gregory Elliott. *
- *The Structural Transformation of the Public Sphere: An Inquiry into a Category of Bourgeois Society.* Jürgen Habermas. *
- *Class, Codes, and Control.* Basil Bernstein. *
- *Anti-Oedipus: Capitalism and Schizophrenia.* Giles Deleuze and Félix Guattari. *
- *Imperialism and World Economy.* Nikolai Bukharin.
- *Ideology.* Terry Eagleton. *
- *Reading Capital Politically.* Harry Cleaver.
- *The Cultural Contradictions of Capitalism.* Daniel Bell.
- *Schooling in Capitalist America.* Samuel Bowles and Herbert Gintis. *
- *Reproduction in Education, Society, and Culture.* Pierre Bourdieu and Jean-Claude Passeron. *
- *State, Power, and Socialism.* Nicos Poulantzas. *
- *Classes, Power, and Conflict.* (Eds.) Anthony Giddens and David Held.
- *Capitalism, Socialism, and Democracy.* Joseph A. Schumpeter.
- *The Return of the Political.* Chantal Mouffe. *
- *The Politics of Identity: Class, Culture, Social Movements.* Stanley Aronowitz. *
- *Moses Hess: Prophet of Communism and Zionism.* Shlomo Avineri.
- *Marxism and Native Americans.* Ward Churchill and Winona Laduke.

- *Marxism and the Interpretation of Culture.* (Eds.) Cary Nelson and Lawrence Grossberg.
- *Post-Fordism and Social Form: A Marxist Debate on the Post-Fordist State.* (Eds.) Werner Bonefeld and John Holloway. *
- *The End of Organized Capitalism.* Scott Lash and John Urry. *
- *Class: A Guide through the American Status System.* Paul Fussell.
- *Class (Key Ideas).* Stephen Edgell.
- *Working Class Movements in India: 1885–1975.* Sunil Kumar Sen.
- *Love and Theft: Blackface Minstrelsy and the American Working Class.* Eric Lott.
- *Japanese Workers in Protest: An Ethnography of Consciousness and Experience.* Christena L. Turner.
- *Class.* (Ed.) Patrick Joyce.
- *Race Rebels: Culture, Politics, and the Black Working Class.* Robin D. G. Kelly. *
- *Class Warfare: Interviews.* Noam Chomsky and David Barsamian. *
- *Class Counts: Comparative Studies in Class Analysis.* Erik Olin Wright.
- *Proletarian Power: Shanghai in the Cultural Revolution.* (Eds.) Elizabeth Perry, Li Xun, and Mark Selden.
- *Materialist Feminism: A Reader in Class, Difference, and Women's Lives.* (Eds.) Rosemary Hennessy and Chrys Ingraham. *
- *America Besieged.* Michael Parenti. *
- *The Wages of Whiteness: Race and the Making of the American Working Class.* David Roediger. *
- *How Capitalism Underdeveloped Black America.* Manning Marable. *
- *The Unknown City: Lives of Poor and Working-Class Young Adults.* Michelle Fine and Lois Weis.
- *Imperialism: Theoretical Directions.* (Ed.) Ronald Chilcote.
- *Rethinking Working-Class History.* Dipesh Chakrabarty. *
- *Where We Stand: Class Matters.* bell hooks.
- *Cultural Studies and the Working Class: Subject to Change.* (Ed.) Sally Munt.
- *Class War in America: How Economic and Political Conservatives are Exploiting Low- and Middle-Income American Families.* Charles M. Kelly.
- *Growing Up Girl: Psychological Explorations of Gender and Class.* Valerie Walkerdine, Helen Lucey, and June Melody. *
- *Rich Get Richer and the Poor Get Prisons: Ideology, Class, and Criminal Justice.* Jeffrey H. Reiman.
- *Dumping in Dixie: Race, Class, and Environmental Quality.* Robert D. Bullard.
- *The Transnational Capitalist Class.* Leslie Sklair.
- *Reveille for Radicals.* Saul D. Alinsky.
- *Working Together against Homelessness.* Eugene Hurwitz and Sue Hurwitz.
- *The Snarling Citizen.* Barbara Ehrenreich. *
- *Queerly Classed: Gay Men and Lesbians Write about Class.* Susan Raffo.
- *Forbidden Workers: Illegal Chinese Immigrants and American Labor.* Peter Kwong. *
- *Social Movements in Advanced Capitalism: The Political Economy and Cultural Construction of Social Activism.* Steven M. Buechler.
- *Masses, Classes and the Public Sphere* (Eds.) Mike Hill and Warren Montag.
- *Spirits of Resistance and Capitalist Discipline.* Aihwa Ong.
- *Spaces of Capital: Towards a Critical Geography.* David Harvey.

- *Strange Love: Or How We Learn to Stop Worrying and Love the Market.* Robin Truth Goodman and Kenneth J. Saltman.
- *We Make the Road by Walking: Conversations on Education and Social Change.* Myles Horton and Paulo Freire. *
- *The Hidden Curriculum and Moral Education.* (Eds.) Henry Giroux and David Purple.
- *Teachers and Texts: A Political Economy of Class and Gender Relations in Education.* Michael W. Apple.
- *Making Progress: Education and Culture in New Times.* Dennis Carlson.
- *Ghetto Schooling: A Political Economy of Urban Educational Reform.* Jean Anyon.
- *School Smart and Motherwise: Working-Class Women's Identity and Schooling.* Wendy Luttrell.
- *Class Issues: Pedagogy, Cultural Studies, and the Public Sphere.* (Ed.) Amitava Kumar. *
- *The University in Ruins.* Bill Readings. *
- *The Knowledge Factory: Dismantling the Corporate University and Creating True Higher Learning.* Stanley Aronowitz. *

Insightful books on science, technology, and nature

- *Against Method.* Paul Feyerabend. *
- *Machines as the Measure of Men: Science, Technology, and Ideologies of Western Domination.* Michael Adas.
- *Feminism Confronts Technology.* Judy Wajcman.
- *Rethinking Technologies.* (Ed.) Verena Andermatt Conley. *
- *Unstable Frontiers: Technomedicine and the Cultural Politics of "Curing" AIDS.* John Nguyet Erni.
- *Science Wars.* (Ed.) Andrew Ross. *
- *Is Science Multicultural.* Sandra Harding. *
- *The Science Studies Reader.* (Ed.) Mario Biagioli.
- *Culture on the Brink: Ideologies of Technology.* (Eds.) Gretchen Bender and Timothy Druckrey. *
- *Women Internet: Creating New Cultures in Cyberspace.* (Ed.) Wendy Harcourt. *
- *Doing Science & Culture.* (Eds.) Roddey Reid and Sharon Traweek.
- *Modest-Witness, Second-Millennium: Femaleman Meets Oncomouse: Feminism and Technoscience.* Donna J. Haraway.
- *The Visible Woman: Imaging Technologies, Gender, and Science.* (Eds.) Paula A. Treichler, Lisa Cartwright, and Constance Penley.
- *Cyber-Marx: Cycles and Circuits of Struggle in High-Technology Capitalism.* Nick Dyer-Witherford.
- *Reading Digital Culture.* David Trend. *
- *The Mismeasure of Man.* Stephen J. Gould. *
- *Impure Science: AIDS, Activism, and the Politics of Knowledge.* Steven Epstein.
- *Stolen Harvest: The Hijacking of the Global Food Supply.* Vandana Shiva. *
- *Dying from Dioxin: A Citizen's Guide to Reclaiming Our Health and Rebuilding Democracy.* Lois Marie Gibbs.
- *Bleeding the Patient: The Consequences of Corporate Health Care.* David Himmel Stein and Steffie Woolhandler.
- *Dying for Growth: Global Inequality and the Health of the Poor.* (Eds.) Jim Yong Kim, Joyce V. Millen, Alec Irwin, and John Gershman. *

- *Geography and Social Movements: Comparing Anti-nuclear Activism in the Boston Area.* Byron A. Miller.
- *The Sun Betrayed: A Report on the Corporate Seizure of U.S. Solar Energy Development.* Ray Reece.
- *Timber Wars.* Judi Bari.
- *Water Wars: Pollution, Profits, and Privatization.* Vandana Shiva.
- *The New Resource Wars: Native and Environmental Struggles against Multinational Corporations.* Al Gedicks and Winnona Laduke. *
- *Ecological Economics: A Practical Programme for Global Reform.* The Group of Green Economists.
- *Ecological Imperialism: The Biological Expansion of Europe, 900–1900.* Alfred W. Crosby.
- *Capitalism, Socialism, Ecology.* Andre Gorz.
- *Ecological Enlightenment: Essays on the Politics of the Risk Society.* Ulrich Beck.
- *Avoiding Social and Ecological Disaster: The Politics of World Transformation.* Rudolph Bahro.
- *Earth for Sale: Reclaiming Ecology in the Age of Corporate Greenwash.* Brian Tokar.
- *Designing the Green Economy: The Postindustrial Alternative to Corporate Globalization.* Brian Milani.
- *Dangerous Intersections: Feminist Perspectives on Population, Environment, and Development.* (Eds.) Jael Silliman and Ynestra King.
- *Ecofeminism: Women, Culture, Nature.* (Ed.) Karen J. Warren.
- *Secrets and Lies: The Anatomy of an Anti-Environmental PR Campaign.* Nicky Hagen and Bob Burton. *

Part II: Representational Politics

Introductory texts

- *McLuhan for Beginners.* W. Terrence Gordon.
- *Introducing Semiotics.* Paul Cobley and Litza Jansz.
- *Introducing Baudrillard.* Chris Horrocks and Zoran Jevtic.
- *Representation: Cultural Representations and Signifying Practices.* (Ed.) Stuart Hall. *
- *Cultural Studies and the Study of Popular Culture: Theories and Methods.* John Storey.
- *Media Semiotics: An Introduction.* Jonathan Bignell.
- *We the Media: A Citizen's Guide to Fighting for Media Democracy.* (Ed.) Julie Winokur.
- *Of Cigarettes, High Heels, and Other Interesting Things: An Introduction to Semiotics.* Marcel Danesi.
- *Networks of Power: Corporate TV's Threat to Democracy.* Dennis W. Mazzocco.
- *Prime Time Activism: Media Strategies for Grassroots Organizing.* Charlotte Ryan.
- *Jamming the Media: A Citizen's Guide, Reclaiming the Tools of Communication.* Gareth Branwyn.
- *Watchdog Journalism in South America: News, Accountability, and Democracy.* Silvio Waisbord.
- *Micro Radio and Democracy – (Low) Power to the People.* Greg Ruggerio.
- *The Habits of a Highly Deceptive Media: Decoding Spin and Lies in Mainstream News.* Norman Solomon.

- *Making the News: A Guide for Nonprofits and Activists.* Jasan Saltman.
- *Notes from the Underground: Zines and the Politics of Alternative Culture.* Stephen Duncombe.
- *Culture Jam: The Uncooling of America.* Kalle Lasn.
- *It's the Media Stupid.* John Nichols and Robert McChesney.
- *Cyberspace: First Steps.* (Ed.) Michael Benedikt.

Taking the next step

- *Questioning the Media: A Critical Introduction.* (Eds.) John Downing, Ali Mohammad, and Sreberny Mohammad.
- *How to Read Donald Duck: Imperialist Ideology in the Disney Comic.* Ariel Dorfman and Armand Mattelart. *
- *Flaunting It: A Decade of Gay Journalism from "The Body Politic."* (Eds.) Ed Jackson and Stan Persky.
- *Taking the Risk out of Democracy: Corporate Propaganda Versus Freedom and Liberty.* Alex Carey. *
- *Manufacturing Consent.* Edward S. Herman and Noam Chomsky. *
- *The Cinema of Apartheid: Race and Class in South African Film.* Keyan Tomaselli.
- *Cracked Coverage: Television News, the Anti-Cocaine Crusade, and the Reagan Legacy.* Jimmie L. Reeves and Richard Campbell.
- *PR: A Social History of Spin.* Stuart Ewen.
- *Challenging Codes: Collective Action in the Information Age.* Alberto Melucci.
- *Doing Cultural Studies: The Story of the Sony Walkman.* Paul du Gay, Stuart Hall, Linda Janes, Hugh Mackay and Keith Negus. *
- *Real Majority, Media Minority: The Costs of Sidelining Women in Reporting.* Laura Flanders.
- *Wizards of Oz: Behind the Curtain of Mainstream News.* Norman Solomon and Jeff Cohen.
- *Arab and Muslim Stereotyping in American Popular Culture.* Jack G. Shaheen. *
- *Media and Cultural Regulation.* (Ed.) Kenneth Thompson. *
- *Consumer Boycotts: Effecting Change through the Marketplace and the Media.* Monroe Friedman.
- *Rich Media, Poor Democracy: Communication Politics in Dubious Times.* Robert McChesney. *
- *All Things Censored.* Mumia Abu-Jamal, (Ed.) Noelle Hanrahan.
- *Megamedia: How Giant Corporations Dominate Mass Media, Distort Competition, and Endanger Democracy.* Dean Alger.
- *Citizen Muckraking: How to Investigate and Right Wrongs in Your Community.* The Center for Public Integrity.
- *Drive-By Journalism: The Assault on Your Need to Know.* Arthur Rowse.
- *Derailing Democracy: The America the Media Don't Want You to See.* David McGowan.
- *Censored 2001.* (See annually.) Peter Phillips. *

Put on your seatbelt

- *Walter Benjamin Selected Writings: 1927–1934.* (Eds.) Marcus Paul Bullock and Michael W. Jennings. *

- *The Culture Industry: Selected Essays on Mass Culture.* Theodor Adorno. *
- *Mythologies.* Roland Barthes. *
- *Understanding Media: The Extensions of Man.* Marshal McLuhan. *
- *The Field of Cultural Production.* Pierre Bourdieu. *
- *Simulacra and Simulations.* Jean Baudrillard. *
- *The Society of the Spectacle.* Guy Debord. *
- *A Theory of Semiotics.* Umberto Eco.
- *Media Matters: Everyday Culture and Political Change.* John Fiske. *
- *The Ideology of the Information Age.* (Eds.) Jennifer Daryl Slack and Fred Fejes.
- *The Media Reader.* (Eds.) Manuel Alvarado and John Thompson.
- *Language in the News: Discourse and Ideology in the Press.* Roger Fowler.
- *Testimony: Crises of Witnessing in Literature, Psychoanalysis, and History.* Shoshana Felman and Dori Laub.
- *Black Looks: Race and Representation.* bell hooks. *
- *The Codes of Advertising: Fetishism and the Political Economy of Meaning in Consumer Society.* Sut Jhally. *
- *African Cinema: Politics and Culture.* Manthia Diawara.
- *White Screen/Black Images.* James Snead.
- *Nation, Culture, Text: Australian Cultural and Media Studies.* (Ed.) Graeme Turner.
- *Make-Believe Media: The Politics of Entertainment.* Michael Parenti.
- *Television, Audiences and Cultural Studies.* David Morley. *
- *Getting the Message: News, Truth, and Power.* John Eldridge.
- *Decoding Advertisements: Ideology and Meaning in Advertising.* Judith Williamson.
- *Media-tions: Forays into the Culture and Gender Wars.* Elayne Rapping.
- *Gender, Race, and Class in Media: A Text-Reader.* (Eds.) Gail Dines and Jean M. Humez. *
- *Fear of the Dark: "Race," Gender, and Sexuality in the Cinema.* Lola Young.
- *Watching Race: Television and the Struggle for the Sign of Blackness.* Herman Gray. *
- *Symbolic Interactionism and Cultural Studies: The Politics of Interpretation.* Norman K. Denzin. *
- *Unthinking Eurocentrism: Multiculturalism and the Media.* Ella Shohat and Robert Stam. *
- *Media Culture: Cultural Studies, Identity, and Politics between the Modern and the Postmodern.* Douglas Kellner. *
- *Approaches to Media: A Reader.* (Eds.) Oliver Boyd-Barrett and Chris Newbold.
- *Picture Theory: Essays on Verbal and Visual Representation.* W. J. T. Mitchell.
- *Cultural Producers in Perilous States: Editing Events, Documenting Change.* (Ed.) George E. Marcus.
- *The Communication Theory Reader.* (Ed.) Paul Cobley.
- *Policing Desire: AIDS, Pornography, and the Media.* Simon Watney.
- *Covering Islam: How the Media and Experts Determine How We See the Rest of the World.* Edward Said. *
- *Feminist Television Criticism: A Reader.* (Eds.) Charlotte Brunsdon, Julie D'Acci, and Lynn Spigel.
- *Cultural Studies and Communications.* (Eds.) James Curran, David Morley, and Valerie Walkerdine.
- *Media Discourse.* Norman Fairclough.

- *Media Making: Mass Media in Popular Culture.* (Eds.) Lawrence Grossberg, Ellen Wartella, and D. Charles Whitney.
- *Living Room Wars: Rethinking Media Audiences for a Postmodern World.* Ien Ang. *
- *Home, Exile, Homeland: Film, Media, and the Politics of Place.* (Ed.) Hamid Naficy.
- *Living Color: Race and Television in the United States (Console-Ing Passions).* (Ed.) Sasha Torres. *
- *The Columbia Reader on Lesbians and Gay Media, Society, and Politics.* (Eds.) Larry P. Gross and James D. Woods. *
- *The Cinematic Society: The Voyeur's Gaze.* Norman K. Denzin.
- *Sailing on the Silver Screen: Hollywood and the U.S. Navy.* Lawrence Suid.
- *The Film Studies Reader.* (Eds.) Joanne Hollows, Peter Hutchings, and Mark Jancovich.
- *Reinventing Film Studies.* (Eds.) Christine Gledhill and Linda Williams.
- *The Material Ghost.* Gilberto Perez.
- *Mystifying Movies.* Noell Carroll.
- *Emancipation, the Media, and Modernity: Arguments about the Media and Social Theory.* Nicholal Garnham.
- *Visual Culture Reader.* (Ed.) Nicholas Mirzoeff.
- *Twilight Zones: The Hidden Life of Cultural Images from Plato to O. J.* Susan Bordo.
- *The Secret Politics of Our Desire: Innocence, Culpability and Indian Popular Cinema.* Ashis Nandy.
- *Media and Cultural Studies: Keyworks.* (Eds.) Meenakshi Gigi Durham and Douglas M. Kellner. *
- *Media Studies: A Reader.* (Eds.) Paul Marris and Sue Thornham. *
- *Propaganda, Inc.: Selling America's Culture to the World.* Nancy Snow.
- *The Decline and Fall of Public Broadcasting: Creating Alternatives to Corporate Media.* David Barsamian. *
- *The Dynamics of Regulation: Global Control, Local Resistance, Cultural Management and Policy: A Case Study of Broadcasting Advertising in the United Kingdom.* George Gantzias.
- *Breaking the News: How the Media Undermines American Democracy.* James Fallows.
- *Nattering on the Net: Women, Power and Cyberspace.* Dale Spender.
- *Cultures of the Internet: Virtual Spaces, Real People, Living Bodies.* (Ed.) Rob Shields.
- *Virtual Culture: Identity and Communication in Cyberspace.* Steven G. Jones.
- *Internet Culture.* (Ed.) David Porter.
- *The Rise of the Network Society.* Manuel Castells. *
- *The Cybercultures Reader.* (Eds.) David Bell and Barbara M. Kennedy.
- *Mapping the Terrain: New Genre Public Art.* (Ed.) Suzanne Lacy. *
- *Mixed Blessings: New Art in Multicultural America.* Lucy R. Lippard.
- *Sights of Resistance: Approaches to Canadian Visual Culture.* Robert Belton.
- *But is it Art? The Spirit of Art Activism.* (Ed.) Nina Felshin. *
- *Zones of Contention: Essays on Art, Institutions, Gender, and Anxiety.* Carol Becker. *
- *Sonia Boyce, Speaking in Tongues.* Gilane Tawadros.
- *Dangerous Border Crossers: The Artist Talks Back.* Guillermo Gomez-Pena. *
- *The Dramatic Arts and Cultural Studies: Education against the Grain.* Kathleen S. Berry.
- *Performing Asian American: Race and Ethnicity on the Contemporary Stage.* (Eds.) Josephine Lee, Michael Omi, and Sucheng Chan.

- *If You Lived Here: The City in Art, Theory, and Social Activism: A Project by Martha Roster.* (Ed.) Brian Wallis.
- *The Chicano Codices: Encountering Art of the Americas.* Patricia Draher and Marcos Sanchez-Tranquilino.
- *An Intimate Distance: Women, Artists, and the Body.* Rosemary Betterton.
- *Trash Aesthetics: Popular Culture and Its Audience.* (Eds.) Deborah Cartmell, Ian Hunter, Heidi Kaye, and Imelda Whelehan.
- *Scars of Conquest/Masks of Resistance: The Cultural Identities in African, African-American, and Caribbean Drama.* Tejumola Olaniyan.
- *Capital Culture: A Reader on Modernist Legacies, State Institutions, and the Values of Art.* (Eds.) Jody Berland and Shelley Hornstein. *
- *Toward a People's Art: The Contemporary Mural Movement.* Eva Cockcroft, John Weber, and James Cockcroft.
- *Cultural Pedagogy: Art/Education/Politics.* David Trend. *
- *Legislative Theatre: Using Performance to Make Politics.* Augusta Boal. *
- *Presence and Resistance: Postmodernism and Cultural Politics in Contemporary American Performance.* Philip Auslander.
- *Unmarked: The Politics of Performance.* Peggy Phelan. *
- *Rituals of Rule, Rituals of Resistance: Public Celebrations and Popular Culture in Mexico.* William H. Beezley.
- *Cultural Representation in Historical Resistance: Complexity and Construction in Greek Guerrilla Theater.* Linda Myrsiades and Kostas Myrsiades.
- *Let's Get it On: The Politics of Black Performance.* (Ed.) Catherine Ugwu.
- *Performativitity and Performance.* (Eds.) Eve Kosofsky Sedgwick and Andrew Parker. *
- *Cruising the Performative: Interventions into Representation of Ethnicity, Nationality, and Sexuality.* (Ed.) Sue-Ellen Case.
- *The Fashioned Body: Fashion, Dress and Modern Social Theory.* Joanne Entwistle.
- *The Culture of Fashion: A New History of Fashionable Dress.* Christopher Breward.
- *Vested Interests: Cross-Dressing and Cultural Anxiety.* Marjorie Garber.
- *Accounting for Tastes: Australian Everyday Cultures.* Tony Bennett, Michael Emison, and John Frow.
- *Academic Discourse and Critical Consciousness.* Patricia Bizzell.
- *Writing Permitted in Designated Areas Only.* Linda Brodkey. *
- *The Routledge Language and Cultural Theory Reader.* (Eds.) Lucy Burke, Tony Crowley, and Alan Girvin.

Insightful reads on persons with disabilities

- *Critical Psychology and Pedagogy.* Edmund Sullivan. *
- *Measured Lies: The Bell Curve Examined.* (Eds.) Joe Kincheloe, Shirley Steinberg, and Arron Gresson. *
- *The War against Children of Color: Psychiatry Targets Inner City Youth.* Ginger Ross Breggin and Peter Breggin. *
- *Madness, Disability, and Social Exclusion: The Archeology of 'Difference'.* (Ed.) Jane Hubert. *
- *Disability and Culture.* (Eds.) Benedicte Ingstad and Susan Reynolds Whyte.
- *Extraordinary Bodies: Figuring Physical Disability in American Culture and Literature.* Rosemarie Garland Thomson. *

- *The Disability Studies Reader.* (Ed.) Lennard J. Davis. *
- *The Body and Physical Difference: Discourses of Disability in Humanities.* (Eds.) David T. Mitchell and Sharon Snyder.
- *Beyond Ramps: Disability at the End of the Social Contract.* Marta Russel.
- *The Disability Reader: Social Science Perspectives.* (Ed.) Tom Shakespeare.
- *Nothing About Us Without Us: Disability Oppression and Empowerment.* James I. Charlton. *
- *Claiming Disability: Knowledge and Identity.* Simi Linton.
- *A History of Disability.* Henri-Jacques Stiker.
- *Disability and the Life Course: Global Perspectives.* (Ed.) Mark Priestley.
- *The New Disability History: American Perspectives.* (Eds.) Paul K. Longmore and Lauri Umansky.
- *Female Forms: Experiencing and Understanding Disability.* Carol Thomas.
- *Education and Disability in Cross-Cultural Perspective.* (Ed.) Susan Peters.
- *Disability and Democracy: Reconstructing Special Education for Postmodernity.* (Ed.) Thomas Skrtic.
- *Inclusive Education: International Voices on Disability and Justice.* (Ed.) Keith Ballard.

Insightful reads on youth(s) resistance and rethinking popular culture

- *Resistance through Rituals: Youth Subcultures in Post-War Britain.* (Eds.) Stuart Hall and Tony Jefferson. *
- *Learning to Labor: How Working Class Kids Get Working Class Jobs.* Paul Willis. *
- *Subculture: The Meaning of Style.* Dick Hebdige. *
- *An Introduction to Theories of Popular Culture.* Dominic Strinati. *
- *Getting Up: Subway Graffiti in New York.* Craig Castleman.
- *Student Politics in America: A Historical Analysis.* Philip G. Altbach.
- *Sold Separately: Parents and Children in Consumer Culture.* Ellen Seiter.
- *Marketing Madness: A Survival Guide for a Consumer Society.* Michael F. Jacobson and Laurie Ann Mazur.
- *Children and the Politics of Culture.* (Ed.) Sharon Stephens.
- *Out of the Garden: Toys and Children's Culture in the Age of TV Marketing.* Steven Kline.
- *Youth in Prison: We the People of Unit Four.* M.A. Bortner and Linda M. Williams. *
- *Pictures of Innocence: The History and Crisis of Ideal Childhood.* Ann Higonnet.
- *Generations of Youth: Youth Cultures and History in Twentieth-Century America.* (Eds.) Joe Austin and Michael Nevin Willard. *
- *The War against Parents: What We can do for Beleaguered Moms and Dads.* Sylvia Ann Hewett and Cornel West.
- *It's No Accident: How the Infant Products Industry Compromises Baby Safety.* E. Marla Flecher.
- *Youth Development and Critical Education: The Promise of Democratic Action.* Richard Lakes.
- *Roots of Civic Identity: International Perspectives on Community Service and Activism in Youth.* (Eds.) Miranda Yates and James Youniss.
- *Youth, Identity, Power: The Sixties Chicano Movement.* Carlos Munoz, Jr. *
- *Cyberpunk: Outlaws and Hackers on the Computer Frontier.* Katie Hafner and John Markoff.

- *Purchasing Power: Black Kids and American Consumer Culture.* Elizabeth Chin.
- *A Century of Childhood, 1820–1920: A Social History of Family Life.* Philippe Ariès.
- *The Tidy House: Little Girls Writing.* Carolyn Steedman.
- *The Case of Peter Pan: On the Impossibility of Children's Fiction.* Jacqueline Rose.
- *Child-Loving: The Erotic Child and Victorian Culture.* James R. Kincaid.
- *We Gotta Get out of this Place: Popular Conservatism and Postmodern Culture.* Lawrence Grossberg. *
- *Children in the House: The Material Culture of Early Childhood, 1600–1900.* Karin Calvert.
- *Sold Separately: Parents and Children in Consumer Culture.* Ellen Seiter.
- *Childhood Conceptions.* Alison James.
- *Vinyl Leaves: Walt Disney World and America.* Stephen M. Fjellman.
- *Playing with Power in Movies, Television, and Video Games.* Marsha Kinder.
- *Crossing: Language and Ethnicity among Adolescents.* Ben Rampton.
- *Childhood: Key Ideas.* Chris Jenks.
- *The Subcultures Reader.* (Eds.) Ken Gelder and Sarah Thornton. *
- *Constructing and Reconstructing Childhood: Contemporary Issues in the Sociological Study of Childhood.* (Eds.) Allison James and Alan Prout.
- *Black Popular Culture.* (Ed.) Gina Dent. *
- *Channel Surfing: Racism, Media, and the Destruction of Today's Youth.* Henry Giroux. *
- *The Children's Culture Reader.* (Ed.) Henry Jenkins. *
- *Cool Places: Geographies of Youth Cultures.* (Eds.) Tracey Skelton and Gill Valentine.
- *Team Rodent: How Disney Devours the World.* Richard Schickel.
- *7 Minutes: The Life and Death of the American Animated Cartoon.* Norman Klein.
- *Youth Culture: Identity in a Postmodern World.* (Ed.) Jonathon S. Epstein.
- *Feminism and Youth Culture.* Angela McRobbie.
- *Cold New World: Growing up in a Harder Country.* William Finnegan.
- *Framing Youth: 10 Myths about the Next Generation.* Mike Males.
- *The Mouse that Roared: Disney and the End of Innocence.* Henry Giroux. *
- *From Barbie to Mortal Kombat: Gender and Computer Games.* (Eds.) Justine Cassell and Henry Jenkins.
- *Daddy's Girl: Young Girls and Popular Culture.* Valerie Walkerdine. *
- *The Making of Citizens: Young People, News and Politics.* David Buckingham.
- *Schooling as Ritual Performance: Towards a Political Economy of Educational Symbols and Gestures.* Peter McLaren. *
- *Power and Criticism: Poststructural Investigations in Education.* Cleo H. Cherryholmes. *
- *Framing Drop Outs: Notes on the Politics of an Urban High School.* Michelle Fine.
- *Multicultural Education as Social Activism.* Christine E. Sleeter.
- *Kinderculture: The Corporate Construction of Childhood.* (Eds.) Shirley R. Steinberg and Joe L. Kincheloe.
- *Ordinary Resurrections.* Jonathan Kozol. *
- *Permitted and Prohibited Desires: Mothers, Comics, and Censorship in Japan.* Anne Allison.
- *Noise: The Political Economy of Music.* Jacques Attali.
- *Rocking Around the Clock: Music Television, Postmodernism, and Consumer Culture.* E. Ann Kaplan.
- *On Record: Rock, Pop, & the Written Word.* (Eds.) Simon Frith and Andrew Goodwin.
- *Diary of a Young Soul Rebel.* Isaac Julien and Colin MacCabe.

- *From Pop to Punk to Postmodernism: Popular Music and Australian Culture: From the 1960s to the 1990s.* Philip Hayward.
- *Rock and Popular Music: Politics, Policies, Institutions.* (Eds.) Tony Bennett, Graeme Turner, and John Sheperd.
- *Rockin' the Boat: Mass Music & Mass Movements.* (Ed.) Reebee Garofalo. *
- *Microphone Fiends: Youth Music & Youth Culture.* (Eds.) Andrew Ross and Tricia Rose. *
- *In Garageland: Rock, Youth, and Modernity.* Johan Fornas, Ulf Lindberg, and Ove Sernhede.
- *Club Cultures: Music, Media, and Subcultural Capital.* Sarah Thornton.
- *Dangerous Crossroads: Popular Music, Postmodernism and the Politics of Place.* George Lipsitz.
- *Discographies: Dance Music, Culture and the Politics of Sound.* Jeremy Gilbert and Ewan Pearson.
- *Performing Rites: On the Value of Popular Music.* Simon Frith.

Introductory texts

- *Bury My Heart at Wounded Knee: An Indian History of the American West.* Dee Brown.
- *The Black Holocaust for Beginners.* S. E. Anderson.
- *Islam for Beginners: A Writers and Reader Documentary.* Nabil Ibrahim Matar. *
- *Black History for Beginners.* Denise Dennis and Susan Willmarth.
- *Narrative of the Life of Frederick Douglas: An American Slave.* Frederick Douglas. *
- *Harriet Tubman and the Underground Railroad: Her Life in the United States and Canada.* Rosemary Sadlier.
- *Book of Life.* Sojourner Truth.
- *Crusade for Justice: The Autobiography of Ida B. Wells.* (Ed.) Alfreda M. Duster. *
- *Malcolm X for Beginners.* Bernard Aquina Doctor. *
- *Black Panthers for Beginners.* Herb Boyd. *
- *Assata: An Autobiography.* Assata Shakur.
- *The Struggle for Freedom: African-American Slave Resistance.* Dennis Wepman.
- *No More!: Stories and Songs of Slave Resistance.* Doreen Rappaport.

Taking the next step

- *The Souls of Black Folk.* W. E. B. DuBois. *
- *Southern Horrors and Other Writings: The Anti-Lynching Campaign of Ida B. Wells, 1892–1900.* Ida B. Wells.
- *Fannie Lou Hamer.* June Jordan.
- *The Price of the Ticket: Collected Nonfiction, 1948–1985.* James Baldwin. *
- *A Call to Conscience: The Landmark Speeches of Dr. Martin Luther King Jr.* (Eds.) Clayborne Carson and Kris Shepard.
- *The Final Speeches of Malcolm X.* (Ed.) Steve Clark. *
- *Blues People: Negro Music in White America.* Leroi Jones.
- *Racial Formation in the United States: From the 1960s to the 1990s.* Michael Omi and Howard Winant. *

- *Chain Reactions: The Impact of Race, Rights, and Taxes on American Politics.* Thomas Byrne Edsall and Mary D. Edsall.
- *Beyond Identity Politics: Emerging Social Justice Movements in Communities of Color.* (Ed.) John Anner.
- *Breaking the Silence: Redress and Japanese American Ethnicity.* Yasuko I. Takezawa.
- *Don't Be Afraid Gringo: A Honduran Woman Speaks from the Heart: The Story of Elvia Alvarado.* (Ed.) Medea Benjamin.
- *Maya Cultural Activism in Guatemala.* (Eds.) Edward Fisher and R. McKenna Brown.
- *Another America: The Politics of Race and Blame.* Kofi Buenor Hadjor.
- *De Colores Means All of Us: Latina Views for a Multi-Colored Century.* Elizabeth Martinez.
- *Black Genius: African American Solutions to African American Problems.* (Eds.) Manthia Diawara, Clyde Taylor, and Regina Austin.
- *Legacy to Liberation: Politics & Culture of Revolutionary Asian/Pacific America.* (Ed.) Fred Ho.

Put on your seatbelt

- *This Bridge Called My Back: Writings by Radical Women of Color.* (Eds.) Cherrie Moraga and Gloria Anzaldua. *
- *Old Nazis, the New Right, and the Republican Party: Domestic Fascist Networks and Their Effect on US Cold War Politics.* Russ Bellant.
- *The Signifying Monkey: A Theory of African-American Literary Criticism.* Henry Louis Gates.
- *The State of Native America: Genocide, Colonization, and Resistance.* (Ed). M. Annette Jaimes.
- *Playing in the Dark: Whiteness and the Literary Imagination.* Toni Morrison. *
- *Culture and Imperialism.* Edward Said. *
- *The Black Atlantic: Modernity and Double Consciousness.* Paul Gilroy. *
- *Reflecting Black: African-American Cultural Criticism.* Michael Eric Dyson.
- *Race, Identity, and Representation in Education.* (Eds.) Cameron McCarthy and Warren Crinchlow. *
- *Confronting Environmental Racism: Voices from the Grassroots.* (Ed.) Robert D. Bullard.
- *Racist Culture: Philosophy and the Politics of Meaning.* David Theo Goldberg.
- *Race Matters.* Cornel West.
- *Welcome to the Jungle: New Positions in Black Cultural Studies.* Kobena Mercer. *
- *Rap Music and Black Culture in Contemporary America.* Tricia Rose.
- *Black Studies, Rap, and the Academy.* Houston A. Baker, Jr.
- *Towards the Abolition of Whiteness: Essays on Race, Politics, and Working Class History.* David Roediger. *
- *The State of Asian America: Activism and Resistance in the 1990s.* (Ed.) Karin Aguilar-San Juan.
- *The Bubbling Cauldron: Race, Ethnicity, and the Urban Crisis.* (Eds.) Michael Peter Smith and Joe R. Feagin.
- *Killing Rage: Ending Racism.* bell hooks.
- *White Guys: Studies in Postmodern Domination and Difference.* Fred Pfeil.
- *How the Irish Became White.* Noel Ignatiev.

- *Lies My Teacher Told Me: Everything Your American History Textbook Got Wrong.* James W. Loewen. *
- *Screening the Los Angeles "Riots": Race, Seeing and Resistance.* Darnell M. Hunt.
- *'Race', Ethnicity and Nation: International Perspectives on Social Conflict.* (Ed.) Peter Ratcliffe.
- *Jews and Blacks: A Dialogue on Race, Religion, and Culture in America.* Michael Lerner and Cornel West.
- *Whiteness: A Critical Reader.* (Ed.) Mike Hill.
- *Displacing Whiteness.* Ruth Frankenberg. *
- *The Politics of Multiculturalism in the New Europe: Racism, Identity, and Community.* (Eds.) Tariq Modood and Pning Werbner. *
- *White.* Richard Dyer. *
- *Racism in a Racial Democracy: The Maintenance of White Supremacy in Brazil.* France Winddance Twine.
- *Like a Hurricane: The Indian Movement from Alcatraz to Wounded Knee.* Paul Smith and Robert Allen Warrior.
- *Yo' Mamas's Disfunktional: Fighting the Culture Wars in America!* Robin D. G. Kelley. *
- *Nga Patai: Racism and Ethnic Relations in Aotearoa/New Zealand.* Nga Patai.
- *The House that Race Built.* (Ed.) Wahneema Lubiano.
- *Anything We Love Can Be Saved: A Writer's Activism.* Alice Walker.
- *The Tyranny of the Majority: Fundamental Fairness in Representative Democracy.* Lani Guinier.
- *The Great White Flood: Racism in Australia: Critically Appraised from an Aboriginal Historico-Theological Viewpoint.* Anne Pattel-Gray.
- *Freedoms Given, Freedoms Won: Afro-Brazilians in Post-Abolition Sao Paulo and Salvador.* Kim D. Butler.
- *Speaking Truth to Power: Essays on Race, Resistance, and Radicalism.* Manning Marable.
- *Cultures in Babylon.* Hazel V. Carby. *
- *White Politics and Black Australians.* Scott Bennett.
- *The Beast Reawakens: Fascism's Resurgence from Hitler's Spymasters to Today's Neo-Nazi Groups and Right-Wing Extremists.* Martin A. Lee.
- *Trans-Pacific Racism and the US Occupation of Japan.* Yukiko Koshiro.
- *Racial Politics in Contemporary Brazil.* (Ed.) Michael Hanchard.
- *White Racism: The Basics.* Joe Feagin, Hernan Vera, and Pinar Batur.
- *White Papers Black Marks: Architecture, Race, Culture.* (Ed.) Lesley Naa Norce Lokko.
- *Race/Sex: Their Sameness, Difference and Interplay.* (Ed.) Naomi Zack.
- *Chicana/o Latina/a Cultural Studies: Transnational and Transdisciplinary Movements.* (Eds.) Lawrence Grossberg, Angie Chabram-Dernersesian, and Della Pollock. *
- *Global Critical Race Feminism: An International Reader.* (Ed.) Adrien Katherien Wing.
- *Islam.* Richard W. Bulliet.
- *The Islamic Threat: Myth or Reality?* John L. Esposito. *
- *Indigenous Mestizos: The Politics of Race and Culture in Cuzco, Peru, 1919–1991.* Marisol de la Cadena.
- *Afro-Cuban Voices on Race and Identity in Contemporary Cuba.* (Ed.) Pedro Perez-Sarduy.
- *The Crusade for Justice: Chicano Militancy and the Government's War on Dissent.* Ernesto B. Vigil. *

- *Theories of Race and Racism: A Reader.* (Eds.) Les Back and John Solomos.
- *Race Relations in Britain: A Developing Agenda.* (Eds.) Tessa Blackstone, Bhikhu C. Parekh, and Peter Sanders.
- *Rethinking Multiculturalism: Cultural Diversity and Political Theory.* Bhikhu C. Parekh. *
- *Yellow: Race in America Beyond Black and White.* Frank H. Wu.
- *Defining and Designing Multiculturalism.* Pepi Leistyna.
- *Cultural Criminology.* Jeff Ferrell and Clinton R. Sanders.
- *Criminal Injustice: Confronting the Prison Crisis.* (Ed.) Elihu Rosenblatt.
- *No More Prisons.* William Upski Wimsatt.
- *No Equal Justice: Race and Class in the American Criminal Justice System.* David Cole. *
- *Lockdown America: Police and Prisons in the Age of Crisis.* Christian Parenti. *
- *States of Confinement: Policing, Detention, and Prisons.* (Ed.) Joy James. *
- *Race to Incarcerate.* Marc Mauer and the Sentencing Project.

Part IV: Gendered Identities in the Realm of Patriarchy

Introductory texts

- *Introducing Feminism.* Susan Alice Watkins, Marisa Rueda, and Martha Rodriguez.
- *Black Women for Beginners.* Saundra Sharp.
- *Introducing Postfeminism.* Sophia Phoca and Rebecca Wright.
- *Domestic Violence for Beginners.* Alisa Del Tufo and Barbara Henry.
- *In Our Time: Memoir of a Revolution.* Susan Brownmiller.
- *WOW: Women on the Web: A Guide to Gender-Related Resources on the Internet.* Helen Fallon.

Taking the next step

- *The Subjection of Women.* John Stuart Mill.
- *The Women's Bible.* Elizabeth Cady Stanton.
- *Ella Baker: Freedom Bound.* Joanne Grant. *
- *Righteous Discontent: The Women's Movement in the Black Baptist Church 1880–1920.* Evelyn Brooks Higginbotham.
- *Women and Labor.* Olive Schreiner. *
- *The Traffic in Women: And Other Essays on Feminism.* Emma Goldman. *
- *Disorderly Conduct: Visions of Gender in Victorian America.* Caroll Smith Rosenberg.
- *The Black Woman.* (Ed.) Toni Cade Bambara. *
- *Black Women, Writing, and Identity.* Carole Boyce Davies.
- *Woman's Legacy: Essays on Race, Sex, and Class in American History.* Bettina Aptheker.
- *Home Girls: A Black Feminist Anthology.* (Ed.) Barbara Smith.
- *All the Women are White, All the Blacks are Men, But Some of Us are Brave: Black Women's Studies.* (Eds.) Gloria Hull, Patricia Bell Scott, and Barbara Smith. *
- *Daring to Be Bad: Radical Feminism in America, 1967–75.* Alice Echols and Ellen Willis.
- *Women Activists: Challenging the Abuse of Power.* Anne Witte Garland.
- *Common Differences: Conflicts in Black and White Feminist Perspectives.* Gloria I. Joseph.

- *Black Women in White America: A Documentary History.* (Ed.) Gerda Lerner.
- *Black Women in America.* (Ed.) Kim Marie Vaz.
- *Feminism and Black Activism in Contemporary America.* Irvin D. Solomon.
- *American Manhood: Transformations in Masculinity from the Revolution to the Modern Era.* E. Anthony Rotundo.
- *Women, Aids & Activism.* The ACT UP/NY Women and Aids Book Group. *
- *Under Attack, Fighting Back: Women and Welfare in the United States.* Mimi Abramovitz.
- *Women of Color in US Society.* (Eds.) Maxine Baca Zinn and Bonnie Thornton Dill.
- *Affirmative Acts: Political Essays.* June Jordan. *
- *Community Activism and Feminist Politics: Organizing Across Race, Class, and Gender.* (Ed.) Nancy A. Naples.
- *Women's Activism in Contemporary Russia.* Linda Racioppi and Katherine O'Sullivan.
- *The Pro-Choice Movement: Organization and Activism in the Abortion Conflict.* Suzanne Staggenborg.
- *Gender and the Politics of History.* Joan Wallach Scott.
- *Engendering Democracy in Brazil: Women's Movements in Transition Politics.* Sonia E. Alvarez.
- *Women's Voices, Women's Power: Dialogues of Resistance from East Africa.* Judith M. Abwunza.
- *Radical Feminism: A Documentary Reader.* (Ed.) Barbara A. Crow.
- *Autobiography as Activism: Three Black Women of the Sixties.* Margo V. Perkins.
- *Dear Sisters: Dispatches from the Women's Liberation Movement.* (Eds.) Rosalyn Baxandall and Linda Gordon.
- *The Personal and the Political: Women's Activism in Response to the Breast Cancer and AIDS Epidemics.* Ulrike Boehmer.
- *Global Feminism Since 1945: Rewriting Histories* (Ed.) Bonnie G. Smith.
- *The Feminist Memoir Project: Voices from Women's Liberation.* (Eds.) Rachel Blau Duplessis and Ann Snitwo.
- *Fighting Words: Black Women and the Search for Justice.* Patricia Hill Collins. *
- *Other Kinds of Dreams: Black Women's Organizations and the Politics of Transformation.* Julia Sudbury.
- *The Whole Woman.* Germaine Greer.
- *Ar'N't I A Woman?: Female Slaves in the Plantation South.* Deborah Gray White.
- *Challenging Democracy: International Perspectives on Gender, Education, and Citizenship* (Eds.) Madeleine Arnot and Jo-Anne Dillabough.
- *Tales of the Lavender Menace: A Memoir of Liberation.* Karla Jay.
- *The World Split Open: How the Modern Women's Movement Changed America.* Ruth Rosen.
- *The Challenge of Women's Activism and Human Rights in Africa.* (Eds.) Diana Joyce Fox and Naima Hasci.
- *Walking on Fire: Haitian Women's Stories of Survival and Resistance.* Beverly Bell and Edwidge Danticat.
- *Japan's Comfort Women: The Military and Involuntary Prostitution during War and Occupation.* Yuki Tanaka and Susan Brownmiller.
- *Global Democracy, Social Movements, and Feminism.* Catherine Eschle.
- *Women's Activism and Globalization: Linking Local Struggles and Transnational Politics.* (Eds.) Nancy A. Naples and Manisha Desai.

Put on your seatbelt

- *The Second Sex.* Simone de Beauvoir. *
- *The Feminine Mystique.* Betty Friedan.
- *Sexual Politics.* Kate Millett.
- *The Dialectic of Sex: The Case for Feminist Revolution.* Shulamith Firestone.
- *Speculum of the Other Woman.* Luce Irigaray. *
- *The Laugh of the Medusa.* Hélène Cixous. *
- *Of Woman Born: Motherhood as Experience and Institution.* Adrienne Rich. *
- *The Mermaid and the Minotaur: Sexual Arrangements and Human Malaise.* Dorothy Dinnerstein.
- *Sexist Language: A Modern Philosophical Analysis.* Mary Vetterling-Braggin.
- *Lesbianism and the Women's Movement.* Charlotte Bunch.
- *The War against Women.* Marilyn French.
- *Hysteries: Hysterical Epidemics and Modern Culture.* Elaine Showalter.
- *The Kristeva Reader.* (Ed.) Toril Moi. *
- *Women, Race, and Class.* Angela Davis. *
- *In Other Worlds: Essays in Cultural Politics.* Gayatri Chakravorty Spivak. *
- *Pornography: Men Possessing Women.* Andrea Dworkin.
- *Alice Doesn't: Feminism, Semiotics, Cinema.* Teresa de Lauretis. *
- *Sexual/Textual Politics: Feminist Literary Theory.* Toril Moi.
- *Man Made Language.* Dale Spender. *
- *Feminist Theory: From Margin to Center.* bell hooks. *
- *Loving with a Vengeance: Mass Produced Fantasies for Women.* Tania Modleski.
- *The Science Question in Feminism.* Sandra Harding.
- *The Pirate's Fiancee: Feminism Reading Postmodernism.* Meaghan Morris.
- *Specifying: Black Women Writing the American Experience.* Susan Willis. *
- *The Feminist Reader: Essays in Gender and the Politics of Literary Criticism.* (Eds.) Catherine Belsey and Jane Moore.
- *Feminism/Postmodernism.* (Ed.) Linda J. Nicholson.
- *A Dream Compels Us: Voices of Salvadoran Women.* (Eds.) New Americas Press.
- *Woman, Native, Other.* Trinh T. Minh-Ha.
- *Unruly Practices: Power, Discourse, and Gender in Contemporary Social Theory.* Nancy Fraser. *
- *Black Women Novelists: The Development of a Tradition.* Barbara Christian. *
- *Invisibility Blues: From Pop to Theory.* Michele Wallace. *
- *Gender Trouble: Feminism and the Subversion of Identity.* Judith Butler. *
- *Third World Women and the Politics of Feminism.* (Eds.) Chandra Talpad Mohanty, Ann Russo, and Lourdes Torres. *
- *Inessential Woman: Problems of Exclusion in Feminist Thought.* Elizabeth V. Spelman.
- *Reading the Romance: Women, Patriarchy, and Popular Literature.* Janice Radway. *
- *Beyond Accommodation: Ethical Feminism, Deconstruction, and the Law.* Drucilla Cornell. *
- *Simians, Cyborgs and Women: The Reinvention of Nature.* (Ed.) Donna Haraway. *
- *After Patriarchy: Feminist Transformations of the World Religions.* (Eds.) Paula M. Cooey, William R. Easkin, and Jay B. McDaniel.
- *Feminists Theorize the Political.* (Eds.) Judith Butler and Joan Scott. *
- *Daughters of the Dust: The Making of an African American Woman's Film.* Julie Dash.

- *Ludic Feminism and After.* Teresa L. Ebert. *
- *Backlash: The Undeclared War against Women.* Susan Faludi.
- *The Woman in the Body: A Cultural Analysis of Reproduction.* Emily Martin.
- *Latina Politics Latino Politics: Gender, Culture, and Political Participation in Boston.* Carol Hardy-Fanta.
- *Chicana Feminist Thought: The Basic Historical Writings.* (Eds.) Alma M. Garcia and Mario T. Garcia.
- *Cultural Resistance: Challenging Beliefs about Men, Women, and Therapy.* (Ed.) Kathy Weingarten.
- *Sexing the Sex: Gendered Positions in Cultural Studies.* Elspeth Probyn.
- *The Essential Difference.* (Eds.) Naomi Shor and Elizabeth Weed. *
- *Volatile Bodies: Toward a Corporeal Feminism.* Elizabeth Grosz.
- *No More Nice Girls: Countercultural Essays.* Ellen Willis. *
- *Food for Our Grandmothers: Writings by Arab-American and Arab-Canadian Feminists.* (Ed.) Joanna Kadi.
- *Last Served: Gendering the HIV Pandemic.* Cindy Patton. *
- *Male Impersonators: Men Performing Masculinity.* Mark Simpson.
- *Nomadic Subjects.* Rosi Braidotti.
- *Reconstructing Womanhood: The Emergence of the Afro-American Woman Novelist.* Hazel Carby.
- *Feminist Contentions: A Philosophical Exchange.* (Eds.) Seyla Benhabib, Judith Butler, Drucilla Cornell, and Nancy Fraser. *
- *Beyond the Masks: Race, Gender, and Subjectivity.* Amina Mama.
- *Resident Alien: A Feminist Cultural Criticism.* Janet Wolff.
- *Reproductive Rights and Wrongs: The Global Politics of Population Control.* Betsy Hartman.
- *The Challenge of Local Feminisms: Women's Movements in Global Perspective.* (Ed.) Amrita Basu. *
- *Scattered Hegemonies: Postmodernity and Transnational Feminist Practices.* (Eds.) Inderpal Grewal and Caren Kaplan.
- *The New Victorians: A Young Woman's Challenge to the Old Feminist Order.* Rene Denfeld.
- *Words of Fire: An Anthology of African-American Feminist Thought.* (Ed.) Beverly Guy-Sheftall.
- *Comparative State Feminism.* (Eds.) Dorothy McBride Stetsupy and Amy Mazur.
- *Verbal Hygiene.* Deborah Cameron.
- *Space, Place, and Gender.* Doreen Massey. *
- *Subversive Women – Women's Movements in Africa, Asia, Latin America, and the Caribbean.* (Ed.) Saskia Wieringa. *
- *Fictions of Feminist Ethnography.* Kamala Visweswaran.
- *Feminist Genealogies, Colonial Legacies, Democratic Futures.* (Eds.) Jacqui Alexander and Chandra Talpade Mohanty. *
- *Race, Gender, and Work: A Multi-Cultural Economic History of Women in the United States.* Teresa Amott and Julie Matthaei.
- *Dangerous Women: Gender and Korean Nationalism.* (Eds.) Elaine H. Kim and Chungmoo Choi.
- *Hard Looks: Masculinities, Spectatorship, and Contemporary Consumption.* Sean Nixon. *
- *Amazon to Zami: Towards a Global Lesbian Feminism.* (Ed.) Monika Reinfelder.

- *Race, Class, Gender.* (Eds.) Margaret L. Andersen and Patricia Hill Collins.
- *Changing Our Own Words: Essays on Criticism, Theory, and Writing by Black Women.* (Ed.) Cheryl A. Wall.
- *When and Where I Enter: The Impact of Black Women on Race and Sex in America.* Paula Giddings. *
- *Dragon Ladies: Asian American Feminists Breathe Fire.* (Ed.) Sonia Shah.
- *Intersecting Voices.* Iris Marion Young.
- *Writing on the Body.* (Eds.) Katie Conboy, Nadia Medina, and Sarah Stanbury.
- *Kinship, Identity, and Native Womanism.* Jaimes Guerrero.
- *Feminist Social Thought.* (Ed.) Diana Tietjens Meyers.
- *Women Transforming Politics: An Alternative Reader.* (Eds.) Cathy J. Cohen, Kathleen B. Jones, and Joan C. Tronto. *
- *Transitions, Environments, Translations: Feminisms in International Politics.* (Eds.) Joan W. Scott, Cora Kaplan, and Debra Keates.
- *Postfeminisms: Feminism, Cultural Theory and Cultural Forms.* Ann Brooks.
- *Body and Flesh: A Philosophical Reader.* (Ed.) Donn Welton.
- *Language and Gender: A Reader.* (Ed.) Jennifer Coates.
- *Redirecting the Gaze: Gender, Theory, and Cinema in the Third World.* (Eds.) Diana Robin and Ira Jaffe.
- *Borders and Boundaries: Women in India's Partition.* Ritu Menon and Kamla Bhasin.
- *Women's Lifeworlds: Women's Narratives on Shaping Their Realities.* (Ed.) Edith Sizoo.
- *Women, Islam and the State.* (Ed.) Deniz Kandiyoti.
- *Nwanyibu: Woman Being and African Literature.* (Eds.) Phanuel Akubueze Egejuru and Ketu H. Katrak.
- *Reconcilable Differences: Confronting Beauty, Pornography, and the Future of Feminism.* Lynn S. Chancer.
- *Female Stories, Female Bodies: Narrative, Identity, and Representation.* Lidia Curti.
- *Feminist Theory and the Body: A Reader.* (Eds.) Janet Price and Margrit Shildrick.
- *Between Women and Nation: Nationalisms, Transnational Feminisms, and the State.* (Eds.) Caren Kaplan, Norma Alarcon, and Minoo Moallem. *
- *Feminisms and Internationalism.* (Eds.) Mrinalini Sinha, Angela Woolacott, and Donna Guy.
- *Black Body: Women, Colonialism, and Space.* Radhika Mohanram.
- *Two-Spirit People: Native American Gender Identity, Sexuality, and Spirituality.* (Eds.) Sue-Ellen Jacobs, Wesley Thomas, and Sabine Lang.
- *Changing Ones: Third and Fourth Genders in Native North America.* (Ed.) Will Roscoe. *
- *Feminism and Cultural Studies.* (Ed.) Morag Shiach.
- *Maneuvers: The International Politics of Militarizing Women's Lives.* Cynthia Enloe.
- *The Male Body: A New Look at Men in Public and in Private.* Susan Bordo. *
- *Transformation: Thinking through Feminism.* (Eds.) Sara Ahmed, Jane Kilby, Celia Lury, Maureen McNeil, and Beverly Skeggs.
- *Ideologies and Technologies of Motherhood: Race, Class, Sexuality, Nationalism.* (Eds.) Helen Ragone and France Winddance Twine.
- *Race, Class, and Gender.* (Ed.) Margaret Andersen.
- *Global Feminisms: A Survey of Issues and Controversies.* (Ed.) Bonnie Smith.
- *Global Sex Workers: Rights, Resistance and Redefinition.* (Eds.) Kamala Kempadoo and Jo Doezema.
- *Female Sexualization: A Collective Work of Memory.* Frigga Haug.

- *Theorizing Feminism: Parallel Trends in the Humanities and Social Sciences.* (Eds.) Anne Hermann and Abigail J. Stewart.
- *Feminism: Critical Concepts in Literary and Cultural Studies.* (Ed.) Mary Evans.
- *Sexuality, Gender, and the Law.* William N. Eskridge, Jr. and Nan D. Hunter.
- *Scratching the Surface: Canadian Anti-Racist Feminist Thought.* (Eds.) Enakshi Dua and Angela Robertson.
- *Infertilities: Exploring Fictions of Barren Bodies.* Robin Truth Goodman.
- *Sapphic Slashers: Sex, Violence, and American Modernity.* Lisa Duggan.
- *Shadowboxing: Representations of Black Feminist Politics.* Joy James. *
- *Black Venus: Sexualized Savages, Primal Fears, and Primitive Narratives in French.* T. Denean Sharpley-Whiting.
- *Black Feminist Cultural Criticism.* (Ed.) Jacqueline Bobo. *
- *Challenging Democracy: International Perspectives on Gender, Education, and Citizenship.* (Eds.) Madeleine Arnot and Jo-Anne Dillabough.
- *Voicing Chicana Feminisms: Young Women Speak Out on Sexuality and Identity.* Aida Hurtado. *
- *Global Critical Race Feminism: An International Reader.* (Ed.) Adrien Katherine Wing.
- *An Ethics of Dissensus: Postmodernity, Feminism, and the Politics of Radical Democracy.* Ewa Plonowska Ziarek.
- *Alternatives: Black Feminism in the Postimperial Nation.* Ranu Samantrai.

Part V: Heterosexism and Homophobia: Critical Interventions

Introductory texts

- *Who's Who in Gay and Lesbian History: From Antiquity to World War II.* (Eds.) Robert Aldrich and Garry Wotherspoon.
- *Who's Who in Contemporary Gay & Lesbian History: From World War II to the Present Day.* (Eds.) Robert Aldrich and Garry Wotherspoon.
- *We are Everywhere: A Historical Sourcebook in Gay and Lesbian Politics.* (Eds.) Mark Blasius and Shane Phelan.
- *The Body for Beginners.* Dani Cavallaro.
- *Queer Theory: An Introduction.* Annamarie Readings.
- *A Legal Guide for Lesbian and Gay Couples.* Hayden Curry, Denis Clifford, and Frederick Hertz.
- *Try This at Home! A Do-It-Yourself Guide to Winning Lesbian and Gay Civil Rights Policy.* Matthew A. Coles.
- *Historical Dictionary of the Gay Liberation Movement.* Ronald J. Hunt.

Taking the next step

- *Sister Outsider: Essays and Speeches.* Audre Lorde. *
- *Sexuality in Western Art.* Edward Lucie-Smith.
- *The Body: Classic and Contemporary Readings.* (Ed.) Donn Welton.
- *Lesbian and Gay Studies: A Critical Introduction.* (Eds.) Andy Medhurst and Sally Munt.
- *Sex Wars: Sexual Dissent and Political Culture.* Lisa Duggan.

- *The Rise of a Gay and Lesbian Movement.* Barry D. Adam.
- *AIDS: Activism and Alliances.* (Eds.) Peter Aggleton, Peter Davies, and Graham Hart.
- *The Global Emergence of Gay and Lesbian Politics: National Imprints of a Worldwide Movement.* (Eds.) Jan Willem Duyvendak, Andre Krouwel, and Barry D. Adam. *
- *The Pink and Black: Homosexuals in France Since 1968.* Frédéric Martel.

Put on your seatbelt

- *Eros and Civilization.* Herbert Marcuse. *
- *The Pleasure of the Text.* Roland Barthes. *
- *The History of Sexuality, Volumes 1, 2, & 3.* Michel Foucault. *
- *In the Life: A Black Gay Anthology.* (Ed.) Joseph Beam.
- *AIDS: Cultural Analysis/Cultural Activism.* (Ed.) Douglas Crimp. *
- *One Hundred Years of Homosexuality and Other Essays on Greek Love.* David M. Halperin.
- *Displacing Homophobia: Gay Male Perspectives in Literature and Culture.* (Eds.) Ronald Butters, John M. Clum, and Michael Moon.
- *Hidden from History: Reclaiming the Gay and Lesbian Past.* (Eds.) Martin Bauml Duberman, Martha Vicinus, and George Chauncey, Jr. *
- *Lesbian Texts and Contexts: Radical Revisions.* (Eds.) Karla Jay and Joanne Glasgow.
- *Passions of the Cut Sleeve: The Male Homosexual Tradition in China.* Bret Hinsch.
- *Inside/Out: Lesbian Theories, Gay Theories.* (Ed.) Diana Fuss. *
- *Bi Any Other Name: Bisexual People Speak Out.* (Eds.) Loraine Hutchins and Lani Kaahumani.
- *Neither Man nor Woman: The Hijras of India.* Serena Nanda.
- *Our Lives: Lesbian Personal Writings.* (Ed.) Frances Rooney.
- *Sexual Dissidence: Augustine to Wilde, Freud to Foucault.* Jonathan Dollimore.
- *The Great Mirror of Male Love.* Ihara Saikuku.
- *Before Sexuality.* (Eds.) David M. Halperin, John J. Winker, and Froma I. Zeitlin.
- *Gay Roots: 20 Years of Gay Sunshine: An Anthology of Gay History, Sex, Politics, and Culture.* (Ed.) Winston Leyland.
- *Nationalisms and Sexualities.* (Eds.) Andrew Parker, Mary Russo, Doris Sommer, and Patricia Yaeger.
- *Epistemology of the Closet.* Eve Kosofsky Sedgwick. *
- *Making Trouble: Essays on Gay History, Politics, and the University.* John D'Emilio. *
- *New Lesbian Studies: Into the Twenty-First Century.* (Eds.) Bonnie Zimmerman and Toni H. McNaron.
- *Out of the Closets: Voices of Gay Liberation, the Twentieth Anniversary Edition.* (Eds.) Allen Young and Karla Jay.
- *Gay American History: Lesbians and Gay Men in the USA: A Documentary History.* Jonathan Ned Katz.
- *Defiant Desire: Gay and Lesbian Lives in South Africa.* (Eds.) Mark Gevisser and Edwin Cameron.
- *The Straight Mind and Other Essays.* Monique Wittig.
- *The Lesbian and Gay Studies Reader.* (Eds.) Henry Abelove, Michele Aina Barale, and David Halperin. *
- *Bodies that Matter: On the Discursive Limits of Sex.* Judith Butler. *
- *The Matter of Images: Essays on Representation.* Richard Dyer. *

- *Fear of a Queer Planet: Queer Politics and Social Theory.* (Ed.) Michael Warner.
- *The Practice of Love: Lesbian Sexuality and Perverse Desire.* Teresa De Lauretis. *
- *Companeras: Latina Lesbians.* (Ed.) Juanita Ramos.
- *Entiendes?: Queer Readings, Hispanic Writings.* (Eds.) Emilie Bergmann and Paul Julian Smith. *
- *Living the Spirit: A Gay American Indian Anthology.* (Ed.) Will Roscoe.
- *Nice Jewish Girls: A Lesbian Anthology.* (Ed.) Evelyn Torton Beck.
- *Homographies: Essays in Gay Literary and Cultural Theory.* Lee Edelman.
- *Power and Community: Organizational and Cultural Responses to AIDS.* Dennis Altman.
- *Autobiography, Politics and Sexuality: Essays in Curriculum Theory 1972–1992.* William Pinar.
- *Boyopolis: Sex and Politics in Gay Eastern Europe.* Stan Persky.
- *Sexual Justice: Democratic Citizenship and the Politics of Desire.* Morris B. Kaplan.
- *Creating Change: Sexuality, Public Policy, and Civil Rights.* (Eds.) John D'Emilio, William B. Turner, and Urvashi Vaid.
- *Queer Theory/Sociology.* (Ed.) Steven Seidman. *
- *Femininity Played Straight: The Significance of Being Lesbian.* Biddy Martin.
- *Mirage: Enigmas of Race, Difference, and Desire.* Kobena Mercer, Catherine Ugwa, and David A Bailey. *
- *Split Britches: Lesbian Practice/Feminist Performance.* (Ed.) Sue-Ellen Case.
- *Virtual Equality: The Mainstreaming of Gay and Lesbian Liberation.* Urvashi Vaid.
- *Male Colors: The Construction of Homosexuality in Tokugawa Japan.* Gary P. Leupp.
- *The Gender/Sexuality Reader: Culture, History, Political Economy.* (Eds.) Roger N. Lancaster and Micaela Di Leonardo.
- *Islamic Homosexualities: Culture, History, and Literature.* Stephen O. Murray and Will Roscoe.
- *Invented Identities: Lesbians and Gays Talk about Migration.* (Ed.) Bob Cant.
- *Feminism Meets Queer Theory.* (Eds.) Elizabeth Weed and Naomi Schor.
- *The Queer Question: Essays on Desire and Democracy.* Scott Tucker.
- *Q&A: Queer in Asian America.* (Eds.) David L. Eng and Alice Y. Hom.
- *Third Sex, Third Gender.* Gilbert Herdt.
- *Private Affairs: Critical Ventures in the Culture of Social Relation.* Phillip Brian Harper.
- *Dangerous Liaisons: Blacks, Gays, and the Struggle for Equality.* (Ed.) Eric Brandt.
- *Out for Good: The Struggle to Build a Gay Rights Movement in America.* Dudley Clendinen and Adam Nagourney.
- *The Pleasure Principle: Sex, Backlash, and the Struggle for Gay Freedom.* Michael Bronski.
- *Hispanisms and Homosexualities* (Eds.) Sylvia Molloy and Robert Irwin.
- *The Other Side of Silence: Men's Lives and Gay Identities: A Twentieth-Century History.* John Loughery.
- *Exile and Pride: Disability, Queerness, and Liberation.* Eli Clare. *
- *Bisexuality and the Eroticism of Everyday Life.* Marjorie Garber. *
- *Sociolegal Control of Homosexuality: A Multinational Comparison.* (Eds.) D. J. West and Richard Green.
- *Queer Diasporas.* (Eds.) Cindy Patton and Benigno Sanchez-Eppler. *
- *Margaret Mead Made Me Gay: Personal Essays, Public Ideas.* Esther Newton, William L. Leap, and Judith Halberstam.

- *Creating Change: Sexuality, Public Policy, and Civil Rights.* (Eds.) John D'Emilio, William B. Turner, and Urvashi Vaid. *
- *Just Sex: Students Rewrite the Rules on Sex, Violence, Activism, and Equality.* (Eds.) Jodi Gold and Susan Villari.
- *Feminism, the Family, and the Politics of the Closet: Lesbian and Gay Displacement.* Cheshire Calhoun.
- *Beyond Carnival: Male Homosexuality in Twentieth-Century Brazil.* James Naylor Green.
- *A Genealogy of Queer Theory.* William B. Turner and Robert Dawidoff.
- *Thinking Queer: Sexuality, Culture, and Education.* (Eds.) Susan Talburt and Shirley R. Steinberg.
- *Sexual Identities, Queer Politics.* (Ed.) Mark Blasius.
- *Dear Uncle Go: Male Homosexuality in Thailand.* Peter Jackson.
- *Beauty and Power: Transgendering in the Southern Philippines.* Mark Johnson.
- *Marxism, Queer Theory, Gender.* (Eds.) Mas'ud Zavaradeh, Donald Morton, and Teresa L. Ebert. *
- *Living Out Loud: A History of Gay and Lesbian Activism in Australia.* Graham Willet. *
- *Disidentifications: Queers of Color and the Performance of Politics.* Jose Estaban Munoz *
- *How to Have Theory in an Epidemic: Cultural Chronicles of AIDS.* Paula A. Treichler. *
- *A Nation by Rights: National Cultures, Sexual Identity Politics, and the Discourse of Rights.* (Eds.) Carl F. Stychin and Shane Phelan.
- *Sex Changes: The Politics of Transgenderism.* Pat Califia. *
- *Pomosexuals: Challenging Assumptions about Gender and Sexuality.* (Eds.) Carol Queen and Lawrence Schimel.
- *Unspoken Rules: Sexual Orientation and Women's Rights.* Rachel Rosenbloom and Charlotte Bunch.
- *Female Desires: Same-Sex Relations and Transgender Practices Across Cultures.* (Eds.) Evelyn Blackwood and Saskia E. Wieringa. *
- *Gender Outlaw: On Men, Women, and the Rest of Us.* Kate Bornstein.
- *Pure Resistance: Queer Virginity in Early English Drama.* Theodora A. Jankowski.
- *Queering the Color Line: Race and the Invention of Homosexuality in American Culture.* Siobhan B. Somerville.
- *The Invention of Heterosexuality.* Ned Katz.
- *Freaks Talk: Tabloid Talk Shows and Sexual Nonconformity.* Joshua Gamson.
- *Sexual Strangers: Gays, Lesbians, and Dilemmas of Citizenship.* Shane Phelan.
- *Laboring for Rights: Unions and Sexual Diversity across Nations.* (Ed.) Gerald Hunt.
- *Global Sex.* Dennis Altman. *
- *Different Rainbows.* (Ed.) Peter Drucker. *

Index

Note: Information in notes is signified by *n* followed by the note number.

CPSIA information can be obtained at www.ICGtesting.com
Printed in the USA
BVOW080841301211

279505BV00004B/4/P